KISS

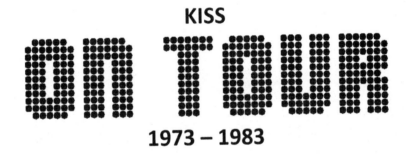

ON TOUR

1973 – 1983

By Julian Gill

In memory of Neil Bogart, William M. Aucoin, and Sean Delaney: Visionaries, dreamers and believers in the impossible, without whom...

Dedicated to the numerous road warriors who kept the band on the road and more importantly did the work to put them on the stage!

Contents

Introduction 9

The Beginning 11

In The Clubs 13

First KISS 33

Hotter Than Hell 83

Dressed to Kill 107

Alive! 137

Destroyer 171

Rock and Roll Over 209

Love Gun 247

KISS Alive II 269

Dynasty: The Return of KISS 297

Unmasked 333

1981/2 "Elder" Intermission 355

10th Anniversary Tour 361

Introduction

"KISS on Tour" is a KissFAQ series title that had been in print in physical format for some years. The most recent volume covers the years 1998–2014 (which included several appendices of earlier tours). However, for much of the past two decades an independent work covering the full KISS touring history has been under development for a "KISS Live Focus;" and as part of the touring section for the KissFAQ, and successor KISSMONSTER, websites. This extract, from what currently weighs in at over 875 pages in U.S. letter format (8.5 × 11"), is a more economically viable method of delivering an investigation of the band's performances gearing it to a specific period of the band's history. This volume covers the period as KISS attempted to establish themselves and escape from the clubs through the end of the initial make-up era.

Unlike the excellent "KISS Alive Forever," which this doesn't attempt to be a replacement for, this work doesn't include interview segments with those associated with the band during the period. Instead, as a supplement, the focus on the touring history during this period is based on the reviews of the band and the perception by which they were held contemporaneously. For every "bad review" or overly artistic negative word used against the band, I hear a Gene Simmons growl attesting to the fact that the band seldom gave those critics any credence. They simply continued to rock and roll all night for many years after the newsprint that held those reviews had rightfully decomposed in landfills! The grammar and copy of those reviews has not been corrected, deliberately, so that the original author's intent remains intact...

As is the nature with any documentary effort such as this, it can never be a static work considered complete or absolute — and it would be beyond arrogant to suggest so. There is always new information or details surfacing. It is instead a current "frozen state" of a long-term project that will never cease, be it by this archivist or by others...

Usage of some terms in this work:
Other act(s) simply refers to other bands that shared the bill with KISS, either as a headliner (HL) or as an opener. By the time the band's headlining status is established then the (opener) tag is dropped from the other acts. Generally, the other acts are listed in order of appearance on a bill (where known). Reported audience is the attendance figure for a show gathered either from industry publications, internal band audit documents, or in worst case from newspaper review estimates. Where not known the venue capacity is provided as an alternative for measurement of scale. Within those figures there is always scope for differences due to venue configuration or numbers of tickets offered for sale. If KISS cancelled an appearance on a bill, which still went ahead, then that status is noted with "KISS CANCELLED." If the whole show was cancelled or postponed then those are also noted. In regards to audio and/or video noted for shows, the quality judgment is subjective — new shows, recordings with improved quality or alternate sources sometimes surface leaving quality very much in the eye/ear of the beholder and whatever "version" they might have. AUD refers to audience sourced, while SBD or PRO refer to audio/video captured via the soundboard or professionally filmed.

The Beginning

November 20/28, 1972 - 5th Avenue & 23rd Street Loft, New York City, NY
Other act(s): None.
Reported audience: <5
Set list: Deuce / Strutter / Firehouse
Notes:
- This showcase was essentially the final nail in Wicked Lester's coffin and marks the birth of an unnamed new band. Two dates were purportedly scheduled for the band to play showcases for Epic Records, to present the band's new concept. It's not clear whether both dates were used or simply one (the former being the more obvious choice unless they also performed for other labels).
- As a trio, Gene, Paul, and Peter invited Epic president Don Ellis and A&R man Tom Werman to their rehearsal loft to hear them play some of the new material they had been working on. Rather than impressing him, they alienated him to the point of ultimately severing all ties with their former record label. Gene recalled the disaster: "We played 'Firehouse' and at the end of the song we start ringing this bell, and Ellis thinks it's a real fire. So Paul runs over to the corner and grabs a red pail with the word 'fire' on it, and goes over and throws it at Don, who freaks as a bucketful of confetti goes all over the place. He gets up and starts to walk out, saying, 'Okay, thank you, I'll call you.' As he's heading out the door, he trips and falls. Then, Peter's purportedly drunken brother, who was sitting behind Don, throws up on his foot. We never heard from him again" (KISStory).
- The trio appeared in basic white face indicating that the genesis of the concept was in place. There were no make-up designs or leather costumes...

(KISS rehearsing sans make-up, late-1973. A few frames are all that survives from an over-written video, but enough for a glimpse provided by this composite of 5 frames. Where's Waldo?)

In The Clubs

When KISS played their debut concert at the Coventry in Queens, New York, on Tuesday January 30, 1973, they already had plenty of original material from which to construct their set. Most of their songs had been worked on throughout the fall of 1972 before Ace Frehley's addition to the band in late-December. Where various dates have been thrown around throughout the years, Lydia Criss has been adamant that Ace had joined the band by Christmas 1972. In fact, with the timing of Paul's two Village Voice ads, it seems to make the most sense with the auditions starting within days of the publication of the first ad. The band, then a trio (following Peter Criss' addition), had performed a showcase for Epic Records towards the end of November 1972, just a week before Paul placed the ad for a lead guitarist. Where that showcase may have been the final nail in Wicked Lester's coffin it ultimately represented the birth of a new band.

LEAD GUITARIST WANTED
with Flash and Ability. Album Out
Shortly. No time wasters please.
Paul 268-3145.

(Village Voice ad which appeared in both Dec. 7 and Dec. 14, 1972 issues)

Those first sets in January 1973 saw the band transitioning from Wicked Lester and becoming a new band. They included songs from Wicked Lester such as "Love Her All I Can," "She," "Simple Type," and "Keep Me Waiting." Also performed were "Deuce," "Watchin' You," "Want You Beside Me" (aka "Life In The Woods"), "Baby, Let Me Go" (aka "Let Me Go, Rock 'N Roll"), "Firehouse," and "Black Diamond." Without refinement, on stage or visually, these are the basic building blocks for the construction of the band. In the beginning they are crude, but there is an unending self-belief, an unrelenting desire to succeed. Failure is not an option...

"Deuce" had been the first original song that Paul "Ace" Frehley had played with the band at his audition (followed by "Firehouse") so its importance to the KISS canon is again solidified. Gene has insisted that when he booked this gig the band was still using the Wicked Lester name, though print advertising closer to the date of the show clearly lists KISS. Whenever the actual renaming of the band took place it had certainly been finalized in time for the ad for the shows to appear in the February 1 edition of Village Voice — it is possible to surmise that the band came up with their name in-between booking the show and the ads being placed by the venue. Regardless, few people came to see the band and the audience consisted mainly of those connected to the band, including Peter's wife and Gene's then girlfriend. Paul recalled, "There were literally five people in the place. I'll tell ya, there's nothing like playing 'Strutter' [Ed. Note that "Strutter" wasn't performed at the first gig, though the point Paul is making is clear] for a bartender and four barmaids" (Guitar World Legends #14). However, KISS were at least doing what Gene and Paul had always wanted — playing sets of original material rather than the covers they'd ended up having to include in sets (albeit the few sets Wicked Lester performed) and on the Wicked Lester album.

That the band's first three shows (1/30 – 2/1) weren't well attended is hardly surprising since they were booked during the middle of the work week (Tues/Wed/Thurs), rather than popular Fri/Sat schedule. It didn't matter, for every story there has to be a beginning and in the case of KISS their creating a monster from such beginnings makes for a better telling of that story. Competing with the band that first night was Bruce Springsteen opening for Biff Rose at Max's Kansas City while Peter's former band-mate Stan Penridge was performing with his band St. Elmo's Fire at Folk City. Ronnie Dio's Elf was at Bananafish Park in Bay Ridge. With a lack of audience these first shows allowed the band to transition from rehearsal loft band to venue stage in a somewhat gentle manner.

The band certainly didn't look like the immediately recognizable KISS at this point — with makeup guises, characters and costumes. In the beginning the band had done a certain amount of visual experimentation from the basic plain mime "white" face to the more "street" glam look similar to the New York Dolls. For the first show Paul wore jeans and a sports jacket over his Mom's glitter shirt; Ace a white turtle-neck and jeans; Peter, a blue shirt and red pants; and Gene brown bell-bottoms and white sailor-suit top. Of the four only Gene wore any substantial amount of makeup, having a coat of white-face with black "splotches" around the eyes looking more like a prostitute who'd been crying. It was nothing like his later "demonic" design. The three known January 1973 photos of the band make it clear that while they may not know what they're doing they're definitely going to explore something different with their appearance. Following the third show the band retreated to their rehearsal loft to continue working on the material and their look. For Gene the image was a challenge. He recalled, "We couldn't fit into the glitter scene, the whole New York Dolls and Lou Reed thing, which had underpinnings of androgyny and sexual ambiguity, of gayness. I'm 6-2, and I'd just look like a football player in a tutu. I don't make a convincing homosexual. So to make our statement, we opted for makeup" (Jonathan Takiff, Knight-Ridder Newspapers, 10/10/96).

With KISS only playing sporadically throughout 1973 more attention would be paid to the band rehearsing and refining new material. At the occasional shows the band was able to book new material would be dropped into the set. One early addition was a cover of the Moody Blues' "Go Now," which Paul Stanley has commented was regularly performed by KISS during their club days. Furthermore, he has suggested that the song was recorded in some lower form by the band. This could mean that it was recorded live, or at least as a very rough demo. The band would never properly record the song having never transformed it properly into an acceptable KISS arrangement. It is possible that the song was recorded rough during the Bell Sound Studios demo sessions prior to the recording of the first album, though that is conjecture and it certainly is not included amongst the surviving Bell Sound demos. It is interesting to note that the original version of the song was one of the earliest Moody Blues songs, well before key member Justin Hayward became involved in the band...

When KISS recorded their demo in March 1973 engineer Eddie Kramer chose the five songs which would be recorded during the demo session. To his ears these 5 songs represented the best, or at least stand-outs, of the 15 songs he heard when the band had auditioned for him at their rehearsal loft. These were the songs which had reached a certain level of maturity with both their arrangements and execution, though Eddie wasn't exactly blown away with the band musically. According to Eddie, "they weren't really good musicians at all in those days, as good as a unit they became, but certainly in the early stages Ace really impressed me. Ace was the sound of KISS, more so that the others. He lent a certain over-the-edge, over-the-top kind of feel" ("KISS This" fanzine, 1/94). It is apparent that the songs they chose to record were the core KISS songs to that point (and some might argue even to this day), within the limitations of the studio time they had available: "Deuce," "Strutter," "Black Diamond," "Watchin' You," and "Cold Gin."

Three of the songs on the demo had been performed live at the band's debut concert, and it is likely that the others had also been in sets at the few shows played between January 31 and March 13, when the demo was completed (KAF). Since the band had played shows at the Daisy on March 9-10, it would seem most likely that the demo was recorded from Sunday March 11 to Tuesday March 13, however the gaps in KISS' show schedule leave open the possibility that the demo was recorded during February or early March, with the finished reel being completed (mixing) on the 13th. Regardless, KISS performed a 15 song private showcase for Eddie Kramer at some point prior to his agreeing to engineer their demo. Also present at this showcase were Ron Johnsen and his wife Joyce. Ron recalled, "When the band started to play, we all had to put cotton in our ears because it was so unbelievably loud. Joyce ended up passing out; she just collapsed and fell right down on the floor" (KISStory).

Lew Linet, who had managed Gene and Paul in Wicked Lester, was still nominally involved with the band during the early part of 1973, though by all accounts he didn't have much faith in the image or music the band were pursuing (having been a folk festival organizer one couldn't go much further away from that style than KISS were moving). He recalled, "They would rehearse on 23rd Street in the city and I realized that two hours out of their three-hour rehearsals were being spent sitting there with crayons and face paint. I still think they're a few on the nicest guys I ever met, but I really wasn't into that type of thing." J.F. Murphy & Salt (signed with Elektra in 1972) had been one of his earlier clients so he simply called one of the clubs where they had performed when he couldn't get the band any bookings locally (Behind The Mask - The New York scene was purportedly limited by the number of clubs where bands could play original material). The Daisy, a club located in Amityville, Long Island, became the second venue where KISS played. Owned by Sid Benjamin, Gene described the club concisely: "It was a drinking club, with cheap beer and a biker crowd. It was the kind of place where you might see a pregnant woman with a drink in one hand and a cigarette in the other. It didn't matter to us what the places were like or how big the crowds were" (KISS & Make-up). According to Paul, it "was no bigger than a living room. We played for 60 people who thought we were out of our minds. They came back the next night to see if we were really what they remembered. We'd sit in the office answering the phone: 'There's an amazing band called KISS playing tonight — you've got to see them'" (Faces Metal Muscle #1, Spring 1986)!

Sid took Lew's advice and hired the band without an audition. From early on in their career KISS were willing to do whatever it took to get people to come to their shows and hype themselves. By the time KISS played the Daisy, the evolution of the makeup had continued. By early March Ace was simply using his silver eye design without the rest of the white facial makeup. Paul would still be very glammed out with more facial rouge and eye-liner. During the early phase of experimentation the band used zinc-oxide cream which was easily available from pharmacies, though later they'd use clown white by Stein or Max Factor. As shown in Lydia Criss' famous photograph of the band with Sid at the Daisy (KISStory p. 26) Gene and Peter are using the full white face designs which are approaching their final form. Sid's daughter Patti had worked with Gene refining his design and incorporating a widow's peak (the V-shaped design pointing down from the center of the forehead). Only Paul remained the New York "doll," heavy on the rouge. The Daisy was the real proving ground for the band through June 1973 where they performed their originals and determined what they'd be as a live act.

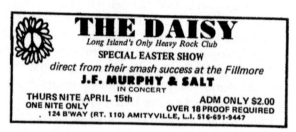

As part of defining themselves the band were determined to do whatever was necessary to find success. The sent out fake press-releases to try and garner interest, due in part to their existence on the periphery of a music scene. Playing the Daisy the band also answered the club's phone and hyped themselves on the unsuspecting callers. The press-releases campaign did ultimately work. According to Sean Delaney, "Gene had sent us a phony press release and press packet. Listing all the places they had been playing and reviews of their performances. All were bogus. I remember laughing and telling Bill, 'if they have gone to this extent to get our attentions, let's go see them'. And we did" (JG). As the year progressed the band started to play shows with other bands, returning to the city from their provincial development excursion. In order to gain a fan base KISS needed to expand their audience so in May 1973 they played a gig opening for Queen Elizabeth (which featured Wayne/Jayne County) and The Brats at the Brat's 8th floor Bleecker Street Loft (rented by bassist David Leeds) in Greenwich Village. These shows at the loft were more organized parties that the Brats hosted on a regular basis. Nothing about the loft was impressive. It was bare, with white-washed walls and uncovered floors, with industrial equipment from its day use installed. While the two bands only appeared on three bills together the final of these (July 13) was the first "Rock And Roll Ball" showcase KISS had put together.

The Brats were one step ahead of KISS at the time, having played their debut gig at the Hotel Diplomat, opening for the New York Dolls, on March 16, 1973. With connections to the Dolls and Alice Cooper they were part of the more legitimate glam scene and benefited from resources KISS lacked (though they still played clubs such as the Coventry and the Mercer Arts Center). Part of this was a result of the band having some "names" involved in the group. The Brats had formed in 1972 by guitarist Rick Rivets. He had, more importantly, co-founded the New York Dolls with Johnny Thunders and Arthur Kane in 1971. After leaving the Dolls in February 1972, being replaced by Sylvain Sylvain, Rick started looking to put a new band together. The Brats contained similar elements to the Dolls and in general to the glam scene of the early 1970's with their platform shoes. For a short time in early

1973 the band's lineup included Ron Blanchard on guitar, though he soon left to form the band Rags (this band would also play with KISS opening for them at their final shows at the Coventry in December 1973). The band would add Anton Timps on lead guitar during the summer of 1973 but his initial tenure in the band would last just over a year. In contrast with KISS, the Brats played a mix of originals and covers at the time.

> Meanwhile, **Ron Johnsen** has been producing and engineering a flurry of sessions there, beginning sometime back with work on the **Bloontz** LP with engineer **Bernie Kirsh,** for Evolution. That project has been succeeded by Johnsen's sessions with **Kiss, Mr. Gee Whiz** (for Dick James) and **Huberlux,** another James date. Also completed there: **Lynn Christopher's** album, produced for Paramount Records by Johnsen.
>
> The Lady has also been involved in **Flipside,** the 13-program television series produced by **Marks-Aucion** (that being Howard Marks and Gui Aucion) **Productions** via Subsid Directions Plus. Aucion will direct and produce, Marks will serve as executive producer and **Joyce Biawitz** is associate producer.

(First known mention of the band in the U.S. national press... Two paragraphs, such a confluence of names that would become so important to the band. Billboard, Apr. 7, 1973)

Wayne County, on the other hand, was the transsexual (later Jayne County) lead singer of the punk band Queen Elizabeth. Wayne was part of the Max's Kansas City scene and also played other gigs with the Dolls. Gene recalled one of the early gigs, "We played with The Brats and Wayne County in The Loft, 52 Bleecker Street. We were not the headliners, we were third on the bill. And I'd have to say, without being too humble about it, that we chewed them up and spit them out — although we didn't know it at the time. And we just came out and we came off like a British band, like Sabbath meets The Who meets something, I don't know what. And it wasn't planned. It was just that those songs were in us. And we were not even aware that we looked different. It's like the makeup, we never think about it. And then afterwards we saw photos of us and we looked at them and said, 'wow, we thought they looked weird, look at us!' We looked like we just landed from Mars. And we had the platforms then too. March '73" (KISS PR, 1/28/93). The whole way the band operated, even at this early stage of their career, set them apart from their peers. Other material was gradually added to the band's repertoire during the year including "Strutter," "Let Me Know," "Acrobat," and "100,000 Years." Some of these songs are listed on the reel recording displayed in KISStory from a show at the Daisy which included "Firehouse," "Life In The Woods," "Simple Type," "Acrobat," "Deuce," "100,000 Years," and "Black Diamond." The date of the recording has caused some confusion, but it is now believed to have been recorded in June (KAF) due to some of Paul's stage commentaries.

During the year the band underwent a visual evolution as their makeup designs developed into more fully realized forms. By March 1973 Gene, Peter, and Ace would have their basic make-up designs in place, though they'd still be performing in street clothes. By the late Spring Paul had finally added his "star" design and the costumes were coming together. He'd initially try the design out using Maybelline waterproof eyeliner, though "it would crack because it's only meant to draw a line around your eye, not a star" (Guitar World Legends #14). Gene would usually play in a black T-shirt, either with a KISS logo or skull and cross-bones design, with black leatherette pants. He'd sometimes use a black biker jacket. Ace would also play with a black KISS T-shirt though also had a black custom shirt with a gold spread eagle-wings design sewn on the front. During the final club shows of December 1973 he'd wear a black T-shirt with "ACE" designed in sequins. Paul, when he kept a shirt on would often wear a black T-shirt, though also wore a biker jacket with the pants he'd made for himself. Peter would dress for comfort often wearing basic loose tops (black tank tops), later with blue jean shorts over black tights. One of the bands on stage at the Coventry that December night was named Flaming Youth, which later provided some inspiration for a KISS anthem...

In the calendar year of 1973 KISS performed just 25 gigs, starting in a club and culminating as making their industry debut as the unlisted opening act on the bill of a major act at the Academy of Music. They solidified a core catalog of material that launched their sound on the world and forged the foundations of their live performance and stage choreography that would carry through much of their career. Those first gigs are detailed below...

(In very small print, a humble beginning, introducing... KISS!)

January 30, 1973 - Popcorn Pub/Coventry, Queens, New York City, NY
Promoter: Paul Sub
Other act(s): None.
Reported audience: ~10 / 700
Set list: (Early Set) Deuce / Watchin' You / Love Her All I Can / She / Simple Type / Keep Me Waiting / Want You Beside Me / Baby, Let Me Go / Firehouse / Black Diamond
(Late Set) Deuce / Love Her All I Can / She / Want You Beside Me / Simple Type / Keep Me Waiting / Baby, Let Me Go / Watchin' You
Notes:
- According to legend, KISS had been booked into their first show while still called Wicked Lester.
- The Coventry, located at 47-03 Queens Boulevard, in the Sunnyside area of Queens, was something of a glam haven for bands playing original material — bands that often couldn't get gigs elsewhere were nearly guaranteed a slot. Other better known acts playing at this club included the New York Dolls, Dictators, and Brats.
- The club, known as "Popcorn Pub" was changing its name to "The Coventry." It was a central venue to the New York glitter scene outside of the better known Max's/Mercer Arts venues. There were few pretenses about the joint. Bands showed up and played no-frills rock 'n' roll. "The Popcorn Pub is a mere Frisbee fling into Queens, situated in a neighborhood that seems to consist mostly of wrestling arenas, cut-rate appliance stores, and used car lots. Originally an Irish dancehall and more recently a greaser bar (the jukebox stocks the Platters' 'Only You' and Frank Sinatra right alongside the Stones' 'Bitch'), the Popcorn has now been taken over by Betty Smyth, former operator of the Village Gaslight and a familiar figure on the Village folk scene for close to a decade. Larger and more comfortable than the Gaslight, the room has much better acoustics and the added bonus of a free-flowing liquor license" (Village Voice, 9/14/72).
- Essentially, no one came to the show other than girlfriends, wives, friends, and original roadies Eddie Solan, Joey Criscuola, Bobby McAdams, and the bar staff who had to be present.
- The band was not wearing their full trademark make-up yet...

January 31 - Coventry, Queens, New York City, NY
Promoter: Paul Sub
Other act(s): None.
Reported audience: (700 capacity)
Set list: Unknown.

February 1 - Coventry, Queens, New York City, NY
Promoter: Paul Sub
Other act(s): None.
Reported audience: (700 capacity)
Set list: Unknown.
Notes:
- After a not particularly encouraging beginning, KISS won't play again for over a month. Instead the band concentrates on rehearsing and refining their material. And working!
- In the interim Peter quits the band; but soon returns. The band's image starts to develop...

March 9 - The Daisy, Amityville, Long Island, NY
Promoter: Sid Benjamin
Other act(s): None.
Reported audience: ~80
Set list: Unknown.
Notes:
- KISS got the gigs at The Daisy, located at 124 Broadway (Route 110), as a result of owner Sid Benjamin doing their former Wicked Lester and then current KISS manager, Lew Linet, a favor. He gave the band a slot without the benefit of an audition. Billy Joel (with his early band Attila) and the Stray Cats were other well-known bands to play the club.
- Lew had other bands that played at the Daisy and since KISS couldn't get any gigs in the city they needed to look further afield to hone their performance skills.
- The venue "was no bigger than a living room," (Metal Muscle #1, Spring 1986) according to Paul, but the beer was 35c. Crowds were generally well under 100 and the band used Sid's office to hype their performances to people calling in.
- During their time playing the Daisy the band's make-up and stage show started developing.

March 10 - The Daisy, Amityville, Long Island, NY
Promoter: Sid Benjamin
Other act(s): None.
Reported audience: ~150
Set list: Unknown.
Notes:
- At one of these shows Lydia Criss took the famous photograph of the band posing backstage with the club owner.
- Following this second group of shows KISS hit the Electric Lady Studios (completed March 13) to record their 5 song demo featuring "Deuce," "Cold Gin," "Strutter," "Watchin' You," and "Black Diamond," engineered by Eddie Kramer.
- In the April 7 edition of Billboard Magazine KISS receive what is probably their first ever national press mention - in a column that also mentions future managers Bill Aucoin, Joyce Biawitz, and business manager Howard Marks.

April 13 - The Daisy, Amityville, Long Island, NY
April 14 - The Daisy, Amityville, Long Island, NY
Promoter: Sid Benjamin
Other act(s): None.
Reported audience: Unknown.
Set list: Unknown.

Notes:
- By the time these shows were advertized, the flyers included the infamous photo of the band posing with club owner Sid.
- This photo shows Gene and Peter in full white face, with the beginnings of their "Bat Demon" and "Cat" designs. Ace's face is more powered, but his basic silver design is more developed than the other two. Paul is still sporting a heavy drag look with eyeliner, rouge, and lipstick; even though he'd experimented with full white-face while the band were still a trio in the privacy of their rehearsal space.
- There are still no costumes...

(Two ads from the "Village Voice")

May 4 - 54 Bleecker Street Loft, New York City, NY

Promoter: The Brats
Other bands: Queen Elizabeth (HL), The Brats
Reported audience: ~300
Set list: Unknown.
Notes:
- This show marked the first time KISS played on a "bill" with other acts. They agreed to play for free and even supplied the sound system. The Brats had been formed by New York Dolls founding member Rick Rivets in 1972 after he left that band.
- The 8th floor loft was The Brat's rehearsal space and they advertized the shows on a BYOB (Bring Your Own Booze) basis with $1 admission. The performance space was directly on the floor of the factory with a rope used to separate the audience from the performers.

- Engineer/producer Eddie Kramer reportedly attended this show; as did many members of bands from the New York music scene of the time. The show was reviewed in the Village Voice, but there was no mention of KISS' set, only "A man in a cowboy hat makes a last-minute adjustment on the tripod of his half-inch video camera" (5/31/73). If only, though in all likelihood he would have been filming Wayne's set...

May 26 - Lamont Hall, Sneaden's Landing, Palisades, NY
Promoter: RA Johnsen, Inc.
Other act(s): Bloontz, Pat Rebillot Quintet
Reported audience: ~200
Set list: Unknown.
Notes:
- This was a Library benefit show organized by Ron Johnsen at a venue in near the town of Orangetown in Rockland County (on the boarder of New Jersey). The benefit raised around $1,500
- Members of Bloontz, and Pat Rebillot, had also performed on Lyn Christopher's album.
- Eric Troyer, who later appeared on Gene's solo album, attended this event.

June 1 - 54 Bleecker Street Loft, New York City, NY
Promoter: The Brats
Other bands: The Brats (HL)
Set list: Unknown.
Notes:
- All four members of KISS now sport their facial make-up designs, though throughout the rest of the pre-Aucoin shows Paul would sometimes revert back to "Dolls" face. Gene's "Demon" eyes have grown and are developing while both Peter and Ace are close to their final forms, though Ace is still light on the clown white.
- Costumes are somewhat developing: Ace has his "eagle" shirt, Paul wears a black T-shirt with KISS logo in sequins, and Gene has a skull & crossbones black T-shirt. Peter's wearing gold hot pants...

June 6 - Dynamic Studios, New York City, NY **REHEARSAL
Notes:
- KISS booked some studio time to rehearse new songs for the set. Hopefully a tape-recorder was running...

June 8 - The Daisy, Amityville, Long Island, NY
June 9 - The Daisy, Amityville, Long Island, NY
Promoter: Sid Benjamin
Set list: Unknown.
Notes:
- Since KISS had rehearsed new material prior to these shows it seems likely that some new songs were added to the set. Which those songs may have been is currently unknown.
- From a local review: "At first no one out here [Ed. Long Island] knew what to make of KISS. Now no one thinks about it. They just do it. Wall-to-wall fans... Noted on the wall of the ladies room: 'We love Ace'" (Fred Kirby, Variety, 6/12/73).
- In the June 9 issue of Billboard Magazine there is a more potent foreshadowing of the future for KISS: Neil Bogart, Bill Aucoin, Joyce Biawitz and Howard Marks mug for the

camera following Neil's appearance on Bill's "Flipside" television series. The stars are starting to align...

June 15 - The Daisy, Amityville, Long Island, NY
Promoter: Sid Benjamin
Set list: Unknown.

June 16 - The Daisy, Amityville, Long Island, NY
Promoter: Sid Benjamin
Set list: (Early Set) Nothin' to Lose / Firehouse / Life in the Woods / Simple Type / Acrobat / Deuce / 100,000 Years / Black Diamond
(Partial Late Set) Strutter / Watchin' You / Sunday Driver
Notes:
- Recorded and mixed by Eddie Solon on a nine-channel 27 input Peavey Sound System. In KISStory the date 8/25/73 is attributed, though the authors of "KISS Alive Forever" suggest that the date is incorrect; due to one of Paul's raps mentioning Father's Day (which would have fallen on 6/17/73).
- This and the partially surviving second set are probably the earliest surviving KISS live audio recordings. Only "Acrobat" has been released from this show, on the 2001 Box Set, the rest of the SBD recording leaked on 12/21/2013.

July 13 - Crystal Ballroom @ Hotel Diplomat, Manhattan, New York City, NY
Promoter: KISS/Brats
Other act(s): The Brats (HL), Planets (opener)
Reported audience: ~450/1,000
Set list: Unknown.
Notes:
- The Hotel Diplomat was located at 108 West 43rd Street and had previously been a clubhouse of the Benevolent & Protective Order of Elks NY Lodge #1. By the 1960s concerts started being hosted at the venue's ballroom, and by the early 1970s acts performing there included Teenage Lust, Uncle Buck, New York Dolls, Jackie Curtis, Shaker, Satan, Magic Tramps, Harlots of 42nd Street, and the Brats. In other words, many bands from the glitter scene that KISS were on the periphery of. More importantly, perhaps, both Gene and Ace had attended Dolls gigs at the Diplomat (Barney Hoskyns, Glam! Bowie, Bolan and the Glitter Rock Revolution). That made it the perfect venue for them.
- The three bands funded the show 40/40/20 and agreed to split the proceeds by the same ratio at the end of the night with one representative from each band to supervise collection of admissions. Paul rented the venue for a fee of $450.
- The band used this show as a showcase for prospective talent scouts selectively invited. They were dressed in all-black (tops at least), each wearing their make-up designs.
- The Planets included guitarist Binky Phillips who later helped Gene record demos such as "Rotten to the Core."

(Three further ads from the Village Voice)

August 10 - Crystal Ballroom @ Hotel Diplomat, Manhattan, New York City, NY
Promoter: KISS
Other act(s): Street Punk, Luger
Set list: Unknown.
Notes:
- KISS meets their future manager Bill Aucoin at this second "showcase" show.
- From a local review: "From the plethora of Gotham glitter-rock acts, comes KISS, who already outshine most of the others in clean, pulsating rock and roll, high in volume and excitement. Facial makeup is more weird than fey. Set momentum is unrelenting and solid. Although all tackle vocals, lead usually falls to bass guitarist Gene Simmons, most ghoulish in appearance. Heavy black makeup around his eyes and white on rest of face is bat-like. His mugging is a theatrical plus, as is his vocal ability. Paul Stanley, who shares lead guitar with Ace Frehley, also usually shares vocals, but all four aid in that department. Drummer Peter Criss even makes screaming fun for the outfit. While Simmons is the most extreme visually, all have some kind of mask effect around their eyes and satiny garb. Simmons removes a black jacket to reveal a black T-shirt with silvery skull and cross-bones. But it's in the music that KISS catches hold and never let's go. They are the only headliners in the irregular show policy of this midtown hotel (HOTEL DIPLOMAT) who have drawn good crowds, indicating KISS is building a local following" (Fred Kirby, Variety, 8/22/73).
- In 1973 Street Punk included Donnie Nossov (Bass), Nicky Martin (Guitar), Jon Montgomery (Vocals), Charlie Davidman (Drums), though the band fell apart before they could take the next step. Jon put a new version of the band together the following year when he was recruited as a vocalist for a band that included Phillip Brown (Guitar), Steve Fitzgerald (Drums), and Jimmy Haslip on bass. That last player's name should set off alarm bells for his work with pre-KISS Bruce Kulick and session work on a 1982 KISS album.

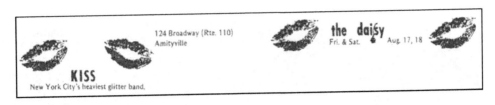

August 17 - The Daisy, Amityville, Long Island, NY
August 18 - The Daisy, Amityville, Long Island, NY
Promoter: Sid Benjamin
Set list: Unknown.

August 24 - The Daisy, Amityville, Long Island, NY
August 25 - The Daisy, Amityville, Long Island, NY
Promoter: Sid Benjamin
Set list: Deuce / Cold Gin / She / Love Her All I Can / Nothin' to Lose / Watchin' You / Let Me Know / Black Diamond / Acrobat / Strutter / 100,000 Years / Simple Type / Baby, Let Me Go
Notes:
- It's really not clear when (or even if) this set was performed. It comes from a Paul Stanley set/rap list sold at the 2001 Butterfields auction, but would have likely fallen in the June-August period since it still included Wicked Lester material.
- It is arbitrarily placed on this date, since it really doesn't compare with the known set list from June where the band was playing two shorter nightly sets. It is possible, that the list was simply a "plan" for a night's single set and was never used...

August 31 - Coventry, Queens, New York City
September 1 - Coventry, Queens, New York City, NY
September 2 - Coventry, Queens, New York City, NY **CANCELLED
Promoter: Paul Sub
Other act(s): Wild Honey & The Dogs
Reported audience: Unknown
Notes:
- These shows marked KISS' final pre-Aucoin commitments. The final show didn't take place, possibly because of a scheduling conflict with a Jerry Lewis Labor Day telethon benefit event (see ad below).
- The August 31 date was the first show that Peter "Moose" Oreckinto worked with the band.
- From a mainstream review: "KISS is a four-piece glitter-rock group whose music is characteristically loud, loud, loud, and whose members look like Lance Loud on a nightmarish bender. Glitter-rock has to be considered as theatre first and music second. The music is fairly simple, some songs don't use more than two chords, but that's okay if they're the right chords. The show is more complex..." (Stanley Mises, New York Sunday News, 9/16/73).

September 2? - 23rd Street Rehearsal Loft, New York City, NY **REHEARSAL

Set list: Strutter / Firehouse / Watchin' You / Let Me Know / Life in the Woods / Acrobat
Notes:
- As noted in KISS Magazine #2 ("Into the Vault by Jeff Suhs), the band recorded one of their rehearsals, probably for their then forthcoming showcase. Some stage banter during the recording suggests that Richie Wise may have been in attendance.
- This recording leaked via Japanese bootleg Zodiac in 2014.

September 2? - LeTang Studios, Manhattan, New York City, NY **SHOWCASE

Reported audience: <40
Partial set list: Life in the Woods / Firehouse
Notes:
- This was a private showcase conducted for Neil Bogart, producers Kenny Kerner and Richie Wise, and members of the press. Other record executives and one Sean Delaney were also present...
- Henry LeTang was a noted choreographer who had a studio in Manhattan which was rented for the occasion.
- Band members went into the audience and made them clap during "Life in the Woods" and used the fire-pail confetti gimmick at the end of the final song.

September 24 - Bell Sound Studios, New York City, NY **STUDIO LIVE SESSION
September 25 - Bell Sound Studios, New York City, NY **STUDIO LIVE SESSION

Songs recorded: Let Me Know / Nothin' to Lose / Acrobat / Firehouse / 100,000 Years / Baby, Let Me Go
Other songs possibly recorded: She / Love Her All I Can / Simple Type / Keep Me Waiting / Life in the Woods / Strutter / Deuce / Black Diamond / Go Now / Watchin' You / Cold Gin
Notes:
- The Bell Sound demos were essentially a quick and dirty recording of KISS' then song catalog done live in the studio, during a two day period. Studio time was booked in two four-hour blocks between 1-5:00PM daily. The songs retained their original live arrangements.
- The purpose of the recording was to provide producers Kenny Kerner and Richie Wise an overall idea of the band's material for consideration and selection of what would be recorded for the debut album.
- Four songs of the six known surviving recorded tracks were released on KISS' "Box Set" (2001), the rest is pure conjecture of what is known to have been in the band's sets at the time and may or may not have been recorded. It is included here since it is essential a live recording, albeit in a studio.

October 28 - Club Nowhere, Brooklyn, New York City, New York **INFINITY

Notes:

- Not KISS, but Peter Criss. This date/venue marked his final non-KISS gig. He had performed more non-KISS shows throughout 1973 than KISS had, mainly with his 50's "greasers" band Infinity. That band included buddy Joey Lucenti (who had also been in Sounds of Soul) and Tommy Dimitri.

October 31 - Coventry, Queens, New York City, NY **RUMORED SHOW

Notes:

- This show is suggested by some to have occurred. However, it dates around the time that the band were entering the studios to record their debut and must be considered erroneous. An ad in Village Voice for that night (see above) indicates that Isis was playing the club.

December 21 - Coventry, Queens, New York City, NY

Promoter: Paul Sub

Other act(s): ISIS, Rags (opener), City Slicker (opener)

Reported audience: 300

Partial set list: Deuce / Cold Gin (incomplete)

Notes:

- As an article in Creem succinctly stated: "Now, Coventry features the Brats, KISS, and Teenage Lust off and on, with a string of mediocre Queens bands on the off-nights." This December 1973 article by Dave Marsh provided an excellent view of the then current glitter scene in New York City. He was somewhat more mixed in describing the band: "This group looks as if it just stepped out of the underground movie Pink Flamingos, leading me to believe that I was right all along in thinking that the glitter craze was an ugliness contest. But KISS' music sounds as if it is the most thought-out, controlled sound around, and the stage show is just as professional" (Creem, 12/73).

- While this show was also videoed, like the 12/22 gig, only 7:22 worth of two songs has survived on the tape; these have yet to be released. A few frames of the overwritten tape show the unmasked band rehearsing ("Into the Vault by Jeff Suhs), though not enough to provide a moving image (the below is a composite of 5 frames).

- Guitarist, Ron Blanchard, had been a member of the Brats in early 1973 but left to form Rags with vocalist Joe St. John, Joe Valentine (guitars), Steve Fraser (bass), and Don De La Pena (drums).

December 22 - Coventry, Queens, New York City, NY

Promoter: Paul Sub

Other act(s): ISIS, Rags (opener), City Slicker (opener)

Reported audience: 300

Set list: Deuce / Cold Gin / Nothin' to Lose / Strutter / Firehouse / Let Me Know / 100,000 Years / Black Diamond / Baby, Let Me Go

Notes:

- Finishing where they started, KISS' last gig in the clubs — until 1988. Gene breathes fire, though it was long rumored that he hadn't done so in the clubs!
- Performance filmed and recorded by Aucoin and released on KISSology VOL. III, though it was only recorded to ensure that the stage show was ready for the Academy of Music gig. The "KISSology Vol. 1" DVD "Easter Egg" suggests that the performance of "Deuce" is from this show, but it's from the following night's show and lacks the "In Concert" info bit prior to the band's introduction.
- It was long known that the band had filmed their final club shows, though the recordings didn't surface until 2004; at which time Bill Aucoin registered the copyright of the video!
- Like the 12/31 "Academy of Music" show, "100,000 Years" still includes the fourth verse.
- By 1975 the Dolls were still playing the Coventry. So was Cyndi Lauper, as a member of Doc West, cutting her teeth performing in the same way KISS had, while the glam/glitter movement died out. KISS, of course by that time, was moving up in the world...

December 23 - Coventry, Queens, New York City, NY **CANCELLED

Promoter: Paul Sub

Other act(s): ISIS, Rags (opener), City Slicker (opener)

Notes:

- This final club show was cancelled. The debate remains about who was the headlining act for these shows, not that it's ultimately important in a club. Both ISIS and KISS claim the honors...

December 31 - Academy of Music, New York City, NY

Promoter: Howard Stein

Other act(s): Blue Oyster Cult, Iggy Pop, Teenage Lust

Reported audience: ~3,000

Reported gross: $22,000

Set list: Deuce / Cold Gin / Nothin' to Lose / Firehouse / Let Me Know / 100,000 Years / Black Diamond

Notes:

- This show was KISS' professional industry debut (for which they earned $250) and marked the first occasion they performed with their iconic 4x10' lighted "KISS" logo. The logo was a surprise gift from manager Bill Aucoin designed and built by Mark Ravitz. This was also the last time that Eddie Solan ran the band's soundboard. In a 1979 interview Gene recalled this show: "We only had 30 minutes of time, but all that I know is that we had that killer instinct. We wanted to chew up and spit out every band out there! The kids went nuts and it's pretty much the same now. We're out there to kill" (Knight Rider News Wire, 1979). The main acts played two shows, one at 8PM the second at 11:30. KISS was only invited to perform at the first.

- "100,000 Years" still featured the original arrangement retaining the later discarded 4th verse. "Baby, Let Me Go" was on also the set list, but not performed. From their club debut in January 1973 both "Deuce" and "Black Diamond" retained their respective set opening and closing positions.

- Gene set his hair on fire, though it wasn't his first public fire-breathing attempt as had been long rumored. According to one contemporary review of the New Year's Eve show, it "almost proved disastrous as the hair of bass guitarists/lead vocalist Gene Simmons, weirdest in make-up, caught fire. A roadie quickly covered it without a note being missed" (Kirby, Fred - Variety, 1/2/74). He also injured a patron in the audience with his flash paper routine.

(So far down the bill to not merit a mention in the show ad, the professional debut of KISS!)

- The band were even mentioned in a mainstream media review of the show: "After a fiery opening set by KISS (an "American Black Sabbath" on Neil Bogart's new Casablanca label) and the ribald antics of Teenage Lust, the Stooges assaulted the audience with wave upon wave of material from Raw Power" (Rolling Stone #153, Jan. 1974, Gordon Fletcher). It was at least a mention of the band's name. Melody Maker US correspondent, Chris Charlesworth, also covered the show: "KISS dress in costumes from the classic American comic books; bat uniforms to be precise. The bass player wears bats' wings and all four are caked in make-up: to say they were disciples of the devil would not be an understatement. The music is both loud and heavy; pretty simple, riff based rock and roll with a very steady funky beat to it. Variation of mood is not their forte, although what they play is effective enough. There are no hitches apart from a mike that fails midway through the set. The climax to their act is brash and spectacular and not a little borrowed from Arthur Brown. The closing number, 'Firehouse,' I think, ends with clouds of dry ice puffing from amps, flashing lights all round them and a display of fire-eating by the bass player. He even chucks a few loose flames out in the general direction of the audience and one fiery mass appears to land on an unfortunate youth's head. He's carried out holding his face in his hands but few seem to notice." (Melody Maker, 1/12/74).

- From a trade review: "KISS, the first group signed to former Buddah maven Neil Bogart's new Casablanca, are a local glitter band which has more or less adopted the glitter to cash in on the current fad. A huge neon sign of their logo served as a backdrop for their set, which most closely approximated the style of Black Sabbath several years ago with little of the style, imagination, or volume of that group... Hopefully Bogart has teamed them with a good producer because they definitely need something more than paint" (Performance Magazine).

- Photos, shot by Bob Gruen, at the show were featured in a "KISS at Midnight" feature in the June 1974 "Rock Scene" magazine issue.

- The sound quality of the circulating AUD recording is generally poor though slightly less generated (or more "processed" copies seem to crop up regularly).

January 8, 1974 - Village East, New York City, NY
Promoter: Casablanca Records/Warner Bros. Records
Other act(s): None.
Reported audience: Unknown.
Set list: Unknown.
Notes:

- In preparation for touring, and to refine their stage show and presentation, Neil Bogart rented the closed former Fillmore East venue, then formerly owned by Bill Graham, where the band rehearsed throughout Dec/Jan. Located at 105 Second Avenue at East 6th Street in Manhattan, the Fillmore East had witnessed its final paying audience on June 27, 1971.

- This show was a more of a showcase for the press and booking agents including members of other bands and member's parents. Johnny Winter, Alicen (sic) Steele, and Scott Muni were name-dropped on the invite as possibly attending. However, people were also invited in off the streets to see the band to provide a more appealing audience for the band to perform to. Also invited was one J.R. Smalling, who was being courted to work with the band as they prepared to head out on the road. He joined Peter "Moose" Oreckinto and Sean Delaney who formed the core of the original road crew.

- The band only played for around 20 minutes, but it was one of two shows Paul performed wearing his alternate "bandit" makeup design.

- The showcase was mentioned in Rolling Stone #154, including the picture of Neil Bogart in make-up chained to the KISS contract: "Neil Bogart, ex-co-head of Buddah, has signed a couple of acts to his new Casablanca label: the Parliaments and KISS. The latter did a special dress rehearsal at Fillmore East January 8th for agents and some press. The four KISSers play very heavy, loud and ultimate monotonous rock in the Black Sabbath tradition; they wear sheet-white make-up and black leather and studs. Midway through their act, dry ice overtakes the stage and the bassist flashes a flaming torch in the air. And they finish in a rain of firecrackers. A sure crowd-pleaser. For crowds of kiddies, that is..."

January 26 - Academy of Music, New York City, NY
Promoter: Howard Stein
Other act(s): Fleetwood Mac (HL), Silverhead (opener)
Reported audience: ~3,400
Set list: Unknown.
Notes:
- Less than a month following their industry debut, KISS were back in action for their first proper gig of the year. Paul's make-up design is still in flux and this is the second and final show he played wearing the "bandit" design. This time they earned $750 for what Paul described as "one more small-scale tune-up show" (Face The Music).
- This show is more notable for the "Fleetwood Mac" in question being the "New" band featuring Elmer Gantry, Kirby Gregory, Paul Martinez, John Wilkinson, and Craig Collinge — not names easily recognizable when thinking "Fleetwood Mac." Drummer Mick Fleetwood had purportedly quit the band the week before the tour commenced, though in the press the manager made it clear that he owned the rights to the band's name.
- British band Silverhead, fronted by Michael Des Barres, was booed heartily by a generally blues-oriented crowd. They were at the tail end of their career with bassist Nigel Harrison later hooking up with Blondie and Des Barres forming Detective (and touring with KISS). In the New York Times review (3/28/74) of the show KISS didn't gain any mention, though it was noted that Silverhead was forced to extend their set to 90 minutes. Hours later, a few members of Fleetwood took to the stage and played an instrumental set without their singer (he'd come down with laryngitis). That is, what little audience hadn't accepted the promoter's offer of a refund and already gone home.
- From a mainstream review (which ignored completely Fleetwood Mac): "KISS, a native New York group about to embark on the concert circuit after playing local bars for over a year, opened the show. Their set proved to be a lot more ear shattering than it was earth shattering. Wearing black leather and studs, and white theatrical make-up, they rely heavily on visual effects but the shock value of their act does little to compensate for the lack of musicianship. Their set climaxed with the drummer soaring high above the stage on a hidden hydraulic life while synchronized magnesium flares are ignited and the bassist arches a flaming torch in the air" (Billboard, 2/9/74). They say that any press is good press!

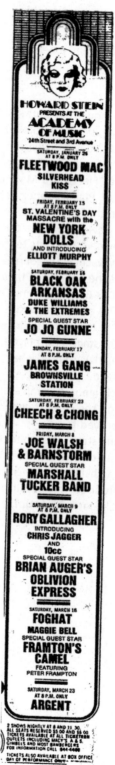

(So many suspects in one ad! How many of these bands would KISS perform with over the next year?)

First KISS

For KISS, the transition between club and touring band took place rapidly. Following their final performances at the Coventry in December 1973 they wouldn't return to club environments until 1988 and essentially hit the road as a professional touring act. They'd performed just 24 club shows during the previous year. While there were a couple of additional shows, between the band's industry debut on New Year's Eve '73/74 and commencing touring activities in early Feb. 1974, these don't really qualify as being part of a scheduled tour — those shows are included at the end of the "Club Era" section and include the January 8 showcase at the briefly re-opened Village East (formerly Fillmore East), at which the band had been rehearsing since December; and a return visit to the Academy Of Music on January 26. The band signing with the booking agency American Touring International (ATI) on February 1 coincides nicely as a marker separating the periods. Following the conclusion of the club era, it's somewhat surprising that KISS's first tour proper didn't even take place in the United States; or anywhere near to their home base of New York City. Instead, they headed to the great white north, Canada, departing New York City on February 3. This activity indicates the ethos with which the band would tour for the rest of the year: Have gig? Will travel! Simply put, the band was willing to do anything to get themselves in front of an audience.

While only comprised of three shows over four nights these dates do qualify as a proper tour, even if KISS were only filling in for another act. The Canadian dates were also an important opportunity to road test the whole act, from crew to band to stage-show. KISS urban legend as this short Canadian tour as being the result of the Mike Quatro Jam Band cancelling dates. According to Paul, "They needed a last minute replacement for Mike Quatro, Suzi Quatro's brother. Three shows, three cities. The first night in Edmonton was OK, but then we were booked into high school cafeterias. Our road crew took the lunchroom tables and gaffer-taped them together. That was our stage" (The Star, 9/14/13). It should be noted that Mike had performed in Ottawa on Feb. 2, opening for Crowbar for an audience of 4,000, so it was more likely a case of his cherry-picking more financially appealing dates. Whatever the case, bringing talent to Canada was a challenge in early 1974. Whether it was the 10% "amusement" tax on gross receipts hitting promoters, or the acts themselves being reticent to travel north, many shows were announced, rescheduled, reformatted and then often cancelled with less than acceptable excuses. Winnipeg, as a market, seemed to fall victim to this more than other cities losing acts such as the Stooges ("faulty equipment"), Nazareth and Status Quo (Francis Rossi "was felled by a bout with pleurisy") in the period surrounding KISS's visit — fans were desperate for international entertainment, or simply entertainment that showed up on schedule! Whatever the case for KISS, it was an opportunity, though one that occurred during a period of extremely poor weather, particularly in Manitoba.

Gene has suggested that the band were undertaking a grueling touring schedule in early 1974, commenting, "Our touring schedule was so intense that by the time we got to the West Coast, we were doing five or six shows a week" ("KISSology" liner notes). That, unfortunately, is not entirely accurate. Actually, it's not accurate at all... Following the final

Canadian show in Winnipeg, on Feb. 8, the band's next scheduled date would be opening for Rory Gallagher and the "new" Fleetwood Mac in Long Beach on Feb. 17. While travel and rehearsals were certainly part of the interim period, the band weren't yet doing what Gene has suggested. The California date, though, was the band's first appearance on the U.S. West Coast as Neil Bogart and Casablanca Records put down the label's roots at 1112 N. Sherbourne Drive in Los Angeles. The Californian visit was more about rehearsals and the filming of the band's appearance for Dick Clark's "In Concert" television show. The opening slot in Long Beach and even the brief showcase at Casablanca's "coming out" party at the Century Plaza Hotel were negligible in relation to the exposure that the band hoped to gain from a major national television appearance. It was an absolute coup for the band at that stage of their career. Other than aborted participation in Richard Nader's Music World Expo Seventy trade fair at Madison Square Garden in early March, the band simply prepared to hit the road properly.

Hitting the road was no easy task, as the band's earliest itinerary demonstrates. From the first show, opening for Redbone on Mar. 22, the band opened for Argent the following night, and then Aerosmith the next. While the differing headliners were a result of the vagaries of touring, with acts flipping shows and venues; and as band members have succinctly explained they were simply getting gigs wherever they were available during this period. It was "estimated that when the band first "began the group was spending $6,000 – $7,000 a week. As the tour progressed expenses increased to $7,000 – $8,500 per week" (Billboard, 5/21/77). KISS needed to be on the road working! A fourth consecutive show was a headlining two set stand at the Bayou in Washington DC, famed as one of the band's earliest shows recorded fully from the audience. While in Washington the band filmed what would have been their second TV appearance for the WDCA channel 20 "Barry Richards' Rock 'N' Soul" show. Barry had hosted several "free-form" shows in the region, though sadly many of the tapes from the shows are missing or degraded. It's not known what KISS performed, or whether it was live or lip-synced — some of the performances from his "Turn-On" show were live, and as some of the performances on his 2006 DVD attest, he often married up acts with interesting partnerships (the Byrds backing Fats Domino or Zephyr backing Little Richard). While not including KISS, the DVD does give one the sense of the show's format and Barry's style, and features some incredible performances by the likes of Rory Gallagher and the Bob Seger System for fans of music from the era. As is obviously the case with any early KISS video, the prospect of anything remaining from their taping is enticing (even a screen capture)!

The band was back in the larger club venues by Mar. 29 opening for Renaissance in Asbury Park, NJ. This hodge-podge of dates was simply a reactive holding-pattern, generally considered a result of Argent, with whom the band had planned on touring, delaying many of the dates at the beginning of their itinerary. The announcement of Russ Ballard leaving the group following the conclusion of the tour may have been a contributing factor — he'd decided to quit during the prior U.K. leg. Equally possible for the delay were changes at American Talent International (ATI), KISS' booking agency, who had pruned their talent roster in March, dropping 25 of their 65 active acts. ATI executive vice president Ira Blacker explained the change, "It wasn't done in terms of marketability. It's the maturation of an organization, a relatively young one, to the point where we are no longer looking for those lesser acts... [The change would] further benefit the remaining acts and give even more attention to this smaller and more select group" (Billboard, 3/16/74). Getting KISS on that agency should be considered another coup with them being unproven as a commodity at that point. According to Bogart, "Casablanca spent a lot of money to introduce them to its present agency, ATI. Judging them only on their tape performance, ATI booked them across the U.S." (Billboard, 5/21/77). An additional factor to be considered in the period was the international energy crisis which certainly had a negative impact on tours. With the oil embargo being lifted in March 1974 many markets were still impacted and recovery was a slow process with Sunday gas sales remaining suspended throughout the year. While the overall impact was greater in Europe, it was still of concern in the U.S. Whatever the case, the band were on the road, and participated in KSHE's 1974 "Kite Fly" in St. Louis on Mar. 31. The associated concert likely saw the band performing to their largest ever U.S. audience for many years, estimated anywhere between 40,000 – 105,000 attendees, before having even conducted a fully scheduled tour of the country!

The band followed this appearance with a three-show stretch opening for Irish blues guitarist Rory Gallagher (check out the previously mentioned Barry Richards' DVD for a great representation of Rory from the period). Better known for his live performances (his 1974 album was "Irish Tour '74," a live release) the contrast between he and his opening act was stark. At the first show, in Cleveland, OH, on April 1, both bands sets were recorded by venue radio partner WMMS for their "Nights Out At The Agora" broadcast, though only Rory's aired. For many years KISS' set was assumed to have not been recorded or to have been lost, though it has surfaced in recent years — albeit in a butchered form with most of the integral stage raps removed. Regardless, it's another pre-FM recording for fans to enjoy from the band's earliest era and the sonics of the show are absolutely outstanding, as is the performance. Unfortunately, following an incident in which Peter was left unconscious in a cloud of smoke from the band's show climax; he was briefly hospitalized forcing the cancellation of the following night's gig in Toledo.

Back on the tour in Columbus, OH on April 3, that night's show was more about the severe weather conditions affecting the region. Tornados had already hit Cincinnati, and parts of Akron were under threat of flooding. Additional tornado watches were issued in many places. The April 3 show is more memorable for occurring soon after a F5 tornado had ripped through nearby Xenia (in between Columbus and Cincinnati) causing considerable destruction and 35 deaths and hundreds of injuries. Stormy and unstable weather continued throughout the evening and KISS's performance was interrupted by a power-outage. One patron recalled Gene taking candles from the on-stage candelabra and handing them to audience members in what must have been a surreal and somewhat demonic scene! Following what had essentially been a stable period of shows, the band's itinerary becomes rather bumpy. An April 4 show with Badfinger in Warren, OH was cancelled. The circumstances are not entirely clear and this date might fall into the "temp hold date" category. Also on the itinerary was a headlining April 6 show in Fort Wayne, IN. This show did not take place with an April 5 show by Genesis being moved from the Embassy Theatre to the National Guard Armory that KISS had planned to use.

The March KSHE-AM "Kite Fly," Barry Richards' show, and more importantly, the national ABC "In Concert" broadcast were indicative of Casablanca's initial strategy for attempting to break the band to a wider audience during this period. It was more about fast-tracking the band's development and getting them in front of the largest audiences possible; rather than going the slow-burn route of touring and working the band up the entertainment food-chain. With such a visually unique image and outrageous live presentation a subtle approach was probably pointless. While a broadcast of "Nights Out At The Agora" had failed, Casablanca worked with or manipulated other appearances, such as the "Kite-In and Balloon Fly" in Detroit on April 7. As KISS's second show with Aerosmith headlining, the event received plenty of regional press coverage; unfortunately mostly negative due to the weather impacting the outdoor component of the event and poor attendee behavior providing a focus. Again, it was important to the band that there was a radio broadcast of the show due to the broader audience they could gain in lieu of radio play of material from the album. The same was the case for the show at Muther's Music Emporium in Nashville on April 15. It is likely that this show was broadcast on local radio as part of WMAK-AM station's "Coyote Concert" series, or that it had initially been scheduled as such, with DJ "Coyote" McCloud hosting the show.

The third of the early radio broadcasts took place on April 18 when the band's Memphis appearance aired locally on the club's radio partner WMC FM-100. The band's second major national TV broadcast was filmed in Philadelphia on April 24, for the Mike Douglas Show, which included the infamous interview with Gene during which he unsuccessfully attempted to go head to head with seasoned comedienne Totie Fields. Paul recalled, "This, however, did not look like fun. This wasn't an audience I thought I could win over, and I had no desire to go out and get ridiculed... Gene went out. He didn't know what to say and described himself as 'evil incarnate' and stuck out his tongue. Totie... dismissed him as a nice Jewish boy, despite the demon get-up. He came off pretty goofy" ("Face The Music"). The appearance was uncomfortable and Totie was merciless with the inexperienced Gene. It is a great opportunity to see a band member such as Gene before he had mastered the skills on that side of the trade, even if his naivety and awkwardness is uncomfortable.

The broadcast also provides a great opportunity to see the evolution of the KISS costumes, with Ace having discarded his simple leather top with the more artistic inverted-V shell with decorative fringe and thick decorative belt. Paul, too, now features a silver-lapelled (and cuffs) leather jacket with starts on the arms. Gene's plain black t-shirt is replaced with a skull t-shirt under the bat-wings, though he is now sprouting shoulder-horns. Months earlier, on ABC's "In Concert," Paul's leather jacket was plain leather, with a few barely noticeable studs, while Ace's plain leather top was enhanced with a lightning bolt across the chest. His thin decorative belt could have been stolen from Steven Tyler's closet. On the road the band was changing, continuing to revise and enhance their appearance and that of the stage set — it would essentially remain based on the same elements until the "Destroyer" tour. The lighted KISS logo would be placed wherever it could safely fit, sometimes hung behind the band and others to either side of the stage. The obligatory fire-engine lights were central to that song's performance. The backline of Marshall Amplifiers was a mix of working models and shells to give the appearance of more equipment than the band actually had. Probably the most important gimmick was the chain-link driven drum riser used for the show's culmination. The drum platform was bordered with a metallic-colored tassel fringe.

The Mike Douglas Show also featured the Florida kissing contest winners and served to promote the then forthcoming national event. If any promotional effort stands out for the first KISS tour then the Warner Bros. sponsored "kissing contests" drew the most national press throughout the April − June period. Co-sponsored by local radio station WSHE in

Florida, the "Great Fort Lauderdale Beach Smoochathon" kicked off on April 21, with 40 pairs of contestants vying for an all expenses paid trip to Toronto to see KISS, gift cards, travelers' checks, and four free years of hairstyling. After 76 hours only 4 pairs of contestants remained, with Vinnie Toro and Louise Heath ultimately winning (with a duration of 96 1/2 hours). The success of the concept surprised Warner regional marketing manager Mike Gilreath who had initially thought that couples wouldn't last more than a day. While the initial inspiration for the contest had come from Warner Bros., Casablanca persuaded them to expand the format and take it national with the regional champs all competing for a grand prize in a national "KISS off." WMAK DJ Scott Shannon in Nashville recommended the band record a cover of "Kissin' Time," a 1959 hit for Bobby Rydell, which they re-wrote mentioning many of the participating cities in the lyrics. The 12 major-market regional contests kicked-off on May 11 with many top-40 local radio promoters combining the events with fund-raisers for various charities.

The national finals of the "KISS-OFF" began at the Woodfield Shopping Center in Schaumburg, IL on June 8 (originally it had been scheduled for the Memorial Day weekend). The band attended a press-conference at the beginning of the event and signed autographs. Playboy bunnies were expected to be on hand to sell kisses for charity along with appearances by other guests including Jan Murray and Joel Gray. Seven couples remained after the first day, and just four were still in the running by Tuesday. When the contest reached 100 hours just two couples remained, though ultimately a Florida couple Louise Heath and Vinnie Toro, boosted by their use of yoga, were declared winners after 114 hours. Their record didn't last long and was toppled later that month in Fresno, CA... Toro and Heath cashed in their grand prize for a $1,000 equivalent to help friends who had lost their home to fire — an action that had helped persuade the contest's runner-up couple to concede. By the end of the contest, some $5,400 had been raised for charity. It was this promotion that contributed to the band becoming known as the "hype of the year" for 1974, and while it didn't translate into a hit single it did expand airplay in large markets and at least get the word out about the band.

Even as the promotions kicked off, the band continued touring. On the road KISS incorporated the new song into the set during the period, one of the few "holy grails" remaining to surface in some format. A long-delayed opening slot for Argent finally kicked off on May 2, in Grand Rapids, MI, though the band were thrown off the tour the following night after their performance in St. Louis (allegedly for playing encores for which they had been forbidden). With a week off, gigs in smaller venues were lined up to keep the band working, but the band hooked up with Savoy Brown and Silverhead by May 12, for a couple of shows, prior to Manfred Mann replacing Silverhead. The bands toured together through Canada and the West Coast with Savoy Brown and KISS heading up to Alaska for two shows in early June. This time is more notable for Savoy Brown running into trouble in Lethbridge for trashing their hotel room, rather than anything of particular note occurring for KISS. Reports of the audience booing the headliners after witnessing KISS's set might help explain Savoy's post-show mood. Other highlights from this period include the band receiving their classic Patrick MacDonald review in Seattle and having their set broadcast in Long Beach on May 31. Their show at San Francisco's Winterland the following day was also likely filmed, but was presumably "lost" over the years. Shows in Flint, Cleveland and Toronto with fellow glamsters, the New York Dolls, followed before the band returned to a holding pattern with some smaller headlining shows; culminating with a four-night stand at Alex Cooley's Electric Ballroom in Atlanta in late June.

Following the Atlanta run the band cancelled two weeks' worth of shows to allow Paul to recover from health issues. By July 11 the band he had recovered and the band hooked up with Blue Oyster Cult to continue touring activities, travelling through southern states through the end of the month. Towards the end of the month, the band took the opportunity to hit the studio to record some demos for the next studio album, which was scheduled to be recorded during August. At the recently upgraded Minot Sound Studios in White Plains they laid down versions of "Mainline," "Parasite," "All The Way," and "Who's Your Baby," all of which would be released on "Hotter Than Hell." While Paul has suggested that much of the material for the sophomore album was written while the band were in Los Angeles recording the album, which clearly was not the case (as this session proves) there was most certainly material written or finished there. Other material was being considered for the album and had been in the band's live set for some time, notably "She" and "Baby, Let Me Go." Both songs were present in the last known tour recording, prior to the "Hotter than Hell" studio break, in South Bend, IN on August 3. It is also during the July demo session period that another major mystery remains. The band's travel itinerary shows them travelling to Charlotte, NC on July 20, and staying overnight, and then staying the following night in Glen Burnie, MD. No shows have been discovered as occurring in either of these locations, so it may simply be a case that the band returned to New York to rehearse for the demo session. Or there are two mystery shows...

Around the recording of "Hotter than Hell," the band still had touring activities that fall more within the context of the "First Tour" (since the second album hadn't been released). Most notable of these dates is the band's appearance in London, Ontario on July 25. This show marked the first of many times that Canadian rockers Rush opened for KISS. It was also the only performance of that band with KISS where their lineup still included original drummer John Rutsey — it was also one of his very last appearances with the band. As soon as recording was completed the band was back on the road, picking up where they had left off — with a brace of shows in Canada. A final pair of dates with Blue Oyster Cult followed, before the band returned to the Electric Ballroom for another four-night stand. A show in St. Louis, opening for Steppenwolf, was cancelled when the band were banned from using their effects. I final series of shows took the band from Detroit to Houston where the tour ultimately concluded on Oct. 4. Interesting in this period is the band opening for Billy Preston in Evansville and having their influence, Roy Wood, open for them in Detroit. Most unfortunately, no set lists are known from this final run of dates. The band would have less than two weeks break before touring in support of the next album commenced...

The first KISS tour may have been a bit of a hodge-podge of varying strings of shows cobbled together, but it would be impossible to not consider the period a major success for the band. Considering their status — as a new band they essentially had none and were on the ground-floor of their professional development — they were the direct beneficiaries of Neil Bogart's connections within the industry, Bill Aucoin's determination, a road crew's loyalty and no small amount of luck. With two major national TV and multiple radio broadcasts they successfully transmitted their image, name and music to a wider audience, even if the result wasn't a massive sales level for the first album. Exposure was everything, and the KISS-a-thon received impressive national press coverage, even if many of the local reviews of their appearances were less than stellar. They likely could not have had a better start to their career, though for the rest of 1974 the road would become more bumpy due to matters beyond the band's control...

February 5 - Dinwoodie Lounge @ University of Alberta, Edmonton, AB, Canada
Promoter: Scenemaker Productions
Other act(s): Barbarossa
Reported audience: 135 / 620 (21.77%)
Notes:
- KISS's first concert outside of the United States, even before their debut album had even been released. Procol Harum had recorded their seminal album, "Procol Harum Live in Concert with the Edmonton Symphony Orchestra" at this venue in 1971.
- Peter's drum-levitating effect was not used for these Canadian dates due to logistical issues. The band, along with Sean Delaney, Cris "Antman" Griffin, J.R. Smalling, Peter "Moose" Oreckinto and Bill Aucoin, flew to Edmonton via Toronto.
- While in Edmonton KISS record radio IDs for CHED-630 during an early morning interview at the station. This may well have been the band's first radio appearance.
- Gene recalled this show as the location of his first groupie experience: "I had my first authentic groupie, a girl with green hair... She didn't know who KISS was. We were just a rock band. I grabbed her, and she spent the night with me. I was in heaven. This girl was spending the night with me just because I was in a band" ("KISS & Make-Up"). He'd also acknowledge her on his 1978 solo album credits list, the first of many...
- The promoter only sold 46 tickets for the show — the rest of the audience was non-paying complimentary guests ("Nothin' to Lose").

February 6 - Jubilee Auditorium, Southern Alberta Institute of Technology, Calgary, AB, Canada
Promoter: Scenemaker Productions
Other act(s): Barbarossa
Reported audience: 161 / 800 (20.13%)
Notes:
- During the drive from Calgary to Winnipeg "Antman" accidentally drives the equipment truck into a snow-filled ditch during a blizzard... They have to wait until the following morning to be towed out, but ultimately make it to the next show.
- Photographer and SAIT photojournalism instructor Frank Shufletoski took some incredible photos at this show.

February 8 - Taché Hall @ University Of Manitoba, Winnipeg, MB, Canada
Promoter: UOM/Frank Wiepert (Program Director)
Other act(s): Mood Jga Jga (opener)
Reported audience: ~1,100
Partial set list: Firehouse
Notes:
- A free concert part of the University's "Festival of Life and Learning."
- From local press: "The big action this week, of course, is on the University of Manitoba campus today until Friday. Dozens of great films, many guest speakers, exhibits and displays and music of all sorts will be featured from morning until midnight. Don't forget the special concert Friday evening featuring KISS, a New York glitter band which has been winning raves around the United States" (Winnipeg Free Press, 2/6/74). Amusing since the band hadn't played outside of New York until this mini-Canadian tour! Mood Jga Jga was a Canadian acid/folk/jazz rock band that included former Guess Who guitarist Greg Leskiw.

- From a college news paper report: "It's pretty easy to be a rock star. You don't need talent. Just money" (The Manitoban, 2/11/74)...
- After each song a heckler in the audience demanded that the band play some rock 'n' roll. Paul eventually retorted, "What do you think this is? Opera?" Another audience member threw cans at stage: "The objects missed their mark... but somehow caused one of the group's roadies to tip over a container of kerosene. If during the course of the show you happened to notice someone scurrying around trying to wipe up a number of wet spots on the stage" (Winnipeg Free Press, 2/13/74)...
- From a local review: "As for KISS, the group turned out to be the original heavy metal kids, as a jam-packed crowd observed. The group's repertoire consisted entirely of original metal rockers, with influences ranging from Silverhead and MC5 to, on occasion, even Black Sabbath. The band utilized a number of visual effects, most notably smoke bombs and dry ice on a song called 'Firehouse.' There were flashing lights and a special drum platform attached to a hydraulic lift which elevated the drummer and his entire kit some five feet into the air during the final number of the evening. The entire group, which has been classified as one of New York City's heaviest, appeared onstage in whiteface, which seemed to shock many in the crowd. As could be expected, most of those in attendance sat on their hands for the majority of the show, but since when is that newsworthy" (Winnipeg Free Press, 2/11/74)?
- One of KISS' early roadies Eric Weinstein, who worked at this gig, went on to roadie for the Dictators.

February 17 - Civic Auditorium, Long Beach, CA
Promoter: Pacific Presentations
Other act(s): Rory Gallagher (HL) & Fleetwood Mac
Reported audience: 4,000 **SOLD-OUT
Reported gross: $22,000
Notes:
- From a local review: "Fleetwood Mac has sacrificed artistic pursuits in search of big bucks. The 'New' Fleetwood Mac — that is, minus Mick Fleetwood and his entire band — has taken to the concert trail with a catalog of mediocre versions of compositions by other groups. That concert trek led to Long Beach Sunday night with the Mac's disputable new sound with Elmer Gantry, lead singer, Kirby, on guitar, Paul Martinez, bass, John Wilkinson, piano and Craig Collinge, drums. The near-capacity crowd was subjected to irrelevant selections, sadly lacking in spontaneity. I felt the inexperienced Fleetwood Mac was filling in a time slot instead of entertaining. The first group, KISS, far out-distanced the top-billed Mac, with an offering of hard-pounding rock and roll. If they lacked polish, they made up for it with an energetic approach to their music. They're young and a group worth watching. Booking Fleetwood Mac's new sound between solid rockers like KISS and Rory Gallagher was like inserting a dead spot into a storm" (Long Beach Press-Telegram, 2/19/74).
- Other attendee reports from the show indicate that KISS was solidly booed off stage by the partisan crowd who wanted Rory and Rory only! Unfortunately, his mic blew out during his set forcing him to end the set with an extended instrumental. Paul recalled the challenge faced by the band in the early days: "We had a lot to prove, and we took a lot of abuse and an opening act for people like Rory Gallagher and those purist blues bands. We'd come out on stage, and all hell would break loose. People would be laughing at us and shouting very unfriendly things" (Lakeland Ledger, 9/9/79)...

- The 8mm footage once attributed to this date has since been determined to have more likely been from the April 13 show in Detroit.
- One paper reported an audience of 8,000, the figure above comes from Performance Magazine.

February 18 - Los Angeles Room @ Century Plaza Hotel, Los Angeles, CA
Promoter: Casablanca Records/Warner Bros. Records
Reported audience: 200+
Notes:
- Casablanca's official West Coast opening included a 20-minute showcase set by KISS and dress/decoration by Gibson & Stromberg with the theme "A Night in Morocco" with the requisite parallels to the movie "Casablanca" including prop camels.
- From trade press: Bogart "is introducing Casablanca's idea of lavish fun to the West Coast music community Monday (18). A hotel ballroom is to be transformed into Rick's Cafe, from the classic 'Casablanca' film as guests are greeted by doubles of Humphrey Bogart and Dooley ('As Time Goes By') Wilson. The bash also serves to introduce the label's latest artists, 'KISS,' a New York hard rock group that performs in painted facial make-up and has a levitating drum set plus a lead singer who does fire-eating between vocals" (Billboard, 3/2/74).
- Guests included Alice Cooper, who made his famous, "All these guys need is a gimmick," quip. Others include Iggy Pop, Alison Steele, Hugh Masakela, Artie Wayne, Cecil Holmes, Allan Rinde (CBS Records) and Dick Clark.
- From a trade review: "Just when things were getting really good, the roulette wheels ground to a halt and KISS took the stage. This group represents an evolutionary cul-de-sac in the realm of glitter sadism groups. The makeup is truly incredible. As for the music, it literally shook the room — people at our table were yelling 'louder! louder!' — and for the grand finale, the drummer's platform levitated. Whether the group itself, and the label, will get off the ground equally, well we'll undoubtedly know as time goes by" (Performance Magazine).
- From a mainstream review: "Casablanca Records' party for glitter-rocking KISS and celebration of the new Neil Bogart label's L.A. arrival turned the Century Plaza ballroom into a replica of 'Rick's Cafe' from the classic 'Casablanca' film. Guests got $1,000 of fake money to play at the gaming tables and the night's biggest winner got the original prop 'Maltese falcon' (Billboard, 3/2/74). The party was also mentioned in Rolling Stone #157, with a brief mention concerning the band: "...It would have been quite a pleasant interlude were it not for the performance of KISS, a rock band with the dubious distinction of being Casablanca's first signing. The KISS set was brief, and, mercifully, they did not play it again" (Rolling Stone, 3/28/74).

February 20 - SIR Studio C, Hollywood, CA **REHEARSAL
Notes:
- The band had a scheduled 5 hour rehearsal, presumably in preparation for the following day's TV filming.

February 21 - Aquarius Theater, Los Angeles, CA **TV FILIMING
Promoter: Dick Clark Productions / ABC Television
Dick Clark's "In Concert" TV filming
Set list: Deuce / Nothin' to Lose / Firehouse / Black Diamond

Notes:
- There really isn't much to say about this TV performance, which most KISS fans will have seen repeatedly. Regardless, it's a very important part of KISStory, regardless of how many times it's been seen before as the band's first national television appearance. "In Concert" was a late Friday night broadcast that ran 1972-75 featuring multiple genres of musical acts. Other guests on the episode (#30) included Foghat, Melissa Manchester, Redbone (see 3/22/74 concert), and Kool & the Gang.
- The short set had long circulated unofficially, with the exception of "Deuce," which at this point is assumed to have been lost. First broadcast on March 29, 1974, the set was officially released on the "KISSology Vol. 1" DVD in 2006.

Major Houk: Campaign of '74: Inside look at the Detroit Tigers training camp to see the team's new manager, Ralph Houk; 8:30 p.m. 4.

CBS Reports: A hard look at America's institutions of higher learning; 10 p.m. 2.

Wide World of Entertainment: Kiss, a rock group known for its stylized makeup and onstage theatrics, performs at 11:30 p.m. on 7. (One member is shown.)

Kiss Member

(An early promo photo provided to the press — One example of its use from the Detroit Free Press, 3/29/74).

March 1 – 3 - Madison Square Garden, New York City, NY **CANCELLED
Promoter: Richard Nader / Happy Medium Shows, Inc.
Notes:
- KISS was booked to appear at the Music World Expo Seventy which would have been an "all industry, consumer-oriented" trade fair. Plans for the event dated back to the autumn of 1973: "Nader plans to have a small theater available during the event. Each record company would be allotted so many hours of programming. 'They can check the audience response to new talent'" (Billboard, 9/15/73). It's not clear on which date KISS would have been scheduled to perform on, but 5 shows per day were planned during the event.
- More interesting, was the prospect of an "audio-visual" tape of KISS planned to be shown at Casablanca's exhibit. Nader's "Real Rock Productions" were interested in videocassette and video disk market emergence something that may have dove-tailed nicely with Neil Bogart and Bill Aucoin's media interests. Direction Plus had mooted a related scheme in

January, "A program to place filmed mini-concerts featuring top recording acts in upwards of 7,000 movie theaters throughout the U.S... The music shorts, from 10 to 15 minutes in length, will be geared to tie-in with major national advertising accounts working through MPA [Motion Picture Advertising]... Along with the promotional mileage for the artists involved, participating labels will get a courtesy credit tag at the end of the film. Consideration is also being given to 'possible' retail tags, said Biawitz. The national advertisers will have two 60-second spots, one at the film's opening and one at its end. Discussing the film itself, Biawitz stated that the format will be 'flexible' and will incorporate taped 'live' performances, as well as interviews and background information on the artist. She also noted that plans call for the eventual showing of anywhere from three to six different films at any one time" (Billboard, 1/26/74).

March 22 - Valley Forge Music Fair, Devon, PA
Promoter: Music Fairs, Inc.
Other act(s): Redbone (HL)
Reported audience: (2,800 capacity)
Notes:
- There has been the suggestion that Argent may have been on this bill, perhaps due to the lineup for the following night's show. It is not beyond the realm of possibility, even with Argent performing at the late night show at the Tower Theater in Upper Darby, PA (with Soft Machine) just 13 miles away, on the same night. A review from that show indicates: "The late starting time grew later because of difficulties in the sound system, but the packed house at the Tower voiced little opposition to the wait... Rod Argent said the group had come to this country to perform at the Academy of Music in New York (Bucks County Courier Times, 3/24/74). Could the "difficulties in the sound system" be indicative of some challenge resulting from moving the band's equipment from Devon to Upper Darby in time for the midnight show? We may never know, though it doesn't seem likely...
- Print ads for the Devon show only list Redbone, "A hard-driving group which grinds out its music with a soul-ish feeling. A group which has been in existence for the past couple years, and receiving acclaim from its outset, Redbone never leaves the audience wanting" (Bucks County Courier Times, 3/19/74). Furthermore, the Californian/Native American rock/fusion band was scheduled to have played 7pm and 10:30pm sets, so it is possible that if KISS did play this date (it is on an itinerary from the period) that they also played two opening sets.
- Redbone was also later featured on the same episode of Dick Clark's "In Concert" with KISS...

March 23 - Academy of Music, New York City, NY
Promoter: Howard Stein
Other act(s): Argent (HL), Redbone
Reported audience: (3,400 capacity)
Notes:
- This early show was first advertized in the final third of January, though initially only with Argent noted. Nazareth cancelled several weeks prior to the show (ads noted such as early as the first week of March), but had appeared in advance print ads, as had Graham Central Station in place of Redbone. KISS wasn't mentioned in ads until Mar. 14. Argent had recently arrived from the U.K. leg of their "Nexus" tour.
- A second concert was held at the venue starting at midnight with Renaissance, Soft Machine, and Eleventh House (featuring Larry Coryell).

- From a local review: "Rock groups do not travel light, and six of them — heavily amplified and some decked out with special equipment — caused jams backstage and delays out front at the Academy of Music on East 14th Street on Saturday night and well into Sunday, thus giving their audience an eight-hour composite of the state of the art.

But if rock groups take their time setting up, rock audiences don't let it bother them. An hour's wait between two performing groups aroused mere sporadic clapping of hands. An 80-minute delay in the start of the second concert elicited barely any criticism, and the appearance of the final group, Renaissance, at 4:25 a.m. yesterday was greeted with as much enthusiasm as the opener, KISS, at 8:20 p.m. Saturday. All this bears out the theory that a basic-rock-music audience sees itself as much an event as what happens on stage. KISS (dressed midway between kabuki players and Spiderman) let loose sirens, fireballs, dry ice fumes, smoke bombs, and as a climax a drummer with full gear ascended 8 feet on a special platform. This was all sound and fury, signifying yet another plastic and empty rock quartet" (New York Times, 3/25/74).

March 24 - DAR Constitution Hall, Washington, D.C. **KISS CANCELLED
Promoter: Dick Klotzman
Other act(s): Argent (HL)
Notes:
- This show was cancelled with enough notice for KISS to get the opening slot for Aerosmith's Baltimore show. It is not known whether this show went ahead with a different opening act or was nothing more than a temp hold date (it doesn't appear to have been

advertized locally). Percy Faith was advertized as performing at the venue in the afternoon, which theoretically could have left it available for an evening concert booking. There has been the suggestion that a tour with KISS opening for Savoy Brown and Argent was scheduled to commence on Mar. 26, 1974, but was cancelled due to Argent experiencing U.S. work clearances. That explanation seems odd, in terms of the known timeline for the bands involved, with Argent having successfully worked in the U.S. for a Mar. 22 show at the Tower Theatre in Tower Theater in Upper Darby, PA with Soft Machine, and the Mar. 23 Academy of Music show at which KISS opened. These two dates are beyond doubt, though could well have been contingencies and/or replacements for the cancelled tour provided by their booking agent, ATI.

There are certainly issues which could have affected a prospective tour. Savoy Brown had been scheduled to tour with Deep Purple from early February (8th). However, that run of dates was postponed due to an unspecified "illness." Instead, the shows were rescheduled — starting in early March and running through Apr. 9. With tickets for the original dates having gone on sale in the first half of December 1973 there was an overall plan for the British band's touring activities. It seems likely that it was intended that Savoy Brown complete their run with Deep Purple by the end of February, sometimes after which they would have toured with Argent; and possibly KISS. As far as Argent were concerned, with the release of their "Nexus" album, they first toured the U.K. (with the John Verity Band), from Jan. 31 through Mar. 14. That left a week gap for preparation and travel to the U.S. for the two confirmed shows. Followed by which they could have scheduled an additional run of shows.

March 24 - Painter's Mill Music Fair, Owings Mill (Baltimore), MD
Promoter: Key Productions
Other act(s): Aerosmith (HL), Redbone
Reported audience: (2,400 capacity)
Notes:
- This show may well have been mentioned in the European Stars & Stripes piece: "In Baltimore, the KISS combo warmed up its audience with its spectacular fire act by almost setting the hall aflame, with fans shouting for more" (4/20/74). Peter also later recalled a show in Baltimore that went amiss: "Baltimore — we played in Baltimore. And the people dug it so much when Gene spit the fire, then lit a part of the place, started burning it" (UPI, 4/75). Whatever the case, it became a foundation for legend that the band themselves enjoyed telling, with Paul recounting, "We were playing a number and suddenly there's a fire in the balcony. Kids gathered around it and were chanting like at a ceremonial magic rite — they'd started it" (NME, 2/1/75). Ironically, the theater did eventually burn down... in 1991, when burglars used an acetylene torch to break into the venue and open a safe.
- KISS became the opening act for this show when Badfinger purportedly pulled out and Aerosmith was promoted to the headliner slot. However, it should be noted that Badfinger had already performed at Painter's Mill on March 1 (a bootleg of that performance circulates), and had also just completed a run of dates at Alex Cooley's Electric Ballroom in Atlanta, GA on the evening of March 23. They instead performed in Little Rock, AR on March 24, allowing them an additional day for the 1000+ miles travel/rest prior their next scheduled show: The Bayou in Georgetown, DC on March 26; the day following KISS's performances at the same venue! KISS appeared in a tiny mention on Badfinger's Mar. 26 concert flyer for that venue. Interestingly, at the end of 1974 Badfinger entered the studio

to record what would become their final album with singer/guitarist Pete Ham. KISS's producers, Kenny Kerner and Richie Wise, were engaged for the project though it ultimately remained unreleased until 2000 following his April 1975 death.

- Joe Perry recounted watching KISS at this show in the "Behind the Mask" book (2003).

March 25 - Bayou Theater, Georgetown, Washington, D.C. **Two shows
Promoter: Barry Richards
Other act(s): None.
Reported audience: (~500 capacity)
Set list: (Early show) Unknown
(Late show) Deuce / Strutter / She / Firehouse / Acrobat / Let Me Know / Black Diamond / Baby, Let Me Go
Notes:
- KISS played two sets this night, at 8:30 and 10:30PM, the latter of which circulates as a reasonable AUD recording. The Bayou was an unglamorous hole-in-the-wall club that looked more like an "unfinished basement" according to one 1974 patron.
- From a local review: "KISS assaulted the Bayou last night. This group is not just uncomfortably loud, it is abusively loud, and the only possible explanation is that they have invested their money in aspirin stock. KISS's loudness is only half their blatant plan of attack. The other half involves what some people would call rock theater. It is patently less offensive that the electric pandemonium which masks the good rock and roll potential of the band... The band's stylized movements are very much akin to the orchestrated steps of club bands in the '60s. It just looks different, because the costumes and the themes of the songs reflect the sexual ambivalence of the '70s. Musically, KISS is better than some similar bands. That's like telling a gourmet that bread and water is better than stale bread and water" (The Washington Star-News, 3/26/74). Peter Criss was featured in the sole live photo accompanying the review.
- Random venue facts: U2 played their second ever U.S. show (12/7/80) and Guns 'N' Roses filmed their "Welcome To The Jungle" video (The Washington Times, 12/31/98) at the venue. U.S. personality "Mr. T" also worked there as a bouncer.

March 26 - Arena, Winnipeg, MB, Canada **KISS CANCELLED
Promoter: Jerry Shore / Joel Brandes / Bruce Rathbone
Other act(s): Savoy Brown (HL), Fleetwood Mac, Argent, Kathy Dalton (opener)
Reported audience: ~5,500
Notes:
- There has been some suggestion that this March 26 date involved KISS in some way, forming part of Argent's delayed U.S. tour (due to the date that appears on Gene's hand-written touring log in KISStory). It seems somewhat questionable, since the show was initially announced as an "all-British package" (Winnipeg Free Press, 1/19/74) with Savoy headlining in January. However, the show soon ran into problems, though when the tickets went on sale on Feb. 10, the acts remained the same (Winnipeg Free Press, 2/6/74 — which also included a brief single line mention of KISS's Feb. 8 show). By Feb. 18 Fleetwood Mac had been nationally unmasked by Rolling Stone magazine, as a "fake" touring entity that included none of the expected members; the promoters approached ATI to confirm whether Mick Fleetwood remained a member (their requirement for a booking of the band to stand). By Mar. 2, only Savoy Brown remained from the original bill, with Blue Oyster Cult, Captain Beyond and Hawkwind replacing the other three acts. By the following week

Flash Cadillac and The Continental Kids and Tucky Buzzard had replaced the two opening acts. When the show did take place, Tucky Buzzard (who were also on tour with Deep Purple and Savoy Brown at the time) didn't appear, but both Blue Oyster Cult and Flash Cadillac did. The point, not a single press mention of KISS in relation to this show throughout the two months of drama.

March 27 - Duluth, MN **CANCELLED
Other act(s): Savoy Brown (HL), Argent
Notes:
- Another date that appears on Gene's hand-written touring log in KISStory that did not take place. The 430 miles from the previous show would not have been much fun for the crew, but was not insurmountable in terms of routing logistics. However, the band remained in the Washington area for the filming of their Barry Richards Show appearance.

March 27 - WDCA-TV Studio, Washington, D.C. **TV FILMING
Promoter: WDCA TV
Barry Richards Show
Notes:
- While the set or song performed at this 6pm taping is unknown, KISS filmed an appearance for Barry Richards' WDCA local television show "Rock 'N Soul," which usually aired Saturday nights at 9:30 p.m. It is likely that the performance was lip-synched ("KISS Alive Forever") and could have been broadcast as early as Mar. 31. That night's guest was advertized as Alice Cooper, so it would have been too perfect a coincidence in terms of the band being paired with one of their inspirations; though it could simply have been a re-broadcast of earlier material filmed for Barry's "Turn On" show. The Apr. 5 show featured Badfinger who had been taped at Thomas Jefferson High School gym in Frederick, MD on Feb. 24.

March 29 - Sunshine In Concert Hall, Asbury Park, NJ
Promoter: Friendship Productions
Other act(s): Renaissance (HL), Truth
Reported audience: 2,000 **SOLD-OUT
Notes:
- Scheduled opener 10CC had the flu and had returned to England. Later, 10CC's absence was explained simply as the band "did not show up" (Asbury Park Press, 6/19/74). Local, and essentially the house band, Truth, replaced them on the bill. KISS performed first. During this period agent Herbert Fleischer was booking fictitious shows at the venue. He'd eventually be charged with 13 counts of fraud for fake shows involving acts such as J. Geils Band, Blue Oyster Cult, Sha Na Na, Edgar Winter and Wishbone Ash (pleading guilty in Sept. 1976). Fleischer was ultimately evicted from the premises in January 1975.
- From a local review: "Last night Sunshine In opened its 1974 season with a sellout crowd and a better-than-average show... Glitter rock is rapidly becoming the most sought after rock genre in the music business today. Fist it was Alice Cooper and David Bowie. Now there is KISS with its penetrating theatrics, wall-to-wall amps, and its comic book-like facial makeup. The music they play is basic rock 'n' roll with a definite emphasis on loudness. They probably could make it as a straight forward rock group but the additional stage show makes the act much more explosive and potent. One of their most rousing numbers, 'Firehouse,' features clouds of dense smoke, fire engine sirens and red lights revolving

above the amps, and flame-throwing flares which exploded on stage at the peak of the performance. All this is done in a professional manner but it took much of the concentration away from their music" (Asbury Park Evening Press, 3/30/74).
- After their performance the members of the band unsuccessfully attempted to watch the broadcast of their first television performance. Unfortunately a storm made it nearly unwatchable.

March 29 - Winterland, San Francisco, CA **CANCELLED
March 30 - Winterland, San Francisco, CA **CANCELLED
Promoter: Bill Graham Presents
Notes:
- These shows were replaced by concerts by the Eagles, Cold Blood and Journey (29th) and Black Oak Arkansas, Jo Jo Gunne and Journey (30th).
- These dates, plus Spokane, WA (4/1), Fresno, CA (4/4), Portland, OR (4/5), Seattle, WA (4/6), Memphis, TN (4/12) and Little Rock, AK (4/13) were listed in the Performance Weekly magazine and the "Performance" section of Rolling Stone #158 (April 11, 1974) which also included a review of the debut album. Only one of these dates is known to have taken place (without KISS's involvement — Savoy Brown at the North Hall Auditorium in Memphis).

March 31 - Aviation Field, Forest Park, St. Louis, MO
Promoter: KSHE-AM / Shelley Grafman
Other act(s): Thirteenth Floor
Reported audience: 40,000 – 105,000
Notes:
- The 1974 KSHE "Kite Fly" was one of the biggest audiences KISS has performed to, even to the current day. The show was reported as having an estimated audience of 100,000 in Billboard Magazine (Apr. 20, 1974).
- The band's appearance was plagued by technical issues with the generators provided being deemed insufficient for the show and no hydraulics being available for Peter's drum kit riser. JR Smalling was nearly unwilling for the band to perform, but in the end they went on in daylight faced with the ultimatum from the promoter, "Play or go home." Rush performed at the event the following year.
- From a local review: "People were everywhere. Of the 105,000 people at the park Sunday, which incidentally was the biggest recorded crowd ever at Forest Park at one time... By 3 o'clock, the crowd was ready for music. A local group called the Thirteenth Floor played various popular songs including several by The Steve Miller Band and Santana. They were followed by KISS, who was described by KSHE radio as being the top group in Los Angeles. KISS smacked the audience with hard rock and bizarre costumes. The group was dressed mainly in black, although the bass guitarist brightened up his outfit with knee high silver platform boots. The members of the group had also painted their faces with white makeup and encircled their eyes with various designs ranging from bats to golden stars" (UMSL Current, 4/4/74). Strong winds in the afternoon explain why, in some of the circulating photos from the event, it appears the precariously stacked backline amps are being held up by the roadies.

April 1 - The Agora, Cleveland, OH
Promoter: In-house / WMMS
Other act(s): Rory Gallagher (HL)

Reported audience: <1,000 / 1,250 (80%)
Set list: Deuce / Strutter / Cold Gin / She / Firehouse / Nothin' to Lose / 100,000 Years / Black Diamond
Notes:
- Dates 4/1 – 4/4 were publicized in Billboard Magazine (4/6/74).
- Peter was asphyxiated at the end of the show when the drum riser got stuck up by the ceiling, in the residual fumes from the show effects, resulting in him passing out. He ended up in the Vincent Charity Hospital. Club owner Henry LoConti Sr. recalled, "It was a night I'll never forget. All of a sudden, the drums stopped. I look up, and I see this hand dangling off the edge of the platform. The other guys just kept playing" (Plain Dealer, 2/26/06)!
- Gene also recalled this show in Cleveland's local Scene magazine, "We opened for Rory Gallagher. And the audience was not ready to see us. When the announcer started introducing us he got as far as 'Now from New York,' before everybody started booing. They wanted to see Gallagher and not some rock 'n' roll band that they never heard of before. But after we were done, they called for two encores" (The Scene, 6/20/74).
- "Nights Out At The Agora" was a collaboration between the Agora and local radio stations, in Cleveland's case, WMMS 101-FM, that recorded live sets from artists and offered those shows to partner radio stations for broadcast. "If a radio station wants to put on the hour, we send the tapes weekly and the station makes a commitment giving the show a certain amount of promos... plus they give the network three spots in the body of the show which the network can either use or sell. The station benefits because they keep three spots. And in Cleveland it's WMMS jocks that emcee our shows. And we tend to advertise on the stations that are running our shows" (Radio Report, 11/23/78). The operation eventually developed into a local TV broadcast, "On Stage at the Agora," also simulcast on radio, through which mostly new acts were featured (early on). The show ran 1974 – 84.
- This show circulates as a pre-FM SBD (in other words copies from the station reels versus copies from a broadcast of the reels); unfortunately, at some point most of the raps during the show were edited out. Of those that remain, Gene does somewhat embarrassingly address the audience at one point asking, "How many people we got here? A hundred? Are you ready to rock?" in an unconvincing and rather awkward manner.

April 2 - The Agora, Toledo, OH **KISS CANCELLED
Promoter: In-house / WMMS
Other act(s): Rory Gallagher (HL)
Reported audience: (1,800 capacity)
Notes:
- While KISS scratched this gig due to the drama of the previous night show's ending, Rory went ahead and performed.

April 3 - The Agora, Columbus, OH
Promoter: In-house / WMMS
Other act(s): Rory Gallagher (HL)
Reported audience: (2,000 capacity)
Notes:
- Due to a power outage caused by a local storm during the show, one patron recalled Gene taking candles from the on-stage candelabra and handing them to audience members while the band performed. When power was restored KISS concluded their set and Rory performed.

April 4 - W. D. Packard Music Hall, Warren, OH **CANCELLED

Promoter: Starshine Productions
Other act(s): Badfinger (HL)
Reported audience: (2,500 capacity)
Notes:
- Badfinger was imminently to commence recording of their "Wish You Were Here" album at Caribou Ranch Studios in Colorado, and had just completed a three-night stand in Boston the night before, so it's unclear whether this was a "KISS cancelled" or "gig cancelled" situation. Regardless, Badfinger played their final U.S. date with Pete Ham in Chicago the following night.

April 4 - Nordic Arena, Hartland, MI **ERRONEOUS LISTING

Promoter: Brass Ring Productions
Other act(s): Mike Quatro Jam Band, Smack Dab (opener)
Reported audience: (4,000 capacity)
Notes:
- This show is sometimes attributed to the "KISS" tour. However, as concert flyers clearly indicate, the show was scheduled on a Friday, which means 1975 rather than 1974.

April 5 - Embassy Theater, Fort Wayne, IN **ERRONEOUS LISTING

Other act(s): Genesis (HL)
Notes:
- An ad in the 4/3/74 edition of the Fort Wayne News Sentinel erroneously listed the band opening for Genesis. A correction was noted in the following day's edition and the review of the show doesn't mention any opening act.

April 6 - National Guard Armory, Fort Wayne, IN **CANCELLED

Promoter: Bill Overman
Other act(s): Babe Ruth (opener)
Notes:
- According to their 3/21/74 itinerary KISS was scheduled to play a date at this venue with opening band Babe Ruth. The April 6th date was scratched from the itinerary, while the Genesis show did go ahead (and was taped) it had nothing to do with KISS. However, the Genesis gig was moved from the Embassy Theater, which had been found unsafe by Fire Marshalls, to the Armory. Make sense?

April 7 - Belle Isle Pavilion, Detroit, MI

Promoter: WABX / Steve Glantz Productions
Other act(s): Aerosmith (HL), Mojo Boogie Band, Michael Fennelly
Reported audience: 5,000 **SOLD-OUT
Reported gross: $4,850
Set list: Deuce / Strutter / She / Firehouse / Nothin' to Lose / Cold Gin / 100,000 Years / Black Diamond / Baby, Let Me Go
Notes:
- The WABX-FM "Kite-In and Balloon Fly" was an annual grassroots event in 1968, but quickly grew to require much larger venues that could accommodate thousands. Billboard reported that "all kites bear the KISS logo" (4/13/74). The station broadcast both the Aerosmith and KISS sets, though KISS performed during daylight and was introduced as a

"most unusual band." The annual "Kite-In" was actually cancelled with poor weather, including rain and snow, forcing postponement until April 21. However, since some among the 3,000 young folk who did turn up for the event caused $2,000 damage inside the Belle Isle Casino the local Common Council banned WABX from sponsoring any further "Kite-Ins" in Detroit parks (Detroit Free Press, 4/12/74). The concert raised $7,000 towards the clean-up of Belle Isle.

- Aerosmith didn't hang around following the show, and opened for Three Dog Night the following night in Portland, OR.

- For many fans this is the king of early performances — simply for the quality of the surviving source material. Since the show was broadcast on radio pre-FM reels have survived. The low gross is a result of tickets being sold for 0.97c, the radio station's frequency.

April 8 - University Center Ballroom @ NIU, DeKalb, IL
Promoter: Northern Illinois University
Other act(s): Conqueror Worm (opener)
Reported audience: (5,000 capacity)
Notes:
- This event was billed as the "Ed Paschke Memorial Glitter Ball." A costume contest took place between act switch-over at 10:30PM.
- Conqueror Worm was a Chicago based act, fronted by singer/guitarist Paul Suszynski, and had opened for many major acts including Cream, Howlin' Wolf, and Moody Blues.
- From a local review: "The emcee announced that the feature group, KISS, who have one LP out on Warner-distributed Casablanca label and appeared recently on ABC's 'In Concert' series would appear at midnight. This was greeted amongst groans of those who had to set alarm clocks for 7 a.m. to prepare for psych tests and whatnot on Tuesday morning. A militia of roadies set up the stage for KISS, which was equipped with a lights 8' x 4' sign with the group's logo. The lights on the sign were turned on when the group entered the stage, and were a marvelous parody of the neon urban commercial jungles that Illinois residents encounter in Chicago, as do KISS in their native New York. Its four members emerged onto the stage, immersed in white makeup and wearing black leather and high platform boots. Some looked like glitter equivalent Hells' Angels; others looked like decadent versions of Batman and Robin. Their music was loud, hard, and sexual — no more extreme than the evening's outlook" (Northern Star, 4/10/74).
- KISS travelled to Detroit the following day and remained in the city until April 13.

April 12 - Auditorium North Hall, Memphis, TN **KISS CANCELLED
Other act(s): Savoy Brown (HL)
Notes:
- This was the only show from a series of shows scheduled between March 26 and April 13 with Savoy Brown to actually take place, even though KISS had cancelled. Argent had originally been scheduled to headline.

April 12 - Michigan Palace, Detroit, MI
Promoter: Steve Glantz Productions
Other act(s): Blue Oyster Cult (HL), Suzi Quatro
Reported audience: 5,000 **SOLD-OUT
Notes:

- The April 5, 1974 issue of Ann Arbor Sun, and some other early ads, had Nazareth listed as second on the bill to BOC for both shows, though they didn't perform.
- At a time when Detroit native Suzi Quatro was topping the U.K. charts with "Devil Gate Drive," she was very much non-mainstream in the U.S. with her self-titled album (Bell 1302) eventually reaching #142 on Billboard Top-200.
- Both shows were reported as sold-out in advance.

April 13 - Michigan Palace, Detroit, MI
Promoter: Steve Glantz Productions
Other act(s): Blue Oyster Cult (HL), Suzi Quatro
Reported audience: 5,000 **SOLD-OUT
Partial set list: Deuce / Strutter / She / Firehouse / Nothin' to Lose / Cold Gin / Acrobat
Notes:
- This date was advertized in February as a Blue Oyster Cult show with Captain Beyond as the opening act.
- Probable set list. Footage from this show was filmed in silent Super8 (8mm). The footage came from a 27 minute source that was originally auctioned on eBay in 2000 and purchased by Jack Sawyers ("Tale of the Fox" video). It was in circulation by 2003. "Acrobat" was eventually released on the "KISSology Vol. 1" DVD though the video remains grainy. It has been synched with audio from the FM broadcast from Lafayette's Music Room in Memphis, TN, on April 18 and other 1974 shows. For some the footage is better on the 2001 unofficial "The Vintage" DVD where 17 minutes were released. For many years this footage was attributed to Long Beach (Feb. 17, 1974), but analysis of the footage and comparison with known photos of both venues has led experts to believe that the April 13 Michigan date is correct.

April 14 - Beggar's Banquet, Louisville, KY
Promoter: Jim Goodwin
Other act(s): Thunderhead
Reported audience: ~400
Notes:
- KISS was paid a flat fee of $400 for this show. The opening act had been arrested at the venue a few days prior, after their former manager had accused them of stealing their own PA. They were released and the charges were eventually dropped.
- Located at 3rd & Market Streets in Louisville, the club was located in the former Loevenhart's clothing store and had opened in July 1972.

April 15 - Muther's Music Emporium, Nashville, TN
Promoter: Sound Seventy Productions
Other act(s): Max Onion
Reported audience: (1,500 capacity)
Notes:
- This show was for a local radio (WMAK-AM) station's "Coyote Concert" series. Muther's was a venue that opened in December 1973 owned by Joe Sullivan (a president of local promoter Sound Seventy Productions) and Bill Bingham. Seating ranged from 800 to 1,500 (with tables and chairs removed). Equipped with a 20-channel console, "Sullivan is planning live radio broadcasts with, most likely, an FM network covering the major metropolitan areas of the state... Sullivan's concept is that relatively unknown acts can be exposed

through his facility, and then brought back at the auditorium" (Billboard, 12/15/73). While the facility didn't survive for more than six months it did host numerous acts including Bruce Springsteen, Ted Nugent and BTO during its short life.

April 16 - Muther's Music Emporium, Nashville, TN
Promoter: Sound Seventy Productions
Other act(s): Max Onion
Reported audience: (1,500 capacity)
Notes:
- A normal format show without the local radio involvement.

April 17 - Lafayette's Music Room, Memphis, TN
Promoter: Overton Square, Inc.
Other act(s): Kathi McDonald (HL)
Notes:
- Headliner McDonald had released her debut, "Insane Asylum," album via Capitol Records earlier in the year. McDonald started out her career as an "Ikette" backing Ike & Tina Turner, before essentially becoming Janis Joplin's replacement in Big Brother & The Holding Company. She later contributed vocals to numerous artists' sessions including Joe Cocker's "Mad Dogs and Englishmen" and the Rolling Stones' "Exile on Main St."
- From an attendee: "By this time, the jam-packed Square had created a burgeoning local music scene that went for three blocks in either direction. At one point, there were at least a dozen clubs within walking distance featuring hometown pickers — 13, if you counted Yosemite Sam's. Lafayette's was filled with curiosity seekers when Kiss shook the stage. I stood in the back, and when Kiss cranked up, it was like being cuffed across the ear. The band wasn't halfway through their grotesque routine when the audience started jamming the exits. Kiss cleared out Lafayette's in 30 minutes. Wanna know why? There were 10 local bands on the street with better musicians than Kiss, and they didn't need stage make-up to get the message across. Kiss made no waves here and were considered to be a short-lived novelty act, reeking of desperation" (Memphis Flyer, 5/21/15).

April 18 - Lafayette's Music Room, Memphis, TN
Promoter: Overton Square, Inc.
Other act(s): Kathi McDonald (HL)
Set list: Deuce / Strutter / Firehouse / She / Nothin' to Lose / Cold Gin / 100,000 Years / Black Diamond / Acrobat
Notes:
- Broadcast on with the club's radio partner WMC FM-100. One is left wondering whether "Baby, Let Me Go" was excluded from the broadcast. By August 1974 WMC program director Mike Powell had left the station to launch Media Masters, a communications firm that aimed to get shows recorded at the venue into syndication. This venue would be the primary recording venue.
- Notable for the obvious inclusion of "Acrobat," though in this case only the second "jam" part is performed as an encore. The circulating recording is very reasonable, though the inclusion of that song, partial or not, outweighs any audio quality issues such as tape-flutters and drop-outs.

April 19 - Aragon Ballroom, Chicago, IL
Promoter: Wayne Mackie Productions
Other act(s): Quicksilver Messenger Service (HL), Flying Saucer, Les Variations
Reported audience: ~2,000 / 5,000 (40%)
Reported gross: $12,000
Notes:
- One itinerary suggested that Aerosmith and Roxy Smith were also on this bill. They weren't.
- KISS reportedly performed until midnight with the headliner performing until nearly 3am!
- From a local review: "KISS. How can they miss? You name it, they've got it. Faces painted like demons from rock 'n' roll hell, with fire and brimstone music to match. Smoke and fire, from seven burning candles which preceded them onstage Friday night at the Aragorn to the very literal fiery finish with which they wound up. One of the singer-guitarists spits on stage; another drools fake blood from rouged lips. And the thing is, it works pretty well. KISS, a guitars-and-drums quartet out of New York with all the attendant hype that seems to accompany any glitzy group from Gotham these days, has all the trappings that usually mean there's nothing else there. Except this time everything fits — the staging suits the music and the masks are part of the excitement rather than a protective covering to hide the fact there's nothing behind them. The music to that matches all the antics, as you might well imagine, is hardly sophisticated or subtle" (Chicago Tribune, 4/22/74). This review was incorporated into the band's first press-kit.

April 20 - Civic Center, Charleston, WV **KISS CANCELLED
Promoter: National Shows
Other act(s): ZZ Top (HL), Peter Frampton's Camel
Notes:
- KISS was replaced on this bill by Tim Buckley by April 14. Since the show was still being advertized locally the day prior to scheduled date it seems likely that it was more than a "temp hold date." However, no review has been located yet...

April 21 - Flashes, Charlotte, NC
Promoter: Rod Guion
Other act(s): Ritual
Notes:
- Sean Delaney's "Hellbox" recounts a story, possibly occurring at this venue (though he names it Joker's Club — whereas the name provided here comes from the band's itinerary), where he threw the opening act off the bill for attempting to upstage KISS with similar stage gimmicks. Similarly, in certain itineraries the venue is simply listed as "The Flash."

April 26 - Victory Theater, Toronto, ON, Canada **CANCELLED
Promoter: SRO Productions
Other act(s): Unknown.
Notes:
- This show was also supposed to have been the KISS show that was part of the grand prize for Ft. Lauderdale WSHE radio's "kissathon" contest. Two shows were originally scheduled, one at 7:30 and the second at 11p.m. Original headliners Argent cancelled their participation in the show on Apr. 19, though the KISS show remained booked until Apr. 25 when it was cancelled due to "uncertainty in getting a flight from New York due to airport strike troubles" (Toronto Star, 4/26/74).
- Most of the dates cancelled between April 26 and May 1 KISS had been scheduled as the opening act for Argent who delayed the start of their tour, and KISS's promotional schedule (recording and TV appearance filming). They were published in trade magazines in the famous ad featuring Gene breathing fire titled "KISS IS SENDING THE COUNTRY UP IN SMOKE."

April 26 - Bell Sound Studios, New York City, NY **SESSION
Notes:
- Recording of "KISSin' Time" with producers Kenny Kerner and Richie Wise, for use as part of the continued Casablanca promotional event... The single was mixed on April 30.
- After the trial-run in Ft. Lauderdale in April, "twelve major-market top 40 radio powerhouses have signed up for the kissing marathon promotion on Casablanca Records' KISS group and their single, 'Kissing Time.' Finals will be hosted May 25 by WCFL-AM in Chicago. Winners get an eight-day cruise to Acapulco after attending the KISS concert at Long Beach Auditorium May 31" (Billboard, 5/18/74).

April 27 - Pucillo Gymnasium @ Millerville State College, Millerville, PA **POSTPONED
Promoter: Dick Klotzman
Other act(s): Argent (HL)
Notes:
- This show was rescheduled for May 5. Date change reported in the college's "The Snapper" (4/24 issue).

April 27 - Capitol Theater, Passaic, NJ
Promoter: John Scher
Other act(s): Blue Oyster Cult (HL), Ross (opener)
Reported audience: (3,200 capacity)
Reported gross: $10,298
Notes:

- Photographer Waring Abbott shot this show. Additionally, two future KISS employees were working at the Capitol at the time: John Harte and Rick Stuart. Roadie Mick Campise attended this show and was hired in time to work with the band in time for their "Mike Douglas Show" appearance. Opener Ross wasn't mentioned in print ads, but was noted on a press pass from the event.

April 28 - Performance Center, Cambridge, MA **CANCELLED
Other act(s): Argent (HL)

April 29 - Watch Tower, Reading, PA **CANCELLED
Promoter: Rose Concerts
Other act(s): Argent (HL)

April 29 - Studio A, KYW-TV Studios, Philadelphia, PA **TV FILMING
Mike Douglas Show TV Filming
Reported audience: 120
Set list: Firehouse
Notes:
- This show has previously circulated and was heavily edited on "KISSology Vol. 1" DVD. It remains somewhat infamous for Gene's run-in with comedienne Totie Fields, and her hilarious "nice Jewish boy" comment. Other guests on the show included Robert Klein, singer Eartha Kitt, Ben Hunter, and Dr. Joyce Brothers. The whole of the broadcast segment was released in 2003 on the unofficial "Lost 1976 Concert" DVD.
- First broadcast on May 21, 1974.

May 1 - Decker Gymnasium @ Mansfield State College, Mansfield, PA **CANCELLED
Promoter: Concert East Associates
Other act(s): Argent (HL)
Notes:
- This show was likely cancelled for the same reasons as an earlier attempt to bring the Ohio Players to the college: Money. The College Union Board had tried to schedule a Mar. 30 show with that band, but had only sold 12 tickets, leaving too much of a gap for the board to cover. While they cancelled that event, the cancellation of the contract still cost them $1,900, wiping out funds for the rest of the semester.

May 2 - Thunder Chicken Rock Theater, Comstock Park (Grand Rapids), MI
Promoter: Rebel Promotions, Inc.
Other act(s): Argent (HL)
Reported audience: (750 capacity)
Notes:
- The first show of the delayed tour opening for Argent. Gene recalled, "We were novices compared to them, and as the junior band we had to follow lots of arbitrary rules, one of which was the no-encore rule. According to Argent, we could go out there and play only eight songs, and then we had to close up shop. The only problem was that the audiences wanted us for longer than that. Argent fixed that by shutting off our power after eight songs" ("KISS & Make-up").
- The Thunder Chicken, also known as the Thunder Bird Dinner Theater, was run by Dick Bichler and located on Alpine Avenue in Grand Rapids.

May 3 - Ambassador Theater, St. Louis, MO
Promoter: Ron Powell Productions
Other act(s): Argent (HL)
Reported audience: (3,006 capacity)
Notes:
- KISS was thrown off the Argent tour following this show. Gene explained: "During one show our set went well as usual, and the audience was in a frenzy. We got to the end of our eighth song, and they were screaming as loud as they could, and we all braced for the lights to go dead — but they didn't. They stayed on. So we played an encore, and the crowd was still screaming. At that point we really didn't have any more songs, so we actually went back and replayed some of the songs from earlier in the set. Finally, after the third or fourth encore, we came off, drenched in sweat, completely confused about Argent's change in heart. It turns out that we owed our good luck to Junior Smalling, who had gotten into a little argument with Argent's road manager and pushed him into an anvil case and locked it shut. Needless to say, we were thrown off that tour too" ("KISS & Make-up").

May 4 - Alexander Memorial Coliseum @ GA Tech, Atlanta, GA **KISS CANCELLED
Promoter: Alex Cooley, Inc.
Other act(s): Blue Oyster Cult (HL), Manfred Mann's Earth Band, Hydra (opener)
Reported audience: (9,000 capacity)
Notes:
- Nazareth was initially also on this bill. KISS arrived late and was bumped from the bill by the headliner.

May 5 - Pucillo Gymnasium @ Millerville State College, Millerville, PA **CANCELLED
Promoter: Dick Klotzman
Other act(s): Argent (HL)
Notes:
- Rescheduled from the postponed April 27 date, this show ultimately didn't take place. The show was still being advertized in the university's student press (The Snapper) on May 1, though with no mention of KISS or any opening act.

May 6 - Embassy Hotel, Windsor, ON, Canada **CANCELLED
May 7 - Embassy Hotel, Windsor, ON, Canada **CANCELLED
Notes:
- These shows were canceled due to the venue's stage being deemed too small.

May 7 - Hillcrest Penthouse Ballroom, Mt. Clemens, MI **UNCONFIRMED
Promoter: Howard Tyner
Notes:
- With a capacity of 1,100 this venue would have seemed an ideal one for a KISS concert at this stage of their career. However, the "Penthouse Ballroom" was located in the clubhouse on a golf course, possibly a less than ideal local for a KISS concert, and it was a very popular for upscale local weddings. While this date appeared on the band's 4/8/74 itinerary, it is unconfirmed as having taken place and likely never took place.

May 9 - The Joint in the Woods, Parsippany, NJ
Promoter: in-house

Other act(s): Sweetwater
Reported audience: (1,800 capacity)
Notes:
- A headlining show. Some itineraries have KISS opening for Manfred Mann at the Tower Theater in Upper Darby, PA on this day, though that show bill only included Argent and Manfred Mann. Argent had played this NJ venue the prior night while Manfred Mann was scheduled on their own on May 11 (though a later ad replaces them with New York City on that date). However, in the May 4 issue of Billboard, Brian Auger was scheduled to perform at the venue...
- It's not clear whether the Sweetwater that opened for several acts during this week was the same "Sweetwater" that had been the first scheduled band to perform at Woodstock in 1969 (Richie Havens was the first actual performer). Vocalist Nancy "Nansi" Nevins, who had been injured in a car accident in early 1970 and damaged her voice, was touring as a solo act on the West Coast at the time. She had endured four years of vocal rehabilitation and released a solo album in 1975.

May 10 - W. D. Packard Music Hall, Warren, OH **CANCELLED
Reported audience: (2,500 capacity)
Notes:
- This show was listed in several trade publications. Members of the original KISS crew have alluded to driving to this show and it being cancelled.

May 11 - Montgomery County Country Club, Blue Bell, PA **CANCELLED
Promoter: Student Center Board
Other act(s): Argent (HL)
Notes:
- This show was cancelled when the student union was unable to raise enough funds for the concert. According to Doug Bazzel, "concert coordinator, the contract with Argent couldn't be signed until the Student Center Board had enough money for the concert. Then there wasn't enough time to provide the technical, staging and production requirements for the concert. Items such as a concert grand piano, which had to be perfectly tuned, and a fork lift truck were to be provided for the group, which caused problems for the concert plans" (Montgazette, 4/26/74).

May 12 - Agora, Columbus, OH **KISS CANCELLED
Promoter: In-house/WMMS
Other act(s): Argent (HL)
Notes:
- Another show that fell victim to the band getting kicked off Argent's tour.

May 12 - Benjamin Yack Recreation Center, Wyandotte, MI
Promoter: Brass Ring Productions
Other act(s): Savoy Brown (HL), Silverhead (opener)
Reported audience: 2,400 / 3,000 (80%)
Reported gross: $12,000
Notes:
- This Detroit area show was criticized by local government council members due to "alleged problems caused by concert-goers drinking and smoking" and the condition the

venue was left in following the concert (Wyandotte News Herald, 5/22/74), though the venue manager defended the audience stating that the mess was really no different from other events they hosted. KISS was not explicitly mentioned, though further concerts during the summer weren't finalized due to the concerns over behavior.

- According to Paul, "It was our first show opening for Savoy Brown and we came waking out of the dressing room (in costume) and these guys (in Savoy Brown) were just in hysterics, laughing at us. And I could understand it, coming from their (English working-class) backgrounds. When we left the stage and half the audience left, too, we had some new-found friends in a blues band called Savoy Brown. My philosophy has always been, as far as the bands we played with: 'I love you, until I walk out on the stage, and then my job there is to win.' That's ultimately what this is about" (San Diego Union-Tribune, 8/10/12).

May 13 - Agora, Cleveland, OH **KISS CANCELLED
Promoter: In-house/WMMS
Other act(s): Argent (HL)
Notes:
- An April ads in Cleveland's Plain Dealer newspaper lists Chase as the opening act for this show. By May 3 the second act is simply a "special guest" with Chase still in the opening slot. Oddly, in the May 13 issue of the Toledo Blade this show is advertized as being scheduled for May 14, calling into question the date in Toledo (though it could be an error).

May 14 - Renaissance Valentine Theater, Toledo, OH **KISS CANCELLED
Other act(s): Argent (HL)
Notes:
- The last of the shows from the "lost" tour with Argent.

May 14 - Frasier Hockeyland Arena, Fraser, MI
Promoter: Brass Ring Productions
Other act(s): Savoy Brown (HL), Silverhead (opener)

Reported audience: 2,170 / 3,400 (63.82%)
Notes:
- Paul recalled, "We opened for a midlevel British blues band called Savoy Brown at a jam-packed ice-skating rink in Michigan. Some of the guys in the band had never seen us, and they came to the side of the stage as we started playing and laughed in full view of us. I was laughing inside, though, because I knew how tough it was to follow KISS. And sure enough, they may have been laughing during our set, but they were crying when half the audience left during theirs. They changed their tune after that" ("Face The Music").

May 16 - Centennial Concert Hall, Winnipeg, MB, Canada

Promoter: The Autumn Stone Company, Ltd. / Rock Manitoba / Frank Weipert
Other act(s): Savoy Brown (HL), Manfred Mann's Earth Band
Reported audience: ~1,500 / 2,305 (65.08%)
Partial set list: Firehouse / Black Diamond
Notes:
- While two of these dates had appeared in the earlier trade full-page ad, the Canadian dates were expanded in scope: "Casablanca group KISS will make a short tour of Western Canada starting at the Centennial Hall in Winnipeg on Thursday (16) then moving to the Kinsman Field house, Edmonton Friday (17): Saskatchewan Arena, Saturday (18); Exhibition Pavilion, Lethbridge, Sunday (19): and Foothills Arena, Calgary, Monday (20). WEA is distributing the first KISS album in Canada" (Billboard, 5/25/74). However, the revised itinerary had been publicized in the previous issue.
- "Two nights later, the scene shifted to the Centennial Concert Hall, where KISS and Manfred Mann's Earth Band raised the roof several times during the course of the evening. KISS, New York's glitter-rock sensation, received rather mixed reactions from a crowd of about of 1,500 people. Quite bluntly, you either like the group or despise it — there's no room for indifference with this band. KISS relies heavily on visuals such as the dry ice fog it turns loose during Firehouse and its standard closing number, Black Diamond, which finds drummer Peter Criss and his entire drum kit being elevated some six feet into the air while the rest of the group goes slightly crazy. There's not one wasted motion in KISS's set. Every toss off the hair, every excruciating solo which lead guitarist Ace Frehley coaxes from his instrument serves a purpose. Even the outrageous attire and facial makeup sported by the group's four member's (bassist Gene Simmons looks like some sort of demented Raggedy Ann doll in drag) is there for a reason — to capture the audience's attention. Many people probably didn't like it but then that's not my problem. As things turned out, the show proved to be a study in contrasts of a sort. Whereas KISS relied so much on the visual impact of its performance, Manfred Mann's all too brief set proved to be a terrific audio experience. As good as the Earth Band's albums are, the group's stage show manages to surpass many of its recorded accomplishments" (Andy Mellen, Winnipeg Free Press, 5/74).
- A Winnipeg press article from 6/8/74 notes: "Cable Channel 9 will feature videotape footage of KISS' recent performance, along with shots of the group arriving at Canadian Customs on a special midnight edition of Tea with Lee this Tuesday." That would make the original broadcast date of whatever that footage was June 11, 1974... Some of this footage was probably rebroadcast on 10/10/74 on the same show.
- An earlier article details: "I'd recommend tuning in this Thursday's special edition of Tea with Lee on cable Channel 9. The show, which is scheduled for 10:30 p.m., will feature some of the musical highlights of that particular concert, along with interviews with band members and some behind the scenes shots. I had an opportunity to view several hours of

the unedited video tape for the show over the weekend, and I think it should make quite an interesting program once the proceedings have been edited into some sort of order. What I would really really like to get my hands on its a print of the film taken by photographer Pat Dundance just as KISS's limousine pulled into the Holiday Inn late Wednesday. The looks on some bystanders' faces when the group trucked into the lobby in full makeup were simply priceless. To look at their expressions you would have thought that the end of civilization had arrived in the form of four normal New York City lads who jumped on the glitter-rock bandwagon to garner some notoriety and consequently a bit of the fame and fortune theirs for the grabbing in the rock and roll game" (Winnipeg Free Press, 5/21/74). That broadcast date would be 5/23.

May 17 - Kinsmen Fieldhouse, Edmonton, AB, Canada
Promoter: The Autumn Stone Company, Ltd. / Rock Manitoba / Frank Weipert
Other act(s): Savoy Brown (HL), Manfred Mann's Earth Band
Reported audience: 6,000 / 7,000 (85.71%)
Reported gross: $21,838
Notes:
- From a trade review: "New York's theatrical rock group KISS returned to Edmonton last week, and as expected, took the city by storm... it was KISS who brought down the house with its music and a barrage of fireworks and smoke bombs" (Performance Magazine).

May 18 - Saskatchewan Arena, Saskatoon, SK, Canada
Promoter: John Fredrickson
Other act(s): Savoy Brown (HL), Manfred Mann's Earth Band
Reported audience: 1,950 / 5,000 (39%)

May 19 - Exhibition Pavilion, Lethbridge, AB, Canada
Promoter: The Autumn Stone Company, Ltd. / Rock Manitoba / Frank Weipert
Other act(s): Savoy Brown (HL), Manfred Mann's Earth Band
Reported audience: (3,100 capacity)
Reported gross: $7,135
Notes:
- 115 tickets for the show were stolen from a local ticket outlet prior to the show. A notice was placed in the Lethbridge Herald on May 18 warning that tickets numbered 85 – 200 would not be honored at the show.
- While staying at the Holiday Inn Savoy Brown caused some C$700 damage to their room though no charges were pressed when they paid restitution...
Promoter Ron Sakamoto recalled booking the band, "When I got their press kit, I thought, 'Wholly moley.' They were different. They were an extremely good show band. They were one of the first theatrical, all-out show bands out there with their costumes and everything... The headliner of that tour was still Savoy Brown, then Manfred Mann and then KISS which didn't have as much equipment as I'm sure they used in the United States. But they were as big as we could get. They made it work, and it was still fantastic" (Celebrity Access).

- From a local review: "KISS, while the least musically impressive group at the concert, was by far the most visually entertaining, with a variety of stage devices, such as heavy makeup, smoke bombs and fire-breathing, being employed. On record one might expect them to be unimpressive, but their l.p. 'KISS' (Casablanca NB-9001) is a fairly good set of straight hard rock material in the Humble Pie tradition" (Lethbridge Herald, 6/15/74).

May 20 - University of Calgary, Foothills Arena, Calgary, AB, Canada
Promoter: Lucifer Productions
Other act(s): Savoy Brown (HL), Manfred Mann's Earth Band
Reported audience: ~2,800
Notes:
- This show was originally scheduled for the 2,000 capacity Father Bauer Arena.
- From a local review: "A minor has-been, a possible could-be and a definite will-never-be provided almost four hours of loud, wall-to-wall rock music for an audience of 2,800 at the Foothills Arena Monday night... As for KISS, this quartet's music can be best described as lobotomy-rock. Theatrics is the name of the game, and KISS ornaments its infantile thumb-sucking music with lotsa kicks for the glitter crowd... The boys in the band also wear make-up and costumes that look like old Zorro outfits with sequins sewed on... When called out for an encore, one member of KISS shouted 'Thank you, Calgary. We'll be coming back.' Next time KISS will be on its own and will no doubt sell out the house. Isn't that sweet, damn it all" (Calgary Herald, 5/21/74).

May 23 - Warnor's Theater, Fresno, CA **CANCELLED
Promoter: Get Down Productions
Other act(s): Savoy Brown (HL), Manfred Mann's Earth Band
Reported audience: (2,000 capacity)
Notes:
- This show was among several cancelled at the venue during May due to a local perception of high ticket prices ($5) resulting in poor sales.

May 24 - Paramount Northwest Theater, Portland, OR
Promoter: Get Down Productions
Other act(s): Savoy Brown (HL), Manfred Mann's Earth Band
Reported audience: ~2,500 / 3,060 (81.7%)
Notes:
- From a local review: "If it takes three bands on the bill to get the rafters shaking at the Paramount Northwest theater then that formula worked Friday night. The three groups had something for everybody and the theater had about 2,500 bodies to enjoy them... If the [latter] two bands were into musicians staging and gimmicks, then the first group, four New Yorkers collectively called KISS, took up the slack while playing all up tempo, slashing rock. There was a punk-rock effect for most of the band's set but also, for most of it the audience found standing up easier. The rhythms were intense, highly disciplined in a maddening way and the result of close cooperation between the bass and drums" (Oregonian, 5/26/74).

May 25 - Paramount Northwest Theater, Seattle, WA
Promoter: Get Down Productions
Other act(s): Savoy Brown (HL), Manfred Mann's Earth Band
Reported audience: (2,997 capacity)

Notes:
- From a local review: "The show started with KISS, a very flashy glitter band that tries to make up in theatrics what it lacks musically. That's a tall order... The band's music is strictly on the moron level being made up of a series of simple chords any child could learn and lyrics that are just there because they rhyme. But who listens to the music? It's the extreme loudness and the flash that counts and a lot of the audience Saturday night went along with it and actually gave the band a standing ovation. I hope the four guys who make up the group, whose names don't matter, are putting money away for the future. The near future. Because KISS won't be around long. Flash doesn't last" (Seattle Daily Times, 5/27/74).

May 26 - J.F.K. Pavilion, Gonzaga University, Spokane, WA
Promoter: Concerts West
Other act(s): Savoy Brown (HL), Manfred Mann's Earth Band
Reported audience: ~4,000
Notes:
- This concert was part of Expo '74 and was reported as being near capacity.
- From a local review: "The first group of the evening was KISS, an assortment of four grotesquely made-up faces that performed neither with class nor flash. Although putting on a better show than Manfred Mann, they really should leave such antics to Alice Cooper" (Spokesman Review, 5/27/74).

May 27 - St. Martin's Capitol Pavilion, Olympia (Lacey), WA **UNCONFIRMED
Promoter: L&M Productions
Other act(s): Savoy Brown (HL), Manfred Mann's Earth Band
Notes:
- This show appears on the band's May 20th itinerary, but can't be confirmed as having taken place. Concert flyers do exist, but their providence is unknown. More likely than not, this show was cancelled.

May 28 - Garden Auditorium, Vancouver, BC, Canada
Promoter: Accident Productions
Other act(s): Savoy Brown (HL), Manfred Mann's Earth Band
Reported audience: 1,824 / 2,600 (70.15%)
Reported gross: $9,558
Partial set list: Deuce / Firehouse / Kissin' Time / Black Diamond
Notes:

- While KISS was booed by the partisan crowd, this is one of the few confirmed occasions "Kissin' Time" was performed.
- From a local review: "Much ... six-foot flashing KISS logos, dry-ice smoke, chiaroscuro facials, vomiting blood, fire-throwing, magnesium flashes, six-inch heels, leather and studs... later, KISS postured and posed their way through an ear-shattering, gut-spilling hour-long barrage on my unfortunate five senses... The music was secondary to the pizzazz. A pretty fourth-rate secondary at that... Their rock is loud and rude, but lacking the sincerity needed to make it a success. Anyway, who cared? We were so engrossed in following the band's antics that, if we could, we tried to avoid the pounding wall-to-wall, roof-to-floor amplification" (Georgia Straight Magazine, 5/30 – 6/6/74). The bands were interviewed by reviewer Robert Geldorf after the show at Oil Can Harry's. The interview appeared in Georgia Straight Magazine (Issue 6/6-6/13/74).
- The following day the band flew to Los Angeles.

May 30 - Sports Arena, San Diego, CA
Promoter: Concert Associates
Other act(s): Savoy Brown (HL), Manfred Mann's Earth Band
Reported audience: (15,000 capacity)

May 31 - Long Beach Auditorium, Long Beach, CA
Promoter: Pacific Presentations
Other act(s): Savoy Brown (HL), Manfred Mann's Earth Band
Reported audience: 3,600 / 4,400 (81.81%)
Reported gross: $18,000
Set list: Deuce / Nothin' to Lose / She / Firehouse / Strutter / 100,000 Years / Black Diamond / Baby, Let Me Go
Notes:
- Of any early KISS show, this recording of this one is perhaps the most famous having been the source material for the classic "Fried Alive" bootleg, courtesy of a KNAC-FM broadcast of the set. However, quality does vary from very reasonable to nearly excellent depending on the source (there is also an AUD version).

June 1 - Winterland Ballroom, San Francisco, CA
Promoter: Bill Graham Presents
Other act(s): Savoy Brown (HL), Manfred Mann's Earth Band
Reported audience: 2,300 / 5,000 (46%)
Reported gross: $10,700
Notes:
- This show was filmed by the in-house filming crew, but the tapes were supposedly "lost" to fire in the 1980s. However, there is more than circumstantial evidence that the tapes do still exist and are in the hands of more than one private collector.
- It seems likely that "Kissin' Time" would have been in the set around this time.
- Paul received his iconic "rose" tattoo at Lyle Tuttle's studio in Los Angeles earlier that day!

June 2 - Sun-Sundowner Drive-In Theater, Anchorage, AK
Promoter: Nebula Productions
Other act(s): Savoy Brown (HL), Flight (opener), Island (opener)
Reported audience: ~3,000

Notes:
- The concert started around 2 hours late and went until 1:30AM. 4 people were arrested at the show. This show was noted as taking place at the Roller Rink in Billboard Magazine (6/1/74).

June 4 - Bakersfield House, Eielson Air Force Base, Fairbanks, AK
Promoter: Nebula Productions/Eielson A.F.B.
Other act(s): Savoy Brown (HL)
Notes:
- The AFB held an "open-house" the day of this show!
- From a local attendee: "Dear Editor: I am one of the many disappointed persons who attended the Savoy Brown/KISS concert. Being held on a Tuesday night — a total of 52 miles down the highway round trip — spoiled it from the beginning. The changing of the concert time made it almost impossible for working people to attend. Savoy Brown did not even start to play until almost 12:30 a.m. The radio announced that the doors would be opening first at 10 p.m., then at 9:30 p.m., which was false. By the time my sister and I arrived, at 9:15 p.m., the doors were open and all of the good seats had been taken. The acoustics were horrible, making the sound all distorted and the volume almost unbearable. Anyone who has ever clapped his hands inside a hangar knows how bad just that sound is — let alone amplified instruments. Many of the people attending the concert were thirsty inside the hot structure only to be told that they could buy pop at one of two places — at Pete's Place miles down the road, or at the PX where you have to have a military ID. I am by no means knocking any of the groups — they are probably fantastic. I just think that it is too bad that poor planning ruined what could easily have been one of the best concerts Fairbanksans have ever heard. Fairbanks has been deprived of good concerts long enough. We are just as deserving of opportunities for quality entertainment as are people living in larger cities" (Fairbanks Daily News-Miner, 6/74).

June 6 - Terrace Ballroom, Salt Lake City, UT **CANCELLED
Promoter: United Concerts
Other act(s): Queen (HL), Dino Valenti
Notes:
- Queen's U.S. tour in support of "Queen II" had to be cancelled due to Brian May becoming ill in New York on May 12 (after a series of dates opening for Mott the Hoople at the Uris Theater). The press reported that he needed a month's recuperation from hepatitis during which time he wrote material for what became the "Sheer Heart Attack" album.

June 7 - Western Idaho Fairgrounds, Boise, ID **CANCELLED
Promoter: United Concerts
Other act(s): Queen (HL), Dino Valenti

June 8 - Allen Theater, Cleveland, OH **POSTPONED
Promoter: Belkin Productions
Other act(s): New York Dolls (HL)
Notes:
- Rescheduled for June 14 in on May 30, due to a "mix-up in scheduling" (Plain Dealer, 5/31/74).

June 10 - Central States Fairgrounds, Rapid City, SD **CANCELLED
Promoter: Mike Chambers
Other act(s): Styx (HL)
Notes:
- This was one of a trio of shows Styx booked on the strength of the initial performance of "Lady" (from their 1973 "Styx II" album) which had transformed the song into a regional hit. Because they were at an early stage of their career they didn't have a booking agent or the business setup of an established group, and it took a further year for that song to take off.
- According to the original KISS Krew, this show was cancelled due to poor weather conditions at the venue.

June 12 - I.M.A. Auditorium, Flint, MI
Promoter: Brass Ring Productions
Other act(s): New York Dolls (HL)
Reported audience: 2,112 / 5,300 (39.85%)
Reported gross: $12,686
Notes:
- Considering the inspiration the Dolls had been for KISS, this gig is an important meeting of two seminal bands and more surprising for having not occurred in 1973.
- From a local review: "KISS played tight well-arranged songs with long drawn-out endings accented with flashing smoke bombs. Most of the songs are rather simple, and the leads seem to repeat the same two-note phrase over and over. All four members sing, and their harmonies, though simple, are good. But their strengths are their act and their odd

costumes. Stanley said the band has caused near-riots in Detroit, and pointed to a lot of jewelry around his neck and on his hands. All of it was thrown to him on stage by enthused fans" (Flint Journal). The same review indicated an audience of 1,464.

June 13 - Ice Arena, Grand Rapids, MI **UNCONFIRMED

Promoter: Brass Ring Productions
Other act(s): Unknown.
Notes:
- This show appears on an itinerary dated June 3, which also reflected the change of the Flint date with the New York Dolls; but remains unconfirmed as to taking place or not. It may even have been a temp hold date. In terms of the travel were the show cancelled it certainly saved a couple of hundred of miles of driving for the road crew!

June 14 - Allen Theater, Cleveland, OH

Promoter: Belkin Productions
Other act(s): New York Dolls (HL)
Reported audience: (2,500 capacity)
Notes:
- Rescheduled from June 8. The band were interviewed by the local "Scene" magazine (the interview appears in the 6/20-26 issue) prior to their set. Peter mentions the prospect of going out on tour with Rod Stewart in August, followed by a European tour. Ace, who was not present, was reportedly "out shopping for clothes."
- From a local review: "KISS came on with a malfunctioning P.A. system, but it was repaired during the first song. Once this was fixed, they were received enthusiastically. People were screaming and whistling after each song. For a new group with only one LP to work from, they're pretty good... KISS plays damn good music; fast, loud and raunchy (The Scene, 6/20/74). In the same feature Peter mentions going on tour with Rod Stewart, and then Europe, later in the year — obviously neither happened.

June 15 - Sunshine In Concert Hall, Asbury Park, NJ **POSTPONED

Promoter: Bob Fisher / in-house
Other act(s): Larry Coryell & Eleventh House (HL), Truth (opener)
Reported audience: (2,000 capacity)
Notes:
- Though KISS had already rescheduled their appearance at this venue for June 17, allowing them to perform in Toronto with the New York Dolls, the adjusted line-up show was postponed at the last moment and was rescheduled for July 6.

June 15 - Massey Hall, Toronto, ON, Canada

Promoter: Encore Productions / Martin Onrot, Inc.
Other act(s): New York Dolls (HL)
Reported audience: (2,675 capacity)
Notes:
- Footage filmed of both acts at this show was broadcast on CBC in 1974 as part of a feature on glitter rock.
- WEA Canada was still actively promoting the debut album at this show and "arranged for a promotion to surround the Toronto appearance of Casablanca recording artists, Kiss. Four models were hired and dressed in black leotards with Kiss makeup. They were then

chauffeured around town in to key dealers and radio stations, passing out red wax lips" (Billboard, 7/13/74).

- From a local review: "It was an old-fashioned battle of the bands Saturday night at Massey Hall in the middleweight freak division. The antagonists: the New York Dolls, headliners, back in town for the second time in less than a year, a band reputed to combine gay abandon with street punk rock 'n' roll; KISS, the opening act, a brand new group whose show is said to be literally explosive. The results: a draw based on judging in three areas — music, presentation and credibility. The breakdown: Musically, KISS plays very simple, very loud rock 'n' roll. On record, good production enables the listener to distinguish between songs which sound very similar. They're all up-tempo and based on a catchy repeated guitar riff. In the somewhat distorted atmosphere of Massey Hall, the songs became indistinguishable from one another. KISS was half way through Strutter before I realized they had stopped playing Firehouse... KISS, on the other hand, is a totally plastic band. The group is a tribute to the imaginative powers and organizational ability of its manager, Neil Bogart. It doesn't matter that the players' makeup hides their faces because they are only marionettes anyway" (Toronto Star, 6/17/74).

June 17 - Sunshine In Concert Hall, Asbury Park, NJ

Promoter: Bob Fisher / in-house

Other act(s): Truth (opener)

Reported audience: (2,000 capacity)

Notes:

- Originally scheduled to take place with KISS opening for Eleventh House featuring Larry Coryell and Truth on June 15. In the June 13 issue of the Village Voice KISS' June 17 show was advertized offering a free ticket to purchasers of tickets to the June 15 Eleventh House show, and apology for the rescheduling of that show.

- From a local review: "The entertainment provided by KISS more than made up for the cancellation [of Coryell]. This was KISS' second appearance at the Sunshine In in less than three months but the excitement that surrounds the group's stage show was still fresh and full of energy. KISS is based in New York City and is part of the new rock genre appropriately called 'glitter rock.' The stage antics of the band is just as important as the music as seen by the complicated facial makeup, the penetrating theatrics and the Hollywood-like wardrobe that is so much a part of KISS... The heavy and outstandingly loud rock music supply the concertgoer with more than enough entertainment. It may not be Larry Coryell, but people that receive free passes can't be choosy. So far KISS has attained a following only with the glitter crowd, but within the month they will release a single, 'Strutter,' to test whether or not Top 40 listeners are ready for the flamboyance of glitter rock" (Asbury Park Press, 6/19/74).

June 19 - Electric Ballroom, Atlanta, GA
Promoter: Alex Cooley
Other act(s): Outlaw
Reported audience: (1,100 capacity)
Notes:
- Gigs in Atlanta, GA (6/19 – 22), Greenville, SA (6/25), Charlotte, NC (6/26), Alexandria, VA (6/30) and Indianapolis, IN (7/3) were also noted in Rolling Stone #164.

June 20 - Electric Ballroom, Atlanta, GA
Promoter: Alex Cooley
Other act(s): Outlaw
Reported audience: (1,100 capacity)
Notes:
- The AUD recording that circulates attributed as this show is fake/incorrectly attributed (it's actually an edited version of the earlier Detroit show).

June 21 - Electric Ballroom, Atlanta, GA
Promoter: Alex Cooley
Other act(s): Outlaw
Reported audience: (1,100 capacity)

June 22 - Electric Ballroom, Atlanta, GA
Promoter: Alex Cooley
Other act(s): Outlaw
Reported audience: (1,100 capacity)
Notes:
- After this show Paul was sick from June 23 – July 5 forcing the band's cancellation of their involvement in all shows during the period, predominately when they would have been opening for Blue Oyster Cult and Nazareth. Paul's ailment was reported as strep throat in Billboard (7/13/74).
- Alex thanked the band in a letter dated June 25: "Just a note to thank you for your dynamic performance at the Electric Ballroom. You really put the energy back in rock and roll. I certainly hope Paul is feeling better and is well on the way to recovery."

June 23 - Sportsdrome Speedway, Clarksville, IN **KISS CANCELLED
Promoter: Starship Enterprises / Mid-Atlantic Concerts
Other act(s): Quicksilver (HL), Nitty Gritty Dirt Band, Canned Heat, Roger McGuinn, Maggie Bell
Reported audience: ~10,000
Notes:
- The Ohio Valley Summer Jam.

June 25 - Memorial Auditorium, Greenville, SC **KISS CANCELLED
Promoter: Beach Club Promotions
Other act(s): Blue Oyster Cult (HL), Nazareth, Lynyrd Skynyrd

June 26 - Hampton Roads, Coliseum, Hampton, VA **KISS CANCELLED
Promoter: Gabbo / Webb Concerts
Other act(s): Blue Oyster Cult (HL), Maggie Bell

June 27 - Salem-Roanoke Valley Civic Center, Salem, VA **KISS CANCELLED
Promoter: Gabbo / Webb Concerts
Other act(s): Blue Oyster Cult (HL), Maggie Bell
Reported audience: 2,295
Notes:
- Some 150 attendees took up the offer for refunds for their tickets after KISS's cancellation of their set was announced (Roanoke Times, 6/28/74) though ads closer to day of show had removed the third band billing.

June 28 - Park Center, Charlotte, NC **KISS CANCELLED
Promoter: Kaleidoscope Productions
Other act(s): Blue Oyster Cult (HL), Brownsville Station, Nazareth

June 29 - Civic Center, Asheville, NC **KISS CANCELLED
Promoter: Kaleidoscope Productions
Other act(s): Blue Oyster Cult (HL), Brownsville Station, Nazareth
Reported audience: ~4,000 / 7,654 (52.26%)
Notes:
- Event billed as the "first rock happening" at the venue due to it being the first rock concert hosted by the venue (which had then only recently opened).

June 29 - Sunshine In Concert Hall, Asbury Park, NJ **POSTPONED
Promoter: Bob Fisher
Other act(s): Blue Oyster Cult (HL), Nazareth
Reported audience: (2,000 capacity)
Notes:
- This show was advertized locally in early June. The show was moved to the new (larger) Casino Arena venue and rescheduled for July 5 without Nazareth and Aerosmith opening in place of KISS.

June 30 - Alexandria Roller Rink, Alexandria, VA **KISS CANCELLED
Promoter: Entertainment Concept Corporation / Barry Richards
Other act(s): Blue Oyster Cult (HL), Nazareth
Reported audience: **SOLD OUT
Note:
- While not KISS related at the time, on this night in Port Chester, NY caught fire when a thief attempting to cover his tracks set fire to an adjacent property. The club was quickly engulfed in flames, and the band playing, Creation including future KISS drummer Eric Carr, struggled to escape the fire and help patrons flee. Two band members, vocalist George Chase and organist Damon DeFeis, perished along with 22 others.

July 1 - Pine Knob Music Theater, Pine Knob, MI **KISS CANCELLED
Promoter: Nederlander Productions
Other act(s): Blue Oyster Cult (HL)
Reported gross: $12,700
Reported audience: (6,000 capacity)

July 2 - Thunder Chicken Rock Theater, Comstock Park, MI **KISS CANCELLED
Promoter: Rebel Promotions, Inc.
Other act(s): None.
Reported audience: (750 capacity)
Notes:
- A contract for this headlining show had been signed June 12. Unfortunately the show fell within the period Paul was ill and was cancelled. This show would not have been with Blue Oyster Cult — they had a show scheduled at the Ohio Theater in Columbus.

July 3 - Convention Center, Indianapolis, IN **KISS CANCELLED
Promoter: Sunshine Promotions
Other act(s): Blue Oyster Cult (HL), Nazareth
Reported audience: (12,000 capacity)

July 4 - Chilhowee Park Amphitheater, Knoxville, TN **KISS CANCELLED
Promoter: Concerts South
Other act(s): New York Dolls (HL), Nazareth
Reported audience: 3,000 **SOLD-OUT
Notes:
- Billed as "Summer Jam #2, Glitter Rock Special."

July 5 - Independence Hall, Baton Rouge, LA **POSTPONED
Promoter: Beaver Productions

Other act(s): Blue Oyster Cult (HL), Nazareth
Notes:
- This show was rescheduled for July 16, though with the New York Dolls replacing Nazareth on the bill.

July 5 - Parthenon Theater, Hammond, IN **KISS CANCELLED
Other act(s): Rare Earth (HL), Nazareth

July 6 - Eagle Stadium, Chattanooga, TN **KISS CANCELLED
Promoter: Concerts South
Other act(s): Rare Earth (HL), Blue Oyster Cult

July 7 - West Tennessee State Fairgrounds, Jackson, TN **KISS CANCELLED
Promoter: Celebration Productions
Other act(s): Blue Oyster Cult (HL), Nazareth, Larry Raspberry & the Highsteppers
Notes:
- Suggested to have been a regional band, Larry Raspberry had already performed on Dick Clark's "In Concert" and American Bandstand; and would be on Don Kirshner's "Rock Concert" later in the month.

July 8 - Ellis Auditorium, Memphis, TN **KISS CANCELLED
Promoter: Alex Cooley, Inc.
Other act(s): Blue Oyster Cult (HL), Nazareth

July 11 - Auditorium, West Palm Beach, FL
Promoter: Performance Associates
Other act(s): Blue Oyster Cult (HL), Nazareth
Reported audience: (5,000 capacity)
Notes:
- First show with KISS rejoining the tour.

July 12 - Jai Alai Fronton, Orlando, FL
Promoter: L&S Productions
Other act(s): Blue Oyster Cult (HL), Nazareth
Reported audience: 2,350 / 3,500 (67.14%)
Reported gross: $14,000
Notes:
- While Uriah Heep and Isis were also advertized on the bill, at least the former didn't perform — a concert attendee recalled the all-female Isis performing at the show, though there is no concrete evidence to confirm that assertion. A separate report in Performance Magazine listed an attendance of 2,300 and gross of $15,000.

July 13 - Curtis Hixon Hall, Tampa Bay, FL
Promoter: Gulf Artists
Other act(s): Blue Oyster Cult (HL), Nazareth
Reported audience: 2,000 / 7,400 (27.03%)
Reported gross: $10,000
Notes:

- The attendance for this show was reported in Performance Magazine and in local press.
- From a local review: "A sparse, spacey jeans and halter to crowd of around 2,000 turned out for more than four hours of noisy, conventional rock and roll Saturday at Curtis Hixon... KISS came on first, all volume and hard-rock beat, with the usual unintelligible lyrics and all the traditional rock band touches of eight years ago, complete with fireworks and fog machines and assorted pyrotechnics. Dealing strictly in noise, including the vocals, this is what the crowd down front, clapping and stomping and cheering, came for: hard rhythm, crushing decibels, basic, unsophisticated music that is little more than noise with a beat. KISS managed to update itself a bit by tossing in a few Alice Cooper touches — pancake makeup, a little fire-eating, and some dribbly red stuff from the mouth of the bass guitarist" (Evening Independent, 7/15/74).

July 14 - Municipal Auditorium, Birmingham, AL
Promoter: Alex Cooley, Inc.
Other act(s): Blue Oyster Cult (HL), Nazareth
Reported audience: (6,000)
Notes:
- After staying overnight in Birmingham, the band flew to Baton Rouge via New Orleans.

July 16 - Independence Hall, Baton Rouge, LA
Promoter: Beaver Productions
Other act(s): Blue Oyster Cult (HL), New York Dolls
Reported audience: ~4,000
Reported gross: $14,000
Partial set list: Deuce / Strutter / She / Firehouse / 100,000 Years / Black Diamond / Baby, Let Me Go
Notes:
- This was the rescheduled show from the July 5 which was reported as "near capacity."
- There were some 24 arrests, primarily for drugs offences, at this show.
- Quite possibly a partial set, since it seems likely that "Baby, Let Me Go" would have closed the set. Paul doesn't interact with the audience until the intro to "She:" "We're going to slow it down a little. This is called 'She.'" Changes in the sound of the tape in between "She" and "Firehouse" suggest that "Nothin' to Lose" may have been performed but edited out of the tape that circulates. Regardless the AUD recording is very reasonable, even with fluctuations and drop-outs. BOC's set also circulates from this show. Interestingly, Gene's mic is much louder at the beginning of "Strutter" with him singing the first few lines of the song in place of Paul.

July 17 - Warehouse, New Orleans, LA **CANCELLED
Promoter: Beaver Productions
Other act(s): Lou Reed (HL), New York Dolls
Reported audience: (3,500 capacity)
Notes:
- Located in an 1850's era cotton/coffee warehouse, on Tchoupitoulas Street, this venue was famed for its wooden construction with brick facade. There is no evidence that this show took place — even without the involvement of KISS.

July 17 - Electric Ballroom, Atlanta, GA
Promoter: Alex Cooley, Inc.
Other act(s): Fat Chance
Reported audience: (1,100 capacity)
Partial set list: Strutter
Notes:
- After the previous month's four-night stand, KISS returned for an additional brace of shows.
- From a mainstream review: "KISS hit them hard right from the first song with ultra-loud slashing riffs, tightly done harmonies, and furious vocal/guitar interplay. The big difference between KISS and most of their ilk is that on a song like 'Strutter' they are perfectly in tune and each member is adept on his instrument, the vocal delivery from rhythm guitarist Paul Stanley and Gene Simmons is unusually good. In short, they produce juggernaut powerful music instead of ear-shattering junk. Lead guitarist Ace Frehley's piercing runs above Stanley's rhythms, Simmons' volatile bass figures and Peter Criss' rapid-fire drumming make for stuff that sticks rather than oppresses" (Phonograph Records, 8/74).

July 18 - Electric Ballroom, Atlanta, GA
Promoter: Alex Cooley, Inc.
Other act(s): Fat Chance
Reported audience: (1,100 capacity)
Notes:
- The band stayed overnight and flew to Fayetteville the following day.

July 19 - Cumberland County Memorial Auditorium, Fayetteville, NC
Promoter: Beach Club Booking
Other act(s): Blue Oyster Cult (HL), Nazareth, Glass Moon (opener)
Reported audience: (7,000 capacity)
Partial set list: Firehouse
Notes:
- The New York Dolls had been scheduled to play, but cancelled and were replaced by Glass Moon, a band from Raleigh, NC. The band drove the 120 miles to Charlotte the following day.

July 20 - Charlotte, NC **UNCONFIRMED
Notes:
- Travel documents indicate that the band was scheduled to be staying at the Holiday Inn, in Charlotte, but no evidence of any show has yet been uncovered. The band were scheduled to fly to Washington National airport at lunchtime the following day, and then drive the remaining 32 miles to Glen Burnie. Presumably the road crew would have driven the 435 miles between Charlotte and Baltimore.

July 21 - Baltimore, MD **UNCONFIRMED
Notes:
- Travel documents indicate that the band was scheduled to be staying at the Holiday Inn, in Glen Burnie, a suburb of Baltimore, but no evidence of any show in this area has yet been uncovered. The band may simply have returned to New York to rehearse for the July 23 demo session.

July 23 - Minot Sound Studios, Inc., White Plains, NY **RECORDING SESSION
Notes:
- The band recorded demos of "Mainline," "Parasite," "All The Way," and "Who's Your Baby" (later re-titled "Got to Choose"). According to studio documentation the band were charged a meager $305.74 for the session.

July 25 - Centennial Hall, London, ON, Canada
Promoter: Mister Sound / CJOM-FM
Other act(s): Rush, Ronny Legge (opener)
Reported audience: (1,854 capacity)
Notes:
- The band received a flat fee of $2000.00 for this show as noted on a contract dated July 15.
- The first show KISS played with Canadian band Rush and the only show they played with that band's original drummer John Rutsey — he was replaced by Neil Peart soon afterwards with this performance marking his last appearance with the band. They had recently signed with the same booking agency as KISS, American Talent International (ATI), and were planning a U.S. tour for September... The band had started their breakout in the U.S., having sold 7,000 copies of their debut album in Cleveland alone, versus 5,000 copies across the whole of Canada!
- According to promoter Nick Panaseiko, Rush impressed KISS so much at this gig that their performance set the stage for their many additional opening slots with the band over the next year.

August 3 - Convention Expo Center, Indianapolis, IN
Promoter: Sunshine Promotions
Other act(s): Blue Oyster Cult (HL), James Gang, Chris Jagger (opener)
Reported audience: 7,950 / 12,000 (66.25%)
Reported gross: $41,500
Notes:
- Performance Magazine noted the band entering Record Plant studios in Los Angeles for the August 3 – 30 period.

August 4 - Morris Civic Auditorium, South Bend, IN
Promoter: Sunshine Promotions
Other act(s): Blue Oyster Cult (HL)
Reported audience: (2,483 capacity)
Set list: Deuce / Nothin' to Lose / She / Firehouse / Strutter / 100,000 Years / Black Diamond / Baby, Let Me Go
Notes:
- Nazareth had been scheduled to perform, but did not.
- This show was recorded by a member of the audience via Superscope CS200 stereo cassette recorder with built-in mics.
- KISS' PA went out during "100,000 Years," but the band kept playing.
- This was the final show prior to the band entering the studios to record the "Hotter than Hell" album in Los Angeles.

August 31 - Raceway Park, Englishtown, NJ **CANCELLED
Promoter: Madison Township Raceway Park, Inc.
Other act(s): Faces (HL) Graham Central Station, Blue Oyster Cult, Styx
Notes:
- From local press: "Resistance by townships, property owners and law enforcement officials has limited the number of post-Woodstock outdoor rock festivals of the 300,000-people sort. But less ambitious events, both outdoors and indoors, still abound, and the New Jersey summer pop season will get under way tonight and tomorrow night with concerts by the Allman Brothers Band at the Roosevelt Stadium in Jersey City.... Potentially, the biggest site in the state is the Madison Township Raceway Park in Englishtown. The track is offering an opening concert June 15 of Sly and the Family Stone, and the Climax Blues Band, and has permission from the town to present three additional concerts. A ticket cutoff of 25,000 has been set for Sly's concert, but the promoters hope to expand that figure for later events... Tentatively, there will be five-band Labor Day weekend show on Aug. 31 headlined by Rod Stewart and Faces. Raceway Park, a 300-acre drag-racing facility, will be surrounded by a six-foot cyclone fence manned by mounted policemen and dog patrols, track officials said" (New York Times, 6/7/74).
- KISS' participation in this event was noted in Billboard, Aug. 31, 1974. The event was still being advertized as late as Aug. 25 (New York Times).

September 2 - Olympia Stadium, Detroit, MI **CANCELLED
Promoter: Bob Bageris / Bamboo Productions
Other act(s): Faces (HL), Haystacks, Blue Oyster Cult
Notes:
- Both the Aug. 31 and Sept. 2 festival dates appeared in KISS's June 3 itinerary and numerous trade publications well in advance of the planned dates, leaving much time for plans and availability for many of the acts involved to change. Plans for the Faces touring the U.S. fell through and they wouldn't return until Feb. 1975.

September 13 - Sir Wilfrid Laurier Theater, Kitchener, ON, Canada
Promoter: SRO Productions
Other act(s): Fludd (opener)
Reported audience: (1,500 capacity)
Reported gross: $4,710
Notes:
- The return to touring following the recording of "Hotter than Hell."
- From a local review: "Utilizing painted faces, flare rockets, glittery leather outfits, fire alarms and semi-synchronized spasticity, KISS invokes a strong initial and visual reaction but another bunch of 'pretty faces' does not make a concert. Technically, KISS has mastery of approximately five chord progressions and the intricate but not forgotten 4/4 beat. Versatility, subtlety and variety are not noticeably absent in KISS. What is noticed and felt is the Neanderthal rock that overpowers the body's natural defense system; it is transmitted in the upper decibel range and demands the body react to it (mind use was optional at this concert). KISS, not being musical or lyrical innovators, appeal to the latent, primitive emotions of the audience and project semi-sexual images (partially naked bodies and wagging foot-long tongues) while heightening their violent music with the audience's energy level" (The Cord Weekly, 9/19/74).

- Additional shows in Toronto, ON (9/14), Atlanta, GA (9/20), Louisville, KY (9/27) and Detroit, MI (9/28) were noted in Rolling Stone #170.

September 14 - Victory Theater, Toronto, ON, Canada **two shows
Promoter: SRO Productions
Other act(s): Fludd (opener)
Reported audience: 1,035 / 1,200 (86.25%)
Reported gross: $5,175
Notes:
- From a local review: "KISS was adequate as an opening band when it appeared in Toronto a few months ago, starting off the show for the New York Dolls. It was amusing as a momentary aberration, four fellows in black leather and makeup who produced a lot of noise and smoke and then disappeared. I didn't even bother to hope forever. But as the climax of an evening, Saturday night at the Victory Theater, KISS was a waste of time. I dozed occasionally while waiting for the band which condescended to appear at a quarter to one in the morning for a late show scheduled to start at 10 p.m. KISS offered little to keep anyone awake even after it appeared. Oh yes, there was pure volume. The sound system could have adequately filled Maple Leaf Gardens and was vastly more than required for the 1,500-seat Victory, but one can, with practice, sleep through the drone of the most unremitting heavy metal rock 'n' roll" (Toronto Globe & Mail, 9/16/74).
- Local band Fludd released their Adam Mitchell produced third studio album, "Great Expectations," in 1975...
- While in Toronto the band filmed an interview on the local City TV "Boogie Dance Show." It's doubtful that they performed, and if they did it was likely lip-synced. Any tapes of the band's appearance have yet to surface...

September 15 - Thomas Fieldhouse, Lock Haven, PA
Promoter: Fang Productions
Other act(s): Blue Oyster Cult (HL), Rush (opener)
Reported audience: (3,000 capacity)

September 16 - Paramount Theater, Wilkes-Barre, PA
Promoter: in-house
Other act(s): Blue Oyster Cult (HL), Rush (opener)
Reported audience: (2,000 capacity)

September 18 - Electric Ballroom, Atlanta, GA
Promoter: Alex Cooley, Inc.
Other act(s): Rush, Fat Chance (opener)
Reported audience: (1,100 capacity)
Notes:
- A promo for the band described them as: "With a background in the theater, the members of New York rock and roll group KISS see their stage make-up, theatrical effects (explosions, rising platforms, etc.) not as 'glitter rock' but simply as an extension of their own fantasy life. You can make up your own minds...)"
- Alex Cooley recalled, "They were almost like our house band in '74 [laughs]. Atlanta audiences took to KISS very early and they became one of Atlanta's favorite bands. They

caused extreme excitement during their shows here. People ate it up and everybody was on their feet through the whole set" ("Nothin' To Lose").

September 19 - Electric Ballroom, Atlanta, GA
Promoter: Alex Cooley, Inc.
Other act(s): Rush, Fat Chance (opener)
Reported audience: (1,100 capacity)

September 20 - Electric Ballroom, Atlanta, GA
Promoter: Alex Cooley, Inc.
Other act(s): Rush, Fat Chance (opener)
Reported audience: (1,100 capacity)

September 21 - Electric Ballroom, Atlanta, GA
Promoter: Alex Cooley, Inc.
Other act(s): Outlaws, Fat Chance (opener)
Reported audience: (1,100 capacity)
Note:
- KISS filed in for the group Nektar who had cancelled their appearance. The originally scheduled openers remained on the bill.

September 27 - The Ambassador Theater, St. Louis, MO **KISS CANCELLED
Promoter: Ron Powell / Panther Productions
Other act(s): Steppenwolf (HL), Pavlov's Dog
Reported audience: 4,400 / 6,012 (73.19%)
Notes:
- There was no mention of KISS in Steppenwolf's listing for this show in the Sept. 28, 1974 issue of Billboard Magazine. KISS's cancellation was reported in the Feb. 1975 issue of Circus Magazine: "When KISS turned up as guest stars to the reformed magic carpet riders in St. Louis recently, John Kay took it upon himself to censor the Gotham rockers' flashy, theatrical show. Steppenwolf denied Peter Criss his rocketing drum routine, as well as the various displays of fire-eating and blood-splitting by which KISS barbecue their fans' brains." Steppenwolf played two shows that night.

September 27 - Commonwealth Convention Center, Louisville, KY **CANCELLED
Other act(s): Rush (opener)
Notes:
- Louisville, KY (9/27), Detroit, MI (9/28) and Jacksonville, AL (10/1) were noted in Rolling Stone #171.

September 28 - Michigan Palace, Detroit, MI
Promoter: Steve Glantz Productions
Other act(s): Roy Wood & Wizzard (opener)
Reported audience: (5,000 capacity)
Notes:
- Paul recalled Roy opening for KISS: "We also got to take a few heroes of mine out on tour with us. That fall of 1975 we had both Slade and Wizzard, the band fronted by Roy Wood of the Move, open shows for us. Roy Wood's band created an eccentric version of Phil

Spector's wall of sound. His bass player wore roller skates. They were booed offstage. Afterwards I told Roy what a huge influence he had been on me. He was still shell-shocked from getting booed, and I was disappointed not to get much of a reaction from him" ("Face The Music").

- Gene and Roy were interviewed on Detroit radio and Gene purportedly copped to the inspiration taken from Roy's band into KISS' show ("Behind the Mask").

September 29 - Roberts Municipal Stadium, Evansville, IN **POSTPONED
Notes:
- This show was postponed, according to the promoter, due to the vehicle transporting the headliner's equipment from Pennsylvania being involved in an accident caused by poor weather. The concert was held the following night.

September 30 - Roberts Municipal Stadium, Evansville, IN
Promoter: Roger's Attractions
Other act(s): Billy Preston (HL), Rush (opener)
Reported audience: (13,600 capacity)
Notes:
- Billy was riding a hit single, "Nothing from Nothing" from his "The Kids & Me" (A&M SP-3645) album. The song topped the Billboard Hot 100 chart the following month (Oct. 19).

October 1 - Leone Cole Auditorium, Jacksonville, AL
Promoter: Jackson State University SGA
Other act(s): Rush (opener)
Reported audience: ~1,000 / 5,500 (18.18%)
Notes:
- From a local review: "As expected, KISS made professional use of their make-up lights and unique sounds to produce an experience to please the most freaky freak. The crowd moved forward, while others simply stood in their chairs to view the spectacle. As time passed, the act became so unreal that reality seemed in danger of slipping away. The presence of Mickey Mouse, Frankenstein or Dracula onstage would have mattered little to the audience or KISS! As if in a whirlwind, the crowd was swept first to their feet, then to come faraway place, perhaps the Twilight Zone.

Yes, perhaps it was the Twilight Zone. Where else would one find all listed above and much more that becomes quite impossible to remember. Or even those things one might wish to forget. For example, the blood dripping from the guitarist's mouth at the height of a song. Or the fancy garb, used to clue the onlookers in that KISS wasn't any ordinary group. Those who attended the KISS concert were treated to the freakiest show Jacksonville will see for a long time" (Jacksonville State University Chanticleer, 10/7/74).
- The show lost the promoter $2,500, who had budgeted some $8,000 to stage the show (to the complaint of some students who suggested the money could have been better spent on bands they'd actually heard of).

October 4 - Music Hall, Houston, TX
Promoter: Bobby Lewis / Bruce Dyson
Other act(s): Rush (opener)
Reported audience: (3,000 capacity)

Notes:

- Following this show the band took a two-week break before commencing the touring cycle in support of "Hotter than Hell."

Hotter Than Hell

Where to place the break between the "KISS" tour and "Hotter than Hell" might be a slightly contentious question. After the final shows in August 1974, before the band went into the studio to record the new album? After the cluster of shows the band performed between the end of September and early October? Or after the break following that second mini-tour? With so few known set lists or accurate reviews from the period it's impossible to currently identify where the first appearance of material from the new album really occurred — at that would provide the most useful "split" point to separate the tours. One might as well say that they kicked off the "Hotter Than Hell" tour at the Thunder Chicken on October 17, since it sounds good! It also makes sense in that the band had been back in New York City for nearly two weeks and had been on a break from the touring cycle. For all of the problems that archivists have with the tour, fans are fortunate that a recording of the tour's second show, at the Parthenon Theater in Hammond, IN on Oct. 18, circulates. This show provides evidence of "Got To Choose" and "Parasite" as the (currently) earliest known additions of material from the new album to the set. Naturally, the oft performed "Baby, Let Me Go" was retained in the set albeit with a new title: "Let Me Go, Rock 'N' Roll."

As for the tour, it was much as case of continuing what the band had been doing in the late summer — getting the band and material in front of as many people as possible and keeping the money-eating machine moving across the country. Without being attached to an established major-name tour. There is little, in general terms of the band's costumes or staging, to differentiate the "Hotter Than Hell" tour from the second half of the previous outing. However in terms of logistics, Paul recalled that the band members, "had switched to flying commercial flights from gig to gig, getting picked up and driven to and from hotels, while the gear caught up with us by truck and met us at the venue. We had also moved up to Holiday Inns instead of roadside motor lodges. It was easy to think we'd won the lottery as I put another quarter in the vibrating bed each night" ("Face The Music"). Casablanca's divorce from Warner Bros. most certainly had an effect on the overall finances surrounding the band, and the focus the label had on its roster, as Neil worked to shore up the independent distribution his label required. The label still advanced the band money where possible, but it was unlikely that that anything monetarily substantial had been recouped from Casablanca's investment in multiple studio sessions, advertizing and promotion, or any of the numerous other elements on the business side of rock and roll. The band's sales had been meager to date. As tight as money may have been, Direction Plus produced a TV commercial for the band in October 1974, utilizing live video filmed earlier in the year for an abandoned promotional film. Direction Plus had planned a bold move to place musical short mini-concerts running 10 – 15 minutes (almost expanded commercials) in some 7,000 movie theaters nationwide. The concept had been something of an evolution from the "Flipside" syndicated show, with the purpose of "combining both hard-sell and entertainment factors" (Billboard, 1/5/74). KISS's proposed episode ran 11 minutes and would have to count as yet another in a long list of "holy grails" from the band.

In some ways there was a regression during the "Hotter Than Hell" period to the more haphazard touring of the early part of the year, with the routing initially being more fragmented than it had been at the end of the previous cycle. Initially, the tour feels more like April 1974, a hodge-podge of dates cobbled together to keep the band on the road and gaining exposure wherever possible — rather than a logically sequential progression. One can imagine a member of the road crew measuring the distance between cities to determine whether a schedule was humanly possible. And while the band might have graduated to flying, their equipment still had to make the often brutal trip by road following the tear-down after a night's show. Larry Harris recalled the band's efforts on the road, "I would go on the road with them for a few days at a time, acting as an advance man of sorts, lining up promotion, schmoozing with my radio contacts and any other local media that would talk with me. These trips were never very long. While I didn't have to deal with the rigors of performing or sleep on tour buses, I was still exhausted after just a few days of touring. KISS had done this for months on end, and they showed no signs of fatigue. The band seemed to feed off the grueling lifestyle rather than letting it feed off them. Their commitment inspired everyone at the label" ("And Party Every Day: The Inside Story of Casablanca Records"). Unlike the "First KISS" tour, there were no major TV appearances, at least on a national level such as "In Concert" or the "Mike Douglas Show," which had provided broad exposure in the U.S. earlier in the year. Nor were there any label-backed promotions — "Kissin' Time" had been a perfect storm, but conversely it is questionable how much impact it really had on the band's fortunes. It's likely something impossible to quantify without delving into the subjective, or cliché — any press coverage is good, right?

By the end of November touring had settled down into a more structured routine with the band taking the middle slot on a Black Oak Arkansas package that included the James Montgomery Band as the opener. If Southern rock had an analogue of KISS, sans makeup, then the high-octane Black Oak fronted by the energetic Jim Dandy may well have come close to fitting that definition at the time. The run of dates was over within a couple of weeks and the period is something of a black hole for concrete details. Few of the available reviews mention any act on the bill other than the headliner, who had more than enough antics in their stage-show to go up against their opener — not least the popularity they were enjoying through the year. The rest of December remained the ubiquitous hodge-podge, though with the band opening at larger venues for the likes of REO Speedwagon or Z.Z. Top. If nothing else, the band's return to a sold-out Michigan Palace in Detroit cemented their support base in the region and could be considered triumphant. Those pre-Christmas shows reunited them with openers Rush who would become regular touring partners the following year. More notably, as the year drew to a close, was the band's first real run-in with the consequences of the inherent dangers of their stage-show. For whatever reason, at their December 30 show in Springfield, IL, an explosion of Peter's drumstick shooter effect nearly took off the hand of roadie Peter "Moose" Oreckinto.

Mirroring the album's performance, the "Hotter Than Hell" tour drew to a rapid conclusion in the early part of 1975 with the band being requested, by Casablanca President Neil Bogart, to return to the studio to record another album. Without radio airplay or national promotion the band had not taken more than a minor step up the rock 'n' roll food-chain with their sophomore offering. However, the seeds had been planted...

October 14, 1974 - CBS Studios B, New York City, NY
NARAS Oct '74 Chapter Meeting
Other act(s): Dick Hyman-Ted Sommer Trio
Notes:
- At the October meeting of the New York chapter of the Recording Academy (NARAS), moderated by Allison Steel, the members of KISS and Wayne County joined the panel for a discussion on the topic "Superstar or Superstud? (The visual vs the musical)." Other panelists included Jobriath's manager Jerry Brandt; producer-writer, Michael Cuscuna; and publicist Connie De Nave. Music will be supplied by the Dick Hyman-Ted Sommer Trio" (Billboard, 10/19/74). This event seems to have gone ahead with KISS being explicitly mentioned in a George T. Simon article in the Dec. 14 edition of Billboard: "At the October membership get-together of the New York chapter of the Recording Academy (NARAS), a visitor attending his first such meeting in several years murmured loudly enough for those nearby to hear, "is this really a NARAS meeting?" Prodded further by his neighborly eavesdroppers, he intimated that he's always thought these were rather stodgy affairs. "But now what do I see? Four members of KISS preening away, and a guy in a dress and, I presume, wearing a wig (Wayne County), camping and pouting his way to Queendom come" (Billboard, 12/14/74)"

The Oct. 19 issue of Billboard noted that this NARAS discussion ("Superstar or Superstud" The visual versus the musical) was going to be held at CBS Recording Studio B on Oct. 15. In the Oct. 26 issue it was reported as taking place on Oct. 14 with topics such as "Superstar vs. Superstud And Homosexuality in music — Is it a turn-on or a turn-off and "Theatrics in Music" on Oct. 14 at Columbia Recording Studio B. Quite a few pictures of the band, with Wayne Country, exist and have been printed in the press.

October 16 - North Hall Auditorium, Memphis, TN **NOT SCHEDULED
Notes:
- Because of Rush's touring activities with KISS during this period there has often been the incorrect assumption that the bands played this venue together. From the majority of sources so far uncovered, none of which are of the quality required to make a definitive statement, it appears that only Rush performed at this show — likely opening for Hawkwind with whom they were touring at the time. As a KISS concert it remains highly improbable... The first show publicized for what would be the "Hotter than Hell" tour was initially scheduled to take place in Hammond, IN. It ultimately became the second gig when another show was bumped up the schedule.

October 17 - Thunder Chicken Rock Theater, Comstock Park (Grand Rapids), MI
Promoter: Rebel Promotions, Inc.
Other act(s): None
Reported audience: (750 capacity)
Notes:
- This show was originally scheduled for the 22nd, but was moved to accommodate a second show at The Brewery being added to the itinerary. Rush, who were originally scheduled to open the 22nd show were playing a headlining gig at the Travis Street Electric Company in Dallas, TX; so did not perform.
- Considering the size of the club there was most likely a local or no opening act.

October 18 - Parthenon Theater, Hammond, IN
Promoter: S&J Productions
Other act(s): Unknown.
Reported audience: (2,500 capacity)
Set list: Deuce / Strutter / Got to Choose / Firehouse / She / Nothin' to Lose / Parasite / 100,000 Years / Black Diamond / Let Me Go, Rock 'N' Roll / Cold Gin
Notes:
- On the band's earliest itinerary for this period, dated 9/23/74, this show was listed as the first for the new leg of touring with Rush opening. However, Rush was actually opening for Hawkwind at Soldiers & Sailors Memorial Hall in Kansas City, MO this night.
- The second show of the "Hotter than Hell" tour and first major known change to the set list in over a year with the appearance of material from the new album in the set. With "Let Me Go, Rock 'N' Roll" having long been performed, the set adjustment was a cautious one. Because sets are unknown for the return to touring following the recording of the new album it's not precisely known when the new material started entering the set.
- A partial SBD recording from this show exists, but is missing the first two songs and begins with an in-progress "Got to Choose." It was one of the more exciting "leaks" during 2010, even with the inherent imperfections, providing an early glimpse of the integration of material from the new album.

October 19 - Renaissance Valentine Theater, Toledo, OH
Promoter: Brass Ring Productions
Other act(s): Rockets
Reported audience: (1,285 capacity)
Notes:
- Hosting weekend rock concerts at the venue was a last gasp attempt by the management to save the venue, though by December 1974 the Renaissance Corp. had gone into receivership.

October 21 - The Brewery, East Lansing, MI
Promoter: In-house / Boogie Bill Smith
Other act(s): None
Reported audience: ~1,000 **SOLD-OUT
Set list: Same as Oct. 18
Notes:
- More of a nightclub than a concert venue, The Brewery was a major part of the music scene for Michigan State University in the era, and just about any band touring at the time made the venue a stop on their itinerary. Technically the venue's capacity was 700, but it was often substantially oversold — especially for major national acts. According to State News reporter Jack Bodnar, who was a fixture at the venue covering live events, "Whether you were drinking, doing something else or just getting off on the music at the Brewery, it was incredibly memorable. Nobody went to the Brewery and only had a good time, they had a great time. It was one of those too-good-to-last places" (Lansing City Pulse).
- From a local review: "Surprisingly, KISS has strong enough pull in East Lansing to sell out the Brewery for two consecutive nights — though this might be easily explained when one considers the group's rising popularity in Detroit. In fact, only a Detroit crowd could have loved this band on Monday night, as it pioneered new loudness levels previously only

reached by the legendary Blue Cheer. At uniform blast intensity, KISS drove the very rowdy crowd to near ecstasy" (State News).
- A great soundboard recording of this show circulates. Unfortunately, currently the bulk of the remaining dates on the tour are devoid of archival recordings.
- Considering the size of the club there was most likely a local or no opening act.

October 22 - The Brewery, East Lansing, MI
Promoter: In-house / Boogie Bill Smith
Other act(s): None
Reported audience: ~1,000 **SOLD-OUT
Notes:
- One series of newspaper ads for this show listed an incorrect date for the show, November 22.
- From a local review: "If there were any power shortages around East Lansing Tuesday night, they were probably caused by the high energy party at the Brewery that featured KISS. The band rocked the entire building and everyone in it... Although their makeup and costumes made them look like they were fresh off a science fiction movie set, or possibly a little early for Halloween. Their overall show was really good. Their music was tight, the showmanship excellent, except for the unnecessary spitting and drooling of 'blood' at one point by bass guitarist Gene Simmons... Except for a slight problem with feedback at one point the only real complaint one could have with the show was the deafening volume of the music, which in itself was bad enough but it almost made it impossible to hear the vocals without plugging your ears" (State Journal, 10/26/74).

October 25 - Capitol Theater, Passaic, NJ
Promoter: John Scher
Other act(s): Golden Earring (HL), John Hammond (opener)
Reported audience: (3,200 capacity)
Notes:
- This show was originally advertized as Golden Earring opening for the Climax Blues Band who had to pull out of the gig. On this occasion the KISS logo was located on the right of the stage.

October 26 - Veterans Memorial Coliseum, Cedar Rapids, IA **KISS CANCELLED
Promoter: Celebration Concerts
Other act(s): REO Speedwagon (HL), third act
Notes:
- While this show appeared as part of an ad for a REO Speedwagon, Focus, and Blue Oyster Cult "Battle of the Bands" in Des Moines on October 28, it remains unlikely to have included KISS. With the previous night's show in Passaic it seems unlikely, but not impossible, that the crew could have handled a 1,000+ mile drive followed by 650 miles back east the following day. The only thing that is definite is that a concert took place at the venue on this night (an attendee was arrested for disorderly conduct though no specific review has yet been located).

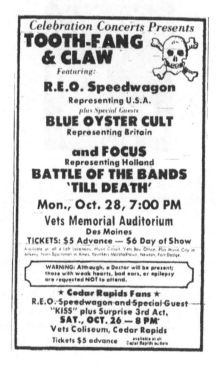

October 27 - Tomorrow Club, Youngstown, OH
Promoter: In-house
Other act(s): Cannonball (opener)
Reported audience: (2,142 capacity)
Notes:

- The Tomorrow Club had only opened on October 20, and by the time KISS performed there had already hosted the Michael Stanley Band, Golden Earring and Focus. Ted Nugent and The Amboy Dukes performed the following week.

October 30 - Agora Ballroom, Columbus, OH
Promoter: Agora Presents
Other act(s): Frijid Pink (opener)
Reported audience: (2,000 capacity)
Notes:
- This show was billed as an over-18 only Halloween party. With similarities to Blue Cheer or the MC5, Frijid Pink were a Detroit band who had a 1970 hit with a heavily distorted cover of "House of the Rising Sun." None of their other singles ever repeated that success and numerous lineup changes followed, but their history does include having Led Zeppelin as an opening act!

October 31 - Peru Circus Center Building, Peru, IN
Promoter: B&E Productions
Other act(s): Stone Wall
Reported audience: (1,000 capacity)
Notes:
- Some old KISS concert lists included a listing for a 10/31/73 show included opening act Stone Wall. Due to the concert flyer being of similar style to some early KISS club flyers (even including the phrase "Rock & Roll Party") it seems likely there was some confusion, between this show which did take place, albeit a year after the club era.
- A local press article mentioned the band's contract rider: "When KISS came to Peru recently to play a concert there, they required in their contract before the concert, a set price and 40 percent of the gate, 150 pounds of dry ice, two super-troopers for lighting, a PA system, a grand piano, a bottle of Seagrams VO, a case of beer, transportation to and from the airport, a body guard, 48 Cokes, 48 7-Ups, 10 cups of tea, a jar of mayonnaise, Swiss and American cheese, white and rye bread, coleslaw; four different kinds of fresh fruit, roast beef, ham and turkey with white and dark meat. Needless to say the group lives well" (Logansport Pharos Tribune, 4/6/75).

November 2 - Maine West High School, Des Plaines, IL
Other act(s): Smokehouse
Notes:
- This show was held in the Herman L. Rider Memorial Gymnasium. Sources suggest that the school won a contest and the prize was KISS performing.
- Smokehouse's line-ups had included numerous musicians throughout their early history, notably Steve Gaines who later joined Lynyrd Skynyrd. The two bands would play together again the following year with another young guitarist in their line-up...

November 3 - Duluth Arena, Duluth, MN
Promoter: Yanqui Productions, Inc.
Other act(s): Dr. John, Easy Steam (opener)
Reported audience: (7,765 capacity)
Notes:

- The Raspberries were originally on this eclectic bill but were replaced by local progressive rock band Easy Steam.

November 7 - Sunshine In Concert Hall, Asbury Park, NJ **TEMP HOLD DATE
Promoter: Bob Fisher
Notes:
- This date was listed in the band's Sept. 23 itinerary, and would have been the first show following a short touring gap. In some trade publications the show was alternatively scheduled for Nov. 9. Regardless, the band's appearance was rescheduled for Nov. 16, likely due to the St. Louis show.

November 7 - Kiel Auditorium, St. Louis, MO
Promoter: KSHE-FM Promotion
Other act(s): Heartsfield (HL), T-Rex (opener), Neil Merryweather & the Space Rangers (opener)
Reported audience: 10,586 **SOLD-OUT
Notes:
- This show was part of KSHE radio's "7th Anniversary Party of Real Rock Radio." KISS was not billed as the headliner; nor was T-Rex mentioned in some print ads. Heartsfield was a country-rock act. The band flew in from New York on the day of the show.
- From a local review: "Good Theater — most rock groups do not know the meaning of it. However, a New York quartet called KISS provided the sell-out house at Kiel Auditorium with plenty of it last night. The New Yorkers were one of four groups that entertained at the KSHE-FM promotion, but they were a grotesque head and shoulders above the rest. Their part of the program opened in semi-darkness, illuminated only by several candles. Then flash powder explosions lit each side of the stage as the spotlights revealed the musicians in all their eerie glory. White and black painted faces, weird clothes, tights and high-heeled boots added to the fascinating and well coordinated choreography that smacked of devil dancing" (St. Louis Post-Dispatch, 11/8/74).

November 8 - Aragon Ballroom, Chicago, IL
Promoter: Jam / Celebration Production
Other act(s): UFO (opener), T-Rex (opener)
Reported audience: (5,000 capacity)
Notes:
- All four acts are listed in print advertisements for the show. The band flew into Chicago at lunchtime on the day of the show. T-Rex was replaced by KISS as the headliner the week of the show. Hydra isn't mentioned in the review.
- From a local review: "Call this New York quartet gimmicky, and nobody can argue. Call their music crude, and you'd call it right. But there's a place for that sort of thing, and when you're in the mood for it, you've got to call KISS killers as well. When they appeared at the Aragon earlier this year, they were unknown. But the word's apparently gotten around, because when KISS returned to the Aragon Friday to headline a triple bill, the place was packed. KISS doesn't just perform. They stage an assault, visually as well as musically. The music's hardly great; with three guitarists and a drummer they produce a sound that's loud, crude, heavy crash and thunder rock 'n' roll as unsubtle and unsettling as the 'blood' that drips vulgarly from a mouth at one point or the flashes of flame that punctuate song after song. But they handle it all well, and the gimmicks mesh with the music from the start to

the fireworks finale. KISS has psyched out its audiences perfectly; they cater to current tastes and come up with a show that's hellishly good fun. Given these credentials, how on earth can KISS miss" (Chicago Tribune, 11/11/74)?

November 10 - Pioneer Gymnasium @ Delta College, Saginaw (University Center), MI
Promoter: Peter Cavanaugh/WTAC
Other act(s): Skyhook (opener)
Notes:
- The band flew into Saginaw during the afternoon the day prior to the show.
- From a local review: "Being as I had in my possession a press pass and being as there was nothing else to do, I attended Delta's KISS concert. Truthfully, I must say I wasn't expecting much... and got what I expected. Shades of BTO, I ain't seen nothin' yet. I though perhaps I'd be getting two for the price of one — attend a concert, see a circus. However, someone forgot to bring the concert. Sarcastic, yes, for a music review, but then, there was no music to review. What there was consisted of four Linda-Blairs-in-drag amusing the audience with such cutesy-pie antics as fire-eating, blood spitting, and light flashing. Oh, wailing and gnashing of teeth, oh sackcloth and ashes, let me out" (Delta Collegiate, 11/26/74).

November 12 - Municipal Civic Auditorium, Minot, ND
Promoter: Galaxy Productions
Other act(s): Clowns (opener)
Reported audience: 1,085 / 5,059 (22.45%)
Reported gross: $4,571.50
Notes:
- The band flew into Minot, via Chicago, the evening prior to the show. They returned to New York City the following day, via Minneapolis, arriving in the late-evening.

November 16 - Sunshine In Concert Hall, Asbury Park, NJ
Promoter: Bob Fisher
Other act(s): Mercury, Fantasy (opener)
Reported audience: (2,000 capacity)
Notes:
- Fantasy included Peter Baron, a former guitarist for Leslie West's Wild West Show. Following this show the band took a brief break.

November 21 – Roberts Municipal Stadium, Evansville, IN **KISS CANCELLED
Promoter: Roger's Attractions
Other act(s): Black Oak Arkansas (HL)
Notes:
- Late September ads included KISS as the opening act. By early November, with KISS instead opening for Foghat in Cedar Rapids, the line-up for this show had changed to include openers Montrose and the James Montgomery Band.

November 21 – Veteran's Memorial Coliseum, Cedar Rapids, IA
Promoter: Celebration Concerts
Other act(s): Foghat (HL)
Reported audience: (4,168 capacity)
Notes:

- On KISS's Nov. 4 itinerary the headliner is listed as Black Oak Arkansas. However, press ads for the show from the same time period detail the headliner as Foghat with Black Oak holding court in Evansville, the originally scheduled date including KISS. Black Oak had performed in Cedar Rapids with Jo Jo Gunne and the James Montgomery Band on Nov. 10.

November 23 - Alexander Memorial Coliseum @ GA Tech, Atlanta, GA
Promoter: Alex Cooley, Inc.
Other act(s): Black Oak Arkansas (HL), James Montgomery Band (opener)
Reported audience: (5,000 capacity)
Notes:
- A brief review of the show in the Great Speckled Bird (1/2/75) makes absolutely no mention of KISS, though first-hand accounts do recount them performing. The only other act noted as performing is the James Montgomery Band. It's unclear whether Trapeze, who were advertized as late as Nov. 21 performed in the middle of the bill.

November 24 - Carolina Coliseum, Columbia, SC **CANCELLED
Promoter: Entertainment Concepts
Other act(s): Black Oak Arkansas (HL)
Reported audience: (13,500 capacity)
Notes:
- Instead of a concert, a three-day antiques show and sale was held at the venue, ending at 6 p.m. on Nov. 24 (which would not have left time to transition to a concert at the venue that same evening). Black Oak performed at the Freedom Hall Civic Center in Johnson City, TN, with Foghat and The Stampeders on Nov. 26.

November 27 - Memorial Auditorium, Greenville, SC
Promoter: Beach Club Booking
Other act(s): Black Oak Arkansas (HL), James Montgomery Band (opener)
Reported audience: (7,500 capacity)

November 28 - Charlotte Coliseum, Charlotte, NC
Promoter: Kaleidoscope Productions
Other act(s): Black Oak Arkansas (HL), James Montgomery Band (opener)
Reported audience: (13,000 capacity)

November 29 - Gaillard Municipal Auditorium, Charleston, SC
Promoter: Beach Club Promotions
Other act(s): Black Oak Arkansas (HL), James Montgomery Band (opener)
Reported audience: (2,734 capacity)
Notes:
- Incorrectly listed as Camden, SC in the band's Nov. 4 itinerary.
- There was not a single mention of any other acts than the two main performers in local press leading up to this show; nor in the review of the concert (Charleston Evening Press, 12/2/74). On the tickets only the James Montgomery Band received any billing, though in the press the day prior to the show, Canadian act, the Stampeders, were also advertized. Whatever the case, there was enough reason for minor opening acts to not receive any mention. Black Oak had had a stunning year with their self-titled album going gold and three other albums performing solidly. In a trade ad they celebrated the year, noting

performances to 1,211,377 fans with a gross income of over $2,000,000.00 from 127 U.S. concerts (Billboard, 11/30/74).

November 30 - Cumberland County Civic Auditorium, Fayetteville, NC
Promoter: Beach Club Booking
Other act(s): Black Oak Arkansas (HL), James Montgomery Band (opener)
Reported audience: (7,000 capacity)

December 1 - Civic Center, Asheville, NC **CANCELLED
Promoter: Beach Club Booking
Other act(s): Black Oak Arkansas (HL), Stampeeders (opener)
Reported audience: (7,646 capacity)
Notes:
- This show was cancelled due to heavy snow and icy conditions in western North Carolina.
- There has been the suggestion that KISS were thrown off the Black Oak tour due to the band's effects burning the headliner's backdrop during the "Black Diamond" finale, but there were no additional shows scheduled with them following this date. Peter recalled, "I blew Black Oak Arkansas' curtains down. I put two holes through them with my fire-shooting sticks. I didn't really do it on purpose — they're really nice guys. I just shot 'em, and they just happened to burn their curtains down" (Gulcher, 1/76).

December 6 - Van Meter Auditorium @ Western Kentucky University, Bowling Green, KY
Promoter: Associated Student Government / Ron Beck / Tom LaCivita
Other act(s): None.
Reported audience: ~1,100
Notes:
- KISS were booked as a replacement for a cancelled Al Stewart show, due to him encountering immigration issues in November. William F. Buckley, Jr., was scheduled to deliver a speech, "Some of the Problems of Freedom," in the auditorium at 1p.m. The show was reported near capacity.
- From a local review: "The group's style and vivacity rather startled some with their smoke bombs and fire-eating antics. Quite a number of students, however, were very pleased with the effort. It seemed to be just what the protesting students had in mind when they called for groups that are of interest to the students. The outlandish theatrics of the four-man group entertained a capacity crowd in Van Meter Auditorium, but for several in the audience, the band's thunder rock was about as enjoyable as a direct hit by a bolt of lightning. KISS was very entertaining, theatrically. Whiteface makeup and leather bat wings enhanced the macho image and the fantastic stage antics of the group. Aside from being too loud, the concert was too short for the price paid, and musically short in many ways.

KISS came up short in musical complexity, '100,000 Years' was the most complex song performed, and it was complex because it had a two-chord introduction. Bassist Gene Simmons provided the most deviant entertainment of the group. He didn't sing much, but he did simulate vomiting in the middle of one of the group's better numbers. He dripped 'blood' over Van Meter's stage and the screaming fans on the front row. The hallowed stage of Van Meter, where sedate lecturers had spoken and lively theatre productions had been performed, was deflowered with the KISS performance. Accustomed to intelligible voices, the auditorium was filled with undecipherable sounds amid a strange, blue smoky haze.

Beck said that he would never participate in booking 'this kind of act' for Western again because the show contained 'no educational value for students.' He said the show left him with an 'empty feeling'" (WKU 1975 Talisman).

December 8 - Roberts Municipal Stadium, Evansville, IN
Promoter: Sunshine Promotions
Other act(s): ZZ Top (HL), Point Blank (opener)
Reported audience: (12,600 capacity)
Notes:
- The first KISS concert attended by future KISS Army Commander in Chief Bill Starkey. He was taken by his father, "a warehouse 'expeditor' for Columbia Records in Terre Haute, where millions of vinyl records were pressed and distributed during the last half of the 20th century. He gave Bill his first KISS record, a self-titled release from February 1974" (Indy Star, 4/6/14).

December 10 - Palmer College Alumni Auditorium, Davenport, IA
Promoter: Celebration Concerts
Other act(s): ZZ Top (HL), Point Blank (opener)
Reported audience: (4,320 capacity)
Notes:
- Palmer College was primarily a chiropractic school.

December 11 - Meadowbrook Theatre Restaurant, Cedar Grove, NJ **TEMP HOLD DATE
Promoter: Meadowbrook Productions
Reported audience: (700 capacity)
Notes:
- While this show was noted in the band's Dec. 2 itinerary, the facility had gone out of business in October, due to the ubiquitous "economic problems," which translated into reality was a result of a strike caused by a conflict in wages between the staff and management during a contract negotiation. A separate newspaper article suggests that the venue was still shuttered in December. Regardless, any booking on the east coast would have made little sense with the emerging mid-western dates that eventually surrounded it. Like the Thunder Chicken, the venue mixed various productions with dining.

December 12 - I.M.A. Auditorium, Flint, MI
Promoter: Brass Ring Productions
Other act(s): ZZ Top (HL)
Reported audience: 4,100 / 5,300 (77.36%)
Reported gross: $27,148
Notes:
- This was apparently a last-minute show with just nine days of advertizing and tickets on sale.

December 13 - Mary E. Sawyer Auditorium, La Crosse, WI
Promoter: Hole in the Wall Productions
Other act(s): Eddie Boy Band (opener)
Reported audience: (4,100 capacity)
Notes:

- Some ads also detail Tongue as an opening act.

December 18 - La Porte Armory, La Porte, IN
Promoter: Schizoid Productions
Other act(s): Scream (opener)

December 20 - Michigan Palace, Detroit, MI
Promoter: Steve Glantz Productions
Other act(s): Rush, Fancy (opener)
Reported audience: 5,000 **SOLD-OUT
Notes:
- The promoter held a reception in the Palace's Mezzanine Lobby following the show to celebrate Peter's birthday. Steve Glantz was a young and hungry promoter who had teamed with the Michigan Concert Palace's owner, Dr. Leo Speer, to bring rock concerts to what was described as a "majestic but deteriorating theater" (Detroit Free Press, 3/23/75). His first year was marred with fines for fire code violations and accusations of overcrowding.

December 21 - Michigan Palace, Detroit, MI
Promoter: Steve Glantz Productions
Other act(s): Rush, Fancy (opener)
Reported audience: 5,000 **SOLD-OUT
Reported gross: $51,000 **both shows
Notes:
- Both concerts were reportedly over-sold by a total of 200 tickets.

December 22 - London Arena, London, ON, Canada
Promoter: Nick Panaseiko Productions/CJOM-FM
Other act(s): Joe, DJ Ronny Legge (opener)
Reported audience: (2,000 capacity)
Notes:
- According to Lydia Criss (in "Sealed With A KISS"), Peter was busted for possessing valium and Darvon (a narcotic pain reliever) tablets, and was prevented from importing them into Canada. He wasn't arrested or charged with any crime.
- This show started nearly 3 hours late. Promotion for this concert included a store display that may have featured the first use of the phrase "Merry KISS-mas."
- From a local review: "KISS is a tight well rehearsed band with some excellent musical ideas. Unfortunately, the ability to hear any of this is lost in the incredible amount of distortion which is created by KISS' pain-inducing volume level. I am not at all against loud music but I do not appreciate pain under any circumstances. They can only be appreciated by hearing them on a recording. KISS has something to offer musically but the glitter and whiteface is on its way out and if the group is to remain alive, it must change and face the future that one of its members is supposed to represent" (London Free Press, 12/23/74).
- 6:28 of silent Super 8mm footage surfaced in 2009 which included Joe performing and the band meeting KISS backstage.

December 23 - Paramount Theater, Wilkes-Barre, PA
Promoter: Fang Productions
Other act(s): Kenny Kramer (opener)

Reported audience: (2,047 capacity)
Notes:
- Kenny was a comedian. Paul recalled him, "our opening act was a circus juggler. He rode a unicycle and people in the audience tried to knock him off by throwing coins at him. Now, I had seen strange bills in the late 1960s and early 1970s — things like Led Zeppelin and Woody Herman's orchestra. That sort of thing was considered hip. But putting some poor soul onstage on a unicycle before KISS? It was tough enough for a regular band to open for us" ("Face The Music").
- Moose recalled getting busted in New York State, while driving from the previous night's show in Ontario, for carrying flash-paper — considered a gambling tool in the state, but used by the band for Peter's exploding drum stick effect. He'd eventually get off with a small fine. The drum sticks would cause bigger problems a few days later...

December 26 - Civic Center Auditorium, Grand Rapids, MI **KISS CANCELLED
Promoter: Rainbow / Celebration Productions
Other act(s): REO Speedwagon (HL)
Reported audience: (4,599 capacity)
Reported gross: $34,560
Notes:
- KISS cancelled their performance due to a snowstorm.

December 27 – Veteran's Auditorium, Des Moines, IA **KISS CANCELLED
Promoter: Celebration Concerts
Other act(s): Wishbone Ash (HL)
Reported audience: (12,216 capacity)
Notes:
- KISS was replaced by Brownsville Station a week prior to the show.

December 27 - Memorial Coliseum, Fort Wayne, IN
Promoter: Sunshine Promotions
Other act(s): REO Speedwagon (HL), Quicksilver Messenger Service
Reported audience: (13,000 capacity)
Reported gross: $38,756
Notes:
- From a local review: "Let's face it. It is insane for a group of men dressed like bats and gargoyles to sling fire and fake blood around the stage and then say they are playing good old, down home rock 'n' roll. If that's rock 'n' roll, then I'm David Bowie. KISS, the New York 'theatrical rock' group dressed like bats and gargoyles, won second place in the crowd's heart Friday night, but they were a distant second to hard, loud and surprising intricate REO Speedwagon" (Fort Wayne News-Sentinel, 12/28/74).

December 28 - Convention Expo Center, Indianapolis, IN
Promoter: Sunshine Promotions
Other act(s): REO Speedwagon (HL), Quicksilver Messenger Service, Hydra (opener)
Reported audience: (12,000 capacity)
Reported gross: $68,592
Notes:

- When this show was initially announced it was scheduled for Market Square Arena. The following week Rush as added as an opener and moved to the Convention Center, while a competing promoter still advertized REO at the then recently opened Arena on the same night. By December 15 the lineup had changed to its final form.
- The second KISS concert attended by future KISS Army Commander in Chief Bill Starkey which his mom takes him to. KISS actually performed after REO had completed their set and many of the patrons had departed. Paul recalled, "They decided they want to go on after us, which was wise. They figured the way to let us go quietly into the night was to not announce it and to have us go on after them — and nobody would be left at the show. Didn't happen. We're not a band that you can stop" (Indy Star, 5/17/14).

December 29 - Performing Arts Center, Milwaukee, WI **KISS CANCELLED
Promoter: Daydream Productions / Randy McElreth
Other act(s): REO Speedwagon (HL)
Reported audience: (2,331 capacity)
Reported gross: $19,912
Notes:
- While KISS didn't appear, REO performed two shows this night.

December 29 - Morris Civic Auditorium, South Bend, IN
Promoter: Sunshine Promotions
Other act(s): Quicksilver Messenger Service, Hydra (opener)
Reported audience: 2,483 **SOLD-OUT
Reported gross: $13,640
Notes:
- KISS had originally been scheduled as the opening act for a REO Speedwagon show at Milwaukee's PAC, but canceled in favor of a headlining show.

December 30 - Illinois State Armory, Springfield, IL
Promoter: A Whatever Production
Other act(s): Mike Quatro Jam Band (opener)
Reported audience: (5,381 capacity)

Notes:
- At this show Moose nearly blew his hand off during the opening act's set while preparing Peter's drumstick shooter effect. The audience thought the explosion was part of Mike Quatro's set and applauded. Causing other injuries, Moose was rushed to a local hospital where surgeons were able to save his hand. Moose was in hospital until Jan. 6 and his recuperation took many weeks.

December 31 - Memorial Coliseum, Evansville, IN
Promoter: Roger's Attractions
Other act(s): Raspberries (opener)
Reported audience: (4,055 capacity)
Notes:
- While Rush were listed as the opening act in print advertisements they did not perform and were replaced by the Raspberries. At the time the Raspberries included guitarist Wally Bryson who'd form the band Tattoo following their split in April 1975. One of the songs from their 1976 debut album (Prodigal), "Give It to Ya Easy," circulated as a so-called Wicked Lester demo for many years.

January 7, 1975 - Pavilion, Lethbridge, AB, Canada
Promoter: Gold & Gold Brimestone Productions
Notes:
- The band flew into Lethbridge via Toronto on the day of show.

January 9 - Commodore Ballroom, Vancouver, BC, Canada **two shows
Promoter: Accident Productions
Other act(s): The Sam Hurrie Band (opener)
Reported audience: (1,000 capacity)
Notes:
- Originally, the opening act had been billed as Sam Hurrie's Diamond Reo, but due the existence of a band in New York already named Diamond Reo a change was required. Shows were scheduled at 9 and 11 p.m.
- "Strange Ways" was reportedly performed at the second show this night, indicating that it may have been in other sets during the period.

- From a local review: "And KISS members are not totally inept as musicians. The sound is the usual wall-of-guitars, Rolling Stones as diluted by Bachman-Turner Overdrive, and yet underneath the hard-rock exterior beats a heart of solid pop. 'Nothin' To Lose' sounded like the Beatles playing a little loud... All true rock fans must recognize KISS for what it is, a healthy counterweight to the creeping intellectualization of rock. But any moron can understand the police sirens and flashing red lights and flame-throwing that makes up KISS' act, any moron at all. Remember, they once laughed at Alice Cooper" (Vancouver Sun, 1/10/75).

January 10 - Paramount Northwest Theater, Portland, OR

Promoter: Get Down Productions
Other act(s): Ballin' Jack (opener)
Reported audience: ~2,700 / 3,060 (88.23%)
Notes:
- From pre-show press: "Music and show business sometime become so intertwined it's hard to tell which is which someone like David Bowie manages to do both admirably, entertaining with production as well as music. So, where do you put a band and called KISS? Last time I saw, and heard, KISS, the quartet of New York rockers put on a visually satisfying show that lacked a bit in the music department. However, reviews from around the country the past several months have given the group credit for playing music, too. Whatever your choice, music or visuals, KISS will have it on display when the group comes back to Portland's Paramount Northwest theater at 8p.m. Friday, Jan. 10. Their rock is the down-to-earth heavy sort, with multi-decibels of volume guaranteed to keep the listener from nodding off" (Oregonian, 1/8/75).
- From a local review: "Pronounce the same three words in a raspy shout about once every 10 minutes: 'Rock and roll.' The effect on a crowded theater of young people 15 to say 19 can be ominous quiet or it can lead to pandemonium. Friday night at the Paramount Northwest Theater, the latter effect was the norm for the 2,700 kids crammed into the hall, most of them on their feet or chairs, as America's latest contribution to showbiz rock — read glitterpunk — returned to Portland. The band is called KISS and it is four guys dolled up in black tights with various vinyl accouterments such as thigh-high boots, breast-plates and capes. They top off the costumes with black and white makeup in bizarre patterns that are a mixture of Satanism, superhero comics and kabuki. There's also a bit of eroticism and, judging from the number of young ladies dressed in 'backstage superstar hip' apparel screaming from the audience, a certain amount of sex appeal joins the aura surrounding KISS ...

With 75 minutes of bizarre behavior from the band, who needs music? Well, without it, it would have been tough. These four fellows may not be the best musicians in rock and roll — there, I've said it again — but they lay down a solid torrent of boogie. No instrumental fireworks, no absorbing solos, just a lot of heavy rhythm that fills your head and moves your feet. It would be easy to say, take away the makeup and costumes and what have you got left? Four rock and roll musicians with a lot of guts. But wait a minute. It was fun. There were no slow tunes to spoil the highs. It was mind-bending with gimmicks" (Oregonian, 1/11/75)...

January 11 - Medford National Guard Armory, Medford, OR

Promoter: Rock 'N' Roll Productions

Other act(s): Arosa (opener)
Reported audience: (2,500 capacity)
Notes:
- Pre show press described the band as being known "for its Alice Cooper-style stage show, featuring fire breathing guitar players, levitating drummers and laser beams" (Medford Mail Tribune, 1/10/75).

January 12 - Paramount Northwest Theater, Seattle, WA
Promoter: Get Down Productions
Other act(s): Ballin' Jack (opener)
Reported audience: ~1,500 / 2,997 (50.05%)
Notes:
- A brief mention in Highline College's Thunder World (2/7/75) suggested that local act Ballin' Jack's act had bombed opening for KISS. The band had been active since 1969, but ultimately had never managed to break nationally.
- Both the Portland and Seattle shows were reviewed in the Seattle Times (1/13/75): "Nobody who was at the Paramount last night will remember the music. That's the least important thing about KISS. Their music is basic rock riffs and lots of repetition... What people will remember are the explosions, the dry-ice smoke, the flashing lights, the leather and metal costumes and the face makeup of the band members." That reviewer was the same person who had suggested the previous year, "... KISS won't be around long. Flash doesn't last" (Seattle Daily Times, 5/27/74).

January 14 - Lane County Fairgrounds, Expo Hall, Eugene, OR **CANCELLED
Reported audience: (2,750 capacity)
Notes:
- Better known as a venue for hosting boxing, this show (which appears on some itineraries) does not seem to have taken place.

January 17 - Long Beach Arena, Long Beach, CA
Promoter: Pacific Presentations
Other act(s): Wishbone Ash (HL), Camel (opener)
Reported audience: 6,270 **SOLD-OUT
Notes:
- The show was noted in Performance Magazine as selling out a 2/3 venue configuration (capacity 9,000).
- From a local review: "How can you follow theatrics like whiteface Kabuki makeup, black stars, sequins, Buck Rodgers space pants, fog bombs engulfing the stage and fire-spitting smoke stacks? Easy, just play some good old rock sounds. Find a balanced effort. Feature good musicians. And forget the gimmicks. The rest takes care of itself. And this is exactly what Wishbone Ash did Friday night at the Long Beach Arena. They played their gig and left the games to the group with the least talent — KISS... KISS, billed as a hot band of fire, was more balcony bologna hiding behind a mask of glittering trickery. For the KISS... the makeup is an extension of collective fantasies. Unfortunately they never say what kind of fantasies produce music which would make a decibel meter blink. Music loud enough to turn the arena into a blur. Music with enough energy to make you forget what it is that you're listening to... and that is the reason for going to a concert. To listen. KISS explodes with sound. Too bad it's not worth picking up the pieces" (Long Beach Independent, 1/21/75).

- From another local review: "Preceding Wishbone Ash was KISS, the latest to wear the 'band you love to hate' tag. The Gotham goblins were loved by the audience and hated by this reviewer, who finds KISS' rip-off riff-rock and rough-tough posing offensive and obnoxious. But that's probably the idea" (Los Angeles Times, 1/21/75).

January 18 - Swing Auditorium, San Bernardino, CA
Promoter: Pacific Presentations
Other act(s): ZZ Top (HL)
Reported audience: ~7,900 / 10,000 (58%)
Notes:
- From a local review: "Looking like a combination of Batman, Dracula and the Exorcist, New York City's KISS rocked a full San Bernardino Swing Auditorium last Saturday night. KISS looked like nothing seen before on a rock 'n' roll stage (not even Alice, Bowie, or the N.Y. Dolls) in their black leather suits and black and white painted face masks. After blasting out a couple of new electrifying songs from their recent infectious 'Hotter than Hell' album, everyone got on their toes. With influences of the heaviest British metal rock, KISS presented a uniquely different sound and sound of their own, as they showed with their version of Humble Pie's 'Firehouse'" (University Times, 1/21/75). The review reported an attendance of ~5,800.
- From an industry review: "KISS, who opened to a very enthusiastic crowd themselves, let their brand of heavy metal hard rock and unique makeup and clothes speak for them, though three times they exhorted the audience to 'Get it on!' Their theatrics and loudness worked to their advantage and they paced themselves well enough to earn two encores for themselves. Make no mistake, the crowd had already gotten down before reaching the Swing in good ole San Berdoo" (Cashbox, 2/1/75).

January 19 - Golden Hall Community Concourse, San Diego, CA
Promoter: Jim Pagni
Other act(s): Wishbone Ash (HL), Camel (opener)
Reported audience: ~3,000 / 3,200 (93.75%)
Notes:
- Gene's fire-breathing routine was apparently prevented by the local Fire Department on safety grounds.
- From a local review: "Picture four frizzy-haired Flash Gordons, for example, possessed by demons, wearing Kabuki makeup and now forming a rock 'n' roll band. Thus you have the members of KISS, a New York quartet that performs in white-face wearing black outer-space costumes apparently salvaged from some early science fiction movie. Costumes and choreographed hair-tossing aside, KISS' brand of straight-on, loud, hard rock became a bit monotonous toward the end of a 45-minute set, lacking as it did any variety or change of pace. Number after number built to one crescendo atop another until the eardrums were numb. The one exceptional moment came on a flashy solo by lead guitarist Ace Frehley that evoked thunder-and-lightning images. Advance publicity said one of the group's members spits fire during the act, but the musicians complained that the Fire Department had nixed the idea; perhaps the gimmick would have lent some interest to the noise" (San Diego Union, 1/20/75).

January 21 - Regis College Field House, Denver, CO **KISS CANCELLED
Promoter: Fey Presentations

Other act(s): Wishbone Ash (HL), Camel (opener)
Reported audience: (3,000+ capacity)
Notes:
- While this show at a Jesuit University was cancelled, KISS remained in Los Angeles and wrote/rehearsed material for a new studio album at SIR Studios B.

January 23 - Terrace Ballroom, Salt Lake City, UT **KISS CANCELLED
Other act(s): Wishbone Ash (HL), Camel (opener)
Reported audience: **SOLD-OUT
Notes:
- This show doesn't appear on KISS itineraries from the period, but did take place. There may be a certain amount of assumption that KISS was involved due to the lineup of the previous few shows. This show certainly took place without them, suggesting (if they were on the bill) that they had cancelled in favor of the Los Angeles rehearsals.

January 24 - Tucson, AZ **TEMP HOLD DATE
Notes:
- Penciled in on a couple of itineraries (one with the date as the 23rd, the other for the 24th), this date did not take place.

January 24-25 - Studio A, Larrabee Studios, Los Angeles, CA **RECORDING SESSION
Notes:
- During two days of sessions the band recorded "Burning Up With Fever," "Anything For My Baby," "Mistake" and "Rock And Roll All Nite." An acetate of a 1/29 mix, running 2:29, was produced and titled "I Wanna Rock N' Roll All Day And Party All Nite." Neil Bogart was reported as producing the session (Billboard, 2/15/74). All of the rough mixes of these songs have leaked in recent years.

January 26 - Selland Arena, Fresno, CA
Promoter: Pappa Productions
Other act(s): ZZ Top (HL), Wishbone Ash
Reported audience: (7,410 capacity)

January 31 - Winterland, San Francisco, CA
Promoter: Bill Graham Presents
Other act(s): Eli, Third Rail (opener)
Reported audience: 5,400 **SOLD-OUT
Set list: Deuce / Strutter / Got to Choose / Hotter than Hell / Firehouse / Watchin' You / Nothin' To Lose / Parasite / 100,000 Years / Black Diamond / Cold Gin / Let Me Go, Rock 'N' Roll
Notes:
- Tickets for this show cost $2/2.50.
- Fans often debate what version of this video is better, the official release or fan "remasters." However, all versions have similar tape glitches at the beginning of "Deuce," throughout other songs, and an abbreviated version of "Let Me Go, Rock 'N' Roll" that's missing a significant section during the jam, indicative of damage to the master. The "KISSology" version simply fades out while fan versions return for the end of the show stage rap from Paul.

- From a local review: "KISS takes the cake. The ludicrous hard rock quartet that appeared Friday at Winterland may be the most crass, most worthless rock band to run through town in years. A blitz of radio promotion and record store giveaways preceded KISS into San Francisco and more than 1,000 curious spectators showed up for the concert... The music the band played contained few, if any, moments of interest — mostly just a drone of monotonous power chords. To create excitement, KISS performed a number of stunts — like the fire-breathing bass player or hoisting the drum set up above the band during a number. Bombs, dry ice fogs, sirens, various fires and explosions punctuated the entire set. A neon light display of the band's name hung above the stage. Lighting was unbelievably simple-minded. The band leaped out of total darkness to sudden brightness at the beginning of every number. The musicians themselves moved like programmed automatons, who had been told about rock bands but never actually seen one. The entire performance was silly (but not funny) and barely worth dignifying by comment" (SF Chronicle, 2/3/75).
- This show was professional filmed by the in-house crew in b/w and released in full on the KISSology Vol. 1 DVD, though it had long circulated among fans.

February 1 - Civic Center, Santa Monica, CA
Promoter: Fun Productions
Other act(s): Jo Jo Gunne (HL), Yesterday & Today (opener)
Reported audience: 3,000 **SOLD-OUT
Reported gross: $17,500
Notes:
- From a local review: "Many of the customers were greased, lubed and attired in emulation of the second-billed act. KISS, and their demonstrative prejudice, sealed the fate of the alleged headliners early on. KISS, as they say in the music biz vernacular, is a 'monster,' which blows real smoke, wears real leather and lots of kabuki make-up... The kissers storm on stage like maniacs, four starving grave-robbers seething with black malevolence. No accusations of subtlety can be leveled here, as the group performs once dance macabre after another, the hard rock a persistent whip-song" (Los Angeles Free Press, 2/14/75).
- From another local review: "And who should turn up second on the bill once again but — you guessed it — KISS. It must be mentioned that the lads have spawned a whole flock of Kissettes — fans who paint their faces in emulation of their heavy-metal heroes — in the audience, so there's no question but that they're well on their way. Smack" (Los Angeles Times, 2/3/75).
- From a mainstream review: "The loud, flamboyant New York band was heavy on both metal and theatrics, and their unsubtle, heavy-punching show was a big hit with the young crowd, many of whom wore KISS-like makeup in adulation. Their show is a display of thudding, pulsating, weighty sound augmented by demonic black leather costumery, fiery staginess, and wholesome ghoulishness. There's not a lot of differentiation between their songs; they swap around lead vocals. Their musicianship is good but never great, but what they lack in individual precision they make up with togetherness, bonding them in a front that appeals to an extremely youthful crowd" (Billboard, 2/15/75).

February 10 - Lafayette, LA **TEMP HOLD DATE
February 11 - Barton Coliseum, Little Rock, AK **TEMP HOLD DATE
February 12 - Tulsa, OK **TEMP HOLD DATE
Notes:

- Penciled in on the band's 1/5/75 itinerary, these dates (the last two which were noted with REO Speedwagon) didn't take place with any involvement from KISS. New Riders of the Purple Sage opened the show on the 11th and judging from the review of the show it wouldn't have been an environment particularly conducive for a KISS show: A "sit down" rule was in effect due to some shows at the venue having become too rowdy for authorities with local police declining jurisdiction at the state-owned facility. Instead, KISS was already ensconced at Electric Lady Studios in New York City with Neil Bogart working on a new album...

February 20 - Kiel Auditorium, St. Louis, MO
Promoter: Panther Productions
Other act(s): Steve Harley & Cockney Rebel, The Road Crew (opener)
Reported audience: 5,600 / 5,700 (98.25%)
Reported gross: $16,800
Notes:
- The band flew into St. Louis on the day of the show.
- From a local review: "Briton Steve Harley received a quiet introduction to the American rock audience in a concert at Kiel Auditorium last night. He performed well, but the crowd of 5,700 was quiet. In truth, they were bored. They had come to see KISS, a New York quartet that deals in devil dancing set to simple rock music. The New Yorkers, dressed in basic black leather, gave the crowd what it wanted: explosions, smoke and flashing lights. Their showmanship and choreography were well done. Harley was mismatched with the main act" (St. Louis Post-Dispatch, 2/21/75).
- The Road Crew included former members of Bachman-Turner Overdrive's actual road crew who had released a single "The Roadie Song" b/w "Yellow Truck" (Mercury 73631) in January 1975. Both songs were written by Bill Schereck (who was later Angel's tour manager).

February 21 - Aragon Ballroom, Chicago, IL
Promoter: Jam Productions
Other act(s): The James Gang, Man (opener)
Reported audience: 4,276 / 5,000 (88.5%)
Reported gross: $24,716
Partial set list: Black Diamond
Notes:
- From a mainstream review: "Twas the first semi-warm day of the year and the teens were leaning just a little too heavily into the plate glass window next to the Aragon. So when the cherry bomb went off by the curb; well, accidents will happen. It's only rock & roll. Inside, the seething representatives of Chicago's working class freakdom put up with Man, bounced and jounced with the James Gang and blew themselves away with KISS... KISS couldn't miss. The last time they played here was as an emergency top-of-the-bill over former headliners T. Rex. Marc Bolan had done his all — electric star platform, plenty of strobes and a sexual attack on his guitar — but KISS had come out thermoblasting and that bad been that. For their first official headlining, the place was crammed. Word of mouth must have done the trick; it couldn't have been the records (it couldn't!). You know: 'Hey, there's all this fire and he spits blood...' Well, the fire was there, enough of it to pop half the corn in Indiana. There were powder charges, smoke bombs, flamethrowers and other goodies, enough pseudo-napalm to justify the extinguishers tucked nervously around the

apron. And Gene Simmons, the malevolent looking bassist with the sky-high steps, flash kabuki topknot ensemble and 17-inch tongue does indeed slobber something blood-ish when not belching flame. It's this kind of frolic which is the band's open secret. KISS's show depends almost entirely on show, with the music (a combination of Blue Oyster Cult played slow, Black Sabbath played fast) acting as a bottom line for the effects. On this winter eve, they had their automatons-from-hell riff down pat. When rhythm guitarist Paul Stanley and Simmons faced off, it was Star Trek glitter meeting kung fu dancing. Peter Criss' drum kit swathed in smoke during 'Black Diamond,' actually did rise into the air. From the black-and-chrome costumes to those blinding bombs, everything KISS did was custom-tailored for neon-loving, volume-eating rockers. Of course, the crowd responded in kind. Audiences toss roses at Melanie, but tonight's bouquets consisted of M-80s, ladyfingers, and just plain firecrackers" (Rolling Stone #184, Apr. 1975).

February 22 - The Omni 41, Schererville, IN
Promoter: Celebration/Jam Productions
Other act(s): The James Gang, Pez Band (opener)
Reported audience: 4,321 / 6,000 (72.02%)
Reported gross: $24,766
Notes:
- This venue was an ice rink. The Pez Band was a local act that eventually signed to Passport Records.
- This final cluster of three shows wrapped up the "Hotter than Hell" touring cycle, even though recording of "Dressed to Kill" had already been completed. In an issue of Cashbox, dated this day, the new KISS album was promoted as being titled "KISS At Midnight." Neil Bogart commented that planned to release it in time for the 1975 NARM (National Association of Recording Merchandisers) convention in Los Angeles, CA, held Mar. 3 – 6.
- The band returned to New York City the following afternoon.

February 27 - Electric Ballroom, Atlanta, GA **TEMP HOLD DATE
February 28 - Electric Ballroom, Atlanta, GA ** TEMP HOLD DATE
March 1 - Electric Ballroom, Atlanta, GA ** TEMP HOLD DATE
Promoter: Alex Cooley, Inc.
Other act(s): Richard Torrance (opener)
Notes:
- These dates were advertized as late as Jan. 30 in the Great Speckled Bird. The Bird was an Atlanta alternative press publication published 1968 – 1976. KISS was replaced with Bloodrock shows with the Law opening. A pairing with Torrance would have been something of a mismatch with his relaxed singer/songwriter style, of a mellow early Santana vibe.

March 13 - Electric Ballroom, Atlanta, GA ** TEMP HOLD DATE
March 14 - Electric Ballroom, Atlanta, GA ** TEMP HOLD DATE
March 15 - Electric Ballroom, Atlanta, GA ** TEMP HOLD DATE
Promoter: Alex Cooley, Inc.
Other act(s): Pretty Things
Notes:
- These dates were advertized as late as Feb. 20 in the Great Speckled Bird and are included here since they fall in the period before "Dressed To Kill" was released. The Pretty Things

had been scheduled for a headlining run at the venue Mar. 10 – 12, before switching to KISS's opening slot. By early March both acts had been replaced, by Babe Ruth and Cowboy respectively. Having performed at the venue 10 times during 1974, the band never returned as they commenced their ascension up the ladder of success...

Dressed to Kill

KISS' "Hotter Than Hell" tour had somewhat abruptly ended in Santa Monica, CA on February 1, 1975 after which the band returned to New York to complete work on their next studio album. With recording of their third studio album completed, and its release imminent, the band was ready to continue their progression up the musical food-chain on the touring circuit. With pockets of popularity and the continued challenge of placement with suitable headliners the group started to be booked more and more as a headliner in their own right during this period. Before the start of the proper "Dressed To Kill" tour (Kenosha, WI, March 27), the band played two clusters of shows. The first, Feb. 20-22, encompassed three shows in the mid-west: St. Louis, Chicago (a review of this show with Man & James Gang appears in Rolling Stone Magazine #184, Apr. 1975), and Schererville. The second group, a month later, included double-shows at both the Roxy (Northampton, PA) and Beacon Theatre in New York. The fan club mailing for the Beacon show summed up the band's excitement: "Finally we are back on the streets of New York... Now we mean to celebrate, get down and rock 'n' roll!!! We're going to raise hell with fire and thunder on March 21st at a new rock palace called the Beacon Theater" (PR). One of the sets from the latter of these shows has long circulated for fans and was the band's first major headlining concert in their hometown, one that promoter Ron Delsener initially didn't think was going to be a success! In fact, as had been the case with Blue Oyster Cult, there was a role-reversal that took place between the Feb. 1 and Mar. 27 shows. Jo Jo Gunne had headlined the former, but opened for KISS at the latter, as the bands respected each other territories and KISS' label/management were on the hook for the show anyway having offered the promoter a guarantee to ensure he'd not lose anything if the show was a failure (there was no "sure thing" for the band at this stage). The band used that event to invite press and friends to see the new stage show, a critical part of press for the new album.

The importance of the Beacon date was clear to the band, and as preparation 3 warm-up gigs were booked, one in Connecticut and two at the Northampton Roxy in Pennsylvania. Six-miles north of Allentown and around 100-miles from New York City, The Roxy Theatre in Northampton was a must-play venue in the early 1970s. The band, though, were still close to the bottom-rung on their ladder to stardom. Booked by WSAN's Rick Mussleman, playing double-sets had become unusual for the band, but for these two dates they didn't have much choice. Despite only boasting 1,000 seats, the venue had hosted many notable acts including Rush, Golden Earring, UFO, Aerosmith, Bruce Springsteen, and Billy Joel, prior to KISS's appearance there on March 19, 1975. In fact, during one such visit, the latter of those performers, had been inspired to write a now famous song titled "Allentown." Coming off a nearly month long break, an eternity for KISS during this period the band had to work out any kinks in advance. Peter recalled, after the second Northampton show, "We needed to straighten out for Friday... 'Cause Friday's a really big gig, we're having all the DJs come down." With photo-shoots and filming a TV segment with Joe Siegle for a news program, the band's schedule was fully booked (a second Beacon show was added due to the unexpected demand).

Most notable, from this first show of a new phase for the band, is their introduction, which has evolved into "Ladies and gentlemen: The hottest band in the land... KISS." For the first five songs the set is the same as on the previous tour: "Deuce," "Strutter," "Got To Choose," "Hotter Than Hell," and "Firehouse." It's a business-like performance, and any cob-webs seem to have been dusted off by the band's earlier set. Following "Strutter" Paul exclaims, "We thought we had a rowdy bunch for the first show, but I think all the rowdy people are here right now!" Even the small location can't mask the foot-stomping and clapping that seasons this rock and roll party. Paul introduces "She" as being a song from the new album, "This is something I know you haven't heard," even though it had been performed on tours from the clubs into the early stages of "Hotter Than Hell" tour (with few recordings/reviews it was present 10/21/74 but not on 1/31/75). He takes the opportunity to tell the crowd that "Dressed to Kill" is being released the following week. Ace's guitar solo spot returns to the end of this song, where it had been located on those above noted recordings. At less than two minutes it remains a highly-condensed guitar attack. The center piece of the set remains the pulsating "Nothin' To Lose" while a similar set order to January continues with "Parasite," "100,000 Years" (with drum solo and Paul in full rock 'n' roll preacher mode), and "Black Diamond" following. Hallelujah! With the band leaving the stage the audience retains an undiminished high-level of energy stomping and cheering for the return of the band who soon comply. Paul announces, "And some people just think city people know how to rock 'n' roll... Bullshit!" In what was possibly the first ever live performance of the song "C'mon And Love Me" follows, though Paul doesn't specifically allude to anything in its introduction other than it being a song from the new album. Regardless, the band deliver a powerful and competent performance. Standard encore "Let Me Go, Rock 'N Roll" follows with a pulsating rendition stretching nearly six minutes with the extended jams. Following another two-minute break the band return to the stage for the last time, concluding the set with "Cold Gin." It's clear that even at that point the crowd didn't want to go home. With all of the activities surrounding this week it's not surprising that the band cancelled the following night's show at Shaboo in Willimantic, CT. It would have been challenging, with the band and crew's health, to travel the 250 miles from Northampton, and then 150 back to New York City, in any reasonable state of health for the critical Friday.

The Beacon show would team photographer Fin Costello with the band for the first time (He'd later shoot the "Alive!" album cover). Fin recalled, "I had only moved to the U.S. a few weeks before that show and was in at AGI with Peter Corriston [who designed KISS' 'Dressed to Kill' album sleeve] working on the design ideas for the first RAINBOW cover when he asked me if I wanted to see KISS — who were virtually unknown then outside the New York area — at the Beacon just around the corner. I had been shooting the Brecker Bros at Todd Rundgren's studio that afternoon so I had the cameras with me. I have often described it as being akin to the Gates of Hell or Dante's Inferno. They were doing the first number when we came into the back of the theatre and I had never seen anything like it. Smoke, flames, etc. and the audience going ballistic. See the first tour programme for the pictures from that gig. The costume and makeup were perfect for the scary theatrical show they had conceived" (KISS Kollector, 2005).

At the beginning of the tour little changed with the band's costumes showing minor, if any, modifications to those used on previous tours. However, efforts were already underway to take the costuming to the next level as all aspects of the band's operation started to be explored for improvement. Central to the development process was the central factor, the band's appearance. And that meant visually improving the costumes that had started looking rather too road worn. There was one young designer building a reputation for striking and futuristic costumes... Moon Stone was a store theater fashion designer Larry LeGaspi had opened in 1973, appropriately located on Madison Avenue in New York City. While the store was too far ahead of its time to be successful, his work found placement with bands such as KISS, Labelle, and Funkadelic.

If anything, Ace Frehley, was the main beneficiary of Larry's efforts due to his interest in the futuristic spacey "Buck Rodgers" apparel look. Silver discs on the shoulders, a sequin studded body suit (giving a twinkling starry night appearance similar to the ceiling of Larry's store), and puffed-lame lightning bolt that traversed the torso down the sides of the leg, was simply and effective. Slightly lower space boots in silver assisted Ace with his gravity challenges while complimenting the rest of the design with a sense of balance. One only has to look at the cover of "Alive!" and Ace, the central figure, is a visually more complex and striking character than Gene and Paul beside him. Paul's design provided the freedom of movement he needed, with an open-chest (but silver-fringed) bodysuit and improved boots. The plain bodysuit soon had large stars added to it, as did his boots. He accessorized with a feather shoulder-guard and choker, and black forearm gloves. Gene, similarly, was cleaned up rather than undergoing an Ace-level transformation. A heavily studded cod-piece, complete with skull and crossbones, and studded knee-high boots mirrored the aggression with which he attacked his instrument. Elements such as the shoulder spikes and bat-wings carried over from the previous era, and like Paul he wore arm coverings, though his basic black leotard had cut-outs on the thighs. The initial studded books, which incorporated spikes, were soon supplemented with a plainer design with silver knee guards. It is likely that the band members regularly mixed and matched what costume item was readily to hand, and perhaps smelt slightly less pungent than another piece!

Peter's costume received the fewest revisions, with a silver lame-fringed spandex bodysuit replacing the leather outfit he'd used the previous year. He'd wear varying accessories included a leather belt with tiger buckle or studded wrist bands. As a drummer he usually wore normal shoes, painted silver, when behind the kit, but had a pair of knee-high platform boots for photo shoots. The stage show also received few modifications, other than a confetti storm being introduced during the final song. Three or four stacks of amps remained on either side of Peter's drum riser, which was either the levitating variety or static block depending on situation. Flash pots were sometimes placed on top of the amps, or on the stage in front of either stack. Lightning, though, became a more important consideration with the ambience and mood that a designed show could provide. In essence, the band toured with their "Hotter Than Hell" configuration until mid-May, when they debuted their new costumes on May 16 in Detroit. Perhaps it was just a cosmic confluence of fortune that the band's new single, "Rock And Roll All Nite," debuted on the U.S. Billboard Hot 100 singles charts at the same time, opening its run at #96 on in the May 17 issue. While it would only enjoy a modest 6 week run on the charts it was the band's first legitimate single charting without the support of a national kissing contest gimmick.

Where support for "Hotter Than Hell" had not included any national television exposure (other than the limited use of KISS's first TV commercial for the album), the situation was remedied with the band filming an appearance on Burt Sugarman's "Midnight Special" on April 1. Compared with competitors, "In Concert" and Don Kirshner's "Rock Concert," NBC had broader national coverage at the time though in some markets the shows competed against one another directly. Interestingly, performers were paid union scale for their appearances. Perhaps somewhat amusingly, on show producer, Stan Harris described the completion the show faced: "Our show is designed for people from 18 to 35, and there really is nothing else for that age group. Our only competition is sleep, not another show... Many groups and many concert promoters object to doing the show. They figure they will shoot their bolt on TV for relatively nothing — compared to what they would get at a concert — because all our acts work for scale. But I am a pretty good salesman. I try to convince them that they owe it to their fans to do the show. I tell them that many kids in small towns never get to concerts, never get a chance to see them. They should do TV once in a while, just to let their fans see them. Of course, the newer acts clamor to get on, to be seen and heard by a national audience" (The Town Talk, 7/5/75). The first episode, hosted by Flip Wilson and airing July 11, paired the band with Kenny Rankin, Blue Magic, and comedian Franklyn Ajaye. The second appearance, using a rebroadcast of "Deuce," plus "Black Diamond," took place on November 28, 1975 on a show that included Frankie Valli, the Four Seasons, Barry Manilow, and David Brenner. When discussing KISS "Holy Grails," the unaired and presumably lost film for "C'mon And Love Me" (Gooch, Suhs — "KISS Alive Forever") is assuredly one item to be included on that list.

The scheduling of the "Midnight Special" performances is problematic, in terms of its usefulness as a promotional tool during the actual "Dressed To Kill" era. Combined with the hold-over costuming, the initial broadcast date came towards the end of the tour and would have been of negligible impact from that perspective. As a counterpoint, Stan Harris' point that the benefit was more important to newer bands for the exposure, then that exposure was assuredly of benefit to the band, but more for their activities during the second half of the year. And, for that matter, how many new fans in the target demographic might have discovered the band, or experienced their first glimpse of the band performing, as a result of the show? The band were mentioned (briefly) in conjunction with another live performance show, "Night Dreams." The show was initially two 90-minute NBC specials scheduled for Aug. 1 & 8, produced by Art Fisher for Syd Vinnedge Productions was seen by the network as a possible replacement for the "Midnight Special." Executives had seen a decline in viewership, no doubt in part a result by the time-slots the shows were forced to exist in and evolution in tastes of those willing to stay up for the shows. And boredom; there were several shows doing similar things and the format was particularly static and for some uninspired. Compared with the "Midnight Special," the pilots were designed to broaden the appeal with elaborate production including animation, film elements, comedy, and doing more for the acts than simply broadcasting them performing. KISS were initially noted as being included in the second pilot episode, subtitled "Fantasy, Dreams, and Illusions." The format might have proved too eclectic for late night audiences, with the first episode featuring The Spinners, BJ Thomas, David Nelson, Black Oak Arkansas, Tanya Tucker, 10CC, and Father Sarducci. Without KISS's involvement the second pilot included Three Dog Night, Rex Reed, Little Richard, and Slade. No further episodes were broadcast, so if KISS had been involved, they never made it to air.

On the road the band motored through the East Coast and Midwest, with opening act Rush, though they'd occasionally take up mid-ticket slots for larger venues. By mid-May they had reached a turning point, with their new costumes becoming available and plans for the live album having solidified. Aucoin also planned to film segments of the show, fitting in with

Direction Plus' previous ideas for a visual calling card for bands — the promo film. Multimedia mixing of bands and video was still very much a part of Aucoin's vision as part of Direction Plus, and efforts they had attempted the previous year. Bill, Joyce Biawitz, and Neil Bogart were scheduled to present "The Year Of The TV Explosion" at the 1975 NARM Meet on Mar. 5. However, this effort was more about the advertizing of acts during appropriately targeted programming, such as on "The Midnight Special," which Neil used as an example during his presentation. Detroit, though, really marked a turning point for the band and is really the point where the changeover from the "Hotter Than Hell" era takes place.

Cashbox reported in their May 17 edition that the band would record their May 16 concert at Cobo Hall in Detroit for their first live LP. A month later, a show in Cleveland, OH would be recorded, and the following month shows in Davenport, IA and Wildwood, NJ would be captured. The Cashbox piece is interesting in that it suggests that "Dressed To Kill" had sold some 175,000 copies by that point — which would have been an impressive improvement on the band's previous commercial efforts. However, a confidential royalty statement placed the sales at 111,766 through June 30, still an improvement on the previous two albums.

March 19, 1975 - The Roxy, Northampton, PA **two shows
Promoter: Rick Mussleman / WSAN
Other act(s): Passport (opener)
Reported audience: ~1,000 **each show
Early set list: Unknown
Late set list: Deuce / Strutter / Got to Choose / Hotter than Hell / Firehouse / She / Nothin' to Lose / Parasite / 100,000 Years / Black Diamond / C'mon and Love Me / Let Me Go, Rock 'N' Roll / Cold Gin
Notes:
- First known performance of "C'mon and Love Me." It was initially situated in the set as one of the encores. Paul also mentioned "She" as being a song from the new album being released the following week, though it had long been part of the band's set.
- There was no levitating drum riser used for Peter — the venue wasn't tall enough.
- An above average AUD recording of this show circulates. The taper/fan also met the band after the show and captured some interesting interaction with Paul, Gene, and Peter. Paul and Gene only talk briefly, to enquire about the recorder, and introduce the fan to Gene's spider jewelry, before leaving together (Ace had already left). Peter, though, hangs out for nearly 15 minutes chatting enthusiastically and amiably on a variety of topics. He discusses forthcoming television appearances, planned magazine covers, and the Beacon shows. He also mentions how his and Paul's voices are shot and most of the crew has become sick.

March 20 - Shaboo Inn, Mansfield, CT **CANCELLED
- A show in Connecticut was cancelled so that the band could rest up for the Beacon Theater show — which was important with the number of press invited — plus a planned filming for a TV broadcast. Instead, the band participated in a photo shoot...
- The 1,000 capacity Shaboo Inn, owned by Mark Foster and Gary John, was a similar venue to the previous night's gig at the Roxy in Northampton with some surprisingly big names playing there including AC/DC, Cheap Trick, Journey, Aerosmith, and many others. The legendary venue burned down on Friday August 13, 1982, following its closure in May, in a suspected case of arson ending an 11 year run of entertainment and some 3,000 concerts.

March 21 - Beacon Theater, New York City, NY **TWO SHOWS
Promoter: Ron Delsener
Other act(s): Jo Jo Gunne (opener)
Reported audience: ~2,700 **SOLD-OUT

Set list: Same as Mar. 19.
Notes:
- A homecoming of sorts for the band, and certainly an important show in terms of the press and publicity surrounding it. On some early itineraries this show was initially scheduled for Mar. 23. With only one song from the new album, this show is still really more of a "Hotter than Hell" era gig. KISS played two sets (one at 7:30 p.m., the other at 11), with Jo Jo Gunne opening both, so it's not clear which set the circulating AUD recording came from. Just over a month earlier KISS had been opening for Jo Jo Gunne in California — the band broke up soon after this show.
- From a local review: "KISS returned to New York — at the Beacon Theater, Broadway and 74th Street — confirmed its status as a genuine headline group and played the same ordinary rock music as before. But for some reason the effect this quartet has on crowds is quite startling: the whole audience was standing on the seats for the last 45 minutes, an event even in these days of rock emotionalism. Perhaps it is KISS's kabuki-type make-up, the fact that its four members hurl glitter around and have a controlled fascination with fire and smoke that must dishearten any stage manager. Or perhaps the crowd is driven wild by the drummer's finale as he ascends, kit and all, some 20 feet in the air, while lights flash and smoke billows. More probably it is because the musicians of KISS genuinely enjoy their work. It may be overly simple and unpretentious rock, not so much sung as shouted, but KISS communicates a sense of fun and commitment to the music. Whatever the causes, a KISS concert is certainly a high energy arena" (New York Times, 3/23/75).
- From a mainstream review: "As KISS thundered onstage March 21, for the first of two shows, it was clearly a case of 'hail the conquering heroes.' The sold -out crowd of hyperactive 16-year-olds rose to their feet as one, cheering and stomping, and remained standing throughout the band's hour-long set. KISS returned the crowd's fervor with full force, praising their hometown audience, and proved to be one of the most energetic groups on the road. The show had very little to do with actual musicianship, since the band operates at continual pain-level volume.

However, they were mixed well enough to allow for distinguishable vocals, and a few instrumental leads. KISS' message is a direct one — it plays behind a wall of sound, and elicits response according to how familiar one has become with its material. Equal attention was devoted to a full stock of special effects KISS uses onstage. Police lights rotated above their battery of amps, candles flickered in sinister manner off to one side, and bassist Gene Simmons spewed fake blood in a manner that must be seen to be believed. Of course, it's all very silly, the latest extension of shock-rock, if you like. Yet KISS is a band that so well communicates with its audience as to make the sci-fi freak show an understandable, even necessary element of their performance" (Billboard, 4/12/75).
- The show was also covered extensively in a feature in the Sept. 1975 issue of "Rock Scene" magazine along with a spread of the classic "in studio" photos (continued in the Nov. issue).

March 27 - Kenosha Ice Arena, Kenosha, WI
Promoter: Twin Productions, Inc.
Other act(s): Rush (opener)
Reported audience: (4,500 capacity)
Notes:
- Official first date of the "Dressed to Kill" tour, and the band's show first as a headliner (though they'd still take gigs opening for other acts at larger venues). The crew arrived the

day before the show while the band arrived the afternoon of the show. Thin Lizzy was originally the scheduled third act, but couldn't make the show due to weather conditions affecting the Midwest.

- Because of the venue configuration the logo was placed to the side of the stage.

March 28 - Sports Arena, Toledo, OH
Promoter: Bamboo Productions
Other act(s): ZZ Top (HL)
Reported audience: (7,500 capacity)
Notes:
- Following this show the band returned to New York before heading out to Los Angeles on the 30th.

April 1 - NBC Studios, Burbank, CA **TV FILMING
Promoter: Burt Sugarman / NBC
Set list: Deuce / She / Black Diamond / C'mon and Love Me
Notes:
- Directed by Stan Harris. Recorded live for Burt Sugarman's "Midnight Special" television show.
- "She" included Ace's guitar solo. Both it and "Deuce" were broadcast when the show first aired on July 11, 1975 (show #124). "Black Diamond," with a repeat of "Deuce," was broadcast on Nov. 28, 1975 (show #141). "C'mon and Love Me" was never broadcast and its status is currently unknown, though it is presumed to have been lost (Gooch/Suhs — "KISS Alive Forever").
- The video of "Black Diamond" is included in stunning color on the "Burt Sugarman's The Midnight Special Legendary Performances — 1975" DVD released in 2010. On the "KISSology Vol. 1" DVD the video is in black and white, though "She" is in color.

April 4 - Calderone Concert Hall, Hempstead, NY **KISS CANCELLED
Promoter: Concerts East
Notes:
- This date was advertized in the Village Voice in March, but cancelled in favor of the show in Michigan.

April 4 - Nordic Arena, Hartland, MI
Promoter: Brass Ring Productions
Other act(s): Mike Quatro Jam Band, Smack Dab (opener)
Reported audience: 4,000+
Notes:
- Paul wore sunglasses during this and the next two shows due to an eye infection preventing him from applying his star makeup.
- The turn-out for this show, estimated in the press at 4–5,000 patrons, resulted in a furor in which the local Township Board was forced tackle, "An ordinance which will regulate large gatherings... following almost unanimous criticism of the manner in which the concert was handled" (Brighton Argus, 4/9/75). Part of the concern was the venue's hockey seating capacity of 1,500 and the lack of any real determination for the safe capacity for concerts and other events that the venue hosted.
- This show is sometimes erroneously attributed to 1974. However, as concert flyers clearly indicate, the show was scheduled on a Friday, which definitely indicates 1975.
- Mike Quatro was very similar to KISS in some ways. One reviewer noted, "While Quatro is an exceptional keyboard performer, he has compromised his music by excessive use of theatrics in his act. The show included several costume changes as well as smoke machines and an electronic wand that controlled Quatro's synthesizers and doubled as a flame thrower" (Rochester Democrat & Chronicle, 4/5/75). He was also playing shows opening for Kraftwerk during the same period as this KISS show.

April 5 - Community College Auditorium, Williamsport, PA **CANCELLED
Promoter: Media Five Entertainment
Other act(s): Rush (opener)
Notes:
- This show was cancelled when local officials banned the group from using their pyrotechnics, though perhaps the 500 miles travel from the previous gig made the decision easier.

April 6 - G.W.U. Lisner Auditorium, Washington, D.C.
Promoter: Cellar Door Productions
Other act(s): Rush, Heavy Metal Kids (opener)
Reported audience: 1,502 **SOLD-OUT
Reported gross: $7,800
Notes:
- This show was a benefit for the Hillcrest Children's Center.
- Heavy Metal Kids were a U.K. rock act in a similar musical vein to KISS supporting their second album, "Anvil Chorus." By this time they had officially simplified their name to Kids, but invariably ended up being referred to by either name. Following this show Rush headed for a headlining show the next night at Cleveland Agora with Sky King opening.

- Rolling Stone & HOYA writer Gordon Fletcher had backstage passes for the show. According to Larry Harris, "Afterwards, Paul Stanley and Gene Simmons met up with Rolling Stone writer Gordon Fletcher, who insisted that they all go to a local club to check out a band called Angel. Gene was so impressed with the group that after their set he called Neil from a pay phone at the back of the club to pitch them" ("And Party Every Day: The Inside Story of Casablanca Records").
- From a local review: "The music — heavy metal, assault rock, whatever you want to call it — is as simple as anything done by Jerry Lee Lewis or Little Richard. Some groups, such as Queen and Led Zeppelin, and pull it off on record and stage... Both Rush and KISS, the headliner and supposedly one of the upcoming groups in the business, had almost none of the first group's redeeming qualities. Their music was ear-shattering and totally uninspired. KISS, in particular, worked hard at presenting what it thought was a rousing stage show. Smoke bombs exploded, lights flashed, costumes glittered. It was all quite boring, so mechanical that the musicians might as well have been computer-programmed robots. The electronic curtain had dropped. Groups like KISS have to learn that smoke bombs and overpowering sound systems do not a performance make. Some people do love it but even more are beginning to be bored with it. The mechanical stage show has gone to the extreme and it is now time to put the performer back in the performance" (Washington Star, 4/7/75).
- From another local review: "Noise draws a full house like the sea draws lemmings... Looking like leather beings from outer space, KISS, the last and featured attraction, played at a decibel level usually reserved for Atlas rockets during liftoff. Despite their volume, costumes and bank of maniacally flashing lights, the group had no more music to offer than the two bands before them. And that, rest assured, was not much music at all" (Washington Post, 4/7/75).

April 8 - Akron Civic Theater, Akron, OH
Promoter: Belkin Productions
Other act(s): Rush, Heavy Metal Kids (opener)
Reported audience: (2,500 capacity)
Notes:
- In the audience for this show was one young aspiring drummer, Eric Mensinger...

April 9 - Erie County Field House, Erie, PA
Promoter: Belkin Productions
Other act(s): Rush, Vitale's Madmen (opener)
Reported audience: (5,250 capacity)
Notes:
- Joe Vitale was the former drummer for Ted Nugent's Amboy Dukes and had been a member of Barnstorm with Joe Walsh. In late 1974 he released his debut solo album.
- From a local review: "It was like watching a convention of professional wrestlers trying to out-gimmick each other. Oh yes, there was loud music to go along with these antics, so it could be qualified as rock music. But the only thing that makes KISS believable is the knowledge that their positions as the kings of weird rock is only secure until another band comes along to out-weird them" (Erie Times-News).

April 11 - Palace Theater, Dayton, OH
Promoter: Belkin Productions
Other act(s): Heavy Metal Kids (opener)
Notes:
- On the day of show, an ad in the Dayton Daily News erroneously noted Victoria Opera House as the venue for the show.

April 12 - I.S.U. Union Auditorium, Normal, IL
Promoter: A Whatever Production
Other act(s): Rush (opener)
Reported audience: (3,457 capacity)
Notes:
- During the mid-1970s Illinois State University this venue, north of Bloomington, was one of few in the area to catch major talent at the time.

April 13 - Soldiers & Sailors Memorial Hall, Kansas City, KS
Promoter: Cowtown Productions
Other act(s): Golden Earring (HL), Vitale's Madmen (opener)
Reported audience: 3,580 **SOLD-OUT
Reported gross: $18,000
Notes:
- The band flew to Pittsburgh via Chicago the following day.

April 15 - Stanley Warner Theatre, Pittsburgh, PA
Promoter: DiCesare-Engler Productions
Other act(s): Rush, Heavy Metal Kids (opener)
Reported audience: 2,885 **SOLD-OUT
Reported gross: $20,000
Partial set list: Firehouse / Parasite / Black Diamond

Notes:
- The KISS logo was positioned at stage-right for this show.
- The show was advertized as an "at least a three-hour show of high-powered rock-n-roll from three of the freshest movers on the scene today" (North Hills News Record, 4/2/75).
- From a local review: "It was a rowdy crowd that invaded the Stanley Theatre last night, guards at the front door filling carton after carton with bottles and cans of potent liquids. But once the music — all heavy, slam-bang rock 'n' roll — started, all attention was directed toward the stage and no one was disappointed by the 'international battle of the bands' except when it was time to go home... Neither band [Kids & Rush] could match the showmanship or reaction KISS got. These New Yorkers are the weirdest bunch like Stargell is a slugger, but they're first-class rockers the same way... Every one of their dozen songs, including the triple encore was excellent rock 'n' roll, sparked by all-too-infrequent bursts of brilliance from Frehley... It was and evening of real rowdy rock 'n' roll, perfect for blowing of steam. In the mishmash of electronic slop from Europe these days, a barn-burner like this was doubly welcome" (The Pittsburgh Press, 4/16/75).

April 17 - Burlington Memorial Auditorium, Burlington, IA
Promoter: Road Fever Productions
Other act(s): Rush, Heavy Metal Kids (opener)
Reported audience: (2,628 capacity)
Notes:
- Amusingly, KISS was billed as an "electronic rock band" in one ad for the show.

April 19 - Fremd High School Gymnasium, Palatine, IL
Promoter: Prophet Productions
Other act(s): Rush (opener)
Reported audience: ~1,500
Probable set list: Deuce / Strutter / Got to Choose / Hotter than Hell / Firehouse / She / Nothin' to Lose / Room Service / 100,000 Years / Black Diamond / C'mon and Love Me / Let Me Go, Rock 'N' Roll
Notes:
- The show was a fundraiser for a special-events sign the Vikings Booster Club had donated to the school. Original scheduled opening act Rockandy had been dropped from the bill by the day of show.
- One school student recalled the show: "[We] knew something wild happened that Saturday night when during our Monday morning gym class it smelled like we were running inside a giant bong" (Beachwood Reporter, 11/2/11).
- Only the first half of the show was archived, though the taper also recorded the opening band's set (Rush) and the stage banter during the equipment change over. The recording is generally poor, bass-heavy, and probably in need of a new transfer from the master.
- In a circulating recorded conversation with the band, Paul suggested that "Room Service" was going to be performed, and the band practiced it three times during sound-check; as well as doing a bit of a jam of Zeppelin's "Communication Breakdown" and "How Many More Times."

April 21 - Memorial Auditorium, Louisville, KY
Promoter: Sunshine Promotions
Other act(s): Rush (opener)

Reported audience: (2,000 capacity)
Note:
- The day prior to the show the band was advertised as "KILL" locally.

April 22 - Convention Expo Center, Indianapolis, IN
Promoter: Sunshine Promotions
Other act(s): Rush, Status Quo (opener)
Reported audience: (SRO)
Reported gross: $25,054
Note:
- One early ad (in the Primo Times) listed KISS opening for America on this date. The obvious error was corrected to a more realistic bill soon afterwards! Status Quo and Rush had already played gigs together, having sold out the Michigan Palace on Apr. 11.

April 24 - Freedom Hall Civic Center, Johnson City, TN
Promoter: Lyn-Lee Productions
Other act(s): Rush, Heavy Metal Kids (opener)
Reported audience: 4,300 / 8,000 (53.75%)
Reported gross: $20,000
Notes:
- 14 fans were arrested during the show, mainly for public drunkenness, drugs offences, and vandalism.
- From a local review: "It was a small, quiet crowd which came out for the 'shock rock' group KISS last night at Freedom Hall. Police reported fourteen arrests, eleven of them for public drunkenness. Most of the arrests were made outside the hall before the concert started... About 3,000 persons, many of them dressed in glitter costumes as outlandish as the bands', attended the concert" (Kingsport Times, 4/25/75).

April 25 - Charlotte Park Center, Charlotte, NC
Promoter: Kaleidoscope Productions
Other act(s): Rush (opener)
Reported audience: (3,000 capacity)

April 26 - Cumberland County Memorial Arena, Fayetteville, NC
Promoter: Beach Club Promotions
Other act(s): Rush, Atlanta Rhythm Section (opener)
Reported audience: 3,564 / 7,000 (50.91%)
Reported gross: $18,850

April 27 - Richmond Arena, Richmond, VA
Promoter: Century Productions
Other act(s): Rush, Brian Auger & Oblivion Express (opener), M-S Funk (opener)
Reported audience: (5,252 capacity)

WGOE & BEACH CLUB PRODUCTIONS
Presents

KISS

RUSH M S FUNK
SPECIAL GUEST
BRIAN AUGER
&
OBLIVION EXPRESS
SUNDAY, APRIL 27, 8 P.M.
RICHMOND ARENA
TICKETS '5 Advance
'6 day of Show
Tickets available at:
Record Rack Ltd.
Gramophone (Grace & Ashland)
Music City (Southside PLAZA)
Gary's (Willow Lawn)
Album Den
Band Box (Grace)
Festival Seating - Plenty of
Room To Boogie

April 29 - Metro Ice Arena, Lansing, MI
Promoter: Paul Stanley Productions
Other act(s): Salem Witchcraft (opener)
Reported audience: 4,000 / 4,600 (86.96%)
Reported gross: $22,000
Notes:
- While the facility had a maximum capacity of 4,600 only 952 bleacher seats had been installed for the local IHL hockey team's final season in the venue.

April 30 - Franklin County Veterans Memorial Auditorium, Columbus, OH
Promoter: Bamboo Production
Other act(s): Status Quo (opener)
Reported audience: (4,000 capacity)

May 3 - Tower Theater, Philadelphia, PA
Promoter: Midnight Sun Productions
Other act(s): Ted Nugent's Amboy Dukes, Rush (opener)
Reported audience: 1,899 / 3,064 (61.98%)
Reported gross: $12,029
Set list: Deuce / Strutter / Got to Choose / Hotter than Hell / Firehouse / Nothin' to Lose / She / Room Service / 100,000 Years
Notes:
- Archived as an AUD recording, this show cuts off during Peter's solo. It's likely missing "Black Diamond" and "Let Me Go, Rock 'N' Roll." While there's a fair bit of background hiss on the recording the bass levels are reasonable and Paul's raps are clear. It's certainly not a terrible show to listen to, but might be better with a much lower generational copy (if available).

May 6 - Riverside Theater, Milwaukee, WI
Promoter: Daydream Productions
Other act(s): Rush (opener)
Reported audience: (2,450 capacity)
Partial set list: Deuce / Hotter than Hell / Firehouse / Nothin' to Lose / She / Room Service / Rock Bottom / 100,000 Years / Black Diamond / Let Me Go, Rock 'N' Roll
Notes:
- Roughly 5 minutes of silent 8mm footage exists.
- From a local review: "The masochists came out for this one.... But tickets for the KISS and Rush concert should have had a warning from the Surgeon General on the back. Loud you ask? It was so loud my earwax melted. It was so loud Neil Sedaka complained, and he was in the PAC. It was so loud you couldn't hear... I'm sure the legally deaf could've heard this one... The music was only that voluminous to cover up the redundancy and inconsequentiality of it all... KISS was at least entertaining to watch, if not hear... I can only see KISS as a novelty item. There is nothing in their music that hasn't been done better and the costumes and stage props will never carry a group for long" (The Bugle-American, 5/14/75).

May 8 - J.F.K. Gymnasium @ Lewis University, Lockport, IL
Other act(s): Rush (opener)

Reported audience: (2,200 capacity)
- From a local review: "It isn't the music that attracts people to the 'glitter rock' scene, but the circus acts performed. In New York it is said that 'glitter rock' is chic and sophisticated. I guess that I am not chic and sophisticated. 'Glitter rock' belongs in the [same] class with McDonalds, red fingernails, plastic furniture, cheap wine, and pink flamingos" (Lewis University Nexus, 5/15/75).

May 9 - King-Horn Convocation Center @ ONU, Ada, OH
Promoter: ONU King-Horn Center Presents
Other act(s): The James Gang, The Flock (opener)
Reported audience: (5,000 capacity)
Notes:
- Rush had been intended to open, but were replaced by The Flock (who included a violin player). This show includes the currently first noted performance of "Rock And Roll All Nite."
- According to one attendee, "One of the band's handlers approached my fraternity (Phi Kappa Theta) about the possibility of KISS preparing for the concert by utilizing our second-floor restroom facility. The Phi Kap house was just across the street from King Horn and the restroom had a bay of four sinks with a large mirror that was exactly what the band needed to apply their make-up. They spent about two hours just relaxing and talking before and during their preparation. They were very receptive to us. We tried to get them to commit to spending time with us after the concert but they had to be on the road" (ONU).
- The James Gang's set was recorded. Unfortunately the batteries on the recorder ran out afterwards...

May 10 - Wilkes College, Wilkes-Barre, PA **CANCELLED
Reported audience: (2,600 capacity)
Notes:
- This show was cancelled in favor of the larger show with ZZ Top.

May 10 - Capital Centre, Largo (Landover), MD
Promoter: Cellar Door Productions
Other act(s): ZZ Top (HL)
Reported audience: ~13,000 / 18,500 (70.27%)
Notes:
- From a local review: "Whether you dress it in 10-gallon hats and cowboy boots, as Z.Z. Top did, or doll it up with black leather' and platform shoes, the option chosen by KISS, it still boils down to the same thing. Heavy-metal music, on display Saturday night at the Capital Centre, .now comes in several different guises, but always it stresses getting back to basics... But musical variety and inventiveness is not what heavy metal is all about. The key to this whole genre of music can perhaps be found in some very direct song titles. KISS's most warmly received number was called 'Rock 'n' Roll All Night and Party Every Day' [sic]" (Washington Post, 5/12/75). The reviewer was particularly bemused that both acts, neither of which had had a hit album to that point, were able to draw as strongly as they did.

May 11 - Orpheum Theatre, Boston, MA
Promoter: Don Law
Other act(s): Hunter-Ronson (HL), Journey (opener)

Reported audience: ~2,000 / 2,900 (68.97%)
Reported gross: $12,000
Set list: Deuce / Strutter / Hotter than Hell / Firehouse / She / C'mon and Love Me / 100,000 Years / Black Diamond / Rock And Roll All Nite
Notes:
- Ian Hunter was touring his self-titled debut solo album, his first release following his departure from Mott The Hoople. It featured former Bowie "Spiders From Mars" guitarist Mick Ronson and included "Once Bitten, Twice Shy" and "Who Do You Love."
- This was the band's last show before they started performing with their new "Alive!" costumes, stage show, and set.
- The AUD recording from this show is the first that includes what became the band's signature tune, "Rock And Roll All Nite." Unfortunately, the recording is of generally poor audio condition.

May 14 - Michigan Palace, Detroit, MI **REHEARSALS
May 15 - Michigan Palace, Detroit, MI **REHEARSALS

May 16 - Cobo Hall, Detroit, MI
Promoter: Steve Glantz Productions
Other act(s): Diamond Reo (opener)
Reported audience: 12,039 **SOLD-OUT
Reported gross: $74,000
Notes:
- This concert was recorded for "Alive!" The recording of the show was no secret and was mentioned in music press soon afterwards (such as is Cleveland's "The Scene" 6/5 – 11 issue and the May 17 issue of Cashbox). During the summer Casablanca issued basic ads with the album's rear cover crowd photo hyping the then forthcoming release of the album.
- The promoter had installed a new sound system in the arena, completely suspended above the stage, in addition to a second one at floor level. There was also a video screen used to project close-ups of the performance during the show. Video is known to exist from the show.
- Following the concert KISS presented Glantz with a "Rocker-Fellow" award to honor him for all of the support that he had given them throughout their career to date. According to Paul, explaining the award at the time, "He [Steve] treats us with as much respect now as a headlining act as he did last year when we were fourth on the bill" (Performance Magazine, 6/13/75).
- Isolated tracks from "Parasite" from this show were used in the Rock Band 2 game.

May 17 - War Memorial Arena, Johnstown, PA
Promoter: Music Artisan Productions
Other act(s): Rush (opener)
Reported audience: (7,000 capacity)
Notes:
- Jaan Uhelszki, a writer for Creem Magazine, travelled with the band from Detroit and appeared on-stage with them for a few minutes during the show. She wore a make-up design based on the composite on the back of the "Hotter than Hell" album cover. The escapade was recounted in the "I Dreamed I Was Onstage with KISS in my Maidenform Bra" feature in the magazine's August 1975 issue.

May 19 - Civic Center Theater, St. Paul, MN
Promoter: Yanqui Productions
Other act(s): Hydra (opener)
Reported audience: (2,687 capacity)

May 22 - Capitol Theater, Yakima, WA **CANCELLED
Other act(s): Rush (opener)
Reported audience: (1,558 capacity)
Notes:
- This date was actually used by Glenn Yarbrough and the Limeliters who were on their "Reunion '75" tour — the show definitely took place and a review appeared in the local press. However, there are multiple first-hand accounts of the band performing in Yakima with Rush in 1975 (and burning a gym's ceiling), so there could have been an alternative date or venue though there is no mention in local press dating back to early May. Also problematic is JR Smalling's day planner which suggests that the band flew from Yakima to Medford via Seattle during the afternoon of May 23, having arrived in the region in the afternoon of May 21. The theater burned down on Aug. 11.

May 23 - The Armory, Medford, OR
Promoter: Get Down Promotions / S.S.A.
Other act(s): Rush (opener)
Notes:
- The band flew to Medford via Seattle arriving mid-afternoon.

May 24 - Paramount Theater, Portland, OR
Promoter: Albatross Productions
Other act(s): Rush (opener)
Reported audience: 3,000 **SOLD-OUT
Partial set list: Deuce / Strutter / Got to Choose / Firehouse / 100,000 Years
Notes:
- 16mm live footage, and an after show backstage interview with Gene and Paul, was professionally filmed at this show; with some eventually being used on the menu sequences on the "KISSology" DVD set in 2006. Parts were also used in the first episode of the VH-1 series "Heavy: The Story of Metal" broadcast in 2006.
- From a local review: "KISS is certainly a Portland band. Not born in the city, but its appearances have been met with rollicking, capacity houses at the Paramount Northwest theater. Well, Saturday night was no exception... There's something going on every minute onstage; not so much the dramatic outpourings of, say, an Alice Cooper, but in the continual interplay between the four members of the group as they utilize the entire stage for their monster-movie shenanigans. And it's all in fun; there's really little to take seriously in this act. The theater rock effects are handled in a disciplined — if loose — manner while thunderous music practically blows your head away with decibels... Hair flies and bodies shake and KISS works to exhaustion. Musically, it's all rock and roll — and loud. Super loud. Extremely loud..." (Oregonian, 5/25/75).

May 25 - Paramount Northwest Theater, Seattle, WA
Promoter: Get Down Productions
Other act(s): Rush (opener)

Reported audience: (3,000 capacity)
Notes:
- Sadly, it appears that music critic Patrick MacDonald, who had penned legendary reviews about the band's previous visits to Seattle, opted to be in New York to see Bette Midler's "Clams on the Half Shell" revue and ZZ Top at the Felt Forum (he didn't enjoy the latter show).

May 26 - Paramount Theater, Portland, OR
Promoter: Albatross Productions
Other act(s): Rush (opener)
Reported audience: (3,000 capacity)
Notes:
- Due to the sell-out of the first date, a second show was added.

May 27 - Spokane Coliseum, Spokane, WA
Promoter: Get Down Productions & Double-T Promotions
Other act(s): Rush (opener)
Reported audience: 4,000 / 8,000 (50%)
Reported gross: $21,000
Notes:
- From a local review: "The four-man group with fluorescent clothes and make-up looked like the demons one sees on a bad trip. For sheer insanity, KISS out-weirded Alice Cooper. It was not a mellow evening. The group proved that psychedelic sound is still alive. They promised to make the crowd 'sweat,' and that they did. The reverberations have never been louder, nor the smoke heavier in the Coliseum. The big building shook with the hard rock beat" (Spokesman-Review, 5/28/75).

May 28 - Terrace Ballroom, Salt Lake City, UT **CANCELLED

May 29 - Space Center @ Sahara Hotel, Las Vegas, NV **two shows
Promoter: Gary Naseef
Other act(s): Rush (opener)
Reported audience: ~4,000 / 4,200 (at each show)
Notes:
- Two shows were played; at 8pm and 2am. Jefferson Starship was originally on the bill but cancelled.
- From a mainstream review: "Officially dubbed 'Glitter Night' May 29 on the Strip, KISS unleashed controlled chaos in visual explosives and heavy metal rock 'n' roll during two near sell-out shows. Brooklyn born, the four authors of Armageddon dazzled, delighted and devastated hardcore rock fanatics alongside novices in a tightly packaged electronic horror show... Bassist Gene Simmons, outrageously decadent, ignited the tight KISS sound with earsplitting vibes and theatrics. Simmons accidentally singed his hair after breathing fire, a featured show gimmick. Anchorman-leader Paul Stanley provided leaping antics with his lead guitar rhythmically followed by drummer Peter Criss with blitzkrieged beats. Ace Frehley belts out KISS songs in savage simplicity. KISS established a distinctive sound in its Vegas debut as a challenger to the likes of Alice Cooper and the New York Dolls... Although the Space Center sound system coped with the noise attack, the overall effect seemed too loud at times. Youth ushers for promoter Gary Naseef were kept busy monitoring KISS fans,

who rivaled the group's fireworks with their own mini-flashes tossed skyward. The tight-knit packaged and choreography jolted the performance into a rousing climax regarded by steady concert goers as the most professional in the local 10- concert series" (Billboard, 6/14/75).

May 30 - Memorial Auditorium, Sacramento, CA **TEMP HOLD DATE
Notes:
- Listed in an early itinerary in Performance Magazine. Instead, the band conducted interviews at K100, KNAC, and KMET in Los Angeles followed by dinner with Neil Bogart.

May 30 - Shrine Auditorium, Los Angeles, CA **ERRONEOUS LISTING
Notes:
- A show attributed to KISS, Nazareth, and Rush on this date appears to be in error. On that particular night Jeff Beck played the venue with Mahavishnu Orchestra opening. That gig was bootlegged and also reviewed in the local press. JR's date planner includes a scratched out date at the venue for May 31, so it is possible that a show was planned at the venue, but was cancelled in favor of the Long Beach show.

May 31 - Long Beach Arena, Long Beach, CA
Promoter: Pacific Presentations
Other act(s): James Gang (opener)
Reported audience: ~8,000 / 13,933 (57.42%)
Set list: Deuce / Strutter / Got to Choose / Hotter than Hell / Firehouse / She / C'mon and Love Me / Rock Bottom / Nothin' to Lose / 100,000 Years / Black Diamond / Cold Gin / Rock And Roll All Nite / Let Me Go, Rock 'N' Roll
Notes:
- From a local review: "Glitter rock may be starting to tarnish around the edges, but it's still a driving force in rock concerts, as KISS proved in its weekend appearance at the Arena. KISS also proved that a group can take something from everyone and make it work. The four-member hard rock group used David Bowie's unisex jump suits, the Who's clouds of dry ice smoke, white-face makeup from mime and drummer Pete Criss even borrowed a little from Ringo and threw his drumsticks into the crowd. Behind all the showmanship lies a band that is still trying hard to work together and hasn't quite made it. Lead guitarist Ace Frehley spun off some solid solos and had clear lines during many numbers, such as "You've Got to Choose," and "Hotter than Hell."

Frehley was let down by the rest of the group's erratic performance. Vocalist Paul Stanley would sound good and then bad; drummer Criss was pounding hard but not always effectively. Gene Simmons, the bass player, put on a good show although he could have paid more attention to his guitar. The show, however, is what 8,000 standing, cheering, clapping people came to see Saturday night. KISS' style was at its peak during the deafening crescendo near the end of "Hotter than Hell." Smoke came billowing over the stage, colored spotlights swept the audience, Simmons flicked his outrageous lizard-like tongue, police lights blinked and sirens wailed and Stanley scattered glitter over the audience. Simmons, it should be noted, followed along with the group's new image of pursuing a serious rock music style, and didn't spit up chicken blood.

As with Bowie, many of the audience came dressed in black, silver-studded clothes with white-face make-up, like the group they came to see. The James Gang, formerly headliners themselves, preceded KISS — who couldn't have had a better warm-up act. The James Gang plays good, honest hard rock with no frills. "Walk Away," the group's sole monster single, brought in a tight mesh of great bass work, clear lead guitar line, audible vocals and a foundation beat. The guitars especially were effective-no slurring even during the louder solos when most groups get pretty sloppy. Both James Gang and KISS would do all right by varying their unrelenting approach to music. Even Led Zeppelin does a slow track to break things up. But as one glitter rock devotee said: 'Ah, it's all been done before'" (Bob Gore, Long Beach Independent, 6/2/75).

- The show circulates as a generally good AUD recording. It is the first known recording with the band's now classic "You wanted the best..." intro by JR Smalling.

June 1 - The Winterland, San Francisco, CA
Promoter: Bill Graham Presents
Other act(s): Rush, The Tubes (opener)
Reported audience: 2,200 / 5,000 (44%)
Reported gross: $12,000
Notes:
- Tickets for this show $5/6, more than twice the cost of the January show!
- From local press: "THEY'RE CALLED 'KISS' AND THEY'RE LOUD: The rock and roll group KISS will team with The Tubes, a group of favorite Bay Area crazies who play music and present humorous and satirical skits and Rush, a Canadian hard rock trio at Winterland on June 1 at 8 pm" (San Mateo Times, 5/30/75).
- From a local review: "Students of rock and roll cosmetology and *la mode grotesque*, those amusingly nitwit posturings practiced by the likes of David Bowie, Gary Glitter, Alice Cooper and Mick Jagger, were faced with a problem a few nights ago. On one hand, at Winterland, veteran weirdo bands KISS and the Tubes met for the mondo bizarro equivalent of the Gunfight at the OK Corral. Sequins blazing, swigging madly from silver hip-flasks filled with For Brunettes Only, the two groups were expected to set standards for bad taste not to be exceeded outside the political arena in this century" (San Francisco Chronicle, 6/6/75). The regular music critic, Joel Silver, declined to review any portion of the show other than the Tubes' set. As for KISS, they were reduced to a brief mention as a "classless, tasteless band known for its garish theatrics."
- From another local review: "KISS is a New York rock quartet, the Tubes are a Bay Area septet also of rock persuasion — although with a featured vocalist, synthesizer, keyboards plus electric instruments and drums, it provides far more varied sounds than KISS. Both these groups are crazies. Their music often is secondary, on stage, to their antics, their show, their special effects. KISS plays in costumes and makeup that give the appearance of a spaced-out Batman off on a vampire trip. Heavily made-up, with leather-like skin tight costumes (with sparkles and studs), the group plays super loud music, sings unintelligibly

over the din and provides, along the way, a wild stage show... Loud, raw, suggestive and carefully choreographed, KISS is a typical New York product — everything is prepackaged (from platform boots to the comments) to turn a crowd up and on" (San Francisco Examiner, 6/3/75)...
- This show was presumably also filmed by the venue's in-house video system, but the tapes were purportedly lost in a 1985 fire. However, the Tubes' set from this concert exists from Bill Graham's archives...

June 4 - Terrace Ballroom, Salt Lake City, UT **CANCELLED

June 6 - Warnor's Theatre, Fresno, CA
Promoter: Get Down Productions
Other act(s): Rush (opener)
Reported audience: (2,351 capacity)

June 7 - Civic Center Theater, San Diego, CA
Promoter: Fun Productions
Other act(s): Rush (opener)
Reported audience: (2,967 capacity)
Notes:
- Last show with Rush for a while as they headed out on their own Canadian tour in support of "Fly By Night" and then entered the studio to record "Caress Of Steel." Geddy later recalled this final show with KISS: "At the end of our last tour with KISS in San Diego we were gonna dress up as them, put on their makeup, and go out and do our set as them, but what finally happened was an onstage pie fight in front of 6,000 screaming kids. They caught us at the end of our set by surprise, and whole stage was covered in shaving cream and whipped cream. Then it was our turn at the end of their set. All their guitars and drums and machines were completely buried in shaving cream, so their encore sounded just great" (Circus, 4/27/76).

June 11 - Coliseum, Denver, CO **CANCELLED

June 13 - Fairgrounds Pavilion, Tulsa, OK
Promoter: Stone City Attractions
Other act(s): Rare Earth (HL), Point Blank (opener)
Reported audience: ~3,000 / 6,311 (47.53%)
Reported gross: $12,000
Set list: Deuce / Strutter / Got to Choose / Hotter than Hell / Firehouse / She / C'mon and Love Me / 100,000 Years / Black Diamond / Cold Gin / Rock And Roll All Nite
Notes:
- Originally scheduled for the larger Tulsa Assembly Center, KISS was paid a flat fee of $3,500 for this show according to the Apr. 28 ATI contract.
- A SBD recording from this show circulates. "Let Me Go, Rock 'N' Roll" would have been on the set list, but was dropped due to time constraints. It's a generally excellent quality show, though not without some issues in parts, not least lacking the show's intro. There are, however, enough references to "Tulsa" throughout the recording to ensure the location.

June 14 - City Coliseum, Austin, TX
Other act(s): Rare Earth (HL)
Reported audience: (3,500 capacity)
Notes:
- While KISS were billed as the opening act, Rare Earth performed first at this show which started well over an hour late due to "technical difficulties." When Rare Earth did take to the stage at 9:15 p.m. they simply suggested it was due to KISS "having trouble getting their pants on" (Austin Daily Texan, 6/17/75).
- From a local review: "KISS was, to say the least, a portrait of pretentiousness. KISS' bowl 'em over knock 'em out type theatrical show would have been more effective if it was backed by some sort of creative talent. However, the former type of show seemed to be what the predominantly high school aged audience came to hear. KISS appeared to be trying to see how many tricks and gimmicks they could cram into their show to dress up their loud, repetitious heavy rock. Beginning with the ever-popular revolving, reflective globe. KISS quickly moved into their razzle-dazzle attack... KISS' assaults on the eyes and the ears included at least six flashing red lights; smoke generators (used twice); towers of flame; bright, white lights flashed at the audience and loud explosions, in addition to the constant thunderous volume of the band's music.

The volume also succeeded in drowning out practically all of the vocals and most of Ace Frehley's guitar solos, which, when audible, sounded pretty good. During one song, the band stopped long enough for Frehley to play an earsplitting solo that was almost too loud to be heard. Rhythm guitarist Paul Stanley took a five-minute break to conduct a question and answer period with the audience on the fate of rock and roll. I can't help wondering what side KISS took. KISS' No. 1 problem was redundance. Every one of their songs sounded the same, with the same beat and same basic chord structures. It is disappointing that the group did not try to add any variety to their music" (Austin Daily Texan, 6/17/75).

June 15 - Memorial Coliseum, Corpus Christi, TX
Promoter: Stone City Attractions
Other act(s): Rare Earth (HL)
Reported audience: 4,500 / 5,016 (89.71%)
Reported gross: $22,000
Notes:
- From pre-show press: "Joining Rare Earth is a group billed as 'the Sensation of the Year,' KISS, their premiere Corpus appearance. KISS will be armed with their entertainment arsenal, including several powerful neutroid explosive flash pods; two giant blow torches; billowing clouds of white smoke; a giant candelabra; snow machines; a display of giant revolving police lights and sirens; and wal1 to wall amps. Gene Simmons, Paul Stanley, Peter Criss and Ace Frehley combine the unique theatrics and hard-driving rock sound of the group" (Corpus Christi Times, 6/13/75).

June 18 - Sports Arena, Jackson, MI
Promoter: Paul Stanley Productions / Steve Glantz
Other act(s): Salem Witchcraft (opener)
Reported audience: (6,000 capacity)
Reported gross: $16,000

June 20 - Roanoke Civic Center, Salem, VA
Promoter: Philip Lashinsky / National Shows
Other act(s): Montrose (opener)
Reported audience: (11,000 capacity)
Reported gross: $10,000

June 21 - Music Hall, Cleveland, OH
Promoter: Belkin Productions
Other act(s): Journey (opener)
Reported audience: (3,000 capacity)
Partial set list: She / C'mon and Love Me / Let Me Know / Rock and Roll All Nite.
Notes:
- This show was recorded for "Alive!" though it doesn't circulate in full format. Two shows had originally been scheduled at Allen Theater. 16 track mobile recording facilities were provided by Bearsville Studios.
- Both "Let Me Know" and "Rock And Roll All Nite" were used on the King Biscuit Radio Show originally broadcast in November 1975 and mention Cleveland by name. The other two songs noted were mentioned in a review of the show.
- Prior to the show Gene gave a private interview backstage and detailed the band's plans to record a live album, which he mentioned would include a fresh side of studio material — the format later used for "Alive II."
- Journey ought not to be confused with the band that it later evolved into. At this time there was no Steve Perry on vocals. Instead, the band comprised of Gregg Rolie (ex-Santana) on keyboards and vocals, Neil Schon (ex-Santana) on guitars, Aynsley Dunbar on drums, George Tickner on rhythm guitar, and bassist Ross Valory. At the time of this show the band had only released their self-titled, generally progressive rock, album.

June 22 - Civic Center, Charleston, WV
Promoter: Entam, Ltd.
Other act(s): Montrose, Journey (opener)
Reported audience: (8,500 capacity)
Reported gross: $20,000
Partial set list: Hotter than Hell / She / Nothin' to Lose / C'mon and Love Me
Notes:
- From a local review: "Next to KISS, Alice Cooper and the New York Dolls make sense. This group of four men (judging from the bared chests and the Civic Center Sunday, I'd say all four are men), thinks the concert is a costume party and they come dressed to kill. KISS is weird, but its music is solid rock 'n' roll... It's hard to know exactly what to make of KISS, this group with the Halloween makeup and exaggerated motions. They sometimes act as if they're not quite sure what their instruments are for, but when they play them, it's obvious they do... They call KISS the hottest band in America. I'm not sure about that, but they certainly are the weirdest" (Charleston Gazette, 6/23/75).

June 23 - Roanoke Civic Center, Salem, VA **TEMP HOLD DATE
Notes:
- This show appeared on an earlier itinerary in Performance magazine, and with several other dates around the time were changed. This date was ultimately booked for June 20.

June 25 - Convention Hall, Asbury Park, NJ
Promoter: Phil Cohen & Earth Productions
Other act(s): Skyscraper
Reported audience: (3,600 capacity)
Set list: Deuce / Strutter / Nothin' to Lose / Hotter than Hell / Firehouse / She / Rock Bottom / C'mon and Love Me / 100,000 Years / Black Diamond / Cold Gin / Rock And Roll All Nite / Let Me Know
Notes:
- Show unusual for "Let Me Know" being performed as the final encore.
- This show is known to exist as an AUD recording but does not circulate widely. Plans for the "Alive!" are well advanced and shows have already been recorded by Eddie Kramer. From this period several shows circulate, notably the May 31 Long Beach Arena audience recording and June 13 Tulsa soundboard. From the same taper as Northampton, the band's show at Asbury's Convention Center in New Jersey on June 25 was captured. It's immediately apparent that the taper didn't have the optimum location for taping. This show is distant and bass heavy, but more than acceptable as an AUD source from the era. Complete with classic intro, the band rip into a standard DTK era set list with a bombastic rendition of "Deuce." The power and glory of classic era KISS is obvious with free-flowing guitar work and pounding drums.

June 26 - Civic Center Arena, Asheville, NC **TEMP HOLD DATE
Notes:
- This show appeared on an earlier itinerary in Performance magazine, and with several other dates around the time were changed. This date was rescheduled for the following day.

June 27 - Civic Center Arena, Asheville, NC
Promoter: Kaleidoscope Productions
Other act(s): Montrose (opener)
Reported audience: (7,654 capacity)

June 28 - Greenville Auditorium, Greenville, SC
Promoter: Beach Club Productions
Other act(s): Montrose (opener)
Reported audience: (7,500 capacity)

June 29 - Atlanta, GA **TEMP HOLD DATE
Notes:
- This show appeared on an earlier itinerary in Performance magazine, and with several other dates around the time were changed. This date was not rescheduled.

July 1 - Capitol Theatre, Port Chester, NY
Promoter: in-house
Reported audience: (1,800 capacity)
Notes:
- Not to be confused with the John Scher venue of the same name in Passaic, NJ; this venue was located northeast of New York City on the border with Connecticut. The venue was an early adopter of Ticketron, the computerized ticketing system, through owner Howard Stein

in 1971. As was similar with many other venues of the time two shows were hosted nightly, at 8 and 11p.m., until 1971 when city ordinances established a 1a.m. curfew for live entertainment. The theatre ended its life in 1976, following a period as a XXX movie house (though it reopened later in the year under new management with Savoy Brown scheduled for the reopening).

July 5 - Convention Center, Wildwood, NJ **POSTPONED
Notes:
- This show was postponed until July 30 so that KISS could perform at the Florida Jam.

July 5 - Tampa State Fairgrounds, Tampa Bay, FL
Promoter: World Wide Events / Marquee Events
Other act(s): ZZ Top (HL), Johnny Winter, Marshall Tucker Band, Ozark Mountain Daredevils, War, Pure Prairie League (opener), Atlanta Rhythm Section (opener)
Reported audience: ~40,000
Notes:
- This "Florida Jam" event was scheduled to run from 11am through midnight. KISS played third on the bill after PPL and Atlanta Rhythm Section.
- Dr. John was another act mentioned, but apparently did not perform.
- From a local review: "The third band to perform was a four-creature menagerie from England named KISS. Featuring pancake make-up, exotic stars painted around their eyes, and costumes made out of leotards with studs all over them, KISS looks like four guys trying out for bit parts in a movie like 'Dracula Meets the Lizard-Men.' Their bizarre costumes could be all in fun, but unfortunately the fun ends when the band tries to make music out of the two or three chords they are able to play together. KISS probably comes across better at night, since their flashing lights and firebombs seem to be the act's highlights" (St. Petersburg Times, 7/7/75).

July 20 - R.K.O. Orpheum Theater, Davenport, IA **two shows
Promoter: Windy City Productions
Other act(s): Journey (opener)
Reported audience: 4,673 / 5,994 **both shows
Reported gross: $26,110.50
Notes:
- The two sets performed this night were recorded for "Alive" though neither currently circulates. Fedco Audio Labs provided remote recording facilities for this venue and the following show in Wildwood.
- It's known that "Let Me Go, Rock 'N' Roll" on "Alive!" was at least partially sourced from this show due to Gene's shout out, "C'mon Quad City!"
- Isolated tracks from "100,000 Years" from this show were used in the Rock Band 2 game, though sadly the lyric "bitch" is censored from the performance.

July 23 - Convention Center, Wildwood, NJ
Promoter: Phil Cohen and Earth Productions
Other act(s): Mushroom (opener)
Reported audience: (3,200 capacity)

Set list: Deuce / Strutter / Got to Choose / Hotter than Hell (intro only) / She (solo end only) / Nothin' to Lose / C'mon and Love Me / 100,000 Years / Parasite (cuts) / Cold Gin (cuts) / Let Me Go, Rock 'N' Roll (cuts)

Notes:

- "Hotter than Hell," "Firehouse," and "Black Diamond" were purportedly used on the King Biscuit radio show originally broadcast in November 1975, but the quality of the circulating AUD recording is so poor and partial only the classic introduction to "Hotter than Hell" can be matched up definitively: "I got this feelin' when we came flying in this afternoon it was so sunny I thought we were gonna fry alive." Still, the three songs are nearly identical to the "Alive!" album versions, albeit with a different audience track.

- While not a good recording or complete, it is the last of the shows recorded for "Alive!" However, with the quality issues and drop-outs, it really is only for diehards/completists only.

- Isolated tracks from "Deuce" from this show were used in the Rock Band 2 game. The full song features part of the strange intro used at the show (that is heavily distorted in the AUD recording): "So if you want to party with the hottest rock 'n' roll band in the world, you've gotta party with KISS!"

August 2 - Civic Center, Baltimore, MD
Promoter: J.H. Productions
Other act(s): Black Sabbath (HL)
Reported audience: (12,500 capacity)
Notes:

- Black Sabbath's set has circulated for many years as an AUD recording leaving some fans with the hope that KISS's set was also recorded. In the break between shows KISS had been in the studio working on "Alive!"

August 3 - Brown Auditorium, Civic Center, Providence, RI
Promoter: Concerts East
Other act(s): Black Sabbath (HL)
Reported audience: 12,500 **SOLD-OUT
Reported gross: $80,000
Set list: Deuce / Strutter / Hotter than Hell / Firehouse / She / C'mon and Love Me / 100,000 Years / Black Diamond / Cold Gin / Rock And Roll All Nite
Notes:
- KISS' shortened set was a result of their opening for Black Sabbath who was touring in support of their then recently released "Sabotage" album. The show was sold out and the audience reportedly booed heartily when the band's set finished, wanting more of what they'd just experienced!
- From a local review: "To the fans walking out of the Civic Center last Aug. 3, there was no question who the stars were. Headliners Black Sabbath had been blown off the stage by upstart openers KISS. No doubt about it. The New York quartet resembled nothing so much as the randomly violent English Droogs of 'A Clockwork Orange,' ... any group that knocks off Black Sabbath can't be all bad. Or can they" (Providence Evening Bulletin, 12/30/75).
- While a bit distant sounding, the circulating AUD recording has nicely balanced levels. Paul's raps can be a bit difficult to hear, though he's very energetic. The show commonly circulates direct from the master (Maloney) recorded using a Sony TC-110A analog cassette recorder. A new source started circulating in October 2009, also direct from a master (Lampinski) that had been recorded using Sony TC-152SD analog tape recorder and Sony ECM-99 stereo microphone. A nice matrix of the two sources also exists.

August 8 - Onondaga County War Memorial, Syracuse, NY **POSTPONED
Promoter: Steve Glantz Productions
Other act(s): Unknown.
Reported audience: (8,000 capacity)
Notes:
- An ad for this show did appear in the Syracuse-Herald American newspaper on 8/3/75, though no opening act was detailed at the time.
- This show was postponed at the last moment, according to a War Memorial source, due to "the Rolling Stories concert in Buffalo, they were unable to sell tickets" (Syracuse Post-Standard, 8/9/75) — hardly surprising with that show pulling a crowd of 70,000. The show was eventually rescheduled for Oct. 2, 1975.

August 9 - Palace Theater, Albany, NY **TEMP HOLD DATE
Promoter: Steve Glantz Productions
Reported audience: (2,800 capacity)
Notes:
- Gene's concert listing in KISStory notes the Civic Auditorium as the venue, while this show is also detailed in an advance itinerary in Performance magazine, including the Syracuse and Hempstead dates. However, this and the postponed Syracuse date both fall directly in the period when KISS was in the studio working with Eddie Kramer on "Alive!" A band memo

dated July 30 detailed that rehearsals would be conducted with Bob Ezrin, Aug. 11 – 14. However, the band were clearly at Electric Lady Studio on Aug. 11 reworking material for "Alive!" While a schedule from late-July is obviously fluid, the overall evidence, with confirmed concert dates on Aug. 14, suggest that both dates may have been postponed, but only Syracuse was rescheduled. Contrary evidence, a brief mention of Evelyn Knoll, director of the Palace, having booked the band (in the Schenectady Gazette, 8/26/75) provides no concrete evidence that the show actually took place, nor does a brief mention of the then forthcoming show in the local press on Aug. 3 — Unlike the Seals & Croft show on Aug. 10, no proper advertisement or review in the local press has yet been found. Additional documentation suggests the road crew were in New York City attending to mundane tasks.

August 14 - Orpheum Theatre, Boston, MA
Promoter: Don Law
Other act(s): Black Sabbath (HL)
Reported audience: (2,900 capacity)

August 15 - Civic Center, Saginaw, MI
Promoter: Steve Glantz Productions
Other act(s): Flock (opener)
Reported audience: 7,200 **SOLD-OUT
Reported gross: $36,000
Notes:
- An ad trumpeting the sell-out appeared in a trade publication: "First advance sell-out in the arena's history" (9/5/75).

August 16 - L.C. Walker Arena, Muskegon, MI
Other act(s): Flock (opener)
Reported audience: (6,500 capacity)

August 17 - Memorial Stadium, Pekin, IL
Promoter: Len Tramper Presents / A Whatever Production
Other act(s): R.E.O. Speedwagon, Ted Nugent, Smokehouse (opener)
Reported audience: (3,000 capacity)
Notes:
- Regional band Smokehouse included a very young Micki Free, with whom both Gene and Paul would later have musical endeavors (WOW, Crown of Thorns).

August 20 - Carroll's Studio 5, New York City, NY **REHEARSALS
August 21 - Carroll's Studio 5, New York City, NY **REHEARSALS
August 22 - Carroll's Studio 5, New York City, NY **REHEARSALS
Notes:
- Rehearsals scheduled with Bob Ezrin to work on material for the album that ultimately became "Destroyer."

August 23 - Calderone Concert Hall, Hempstead, Long Island, NY
Promoter: Concerts East
Other act(s): The Flock (opener)
Reported audience: 2,435 **SOLD-OUT

Reported gross: $15,000

Set list: Deuce / Strutter / Got to Choose / Hotter than Hell / Firehouse / She / Nothin' to Lose / C'mon and Love Me / 100,000 Years / Black Diamond / Cold Gin / Rock And Roll All Nite / Let Me Go, Rock 'N' Roll

Notes:

- From a trade review: "The Calderone Theater hastily added KISS to their summer concert schedule but the show sold well considering the lack of publicity due to the short notice booking... Unfortunately, the opening act never stood a chance. No opening act would've stood a chance there. The audience was rabid and shouted 'We want KISS, we want KISS' in unison to the embarrassment of The Flock, whose set was interrupted on more than one occasion by the cheers for KISS" (Performance Magazine). This show was an 8 p.m. concert at the venue with Gentle Giant performing the late show at 11:30.

- As an AUD recording, this is one of the best shows to circulate from the late stage of the tour. It circulated for quite a few years before a very nice upgrade surfaced.

August 24 - Harman-Geist Auditorium, Hazleton, PA **TEMP HOLD DATE

Notes:

- There is currently no evidence that this show took place and was anything other than a temp hold that appeared on some of the band's itineraries.

August 25 - State Farm Show Arena, Harrisburg, PA

Promoter: East Coast Concerts, Inc.

Other act(s): R.E.O. Speedwagon (opener)

Reported audience: (7,600 capacity)

August 27 - Sports Center, Owensboro, KY

Promoter: Steve Glantz Productions

Other act(s): Hydra (opener)

Reported audience: (5,000 capacity)

Notes:

- A banner still hangs at the venue commemorating the time KISS performed there, and slightly singed the roof...

August 28 - Convention Expo Center, Indianapolis, IN

Promoter: Windy City Productions

Other act(s): Uriah Heep (HL), Atlanta Rhythm Section (opener)

Reported audience: 13,000 **SOLD-OUT

Reported gross: $72,913

Notes:

- The final date of the "Dressed to Kill" tour.

August 30 - Laurel Harness Raceway, Laurel, MD **CANCELLED

Promoter: Fred Dendy

Other act(s): R.E.O. Speedwagon (HL), The Guess Who, Blue Oyster Cult

Notes:

- This show, which would have been part of a two-day festival, was listed on some itineraries, but ultimately did not take place. Laurel is located midway between Washington D.C. and Baltimore.

- The Howard County Executive denied the promoter a permit for the concert citing one of the band's "histories of past disturbance" (Cumberland News, 8/27/75) coupled with a shortage of police protection for the event. As a result the promoter was forced to cancel the event.

Alive!

In a January 1976 interview Paul suggested, "'Alive!' was like a transitional album, because we knew what we wanted to do, but we needed someone to work with, you see. The whole idea of the live album was to make a cutoff point between old KISS and new KISS, so that people would be able to say, "Oh, that came after the live album.' The live album was the synopsis of everything that went on before; it says, 'Here's what KISS has done to date, now they're gonna go on'" (Bloomington Gulcher, 1/76). The same sentiment is very much true of the tour that supported the album in that it drew a line in the sand between the "old" KISS and the "new" KISS that emerged during the summer of 1976. As a continuation of the "Dressed To Kill" tour, the show essentially presented the live album live in concert. The tour certainly didn't break new ground, other than witnessing the band's explosion in popularity as the album took on a life of its own.

The "Alive!" tour began essentially brought the track-listing from the "Alive!" LP to the stage for audiences to experiences, though throughout there was enough scope in the timing of the show for the band not to have to simply perform the whole album each night. At the currently earliest definitively known show set, at the Tower Theatre in Upper Darby, PA on Oct. 3, LP cuts such as "Parasite," "Watchin' You," and "Rock Bottom" were excluded. Two of these, "Parasite" and "Rock Bottom" would be substituted into the set days later, making the set organic, with non-LP songs such as "Ladies In Waiting" also making appearances. There are unfortunately not a plethora of 1975 shows from the tour from which bootlegs circulate, nor was it the norm for reviews to explicitly mention sets. As a result there is a certain amount of mystery about what the band performed throughout the tour. The Jan. 1976 shows in Detroit are probably best illustrative of the varying sets with "Parasite" and "Ladies In Waiting" alternating, with the former taking precedence until "Destroyer" material started appearing in early March.

The first known performance of "Shout It Out Loud" is currently unknown. It's hardly surprising that, as the first single from the album, that it was the first song performed from the album. Its inclusion was noted in a review of the Mar. 12 show in New Orleans right around the time it was released. By the time a fully validated set is available, from the Mar. 21 show in Miami, it is simply an addition to the set, having not bumped any other song, and is neatly slotted in between "Nothin' To Lose" and "100,000 Years." An identical set would be performed on Mar. 24 in Philadelphia. Two days later "Flaming Youth" is noted as being performed, along with "Ladies In Waiting" and "Rock Bottom." From the available sets it is clear that the tour was anything but static.

The tour was mostly without incident. One notable exception would be the cancelled Dec. 19 show at the Centrum in Cherry Hill, NJ which was initially "postponed" by promoters just days before show-date, even after 6–7,000 tickets had been sold. Initially ads were placed noting that tickets would be honored at a rescheduled date, but ultimately no date was forthcoming and further ads offered refunds. While the promoter suggested that there had been a "conflict over who was staging the KISS concert" (Trenton Evening Times, 3/26/76) Aucoin and ATI were forced to take out ads disavowing any connection with the Camden show, due to the harm the existing tickets still in circulation could cause the promoters of the officially sanctioned show on Mar. 24. Without doubt it was a messy situation, and purchasers of the Camden tickets could only receive refunds by post or visiting a less than desirable location. "Jennifer Productions' Honney is concerned, as a result of phone calls and other inquiries, that holders of the Dec. 19 tickets will think their March 24 concert is the postponed date. And with most of the early buyers from nearby New Jersey, a situation of large numbers showing up at Civic Center here with Centrum tickets is fraught with danger" (Billboard, 3/13/76). Challenges with tickets weren't limited to just the KISS show through the promoter's ticket agency with other events also proving problematic for patrons.

Mirroring the rise of the album the tour started out in September to mediocre audiences, averaging 3,180 patrons. By Oct., as the band transitioned to larger venues, the average attendance had increased to 5,525. By the end of the following month the average audience was approaching 8,000 including a staggering 21,897 at the Capital Center and numerous sold-out shows. KISS had arrived, even if there were still a few markets that hadn't received the memo concerning their success. The hard slog was finally about to pay dividends as the band were transformed from novelty or oddity into zeitgeist status.

September 10 - Memorial Auditorium, Chattanooga, TN
Promoter: Sound Seventy Productions, Inc. / Entam, Ltd.
Other act(s): Slade (opener)
Reported audience: 1,818 / 5,000 (36.36%)
Reported gross: $10,000
Notes:
- This show took place on Slade drummer Don Powell's birthday.

September 11 - Knoxville Civic Coliseum, Knoxville, TN
Promoter: Entam, Ltd.
Other act(s): Slade, Gary Wright (opener)
Reported audience: 4,540 / 6,500 (69.85%)
Reported gross: $25,000

September 12 - Greensboro Coliseum, Greensboro, NC
Promoter: Entam, Ltd.
Other act(s): Slade, Gary Wright (opener)
Reported audience: 3,813 / 5,000 (76.26%)
Reported gross: $21,000
Notes:
- Ex-Spooky Tooth member Gary Wright was not a fan of KISS's music, suggesting that he thought the music was more important than a band's theatrics, but in the case of KISS the theatrics were more important than the music (Daily Tar Heel, 9/24/75).

September 13 - The Scope, Norfolk, VA
Promoter: Entam, Ltd.
Other act(s): Slade, Gary Wright (opener)
Reported audience: 2,727 / 5,000 (54.54%)
Reported gross: $15,000

September 14 - King's College Gym, Wilkes-Barre, PA
Promoter: King's College
Other act(s): Diamond Reo (opener)
Reported audience: ~3,000
Notes:
- From a local review: "After a minute or two into their set it became apparent that KISS's success is not based on their music, but on the package in which they offer it. In a battle of the glitter bands the silver faced freaks would win hands down" (The Crown, 9/18/75).
- From another local review: "Once your ears become accustomed to the heavy metal drone and the initial shock of the theatrics wears off, it becomes obvious that KISS merely offers a simplistic and redundant for rock and roll. The four band members are competent but not original and their solos became a bit boring after a while. KISS is the most arrogant band I've ever seen. No 'thank yous' were uttered even though the audience were on their feet and clapping throughout the set. Whenever they did talk directly to the audience it was about partying and getting high one way or another" (The Wyoming Valley Observer, 9/21/75).

September 21 - Memorial Field, Mt. Vernon, New York **CANCELLED
Promoter: Concerts Promotion International (CPI)
Other act(s): Orleans, John Sebastian, Don McClean, Chris Hillman, and others
Notes:
- This "Summer's End" festival was cancelled, though ads (such as the one below) still appeared in print at the time the show was scheduled to take place.

October 2 - Onondaga County War Memorial, Syracuse, NY
Promoter: Steve Glantz
Other act(s): James Montgomery Band (opener)
Reported audience: (8,000 capacity)
Notes:
- This show was rescheduled from Aug. 8, 1975.

October 3 - Tower Theatre, Upper Darby, PA
Promoter: Midnight Sun Productions
Other act(s): Fallen Angels (opener)
Reported audience: 2,877 **SOLD-OUT
Reported gross: $18,700
Set list: Deuce / Strutter / Got to Choose / Hotter than Hell / Firehouse / She / Nothin' To Lose / C'mon and Love Me / 100,000 Years / Black Diamond / Cold Gin / Rock And Roll All Nite / Let Me Go, Rock 'N Roll
Notes:
- From local pre-show press: "KISS appears in sadomasochistic leather with death-white faces scarred in black paint. The music is atrociously loud, the actions garish. The group is just the thing to convince your cousin in Kansas how decadent the East is" (Philadelphia Inquirer, 9/28/75).
- Peter's mic dropped out during "Black Diamond" and Paul helped out with the vocals.
- An average AUD recording circulates from this show.

October 4 - Capitol Theatre, Passaic, NJ **TWO SHOWS
Promoter: John Scher
Other act(s): Savoy Brown (opener)
Reported audience: (3,200 capacity)
Notes:
- Shows at 8 and 11:30PM were scheduled.

October 5 - Rochester Dome Arena, Rochester, NY
Promoter: Steve Glantz / Concerts East
Other act(s): Black Sheep (opener)
Reported audience: 5,600 **SOLD-OUT
Reported gross: $34,000
Notes:
- Local band Black Sheep included future Foreigner vocalist Lou Gramm and future KISS co-writer Bruce Turgon on bass. Performance magazine reported Slade to be on the bill in one issue and Black Sheep in another. Regardless, Black Sheep were last minute replacements for originally billed openers R.E.O. Speedwagon. This show was the second advance sell-out for the venue.
- From a local review: "In spite of all the hype, KISS is just another punk-rock band from Detroit. If you took the old MC5 and dressed them in greasepaint and leather costumes you would come up with something very close to KISS... It seems that all it takes to turn on a rock audience these days is an over abundance of volume, a basic knowledge of 4/4 time and a few theatrical gimmicks, no matter how hackneyed. That was the formula used by KISS Sunday night. KISS plays a brand of rock and roll that is basic in the extreme. Using a lineup of two guitars, bass and drums, they emphasize the bottom end of their sound, relying on rhythms that are always simple and occasionally catchy. By the end of a song, however, even the catchy rhythms have been pounded into oblivion through endless repetition. The theatrical gimmicks KISS uses are even more trite than their music" (Democrat & Chronicle, 10/7/76).

October 6 - Agricultural Hall, Allentown, PA
Promoter: DiCesare-Engler Productions

Other act(s): R.E.O. Speedwagon (opener)
Reported audience: 4,400 / 4,510 (97.56%)
Reported gross: $25,000

October 7 - Read Fieldhouse, Kalamazoo, MI
Promoter: Western Michigan University Student Concert Committee
Other act(s): Styx, Hammerhead (opener)
Reported audience: (11,000 capacity)
Partial set list: Deuce / Hotter than Hell / Nothin' to Lose / C'mon and Love Me / Parasite / Rock Bottom / Cold Gin / Let Me Go, Rock 'N' Roll
Notes:
- From a local review: "Fulfilling their promise of a horror show, reaching all of the senses with polished precision. This concert, instead of the usual escape from reality, unfolded into a coarse, nightmarish look at what is happening... these four men are setting their own standards and they give a good look at what is ahead around the rock 'n' roll corner. 'KISS' has the talent to provide — or decide — exactly what the heavy metal music followers want" (Kalamazoo Gazette, 10/8/75).
- From another local review: "KISS never let up in their assault on the audience with an assortment of exotic special effects, screeching guitars and satanistic garb. Playing for a total of three encores KISS was like seeing 'The Exorcist' put to rock music. They vibrated and scorched and left the onlooker in a different world" (The Western Herald, 10/8/75).

October 8 - Beacon Theatre, New York City, NY **TEMP HOLD DATE
October 9 - Beacon Theatre, New York City, NY **TEMP HOLD DATE
Notes:
- These shows were listed on some early itineraries, but did not take place due to how the routing of the tour developed. They may well have been erroneous.

October 9 - Cadillac High School Gym, Cadillac, MI
Promoter: Cadillac High School
Other act(s): Double Yellow Line (opener)
Reported audience: ~2,000
Set list:
Notes:
- This legendary performance was conducted in conjunction with the band's highly stage-managed visit to Cadillac, MI. Jim Neff, whose 1974 football team used the "KISS Defense," approached Rock Steady Management about having KISS appear at the KISS themed Homecoming week since the band was popular with the kids.
- Apparently, Gene didn't spit blood during the show on agreement with the school's officials, but did breathe fire. The KISS logo also wouldn't fit in the gym, so the students made one.
- It is purported that much of the band's visit, including the show, was filmed.

October 11 - Veterans Memorial Auditorium, Columbus, OH
Other act(s): Black Sheep (opener)
Reported audience: (3,964 capacity)

October 12 - Veterans Memorial Auditorium, Columbus, OH **TEMP HOLD DATE
Notes:
- The Columbus visit was detailed in a Performance itinerary as a pair of dates, following which the band took a short break during which Peter undertook some primal scream therapy sessions.

October 19 - Sports Stadium, Orlando, FL
Promoter: Steve Glantz Productions
Other act(s): Atlanta Rhythm Section (opener)
Reported audience: (8,000 capacity)

October 20 - Bayfront Center, St. Petersburg, FL
Promoter: Steve Glantz Productions
Other act(s): Bob Seger, Atlanta Rhythm Section (opener)
Reported audience: (8,055 capacity)
Notes:
- In 2013 a full color concert poster advertising this show sold for a whopping $3,125 on eBay. It featured the classic "Peter holding dagger" photo of the band that had been used as the band's first promotional poster.

October 21 - Municipal Auditorium, Mobile, AL **CANCELLED
Reported audience: (10,200 capacity)
Notes:
- This show was still being advertized as on-sale in the Mobile Press-Register, just two days before it was scheduled to take place; even though it had been cancelled weeks earlier. Inexperienced promoters, coupled with low ticket sales, were blamed for the KISS, and other act's cancellations around the time. The facility manager suggested that "most of the tickets are sold the day before or the day of the concert" (Mobile Register, 10/9/75), suggesting that risk-adverse promoters were cutting perceived losses before the shows generally sold at the venue.

October 22 - Municipal Auditorium, Birmingham, AL
Promoter: Steve Glantz Productions
Other act(s): Bob Seger, Atlanta Rhythm Section (opener)
Reported audience: (5,000 capacity)

October 26 - Garrett Coliseum, Montgomery, AL
Promoter: Good Time Productions
Other act(s): Harvest (opener)
Reported audience: (12,528 capacity)
Notes:
- Harvest was a band that included guitarist Tommy Shaw — he'd quit the band within a couple of months of this show and played his debut gig with Styx on Dec. 16.

October 29 - Minneapolis, MN **TEMP HOLD DATE
October 30 - Madison, WI **TEMP HOLD DATE
Notes:

- Many dates, that were ultimately not booked, appeared in an early Performance itinerary for the band.

October 30 - Municipal Auditorium, Nashville, TN
Promoter: Sound Seventy Productions, Inc.
Other act(s): Bob Seger, Montrose (opener)
Reported audience: 5,100 / 8,000 (63.75%)
Reported gross: $27,500
- Photos of Ace and Gene, from this show, were published in the McGavock High School's 1976 year book.
- From a local review: "Thursday's night KISS concert, touted as a Halloween season special, didn't pull may interested parties. However you feel about good ol' basic rock 'n' roll, you have to admire a group who can survive both the heat of stage lighting and a full face of makeup" (Nashville Tennessean, 11/2/75).

October 31 - Kiel Auditorium, St. Louis, MO
Promoter: Ron Powell
Reported audience: 10,584 **SOLD-OUT
Other act(s): Atlanta Rhythm Section (opener)
Notes:
- From a local review: "It was a battle of eardrums and amplifiers as a truly scary rock act, KISS, appeared in Halloween concert at Kiel Auditorium Friday night... The four members of KISS came on like superstars and left the audience, which had spent most of the concert on its feet, drained... Not lost in all the histrionics and special lighting effects was some decent musicianship, although it was hard to comprehend how they could play so well while wagging back and forth like human metronomes. The melody was hard to pick out more often than not, other times it was a steady drone. No one in the group sang that well, but that didn't matter much to the crowd" (St. Louis Post-Dispatch, 11/1/75).

November 2 - Oklahoma City, OK **TEMP HOLD DATE

November 2 - Mary E. Sawyer Auditorium, La Crosse, WI
Promoter: Daydream Productions
Other act(s): Brownsville Station (opener)
Reported audience: 3,187 / 4,100 (77.73%)
Reported gross: $17,899
Notes:
- Some itineraries indicate that this show took place on the 3rd. Flyers indicate otherwise, that it took place on a Sunday, the day before; as does the following review.
- From a local review: "Blood-sucking Count Dracula may have passed into legend, but a group called KISS goes on. Weirdsville... Whatever their thing is, it's loud, kinky, bizarre and weird with a frenetic beat, and uses a sound system that could have called in a deaf Norwegian elk-hound from Viroqua... Unless you were deaf as a post they stimulated you right out of your mind" (La Crosse Tribune, 11/3/75).

November 3 - Levitte, TX **TEMP HOLD DATE
November 4 - Galveston, TX **TEMP HOLD DATE
November 6 - Houston, TX **TEMP HOLD DATE

November 6 - Municipal Auditorium, San Antonio, TX
Promoter: Jam Productions / Concerts West
Other act(s): Mott (opener)
Reported audience: (5,785 capacity)
Notes:
- From local press: "Dear lovers, earthlings, cat people, and victims the masters of living 'Batman' comics are coming to San Antonio. KISS, the band that is very difficult to ignore, will appear at the Municipal Auditorium on Thursday at 8 p.m. KISS will storm the city armed with an arsenal of several powerful neutroid explosive flash pods, relentlessly billowing clouds of white smoke; a giant candelabra; snow machines; a halting display of giant, revolving police lights and sirens; wall to wall amps; exploding drumsticks; rocket firing guitars and a levitating drum kit plus a fire-breathing, blood-drizzling bassist" (San Antonio Light, 11/2/75).

November 7 - Dallas, TX **TEMP HOLD DATE

November 7 - McDonald Gym @ Lamar University, Beaumont, TX
Promoter: Setzer Student Center Council / Redman's Productions
Other act(s): Mott (opener)
Reported audience: ~3,000

November 7 - Swing Auditorium, San Bernardino, CA **TEMP HOLD DATE
Notes:
- Mentioned in a Los Angeles Times Fall season report on Sept. 28, a show as eventually scheduled for Feb. 22 and then postponed until Feb. 26.

November 8 - San Antonio, TX **TEMP HOLD DATE

November 8 - Beacon Theatre, New York City, NY **TEMP HOLD DATE
November 9 - Beacon Theatre, New York City, NY **TEMP HOLD DATE
Notes:
- These shows were listed on some itineraries, but did not take place due to how the routing of the tour developed. As early as August KISS had been mentioned in trade publications as being part of a series of concerts to be hosted by the legendary Radio City Music Hall in New York City, with an anticipated run of dates in November 1975. While nothing came of any plans considered during the "Alive!" tour period the concept of a multi-date stand at the venue was reconsidered during a Nov. 30, 1976 meeting. By that time, however, Bill Aucoin was not particularly interested in pulling the band off the road unless they could earn at least $100,000 for any residency.

November 8 - U.T.A. Texas Hall, Arlington, TX
Promoter: Concerts West
Other act(s): Mott (opener)
Reported audience: (2,625 capacity)
Notes:
- From pre-show press: "This one is for the flashy set. KISS will bombard you with flash pods, giant blow-torches, clouds of white smoke, snow machines, revolving police lights, sirens, wall-to-wall amps, guitars that fire rockets and a fire-breathing bass player. Music, however,

is not guaranteed with KISS and almost improbably with Mott" (Dallas Morning News, 11/8/75).

- From industry press: "Considering their lack of area radio exposure, the songs of KISS were instantaneously recognized by the fans — and each was greeted with adoration. The crowd, for the most part, remained on its feet from the beginning to the bitter end. KISS' material hasn't changed much through the course of several albums, but they've found a successful formula and they appear to be sticking with it. They performed selections from all their records and it mostly seemed like the 'KISS Alive' LP which had gone gold the day before the concert. But the record cannot, despite and exciting full color booklet of photos, duplicate the excitement of KISS' choreography, outfits, make-up, stunts, explosions, flash-pots, and smoke-bombs. And the kids know it. They went wild. KISS are in the process of conquering the few remaining unKISSed territories in the U.S. It is obvious now that they are no longer merely a regionally successful band but are in actuality a national phenomena" (Performance).

November 9 - Long Beach Arena, Long Beach, CA **TEMP HOLD DATE
Notes:
- Mentioned in a Los Angeles Times Fall season report on Sept. 28, shows were eventually scheduled for Feb. 23 – 24.

November 9 - Sam Houston Coliseum, Houston, TX
Promoter: KILT / Concerts West
Other act(s): Mott (opener)
Reported audience: (11,500 capacity)
Notes:
- From a local review: "Theatrical rock and roll made its Coliseum debut as KISS cranked out two hours of manic music and thrills. Flares, flashing lights, fire and sirens an provided effective excitement within the bizarre Sunday night performance, however, the show's near duplication of the group's 'Alive' album detracted from the element of surprise... Ace Frehley was a competent lead guitarist, but his instrument made up as much of the performance as his actual playing. The faster and more furious his playing, the more smoke which seemed to rise off the chords. As if that wasn't enough, it erupted a bright flare from the neck for the climax. In the following song, 'Firehouse,' Frehley performed strongly despite the clouds of billowing smoke, flashing lights, and fire around him. Unfortunately, the group continued the reproduction of their live album down to the conversations with the audience. There were no complex themes in the music, just no-nonsense lyrics about women and raising hell, so to speak. Drummer Peter Criss kept the beat at a moving pace and gave a decent solo during '100,000 Years'" (Houston Daily Cougar, 11/12/75).

November 12 - Toledo Sports Arena, Toledo, OH
Promoter: Steve Glantz Productions
Other act(s): Styx (opener)
Reported audience: 7,500 **SOLD-OUT
Reported gross: $42,000
Notes:
- 200 – 300 fans couldn't get into the sold-out show resulting in a disturbance outside the venue. 13 fans were also arrested during the show for drugs and other offences.

November 14 - St. Bernard Parish Civic Auditorium, New Orleans, LA **TEMP HOLD DATE
Reported audience: (9,000 capacity)
Notes:
- This show was noted in Performance magazine but obviously wouldn't have made sense in terms of routing by the time the tour itinerary solidified.

November 15 - Kansas City, KS **TEMP HOLD DATE

November 15 - Rockford Armory, Rockford, IL
Promoter: Windy City Productions
Other act(s): Rush (opener)
Reported audience: 3,610 **SOLD-OUT
Reported gross: $23,465
Set list: Deuce / Strutter / Got to Choose / Hotter than Hell / Firehouse / She / Ladies In Waiting / Nothin' To Lose / 100,000 Years / Black Diamond / Cold Gin / Rock And Roll All Nite
Notes:
- From a local review: "There were some strange tribal rites at the National Guard armory Saturday night. Hordes of hirsute cultists mobbed the place. Some began collecting not long after sundown. Shortly after 8 p.m. the ceremonies began. Everyone in the place jumped to attention and feet hanging over the edges of the balconies began clacking together. Then a bright spot hit the stage and a long-armed dude opened up with a barrage that sounded like Capone's boys were back in the garage on St. Valentine's Day. Suddenly this hairy devil jumped up with an electric guitar. I think it shorted out though, because he commenced to scream and howl like a bull that didn't clear the barbed wire. Even the Jaycee's haunted house didn't have noises like that. It sounded at one point like someone was torturing a cat backstage... The sound grabs you by the throat as you walk in and twangs on your nervous system like a guitar string. Between the visceral beat that hammers your backbone and the cloudbank of smoke hanging over the audience, it keeps you vibrating for an hour afterward. A steady diet of it will grow hair on your feet... Fans identified the performing artists. The groups have short titles. Saturday night there was Rush and KISS. I couldn't wait for KISS. Rush sent me hunting for a crowbar to pry my eyes back into place" (Rockford Register-Star, 11/16/75).
- Later this evening recordings from Cleveland, OH were broadcast as part of DIR Broadcasting's King Biscuit Flower Hour show. The show primarily featured the Average White Band with just five KISS songs: "Hotter Than Hell," "Firehouse," "Black Diamond," "Let Me Know," and "Rock And Roll All Nite." The first three of these are usually attributed to Wildwood, NJ, but there's no definitive evidence that that's really the case, other than the intro.
- A good AUD recording from this show circulates with a rare performance of "Ladies In Waiting."

November 16 - I.M.A. Auditorium, Flint, MI
Promoter: Mid-West Enterprises
Other act(s): Mott (opener)
Reported audience: 5,300 **SOLD-OUT
Reported gross: $36,193

November 17 - I.M.A. Auditorium, Flint, MI
Promoter: Mid-West Enterprises
Other act(s): Rush
Reported audience: 5,300 **SOLD-OUT

November 18 - McMorran Place Arena, Port Huron, MI
Promoter: Fatso Productions
Other act(s): Rush (opener)
Reported audience: 3,788 **SOLD-OUT
Reported gross: $25,077
Partial set list: Deuce / Strutter / Firehouse / Cold Gin / Rock And Roll All Nite
Notes:
- From a local review: "KISS came, saw and easily conquered a howling, cheering crowd of more than 3,700 teenyboppers and rock lovers Tuesday night at Port Huron's McMorran Place Arena. The black leather and silver-sequined New York City band, whose members resemble mutant escapees from some future shock nightmare, ripped the night air and young ears with their own brand of mega-decibel rock and roll for nearly two hours... For lovers of this sort of armored attack rock and roll — and they are legion — the overall concert effect was of being strapped to a friendly Saturn rocket as it blasted off for Mars. Quite lovely indeed" (Port Huron Times-Herald, 11/19/75). The review also mentions that 12 songs were performed, indicating that the set may have been very similar to that in Rockford days earlier.

November 19 - Glacier Dome, Traverse City, MI **KISS CANCELLED
Promoter: Steve Glantz Productions
Other act(s): Styx (opener)
Reported audience: 5,800 **SOLD-OUT
Reported gross: $28,200
Notes:
- KISS's equipment blew out and the band reportedly only managed three songs following Styx's set at this concert. According to press reports, while Styx was performing their final song an electrical short caused $12,000 of damage to amps, speakers, and lighting. Requiring $35,000 worth of refunds!
- The management of the Dome later blamed KISS for the short-circuit that ended the show, but also installed an upgraded electrical system to power concert backlines. However, the issues affecting the venue were more serious, since the event was dangerously over-sold for the venue.
- The official capacity was 4,154 seats, though the facilities could only handle a maximum 2,451 person capacity at the time. The state fire marshal limited the venue's capacity to that latter figure following the show. Initially there were plans to reschedule the show, but the facilities issues caused the ultimate cancellation.
- The whole situation, plus police seizures of "$1,300 of illegal drugs and paraphernalia from the fans" during the concert beg the question that the "short" might have been seen as a convenient way out of a potentially dangerous situation. No concerts were held at this venue until June 1976 when REO Speedwagon came to town with Head First.
- Cadillac High School Coach Jim Neff attended this show.

November 21 - Hulman Civic University Center, Terre Haute, IN
Promoter: Sycamore Showcase Committee
Other act(s): Rush, Mott (opener)
Reported audience: 10,000 **SOLD-OUT
Reported gross: $60,000
Notes:
- This concert came close to Elvis' then house record of 10,244, but didn't exceed it, though at the time it was the only sell-out of the venue in festival seating configuration (Terra Haute Tribune, 4/17/76).
- Local press reported that two unnamed members of the band were returning to the hotel in Jerry Chaplain's Rolls Royce, following the show, and were involved in a traffic collision that resulted in heavy damage to the beautiful car.
- Mayor William J. Brighton declared the day "KISS Day," whereas "KISS is dedicated to good clean rock and roll at 105 decibels." The mayor didn't present the award to the band personally — that task was relegated to airport superintendant Ray Feiler.

November 22 - International Amphitheatre, Chicago, IL
Promoter: Windy City Productions
Other act(s): Mott, Leslie West Band (opener)
Reported audience: 10,140 / 11,237 (90.24%)
Reported gross: $71,554
Notes:
- From a local review: "Once in a while, you see a rock concert that's so good, you forget that you're risking your life, and you're actually glad to be part of all that craziness. KISS did it for me" (Chicago Sun-Times, 11/24/75).
- From a trade review: "Defused by the stringent fire laws, KISS were not allowed to us any of its explosives, rockets, etc., and had to make do with balloons from the ceiling and snow effects. The audience didn't seem disappointed" (Performance Magazine).

November 23 - Roberts Stadium, Evansville, IN
Promoter: Tom Duncan
Other act(s): Rush, Mott (opener)
Reported audience: 11,200 / 11,000 **OVERSOLD
Reported gross: $67,200

November 26 - Memorial Field House, Huntington, WV
Promoter: Entam, Ltd.
Other act(s): Rush, Mott (opener)
Reported audience: 9,000 **SOLD-OUT
Reported gross: $54,000
Notes:
- Styx was originally scheduled to open.
- From local press: "KISS is a band most people either love or hate. Me, I mostly don't understand them. I saw them in performance here at the civic center and plan to see them next Wednesday when they invade Huntington's Memorial Field House. Maybe this time I'll learn what they're all about. When you first see KISS, you may be overwhelmed by the visuals— the wall to wall amps, the 6-foot high electric KISS sign just above their heads, the weird makeup, their fantastic theatrics. When they begin to play, however, the sound truly

overwhelms. It is loud, raucous stuff. It's an explosion, powerful rock 'n' roll. It is, says one critic, 'mood music — if you happen to be in the mood to blow up buildings or wreck cars.'

I talked with Philip Lashinsky in Huntington before the recent Little Feat/Dave Mason concert and we discussed the KISS show. Lashinsky, who happens to like KISS, still was able to lament the fact the show had then already sold more tickets than the total Little Feat attendance. 'Little Feat is great music,' Lashinsky said. 'I was here for their sound check today, and even it was great.' KISS, of course, puts on a show. There is more to the music than just the music, which means it's interesting to watch as well as being something to hear. As bassist Gene Simmons of the group says, 'We're in show business, aren't we'" (Jim Games, Gazette Mail, 11/23/75).

November 27 - Cumberland County Memorial Arena, Fayetteville, NC
Promoter: Beach Club Promotions
Other act(s): Mott, Styx (opener)
Reported audience: 7,000 **SOLD-OUT
Reported gross: $42,000

November 28 - Civic Center, Asheville, NC
Other act(s): Mott, Styx (opener)
Reported audience: (7,646 capacity)
Notes:
- Due to complaints about the volume, and possible impact on patron's hearing, the volume at this show was measured by authorities. According to measurements reported in the local press 114 decibels were recorded at the back of the arena with peaks of 120 decibels.

November 29 - Charlotte Coliseum, Charlotte, NC
Other act(s): Mott, Styx (opener)
Reported audience: (13,000 capacity)

November 30 - Capital Centre, Largo (Landover), MD
Promoter: Cellar Door Productions
Other act(s): Mott, Styx (opener)
Reported audience: 21,897 **SOLD-OUT
Reported gross: $128,749
Partial set list: Cold Gin / Rock And Roll All Nite / Let Me Go, Rock 'N' Roll
Notes:
From a local review: "The overflow crowd was made possible by the 'festival seating' approach that Washington promoters have been using recently, with the seats on the arena floor removed to permit standing room, and a general admission ticket policy, the Capital Centre's usual 18,786 capacity is raised by several thousand" (Washington Post). In another review, a 'local disc jockey, who admits hating having to play the KISS hit single suggested that, 'It's pure masochism, the kids liked to be abused. I'm appalled people would pay good money for something like that'" (Washington Star, 12/2/75).
- Only the encores from this show circulate on this pro-shot video raising the tantalizing question about whether there's "more." It's reasonable quality footage, and cool due to very close camera work, giving an interesting view of the stage. Audio, or at least the mix, leaves a bit to be desired.

December 2 - Municipal Auditorium, Columbus, GA
Promoter: Entam, Ltd.
Other act(s): Styx (opener)
Reported audience: (5,265 capacity)

December 3 - Civic Center, Dothan, AL
Promoter: Entam, Ltd.
Other act(s): Styx (opener)
Reported audience: (3,500 capacity)

December 5 - The Omni, Atlanta, GA
Promoter: Alex Cooley, Inc.
Other act(s): Leslie West Band, Styx (opener)
Reported audience: (16,700 capacity)
Notes:
- This show was initially advertized for the Fox Theater.

December 6 - Coliseum, Jacksonville, FL
Promoter: Jet Set Enterprises
Other act(s): Styx, Dixie Dregs (opener)
Reported audience: (10,228 capacity)
Notes:
- The Dixie Dregs included guitarist Steve Morse, a jazz-rock outfit from Augusta, GA, whose lineup included Winger's Rod Morgenstein. Steve later replaced Richie Blackmore in Deep Purple.

December 7 - Municipal Auditorium Mobile, AL **TEMP HOLD DATE
Notes:
- A second attempt at the venue didn't result in a solid booking...

December 12 - Onondaga County War Memorial, Syracuse, NY
Promoter: Concerts East
Other act(s): Black Sabbath (HL)
Reported audience: ~7,000 / 8,000 (87.5%)
Partial set list: Nothin' to Lose / Ladies in Waiting / Cold Gin / Rock And Roll All Nite
Notes:
- From a local review: "Although possibly not as popular as several years ago, Black Sabbath still has a strong following, as some 7,000 showed up last night at the War Memorial for their concert. Also on the bill was KISS, who are becoming regular visitors to Central New York. Black Sabbath, who proved to be perfectionists — keeping fans waiting for over an hour while equipment was set up and sound checks were made and remade — is widely acclaimed as the best acid-hard rock group in the business. The concert substantiated this claim. The set last night featured selections from all their top-selling albums, such as 'Hole in the Sky,' 'Snow Blind,' 'War Pigs,' 'After Forever' and 'Don't Start Too Late.' There was nothing fancy about the performance, just driving, dynamic sounds reflecting intricate care for detail. The four British musicians performed compositions with a minimum of theatrics, but rather, placed influence on the music itself. The fans certainly seemed pleased with this arrangement.

Sabbath had somewhat of a hard time pleasing the audience at first, after one of the fastest-rising groups currently, KISS, opened the evening's entertainment. Their stint was more of a theatrical, glittery type that was emotionally exhausting. Bedecked in white-face makeup and utilizing such props as sirens, flashing lights, bellowing smoke and flaming gas torches, the music is definitely better suited to live renditions than recordings. Among the selections offered in their portion of the concert were 'Nothin' to Lose,' 'Ladies in Waiting,' 'Cold Gin' and 'Rock 'n' Roll All Night.'

The grotesque make-up and strange on-stage antics provided a performance touching all the senses. If the music was not brilliant, but certainly loud, the theatrics nevertheless kept your attention and lent KISS its uniqueness" (Syracuse Herald-Journal, 12/13/75).

December 14 - The Orpheum, Boston, MA
Promoter: Don Law
Other act(s): Black Sheep (opener)
Reported audience: 1,700 / 2,900 (58.62%)
Reported gross: $16,600

December 18 - The Palace, Waterbury, CT
Promoter: Koplik & Finkel Productions
Other act(s): Black Sheep (opener)
Reported audience: (3,419 capacity)
Set list: Deuce / Strutter / C'mon and Love Me / Hotter than Hell / Firehouse / She / Ladies In Waiting / Nothin' To Lose / 100,000 Years / Black Diamond / Cold Gin
Notes:
- The show is halted, briefly after Ace's solo following "She," for an announcement to the crowd with a warning from the Fire Marshal about the audience standing on their chairs. After "Black Diamond," another interruption occurs with a request for fans to put away their lighters/matches and not burn the place down. The band then performs what may have been their final song, "Cold Gin," though one source has suggested that the band eventually came back out and performed their encores, but they certainly weren't captured on tape. Contrary to local legend, the band did not set fire to the stage drapery...
- Circulating 8mm footage runs about 14:24, so roughly 1/5 of the show is represented. Regardless of the nature of the footage, captured is Gene setting his hair on fire. The quality of makes it rather difficult to decipher at first glance what may have been performed.
- An average AUD recording from this show became more widely available in October 2013.

December 19 - Centrum, Cherry Hill, NJ **CANCELLED
Promoter: Willow Weep Productions
Other act(s): Steppenwolf, Slade (opener)
Reported audience: (4,416 capacity)
Notes:
- Initially mentioned in Billboard (12/13/75) as a legitimate date.
- Between 6 and 7 thousand tickets were sold for this cancelled concert. When the tour returned to the area in March 1976, the new promoters (Jennifer Productions) had to take out press informing ticket holders that those original tickets would NOT be honored and for holders to obtain refunds from the original promoter. KISS' tour bookers ATI issued an advertisement that announced, "Any announcement of promoters of an alleged

performance, or one to be announced at the Centrum, is false" (Billboard, 3/13/76). Willow attempted to suggest that the date was simply postponed, leading to challenges in March when the Philadelphia concert was seen by ticket holders as a replacement show. What was clear was that there were many un-refunded tickets in circulation at the time. Management and ATI suggested that the date had not been officially booked or sanctioned.

December 19 - Broome County Arena, Binghamton, NY
Promoter: Creative Promotions
Other act(s): Styx (opener)
Reported audience: (6,900 capacity)
Reported gross: $31,064
Notes:
- Styx were performing at the Ohio Theatre in Lima, OH, the night previous, so this may well be a case of an erroneous opening act being advertized. Whatever the case, Styx were certainly back in Binghamton on April 15, 1976 for a bill that included Skyhooks and Uriah Heep. All ads mention KISS/Styx the week of show, though it is possible Rush/Mott opened.
- From a local review: "Don't be discouraged if you are still perplexed after Friday's show, because the KISS list of moods ranged from diabolical to destructive. The six-foot-high electric KISS sign rose for the occasion, and billows of smoke filled the stage as Gene Simmons (bass), Ace Frehley (lead guitar), Paul Stanley (ryhthm guitar) and Peter Criss (drums) began their attack on the extreme boundaries of high-energy rock and roll. KISS included your token drum solo and guitar break, like the other heavies. After this, however, KISS' other stage effects propelled them into a class by themselves" (Press and Sun-Bulletin, 12/21/75).

Creative Promotions & WAAL-FM-99.1 Stereo
present
KISS and special **STYX**
guest stars
The ARENA—Binghamton—FRI., Dec. 19
Tickets: 5.50 Advance — 6.50 Day of show
Available at Arena Box Office, all Kent Drugstores and
Brown's Pharmacy — Deposit

December 20 - Civic Center Arena, Pittsburgh, PA
Promoter: WDVE / DiCesare-Engler Productions, Inc
Other act(s): Rush, Mott (opener)
Reported audience: 15,500 / 17,000 (91.18%)
Reported gross: $87,000

December 21 - Mosque Theatre, Richmond, VA
Promoter: Entam, Ltd.
Other act(s): Mott (opener)
Reported audience: 3,732 **SOLD-OUT
Notes:
- Rush did not perform at this show, instead headlining their own gig in Youngstown, OH; at the Tomorrow Club with Mojo opening.
- From a local review: "If quality were measured in decibels, KISS and Mott would be slugging it out for the title of top band. It isn't and they aren't, but you could have fooled a packed house of howling partisans at the Mosque last night. The two groups are exponents of what used to be called heavy metal, a megalithic, high-volume, high-visuality deviation on the theme of rock 'n' roll. Their music is a medium tempo series of all-together-now whumps on guitars, bass and drums... Lately, KISS has been packing the crowds in with the visual element. The four of them dress up in dada suits, paint their faces and perform under a couple of twinkle balls, while 'KISS' blazes in lights from behind the drummer. Trouble is, they don't spell it right. It ought to be 'KI$$'" (Richmond Times-Dispatch, 12/22/75).

December 26 - Memorial Coliseum, Fort Wayne, IN **CANCELLED
Promoter: Sunshine Productions
Other act(s): Mott, Ted Nugent's Amboy Dukes (opener)
Reported audience: 9,500 **SOLD-OUT
Notes:
- KISS cancelled and the show went ahead with Mott as the headliner. The show was reported as sold-out in advance in the Fort Wayne News-Sentinel (12/24/75). According to local press, only one member of the band was able to get to the venue with the other three being stuck in Toledo due to a snowstorm. They didn't want to fly a charter due to the weather conditions (Fort Wayne Journal-Gazette, 9/5/76).

December 27 - Louisville Gardens, Louisville, KY
Promoter: Sunshine Promotions
Other act(s): Styx, Black Sheep, Santa Claus

Reported audience: 7,200 **SOLD-OUT
Reported gross: $39,600
Notes:
- This show was promoted as the 1st Annual Holiday Festival. A day of show ad had an alternate line-up including Blue Oyster Cult and Mott.
- Two people were arrested trying to sell $313.50 worth of stolen tickets for the show.

December 28 - Morris Civic Auditorium, South Bend, IN
Other act(s): Styx (opener)
Reported audience: (2,483 capacity)
Notes:
- Originally a show at the Nelson Center in Springfield, IL was scheduled on this date.

December 29 - Providence Civic Center, Providence, RI
Promoter: Frank J. Russo
Other act(s): Leslie West Band (opener)
Reported audience: 13,000 **SOLD-OUT
Reported gross: $85,000
Notes:
- Leslie West's opening set was brought to an abrupt end when someone "tossed a burning object into West's long curly hair. A member of the band's road crew rushed to West's side with a towel to smother the burning hair. West played for several seconds after the incident but abruptly ended his set" (UPI).

December 31 - Nassau Coliseum, Long Island, NY
Promoter: Phil Basile / Ron Delsener Present
Other act(s): Blue Oyster Cult, Leslie West Band (opener)
Reported audience: ~13,000 / 17,000 (76.47%)
Reported gross: $129,900
Set notes
- This show is notable since two years to the day prior, KISS had opened for BOC. After the show the band hosted a pool party at the Excelsior Club in Manhattan.
- Following this show the band took a short break to finish the recording of "Destroyer."

January 1, 1976 - Civic Center, Baltimore, MD **TEMP HOLD DATE
Notes:
- Noted on some early itineraries, this date did not take place.

January 22 - Carroll Musical Instrument Rentals, New York City, NY **REHEARSAL
Notes:
- The band conducted an afternoon rehearsal. They were scheduled to take a charter jet to the show the following day. Days earlier, members of the band had jammed at Ashley's in New York City to celebrate Paul's birthday.

January 23 - Grand Rapids, MI **TEMP HOLD DATE
Notes:
- An issue of Performance magazine noted this date, though it was either in error or changed.

January 23 - Erie County Field House, Erie, PA
Promoter: Steve Glantz
Other act(s): Phillippe (opener)
Reported audience: (5,250 capacity)
Notes:
- Popular local progressive rock band Phillippe was engaged by the promoter when the scheduled opener, Lou Gramm's Black Sheep, failed to turn up. However, they may well have had the legitimate excuse as having broken up by that point.
- KISS' pyrotechnics at one point singed the venue's ceiling. The incident grew in stature to the point where they'd nearly burned the place down and was banned from performing there again.

January 25 - Cobo Arena, Detroit, MI
Promoter: Steve Glantz Productions
Other act(s): Back Street Crawler (opener)
Reported audience: 12,600 **SOLD-OUT
Set list: Deuce / Strutter / C'mon and Love Me / Hotter than Hell / Firehouse / She / Ladies In Waiting / Nothin' To Lose / 100,000 Years / Black Diamond / Cold Gin / Rock And Roll All Nite / Let Me Go, Rock 'N' Roll
Notes:
- The band flew in make-up to Detroit, direct from Erie on January 24, to conduct a press conference at the Detroit Airport Hilton. They were given the evening off. Opening act, Back Street Crawler, also flew in from Texas, where they had been completing rehearsals with John "Rabbit" Bundrick. Even if there was a stylistic mismatch between the bands, they had connections with KISS, with two members having been in the Ron Johnsen produced band, Bloontz, who performed with KISS at the Palisades Library benefit concert in May 1973 (and had performed on the Lyn Christopher album). Guitarist Paul Kossoff had been a member of one of Paul Stanley's favorite bands, Free.
- Video from the pro-shot show is missing the presumed encores, but remains notable for the inclusion of "Ladies In Waiting," and Paul knocking his mic over during "Strutter."
- This show was officially released as the third bonus DVD as part of the "KISSology Vol. 1" DVD package offered by "Best Buy."

January 26 - Cobo Arena, Detroit, MI
Promoter: Steve Glantz Productions
Other act(s): Rory Gallagher (opener)
Reported audience: 12,600 **SOLD-OUT
Set list: Deuce / Strutter / C'mon and Love Me / Hotter than Hell / Firehouse / She / Parasite / Nothin' To Lose / 100,000 Years / Black Diamond / Cold Gin / Rock And Roll All Nite / Let Me Go, Rock 'N' Roll
Notes:
- Glantz had booked a limo service, Cole's Coach Service, for the band while they were in Detroit. However, "disagreements ensured, and Glantz's fired Cole's twice in two hectic days. An attorney for Cole's says the company is considering court action. Meanwhile, KISS managers have filed an extortion complaint with police against company president Thomas Cole, claiming he demanded $825 for the return of three luggage pieces that a KISS manager had left in a limousine" (Detroit Free Press, 1/27/76). According to Lydia Criss in

"Sealed With A KISS," items left in the limo that were held hostage were the video tapes of the performances filmed by Kirby/Kelly Productions.
- Complete pro-shot video, versus night 1, though "Parasite" replaces "Ladies In Waiting." Tape issues affect parts of the show as do some audio effects, which may be the result of the band's instruments tuning.
- 13 minutes of silent 8mm footage was shot with the band receiving their RIAA awards.
- This show was officially released on the "KISSology Vol. 1" DVD.

January 27 - Cobo Arena, Detroit, MI
Promoter: Steve Glantz Productions
Other act(s): Rory Gallagher (opener)
Reported audience: 12,600 **SOLD-OUT
Set list: Deuce / Strutter / C'mon and Love Me / Hotter than Hell / Firehouse / She / Parasite / Nothin' To Lose / 100,000 Years / Black Diamond / Cold Gin / Rock And Roll All Nite / Let Me Go, Rock 'N' Roll
Notes:
- Parts of this pro-shot show have been released, on the "KISS My Ass" video. Like the first night the encores are missing from the video. The show was added after the first two sold well.
- The semi-complete video does not generally circulate. It's believed that the reels suffered physical damage that affect their quality, though the "KISS My Ass" videos would seem to suggest that were that the case any damage does not affect the whole available show. Audio from the partial show (also excluding encores), sourced from the video, was released via the "A Detroit Trilogy" bootleg in mid-2015. The quality of the untouched audio and performance is indicative of issues that may have prevented the use of more of the concert.
- The band returned to New York the day following the show for a "Destroyer" album listening session scheduled for January 29.

January 30 - Rose Arena, Mount Pleasant, MI
Promoter: CMU Program Board
Other act(s): Hot Lucy (opener)
Reported audience: 6,000 **SOLD-OUT
Notes:
- The band flew in from New York on the day of show.
- The sold-out audience was the most attendees of a CMU PB event up to that time.
- From a local review: "There was a circus in the Rose Arena Friday night. It wasn't the kind of circus you would take a seven-year-old to, but it certainly shouldn't have been billed as a musical concert... The enthusiastic but orderly audience definitely was fanatical about this current 'fad' group" (Central Michigan Life, 2/2/76)...

January 31 - Hara Arena, Dayton, OH
Promoter: Belkin / Windy City Productions
Other act(s): Leslie West Band (opener)
Reported audience: 8,000 **SOLD-OUT
Reported gross: $44,000
Notes:
- Show sold out in advance with an arena spokesman commenting, that the sell-out "came as a pleasant surprise, but we want to get it across that there'll be absolutely no tickets,

seats or room for anymore persons... don't want anyone getting their hopes up and showing up the night of the show" (Dayton Daily News, 1/26/76).

- From a local review: "Yes, KISS, the ultimate in heavy, pervo, rock groups, played to an adoring mob of boppers, freaks, straights, and even some oldsters (over 30?), and presented one of the most ridiculous, fast-paced, electrifying and hysterical shows ever to hit town. In KISS one finds the worst aspects of every '70's super-mean rock act: Volume bordering on the vomit level, absurd and tasteless costumes and makeup, childish lyrics that deal largely with death and sex, asinine stage antics, and way too many visual stunts. But I love 'em! I am so tired of intensely serious rock-and-rollers who are 'into their music' and unbelievably hip and cool that they come across as a bunch of snobs or — worse yet — musical zombies. Enter KISS like a breath of fresh air" (Journal Herald, 2/2/76).

- According to an internal financial statement, KISS grossed $127,895 from their performance guarantees and percentages for the 6 January shows.

February 1 - Richfield Coliseum, Richfield (Cleveland), OH
Promoter: Belkin Productions
Other act(s): Hydra (opener)
Reported audience: ~13,000 / 17,500 (74.29%)
Notes:
- The show started at least 30 minutes late due to icy local conditions.
- Belkin Productions had planned to run their inaugural charter bus service to this show delivering ticket holding patrons from May's on the Heights in Parmatown to the venue for a $1.50 ticket. Ultimately the idea was abandoned, and the 21 fans who had signed up were instead transported to the show via limo. Another plan of Belkin's, to limit the show to 6,500 tickets was also abandoned...
- From a local review: "It may have been five degrees above zero last night, but it was hotter than Hades at the Coliseum... Bass player Gene Simmons out-did the Devil in his metal costume with bat-wing sleeves and his red-painted tongue. Before the evening was over, the band started flames on stage, flashed lights around an arch above the stage and sent electrical charges to light up silver balls on the Coliseum ceiling, which had been encrusted with flashlight batteries. But unfortunately, "KISS" is almost a near-miss. It has a good basic rock 'n' roll beat, but its songs as so similar that the sounds merge... Lead guitarist Ace Frehley did a standout solo and he didn't have to add smoke to his guitar to make it sizzle. His riffs were razor-sharp" (Plain Dealer, 2/2/76).
- From another local review: "The visual side of KISS's show Sunday was entertaining to say the least as bombs, lights, rising stages, fire sirens and everything but the kitchen sink was employed to deliver the tunes. This, combined with the fireworks and sparklers flying around, produced and exciting time for all, with the exception of any shell-shocked war vets in the house... the hellacious extravaganza probably gave the Coliseum something the hall hasn't had since the last 'Big Time' wrestling card — a good foundation check" (Scene, 2/11/76).

February 4 - Milwaukee Auditorium, Milwaukee, WI
Promoter: Daydream Productions
Other act(s): Point Blank (opener)
Reported audience: ~6,500

Set list: Deuce / Strutter / C'mon and Love Me / Hotter than Hell / Firehouse / She / Parasite / Nothin' To Lose / 100,000 Years / Black Diamond / Cold Gin / Rock And Roll All Nite / Let Me Go, Rock 'N' Roll
Notes:
- From a local review: "There's one guy in the group, the bass player, who's a scream. He's got his hair pulled up into a topknot, triangles painted around his eyes, and he constantly runs his tongue out at the crowd like a bullfrog after a fly. Perhaps he saw the underground film rage 'Pink Flamingoes' and was taken with the character called Divine; because he's a dead ringer for that weirdo drag queen" (Milwaukee Journal, 2/5/76).
- An incomplete average AUD recording from this show exists.

February 5 - Dane County Memorial Coliseum, Madison, WI
Promoter: Daydream Productions
Other act(s): Point Blank (opener)
Reported audience: (10,400 capacity)
Note:
- Cheap Trick was noted as the opening act on a Jan. 21 concerts listing in the Bugle American.

February 6 - Civic Center Theater, St. Paul, MN **two shows
Promoter: Schon Productions
Other act(s): Point Blank (opener)
Reported audience: 2,700 **SOLD-OUT (EACH SHOW)
Reported gross: $16,200
Notes:
- A second show at midnight was added after the first, at 8AM, sold out quickly.
- From a local review: "In the first of its two performances Friday in St. Paul, KISS captivated the youngsters with a 70-minute barrage of histrionics, high energy and heavy metal. To convey their hell-fire and brimstone theme, the musicians, dressed in pseudo-sadomasochism outfits and with paint on their faces, resorted to a panoply of gimmicks: stage fog, smoke and fire bombs, showers of confetti, fire spitting and stage blood drooling from their mouths, strobe lights, red lights, squad car lights, KISS' name in lights, ad infinitum. It's a playful, mock-degenerate hedonism in the spirit of Alice Cooper to which the teenagers, several of whom painted their faces like the musicians', responded with joyous enthusiasm. Yet it was a frantic performance without the spontaneity, vitality and urgency that has made rock — whether glitter, rock and roll or heavy metal — a compelling and valid pop-art form. Rock was never meant to be choreographed, meticuously produced and replicated night after night in the manner that KISS' routine is" (Minneapolis Star, 2/9/76).

February 9 - UT Terrace Ballroom, Salt Lake City, UT
Promoter: United Concerts
Other act(s): Point Blank (opener)
Reported audience: (5,000 capacity)
Notes:
- From a local review: "KISS. Talk about your dark satanic mills. KISS could be the house band in the palace of Ming the Merciless... KISS, which invaded the Terrace Ballroom Monday night, embodies metaphors. The one with the topknot eats fire, drips blood from

his mouth and wags his snake's tongue at the audience. The lead guitarist plays a solo so hot the guitar smokes. These are not metaphors: this is what KISS does. Call it satire: one cannot know their intentions. I liked them, and the crowd shoehorned into the ballroom screamed, waved their arms, jumped, sat on one another's shoulders, smoked grass and had a fine time: a very polite and friendly crowd, I might add" (Salt Lake Tribune, 2/10/76).

February 11 - Portland Memorial Coliseum, Portland, OR
Promoter: Concerts West
Other act(s): Point Blank (opener)
Reported audience: ~11,000 / 13,200 (83.33%)
Notes:
- From a local review: "KISS returned to town Wednesday night with its full line of bizarre shenanigans, science-fiction costumes, and explosive music. The four-piece New York band has finally made the move into larger halls and made its debut in Memorial Coliseum after three previous Portland concerts in the Paramount Theater. In an era of visual rock shows, KISS is probably the flashiest. The band is about as subtle as a firing squad and as loud as an H-bomb. There are overt feelings of violence, as the group's forte is to look menacing... There isn't much mysterious about the band, though. It uses the same fast tempo on all music, hammering the beat home with sledgehammer rhythm in the heavy metal style. The guitarists prowl the stage like loose cats, playing single riffs with that strong beat that is the essence of raw rock and roll. The music is really only part of the show KISS puts on. The power of the band is its use of staging and effects" (Oregonian, 2/12/76).

February 12 - Spokane Coliseum, Spokane, WA
Promoter: Concerts West
Other act(s): Point Blank
Reported audience: (8,000 capacity)
Notes:
- From a local review: "KISS hasn't changed their show much since they were here last May, but no matter. Theirs is the kind of concert worth seeing twice. Bedecked in studs, spikes glitter, and their famous face paint, KISS grabbed the Coliseum crowd's attention last night... Paul Stanley, vocalist and lead guitarist, played his instrument backwards and forwards, on the floor and behind his head, all the while belting out shrill, inaudible lyrics" (Spokane Daily Chronicle, 2/13/76).

February 13 - Paramount Northwest Theatre, Seattle, WA
Promoter: Concerts West
Other act(s): Point Blank
Reported audience: 2,997 **SOLD-OUT
Notes:
- From a local article: "There's no justice in the world when a group like KISS can sell out two shows at the Paramount Northwest (tonight and tomorrow night) and the Kinks couldn't even sell out the first floor last Friday night" (Seattle Times, 2/13/76).

February 14 - Paramount Northwest Theatre, Seattle, WA
Promoter: Concerts West
Other act(s): Point Blank (opener)
Reported audience: 2,997 **SOLD-OUT

Notes:
- From a local review (which in some ways was awkwardly prophetic): "KISS is a sideshow, a carnival act of weirdos doing strange things like spitting fire and blood while flame pots explode and confetti falls like a snow storm... KISS' music is all basic metronomic rock rhythms and constantly repeated catch phrases, or hooks, that are always something simple... Crazy like a fox, as they say in the boardrooms. The band sells lots of tickets and now their records are starting to follow. The bottom line is probably looking pretty good. In fact, the act should be franchised now while it's having its run, like 'Hair' in its heyday. They could have several groups travelling the country doing the KISS routine because it doesn't really matter who the guys are. And the music could be easily learned. They might as well cash in while they can.

The audience for the band is generally young and most of them will grow tired of KISS' monotonous music and act (they've been doing virtually the same thing for years) and go on to something more freaky, if someone can think it up — and don't worry, they will. Right now the band is treated pretty much as a joke — a readers poll in the current Creem voted KISS the second best live group, after the Rolling Stones, and the second worst band, after the Bay City Rollers — and it probably soon will not be 'hip to like them. But then maybe the microboppers will take them over and they'll have a KISS cartoon show on Saturday TV and special KISS issues of 16 Magazine " (Seattle Times, 2/16/76)...
- Patrick MacDonald dropped some legendary reviews on KISS during his career. In his final piece for the newspaper before retiring, Patrick commented, "I know I haven't been the best rock critic, the most knowledgeable or the most perceptive. I'm in the shadow of betters who have influenced me, including Lester Bangs, Dave Marsh, Robert Hilburn and David Fricke. When I was young, I took myself too seriously, and was somewhat aloof and detached. I was so much older then. I'm younger than that now. I've been saying for the past decade or so that I'm finally learning how to do this job." Playfully, he signed off with, "What am I going to do now? Well, of course, I'm going to rock 'n' roll all night and party every day" (Seattle Times, 12/14/08).

February 16 - The Adams Field House, University of Montana, Missoula, MT
Promoter: Albatross Productions / ASUM
Other act(s): Point Blank (opener)
Reported audience: (6,000 capacity)

February 18 - Lane County Fairgrounds Expo Hall, Eugene, OR **CANCELLED
Promoter: Concerts West
Other act(s): Point Blank (opener)
Notes:
- KISS cancelled this show, just hours before it was to start, due to Paul having been "Diagnosed as having strep throat. West said the diagnosis was made Wednesday afternoon in Eugene" (Eugene Register-Guard, 2/19/76). As a result, the band was forced to pay a $5,519 cancellation charge. Several following shows were also affected, though the heavily sold Los Angeles shows were preserved.

February 20 - Civic Auditorium, San Jose, CA **CANCELLED
Promoter: Bill Graham Presents
Other act(s): Slade (opener)

February 21 - The Winterland, San Francisco, CA **CANCELLED
Promoter: Bill Graham Presents
Other act(s): Slade, Point Blank (opener)
Notes:
- Point Blank were an addition to this bill in early February.

February 22 - Swing Auditorium, San Bernardino, CA **POSTPONED
Promoter: Fun Productions / Pacific Presentations
Other act(s): Montrose, Point Blank (opener)
Notes:
- This show was rescheduled for Feb. 26. The show had already sold-out as of Feb. 11, marking the earliest advance sell-out to date for the venue.

February 23 - The Forum, Inglewood, CA
Promoter: Fun Productions / Pacific Presentations
Other act(s): Montrose (opener)
Reported audience: 16,283 / 18,679 (87.17%)
Reported gross: $90,925
Notes:
- While in Los Angeles, Ron Boutwell and Bill Aucoin dined at the Scandia restaurant and were reported in the press as sharing a $750 bottle of 1882 Chateau Lafite Rothschild (Los Angeles Times, 3/4/76). Things were indeed looking up for the band's merchandising...

February 24 - The Forum, Los Angeles, CA
Promoter: Fun Productions / Pacific Presentations
Other act(s): Montrose (opener)
Reported audience: 17,905 / 18,679 (95.86%)
Reported gross: $102,401
Notes:
- This show is reported as selling out in 36 hours, resulting in the addition of a second date on Feb. 23rd. Performance magazine box score reports indicate otherwise, but whatever the case the attendances of both shows were massive.
- From a local review: "It was obvious when KISS first started belching rock 'n' roll fireballs around the country that it would zip straight to the top, and now the time has come. The group headlined at the Inglewood Forum Monday and Tuesday, where it offered a streamlined compendium of every trick in the book, and while the gaudy razzle-dazzle of the show and the intense audience response made for quite a spectacle, there's something a little too pat about the whole affair. Actually, KISS should be admired more for its programming and merchandising than for its music, personality or rock 'n' roll impulses. Despite the sleazy, violent nature of the show, the KISS persona seems to have emerged

from boardroom meetings that distilled essential wants of the rock audience rather than from the more vital route of garage rehearsals and small-time gigs. And despite the brutal heavy-metal attack, the tenets of KISS' act are pure show biz. In its predictability and in its aggressive pandering to youthful tastes, the band is closer to the Osmonds than to its predecessor in outrage, Alice Cooper" (Los Angeles Times, 2/26/76).

February 25 - Convention Center Arena, Fresno, CA **CANCELLED
Promoter: Fun Productions
Other act(s): Slade (opener)
Reported audience: (7,410 capacity)
Notes:
- Band illness was given as the reason for the cancellation of this show (Fresno Bee, 2/25/76).

February 26 - Swing Auditorium, San Bernardino, CA
Promoter: Fun Productions / Pacific Presentations
Other act(s): Montrose, Point Blank (opener)
Reported audience: 7,500 **SOLD-OUT
Reported gross: $45,750
Notes:
- From a local review: "KISS is just the latest of the Ringling Brother's rock-and-roll bands. Their specialty is pyrotechnics, and with their vast assemblage of fireballs, flash and smoke bombs, the Army should consider using the band as a peace-keeping force... Musically, KISS's basic rock and roll crunch chords work well for the blast-furnace visuals, though they rely on echoplexed guitars and phased fuzz" (San Bernardino County Sun-Telegram, 2/28/76).

February 27 - Sports Arena, San Diego, CA
Promoter: Fun Productions
Other act(s): Montrose, Slade (opener)
Reported audience: 13,577 / 14,500 (93.63%)
Reported gross: $77,539
Notes:
- From a local review: "What, no laser beams? No, but KISS blasted its 12,000 hyper-frenetic fans at the Sports Arena Friday night with every other conceivable eyeball-popping visual effect known to rock 'n' roll. A lot of groups, for example, find it effective to climax with spotlight beams reflecting off a revolving mirror ball. KISS opened with TWO mirror balls PLUS a barrage of smoke explosions... When there was time to listen, it seemed that the best musician of the bunch was Criss, who played an electrified solo of some duration and considerable variation and unerringly kept his beat going during a long rap by Stanley... Over the long haul, it will be interesting to see if KISS can last at its present level of popularity. It is, after all, a freak show, basing its appeal primarily on novelty. From here, it can either grow more outlandish from one tour to the next, or perhaps see respectability, a la Alice Cooper" (San Diego Union, 2/29/76).
- The following day the band flew to Hawaii, where they'd remain until Mar. 3.

February 29 - Blaisdell Arena, Honolulu, HI
Promoter: Third Eye Productions

Other act(s): Booga Booga (opener)
Reported audience: (8,639 capacity)
Notes:
- Booga Booga was a comedy act that included James Kawika Piimauna Reiplinger, James Grant Benton, and Ed Ka'ahea.
- During their Hawaiian visit security manager Rick Stuart saved Paul Stanley's life when he decided to jump off a perfectly good boat for some ill-advised ocean swimming.
- This show remains the band's first and only visit to this state.
- According to an internal financial statement, KISS grossed $242,829 from their performance guarantees and percentages from the 15 February shows.

March 4 - Civic Center Music Hall, Oklahoma City, OK
Promoter: Shelly Finkel / Concert Club
Other act(s): Mountain Smoke (opener)
Reported audience: 3,200 **SRO
Reported gross: $18,100
Partial set list: Strutter / Hotter than Hell / Firehouse / Parasite / Nothin' To Lose / Black Diamond
Notes:
- From a local review: "The warm-up group originally scheduled to perform refused to play after seeing the highly vocal audience. They told promoter Ron Nance of the Satellite Ticket Agency they were leaving and departed the hall at 7:40 p.m. Nance had only 20 minutes before show time and finally reached a local bluegrass group called Mountain smoke. The crowd, however, didn't approve of bluegrass and showed it through pure animal reaction. After playing only six songs, one of the Mountain Smoke musicians was struck in the face with a half-filled beer can and the group walked off stage to a jeering, standing ovation" (Tulsa Tribune, 3/9/76).
- Mountain Smoke included a high-school aged Vince Gill would later become a country star in his own right. He was also a member of the band The Flock who opened for KISS. Vince recalled the concert: "The promoters just called and said they needed an opening act at 8 p.m. We were pretty well-known around the area then, and they used us a lot. So we hopped in the car and drove down. I remember seeing the marquee that said KISS was playing, and I thought, 'Hmmm, they must be here tomorrow night.' We played as much as we could, until we realized our lives were in danger. They were throwing beer cans at us. Everybody was booing. I'd never heard 5,000 people booing all at once before. One of the guys got scared, and I told him, 'They can't hurt you with beer cans. They're empty.' Really, it was pretty funny. The best part about it was the guy who wrote the review for the paper the next day. He said, 'It was amazing that Mountain Smoke took it as long as they did, and after they'd had enough, Vince Gill showed what part of his anatomy the crowd could KISS.' And when I did it, the police gave me a standing ovation" (Tulsa World, 1/9/90). Vince also later recalled, "We only lasted about four or five songs. No one believes me, but I was actually laughing my head off. I just couldn't believe the sound of that many people that mad... Why'd I moon them? I didn't actually take any clothing articles off to get this done, but I got my point across. I got a standing ovation from the police... I gave them the international symbol that goes along with it" (Asheville Citizen-Times, 7/21/75).
- From another local review: "KISS did not walk on stage until 9:30 p.m., an hour after Mountain Smoke fled... The visual and audio impact of KISS astounds the senses. They have taken the violence of Alice Cooper and the makeup of David Bowie to arrive at a show wild

enough to cause a commotion such as the Beatles did in the sixties. They're not as good as the Beatles, but the shock puts fans in a fantasy world and they love it" (Oklahoma Journal, 3/5/76).

March 6 - Pershing Municipal Auditorium, Lincoln, NE
Promoter: Ron Powell / Panther Productions
Reported audience: (7,570 capacity)

March 8 - Assembly Center, Tulsa, OK
Promoter: Concerts West
Other act(s): Mountain Smoke (opener)
Reported audience: (8,994 capacity)
Notes:
- From a local review: "KISS, dubbed 1974's 'Hype of the Year' by Rolling Stone magazine, lived up to its designation Monday night... KISS utilizes makeup, smoke and other special effects and theatrics to bolster their act. Strip these items and gimmicks away from this act and there's not a lot left. Just decibels. Maybe, in time, they will mature musically" (Tulsa Tribune, 3/9/76).

March 11 - Von Braun Civic Center, Huntsville, AL
Promoter: Sound Seventy Productions / Concerts West
Other act(s): Albatross (opener)
Reported audience: 9,559 **SOLD-OUT
Reported gross: $52,994

March 12 - The Warehouse, New Orleans, LA
Promoter: Beaver Productions / Don Fox
Other act(s): Van Wilkes (opener)
Reported audience: 3,500 **SOLD-OUT
Partial set list: Hotter Than Hell / Shout It Out Loud / Cold Gin / Rock And Roll All Nite / Let Me Go, Rock 'N' Roll
Notes:
- While still technically the "Alive!" tour material from "Destroyer" had started making its way into the band's set lists — "Shout It Out Loud" had already been released as the first single from the new album and had debuted (at #81) on the Billboard Hot 100 chart in their Mar. 20 issue.
- From a local review: "The crowd was like KISS crowds everywhere; they would have killed if Gene Simmons had said so. A sell-out days in advance, KISS packed the Warehouse without an inch to spare. It was basically a performance of their 'KISS Alive!' album. But hearing it on stereo and seeing it from the front row are two totally different experiences. The sound live was not as good and clear as on their live album which recently turned platinum (a step above gold) but their visual displays and extra onstage instrumentation easily made up for it" (UNO The Driftwood, 3/23/76). The review also mentions several of the songs performed.
- Eddy Allman, from the New Orleans Advocate, wasn't as positive: "KISS' theatrics were the most blatantly decadent forays into retch-rock since Alice Cooper's chicken-killing days. At one point one of the guitarists somehow managed to drench his mouth with a slimy red

goo, much to the delight of those closest to the stage. And what he did with that tongue of his. Absolutely scandalous. Ugh. Please, just go away."

March 13 - Exposition Hall, Mobile, AL
Promoter: Beaver Productions / Don Fox
Other act(s): Dr. Feelgood (opener)
Reported audience: (10,200 capacity)
Notes:
- It's not clear whether originally scheduled opener, Dr. Feelgood, performed at this or any show with KISS, "Gene Simmons, the KISS bass player, will say later of Feelgood that they didn't like their dressing room in Mobile, Ala. 'A fine dressing room,' Simmons says" (Toledo Blade, 4/11/76). In turn that puts in question their participation in the following night's show in Memphis. The band were a British "pub-rock" outfit supporting their second album, "Malpractice."

March 14 - Auditorium North Hall, Memphis, TN
Promoter: Beaver Productions / Don Fox
Other act(s): Target (opener)
Reported audience: 4,361 **SOLD-OUT
Reported gross: $26,166
Notes:
- This show was originally scheduled for Dixon-Myers Hall. Originally scheduled opener, Dr. Feelgood, were replaced by local Southern Rock act Target who had signed with A&M Records to release their self-titled debut album. They included singer Jimi Jameson, who later fronted bands such as Cobra and the better known Survivor (he replaced "Eye of the Tiger" vocalist Dave Bickler). The band also opened for the likes of Black Sabbath during their visit to Memphis.

March 17 - Township Auditorium, Columbia, SC **CANCELLED
Promoter: Beach Club Promotions

March 18 - Memorial Auditorium, Greenville, SC **CANCELLED
Promoter: Beach Club Promotions

March 19 - Coliseum, Macon, GA **CANCELLED
Promoter: Alex Cooley, Inc.

March 20 - Civic Center, Lakeland, FL
Promoter: Beach Club Promotions
Other act(s): .38 Special (opener)
Reported audience: (10,000 capacity)
Notes:
- Dr. Feelgood was replaced on the bill.
- Some 21 people were arrested during this concert, from offences including drugs possession, concealed weapons, public intoxication to "stealing gasoline from cars" (Tampa Tribune, 3/22/76).
- The Knight News Service's Bill Cosford joined the band in Lakeland for a piece that appeared in syndication under the title "KISS Makes It To The Big-Time." He suggested that

Dr. Feelgood didn't perform in Lakeland, having dropped from the tour; "There seems to have been bad feelings between the two bands, even a report that the newer group was 'too good' an opening act for KISS to stomach. But it's hard to tell. The protocol usually demands that the headliner not pay the opener much heed" (Toledo Blade, 4/11/76).

March 21 - Miami Jai-Alai Fronton, Miami, FL
Promoter: Jack Boyle / Cellar Door Productions
Other act(s): .38 Special (opener)
Reported audience: ~5,000 / 5,102 (98%)
Set list: Deuce / Strutter / C'mon and Love Me / Hotter than Hell / Firehouse / She / Parasite / Nothin' To Lose / Shout It Out Loud / 100,000 Years / Black Diamond / Cold Gin / Rock And Roll All Nite / Let Me Go, Rock 'N' Roll
Notes:
- Dr. Feelgood was a late addition to the bill, but as had been the case with other shows did not perform.
- From a local review: "The debate over KISS is going to stay hot for a while. Sunday's KISS concert in the Jai-Alai Fronton only served to reinforce the strident claims on either side, though it may also have made South Florida a bit more aware of the 'phenomenon' that has already become an entrenched, if somewhat bizarre, fact of life in the Midwest and West... Even the band members admit that you can't always make great music while breathing fire or launching rockets from your guitar... The music was simple, occasionally appealing but largely loud and repetitive. But the KISS stage act remained impressive, a ceaseless barrage of entertaining happenings, an assault of special effects used with perfect timing and even restraint... Love 'em or hate 'em. Either way it's fun. But in either case, KISS is hard to ignore" (Miami Herald, 3/23/76). The band were originally scheduled to perform at the new Sportatorium venue, but its opening had been delayed.
- A very good AUD recording from this show circulates.

March 24 - Civic Center, Philadelphia, PA
Promoter: Jennifer Productions / Dick Clark Concerts
Other act(s): The Rockets
Reported audience: 9,810 **SOLD-OUT
Reported gross: $66,231
Set list: Same as March 21.
Notes:
- In the recurring issue with the fake December show at the Centrum, promoters were forced to add a disclaimer to their advertising: "Only tickets purchased expressly for KISS - March 24, 1976 at Philadelphia Civic Center will be honored ... KISS tickets purchased for Centrum concert must be redeemed at place of purchase."
- From a local review: "After the warm-ups finish their number, whatever it is, the entire center moves as one to the refreshment stands, for their only chance to cure the 'munchies.' With four months' worth of waiting coming to an end, there are not many here who bothered to eat all day... And there they are. KISS: Four musicians from New York City, with average songs. But an unforgettable stage show that no other group has yet matched. Blood is dripping from their mouths. Smoking guitars and flame-throwers spit fire 20 feet into the air. Hydraulic drum stand and real sirens" (Wilmington Morning News, 3/28/76)...
- A reasonable AUD recording of this show exists.

March 25 - Cambria County War Memorial Coliseum, Johnstown, PA
Promoter: Silver Bullet Productions
Other act(s): Thee Image (opener)
Reported audience: (6,000 capacity)

March 26 - State Farm Arena, Harrisburg, PA
Promoter: Jennifer Productions
Other act(s): Artful Dodger (opener)
Reported audience: (8,200 capacity)
Partial set list: Flaming Youth / Strutter / Deuce / Ladies In Waiting / C'mon And Love Me / Hotter Than Hell / Firehouse / Rock Bottom / Black Diamond / Cold Gin / Rock And Roll All Nite / Let Me Go, Rock 'N' Roll
Notes:
- The review for the Philadelphia show notes several songs that weren't performed that night, and the reviewer also makes the odd comment, "From then on, forget everything about hearing anything. Just watch. People in Harrisburg won't sleep tonight" (Wilmington Morning News, 3/28/76). This suggests that the reviewer may be mixing two shows in the review — Harrisburg is only two-hours from Wilmington. The Partial set list here is the songs noted in the review, though could obviously be in error on the part of the reviewer.

March 27 - Memorial Auditorium, Utica, NY **POSTPONED
Promoter: Shelly Finkel
Reported audience: (5,986 capacity)
Notes:
- This show was postponed until April 13. In the weeks prior to this show date there appears to not have been a single mention of it in the local press. While this does not provide a definitive answer, it suggests that it was either postponed long before the date or may have initially been a temp hold date. Venue renovation scheduling may have played a part in the date change though concerts did take place during the six-month period the facility was being improved through July 1976. In terms of routing, Harrisburg to Utica would have been a 5 hour drive, and were it skipped then Harrisburg to Springfield was more than 6 hours of

driving, albeit with an extra rest/travel day in between shows. With the lack of solid evidence the reasons for postponement remains in the undetermined (TBC) category.

March 28 - Civic Center, Springfield, MA
Promoter: Koplik & Finkel Productions
Other act(s): Artful Dodger (opener)
Reported audience: 10,395 **SOLD-OUT
Notes:
- From another local review: "Using nearly every pyrotechnic device known to man, the New York group KISS presented a slickly packaged two hours of outrageousness to 10,000 roaring patrons at the Springfield Civic Center Sunday night. The quartet's weird costumes and whiteface makeup almost managed to obscure the concert's biggest outrage: KISS plays horrible music as poorly as any band in memory... As visual, visceral extravaganza, KISS is perhaps unequaled. Next time, the band may take the ultimate step and leave their instruments at home. Sunday night, the music only cluttered up the concert" (Springfield Union, 3/30/76).
- The final show of the "Alive!" tour, of which roughly 10 minutes is archived in silent Super8, the quality of which makes it rather difficult to decipher what may have been performed.
- According to an internal financial statement, KISS grossed $184,861 from their performance guarantees and percentages for the 13 shows performed during March.

(A good year for one taper: Master tapes from Mar. 19 & June 25, 1975, and Mar. 24, 1976 — to think what else might still be out there...)

Destroyer

With the manner in which touring for the "Alive!" was concluded and the recording of the "Destroyer" album, the transition between the two eras is somewhat confused and convoluted. While the recording of the "Destroyer" album had been completed in January the band still had dates scheduled for touring in support of the "Alive!" album. Following the conclusion of the "Destroyer" sessions the band recommenced touring activities on Jan. 23. The first single from the new album, "Shout It Out Loud," was released in early March, so it is hardly surprising that it was the first song from the album to be added to the set list. When precisely is unclear, but it is most certainly present on the recordings available from the Miami and Philadelphia shows on Mar. 21 and 24 respectively. Following the conclusion of the "Alive!" tour in Springfield, MA, on Mar. 28, the band took a two week break to prepare for the next touring cycle. During that downtime, press reports appeared detailing a possible new KISS venture: That the band had formed its own film production company and was planning to acquire the rights to the 1964 musical "The Roar of the Greasepaint — The Smell of the Crowd," the title of which had substantial allusions to the band's stage presentation. It's not clear how the class struggle plot of the story would have been adapted, and it may well be that this was a case of something being misreported.

The band was back on the road by Apr. 11, for another cycle of shows starting in Fort Wayne, IN. While there were several make up dates from the "Alive!" tour, the primary function of this brief touring cycle was to conclude the North American run of dates. The band also made a concerted effort in Canadian markets with opening act Hammersmith (who had released their "Late Night Lovin' Man" single via Mercury Records). Visually, there was not much changed from the "Alive!" tour. Costumes and staging remained the same, though musically the band had started to transition the set in favor of material from the new album. While out on the road "Destroyer" was certified Gold by the RIAA on April 22. This was the band's first studio album to receive a certification and provided all of the motivation required to move the business forward. By mid-April the reorganization of the set was in full swing. "Flaming Youth" is firmly established in the set while "God of Thunder" had also been added. A review of the Apr. 24 show in Ottawa provides the first known mention of the latter song being performed, though at that show Gene unfortunately also encountered another self-immolation event during his fire-breathing routine. "Detroit Rock City" was noted as being present in the band's set during their show in Winnipeg Arena on Apr. 28. However, it is likely that the set was mostly static for the full April run and that all of the songs had been performed (at least at some point) during the period. One date already on the future itinerary was a "School Spirit Contest" sponsored by Chicago's WCFL and Mars Candy company where the school (within a 100 mile radius of Chicago) submitting the most candy bar wrappers collection by Apr. 17 would receive a concert performed by KISS. The winner, River Trails Junior High in Mt. Prospect, IL, was announced at the winner on Apr. 20 with the concert taking place in the school's gym on May 4.

Other than Ace Frehley's wedding, the band was more concerned with their first proper international tour outside of the confines of North America, which was to commence mid-month. Based out of London, the band rehearsed at the famed Sheperton Film Studios in Middlesex on May 12, heading up to Manchester for the first show the following day. The European tour was in some ways a massive step backwards for the band, at least economically and in terms of scale, with their performance gross for the whole tour being a paltry $60,695. Compare that sum for 17 shows performed in Europe with the 12 North American shows in April grossing $181,000. While the venues were far smaller than those to which they had graduated to performing in at home during the prior year. The band had taken a step downwards in many ways during this trek, contrary to how Gene had initially envisaged the tour to take place. In a Feb. 1976 interview with Cleveland's "Scene" magazine he commented, "We keep getting great offers, but we're not going over until it goes over the edge... We really want to go over and do it right. The size of our show is such that we have to get large sums of money to go over there. We don't want to go over and half-fill a hall; we want to fill them all the way" (Scene, 2/12–18/76). While that strategy might have been a failure for the European market, the plan for Japan certainly worked in terms of scale: "We had great offers, in Japan especially, where the promoters were willing to pay all of our transportation, give us the presidential suite and the whole bit. The treatment sounded wonderful, but we wanted to wait just a little bit longer to make sure we're the biggest thing to ever come in there" (Scene, 2/12–18/76).

Most indicative of the band's lowly position in Europe, or lack thereof, was perhaps the band's Paris show being scheduled for 3p.m. in the afternoon, so that the *rabble* could be cleared out in time for Jerry Louis comedic engagement during the evening. Only the Frankfurt and Stockholm shows could be considered to providing engagement grosses anywhere comparable with what the band were earning back at home. The risk to promoters was also palpable, with guarantees as low as $1,000 being offered (Paris). At least the band could report shows in England being sold-out albeit to audiences under 3,000 patrons in most cases. EMI International reportedly spent some "$60,000 on promotion... a general theme being 'lock up your daughters, KISS is coming'" (Billboard, 5/22/76) in the U.K, resulting in "Destroyer" entering the local charts at #37 and rising to #22 soon afterwards. "Alive!" also skirted the charts, though for the U.K. the album was initially only available on cassette at the time of the tour with a LP release pending. "Destroyer" also charted in Sweden where the band's reception was far more positive than had generally been the case elsewhere.

The experience in Europe was humbling for the band. Paul recalled, "Nearly as soon as we landed, I hated it. We had become a big band in the United States. In England and the rest of Europe, we had to prove ourselves all over again. We were back at square one — nobodies. Thank God for the fans. As we had seen back home when we started out, the fans in England were also rabid in their dedication to us. On the other hand, the food was horrible and the transportation archaic. The people who ran things were very stodgy. Merchants took perverse pride in the fact that you couldn't get dry cleaning back for a week. There was no air conditioning, and, if you pleaded, they might begrudgingly put one lone ice cube in a drink for you. These things were badges of honor to the older guard of the British Empire" (Face The Music). Whatever the case the band had at least finally had a taste of the other markets that were going to become increasingly important to them in the coming years. And, for that matter, they had at least finally toured outside of North America. Following a performance to less than 500 in Belgium on June 4, the band returned to the U.S. and continued the frenzied preparations for the proper "Destroyer" tour. Jules

Fisher Associates, who had previously provided assistance to the band with their staging — dating back to 1973 when Fischer acolyte Mark Ravitz designed both the spider-web backdrop for the band and built their original "KISS" logo — were engaged to fully design the new stage set that would be used on the proper U.S. "Spirit of '76" tour. Matters were complex with the staging proving problematic as the crew and designers struggled with scale and technical challenges. At least the band's new costumes had been completed. The band had submitted their designs to Larry LeGaspi in April. The contract for their design and construction notes a cost of $4,775 for the set with Gene's unsurprisingly being the most costly at $1,575.

The $192,000 "Destroyer" stage production was impressive, not simply in comparison with what it replaced but as the quantum leap it represented for the band. The overall design was loosely based on the apocalyptic cityscape theme of the album's cover. Press features promoting the tour regularly described the band destroying a city during the show. Peter's drum riser was complimented with a pair of 6' tall "altar" cats, with glowing eyes, on either side of his kit and a 40" gong. Stairs on either side of the riser led to 10' elevated platforms with faux "crumble wall" fronting hiding the amps and multiple fog machines. At stage-left and right were additional platforms. Ace's raised platform was designed like a lunar landscape, in keeping with his "space" theme, and he would usually perform his solo in this location. Gene's platform was designed like a destroyed demonic Transylvanian castle atop which he'd perform his blood vomiting gimmick. The crumble effect was abandoned as too time consuming, but in essence KISS were going to destroy the stage with their show. Combined, all of the elements transformed the theatrical nature of the performance and gave it a setting versus the dated equipment of its predecessor. The stairs would remain a central theme for KISS stages throughout numerous iterations over the years.

The "God of Thunder" machine was placed directly behind the drums, but in front of the new KISS logo over which was flown the lighting truss. It was seldom used and as infrequently noted in reviews during the tour. Two manned follow spot towers were situated at stage-left and right, with a third toward the rear. According to Mark Ravitz, "The lighting towers had a shape to them and they were custom made. They had a certain shape to them styled after power towers in New Jersey. I was driving on some highway in New Jersey and they had all these electric lines going through the countryside and they were being held up by scaffold towers. The top of them had a certain shape so I played around with the base and gave that a little more of a dynamic shape so they had a little more drama." Other props included the stage tree, obligatory mirror ball and flown lightning bolts. Many of the elements of the stage were hidden, or not immediately obvious looking up from the concert hall floor. Again, Mark recalls, "Unless I'm looking to reveal something it was to be seen. The stage itself didn't have so much on it, but the KISS logo, that's big. You want to see all that — that's upstage. Everything in front of that wants to be a little lower and not as prominent. The spike, the glowing spike for Gene, that was on stage but, unless it's lit up, you're not really aware of it. When it's time for each of those characters to come alive, the set pieces supporting them came alive. Otherwise they're dialed down and something else is highlighted. That's just theatrics."

It is perhaps more interesting and important is the professional transition that occurred following the conclusion of the European tour — a process that would have been well in place well before the band departed. KISS had been preparing to take their business to the next level, on multiple levels. Foremost was the appearance of business/financial managers Glickman/Marks on the scene; with the band signing the legal instruments giving them control over their financial interests on May 5. Their involvement would mark a paradigm shift in the overall operation. Bill Aucoin was partnering with Ron Boutwell with the creation of Boutwell/Niocua (yes, that's "Aucoin" spelt backwards), which would control the merchandising and licensing of KISS product henceforth. The stage show being professionally developed is similarly obvious. All of these factors were indicative of a professionalization of the operation, and there were going to be causalities, namely members of the original road crew, many of whom had been with the band, and had shared the same (if not in some cases worse) struggles the band had faced, as early back as December 1973. There is an overriding theory that change is inevitable, and that the lack of change, or evolution, will result in stagnation and ultimately failure. Having reached a pinnacle the band knew that they had limitations, and most certainly that they were carrying excess baggage in certain areas of their operations. There was going to be nothing pretty about the change; and Mick Campise and Rick Stuart were also left out on the streets as the band prepared for the U.S. tour in a secluded hanger at Stewart International Airport in Newburgh, NY. Paul alludes to possible justifications, "Some of the tour managers were fired because Bill didn't think they were doing a good job; most were ousted because of jealousies within the band — each member wanted the undivided attention of the road manager, or at least a sense of favoritism."

No doubt there were new "voices" in the mix that had self-interest in moving things in new direction, or in the least separating the band from the past, severing those relationships and starting to exert influence and control. JR Smalling, so centrally important to the band for so long, recounted his less than ceremonial dismissal from the band's services following the conclusion of the European tour. Walking in to Aucoin's new Madison Avenue office, he thought he'd be wrapping up the business from the tour as he thought about the next road-cycle. Instead, he was let go. The roots of his dismissal had been cultivated during the European tour purportedly resulting from Peter requiring numerous cortisone shots for arm pain, in order to perform. According to Lydia, "When Peter found out what he had been taking, he was furious. Management denied knowing anything and JR was fired" (Sealed With A KISS). Were any of the changes made without the knowledge of the band? Unlikely, though in essence it was a matter of business with the adoption of a new package of people, who had people that they wanted in the roles. Or people that they felt were better suited to the new vision for the band. Business; and business is seldom kind when it comes to matters affecting the bottom line. Or business; in terms of getting rid of those who collectively may know "where the bodies are buried." That bottom line, by May 1976, was the sole concern of Glickman/Marks, on behalf of the band. They were looking at all aspects of the KISS business operation to determine where money was being lost, or revenue streams were not being maximized or exploited. That was their business, and the tentacles of their reach necessarily enveloped all areas of the operation.

That the road support staff were being pruned is not surprising. Many people had come and gone from the crew in two and a half years, but now a core was gone, or on their way out. Mike McGurl, Rick Munroe, Jay Barth and Craig Blazer followed at the end of the "Destroyer" tour. Peter "Moose" Oreckinto didn't even make it that far. That core had grown with the band, and had come from the same starting point and developed and refined their skills and operation parallel to the same for the band on the musical and performance side. It was a symbiotic relationship, but to the extent that the road crew had bled for the band there was never going to be a happy ending when business reared its unemotional head from whichever perspective. Overall, there had not been that much development to the KISS stage show from the time they first hit the national circuit in March 1974. Sure, things that broke or failed were replaced, repaired or improved, but the overall elements remained the same. Once the European tour had concluded, the planned summer tour stage was a completely different beast in its design and execution. No longer was it just a stage with a few gimmicks, it was a setting, and full production for an even greater visual experience for the attendee. Frankie Scinlaro, who had worked with Alice Cooper (and therefore a similarly sized stage production), was recruited as road manager.

The proper North American "Spirit of '76" summer tour was scheduled to kick-off in Richmond, VA on July 4, though that first date ended up having to be postponed until July 8, after initially being rescheduled for July 1. Ultimately, the first show in Norfolk, VA reported just 6,777 of 11,584 tickets being sold to mark the beginning of the band's new era. Overall, July saw the band tour venues filled to just 67% of capacity which while reasonable was certainly not keeping up with the aspirations for a whole new show and album. A second single from the album, "Flaming Youth," had stiffed on the charts reaching just #74 in early June (though admittedly the band hadn't been on the road in the U.S. at the time and it was more a matter of keeping something fresh for radio play). Its follow-up, "Detroit Rock City," fared even worse when it failed to chart at all. There was regional airplay in pockets where the band's popularity generally carried over from the "Alive!" period, but the band, album and tour were certainly not setting the world on fire. It was almost a case of too little too late when "Beth" changed both the band and record's success. The tour was in its final stretch by that point, but the unexpected success would pay dividends on the following tour. During the final shows of the tour the band's concert-filling performance certainly improved. August saw them performing to roughly 78% capacity. This trend of improvement continued into September, though the poor performance at Varsity Stadium skews the overall figure that would otherwise have grown to over 82% of capacity.

For every new way things were done for the summer tour it still operated in the old way with there being neither experience nor skill to necessarily take the production out on the road. Glickman/Marks knew that and engaged Robert D. Brown to follow the tour and conduct an overall business analysis of the existing tour processes. His task included examining the booking process, production, routing, expenses, ticketing, settlements, promotion and merchandising aspects of the tour. As noted in his report introduction, "the conclusions contained herein are the result of personally attending concerts in Baltimore and Knoxville (small indoor facilities); Indianapolis (large indoor facility); and Anaheim (outdoor/stadium) as well as watching entire set-up operation in Charleston, West Virginia. These on-set experiences were supplemented by conferring with numerous personal resource people throughout the entertainment industry." The report did not paint a pretty picture! In regards to the booking process, production, his findings are hardly surprising when looking at the band's itinerary for the period. They generally played 2–5 shows per week, often in travelling routes that were reminiscent of the city-hopping they'd experienced in 1974. One day a show in Baltimore, the next in Knoxville (525 miles travelled), the next in Charleston (back east 310 miles). Roberts commented, "too few dates were being scheduled per week often times with routing making little logistical sense. It seems the approach was simply to play as many dates and types of facilities as possible. The result was a shotgun approach to the market place lacking a viable game plan."

Roberts also found the number of different types of facilities being booked confusing and problematic. Since they differed in size they forced "constant production adjustments" trying to get the production scaled to different environments where only the 12–20,000 capacity venues ought to have been considered in relation to the band's popularity at that point. The stage show needed to be designed in a manner that was easily adjustable to all types of facilities on the tour, not one in constant need of tweaking for each engagement. Set-up and tear-down also needed to be streamlined. Unnecessary or unworkable elements needed to be jettisoned. One of the most important routing suggestions was to "book the tour in two to three week segments concentrating on a specific regional market." This would lower transport costs and time and allow a greater number of shows on a weekly basis. It would also offer "A system to control production expenses, drops more dollars to the bottom line. And, another plus, it's conducive to better moral for the band and a consistency higher level of performance." In essence, though, it was still all about the money. Keeping the band healthy and happy meant that they could be worked more efficiently during the week resulting in more dollars.

Touring expenses were found to be outrageous with there being far too much equipment being used and too many people travelling with the band. Roberts noted, "Your own rider dictates an astounding stagehand call for all shows, small and large facilities alike. It's over production in the classic sense." Even basics, such as overtime rules for facilities, or avoiding late check outs at hotels, needed to be taken into consideration in order to avoid the unnecessary outlay of funds. Simply put, Roberts recommended taking earlier flights and starting shows earlier if needed to avoid those costs. Simplifying the stage also meant that the number of trucks, people and equipment being transported could be reduced, providing savings. The driving factor for all of this analysis? A total performance gross of $1.5 million for the summer tour was reduced to a net of $340,000 after expenses and commissions/fees — which certainly didn't mean that each band member received a check for $85,000.

Bill Aucoin had been cognizant of certain factors in touring as the band grew, particularly when it came to staying away from stadium shows wherever possible. According to Bill, the band didn't expect to rely on the venues of that scale during the tour. While there would likely have been challenges filling them on a regular basis, he felt that the "indoor show is fairer to the ticket buyer" particularly considering the challenges of presenting the band's show. More importantly, "The best concert sound can be gotten indoors and at a stadium most of the audience is too far away to really see the artists" (Billboard, 5/1/76). For a show on the scale of Anaheim, Eddie Kramer was retained to mix the sound and video projections were utilized. Economically, Aucoin felt that an act could make more from multiple arena engagements rather than a single stadium show, but remained receptive to the idea. He commented, "The staging effects are being designed to work in big stadiums. But in each market along the route, we are looking closely at the comparative advantages between local stadiums and arenas. We won't do an outdoors show unless it makes sense" (Billboard, 5/1/76). Economics also meant that booking stadium shows required the reservation of a rain-date, which in turn affected the routing of the tour and the ability to book other dates. When KISS performed at Anaheim Stadium on Aug. 20 they were joined by multiple opening acts, Ted Nugent, Montrose, and Bob Seger. Drawing a crowd of 42,987 the attractive package compared favorably with other bands: "50,633 was on hand for Rod Stewart and Faces, 47,760 saw the Beach Boys, and another 44,480 took in the Eagles" (Billboard, 5/8/76). An in-depth financial analysis identified poorly performing markets and probably indicated that the band had not yet attained a position where they could fill regularly stadiums, particularly with the subpar showings in Tempe and Toronto. The first stadium show, held at Roosevelt Stadium in early July only drew 13,867 patrons to a 35,000 seat venue, even with openers J. Geils Band, Bob Seger, and Point Blank on the bill. Even that show had been a near-miss, having only shifted 7,000 tickets by a week before it took place — not helped by a murder at a recent show at the venue. While successful, Anaheim had underperformed 20% below maximum gross even with its impressive $437,653 gross. The $35,850 in merchandising gross for the show probably helped assuage any pain from the $112,000 unsold tickets, at least for the band — they'd received a flat $100,000 guarantee for the performance anyway. Whatever the case, the tour did impress some: According to Elton John, "I've walked out of nearly every concert I've seen lately... Except for the KISS concert and Wings" (Lisa Robinson, 7/13/76)...

Members of the original KISS crew were not the only figures jettisoned during the "Destroyer" era, Commander-in-Chief of the KISS Army, Bill Starkey, was unceremoniously marginalized in May with the establishment of the official KISS Army fan club based in Woodland Hills, CA. Run by Jennifer Baker (who was also responsible for Elton John's fan club), who admitted knowing nothing about the band whatsoever when given the task. It seems improbable that the band's management ever had any intention of basing the KISS Army out of the mid-west or placing in the hands of a fan. In experienced hands the fan club was an unmitigated success grossing some $40,000 and growing to a membership of 5,000 in just months (Billboard, 5/29/76). In a June letter to Bill Aucoin, Ron Boutwell had to sheepishly admit, "if you recall our meeting in September of 1975, wherein you forced me to organize and manage a fan club, i.e. the KISS Army, my promise to you at that time was that we would do it and probably end up losing money, or at best, break even. However, the bottom line is that in spite of all my efforts, the fucking fan club has made money ...... too much goddamn money!" Boutwell was well positioned to profit from the partnership demanding a 50/50 split of net with the artists, and during 1976 the business rapidly expanded with not only merchandising KISS, but with other band such as Queen and the Sweet.

During the summer tour the band sold over $220,000 worth of merchandise at concerts, resulting in a net of $53,000. At that point the merchandising line was limited to tour books, 4 T-shirt designs, 3 posters, plus belt buckles and buttons. Things would rapidly escalate, but it utterly validated Aucoin's vision in turning to the obvious merchandising appeal of the band's image. According to Paul, "Bill Aucoin always saw the bigger picture. He could tell that we connected with our fans in a way that far exceeded the norm. He grasped the extent to which people would respond to us beyond the music: he understood the potential of merchandising" (Face The Music). All areas of revenue were ripe for growth, and Glickman/Marks immediately concerned themselves with the economic impact of the band's contract with Casablanca, even though the band had signed a revised one in May 1975 (which even then included the "key man" clause that would become critical years later). Their early proposals for a new contract with Casablanca included signing bonus and rising scale of advances throughout the 5 year lifespan of a contract ultimately resulting in a

$2 million advance in the 5th year. The record company would pay an upfront cost of $50,000 advance for the recording of an album, or $5,000 per single, with two albums being expected per year. A sliding scale of royalties was recommended with the rate reaching 20% for 1,000,000 units and above. Casablanca would also be responsible for providing $1 million per year for advertizing and promotion. In essence, Glickman/Marks had a very good idea of areas that were ripe for the picking. Negotiations soon commenced with Casablanca, bolstered by the late-summer success of "Beth." Aucoin also expanded his commercial endeavors and split his operation into two, Rock Steady Productions and Aucoin Management to deal with the growth, along with the addition of artists such as Starz to his roster.

It could be argued that the loss of experience with the redundancies of the post-European tour period could be blamed on some of the seeming disarray expressed by Roberts concerning the summer tour. Still, there had been a quantum leap in the band's presentation as they attempted to take the next step in their public popularity as a touring act. In the pre-Destroyer period there were many of the same failings for the band on a financial perspective as noted in Roberts' report. There was also the perception of a "homebrew" ethos, where the crew approached each problem individually and solved it step-by-step rather than wholesale reinvention. Their expertise was certainly perfectly tailored to the show they had long been a part of developing and by April 1976 the operation would have been a well-oiled machine — at that level — and it was equally *their* show as much as the band's. For all of the challenges noted for the "Destroyer" tour, many would be directly handled on the following tour which had to take them into account as the band's popularity exploded with the success of "Beth." Still, for those who had departed the organization, it would be bittersweet to not be part of the culmination of the fruits of their labors. Whatever the case, while the band first stumbled and then recovered to secure their star status, they sold 420,092 of 571,812 tickets (73.47%) during the tour's 35 date main section, July 3 through September 12, grossing nearly $3 million. Soon after the conclusion of the tour the band started work on their next studio album, "Rock And Roll Over" (mentioned in early September as being titled "Rock And Roll Forever") while further changes to their operation were considered.

April 11, 1976 - Allen County War Memorial Coliseum, Fort Wayne, IN
Promoter: Sunshine Productions
Other act(s): Artful Dodger
Reported audience: 9,665 **SOLD-OUT
Reported gross: $57,978
Notes:
- An 11,000 SRO crowd was reported by some sources.
- From a local review: "The audience rushed the stage and broke through the barrier in front of the stage with such force that the sage began to buckle. The show had to be stopped — with the kids trying to get backstage to KISS — to repair both the stage and the barrier. Needless to say both were done, and KISS made their fastest exit ever to avoid a second onslaught" (Exclusive to Ben Edmonds Record World, 4/26/76).

April 13 - Memorial Auditorium, Utica, NY
Promoter: Jim Koplik Presents
Other act(s): Ethos
Reported audience: ~4,500 / 5,986 (75.18%)
Notes:
- This show was rescheduled from Mar. 27. Ethos was a progressive rock/folk act from Fort Wayne who released their debut album, "Ardour," via Capitol Records. One of the engineers for the album was Ed Sprigg who also worked with a one Vincent Cusano during the year.
- From a local review: "A maniacal, fiery, furious return to frenzied rock and roll came to the Utica Memorial Auditorium last night with 'KISS' who used a dazzling display of fire and props to get their music across. About 4,500 attended the concert according to Michael Fusco, auditorium manager. The group of four, in clown-faced make-up and tight black costumes accosted the audience with high decibel sounds, sometimes reaching the ear drum cracking level, and a hypnotic intensity which tore through every nerve ending" (Utica Daily Press, 4/14/76).
- The promoters were forced to pay some $2,500 for damages caused to the dressing rooms during the show.

April 14 - Convention Center Auditorium, Niagara Falls, NY
Promoter: Ruffino & Vaughn Productions
Other act(s): Brownsville Station
Reported audience: 9,500 / 12,500 (76%)
Reported gross: $56,000

April 16 - Municipal Auditorium, Bangor, ME
Promoter: Cedric Kushner Productions, Ltd.
Other act(s): Ethos
Reported audience: 6,932 **SOLD-OUT
Reported gross: $39,356
Notes:
- Some 500 patrons were turned away from this show.

April 18 - Moncton Coliseum, Moncton, NB, Canada
Promoter: Donald K. Donald/CPI

Other act(s): Hammersmith
Reported audience: (7,200 capacity)
Notes:
- Opening act Hammersmith had evolved out of earlier bands Shades Of Blond into 49th Parallel, and then into Painter. By early 1976 the band had then recently completed recording their second album, "It's For You" (Polydor), which was scheduled for release in May.

April 19 - Halifax Forum, Halifax, NS, Canada
Promoter: Donald K. Donald/CPI
Other act(s): Hammersmith
Reported audience: ~7,000 **SOLD-OUT
Notes:
- Sean Delaney and Lydia Criss flew into Montreal from New York to meet up with the band.
- From a local review: "Collectively known as KISS, the four nuclear-powered minstrels smashed their way into the hearts of thousands of madly applauding teenagers and pre-teens. There can be no doubt, the effects of this assault on the eyes and ears are mesmerizing, much in the ways the population of Halifax once stood and gazed at the munitions carrier Mont Blanc as it lit up the morning sky before wreaking havoc upon the city. Leveling anything and everything with a megawatt wall of distorted sound, KISS came, saw and according to the crowd's response, conquered Halifax. One might compare it with the Vandals of sacking Rome. We may be thankful that our society has restricted this type of carnage to concert halls, it is a modern day equivalent of the ancient Roman pastime of throwing Christians to the lions at gladiatorial contests" (John Howitt).

April 21 - Forum Concert Bowl, Montréal, QC, Canada
Promoter: Donald K. Donald/CPI
Other act(s): Hammersmith
Reported audience: ~6,000
Notes:
- From a local review: "Dressed in demonic, ghoulish paraphernalia and at no lost for stage gimmickry, the quartet has picked up on the success of Alice Cooper. The group is to Cooper as the Monkees were to the Beatles in the late 1960s... The quartet cranks out a speedily nondescript destructo-rock sound, while strutting about in masks, heavy makeup, leather jumpsuits and boots with heels a foot high" (The Montreal Gazette, 4/22/76).

April 22 - Civic Centre, Ottawa, ON, Canada
Promoter: Treble Clef/CPI
Other act(s): Hammersmith
Reported audience: (10,585 capacity)
Partial set list: Deuce / Stutter / Flaming Youth / Hotter Than Hell / Firehouse / Nothin' To Lose / God of Thunder / 100,000 Years
Notes:
- Gene set his hair on fire during this show. Local act BIM was mentioned in day-of-show advertizing, but apparently didn't perform.
- From a local review: "They were introduced at the Civic Centre last night as the greatest band in the world and, of course, they're not. But they probably don't believe it either. KISS is kids' stuff. Nothing much to do with music, but a lot to do with pure glittery hype. They

are a four-man rock band from the States and pound-out a deafening block of noise. If they dressed in denims and T-shirts and stood under steady spot-lights, their performance would become totally boring after the first couple of tunes. Because of their visual effects, the boredom doesn't set in until the seventh or eighth song. KISS dress in black leotards spiced with glittering sequins, wear boots with 10-inch heels and perform miracles by walking on them. The four members wear make-up that resembles African war paint, jump up and down a lot, tantalize the girls a little bit and (with tongue in cheek one suspects) say 'Look at us we're great.' Bassist Gene Simmons did his famed fire belching trick last night and set his hair ablaze... Despite the grandiose intro, the band has to be given credit for not being completely pretentious" (Ottawa Journal, 4/22/76).

- Nearly 10 minutes of silent 8mm footage circulates from this show. Married to audio from other gigs from the period it confirms that "God of Thunder" was performed with the "Alive!" costumes. Disjointed and partial, it's not possible to determine the definite set order, though it probably flowed similar to the end of the "Alive!" tour.

April 23 - Memorial Auditorium, Kitchener, ON, Canada
Promoter: Donald K. Donald/CPI
Other act(s): Hammersmith
Reported audience: 6,000 / 8,000 (75%)
Partial set list: Hotter Than Hell / Firehouse / Shout It Out Loud / Flaming Youth / Black Diamond
Notes:
- From a local review: "Proving just how easy it is to wield a Hitler-like influence over the malleable masses, the quartet of ghoulishly painted and leather-and-chrome-garbed musicians controlled the crowd's responses with the skill of master puppeteers during a 70-minute performance which bore more a resemblance to a satanic conclave that a rock concert. Substituting a garish circus-sideshow atmosphere for musical artistry, KISS stimulates a mood of aggression and physical excitement that reaches a fever pitch with a variety of on-stage explosions and thundering, percussive riffs of guitars and drums. The

effect, besides being deafening, is to release a kind of mob hysteria, which, if it were ever to get out of the musician's control, could be devastating" (Kitchener-Waterloo Record, 4/24/76). The review mentions that 12 songs were performed, including those listed in the Partial set list.
- Another review in the Waterloo

April 24 - London Gardens, London, ON, Canada
Promoter: Donald K. Donald/CPI
Other act(s): Hammersmith
Reported audience (5,800 capacity)
Partial set list: Deuce / Strutter / Flaming Youth / Hotter than Hell / Firehouse
Notes:
- Silent 8mm footage was filmed at this show.
- Cuts from 5 songs with audio were posted on YouTube in 2009. The video was originally shot by Paul Boyd using a 1/4" AKAI reel to reel system.

April 26 - Maple Leaf Gardens Concert Bowl, Toronto, ON, Canada
Promoter: Donald K. Donald/CPI
Other act(s): Hammersmith
Reported audience: ~10,000 / 18,500 (54.05%)
Notes:
- Billboard reported that Bob Ezrin, Bill Ballard, Donald Tarlton (promoter), and others attended a reception hosted by Quality Records following the show.
- From a local review: "The dry, acrid smell of sulphur filled Maple Leaf Gardens last night as sparklers, torches and almost anything else that would burn were hurled at KISS, the band on stage. This wasn't an act of hostility on the part of the nearly 10,000 people in the audience, one of the largest crowds ever to fill the Garden's concert-bowl set-up. It was just in the swing of things. From the moment KISS started they began blasting back at the crowd. It became an unfair fight, though. The band's arsenal included just about every noise-making and flame-throwing device this side of Cape Kennedy... It would all have seemed simply silly, if not downright stupid, hand not so many chanting, fist-waving fans taken it so frighteningly seriously" (Toronto Star, 4/27/76).

April 28 - Winnipeg Arena, Winnipeg, MB, Canada
Promoter: Donald K. Donald/CPI
Other act(s): Hammersmith
Reported attendance: 10,400 **SOLD-OUT
Partial set list: Deuce / Firehouse / Flaming Youth / God of Thunder / Cold Gin / Black Diamond / Detroit Rock City / Rock And Roll All Nite / Let Me Go, Rock 'N' Roll
Notes:
- Ace and Gene were interviewed by Andy Mellen of the Winnipeg Free Press prior to the show.
- Fans attending the show caused some $3,000 damage to the venue during the concert, which was the last of this leg of touring prior to Ace's wedding and the European tour. While the show sold-out 1,500 tickets were still available for walk-ups on the day of the show. The show set a then record gross for the venue.
- This is the earliest confirmed performance of "Detroit Rock City," but was likely in the set at the start of the April tour.

- From a local review: "For one confusing moment or two, it appeared that the Wednesday night performance of KISS was not such a sellout as had been rumored. At zero hour the Winnipeg Arena parking lot was not yet full, and the seats were rush. But of course. At least half of the 10,000 people inside the Arena were not yet old enough to drive. Nor were they old enough to know music from noise, the real McKISS from Alice Cooper on Star Trek, the Marquis de Sade from A Child's Garden of Puerile Perversities" (Winnipeg Free Press, 4/29/76).

- From another local review: "There's no denying that those in attendance got their money's worth from KISS's surprisingly brief but, effective 50-minute set, which was augmented by three one-song encores in response to several sustained ovations from the assembled fans. KISS's appeal is as much visual as it is musical. The group's outrageous makeup and costumes and an effect-laden stage show add up to one of the most entertaining visual extravaganzas to be found today. Although the group's self-imposed musical limitations have earned it many detractors I thought (the band displayed a lot more inventiveness and originality during its excellent sound check several hours prior to the concert), than It did during the show itself" (Winnipeg Free Press, 5/5/76).

- Press from around the time of this show indicated: "Recently, they created their own theatrical production company and purchased the rights to the Tony Newley musical, 'The Roar of the Greasepaint.' Next you'll be viewing them in two dimension, full-color when Marvel Comics, a bible to those who find little else to get excited about in life, adds KISS to its stable of superheroes" (Stephen Ford (NEA), via Fond Du Lac Reporter, 4/29/76).

- The brief April touring wrap-up was financially beneficial. While the band accepted low guarantees for the Canadian dates ($5,000–5,500) they did will with the added percentages. All told, the band grossed $180,937 from these 12 dates.

May 1 - The Americana Hotel, New York City, NY
Frehley-Trerotola Wedding Reception
Set list: Strutter / Rock And Roll All Nite / Nothin' to Lose
Notes:
- An impromptu unmasked jam took place at Ace and Jeanette's wedding reception using the wedding band's equipment.
- Hand shot footage is reasonable quality for the era, but certainly far from pro-shot! Only one of the songs has been released so far, as an Easter-egg on the "KISSology Vol. 1" DVD.

May 4 - River Trails Junior High, Mt. Prospect, IL **M&M contest concert
Promoter: WCFL/M&M-Mars Candy
Other act(s): None.
Reported audience: ~350
Set list: Unknown.
Notes:
- Chicago's WCFL Radio "School Spirit Contest," which was open to schools within 100 miles radius of the station.
- The school collecting the most candy wrappers by April 17, 1976 (winner announced April 20) would win a KISS concert in their gym. River Trails submitted some 3 million wrappers and facsimiles to win the contest. The school also won $1,000 which they planned to donate to charity.

May 11 - Sheperton Film Studios, Sheperton, MDX, England **TECH REHEARSAL
May 12 - Sheperton Film Studios, Sheperton, MDX, England **REHEARSAL
Notes:
- After arriving in England on May 10 the band were initially based at London's Embassy hotel before travelling to Manchester on the day of the tour's first show. According to Gene, "On the way over to our first English tour, I was struck by the notion that this was the Land Of The Beatles. To me, the English Kings and Queens never meant anything. I have always looked at it as an archaic and rather silly posturing about past glories. But as cultural oddities, I suppose it had its own innocence. Still, I was nervous to set foot on Holy Ground. We got off the jet in full makeup and the fotogs were waiting for us. We came through customs and jumped on street cars at the airport for photo ops. I was aware it was drizzly and grey. I was hoping that would change in the next few days to sunshine. It didn't" (KISS Facebook, 5/15/15).
- The band received low guarantees and no percentages for their four U.K. shows, netting only $16,000 from their performances though with small venue capacities and £1–2.50 ticket prices (which was roughly equivalent to $2.50–5.00 at a time when the band charged around $5.50–7.50 in the U.S.) there wasn't the sort of economics on a scale similar to their home market.

May 13 - Free Trade Hall, Manchester, England
Promoter: Straight Music
Other act(s): Stray
Reported audience: 2,500 **SOLD-OUT
Set list: Deuce / Strutter / Flaming Youth / Hotter than Hell / Firehouse / She / Nothin' To Lose / Shout It Out Loud / Black Diamond / Detroit Rock City / Rock And Roll All Nite / Let Me Go, Rock 'N' Roll
Notes:
- First concert outside of North America. The show was reported as sold-out in press ads. Stray were touring in support of their "Houdini" album released on Pye Records (which eventually became UK distributor for Casablanca Records following the expiration of the contract with EMI mid-year).
-The band filmed interview segments for Granada Television's "So It Goes" show hosted by Tony Wilson. Broadcast on Aug. 21, 1976 the show also included interview bits with the band's special effects coordinator, and backstage and live footage from the concert.
- A below average AUD recording of the full show also circulates.

May 14 - Odeon, Birmingham, England
Promoter: Straight Music
Other act(s): Stray
Reported audience: 2,397 **SOLD-OUT
Notes:
- The show was reported as sold-out in press ads. The band drove in from Manchester at lunchtime for the show.

May 15 - Hammersmith Odeon, London, England
Promoter: Straight Music
Other act(s): Stray
Reported audience: 3,487 **SOLD-OUT

Notes:
- From a local review: "KISS are due on at 9 p.m. but owing to exigencies of G.L.C. fire regulations they don't make it until about 9:40: the natives, not knowing the impossibility of trying to persuade irate officials that fireballs on the side stage are O.K. fun, are understandably restless. The excellent Keith Peacock from Casablanca passes on the information and tells me that KISS had played a blinder at Birmingham the night before. Still, it seems ironic that a band with such a cast iron S.M. reputation, that you wouldn't let your kids within a thousand miles of, are stymied by the safety rules that operate with regard to large concert venues. Could have something to do with the fact that anyone sitting twenty feet from the stage stood a fair chance of having their eyebrows singed...

The girls in front of me with KISS scrawled on their cheeks, and who can't be a day over twelve, aren't that impressed either. Under all the guff I got the feeling that KISS were condescending to the audience. Give 'em what they want and then put the takings in the bank quick. Their moves are professional enough only to gratify the noise lust of the lowest common denominator open to rock. I don't care that they wear their kinetics so far out you know they haven't got a single original lick, but once the energy graph dissipates and you begin to study their ability to even play what simply ideas they do posses, the shortcomings are tremendous. For starters, they ain't even sexy. Ace Frehley moves with the approximate grace of a third degree advanced numbskull. A guitar by rote. It's no surprise to learn that he exists in a permanent heat haze of zonked vacancy. Simmons' bass playing is basic, and that's being kind. He played a one note solo which was good... Stanley's in between raps become more tedious... What with the gear and the noise and the monotony they remind one of vintage Slade except they aren't as competent. Only drummer peter Criss looks like he could get his stash together by doing another kind of music. Besides, his cat whiskers are cute. He has something recognizable as style" (NME, 5/22/76).

May 16 - Hammersmith Odeon, London, England

Promoter: Straight Music
Other act(s): Stray
Reported audience: (3,487 capacity)
Set list: Deuce / Strutter / Flaming Youth / Hotter than Hell / Firehouse / She / Nothin' To Lose / Shout It Out Loud / Black Diamond / Detroit Rock City / Rock And Roll All Nite
Notes:
- The three other shows were sold-out in advance of the first show, and that day tickets were still available for the final U.K. show. It's not known whether it sold-out, though this date was an extra date added after the first three had gone on sale.
- From a local mainstream review: "KISS had everything; every single effect in the book. They had a perfect lighting system; dry ice; smoke bombs; a fire-eater; a huge lighted insignia; sirens; confetti that simulated a blizzard; guitars; drums; EVERYTHING. But what KISS hadn't got at their London Hammersmith Odeon gig on Sunday night was a feeling for the music. They depended on their bland pyrotechnics to win over this English audience and, admittedly, they seemed to do that. But it was all so nauseatingly contrived that, to me anyway, the showmanship meant nothing" (Melody Maker).
- The generally good AUD recording from this show became the famed "KISS Blitz London" bootleg LP. Most copies of this recording exclude the final two songs.

May 18 - Rosengarten, Mannheim, Germany
Promoter: Mama Concerts
Other act(s): Scorpions
Reported audience: ~2,000
- "Hamburg's vice-squad told KISS in no uncertain terms that the short film opening their concerts was obscenity, and that if they tried to show it to local audiences they'd wind up in jail. So KISS elected to project the lamed-down version" (Ray Bearfield, Kingsport-Times News, 7/17/76). Other press reports from the time indicate issues the German authorities had with the "SS" logo at the time, though it would continue to be used on releases by Bellaphon until 1980.
- The Scorpions were still actively touring their "In Trance" album. According to Uli John Roth, Paul had heard the band's "In Trance" album and requested them as the opening act for the German shows.

May 19 - Philipshalle, Düsseldorf, Germany
Promoter: Mama Concerts
Other act(s): Scorpions
Reported audience: (5,450 capacity)
Notes:
- The following day was a travel day, following a press conference in Düsseldorf, with the band flying to Paris in the evening where they stayed at the Hotel de Scibe. May 21 was a day off spent in Paris.

May 22 - L'Olympia Bruno Coquatrix Theatre, Paris, France
Promoter: Albert Koski / Cauchoix Productions
Other act(s): None.
Reported audience: 2,033
Set list: Deuce / Strutter / Flaming Youth / Hotter than Hell / Firehouse / She / Nothin' To Lose / Shout It Out Loud / Black Diamond / Detroit Rock City / Rock And Roll All Nite / Let Me Go, Rock 'N' Roll
Notes:
- An afternoon show with the concert starting at 3PM, with the band having to be out of the venue by 6:30PM, to allow for comedian Jerry Lewis' scheduled performance (he was booked May 18–31).
- Classically this show circulates in the form of the "Stoned in Paris" bootleg LP, though without several of the songs. The final song in the set appears to not circulate in any form and may simply have been lost. Regardless, the show does provide the best AUD recording of the European "Alive/Destroyer" tour, though some copies run too fast.

May 23 - RAI Congrescentrum, Amsterdam, Holland
Promoter: Acket & Mojo Concerts
Other act(s): Finch
Reported audience: 1,400
Set list: Deuce / Strutter / Flaming Youth / Hotter than Hell / Firehouse / She / Nothin' To Lose / Shout It Out Loud / Black Diamond / Detroit Rock City / Rock And Roll All Nite / Let Me Go, Rock 'N' Roll
Notes:
- KISS flew in to Amsterdam from Paris at lunchtime.

- The opening act was a Dutch progressive rock band active 1974–78.
- A generally a good AUD recording circulates from this show. The show was also recorded by VARA (for radio) but deemed unsuitable for broadcast due to quality issues.

May 24 - Stadthalle, Offenbach, Germany

Promoter: Mama Concerts
Other act(s): Scorpions
Reported audience: (3,000 capacity)
Notes:
- Peter Criss recalled some of the on tour madness that followed this show: "We were staying at an old-style hotel and it was the night of Muhammad Ali's big comeback fight versus a German guy named Richard Dunn. While we were watching the fight, I decided to try Jägermeister. I was downing it with beer chasers, and that shit will fuck you up. Our roadie Fritz noticed that the Cat had gone crazy. I was threatening to jump out the window, tear the place up, whatever. So Fritz and J.R. and Campise decided to lock me inside the huge, beautiful antique armoire in my room. They threw me in it and locked the doors.

That gave me flashbacks of being locked in the closet in Catholic school. I started screaming and making growling noises and banging on the doors. Campise told me later that you could literally see both sides of the armoire bust out, the front doors fall off, and the whole thing collapse as I broke my way out. Then I ripped all my clothes off and jumped out the window. There was a two-foot-wide ledge that ran all the way around the hotel. I started scampering around the ledge to the front of the hotel, where there were two huge gargoyles on either side of the main entrance.

I climbed up on the back of the one of the gargoyles, buck naked, screaming, 'Muhammad Ali! Muhammad Ali rules, you fucking bastards!'

The police came in two minutes flat. They threw a blanket over me and dragged me off the gargoyle and back into the hotel room. They told Bill that we'd better be out of Germany in the morning, which was okay since we were scheduled to play Sweden the next day. But we had to pay the hotel $10,000 in damages before we could leave" (Makeup To Breakup: My Life In And Out of KISS).

May 26 - Scandinavium, Göteborg, Sweden

Promoter: EMA Telstar
Other act(s): None.
Reported audience: ~4,500
Set list: Deuce / Strutter / Flaming Youth / Hotter than Hell / Firehouse / She / Nothin' To Lose / Shout It Out Loud / 100,000 Years / Black Diamond / Detroit Rock City / Rock And Roll All Nite / Let Me Go, Rock 'N' Roll
Notes:
- Lydia Criss met up with Peter in Göteborg after flying from New York to Copenhagen on May 24 at his request. For all intents and purposes it was hoped that Lydia would help calm Peter for the remaining dates on the tour.
- According to Lydia, "Throughout the entire show, no one clapped or showed any emotion, and then, at the very end of the concert, the fans went wild, breaking chairs and throwing them onstage at the band. The promoter told us this was the way the fans let you know

they liked you, and he seemed to be right as they reacted similarly at KISS's two remaining shows in Sweden" (Sealed With A KISS).

May 28 - Gröna Lund Tivoli Garden, Stockholm, Sweden
Promoter: EMA Telstar
Other act(s): None.
Reported audience: 15,600 **SOLD OUT
Set list: Deuce / Strutter / Flaming Youth / Hotter than Hell / Firehouse / She / Nothin' To Lose / Shout It Out Loud / 100,000 Years / Black Diamond / Detroit Rock City / Rock And Roll All Nite / Let Me Go, Rock 'N Roll
Notes:
- This show provided the venue with one of its largest attendances of 1976.

May 29 - Falkoner Theater, Copenhagen, Denmark
Promoter: EMA Telstar
Other act(s): None.
Reported audience: ~1,300 / 2,000 (65%)
Set list: Deuce / Strutter / Flaming Youth / Hotter than Hell / Firehouse / She / Nothin' to Lose / Shout It Out Loud / 100,000 Years / Black Diamond / Detroit Rock City / Rock And Roll All Nite / Let Me Go, Rock N' Roll
Notes:
- After staying overnight in Copenhagen, the band took a ferry to Lund for the next show.
- A poor AUD recording circulates from this show.

May 30 - Olympen, Lund, Sweden
Promoter: EMA Telstar
Other act(s): None.
Reported audience: ~2,500
Set list: Deuce / Strutter / Flaming Youth / Hotter than Hell / Firehouse / She / Nothin' To Lose / Shout It Out Loud / 100,000 Years / Black Diamond / Detroit Rock City / Rock And Roll All Nite / Let Me Go, Rock 'N Roll
Notes:
- Paul suggested, prior to the final song, that Ace was going to make his vocal debut — though by singing what is unknown with him having not yet recorded a lead vocal in the studio.
- Recorded on both audio and video.

June 2 - Ludwigsburg, Germany **CANCELLED
Promoter: Mama Concerts
Notes:
- Initially a show in Ludwigsburg was scheduled, and then cancelled with the intention of replacing it with a second Munich date. Ultimately, the show in Zürich was booked and the itinerary was finalized by late-April. The show in Fürth was also considered for this date, but it was moved to June 4.

June 2 - Volkshaus, Zürich, Switzerland
Promoter: Good News Presents
Other act(s): None.

Reported audience: 1,497 **SOLD-OUT
Notes:
- The band enjoyed a day off in Zürich the day before this show. However, a brawl occurred between members of the band's entourage and some locals resulting in the hotel confiscating the band's passports and holding them as collateral against any damages.
- Lydia returns to the U.S. following this show.

June 3 - Circus Krone, Munich, Germany
Promoter: Mama Concerts
Other act(s): Scorpions
Reported audience: (2,800 capacity)
Partial set list: Detroit Rock City
Notes:
- At least one song from this show was filmed (multi-camera) and broadcast on the 3 Szene Musik television show mixed in with backstage footage.
- Lyrically, Paul has issues with the first verse.

June 4 - MTV Grundig Halle, Fürth (Nürberg), Germany
Promoter: Mama Concerts
Other act(s): Scorpions
Reported audience: (1,500 capacity)

June 5 - Musikhalle, Hamburg, Germany **TEMP HOLD DATE
June 6 - Open Air, Mannheim, Germany **TEMP HOLD DATE
Notes:
- Neither of these final German shows were ultimately booked, though both were included in some early tour listings.

June 6 - Ontmoetingscentrum, Harelbeke (Kort Rijk), Belgium
Promoter: Rock Steady Productions
Other act(s): Hoa Bihn
Reported audience: <500 / 1,500 (33.3%)
Notes:
- KISS' final date of the European tour was performed to apparently less than 500 patrons.
- The European outing only grossed the band some $60,695 from 17 shows, compared with three times as much during the 11 April shows. From the venue sizes and audiences it was clear that KISS was not yet economically viable in those markets yet.

June 20 - Hanger E, Stewart International Airport, Newburgh, NY **REHEARSALS
Notes:
- During rehearsals press are invited to witness the new stage show.
- Roughly 30 minutes of static tri-pod shot black and white footage was shot by the band rehearsing "Cold Gin," "God of Thunder," "Rock And Roll All Nite," "Deuce," and "Black Diamond." While nothing exceptional, nor is the circulating tape exceptional quality, viewers do witness Ace jumping on stage and Paul shouting out "George Criscuola" following Peter's drum solo. Additional closer filmed footage from full-scale production rehearsals features the start of the show: "Detroit Rock City," "King of the Night Time World," and "Let Me Go, Rock 'N' Roll" with pyro and costumes.

- The stage production was designed by Mark Ravitz for Jules Fisher Associates and incorporated the ubiquitous mirror ball, flashing lightning bolts, strobe effects, and jewel cluster lights, not to mention Peter's 40" gong and 6' black "altar" cats. The stage set was supposed to emulate the destroyed city featured on the album cover with there being ruined towers, twisted tentacle tree, and other architectural features. Some effects, such as the CSI "Frankenstein" machine (known as the "God of Thunder" machine, originally designed by Kenneth Strickfaden for the 1931 movie) seldom functioned properly, with Jules suggesting that the band's crew were unable to operate it properly. There had been previous accusations of the KISS crew having issues with electrical power with the abandoned November 19 Glacier Dome show being an example: "The problem that started the whole KISS concert quagmire was, the power blow-out, a short circuit that McCann said was caused by lack of knowledge on the part of KISS, not the Dome management" (Traverse City Record Eagle, 6/21/76) — though there's always two sides of the story and PR attempts!

July 1 - Richmond Coliseum, Richmond, VA **POSTPONED
Promoter: Entam, Ltd.
Notes:
- This show was rescheduled for July 8 on June 29. According to local press, "A spokesman for the promoter said yesterday the group asked for the delay citing difficulties in setting up the new production that will be used for the summer tour" (Richmond Times-Dispatch, 6/30/76).

July 3 - The Scope, Norfolk, VA
Promoter: Belkin Productions
Other act(s): Bob Seger
Reported audience: 6,777 / 11,584 (58.50%)
Reported gross: $41,791
Notes:
- From a local review: "Opening its worldwide tour in Scope Saturday night, KISS showed exactly how extravagant a rock 'n' roll show can get. The stage show is so absolutely gaudy that it works. KISS' four members are obviously the gods of glitter and gimmickry. Early and David Bowie are tame in comparison. The band uses almost too many forms of special effect to catalogue" (Virginian-Pilot, 7/5/76).
- Performance Magazine listed an attendance of 6,539/11,500 (56.86%) for this show.

July 4 - Richmond Coliseum, Richmond, VA **RESCHEDULED
Notes:
- The original date for this show announced on June 13 was on the U.S. Bicentennial day, though it was rescheduled on June 16. Local press noted sardonically, "The Bicentennial is safe."

July 6 - Carolina Coliseum, Columbia, SC
Promoter: Beach Club Promotions
Other act(s): Bob Seger
Reported audience: 6,157 / 12,328 (49.94%)
Reported gross: $38,391
Notes:

- Lydia Criss recounts meeting members of her extended family at this show — her uncle was working parking lot security.

July 8 - Little John Coliseum, Clemson, SC **CANCELLED
Promoter: Beach Club Promotions
Reported audience: (10,600 capacity)
Notes:
- There are a variety of reasons that probably help explain the cancellation of this show to be replaced by the rescheduled Richmond date. Other than questions of ticket sales, which are often the most obvious of culprits, tour routing plays a significant part in decisions. The Clemson date made for awkward routing, though certainly nothing the crew couldn't have handled. That being said, the onward travel between Clemson and Jersey City was over 750 miles, more than double the 330 miles between Richmond and Jersey City. Cancelling the Clemson date certainly reduced the wear and tear on the crew and made more sense in pure terms of logistics. However, it should be noted that the Richmond date was hardly a block-buster in terms of ticket sales, so the decision may simply have been one based on early projections in conjunction with routing.

(Third time lucky, Richmond finally took place on July 8)

July 8 - Richmond Coliseum, Richmond, VA
Promoter: Belkin Productions / Entam, Ltd.
Other act(s): Bob Seger
Reported audience: 6,545 / 11,800 (55.47%)
Reported gross: $41,332
Notes:
- That this show had been scheduled for three different dates probably goes some way towards explaining the less than spectacular turn out.
- A firecracker was thrown on the stage after three songs, landing behind Peter, resulting in a 30 minute delay to the show. There were 30 arrests at the show, due mainly to drugs charges.
- Billboard reported an attendance of 6,430 (7/24/76).
- From a local review: " In case you thought that curious hybrid called 'rock theater' was dead, fear not or take no comfort (as you choose). It lives, in the form of KISS, a four-man band that has become the music fetish of contemporary teendom... Musically, it is

negligible, but music is not the point of this show. KISS is a national rage because it is outrageous (the cliché that replaced 'far out' a couple of years ago), because it is louder, showier, rowdier than the competition" (Richmond Times-Dispatch, 7/9/76).

July 10 - Roosevelt Stadium, Jersey City, NJ
Promoter: Monarch Entertainment Bureau
Other act(s): J. Geils Band, Bob Seger, Point Blank
Reported audience: 13,867 / 35,000 (39.62%)
Reported gross: $105,388
Set list: Detroit Rock City / King of the Night Time World / Let Me Go, Rock 'N' Roll / Hotter than Hell / Cold Gin / Shout It Out Loud / Strutter / Nothin' to Lose / Do You Love Me? / Watchin' You / God of Thunder / Flaming Youth / Deuce / Firehouse / Black Diamond / Rock And Roll All Nite
Notes:
- Just the fourth date on the U.S. tour, a rain date was scheduled for July 12. An alternative source reported a gross of $90,135.
- Parts of this show were released as the unofficial "Lost Concert" DVD in 2003. Gene referred to it as being a bootleg at the time, and KISS obtained the copyright of the original 1/2" video the following year. While the black and white video quality isn't the greatest the audio is fine. An audio version of the show, missing the first four songs, has also circulated for several years. The full show does exist on video, but doesn't widely circulate.
- Then account executive for Glickman/Marks (or simply "presence" for them looking after the financial interests), CK Lendt, was introduced to the band at this show at the start of his twelve year adventure with both G/M and the band.

July 11 - Cape Cod Coliseum, South Yarmouth, MA
Promoter: Cross Country Concerts
Other act(s): Bob Seger
Reported audience: 7,200 **SOLD-OUT
Reported gross: $42,814

July 13 - Civic Center, Baltimore, MD
Promoter: L&S Productions
Other act(s): Bob Seger
Reported audience: 6,940 / 12,500 (55.52%)
Reported gross: $47,438
Notes:
- CK Lendt joined the band's touring entourage in time for this show.
- As a promotional gimmick, girls from the Patricia Stevens modeling school were advertised as giving away kisses in the venue's lobby on the night of the show.

July 14 - Civic Center, Charleston, WV **POSTPONED
Promoter: Entam, Ltd.
Notes:
- This show was rescheduled for July 17 in late-June.

July 15 - Civic Coliseum, Knoxville, TN
Promoter: Belkin Productions

Other act(s): Bob Seger
Reported audience: 9,111 / 10,000 (91.11%)
Reported gross: $57,904
Notes:
- Paul was interviewed by WKGH prior to the show.

July 17 - Washington Park, Homewood, IL **TEMP HOLD DATE
July 18 - Washington Park, Homewood, IL **TEMP HOLD DATE
Notes:
- This show (plus obligatory rain-date) was included in an advance itinerary, in Performance Magazine and appear to never have gotten further than being considered. This stadium show was also mentioned in April, in the May 1 issue of Billboard Magazine, but would have made no sense in terms of routing by the time the tour was finalized. For all appearances, from the number of stadiums either considered or booked on the tour, the band were testing the waters to see if their popularity had grown to a level that would allow them to jump to shows of that sort of scale.

July 17 - Civic Center, Charleston, WV
Promoter: Entam, Ltd.
Other act(s): Bob Seger
Reported audience: 9,500 **SOLD-OUT
Reported gross: $62,000
Notes:
- Originally scheduled for July 14.
- From a local review: "The 9,500 people who attended the Bob Seger/KISS concert at Charleston Civic Center Saturday night were treated to one of the loudest, brightest, tightest run (and, parenthetically, best) rock shows this season... From the moment the act began — with explosions on either side of the stage and smoke and lights galore — there was pandemonium. Throughout a long set and four encores — FOUR — the band didn't let up... Ace Frehley's lead guitar rages periodically atop the mass, while Paul Stanley prowls the stage sensually, adding licks almost as the spirit moves. Sitting behind the madness is drummer Peter Criss, expending energy as if he had an endless supply. Criss was playing Saturday night with a fractured thumb. The thumb was wrapped in tape, and he wore no glove on that hand. It didn't interfere with his playing a bit" (Gazette Mail, 7/18/76).

July 19 - Freedom Hall Civic Center, Johnson City, TN
Promoter: Entam, Ltd.
Other act(s): Bob Seger
Reported audience: 8,000 **SOLD-OUT
Reported gross: $51,000
Notes:
- Only 4,000 of the 8,000 tickets had sold by July 17. This show was initially scheduled for July 2.

July 21 - Municipal Auditorium, Nashville, TN
Promoter: Sound 70 Productions
Other act(s): Bob Seger, UFO
Reported audience: 8,233 / 11,000 (74.85%)

Reported gross: $51,752

Notes:

- The first two songs of the set were filmed by local station WNGE Channel 2.

- UFO was advertized as the opening act the week before the show with the concert's start time being changed from 8 to 7pm to accommodate the third act. Ads in late-June only list Bob Seger.

- Billboard reported an audience of 8,300 with a gross of $51,800 (8/7/76). It also noted the opening act as ex-Mountain bassist Felix Pappalardi (who had also become a producer — one whom Gene had invited to the band's Hotel Diplomat showcase in 1973).

July 23 - Rickwood Field, Birmingham, AL
Promoter: Ruffino & Vaughn Productions
Other act(s): Kansas, Bob Seger
Reported audience: 12,616 / 20,000 (63.08%)
Reported gross: $93,476
Notes:

- Two separate stages were used for this show, which was held in what was then (and still is) the oldest surviving professional baseball venue in the U.S.

- Bob Seger proved himself a true road-warrior following this show. He headlined his own sold-out show at the Glacier Dome in Traverse City, MI the following day (with Tantrum opening) after travelling all day from Atlanta, GA.

July 25 - Municipal Auditorium, Kansas City, MO **TEMP HOLD DATE

July 26 - Municipal Auditorium, Kansas City, MO
Promoter: Cowtown Concerts
Other act(s): Artful Dodger, Felix Pappalardi
Reported audience: 8,234 / 11,000 (74.85%)
Reported gross: $55,403
Notes:

- As the band took the stage, "One of the young concert-goers apparently turned on a fire hose at the top of the ramps at the southwest corner of the building, sending a 3-inch high wave of water shooting down the ramps to collect on the hallway floor outside the arena and drip from the ceiling of the Exhibition Hall below" (Kansas City Times, 7/27/76).

- Photographer Richard Galbraith shot photos from the audience and recalled that Felix Pappalardi opened.

July 28 - Kiel Auditorium, St. Louis, MO
Promoter: Ron Delsener Presents
Other act(s): Bob Seger
Reported audience: 6,896 / 10,584 (65.16%)
Reported gross: $95,529 **both nights
Set list: Detroit Rock City / King of the Night Time World / Let Me Go, Rock 'N' Roll / Cold Gin / Shout It Out Loud / Strutter / Nothin' to Lose / Do You Love Me? / Watchin' You / God of Thunder / Rock And Roll All Nite / Deuce / Firehouse / Black Diamond
Notes:

- From a local review: "There's no such thing as the kiss of death. At least, there was no sign of it in the audience of 8,000 at Kiel Auditorium last night as four of rock music's most popular ghouls put on an explosive show. KISS, if you hadn't guessed, is following in the proud tradition of Alice Cooper in suggested musical depravity. The difference is that unlike Alice there is really nothing sickening about the words of the quartet's songs, which mostly are basic one-lyric rockers... Once over the idea that they're anything more than four athletic me in fright suits and high heels, a person can sit back and enjoy the theatrics as long as his ears can take it" (St. Louis Post-Dispatch, 7/29/76).

- A poor quality video circulates from this show. For the quality criticisms, the show is at least a complete "Destroyer" show, even if the details aren't discernible. Shot via a single static camera which is very distant, though the viewer does get the whole of the stage above the heads of the audience. Audio is better, though echo-ey and tinny, and the overall perception of this archive really comes from it not being particularly interesting visually.

July 29 - Kiel Auditorium, St. Louis, MO
Promoter: Ron Delsener Presents
Other act(s): Bob Seger
Reported audience: 8,969 / 10,584 (84.74%)

July 31 - Comiskey Park, Chicago, IL **CANCELLED
Promoter: Windy City Productions
Other act(s): Uriah Heep, Ted Nugent, Bob Seger, Starz
Notes:
- This show would have been Game 2 of promoter's Windy City's "World Series of Rock" concert series. Game 1, scheduled for July 10, included Aerosmith, Jeff Beck, Jan Hammer, and Derringer had drawn some 60,000 patrons. The show was canceled in late July, due to "technical problems connected with switching the show from day to night, but a source close to KISS reports that only about 10,000 seats were sold" (Performance Magazine, 7/30/76). KISS had not wanted to perform during the day, caused be a 6p.m. curfew at the

venue, due to the negative impact playing outside during the day would have on the impact of the show's effects. An early September concert at the smaller (and indoor) Chicago Stadium was suggested as being planned.

July 31 - Toledo Sports Arena, Toledo, OH
Promoter: Belkin Productions
Other act(s): Starz
Reported audience: 7,485 **SOLD-OUT
Reported gross: $49,952
Notes:
- With this show being put together with little time for scheduling, due to the Comiskey Park cancellation, AMI stable-mates Starz were given the opening slot since their debut album had been released a month earlier.
- The $12,750 check the band was due for their performance bounced; though presumably ATI had received 50% of the guarantee for the show ($10,000) prior to the performance!

August 2 - Market Square Arena, Indianapolis, IN
Promoter: Sunshine Promotions
Other act(s): Bob Seger, Artful Dodger
Reported audience: 19,000 **SOLD-OUT
Reported gross: $121,524
Notes:
- From a local review: "It was important to be there, the rock concert. When you are young, you drape experiences about you as if they were medals of war. It certainly wasn't a good musical concert, but, more than 13,000 shrieking teen-age voices paid about $5 apiece to be there on Monday night. It must have been important to be there... The many stage effects do have the effect of camouflage over a less than competent musical act... It was crude, unimaginative rock and roll, but regardless it held the audience in sway. In fact, the entire Market Square Arena was swaying... KISS, did all their big hits, all easily forgettable. Of course, it's not easy to forget that for all of this zaniness, repulsiveness, ridiculousness the members of the band and their record label have probably all become rich" (Franklin Daily Journal, 8/5/76).
- Gene recalled meeting Karen Carpenter while both were staying at the Indianapolis Hilton: "I finally got to meet her. She's my idol; I really think she's sexy. She was on the 13th floor and I was on the 16th floor of the Indianapolis Hilton. I went to her room, and we talked for three hours... about music, about everything. She thinks she's very pure, but she didn't realize that there's a completely different Karen Carpenter that the males of America see. The image of a female sitting behind a drum kit banging away at the drums... I think it's a real fantasy turn-on. She was fascinated. She never thought of it that way before" (Independent Press-Telegram, 8/15/76). The Carpenters had performed the same night as KISS, at the Indiana Convention-Exposition Center.

August 4 - T.H. Barton Coliseum, Little Rock, AK
Promoter: Mid-South Concerts
Other act(s): Bob Seger, Artful Dodger
Reported audience: 7,297 / 10,000 (72.97%)
Reported gross: $45,016
Notes:

- The band flew to Little Rock, via Memphis, late in the evening of Aug. 3.
- From a local review: "The group is especially popular with the younger teenagers, who admire the antics as much as the music. The members of the group break guitars, spit what looks like blood, throw confetti and, during a recent show in Dallas, stomped live chickens in time to the music. At the Little Rock performance, 'KISS' wanted to shoot a stream of fire on stage, but the fire marshal said no" (Arkansas Democrat, 8/7/76). Fortunately, the photos accompanying the review were of better quality...

August 6 - Roberts Municipal Stadium, Evansville, IN
Promoter: Sunshine Promotions
Other act(s): Bob Seger, Artful Dodger
Reported audience: 11,480 / 12,600 (91.11%)
Reported gross: $72,254
Notes:
- Press reports indicated an attendance of 11,353.
- The band flew into Evansville, via Memphis, at lunchtime on the day of show.
- From a local review: "The capacity crowd was on its feet clapping and didn't sit down for the 90 minutes that KISS played. The fans, that ranged from bubble-gummers to acid-rock addicts, heartedly welcomed KISS' production... The stadium crowd saved its longest round of applause for the moment when Stanley announced the playing of 'the rock and roll national anthem,' — 'Rock and roll all night, and party every day.' The song was played to 6-foot bolts of electricity, 20 foot flames, and a layer of smoke that obscured the band from view" (Evansville Courier, 8/7/76).

August 8 - Hara Arena, Dayton, OH
Promoter: Belkin / Windy City Productions
Other act(s): Bob Seger
Reported audience: 8,300 **SOLD-OUT
Reported gross: $53,163
Notes:
- A show in Tampa, FL was originally scheduled on this date.

August 10 - Hirsch Coliseum, Shreveport, LA
Promoter: Concerts West
Other act(s): Bob Seger
Reported audience: 8,033 / 10,000 (80.33%)
Reported gross: $50,789
Notes:
- Billed as the "Rock 'N Roll Destruction Derby!" The band arrived in town during the afternoon of the day before the show.

SPECIAL GUEST: BOB SEGER
August 10, 8:30 PM HIRSCH COLISEUM
$6 ADVANCE GEN. ADMISSION
TICKETS **NOW** AVAILABLE AT ALL STANS RECORDS
PRODUCED BY CONCERTS WEST/KROK

August 11 - Tarrant County Convention Center Arena, Fort Worth, TX
Promoter: Concerts West
Other act(s): Bob Seger
Reported audience: 11,276 / 14,000 (80.54%)
Reported gross: $76,751
Notes:
- The band was charged with $543 for damages to the venue hall.
- In press for the show Gene mentions that the next album will be produced by the same person who had worked on Bad Company's "Run with the Pack" — an album that involved both Ron Nevison and Eddie Kramer.
- The show was reported as 13,000 attendance of 14,000 in Performance Magazine (9/3/76) grossing $79,000.
- From a local review: "Pillars of fire sprouted from for different spots on the stage. Bombs exploded. Lights flashed. Smoke billowed. And the drummer's platform rose 25 feet into the air. Show biz, man. Pure rock 'n' roll show biz. And show biz is as big a part of entertainment as the music itself. But the music wasn't all that bad. In fact, KISS sounded better Wednesday night at Tarrant County Convention Center than I've ever heard them on record. The band never slowed down. They kept a steady pace of hard rock 'n' roll throughout their 75-minute set — deafening, pounding rock 'n' roll... KISS, while not ready to stand alongside the great rock bands of our time, is definitely growing and progressing with its music. But all during the show I kept thinking to myself. Would the Beatles have come over here knowing it would lead to this" (Evansville Courier, 8/7/76)?

August 13 - The Summit, Houston, TX
Promoter: Pace Concerts / Concerts West
Other act(s): Bob Seger, Artful Dodger
Reported audience: 15,196 / 17,000 (89.39%)
Reported gross: $110,530

Presumed set list: Detroit Rock City / King of the Night Time World / Let Me Go, Rock 'N' Roll / Strutter / Hotter than Hell / Shout It Out Loud / Cold Gin / Nothin' To Lose / Do You Love Me? / God of Thunder / Rock And Roll All Nite / Deuce / Firehouse / Black Diamond
Notes:
- Some band confusion reigns during this partial show in the transition to "Shout It Out Loud" which will be of interest to those who exhibit tendencies towards *Schadenfreude*.
- The whole of the pro-shot video is known to exist, but not circulate widely. For many there are too many back/side angles on this. It's also unfortunate that "Nothin' to Lose" cuts mid-song, particularly because the colors of this video are particularly appealing.
- From a local review: "If you shut your eyes real tight — completely blanking out all of those fire-and-smoke drenched visions — then KISS sounded something like a series of explosions in a tin can factory. It was not, in other words, the kind of sound you'd spring on your loved ones — unless, of course, you had a very evil heart and they were heavily insured" (Houston Post, 8/14/76).
- The day following this show the band participated in an in-store appearance at Peaches Records in Atlanta, GA. Some 5,000 fans attended the event with the band selling kisses for 93 cents to raise money for a WZGC-FM93 Muscular Dystrophy charity (and promote the August 29 Atlanta Stadium show).

August 15 - El Paso County Coliseum, El Paso, TX
Promoter: Pace Concerts / Concerts West
Other act(s): Moon Pie Dance Band
Reported audience: 11,000 **SOLD-OUT
Reported gross: $66,400
Notes:
- From a local review: "The program said 'KISS is totally sensuous Thunderous rock... (and lots of visuals) make for a nerve stimulating experience.' And that's what it was like in the Coliseum last night with a crowd of more than 11,000. The band, all in black suits and silver trim, along with silver platform boots coming to mid-thigh were professional in every sense of the word. The show was well choreographed and the script was almost as good. The lights flashed and the smoke poured from different areas of the stage made to look like a castle in ruins... Musically the band gave a tight hard rock show" (El Paso Herald Post, 8/16/76).
- CK Lendt recalled a somewhat scarier version of the show: "I normally walked through the hall before and during the show to check out the crowd and inspect the ticket gates and turnstiles to see that things were going smoothly. But this crowd was frightening. At any moment, somebody could pull out a knife and start on a rampage. The fans were getting increasingly charged up while waiting for KISS to start, and in the darkness of the Coliseum, everything could easily slip out of control... The El Paso concert was a harrowing nightmare of the worst elements of a rock show" (KISS And Sell).
- Moon Pie Dance Band was a country-rock band that included guitarist Randy Jones. Bob Seger was headlining at the Jackson County Fair the night before and would therefore have been unlikely to have been able to travel to El Paso in time.

August 17 - Tempe Stadium, Tempe, AZ
Promoter: Fun Productions
Other act(s): Ted Nugent, Montrose, Bob Seger
Reported audience: 15,913 / 25,000 (63.65%)

Reported gross: $101,477

Notes:

- Lydia Criss recalled a near brawl occurring, during the day-off prior to this show, between Peter and members of Ted Nugent's crew: "KISS went on to their next gig at Tempe Stadium in Phoenix, Arizona. Ted Nugent was one of the opening acts for the gig. Despite playing several gigs with KISS over the years, Ted never once said hello to me, even though he constantly passed me everywhere... While Ted never acknowledged me, his road crew certainly did. It was another hot summer night and we were outside in an area set up for drinking and dancing with rock music playing. I was sitting with Peter and as he got up to get a drink and talk to someone, one of Ted Nugent's road crew members came over to me and asked if I wanted to dance. I politely declined his invitation, but because he had a few drinks in him, he began to get very indignant, eventually calling me a whore. Peter wasn't too far away from us, heard this comment and came running. Naturally a fight started; Peter was furious and wanted to beat the shit out of this guy. Because Peter had a show to perform the next day, one of KISS's security guards jumped into the brawl and stopped it. I was really flattered that Peter didn't think twice before coming to my defense" (Sealed with a KISS).

- From a local review: "The Arizona debut of the rock band KISS was marred by an unruly and sometimes violent crowd, and by the failure of the concert officials to handle the situation. Tempe Stadium's infield, outfield and stands were packed with over 35,000 persons, for the end-of-summer concert August 17 Bob Seger, Ted Nugent and Montrose shared the bill. Most of the crowd gathered well before the 3:30p.m. opening time. Some people tossed bottles over the fence, growing impatient in the dust and hundred-degree weather. When the gate was not opened at 3:30, the crowd forced it down. As the crowd surged through the opening, many people fell and were trampled on amid the broken glass, barbed wire and lost shoes.

Motorcycles and cars joined in the quarter mile dash to the next fence, where tickets were to be taken. Containing the crowd became impossible as people pushed and shoved at the ticket entrance. Tow trucks were brought in to keep the second gate from giving way. A concert official stood atop a tow truck and exchanged obscenities with the crowd as people jumped the fence from the roofs of cars. Finally, the fence was torn down and battle lines were drawn outside the walls of the stadium itself. One large group of tired, ill and discouraged people waited outside what they thought was a proper entrance for over an hour while the first act, Bob Seger was performing inside.

It was 9p.m. before KISS came on. Their show was an extravaganza of loud rock and visual effects from towers of fire and artificial lightning to bassist Gene Simmons blood spitting and fire breathing acts. For the finale of the nearly two-hour show, the drum platform was lifted 20 feet in the air by hydraulic jacks. The show would've beer worth the money if it hadn't cost so many people more than the $6.50 admission. For some, it cost them a trip to the hospital" (Flagstaff Lumberjack, 8/26/76).

August 20 - Anaheim Stadium, Anaheim, CA
Promoter: Fun Productions
Other act(s): Ted Nugent, Montrose, Bob Seger
Reported attendance: 42,987 / 55,000 (78.16%)
Reported gross: $437,653

Set list: Detroit Rock City / King of the Night Time World / Let Me Go, Rock 'N' Roll / Strutter / Hotter than Hell / Nothin' to Lose / Cold Gin / Shout It Out Loud / Do You Love Me? / God of Thunder / Rock And Roll All Nite / Deuce / Firehouse / Black Diamond

Notes:
- Uriah Heep were scheduled to play, but were replaced by Montrose.
- Flo & Eddie hosted the event and introduced the band onstage with their custom, and garish, pseudo-KISS makeup designs and costumes. High-wire daredevil Steve "Unique" McPeak also provided additional entertainment at the show, making a 150-foot-high quarter mile walk above the fans at the stadium, in between acts. A fireworks display closed the event.
- Eddie Kramer was hired to record this show and was assisted by engineer Biff Dawes. An audience recording of the show became one of the early KISS bootlegs as "KISS Destroys Anaheim," though not in the quality that accompanies the DVD. There are some sonic fluctuations throughout the show, but it is generally a storming performance with character. There have been numerous bootleg LP issues from the 70s onwards, some of which are highly sought after.
- This show was one of the top stadium concerts of 1976 (#15). The band also shifted an impressive $35,850.83 worth of merchandise at the show (which represented an impressive 16% of the whole tour's merchandise sold)!

August 21 - Anaheim Stadium, Anaheim, CA **TEMP HOLD DATE
Notes:
- Unused rain date for the Aug. 20 show.

August 22 - Oakland Coliseum Arena, Oakland, CA
Promoter: Bill Graham Presents
Other act(s): Bob Seger, Earth Quake
Reported audience: 9,897 / 14,000 (70.69%)
Reported gross: $63,041
Notes:
- Uriah Heep had been advertized as the opening act but were replaced by local band Earth Quake. Having cut a demo for CBS Earth Quake were rejected and signed with their manager's Berserkley/Playboy label for the release of their "Rocking the World" (1975) and "8.5" (1976) albums.
- Lydia Criss recounted in "Sealed With A KISS" that Peter nearly OD'd prior to this show.

August 27 - Groves Stadium, Winston-Salem, NC **TEMP HOLD DATE
Promoter: Entam, Ltd.
Reported audience: (45,000 capacity)
Notes:
- The summer of '76 provided numerous challenges for promoter Phil Lashinsky. First Wake Forest officials pulled the plug on Sunday shows at Groves Stadium on the campus grounds, resulting in him having to cancel the Who's date on Aug. 1 (they didn't want to play smaller venues). Then two separate shows, with ZZ Top and Aerosmith headlining respectively, failed to draw more than 45% capacity. KISS, who were scheduled to be the fourth big concert date of the summer declined the outdoor venue, preferring to keep their show indoors (perhaps knowing the challenges of presenting the show outdoors AND drawing

enough patrons). As a result Lashinsky opted for the smaller indoor venue, a decision validated with the less than spectacular attendance in Greensboro.

August 27 - Greensboro Coliseum, Greensboro, NC

Promoter: Entam, Ltd.
Other act(s): Point Blank
Reported audience: 11,068 / 17,500 (63.25%)
Reported gross: $71,130
Partial set list: Detroit Rock City / King of the Night Time World / Rock and Roll All Nite / Strutter / Deuce / God of Thunder / Shout It Out Loud / Do You Love Me? / Black Diamond
Notes:
- From a local review: "It's like sitting back and watching Bela Lugosi and it's like seeing a famous movie star come walking down the street. Maybe you've seen a silver-nosed tomcat stalking the alleys or possibly it is what the Martians sent us in exchange for Viking I. Anyway you look at them you see an unusual visual effect. Every time these fellows perform, it is like going to the circus, with all kinds of weird entertainment. Last Friday night, in the Greensboro Coliseum, KISS did everything from spitting blood to making snow. There are no words to describe KISS perfectly. They are a show band that pulls tricks out of their hats so fast that you just stand amazed. With a stage set up like an old horror movie, the only thing lacking was the haunted house, and KISS pranced around the stage with bizarre, teasing dances... The sound was remarkably clear and crisp, and all vocals could be heard. The drums did not overpower and beat the listeners to death. All the voices, however, sounded like a rasping scream. The lead guitar solo became monotonous, showing technical ability but not sensitivity. The drum solo was not extremely long but was musically uninteresting. Their solos, in fact, were no better than any other band's. KISS is beginning to depend too much on their showmanship. Musical ability is much more important today than crowd deception. When KISS returns to their original sound, then they can afford to perfect their show" (Statesville Record & Landmark, 9/4/76).
- 30 fans were arrested during the show for drugs and alcohol violations. Amusingly, the Greensboro Daily News review of the show managed to omit KISS completely and focused instead on opener Point Blank praising their straight-forward approach instead of reliance on gimmicks.

August 29 - Fulton County Stadium, Atlanta, GA

Promoter: Alex Cooley, Inc.
Other act(s): Bob Seger, Johnny & Edgar Winter, .38 Special, & Blue Oyster Cult
Reported audience: 34,489 / 50,000 (68.98%)
Reported gross: $291,292
Notes:
- From a local review: "If you're a rock and roll fanatic, then the low point of your summer was the so-called Summer Starburst concert featuring KISS, Blue Oyster Cult, and Johnny and Edgar Winter, at the Braves Stadium on August 29. Technical problems, poor sound reproduction, unending waits between groups, and an unruly crowd ruined what could have been an excellent outdoor show... The headliners for the show, KISS, leaped onstage after another tedious wait to bombs bursting, giant flames, and lots of smoke. Attired in their standard black leather and makeup, KISS put on a show of high-energy noise that thrilled everyone under sixteen and offended those who know anything about rock and music in general. Any veteran rock fan would note with distaste guitarist Paul Stanley's

attempts at Peter Townshend-type leaps and would simply yawn at bassist Gene Simmons' blood spitting routine. Their entire set showed no redeeming social value whatsoever" (GA Institute of Technology - The Technique, 9/24/76).

September 1 - Notre Dame Athletic & Convocation Center (ACC), South Bend, IN
Promoter: Sunshine Promotions
Other act(s): Bob Seger
Reported audience: 7,525 / 11,500 (65.43%)
Reported gross: $48,912
Notes:
- Billboard reported an attendance of 7,677 with a gross of $47,911 (9/18/76).

September 3 - The Coliseum, Richfield (Cleveland), OH
Promoter: Belkin Productions
Other act(s): Artful Dodger
Reported audience: 15,496 / 18,500 (83.76%)
Reported gross: $102,611
Set list: Detroit Rock City / King of the Night Time World / Let Me Go, Rock 'N' Roll / Strutter / Hotter than Hell / Nothin' to Lose / Cold Gin / Shout It Out Loud / Do You Love Me? / God of Thunder / Rock And Roll All Nite / Deuce / Firehouse / Black Diamond
Notes:
- Usually described as "Cleveland."
- A nice soundboard recording exists from this show. It's really pretty "pure" since not much of the audience is captured. There are sonic fluctuations on the first few songs as recording levels are adjusted, and "Rock And Roll All Nite" cuts at the end. This show is a great opportunity to really hear the band, warts 'n all, performing in the 1970s.

September 4 - Civic Arena, Pittsburgh, PA
Promoter: Dicesare-Engler Productions/Dick Clark Concerts
Other act(s): Bob Seger, Artful Dodger
Reported audience: 11,615 / 12,000 (96.79%)
Reported gross: $76,465

September 6 - Varsity Stadium, Toronto, ON, Canada
Promoter: CPI Presents
Other act(s): Blue Oyster Cult, Artful Dodger
Reported audience: 13,650 / 35,000 (39.00%)
Reported gross: $124,701
Set list: Detroit Rock City / King of the Night Time World / Let Me Go, Rock 'N' Roll / Strutter / Hotter than Hell / Nothin' to Lose / Cold Gin / Shout It Out Loud / Do You Love Me? / God of Thunder / Rock And Roll All Nite / Deuce / Firehouse / Black Diamond
Notes:
- Bob Seger was originally scheduled as the opener, but was replaced by Artful Dodger. A minor "riot" occurred at this show as fans rushed the entrance for the general admission seating trampling some fellow fans. Musical issues occur at the end of "Hotter than Hell" and Ace calls someone an "asshole" during the intro to "Black Diamond," making for an entertaining show.

- KISS also received their Canadian platinum award for "Destroyer" from Quality Records at a reception at Cooly's on Yonge Street after the show...
- From a local review: "KISS, its first-rate sound system turned up to the mega-decibel level, its creepy stage setting looking like something out of a Stan Lee gothic horror comic, and it's special effects department working overtime. KISS' show is a collection of disparate elements which, when thrown together, combine to overwhelm you. Guitars explode. Cannons go off. Strands of lights flicker. And there are assorted explosions as the band's four members prance and strut like comic-book ghouls. And does it matter if none of this has anything to do with what the band's singing about? That despite all the gore, the band's lyrics dwell on having a good time and the joys of rock? Not at all. But, then again, in an army, especially the KISS Army, one isn't meant to think. One is meant to take orders" (Toronto Star, 9/7/76).
- A clinical SBD recording, with barely any audience to be heard, circulates. However, "Rock And Roll All Nite" cuts during Ace's solo into an already in-progress "Deuce."

September 8 - Freedom Hall Coliseum, Louisville, KY
Promoter: Sunshine Promotions
Other act(s): Bob Seger, Artful Dodger
Reported audience: 17,051 / 19,000 (89.74%)
Reported gross: $103,918
Notes:
- Local radio station WKLO held a concert ticket/backstage meet contest with the winners delivered to the venue via limo with DJ Bo Brady.
- From a local review: "The KISS concert, a near-sellout at Freedom Hall last night, proved that rock is still a bull market for bread and circuses. And in the case of KISS, an unimaginative American heavy metal band, you could probably hold the bread. But the circus certainly was impressive. In fact, the show's heroes must have been the KISS stage crew. It coordinated the theatrical mesh of strobes and smoke pots, fireball launchers and bellowing bombs that had the big Fairgrounds barn looking like Dresden after the bombers rolled over it. The young audience loved it" (Louisville Times, 9/9/76).

September 10 - Riverfront Coliseum, Cincinnati, OH
Promoter: Electric Factory Concerts
Other act(s): Bob Seger, Artful Dodger
Reported audience: 13,677 / 18,000 (75.98%)
Reported gross: $82,299
Notes:
- This show was initially scheduled for Sep. 12 (erroneously listed as October in the press), but was changed in early August.
- From a local review: "The four members of KISS never perform sans surrealistic mime makeup. I don't blame them. If I played music as miserably as they do, I would want to be disguised, too. At Riverfront Coliseum Friday evening, KISS' performance managed to chalk up the four big T's: tacky; tawdry; tasteless; and trite. Their light, fire, and explosives shows were tawdry; their posturings tasteless; and the music, trite... The black cat-whiskers and sliver nose adorning the alabaster face of drummer Peter Criss gave him the visage of a cross between Bozo the Clown, a character from 'Westworld,' and Cat Woman... KISS' debacle lasted one hour and 15 minutes. Advertisements for the concert claimed the group

would be on stage for over two hours. This was one occasion when false advertising was a blessing" (Cincinnati Enquirer, 9/13/76).

- From another local review: "KISS is an underground phenomenon in America. And six-feet under they should be. KISS is the worst of the theatrical rock groups. They make Alice Cooper look as mild as Grandma Moses or Whistler's Mother. KISS must realize how weak it is in talent, particularly as musicians and lyric-writers. As entertainers, they might pass for nursery school dropouts. KISS wisely disguises their major flaws, which would he the death of most groups. They do this by hiding behind a facade of loud, distorted music, outrageous theatrical makeup and dress, repulsive gimmicks and tons of extra noise, such as exploding fireworks, smoke bombs and sirens. KISS is a cover-up. Bigger than Watergate. They have only two songs on charts: "Shout It Out Loud" and "Hotter than Hell." They parlayed both headlining a major concert Friday Riverfront Coliseum. Incredibly, 12,000 suckers showed up to witness this freak show. Only Bob Seger and the Silver Bullet Band were worth hearing. Certainly not Artful Dodger. The mob on the arena floor turned just before KISS arrived. They began shoving and fighting to get close to stage. A dozen fans wore their makeup. Most didn't own driver's licenses.

KISS finally came out, in a belch white smoke and bombs. The performers looked like they were ready for Halloween... Lead singer Paul Stanley wore a body suit suitable for a porno flick, was open in front all the way down to sequined crotch. He had white makeup and a black star over one eye. Bass guitarist Gene Simmons, who would later spit blood (from a blood capsule) at the audience and also spit lighter fluid into a flame, was dressed like a creature from the black lagoon. He wore scaly monster shoes and knight's armor. The other two weren't so outrageous. Drummer Peter Criss looked like a poor imitation of a dog, while lead guitarist Ace Frehley looked like he came from Mars. Ironically, the real KISS eventually showed its inner skin, despite all the outer makeup. When the theatricals wore ragged, the real monsters called KISS were exposed. And it was a cosmic joke" (Hamilton & Fairfield Journal News, 9/14/76).

September 11 - Colt Park, Hartford, CT **CANCELLED
Promoter: Contemporary Concerts
Notes:
- There were some massive shows hosted at Hartford's Colt Park in the summer of '76 including Aerosmith, Jefferson Starship/Fleetwood Mac, Grateful Dead, and Peter Frampton. Frampton's show almost didn't go ahead when he fell off the stage and fractured a couple of ribs. The events caused a series of complaints, with more than 20 being arrested at one show for trying to gate-crash and battling police with bottles. Promoters attempted to work with local authorities, who also complained about the amount of mess being left behind following shows. Neighbors had complained about noise and fans loitering. By the time Jethro Tull and J. Geils Band performed in July the number of arrests had increased to 30. While 30,000 paying fans showed up, an additional 15,000 were allowed to watch from a hill overlooking the concert facility. About "two dozen persons were brought in from the show and treated for minor injuries from fights or for intoxication. Police reported two minor stabbings among the fights" (Bridgeport Post, 7/17/76). Later, several men were arrested for a gang rape of one 17-year-old attendee.

On July 26 city officials had met with 40 malcontent neighbors of the concert facility who complained that they felt like prisoners in their homes during concerts. An Aug. 4 Doobie

Brothers concert was moved to the Hartford Civic Center. The council hadn't expected so many concerts, though the promoters promised to increase security at future concerts. The promoter went so far as to negotiate with youth gangs offering them $100 to help "keep order during the Grateful Dead concert" (Bridgeport Post, 8/2/76) on Aug. 2, though the gangs wouldn't be paid until after the show. It wasn't a successful tactic and more than 40 were arrested at the show which also included "numerous injuries and drug overdoses" (Naugatuck Daily News, 8/4/76) in addition to bottle throwing at firemen attempting to extinguish a small blaze set by non-ticket holders outside the venue. On the morning following the concert Hartford's mayor asked the City Council to cancel all remaining concerts at the venue.

While Aerosmith's Aug. 9 show was initially allowed to go ahead, new rules and regulations were implemented by the City Council: Alcohol was banned within the park, non-ticket holders were banned from going anywhere near the park, surrounding streets were blocked by police, sound was controlled by the police, and undercover police were stationed in the audience. Those changes proved moot with the remnants of hurricane Belle, which forced the promoters to move the concert indoors (to the Springfield, MA Civic Center) at the last moment. Perhaps reports of that unruly audience were the final straw, and the Council voted to terminate the contract with the promoters on Aug. 11. "Revoking the contract means the city will have to pay a $25,000 penalty to Contemporary Concerts, the promotion company. The city however, gets to keep about $150,000 equipment the promoters installed in the stadium" (Bridgeport Post, 8/12/76). The Spirit of '76 indeed...

September 12 - Fairgrounds, Allentown, PA **TEMP HOLD DATE
Promoter: Jennifer Productions
Notes:
- This date appeared on early itineraries for the tour, but was apparently never booked.

September 12 - Civic Center, Springfield, MA
Promoter: Koplik & Finkle Productions
Other act(s): Artful Dodger
Reported audience: 8,612 / 10,347 (83.23%)
Reported gross: $54,658
Set list: Detroit Rock City / King of the Night Time World / Let Me Go, Rock 'N' Roll / Strutter / Hotter than Hell / Nothin' to Lose / Cold Gin / Shout It Out Loud / Do You Love Me? / God of Thunder / Rock And Roll All Nite / Deuce / Firehouse / Black Diamond
Notes:
- There were 24 arrests at this show for the usual drugs violations and other breaches of the peace. Six fans didn't even make the show having been arrested en route from Worcester following a barroom brawl at the Keg Room on State Street.
- This was the final show of the "Destroyer" Spirit of '76 tour, at the same venue where the band had performed what might be considered the final show of the "Alive!" touring cycle.
- From a local review: "Those expecting fresh chills from the four grease-painted demons had some laughs instead at the expense of the new KISS equipment. Two pieces of scenery intended to represent a haunted castle and a volcano came off looking like the sets from a junior high pageant. The giant strands of colored lights winked with all the menace of Christmas tree decorations — exactly what they were. Most hilarious was the smoking obelisk at stage right. Was it meant to portray a rocket, or a fiery Bicentennial salute to the

Washington monument" (The Morning Union, 9/14/76)? Fans apparently didn't care for the review and bombarded the paper with their rebuttals for weeks after the show's final notes had been silenced...
- This show circulates a generally poor AUD recording.

(Trade publication ad for the "Destroyer" tour)

Rock and Roll Over

It is generally accepted that "KISS Alive!" was the album that saved KISS's then stalling career. Similarly the live album was also a savior for Casablanca Records at a convenient time when a couple of other roster artists started gaining traction. It's also obvious that "Destroyer" nearly destroyed the band's success before they'd really had more than a taste of fame (but no fortune for the band members quite yet); prior to a certain "throw-away" ballad transforming the band from successes to superstars. It was a near miss, and that album had taken the band far from their comfort zone, both creatively and artistically. Bob Ezrin had pushed them to their limits on an individual and group basis. While the band had willingly agreed to Ezrin's guidance, and all-out sonic experimentation and refinement which resulted in "Destroyer," it was not something they could aspire to on a regular basis. The resulting album, however, alienated a large sector of the original core of '73 – '75 fans — the band's studio sound became ultra-polished rather than raw and somewhat rushed "thunder-rock." The KISS of 1975, into early 1976, was a band whose studio sonic dynamic had changed. An analogy of a caterpillar metamorphosing into a butterfly might be apt, were one writing flowery prose. Discarded was the foundational ethos of trying to capture the band "live" in the studio. The band had been chasing the impossible, trying to present themselves as fans heard them live. "Alive!" proved the futility, the need to accept that they could ultimately never capture that missing magical ingredient that fueled the live performance. No revisionism is required when considering the merits of the albums that preceded "Rock And Roll Over."

It might also be fair to suggest that KISS' success had turned some of the original fans off — they now had to share "their" band with apparent bandwagon-hopping newbies (some of those fans are still bitter). They had been fans of the band before any success made others at least give a second thought to the band. Even the band's members and support personnel weren't absolutely sure about the path they'd taken with "Destroyer," but in the end they probably picked up more new fans than they lost. The humorous point to the overall uncertainty about the product they'd created was obvious by the last minute invitation to Jack Douglas, then Ezrin's assistant, to remix the album and try and salvage something from a perceived mistake. That "remix" was ultimately not required and instead of taking the step back the band took a leap forward. Behind the scenes, with Glickman/Marks entering the picture, out went a majority of the old way of doing things as what had been something of a homebrew organization started its transformation into a properly run business. In early press concerning a new album to follow "Destroyer" the band made it clear that they would return to basics — almost a plea to the fans to take "Destroyer" as an artistic aberration that would quickly be consigned, apologetically, to history. What resulted from the follow-up was another 180 degree turn, a return to the recording ethos of 1973–75, with that analogous "butterfly" dropping dead, as the band reverted to their quest for studio rawness that mimicked their live presentation (on a good day).

"Rock And Roll Over" reunited the band with Eddie Kramer, with whom they'd recorded their first demos during March 1973 and constructed their breakthrough "Alive!" (He had also engineered some other live recordings for them, notably Anaheim '76). His studio work with them provided a taste of what could, and probably should have been, the sound of the first two albums. A cynical voice also suggests that he did exactly that with the band when he re-recorded the material that ultimately became "Alive!" Eddie had turned down live albums with Led Zeppelin and the Rolling Stones to work with KISS (in the studio) at this juncture, but it was probably the right time for him to do so. Yet, Ezrin's imprint was still very much present. However tough the recording experience had been, the band had discovered that more variety in the music could be beneficial. Ezrin's input in the song-writing had also left an indelible mark, even if he was no longer present to provide the extra perspective to the material.

Recording officially commenced at "closed" Nanuet Star Theater in Nanuet, NY on Monday, September 20 and was scheduled to be completed by October 11. The theatre had closed in late-1975 (reopening in May 1978), but was rented out for one-off or other special events. It was also very conveniently located an hour north of New York City, thus not requiring any major relocation for the band and their staff. The weekend of September 18–19 saw the crew and band arriving and acoustic tests being conducted on the environment and equipment. Recording in a theatre was supposed to help capture the live dynamic that proved so popular with the fans. The album was completed at the Record Plant, back in New York City, October 12–17. Final overdubs and mixing took place October 18–24 while the band was in Los Angeles. With Kramer at the helm recording took weeks instead of the months the previous album had taken — though to be fair, there were breaks in the recording schedule.

There was no shortage of ideas or material, and the resulting album was released on November 1, which seems completely insane for an album that had only been completed a week earlier! But it seems likely that the material was very spontaneous and specifically lacking in the refinement that Ezrin brought to the sessions. For the first time in their history KISS was not on tour at the time the album was released. In the meantime there were rehearsals to complete and promotional material to produce. KISS and their core entourage flew to Los Angeles on various days to tape the Paul Lynde Halloween special in late-October. Most of the band arrived on the October 18 (an advance "guard" had arrived on October 12). KISS rehearsed in Hall #5 at ABC Studios in Los Angeles, CA the following day and taped the show during multiple sessions on October 20–21.

KISS' part of the show included minor dialogue bits and the lip-synched performances of "Detroit Rock City" (taped on 10/20), "Beth," and "King of the Night Time World" (both taped on 10/21). For some the choice of material seems off with a new release imminent, however with both the album and single having legs on the U.S. charts it made more sense to stick with what was then current product. Most of the band returned to New York the following day. For promotional purposes to support the album band also appeared on the Burns Media radio show "Rock And Roll Over With KISS." It featured interview segments and sound-bites from members of the band and tour personnel, plus clips of various KISS recordings, not only those from the new album.

Tour rehearsals were booked at Studio B at Studio Instrument Rentals (S.I.R.) in New York City between November 7 and 13. These were followed by the full production rehearsals held at the Camp Curtis Guild Armory (which became the American Civic Center) in Redding,

MA between November 14 and 21, though staff were certainly onsite from Nov. 12 for setup and equipment unloading. Eddie Balandas and Joe Gusti drove up from Boston in a truck carrying the costumes and Peter's stage cats on November 13. For the tour there were only minor revisions made to Gene, Ace, and Peter's "Destroyer" costumes. For the early part of the tour Paul continued to use older costumes, before getting his new one. The new costume was essentially a sleeveless version of the "Destroyer" unitard. During their stay the band and entourage took over the Lord Wakefield Motor Hotel on the shores of Lake Quannapowitt. Tour manager and "Artist Representative," a term which could also be read as "babysitter," was Frank Scinlaro. Billy Miller soon took over from Frank.

Fans are lucky that a couple of recordings of those rehearsals circulate, not just the singular "Take Me" that was included on the "KISS My Ass" video. First is a half-hour tripod shot black and white video that features the band running through "Cold Gin," "God Of Thunder" (including Peter's solo), "Rock And Roll All Nite," "Deuce," "Black Diamond," and "Love 'Em And Leave 'Em." None of that material is particularly staggering, since the band trying to arrange an electric version of "Beth" isn't present, but KISS are without their make-up and costumes. "Love 'Em And Leave 'Em," which was probably filmed separately, wasn't even a performance as such. It's the band working on lip-synching the performance that they'd film for television use during the rehearsals. That song, "I Want You," and "Hard Luck Woman" were professionally filmed for use on Don Kirshner's "New" Rock Concert during the rehearsals. While those songs would have been an indication of what new material was going to debut on the tour they weren't broadcast until May 28, 1977, long after the tour had ended (and they then included an over-dubbed live audience). The 90 minute show also featured Alice Cooper, Burton Cummings performing "I'm Scared," Dorothy Moore, and Casablanca label-mates Angel. KISS was also featured during the 4th anniversary high-lights show. The videos also found use in international markets for promotional purposes and have become accepted as being promos even though their original intent was different.

The commonly circulating audio only version of the tour rehearsals includes: "Detroit Rock City" (incomplete), "Take Me," "Let Me Go, Rock N Roll," "Strutter," "Ladies Room," "Firehouse," "Hard Luck Woman" (incomplete), "Do You Love Me?" (incomplete), "Cold Gin" (several attempts), "Makin' Love," "I Want You," and a more complete and fast-tempo 2:34 arrangement of "Hard Luck Woman." This audio version is usually found in very reasonable sound-quality, though there is some fluctuation. The last song, while complete, is more "muddy" than the rest of the recordings. However, cleaned-up with a bit of audience over-dub, presto, that's what "Hard Luck Woman" sounded like live in concert in 1976! A couple of other audio recordings of the set rehearsals also exist with actual live takes of "Love 'Em And Leave 'Em," suggesting that the song was indeed at least prepared for the tour. There is currently no evidence to prove without any doubt that KISS performed "Love 'Em And Leave 'Em" during the early part of the tour — the sets for the November dates of the tour are unknown — as suggested by Gene. The aforementioned rehearsal takes do seem to point in the direction of it strongly seeming to have least made an appearance or two before being dropped. Audience reaction, set flow, and other factors would likely have needed to have been taken into consideration as the set started the process of refinement.

The "Winter Tour 1976/77" (the official title of the tour, rather than oft mentioned "Spirit of '76 Part II" or other such other variants) kicked-off in Savannah, Georgia on November 24.

The originally intended opening city of Fayetteville, NC was inexplicably changed, though it was rescheduled for later in the tour. The band essentially used the same stage that had been used on the previous tour though it was refined with some stage props not being used. What is clear is that plenty of new material was introduced for the tour. Initially, "Rock And Roll Over" was represented with "Take Me," "Ladies Room," "Hard Luck Woman," "I Want You," and "Makin' Love," which during the early stages of the tour appeared as an encore! Representing 50% of the new album ("Calling Dr. Love" joined the set during the "Love Gun" tour) the amount of new material was impressive and further shifted the band's material away from relying on the pre-"Alive!' albums, particularly for a set that was specifically designed to run around 75 minutes in duration. Perhaps most important was the introduction of "Beth" into the set. By that time the band had no choice but to incorporate the song due to its hit status. Bringing Peter out from behind the drum kit, to sit on a case and sing along to the canned orchestral track, allowed him to connect with the audience in a very personal and somewhat tender manner, again changing the overall dynamic of the band's live show from the pure shock and awe of the earlier years. The band was moving on from their early years, not necessarily maturing, but at least evolving.

Early standards such as "100,000 Years" and "Deuce" were dropped from the set in order to limit the length of the shows and focus the material on the most popular albums at that point. The band and their advisors were very aware and concerned with the product they were selling. There was also less experimentation with the set, though obviously there were changes, but things became very much stream-lined, or perhaps more scripted and choreographed than ever before. By becoming less dynamic, the band were able to present a near identical show night after night ensuring that it didn't matter what city the fans saw the band in. This also helped budgeting for the requisite supplies and streamlined setup and tear-down into a finely choreographed ballet by the crew. With the cost of the show already being high, in comparison with many other touring acts, there was a necessity to take a more business-like approach to both how it was executed and routed. A study of the overall touring methodology have been conducted during the "Destroyer" tour, and while that methodology was new at that point, there were many areas deemed in need of improvement. The '76–77 would be the first opportunity to implement some of the more obvious fixes.

Initially, KISS were joined by higher level local or regional acts such as Graham Parker & The Rumor, Jesse Bolt, the Raisen Band, Blackfoot and even Tom Petty and the Heartbreakers! Opening act for most of December through mid-February was the Uriah Heep. When their stint ended New York punk band and contemporaries of KISS, The Dictators, lead by "Handsome" Dick Manitoba joined to tour. Like KISS, the Dictators had played the Coventry in New York City in their early years and even played on a bill with the Stooges and Blue Oyster Cult months before KISS' own Academy Of Music industry debut! However, the bill was very much mismatched, with the band often being perceived as being some lower life-form when compared with the headliner. It is interesting to point out that the band had a song, "The Minnesota Strip," on their 1978 "Bloodbrothers" album that has more than a few similarities with KISS' later version of Bryan Adams and Jim Vallance's "War Machine." An interesting coincidence, in addition to the band's other shared histories. Other acts to open for KISS during the 1977 section of the tour included Sammy Hagar for three dates, including the Madison Square Garden show where he exposed himself to the audience, and

Legs Diamond. Legs Diamond purportedly crashed a KISS after-show party and persuaded Gene to check them out with him purportedly liking them enough for them to get the final three shows of the U.S. tour.

As previously mentioned, the "Rock And Roll Over" tour discarded much of the material that had comprised the set pre-"Destroyer." In one sense it was understandable: KISS version "1976 Part II" certainly wasn't KISS v.75 or "76 Part I". Of this material "Strutter" survived in the set until early December, with the show at the Mississippi Coliseum (12/3) being the last known performance. At some point soon after that the song was dropped from the set, and it remained absent for the next few years. KISS was full steam ahead as a major act and the past was rapidly falling behind them as they conquered America and the size of their recorded catalog grew. Where fans have heard in the band's heritage era, about the difficulty choosing a set, the same was very much the case in the mid-1970s while they generated two albums worth of new material annually and had fewer songs that could be considered sacrosanct.

The few other audio and video recordings from the tour provide fans with a fascinating look at the period. An early December concert in Memphis, TN, is the earliest currently known full recording from the tour, and one of only two shows from 1976 that was archived in some form — the other being the partial New Orleans, LA from Dec. 4 which surfaced around the same time as Memphis. There is a third if one counts the silent 8mm footage from Jackson, MS on Dec. 3. The show was the sixth of the tour, so its early date makes it a particularly important artifact. What makes either of these recordings fascinating is the inclusion of "Hard Luck Woman" in its original electric backed arrangement. With the single having been released around the time the tour kicked off (backed with "Take Me") it wasn't particularly surprising that the band initially included either song in the set. "Hard Luck Woman" gave Peter another opportunity to shine with material better suited for his vocal style, particularly following the rise of the gravelly voice Bob Seger. The Dec. 2 show also provides a listen to what is currently the earliest performance of "Beth."

The evolutionary state of the set sequence is clear in Memphis: "Detroit Rock City," "Take Me," "Let Me Go, Rock 'N Roll," "Strutter," "Ladies Room," "Firehouse," "I Want You," "Hard Luck Woman," "Do You Love Me?" (which on this occasion had a rather long drum intro section), "Cold Gin" (w/ Ace's solo), a brief Gene bass solo followed by "God Of Thunder" (w/ Peter's solo), "Rock And Roll All Nite," "Beth," "Makin' Love," and "Black Diamond." Unlike shows later in the tour "Nothin' To Lose" and "Shout It Out Loud" were not performed. The positioning of "Makin' Love" as an encore seems odd and somewhat uncomfortable, and it is clear that the set was a work in progress as the band and crew attempted to get things streamlined. This concert is interesting from another point of view: Issues with the audience interrupted the show several times culminating in the local Fire Marshall taking to the stage at one point. The first interruption occurs after "Take Me" with an announcement being made: "The fire marshal wants us to keep the aisles clear. There's broken glass, someone might get hurt and we don't want to stop the show. So please keep the aisles clear!" Apparently the request didn't work and following "Firehouse" there is a several minute delay with the announcer pleading: "Everybody listen up a second! The fire marshal wants the aisles cleared. He's threatening to stop the show." The audience eventually starts chanting "We want KISS" while the announcer pleads for the audience to comply with his request. The interruption only lasts around four minutes, but it's pretty clear the show was close to getting fully stopped. Without further announcement Paul somewhat tepidly starts "I Want You," but the undercurrent of the show leaves the song lacking its usual electricity. It seems the interruption has de-energized the band somewhat. It's also somewhat odd that Paul didn't work any cautions into his raps, very much following the usual script (though they were not necessarily audible on the recording).

As it's the earliest recording known from the tour it provides the earliest known concert recordings of "Take Me," "I Want You," "Ladies Room," and "Makin' Love." The last of these songs started out in an encore position in the set before being re-sequenced to the end of the first third of the show. "Ladies Room" also features a slightly different arrangement, including a breakdown, almost sing-a-long section, on the final chorus. The song soon returned to a form closer to the album recording and more familiar to the fans, but still needed more cowbell. With the guitar style of "I Want You" it's not surprising that "Hard Luck Woman" followed it in the set. The performance is very much a band effort with more obvious backing vocals, notably from Paul. However, Peter sounds very much into performing the song, though it really did slow the set down. Paul seems almost confrontational as he introduces "Rock And Roll All Nite" telling the audience to get up off their seats.

The following night's show at the Mississippi Coliseum in Jackson, MS was also partially archived, in this case on silent 8mm. Focusing mainly on Paul from the photo pit, the dark video has been synched with mismatched audio, leaving collectors unsure about exactly what is featured on the video. It's barely watchable, but is interesting nonetheless. Since the December 4 show in New Orleans show included "Hard Luck Woman," it is likely that was still present in the set list on 12/3. However, the 8mm footage that is available seems to jump from parts of one song to the next. "Firehouse" is certainly present with Paul donning the fire-hat and Gene successfully breathing fire — something he'd not manage a couple of days later in Mobile, AL, when he set his hair on fire. According to variety, KISS completed the first leg o their 1976-77 tour with 22 sold-out concerts in the U.S., grossing $1,600,000 and playing to 233,763 spectators" (Variety, 1/19/77).

What is generally considered to be the first available standard set recording of the tour is from the January 1, 1977 show at Providence's Civic Center in Rhode Island. During December kinks were ironed out of the set and it somewhat stabilized featuring: "Detroit Rock City," "Take Me," "Let Me Go, Rock 'N Roll," "Ladies Room," "Firehouse," "Makin' Love," "I Want You," "Cold Gin" (w/ Ace's solo) , "Do You Love Me? ," "Nothin' To Lose," "God Of Thunder" (w/ Peter's solo), "Rock And Roll All Nite," "Shout It Out Loud," "Beth," and "Black Diamond." That's not a particularly grueling set list, and nine of the songs are post-"Alive!" But it is the form that the set would take for much of the remainder of the tour. In Japan "I Want You" and "Makin' Love" would simply be flipped in performance order with the rest of the set remaining the same.

Considering that the tour concluded at Hampton Coliseum in Hampton, VA on March 7 that's a substantial part of the tour not archived! In fact, according to Curt Gooch and Jeff Suhs' "KISS Alive Forever: The Complete Touring History," some 22 shows out of a tour of 70 equates to around 32% of the tour to remain pretty much shrouded in mystery. Newspaper reviews are not particularly helpful either. The focus of the reviewer is still blinded by the show, rather than them knowing any of the particulars of the band's catalog. Furthermore, the show on March 7 probably had the same set list as the show on January 1 indicating that the set was very much static during this major part of the tour. The last know audio recording from March 5 also has the same set, so it is unlikely that it changed for the final two shows. In fact, from the audience recordings (ROIO) that do circulate most indicate similar sets, though invariably encores and/or other parts of the show may be missing. Hartford, from February 16, is particularly butchered, missing "Firehouse," "Do You Love Me?," "Nothin' To Lose," "Shout It Out Loud," and "Beth," but at least sounds better than the few other audience attempts.

Another particularly interesting show from this period, Johnson City, TN, from February 26, has Paul singing many of Peter's vocal parts. Peter had been involved in a self-inflicted car crash, after the band's show at Nassau Coliseum on February 21. This incident resulted in the postponement of the tour's next scheduled show in Hampton, VA on February 23. At the Nassau show, which had been an extra date scheduled due to MSG selling out and being unable for further booking, Peter's levitating drum had malfunctioned and nearly tipped him and his kit off while descending unevenly — Peter should have been used to that after what he'd gone through during 1973-4! When the tour reconvened in Johnson City, Peter didn't perform "Beth," though he did complete his drum solo. Apart from this show we pretty much hear and see the "same old, same old," not that it would have mattered to fans at the time who didn't travel from show to show or have access to the instantaneous information at our fingertips today.

Most stunning of the "Rock And Roll Over" tour archive is the unfortunately incomplete video from the Jan. 29, 1977 Cobo Arena show; the final and hastily added third show in Detroit (Paul references it as the last of the shows during the introduction to "Let Me Go, Rock 'N' Roll"). On the day of the first show (1/27) the band were interviewed unmasked, though with their backs facing the camera, by Max Kinkel for a local television news feature. It is fitting, perhaps, that this Detroit show is available to collectors, though somewhat sad that the lesser MSG show was featured as a bonus for the KISSology Volume 1 DVD in terms of wider distribution. Professionally filmed to a standard that in the opinion of the author exceeds the previous year's shows, Cobo '77 is sourced from a 3/4" master tape that surfaced on E-bay in June 2006. The other two Cobo shows are also known to exist offering a glimmer of hope that fans will one day get the opportunity to enjoy them too.

That tape was snapped up by a European collector for a bargain $5,000, though the seller, lacking any integrity, immediately started selling DVD copies to others. Once that occurred a free-for-all took place with traders making the video available in as many places as possible for free and reporting the auctions to the E-bay police to get them shut down. The video starts with the band backstage with "Big" John Harte leading them to stage and segues into the band taking to their instruments on a darkened stage. The tape then jumps into an already in progress "Detroit Rock City" (missing the first verse and band intro). The video excludes the encores after "Rock And Roll All Nite," but the clarity and performance is simply staggering. Some believe the show is an equal of Tokyo '77, others believe it blows that show out of the water. If any show can claim to be definitive of this tour, then this is perhaps it, even in its incomplete state. Until, perhaps, the long-rumored video from Largo, MD (Dec. 19) surfaces (if it even exists).

What happened to the Detroit encores? Well, TV-2 in Chicago broadcast a news piece that featured parts of "Black Diamond," "Beth," and the band's closing bows. Filmed from the side-left of stage, camera panning captures the over-head video screen on which the show was originally filmed to be displayed on, indicating that the full show was indeed filmed and displayed. What happened to those sections of missing film? Likely, the film was appropriated for use, such as "Beth" had been for use during the television broadcast of the People's Choice Award on February 10. Oddly, even with that footage having been available for years it did little to dull the excitement when the Cobo show surfaced. Parts of both Denver, CO (1/15) and Chicago, IL (1/22) are also available in silent 8mm video from the tour, but knowing the somewhat static set during January makes these rather less appealing, as does the "die-hard only" seizure causing quality. Amusingly, the show before Denver had been Salt Lake City on January 13. Ace, Chris Lendt, and Ed Balandas, took off for a day in Las Vegas on the 14th, rejoining the band in Denver on the afternoon of the 15th. The other members of the band took a break in Los Angeles for the day. The January 20 show in Lincoln, NE is also archived on audio. The band didn't sing "Happy Birthday" to Paul, but Ace did announce the fact to the audience following "Rock And Roll All Nite." Since no women were around, the band dressed up in drag to mark the event and provide fans with an infamous photo.

Prior to the circulation of Cobo Arena '77, the most complete and common video from the U.S. tour was KISS triumphant headlining return to New York City. Filmed at a sold-out Madison Square Garden on February 18, the full video features: "Detroit Rock City," "Take Me," "Let Me Go, Rock 'N' Roll," "Ladies Room," "Firehouse," "Makin' Love," "I Want You," "Cold Gin" (w/ Ace solo), "Do You Love Me?," "Nothin' To Lose," "God Of Thunder" (w/ Peter solo), and "Rock And Roll All Nite," "Shout It Out Loud," "Beth," and "Black Diamond." While the band have often waxed lyrical about the show being the band's homecoming and it representing the success the band had attained, the performance is sloppy at best and visually the show doesn't compare with Cobo (or the later Budokan show in April). The band celebrated at an after-show bathing party at Parc Health & Swim Club in Manhattan. Seven of the fifteen selections from the 2/18 show were released as the standard bonus disc on initial copies of KISSology Volume 1 in 2006 at least making it somewhat officially available. The band promoted the concert during an interview on local 99X radio on February 17.

Because of one event the "Winter Tour 1976/77" has attained a somewhat infamous and legendary status: As the band ripped into "Detroit Rock City" at the Lakeland Civic Center in Lakeland, FL, on December 12, Ace Frehley managed to electrocute himself and was knocked unconscious on stage when his guitar touched a non-grounded metal railing while descending the stage stairs after losing his balance. The stairs had always been a challenge for Ace, not only due to his sense of balance and awkward boots, and it wasn't unusual for Ace to appear wobbly while slowly descending to the stage. After a short delay Ace deemed himself fit, even with a slightly burned hand, to continue and the band restarted the concert. The rest of the show was not as uneventful as the band would have hoped. Gene set his hair on fire for the second time in a week... The misfortune of Ace's electric adventure wasn't totally negative (sorry, bad pun); it provided him with inspiration for some songwriting and what became "Shock Me." The electrocution incident also resulted in the band investing $25,000 in a radio microphone system, not only to solve the danger issue. KISS became one of the first bands to move to the then new wireless systems for their instruments, during the next tour, giving them additional freedom of movement on stage without further worries of grounding or cables. This sort of technology was perfect for a band who actually tried to use all of the real-estate on stage.

Following the band's U.S. tour the band took a short break before preparing for their first visit to Japan, under the guise of a "Sneak Attack" tour. This mini-tour saw the debut the stage that would be used as the foundation for the "Love Gun" tour later in the year. It was essentially a pruned down version. Many of the extraneous stage "scenes" and effects were simply cut, probably to help manage the costs involved in trucking the bits around and help manage the time it took to set up and rip down the stage. The set list also didn't change much from what had been performed during the American leg of the tour. Office memos that circulate suggest that the band were highly respectful of the vastly different culture they were going to be experiencing for the first time. Communications were traded with promoter Udo Artists asking for translations of stage raps or other phrases to allow Paul a more direct communication with the audience. However, the band was advised that it would be better to simply communicate in English and that the audience would understand it, or at least the sentiment, well enough rather than risk the awkward indirect translations. Departing from JFK in New York on Thursday, March 17, KISS arrived in Japan at 3:40pm following day, flying into Narita International in Tokyo on Pan Am flight #801, christened the "KISS Clipper."

On arrival the band was met with their first hurdle: They had planned to enter Japan wearing their make-up, however Japanese customs officials couldn't compare the band members with their passport photos. The band was escorted to a holding room where they had to remove the make-up for comparison. With that quickly completed they had to reapply their make-up to make it past the surging crowd of fans. Promoter Mr. Udo took the band and entourage for a somewhat sedate dinner that night. With the first weekend spent recuperating from travel at Tokyo's Hotel Okura, touring events didn't commence until Monday 21st. After a weekend of rest and Tokyo sight-seeing the band held a press conference at the Tokyo Hilton before departing for Osaka on All Nippon Airways in the evening.

Tuesday 22 was spent conducting interviews and a photo session with Music Life and other rock magazines. The band also conducted their first rehearsal at Osaka's Bampaku Hall (Expo Hall). Along with additional rehearsals on the 23rd, there were also meetings with the Osaka Police and Fire departments. The band played their first Japanese concert at Osaka's Kosei Nenkin Hall on March 24. The schedule for the day was essentially the same for both shows with sound checks being performed between 3 and 4pm. Opening act Bow Wow hit the stage for a short set at 6:30, followed by KISS at 7:30pm. Following the first show there was a party held for the band on top of their hotel.

On Saturday March 26, the band traveled from Osaka to Kyoto by bus. That night's performance at Kyoto's Kaikan was done without a sound check. Sunday was spent doing assorted sight-seeing and the famed photo session at the Kyoto shrines. In the evening the band took the bullet train to Nagoya. Monday's show was held at Nagoya's Aichi-Ken Taiiku-Kan venue. The schedule was the same as the Osaka shows and the band sound-checked. On March 29 the band returned to Osaka for the evening's show at the Festival Hall, which started at 7pm, but also found time for sight-seeing in the city. The next day the band flew to Fukuoka. Following a late sound-check (4:30-5:30pm) and a stage check with the local fire and police, the band played their 8pm show at Kyuden Taiiku-Kan. Gene and Paul participated in a short jam session at a local club, Honey Pot #2, after the show (Gooch/Suhs – KISS Alive Forever).

Thursday, March 31, was a day off for the band — it was spent traveling back to Tokyo by air. The band played their first show at the legendary Budokan on April Fool's Day. Saturday saw the band playing two shows, one at 4pm the other at 8pm, with television station NHK filming both for domestic broadcast. These shows were also recorded by Eddie Kramer for a planned Japanese only live album. That album would have featured: (Side A) "Detroit Rock City," "Take Me," "Ladies Room," "Do You Love Me?," "Makin' Love," and "I want You;" and (Side B) "God Of Thunder," "Cold Gin," "Beth," "Shout It Out Loud," and "Rock And Roll All Nite." Very representative of the 1976/7 set list, though "Firehouse" had been included on Side-B for a while. Following a day off on April 3, the band played their final Japanese show on April 4. Some members returned to the United States, though Gene remained in Japan. CK Lendt, Peter, and Lydia departed for a holiday in South East Asia visiting Hong Kong, Macau, and eventually Hawaii where they met up with Paul.

As "Rock And Roll Over" passed into history KISS were planning their next assault...

(Memphis, TN 1976 master tape shell — spools removed for repair, baking, and studio transfer)

October 19, 1976 - ABC Studios, Rehearsal Hall #5, Los Angeles, CA **REHEARSAL
October 20 - ABC Studios, Stage #54, Los Angeles, CA **TV-FILMING
October 21 - ABC Studios, Stage #54, Los Angeles, CA **TV-FILMING
Notes:
- The first day was simply rehearsal with the rest of the cast for the Paul Lynde Halloween special. No songs were performed "live" with the actual filming taking place on the other two days. The band, and entourage(including Sean Delaney, John Harte, Frank Scinlaro, Eddie Kramer and Tony Canal, arrived in Los Angeles on Oct. 18. Eddie Balandas, Barry Ackom and Chuck Elias arrived Oct. 17 for support logistics at rehearsals.
- The impact of the Paul Lynde TV broadcast was seminal in American pop-culture, as the Beatles-like Ed Sullivan television appearances of 1964 had been, that had hooked a whole new generation on the band (or more importantly inspired a future generation of musicians). For KISS, having survived their "Destroyer" album with the nitrous-oxide boost provided by "Beth," they were firmly entrenched in their classic period.
- "Detroit Rock City" was filmed on Oct. 20 with both "Beth" and "King of the Night Time World" the following day. The rest of the cast had been rehearsing since Oct. 13 for the special
- This brief interlude, between the end of the "Destroyer" tour (more correctly titled "Spirit of '76 Tour, Part 1"), in Springfield, MA on September 12, and start of the "CanAM Winter Tour, 1976–77" in Savannah, GA, on November 24, provides a neat segue between the two chapters in KISStory.
- Following the filming Gene, Paul and Peter returned to the East Coast on Oct. 22, while Ace and Jeanette took a week's holiday in Hawaii, returning to New York on Nov. 1.

November 7 - SIR, New York, NY **REHEARSALS
November 8 - SIR, New York, NY **REHEARSALS
November 9 - SIR, New York, NY **REHEARSALS
November 10 - SIR, New York, NY **REHEARSALS
November 11 - SIR, New York, NY **REHEARSALS
November 12 - SIR, New York, NY **REHEARSALS
240 West 54th Street
Studio Instrumental Rentals (SIR) Tour Rehearsals
Set list: Detroit Rock City / Take Me / Let Me Go, Rock 'N' Roll / Strutter / Ladies Room / Love 'Em And Leave 'Em / Firehouse / I Want You / Hard Luck Woman / Do You Love Me? / Cold Gin / Makin' Love
Notes:
- The "set list" comes from audio recordings of various rehearsals. It's a guess that these recordings were from the SIR sessions, but in a twisted bit of logic it makes sense that studio rehearsals would be recorded on audio, and stage production rehearsals on video. The songs are in various stages of completion, and some are repeated.
- The audio version is usually found in very reasonable sound-quality, though there is some fluctuation throughout the tape. Not all of these songs have made it into circulation, but it is clear that a hefty six songs from the new album were rehearsed for the new tour.
- Following this series of rehearsals the band took a brief break, including attending Lou Reed's show at the Palladium on Nov. 13, where a photographer reportedly came very close to catching all of the members unmasked.

November 15 - Redding Armory, Camp Curtis Gill, Redding, MA **REHEARSALS
November 16 - Redding Armory, Camp Curtis Gill, Redding, MA **REHEARSALS
November 17 - Redding Armory, Camp Curtis Gill, Redding, MA **REHEARSALS
November 18 - Redding Armory, Camp Curtis Gill, Redding, MA **REHEARSALS
November 19 - Redding Armory, Camp Curtis Gill, Redding, MA **REHEARSALS
November 20 - Redding Armory, Camp Curtis Gill, Redding, MA **REHEARSALS
November 21 - Redding Armory, Camp Curtis Gill, Redding, MA **REHEARSALS
Tour Production Rehearsals
Partial set list: Cold Gin / God of Thunder / Rock And Roll All Nite / Deuce / Black Diamond / Love 'Em And Leave 'Em / I Want You / Hard Luck Woman
Notes:
- Video recordings of these rehearsals circulate.
- During these production rehearsals the band filmed lip-synced versions of "I Want You," "Beth" and "Love 'Em And Leave 'Em" for use as promotional videos internationally. For many in the U.S. their first viewing of these were when they were broadcast on Don Kirshner's "New" Rock Concert with over-dubbed audience on May 28, 1977.

November 24 - Civic Center, Savannah, GA
Promoter: Alex Cooley, Inc.
Other act(s): Graham Parker & The Rumor
Reported audience: 8,000 **SOLD-OUT
Reported gross: $60,000
Notes:
- The opening night of the "Winter Tour 1976/77" in support of the "Rock And Roll Over" album. KISS flew to Savannah the day prior to this show. "Beth" was performed as the second encore marking the first public live performance of the song.
- British rocker Graham Parker was breaking out in 1976, with "The Rumor" including Brinsley Schwartz (guitar) and Bob Andrews (keyboards). Their album, "Heat Treatment," was considered one of the best of 1976 by mainstream media.
- From a local review: "KISS epitomized bizarre. This reviewer was totally 'bizarred-out' by the group's performance. Of course, KISS' music is pedantically pedestrian in that the group's repertoire lacks and semblance of imagination. But their stage theatrics? Mind-boggling! KISS pulled out all the old stops. The flaming guitar replete with excruciating feedback... strobe-like effects with multi-colored confetti being strewn about by massive blowers... a battery of flame-throwing cannons... and the neon KISS logo... *ad nauseum*... In spite of their shortcomings, the members of KISS know how to please their audience" (Savannah Morning News, 11/26/76).

November 25 - Charlotte Coliseum, Charlotte, NC
Promoter: Kaleidoscope Productions
Other act(s): Jesse Bolt
Reported audience: ~13,000 (13,000 capacity)
Notes:
- From a local review: "The whole affair seemed unreal. Here was a rock group that has had little national exposure (few adults have ever heard of it) filling the Coliseum at $6 a ticket... The music was heavy, metallic and deafening. It played upon the youth fears and fantasies: sex, drugs, violence and destruction... Whoever dreamed up this combination concert-stage show knew what he was doing. It was designed to appeal to the hungers of youth and their

desire to escape the demands and oppressions of the real world... In idolizing the members of KISS, young people are responding to a power that delivers them not from fears of the past but from those of the future. After a KISS concert, reality seems to be less threatening" (Charlotte Observer, 11/27/76).

November 27 - J.S. Dorton Arena, Raleigh, NC
Promoter: Kaleidoscope Productions
Other act(s): Raisen Band
Reported audience: ~10,000 (7,000 capacity)

November 28 - Memorial Auditorium, Greenville, SC
Promoter: Kaleidoscope Productions
Other act(s): Climax Blues Band
Reported audience: ~7,000 **SOLD-OUT
Notes:
- From a local review: "When KISS takes the stage, they put on a show. A circus. A carnival side-show... While KISS attacks the crowd with its high-volume music, smoke bombs go off, flares fire to the ceiling, a guitar explodes, a guitar is broken into pieces and flung at the crowd, 10-foot letters spelling 'KISS' light up and four-foot mortars fire confetti into the frenzied crowd... And the crowd — the KISS Army — loves it" (Greenville Piedmont, 11/29/77).
- Less than 2 minutes worth of silent 8mm footage circulates from this show.

November 30 - Municipal Auditorium, Columbus, GA
Promoter: Bash Productions
Other act(s): Tom Petty and the Heartbreakers
Reported audience: (5,265 capacity)

December 2 - Mid-South Coliseum, Memphis, TN
Promoter: Mid-South Concerts/Beaver Productions
Other act(s): Dr. Hook
Reported audience: 12,000 **SOLD-OUT
Reported gross: $73,250
Set list: Detroit Rock City / Take Me / Let Me Go, Rock 'N Roll / Strutter / Ladies Room / Firehouse / I Want You / Hard Luck Woman / Do You Love Me? / Cold Gin / God of Thunder / Rock And Roll All Nite / Beth / Makin' Love / Black Diamond
Notes:
- Ex-James Gang/Deep Purple guitarist Tommy Bolin was initially advertized as the opening act in late-November, before being replaced. Opting to instead open for Peter Frampton and the legendary Jeff Beck in Florida, Bolin died from an overdose of multiple substances on Dec. 4.
- From a local review: "A KISS performance, like the one last night at the Mid-South Coliseum, is not so much a concert as it is a constant stream of short pellets of sound and images... Multi-colored lights bounce off the coliseum walls. Explosions. Smoke. Nobody's sitting down. Every chair is filled with feet... The music is as thick as the red, silver, black and white makeup the band wears. Gut level rock and roll with no quarter asked or given" (Memphis Commercial Appeal, 12/3/76).

- The only complete show from early in the tour that currently circulates — as an average AUD recording. This concert is interesting from another point of view: Issues with the audience interrupted the show several times culminating in the local Fire Marshall taking to the stage at one point. The first interruption occurs after "Take Me" with an announcement being made for the audience to clear the aisles. Apparently the request didn't work and following "Firehouse" there is a several minute delay with the announcer pleading for the audience to comply or the fire-marshal was going to stop the show. As it's the earliest recording known from the tour it provides the earliest known concert recordings of "Take Me," "I Want You," "Ladies Room," and "Makin' Love." The last of these songs started out in an encore position in the set before being re-sequenced to the end of the first third of the show. "Ladies Room" also features a slightly different arrangement, including a breakdown, almost sing-a-long section, on the final chorus. The song soon returned to a form closer to the album recording and more familiar to the fans, but still needed more cowbell. With the guitar style of "I Want You" it's not surprising that "Hard Luck Woman" followed it in the set. The performance is very much a band effort with more obvious backing vocals, notably from Paul. However, Peter sounds very much into performing the song, though it really did slow the set down. Paul seems almost confrontational as he introduces "Rock And Roll All Nite" telling the audience to get up off their seats.

December 3 - Coliseum, Jackson, MS
Promoter: Beaver Productions
Other act(s): Dr. Hook
Reported audience: ~12,000 (7,500 capacity)
Partial set list: Detroit Rock City / Take Me / Firehouse / I Want You / Rock And Roll All Nite / Black Diamond
Notes:
- Partially captured on Super8 (roughly 15 minutes) silent video allowing for the identification of certain songs in the set.
- Paul was interviewed in his hotel following the show for a review in the Clarion-Ledger.

December 4 - Municipal Auditorium, New Orleans, LA
Promoter: Beaver Productions
Other act(s): Blackfoot
Reported audience: (9,000 capacity)
Partial set list: Detroit Rock City / Take Me / Let Me Go, Rock 'N' Roll / Firehouse / Do You Love Me? / Ladies Room / Hard Luck Woman / I Want You / God of Thunder / Cold Gin / Rock And Roll All Nite / Beth / Makin' Love / Black Diamond
Notes:
- This show features one of the final contemporary electric performances of "Hard Luck Woman," a song that was only included in the band's set for a short time during Nov/Dec 1976.
- While the below average audience recording is incomplete, it does provide a second example of "Hard Luck Woman" performed live.
- Roughly 20 minutes of 8mm footage from this show circulates.

December 5 - Municipal Auditorium, Mobile, AL
Promoter: Beaver Productions
Reported audience: (10,200 capacity)

December 7 - Von Braun Civic Center, Huntsville, AL
Promoter: Sound Seventy Productions
Other act(s): Dr. Hook
Reported audience: ~8,738
Notes:
- The first 3,000 tickets for the show were discounted at $6, with the remaining going for $7.50 day-of-show rate.

December 8 - Macon Coliseum, Macon, GA
Promoter: Alex Cooley Inc.
Other act(s): Uriah Heep
Reported audience: 8,000 / 10,242 (78.11%)
Reported gross: $50,000
Notes:
- First show with Uriah Heep opening. This performance would mark John Lawton and Trevor Bolder's debut with Heep.
- From a local review: "A teacher friend was wondering Wednesday how many of her students wouldn't show up Thursday because they might have been arrested. It seems all most all of her ninth-grade class was planning on attending the KISS concert at the Macon Coliseum that evening" (Macon News, 12/10/76).

December 10 - Coliseum, Jacksonville, FL
Promoter: Kaleidoscope Productions
Other act(s): Uriah Heep
Reported audience: 10,000 **SOLD-OUT
Notes:
- This show was reported as sold out in advance.
- From a local review: "KISS and Uriah Heep played to a capacity crowd of nearly 12,000 people at the Coliseum Friday night. Their fans loved it and, surprisingly, so did the parents who brought them. The hall was filled to the hilt with concertgoers sporting KISS T-shirts, carrying KISS posters, and a number of them wearing bizarre make-up closely resembling that of their rock 'n' roll idols — you just weren't 'in' if you didn't have some form of KISS paraphernalia in your possession" (Times-Union And Journal, 12/12/76).

December 11 - Sportatorium, Miami, FL
Promoter: Kaleidoscope Productions
Other act(s): Uriah Heep
Reported audience: 12,943 / 15,500 (78.44%)
Reported gross: $91,323

December 12 - Civic Center Arena, Lakeland, FL
Promoter: Kaleidoscope Productions
Other act(s): Uriah Heep
Reported audience: 10,000 **SOLD-OUT
Partial set list: Detroit Rock City
Notes:
- At this concert Ace was famously electrocuted when touching an ungrounded handrail while descending to the stage. After a short delay the show restated. "When Frehley

touched the railing to help himself come down, he completed an electrical circuit with his guitar and was unable to move. He finally fell several feet to the stage floor but was miraculously unhurt. He went to his dressing room for about 10 minutes and returned to a standing ovation, as the crowd chanted his name" (Charles M. Young, Rolling Stone Magazine).

- The incident led to the band using radio mics to free themselves from completing electrical circuits and remove cables as hindrances during their performances. Within months New York based company Ken Schaffer Group, Inc. had seen a massive increase in acts moving to their wireless Schaffer-Vega Diversity System.

- Gene also set his hair on fire during the show...

December 15 - Memorial Auditorium, Buffalo, NY
Promoter: Festival East Inc.
Other act(s): Uriah Heep
Reported audience: 12,182 / 18,000 (67.68%)
Reported gross: $75,274

December 16 - Onondaga War Memorial, Syracuse, NY
Promoter: Concerts East
Other act(s): Uriah Heep
Reported audience: ~9,200 (SRO)
Partial set list: Firehouse / Do You Love Me? / Beth
Notes:

- From a local review: "KISS entertained a wildly fanatic SRO Memorial Auditorium audience last night with flaming torches, blinding flash pots, thunderous explosions, a snowstorm of confetti, animal antics, and some rock 'n' roll. Music is not the group's specialty spectacles are. KISS is a four-'man' rock group presently enjoying a cresting wave in its career. Members of the group paint their faces with silver, black-and-white makeup and wear black costumes. The group has a fan club called 'KISS Army' and the audience was strewn with KISS Army banners. A few followers painted their faces like the entertainers. The fans got what they wanted last night, a rock show managing to upstage old Alice Cooper and a wild, rollicking rock 'n' roll blitz. The audience was so delighted it called KISS back for four count 'em four encores. 'Beth.' their Top 40 hit, was performed by Peter Criss, the drummer, for the fourth encore. It's a very nice song, with meaning in the lyrics and a good musical score. Unfortunately, none of the other rock music played last night fell into that category. The point is KISS can do some good rock when it wants to, and Ace Frehley (who was made up to resemble something to do with space) is an excellent guitarist. He performed a genuine "acid" rock solo.

The crowd came for the spectacle, and that's what they got. Gene Simmons, disguised as a ghoulish spider-man, excited the audience with his antics goose-stepping around in his knee-high, silver elevator shoes. Paul Stanley, dressed half 'n' half (female and male), does most of the lead singing. He treated fans to pieces of his guitar after he smashed it to smithereens on the stage opting there for one of the more traditional rock spectacles. Watching a performer smash an expensive guitar always excites fans and makes some in the audience wish they could get the instrument in one piece for a souvenir. Peter Criss choose to be made up as a cat. He is the drummer whom the audience sees little of until the grand finale. The stage fills with a foggy groundcover of smoke, as his individual drum stage elevates about 20 feet above the stage and a giant demoniacal banner depicting his made-up face unrolls. The fans roared so loud the group's music was virtually smothered in shrieks.

Other spectacles in the show included a guitar which spewed out little fire-rockets and ignited into flames. Gene Simmons blew fire from his mouth. But, the most startling spectacles were the giant torches, which spewed 20-foot columns of flame in the air. Many of the fire stunts highlighted a song entitled — appropriately enough, 'Firefly.' Thousands showed up by 6 p.m., and auditorium officials let them in the hall at 6:30 p.m., one-half hour early, 'to keep them from getting restless in the streets.' The fans loved every second of the show and rewarded KISS with countless standing ovations. The audience said it all during the chorus of KISS' song 'Do You Love Me?' They screamed, 'Yes.' Uriah Heap opened the concert" (Syracuse Herald Journal, 12/17/76, Terry Lee).

December 18 - Memorial Coliseum, New Haven, CT
Promoter: Cross Country Concert Corp.
Other act(s): Uriah Heep
Reported audience: 9,300 / 11,171 (83.25%)
Reported gross: $66,828
Notes:
- KISS received a $20,000 guarantee for this show. A show at Boston Gardens was originally scheduled on this day.

December 19 - Capital Centre, Largo (Landover), MD
Promoter: Cellar Door Presents
Other act(s): Bob Seger
Reported audience: **SOLD-OUT (18,500 capacity)
Notes:
- Rumored to exist as a pro-shot house feed video.
- On the day of show this concert was noted as being close to a sell-out, so likely was with walk-ups. A brief review in the Washington Star noted an audience of more than 19,000.

December 21 - The Spectrum, Philadelphia, PA
Promoter: Electric Factory Concerts
Other act(s): Bob Seger
Reported audience: 19,500 **SOLD-OUT
Notes:
- This show was advertized as a WFIL charity gig. A collection for toys/gifts for distribution to local hospitals was also held by the radio station at the show.
- From a local review: "KISS has ceased to be a musical group it is a cult with a devoted following which approaches a near religious fervor. Last night the group appeared for the first time at the Spectrum and it was a sell-out. Although the concert was led off by Bob Seeger and Silver Bullet, It was clear early in the going the only attraction which mattered to the people in attendance was KISS. The first thing you notice about the followers of this cultural and musical force is the age. The average age seemed to be the early to mid teens. The second thing you noticed was the absolute devotion they hold for the foursome who wear makeup which make them appear to be more demonic than spiritual leaden. But leaders they are in an esoteric revolt of sorts. A revolt by the young against mores of their

parents. A reverence of the idol of 'King Rock' and the highs and devil-may-care social aura which surrounds it. In its present concept it is all good clean fun. A catharsis whereas the young followers can relieve their frustrations during a thunderous two-hour-plus concert.

If you place KISS on a scale with music on one side and show on the other the scale would have to dip rapidly to the show side. Musically they are an average to slightly-above-average hard rock band but where they surpass any group not playing is in their visual presentation. Flames and smoke seem to shoot from everywhere during the course of a KISS concert. The company manufacturing flash pods will forever be in their debt and the mayhem inflicted upon their guitars is keeping one Japanese firm in business. The group is larger than life to its followers and the process begins with costuming. The members across the stage in stacked platform shoes which automatically give them a surrealistic menacing demeanor. Moving upwards, they feature the skin-tight trappings of most of the performers of the glitter-rock genre but they top this all off with clown white-face makeup. But clowns they are not. The bass player looks more like a lizard with a medical-record-long tongue flicking almost perversely out at the audience. Then you have a feline character and another who almost appears a mixture of he/she. Picture these three prancing around on the front of the stage like a leftover from a bad dream provoked by a pepperoni pizza late at night and you have some idea of the visual image of the group. Then you have the music. It is pure derivative three to four chord rock and roll. It is nothing spectacular but it is tight and it provides a good background for the well-though-out stage movements or vice versa.

The music is constantly driving, the lyrics are of the same rebellious nature as the performers. When you place the music, the theatrics and the pyrotechnics together, it makes for an awe-inspiring and engaging presentation. It is hard to resist the groups' flair. It never ceases working to draw the audience into the show. Because of the outlandishness of the groups' dress and antics, it is easy to go into the concert with a negative attitude about their talent. But its talent lies in a multifaceted grey area. It is more than just another rock band. They are entertainers, manipulators and above all innovators. KISS has its army now but next year it should be the hottest thing on the rock market and then its fans will be legions (John Fisher, Courier Times, 12/22/76).
- Following the show the band and crew headed off for a brief Christmas break.

December 27 - Cumberland County Memorial Arena, Fayetteville, NC
Promoter: Beach Club Promotions
Other act(s): Blackfoot
Reported audience: (7,000 capacity)

December 28 - Roanoke Civic Center, Roanoke, VA
Promoter: Entam, Ltd.
Other act(s): Uriah Heep
Reported audience: 11,000 **SOLD-OUT
Notes:
- From a local review: "Their opening chords — the only three they know — were punctuated by deafening explosions and propane jets spewing flames to the ceiling while smoke enveloped them in an eerie green glow. Unfortunately, the smoke blew away, revealing Gene Simmons... Simmons is the token obscenity for the group. He didn't stand; he crouched with legs far apart, gesturing lewdly to the crowd with an incredibly long tongue that could catch flies... It's a good thing KISS can put on a show because their music

is pure garbage. It is somewhat like trying to make a jack-hammer a musical instrument" (Roanoke World News, 12/29/76).

December 30 - Civic Center, Augusta, ME
Promoter: Ruffino & Vaughn Productions
Other act(s): Uriah Heep
Reported audience: 7,198 **SOLD-OUT
Notes:
- This show was the venue's third fastest sell-out (at the time) behind only Lawrence Welk (1972) and Bob Dylan (1975). It would also have been a victory for local fans since the venue managers felt that the location wasn't suitable for rock concerts and few promoters had been willing to take a chance on a show.
- From a local review: "Hailed by a roaring crowd of stomping, screaming fans, KISS crashed their way onto a smoky stage at the Augusta Civic Center Thursday night. The teen-age crowd shrieked in delight as lights flashed and torches, flamed under eerie stage lights. The KISS members, leaping in mid-air in knee boots with five-inch heels, rocked and writhed in ghastly glee. Vampire-like Gene Simmons and sex symbol Paul Stanley dominated the stage as they stalked back and forth, teasing the audience before them. Simmons, dressed in silver hip boots with dragon heads for feet, shook his Chinaman's topknot and waved his tongue invitingly to the crowd reaching up to him. Stanley, his shirt slit to the waist, pranced around brandishing a glittering, sequin covered guitar. 'Space' Ace Frehley, attired Moon-man style, rocketed around the stage waving a star-studded head. Only drummer Peter Criss, the feline figure, remained stationary throughout the fiery performance, flanked by two huge stone cats.

The crowd, reacting with contented roars to the music pumped out by the quartet, jumped in the air and clapped loudly at the group's theatrics. It was evident that the KISS appeal is due not so much to their hard-pounding, heavy beat rock, as their circus style. At the climax of one song, Simmons blew a huge bolt of fire out of his mouth, a famous trick which precipitated similar attempts by members of the audience. The vampire star also spit blood over the crowd later, while lurking in a greenish glow atop a castle-like structure. Paul Stanley, yelling 'Do you want me?' to upturned faces, strutted alluringly around the stage during one number. Then, much to the girls' delight stripped his skin-tight suit from the upper half of his body. Bending himself over the edge of the stage, he let hundreds of fans' fingers touch his body. Stanley cried, "I love you to death, handsome people here tonight."

Violence and destruction were woven into the freakish show throughout, as KISS stomped menacingly and belted out loud, raucous rock. At one point, following a whining guitar solo, 'Space' Ace Frehley's instrument belched smoke and spit sparks over those standing below. In an unexpected move, Frehley stuck his guitar on a pedestal and set it afire. In a similar destructive display, Stanley smashed his guitar and threw it into the wildly waving audience as a souvenir. Toward the evening's end, tension heightened in the expectant crowd, which was aware of the spectacular stage shows with which KISS culminates their concerts. More and more colored lights passed kaleidoscopically over the group, turning their silver and black bodies, garish green and bright fuchsia. Multi-colored confetti streamed down, as a huge neon 'KISS' sign blinked and flashed. The energy of the group equaled that expressed in their music's thundering tone, which built to a feverish pitch toward the end.

Stanley, obvious spokesman for his cohorts, screamed, 'You know we ain't never been here before and you don't know what to expect when you haven't been to a place. But now I know this is the rock and roll capital of Maine!' The clamorous chords the group belted out were stilled only once during the evening, when Criss sat alone on a stool and sang his hit, 'Beth.' The 7,000-plus in attendance were hushed as the bewhiskered drummer crooned to the crowd in a husky, gravelly voice. "Beth", performed with one singer seated quietly onstage — stood isolated from the rest of the performance. It was KISS' way of proving that even though their style is so unique in the rock world today, they can do the unexpected by giving a more conventional performance.

There was no doubt, however, as KISS exploded with stupendous stage effects in their finale, that the group's success is directly due to their outrageous actions and demented demeanor. A freak show or a three-ring circus has always attracted curious crowds, and KISS uses the formula to its fullest. It was bound to happen the wildest, spaciest group ever has created the craziest rock show of all" (Kennebec Journal, 12/31/76).
- It was reported in the press that KISS had "sold-out the first 22 dates of its ongoing U.S. tour in advance, grossing some $1.6 million from an attendance of 233,763" (Billboard, 1/29/77). However, reported box office numbers from the period paint a slightly less spectacular picture of attendance (still excellent, but less hyperbolic). Between Nov. 24 and Dec. 30 the band received $395,000 in guarantees and an additional $168,954 from gate percentages.
- Sold-out capacity reported as 7,198 in a Waterville, ME Sentinel newspaper article, 1/9/82.

January 1, 1977 - Civic Center, Providence, RI
Promoter: Concerts East/Mark Puma
Other act(s): Uriah Heep
Reported audience: (13,082 capacity)
Set list: Detroit Rock City / Take Me / Let Me Go, Rock 'N' Roll / Ladies Room / Firehouse / Makin' Love / I Want You / Cold Gin / Do You Love Me? / Nothin' To Lose / God of Thunder / Rock And Roll All Nite / Shout It Out Loud / Beth / Black Diamond
- Notes: This show established the "standard" set for the tour, though it's not currently known at what point during December the band had finally settled on this sequence. "Natural Gas" is noted in some early paperwork as the proposed opening act.
- This show circulates as an AUD recording though the end of "Black Diamond" cuts.

January 5 - Taylor Coliseum, Abilene, TX
Promoter: Stone City Attractions
Other act(s): Uriah Heep
Reported audience: 8,956 **SOLD-OUT
Reported gross: $63,000
Notes:
- KISS beat the then house record at the venue that had been held by Elvis and Lawrence Welk. One newspaper article suggested an audience of 9,016. Break-even for the promoter at the venue was generally 6,500. Performance Magazine reported the audience at 8,500 of 8,946 (1/28/77).
- One local "Letter to the Editor" suggested poor organization at the concert and indifference by local authorities. Ticket availability had been delayed following the show being announced (Abilene Reporter-News, 12/19/76).

- A local review of the show: "'The hottest band in the land' they call themselves: KISS, the biggest rock group ever to hit Abilene. They proved it, too, by drawing the biggest crowd the Taylor County Coliseum has ever hosted 9,000 fans, more than even the Elvis Presley concert drew. The KISS fans earned the name 'fans,' reminding us this word is from the same root as the word fanatic. They were frantic — screaming, yelling, cheering, dancing, climbing on each other's shoulders, building human pyramids, crushing those on the front row against the stage and convincing KISS to return for four encores.

I'm not basically a rock fan. I listen mostly, depending on the mood I'm in, to 17th-century chamber music or country and western. Now that's a wide variety, but my tastes never really included rock. Oh, I like the groups on the edge of the dividing line between pop and rock, the group's hard rock fans might call 'bubble gum' like K.C. and the Sunshine Band. But I've never seen the point in hard rock until I heard KISS. Since I don't have a background as a rock music fan, I was not very familiar with most of KISS' songs. I can't name the songs they played, and I very seldom understood the lyrics but it doesn't matter. You don't go to a KISS concert for the lyrics. KISS, Paul Stanley had said, is a party. It's audience participation music. Few if any fans go to a KISS concert to simply sit and listen. In fact, the concert is so designed that it's almost impossible to just sit and listen no matter how hard you try.

KISS' music is not even meant to be listened to, really: not in the usual sense anyway. It is more to be felt. At a KISS concert, you feel the music in two nays literally, through vibrations, and figuratively, through the reaction it causes inside you. There's as much to look at as to listen to with KISS, even if it were not for the interesting spectacle the fans create. KISS skillfully employs thousands of dollars worth of lighting, sets and special effects equipment, creating the most impressive sound and light show I've seen anywhere. Spectacle is the name of their game, and they play it well. Banks of flashing lights, dozens of colored spotlights, six carbon arc spotlights, smoke and fire machines, explosions and even simulated snow were used to create the moods KISS wanted to convey.

The fans were a show in themselves. Since I have had very little experience with rock concerts, I felt very conspicuous and out of place. I stood silently against the wall all night (I never found even one empty seat) just watching. I know half the kids thought I was the local nark. The fans were mostly young certainly more high school than college age. Representatives from all the predominant high school social groups were present the 'freaks,' those one would expect to see at a rock concert; several cowboys; and several of the super-straight, 'clean-cut,' average-kid-next-door types. Most were not dressed in any unusual way, but there were a few strange costumes present. At least three young men had on make-up modeled after the group's make-up.

KISS did, as they promised they would, put on a great show. Taken out of context, many of the group's antics seem strange. But in the context of a concert, everything seems to fit. Everything seems calculated and well planned. Gene Simmons played his satanic lizard image untiringly, always moving in an inhuman crouch, displaying his famous long tongue, and even making a show of vomiting blood. Peter Criss, whose make-up suggests a cat, seemed to fit that image very well always quiet and cool. Paul Stanley, who sang lead more often than any of the others, spent most of the night performing impressive athletic leaps as he sang. Ace Frehley, surprisingly, was the least noticeable, least memorable of the group.

KISS was always sensitive to the audience, felling them out and trying to give them exactly what they wanted. As they went into their series of encores, each time making the audience reach exactly the level of frenzied cheering they wanted before they would return to the stage, everyone seemed to be pretty sure they would come back each time. But then, they weren't really sure. KISS managed to plant enough doubt with them that they did give the frenzied cheers, and light up the coliseum with cigarette lighters to beg the group to come back on. I thought I was going to be disappointed and not get to hear the one KISS song I would recognize Peter Criss' atypical 'Beth.' He sang it, but he saved it for just the right moment the second encore.

As we made the mass exodus to the overflowing parking lot, and as each driver fended for himself to get through the traffic jam (beats me why no police were sent to direct traffic for the largest crowd ever to fill the coliseum maybe they were all busy inside, trying to find a little marijuana), I no longer felt like I didn't belong there. We all had something in common. We had all experienced KISS" (Robert Williams - Abilene Reporter-News, 1/6/77).

And another: "KISS concert traffic orderly, no marijuana arrests made. Lt. Grover Chronister, who was in charge of the police detail al the Taylor County Coliseum Wednesday night during the KISS concert, said the city does not assign police to direct traffic from the parking lot at that time of night. 'The traffic at 11 or 12 at night... all you have is just people leaving.' Once they get on the road, he said, traffic is manageable because at that time of the night, few other people are on the road. Police on duty during a concert are hired by the performers to keep order. Chronister explained. 'When you have 10,000 (in the audience), there's no way you can get out of there in a hurry,' Chronister said 'I know they have a real problem. (But) if we had men working (traffic), it would be a real problem.'

'They didn't start to leave until after 11,' Chronister said. By midnight, when he left, the parking lot was cleared, he said. As for marijuana arrests during concerts, Chronister had told a reporter on Wednesday that making such arrests are incidental to the main purpose of keeping order and safely. The officers don't go looking for people smoking marijuana, he said. But if they notice illegal smoking they do make arrests, he said. There were no arrests for marijuana possession at the KISS concert, police reported" (Abilene Reporter-News, 1/6/77).

January 6 - Assembly Center, Tulsa, OK
Promoter: Concerts West
Other act(s): Uriah Heep
Reported audience: (8,994 capacity)

January 7 - Lloyd Noble Center @ University of Oklahoma, Norman, OK
Promoter: Concerts West
Other act(s): Uriah Heep
Reported audience: (12,540 capacity) **SOLD-OUT
Notes:
- From a local review: "It was the heavy metal children's hour at Lloyd Noble Arena Friday night as KISS assaulted a sellout crowd (average age about 15) with blinding light and ear-splitting explosions. The audience was on its feet throughout this sweaty rock and roll circus

and on the main floor spectators danced and swayed precariously on folding chairs, as the painted, leather-clad quartet performed their usual brand of raucous three-chord music" (Oklahoma Journal, 1/9/77).

January 9 - Henry Levitt Arena, Wichita, KS
Promoter: Feyline Inc.
Other act(s): Uriah Heep
Reported audience: 10,886 **SOLD-OUT
Reported gross: $76,202

January 10 - Civic Center Auditorium, Amarillo, TX
Promoter: Feyline Productions
Other act(s): Uriah Heep
Reported audience: 7,875 **SOLD-OUT
Reported gross: $55,439

January 11 - Tingley Coliseum, Albuquerque, NM
Promoter: Feyline Productions
Other act(s): Uriah Heep
Reported audience: 9,671 / 15,800 (61.21%)
Reported gross: $68,500
Partial set list: I Want You / Do You Love Me? / Beth
Notes:
- A local review of the show: "Almost filled to capacity, Tingley Coliseum Tuesday night was transformed into an arena for members of the KISS Army thousands of Albuquerque teenagers out to take part in a spectacle that included fire pods belching flames 15 feet into the air, mist, confetti and a barrage of well-executed lights. Hosts for the evening were four creatures from New York City that call themselves KISS, decked in heavy silver and black leather with matching face makeup. Their stage was a small planet of gray-black rock and castle facades and slimy trees beneath multicolored rays. Their form of communication was heavy metal rock, a forceful part of the package designed to build the KISS Army of fans and make the group a success. 'I Want You' wasn't a love song, but a recruitment for the KISS Army. The repeated line in 'Do You Love Me?' was more an order than a question and only slightly more subtle than if KISS had asked 'Do You Love Us?'

The numbers that moved along the ego-fantasy of KISS were variations of hard rock riffs with fewer than a handful standing out as more than trashy. The exception was the KISS hit, 'Beth,' which seemed out of place with its slower pace, lack of action and lack of lights. Drummer Peter Criss was the sole performer, rasping out the vocals to the accompaniment of track tapes. But the boundless energy of the performers and the visual effects were otherwise engrossing and apparently successful in transporting the excited crowd to the fantasy plane. The gimmicks blue and orange lightning streaks, smoke, mists, firecrackers, bright bulbs flashing a gigantic 'KISS' and a hydraulically levitated drum stand at times were incredibly effective. It was easy to see why some acts refuse to follow KISS in a concert. Opening act Uriah Heap's rock-out faded quickly in the shadow of KISS glitter. But sooner or later reality will hit the KISS fantasy planet. To survive, KISS will have to develop real music that can stand alone without the lights" (Albuquerque Journal, 1/13/77).

January 13 - Salt Palace, Salt Lake City, UT
Promoter: United Concerts/KCPX
Other act(s): Uriah Heep
Reported audience: 13,700 **SOLD-OUT
Notes:
- Following this show Ace, Chris Lendt, and Eddie Balandas flew to Las Vegas. Paul, Peter, Gene, Paul Mozian, and John Harte went to Los Angeles for the day off. All flew into Denver on the afternoon of January 15.
- 13,700 tickets were put on sale and around 13,400 had sold by January 10 with the unsold tickets being returned to the box office for direct sale.
- From a local review: "A group called KISS performed to a capacity crowd last night at the Salt Palace. Given the average age of the crowd, 13, the answer is even simpler than the questions. While a baby fears falling, and a toddler fears not being loved, today's teenager has only one great fear — the fear of BEING BORED. Anyone who ever doodled through a high school study hall wishing the minute hand were a second hand, so the hour would fly by faster, knows boredom... Not for one minute, not for one second last night was KISS ever boring" (The Deseret News, 1/14/77).
- From a local review: "A KISS show is a series of gimmicks geared to one with a short attention span, i.e., young. Gimmicks is a dirty word in the rock world these days, but it's also entertainment. I doubt there was a genuinely spontaneous move made by and of the members throughout the show. It was as choreographed as 'The Nutcracker,' but the audience knows and expects it. If Simmons had decided *not* to spit blood that night, we would have all felt cheated" (Daily Utah Chronicle, 1/17/77).

January 15 - McNichols Arena, Denver, CO
Promoter: Feyline Productions
Other act(s): Uriah Heep
Reported audience: 16,137 / 17,344 (93.04%)
Reported gross: $110,900
Set list: Detroit Rock City / Take Me / Let Me Go, Rock 'N' Roll / Ladies Room / Firehouse / Makin' Love / I Want You / Cold Gin / Do You Love Me? / Nothin' to Lose / God of Thunder / Rock And Roll All Nite / Shout It Out Loud / Beth / Black Diamond
Notes:
- Partially captured on Super8 silent video in addition to AUD. There are cuts in both "God of Thunder" and during Peter's drum solo.

January 17 - University of North Dakota, Grand Forks, ND
Promoter: Ken Brandt
Other act(s): Uriah Heep
Reported audience: 6,800 **SOLD-OUT

January 18 - Arena, Duluth, MN
Promoter: Vanquish Productions
Other act(s): Uriah Heep
Reported audience: (7,765 capacity)

January 20 - Pershing Auditorium, Lincoln, NE
Promoter: Feyline Productions

Other act(s): Uriah Heep
Reported audience: 8,387 **SOLD-OUT
Reported gross: $57,605
Set list: Detroit Rock City / Take Me / Let Me Go, Rock 'N' Roll / Ladies Room / Firehouse / Makin' Love / I Want You / Cold Gin / Do You Love Me? / Nothin' To Lose / God of Thunder / Rock And Roll All Nite / Shout It Out Loud / Beth / Black Diamond
Notes:
- The band didn't sing "Happy Birthday" to Paul on this occasion, but Ace did announce Paul's birthday to the audience following "Rock And Roll All Nite." Since no women were around, the band dressed up in drag to mark the event and provide fans with an infamous photo.
- A local review of the show: "It's easy to tell when something weird is coming down, but harder to define what it is. A sell-out crowd came to Pershing Auditorium Thursday night to hear KISS, a hard rock band short on talent and long on hype. I didn't understand what I saw there. Why a 14-year old girl would stomp a beer bottle to bits then kick the pieces at strangers I can t grasp why people enjoy tossing flashcubes at the performers. But a lot of people enjoy this band. As early as 3:30pm Thursday, people were waiting outside the auditorium for the concert five hours away. The crowd that eventually filled the place was young, mostly between the ages of 10 and 20. I listened to this crowd. I heard it get more aroused over smoke bomb explosions and fire-breathing stunts than the music. And I realized I didn't know what rock means anymore. This music is meant to impress rather than express emotion. I don't know what happens when a band makes it because it thinks of new ways to be disgusting or because it has the most cornea-searing light show. I wonder what's the limit? KISS performed here last year, another packed house. They have two hit singles — "I Want to Rock and Roll All Night (And Party Every Day)" and "Beth." KISS is one of the few successful practitioners left of what was once called "heavy metal" rock. The music is guitar driven. The sound is muddy but the rhythm will throb your body if you stand still long enough. The band has its models: Gene Simmons busts his guitar to smithereens, something Pete Townsend of The Who used to do. Paul Stanley can rasp deliveries a la Robert Plant of Led Zeppelin, as if sandpaper covered his larynx.

But the music is not the point, the stage show is if it weren't for the greasepaint fire bombs fog screens sirens twirling cheery tops and blinking roller-dome lights KISS would be out on the street, driving cabs in Peoria. KISS has things no one else has. It has Gene Simmons' tongue. When he waggles it about it almost curls under his chin. When KISS appeared on Paul Lynde's Halloween special Simmons was forbidden to stick it out. Simmons can leer better than Snydley Whiplash. His samurai topknot and makeup make him look properly revolting. During one song, Simmons, while mugging disdainfully at the audience, chomped down his teeth and red liquid squirted over his face. Another time, he appeared to suck in fire from a torch, then flame it out his mouth. Stanley kept the audience in frenzy between the numbers by shooting forth this rock-and-roll savior rap, its fervor matching that of a Fire Holiness Baptized Pentecostal evangelist "I know there are people out there who are a little high," he rasps. "YEEEEAAAAH!" says the crowd. "I know some of you have had a little alcohol. Southern Comfort? Tequila?" Judging by the volume of the roar, tequila won hands down" (Deb Gray - Lincoln Star, 1/22/77).

January 21 - Veterans Memorial Coliseum, Des Moines, IA
Promoter: Celebration Productions

Other act(s): Uriah Heep
Reported audience: 14,234 **SOLD-OUT
Reported gross: $93,146
Notes:
- A local review of the show: "KISS is a misnomer. Bludgeon is more like it. KISS is a flat-out, screaming, shattering rock band. Unfortunately, for all their energy, they play really lousy music. No doubt most of the 14,500 young folks who crammed Veterans Memorial Auditorium Friday night would bristle at that. Most of them, on the short end of the 10-to-20-year-old age bracket, thought they were really having a good time. But KISS, one of the country's hottest hard-rock groups, was all theater. Music isn't really part of the show, the smoke bombs, flashing lights and torches were all well and good, but the group bills itself as a musical entourage. The quality of music displayed at the auditorium was about what one would expect from a $100-a-night bar band that had been together a couple of months. It was dominated by the same, two- and three-chord guitar leads, unoriginal bass playing and unheard drumming - interesting, since percussionist Peter Criss had spread before him an array that included no less than eight tom-toms.

The sad part of it all is that KISS apparently can play well, as evidenced by two current hits - "Beth" and "Hard Luck Woman," both palatable tunes. But art is obviously not where KISS is at. Money is. They sold out the hall, at $6.50 a ticket, several days in advance. Tony Abramovich, the auditorium manager, said the crowd was a house record, some 1,000 more than showed up for The Who in December, 1975. Friends had advised, "Don't miss it; it's bad, but it's the loudest and flashiest show ever." Well, they were right about the first part. But any number of local, hack bands play louder, and several top acts have been flashier and more tasteful with their flash. As loud as the sound was, the two droning, monotonous guitars, played (more or less) by Paul Stanley and Ace Frehley, were about all that was audible. The bass and drums were mixed too far into the background, and the vocals were shouts in a canyon.

The costumes were definitely not Edith Head; more like early Chicken Man, or late Halloween. Outrageous, but without the style that marks Alice Cooper or Elton John. In fact, getting right down to the proverbial Bottom Line, there was little redeeming social value about the performance. If anything, the night offered an excuse for thousands of pubescent youngsters to let off all the steam they could generate. So much, in some cases, that they needed a bit of medical aid. The medics at the first-aid room estimated they'd sent half-a-dozen most about 14 or 15 to the hospital for drug overdoses. Recalled one medic: "One guy we sent, he said he'd taken three hits of something, but he didn't know for sure what." And a police sergeant joked about the unfortunate soul at the snack bar: "Passed out right on the lunch counter; can you imagine that? He was eating a hot dog and fell right over into it. Fell into his hot dog, can you imagine that?" Maybe it wasn't a wasted night after all. From the line of Moms and Dads queued up out front to pick up their kids, it looked like KISS made good babysitters" (Jim Healey - Des Moines Register, 1/22/77).

And another: "Not all the excitement was on stage at the KISS rock concert Friday night as police cars and ambulances with flashing lights and wailing sirens made fairly regular trips to Veterans Memorial Auditorium. As of 11 p.m., eight persons in their teens or early 20s had been arrested in or near the auditorium, police said. All but two were arrested on charges of intoxication. One person was charged with possession of drugs, and another with criminal trespass, police said. Also, fire department ambulances were summoned to the auditorium three times during the concert. Two of the patients appeared to have drug reactions, and a woman who is eight months pregnant was taken to a hospital complaining of stomach pains, authorities said. Heavy traffic near the auditorium also was blamed partially for three accidents that happened almost simultaneously in the westbound lanes of the MacVicar Freeway near Pennsylvania Avenue. Ten cars were involved in the accidents but there were no serious injuries, police said. Two of the three westbound freeway lanes were closed to traffic for about 90 minutes after the accidents, which occurred about 7:45 p.m." (Des Moines Register, 1/22/77).

- The venue received $11,947 from the event, comprised of $1,150 facility rental, $1,426 from parking, $7,548.80 from 10% of gross receipts over $15,000, and $1,827.49 from 22% cent of concession sales. According to auditorium manager, Tony Abramovich, not bad for "kids up on a stage, banging around and making a lot noise" (Des Moines Register, 1/28/77).

January 22 - Chicago Stadium, Chicago, IL
Promoter: J. Weintraub / Concerts West
Other act(s): Uriah Heep
Reported audience: (13,000 capacity)
Notes:
- The Chicago Tribune reported that tickets were still available for the show on Jan. 20.
- In the Jan. 22 issue of Billboard Magazine, Casablanca took out an ad trumpeting the success of KISS in 1976: 250,000 copies of "The Originals" sold-out, 1 million copies of the "Beth" single, more than 1.5 million copies sold of "Destroyer" and "Rock And Roll Over" each, and 2 million copies of "KISS Alive!" KISS had arrived...
- This show was partially captured on Super8 silent video.

January 24 - Veterans Memorial Coliseum, Fort Wayne, IN
Promoter: Sunshine Promotions
Other act(s): Uriah Heep
Reported audience: (10,500 capacity)
Notes:
- From a local review: "KISS landed an electric smooch on Fort Wayne's cheek at the Memorial Coliseum Monday night, and the crowd loved it. Machismo was the evening attire as the four brash heavy metalists, faces hidden by heavy makeup, strode on stage amidst exploding smoke bombs and a cloud of dry ice vapors. No Bay City Rollers these boys, although most of the crowd was young. Leady and rhythm guitar, bass and drums pounded out a beat designed to shake the crowd out of the seats, designed by promoters who wanted to make some money" (Fort Wayne News-Sentinel, 1/25/77).

January 25 - Hulman Civic Center, Terra Haute, IN
Promoter: Entam Ltd.
Other act(s): Uriah Heep
Reported audience: 11,100 **SOLD-OUT
Notes:
- From a local review: "Watching KISS is sort of fun. Their outlandish outfits and made-up faces make them look more humorous than evil. My favorite is Gene Simmons, the fire-breathing bass player whose tongue rolls out about a foot or so. He squats at stage right and flutters out his tongue in what is supposed to be a suggestive manner at little girls. He

looks like a retarded frog. KISS music is awful. The lyrics of the songs on all their albums could be printed with this type and might fill up a postage stamp" (Terra Haute Spectator, 2/5/77).

January 27 - Cobo Hall, Detroit, MI
Promoter: Belkin Productions
Other act(s): Uriah Heep
Attendance: (11,597 capacity)
Set list: Detroit Rock City / Take Me / Let Me Go, Rock 'N' Roll / Ladies Room / Firehouse / Makin' Love / I Want You / Cold Gin / Do You Love Me? / Nothin' to Lose / God of Thunder / Rock and Roll All Nite / Shout It Out Loud / Beth / Black Diamond
Notes:
- Before the show the band were interviewed by Rolling Stone writer Charles M. Young for a feature published in the April 7 edition.
- KISS was guaranteed $27,500 for each of the Cobo shows.

January 28 - Cobo Hall, Detroit, MI
Promoter: Belkin Productions
Other act(s): Uriah Heep
Reported audience: (11,597 capacity)

January 29 - Cobo Hall, Detroit, MI
Promoter: Belkin Productions
Other act(s): Uriah Heep
Reported audience: (11,597 capacity)
Set list: Detroit Rock City / Take Me / Let Me Go, Rock 'N' Roll / Ladies Room / Firehouse / Makin' Love / I Want You / Cold Gin / Do You Love Me? / Nothin' to Lose / God of Thunder / Rock and Roll All Nite / Shout It Out Loud / Beth / Black Diamond
Notes:

- Jeanette Frehley flew in and joined Ace for this show.
- Professionally filmed to a standard that in the opinion of the author exceeds the previous year's shows, Cobo '77 is sourced from a 3/4" master tape that surfaced on E-bay in June 2006. That tape was snapped up by a European collector for a bargain $5,000, though the seller, lacking any integrity, immediately started selling DVD copies to others. Once that occurred a free-for-all took place with traders making the video available in as many places as possible for free and reporting the auctions to the E-bay police to get them shutdown.
- Most stunning of the "Rock And Roll Over" tour archive is this incomplete video from the band's final and hastily added third show (Paul references it as the last of the shows during the introduction to "Let Me Go, Rock 'N' Roll").
- It is fitting, perhaps, that this Detroit show is available to collectors, though somewhat sad that the lesser MSG show was featured as a bonus for the KISSology Volume 1 DVD in terms of wider distribution. While incomplete, it is a stunning pro-shot video. Starting with backstage footage of the band heading to the stage (presumably shown on the venue screens), "Detroit Rock City" is joined in progress. The encores are also missing. What is known is that the video for "Beth," from one of the three Cobo shows, was used during the February 10, 1977 broadcast of "The People's Choice" awards show.

February 1 - Milwaukee Auditorium, Milwaukee, WI
Promoter: Daydream Productions
Other act(s): Uriah Heep
Reported audience: 6,156 **SOLD-OUT
Reported gross: $86,719 **both nights
Notes:
- Attendance reported in The Milwaukee Journal (2/2/77) anticipating another capacity crowd for the second show. Both attendance figures are over-capacity what the venue's reported maximum was in that auditorium format (6,000).
- From a local review: "No other rock group in the business electrifies an audience more than KISS. The fans began cheering as soon as the prop men uncovered the elaborate scenery the band used in its act... KISS put on a show that surpassed every piece of rock theatrics seen in Milwaukee. And the fans loved it so much that they spent more time standing on their chairs than sitting on them" (The Milwaukee Sentinel, 2/2/77).
- From a local review: "Gene Simmons — a cross between Genghis Khan and King Kong — lurked menacingly about the stage in his scaly, thigh length platform boots and leathery batlike wings. When he wasn't flicking his painted tongue or grinding his pelvis at the crowd in front of the stage, Simmons pointed defiantly at the crowd, spit or breathed fire. On the lighter side was Paul Stanley, a dainty pixie in white face with a black star over his right eye who pranced about in a silver speckled space suit cut to the navel" (Milwaukee Journal, 2/2/77).

February 2 - Milwaukee Auditorium, Milwaukee, WI
Promoter: Daydream Productions
Other act(s): Uriah Heep
Reported audience: 6,156 **SOLD-OUT
Notes:
- This second show was also reported in some press reviews as sold-out.

February 3 - Brown County Arena, Green Bay, WI
Promoter: Daydream Productions
Other act(s): Uriah Heep
Reported audience: 7,008 *SOLD-OUT
Reported gross: $52,560

February 4 - Dane County Coliseum, Madison, WI
Promoter: Daydream Productions
Other act(s): Uriah Heep
Reported audience: 10,050 *SOLD-OUT
Reported gross: $73,375
Notes:
- From a local review: "How do you describe this kind of act, with its heavy overtones of sadomasochism and horror fantasy? Visually it seems to occupy a space half-way between H.P. Lovecraft's literary monsters and Frank Frazetta's sci-fi drawings. People friendly to KISS call it 'the world's first chrome glitter group,' or the U.S. Steel of the heavy metal bands. Detroit promoter Steve Glantz, who made a pile on them, approvingly called the band's act 'Hitler rock.' A writer in 'Circus' magazine lovingly explained that their power came when they 'combined the flash of the Dolls with the violence of Alice Cooper'" (The Capital Times, 2/5/77).

February 6 - Met Center, Bloomington, MN
Promoter: Schon Productions
Other act(s): Uriah Heep
Reported audience: 16,800 **SOLD-OUT
Reported gross: $104,900
Notes:
- From a local review: "KISS' choreographed, high-energy show last night was not substantially different from its local debut in 1976, although the staging was somewhat more elaborate if not more outrageous... The 75-minute performance was characterized by more spontaneity than last year's, though KISS clearly lacks the finesse, vitality and style demonstrated on stage by its heavy metal colleagues such as Led Zeppelin, Aerosmith and Blue Oyster Cult. KISS' music is merely an assault" (Minneapolis Star, 2/7/77).

February 8 - Auditorium Arena, Omaha, NE
Promoter: Schon Productions
Other act(s): Uriah Heep
Reported audience: 12,000 **SOLD-OUT
Reported gross: $78,000
Notes:
- From a local review: "The KISS Army isn't very disciplined, but its devotion to its leaders goes beyony fantaticsm... This concert, sold out more than a month ago, was as much a stage show as a musical event. It began with the spotlights trained on a revolving, multifaceted mirror high above the arena. After a suitable dramatic pause, the stage lights burst on, to reveal the group in a 'KISS uber alles' pose, arms thrust defiantely up and out, atop a surrealistic set representing mountains and ruins... Wen nothing special was going on, there were plenty of random bursts of flash powder, sheets of flame and confetti sprayed over the crowd to keep everyone diverted" (Omaha World-Herald, 2/10/77).

February 9 - Kemper Arena, Kansas City, MO
Promoter: Contemporary Productions / Chris Fritz / Cowtown Productions
Other act(s): Head East
Reported audience: 14,794 / 17,500 (84.54%)
Reported gross: $103,558

February 10 - McElroy Auditorium, Waterloo, IA
Promoter: Fox Promotions
Other act(s): The Dictators
Reported audience: 7,800 / 8,735 (89.3%)
Reported gross: $54,600 *estimate
Partial set list: Detroit Rock City / Beth / Black Diamond
Notes:
- Head East was originally scheduled to open this show. The Dictators included Mark "The Animal" Mendoza, later of Twisted Sister fame.
- From a local review: "Smoke and fire roll off the stage revealing a lizard-footed creature, spitting blood into a glittering electric guitar. Like Tolkien's Black Riders of Mordor, three other creatures appear, wiggling their tongues out of black and white painted faces. A rock and roll nightmare? No, but the action was real and grossly tasteful, as only KISS can be as they exploded on the McElroy Auditorium stage Thursday evening for 7,800 fans. Black metal gargoyles on stage seemed to glare down on this foursome with a look of approval, as KISS presented their bizarre combination of spectacle and hard rock. The music is hard and tight, and at the extreme volume it is played, it is surprisingly crisp.

Two top-40 hits, 'I'm Gonna Rock and Roll All Night' and 'Shout It, Shout It Out Loud.' were favorites with the crowd. Such excitement as was generated by KISS hasn't been seen since the 60's Beatles hysteria. Tight music by all four, and solos by drummer Peter Criss and guitarist Ace Frehley helped stir the crowd into a constant hubbub. A top-selling band worldwide, KISS has that knowledge that is needed to combine grotesque effects and tricks with their driving rock music. Showers of confetti, glitter, flaming torches, sparks, burnt guitars, explosions... all were perfectly timed with a Hollywood flair. It is hard to discern whether KISS has won its audiences with the bizarre effects, or the music, unique in the rock and roll world. All three guitarists display considerable talent on their instruments, and achieved music and electronic effects simultaneously.

The evening started off slowly as concert-goers were subjected to a five-and-ten version of their white-face idols. The Dictators, garbed in blue jeans, seemed to have trouble keeping their leaping and dancing from interfering with lyrics ('I am diseased'?) and what musical ability they had. A nameless keyboard player appeared to possess what talent there was for the group, who seemed to be crying out, 'But, would you want to precede KISS?' Waterloo has been 'KISSed' with a touch of the grotesque, and they loved it... Maybe this spark-flinging foursome is a rock phenomenon after all" (Waterloo Courier, 2/11/77).
- On this night Lydia Criss received the band's People's Choice Award for "Beth," on their behalf. The awards ceremony, held at the New Longhorn Theatre on Sunset Boulevard, was broadcast live on CBS television.

February 12 - Civic Center, Bismarck, ND
Promoter: Amusement Conspiracy

Other act(s): The Dictators
Reported audience: 8,000 **SOLD-OUT
Reported gross: $48,790

February 13 - Fieldhouse @ Dakota State University, Fargo, ND **CANCELLED
Promoter: Amusement Conspiracy

February 16 - Hartford Civic Center, Hartford, CT
Promoter: Koplik & Finkel
Other act(s): Sammy Hagar
Reported audience: ~9,150 /13,500 (67.78%)
Partial set list: Detroit Rock City / Take Me / Let Me Go, Rock 'N' Roll / Ladies Room / Cold Gin / I Want You / God of Thunder / Makin' Love / Rock And Roll All Nite / Black Diamond
Notes:
- From a local review: "Like a migraine headache, the rock group KISS has to be experience to be believed. (Not a bad simile, actually.) ... The carefully programmed 80-minute show included nearly every cheap and not-so-cheap trick of pop stagecraft: explosions, towers of flame, fake snow, a fire-eating torch bit and a smashing the guitar bit, among others. A picture would truly be worth 10,000 words in describing the performers. (And they are performers more than musicians.) ... Musically, to stretch the use of that word, the act consisted of grinding, pounding, screeching, deafening noise. It was well-rehearsed, however" (Hartford Courant, 2/17/77).
- From a local review: "Not having liked KISS in the past isn't quite accurate: I had always despised them. More to the point, I ignored them; everything about their ungodly theatrics made them seem pathetic, made their music trivial. These were four pop hustlers who were determined not to let a lack of talent keep them from the top. Then along came 'Beth' and 'Hard Luck Woman,' decent songs on anyone's terms, and it appeared that KISS might have something more to offer than ram-it-down-your-throat-rock. Not so. The top forty should sue for misrepresentation. Nothing in last Wednesday's nights concert at the Hartford Civic Center even vaguely resembled the KISS on the radio. In performance, KISS has taken a quantum leap from 3-chord rock right into a new realm — they're a *one note* band. And it tends to be a loud note at that... KISS will keep on having a good time until the KISS Army switches allegiance to something more enduring, like music" (Hartford Advocate, 2/23/77).
- A below average AUD recording circulates. This show is heavily edited and not complete.

February 18 - Madison Square Garden, New York, NY
Promoter: Ron Delsener
Other act(s): Sammy Hagar
Reported audience: 19,600 **SOLD-OUT
Reported gross: $145,000
Set list: Detroit Rock City / Take Me / Let Me Go, Rock 'N' Roll / Ladies Room / Firehouse / Makin' Love / I Want You / Cold Gin / Do You Love Me? / Nothin' To Lose / God of Thunder / Rock And Roll All Nite / Shout It Out Loud / Beth / Black Diamond
Notes:
- This show was always considered to be the moment the band had "made it," at least in their own minds, playing their home town major venue to family and friends.
- From a local review: "The show, what there was to enjoy of it, was turned into an endurance test. Interminably boring guitar, bass and drum solos, rotten slipshod new songs,

imbecilic repetitive stage patter... it was all here for your displeasure. Most of these clowns ate it up though this was the KISS Army, after all, and onstage the generals were heading the attack. The whole place was a battle zone" (Aquarian Weekly, 3/23/77).

- From a local review: "Stumbling in the darkness into a KISS concert, as this well-meaning observer did Friday at Madison Square Garden, might lead on directly to dire meditations on the decline of Western civilization. How else, after all, are we to interpret an entertainment that highlights a bass player spitting 'blood' atop a tower, surrounded by swirls of smoke and bathed in bilios green light, all the while dressed in a black leather and silver costume that makes him look like a diabolical armadillo? And the sight of this apparition evoking a dull, throaty roar of appreciation from the sold-out house, the cries of the multitude overlaid with the treble piping of a large pre-pubescent minority" (New York Times, 2/20/77).

- Sammy Hagar recalled opening for KISS at this show, "People started booing before I walked out. I had never played New York except with Montrose. They didn't even know me. I looked out and the whole place was dressed like KISS. They've all got their makeup on. They were booing and flipping me off... 'F*** you,' I said and dropped my pants, pulled out my d*** and smashed my f***ing '61 Stratocaster to pieces onstage. What an idiot. Demolished this vintage guitar and walked offstage... It was the worst experience I ever had onstage, and it ruined me in New York. They didn't even know who I was. They hated me before they heard me" (Red: My Uncensored Life in Rock).

- The band hosted an after-show party ant the Parc Swim and Health Club in Manhattan following the show.

- Parts of this show were officially released as a non-chaptered bonus disc for the "KISSology Vol. 1" DVD package. While it is pro-shot video there are some camera focus issues that detract, though the show had circulated for many years. The use of video was noted in one mainstream review: "The special equipment used by KISS included a full-size video tape broadcast system, with a large screen positioned well above the stage. Cameras at strategic points caught every facial leer and strutting movement by Paul Stanley and Gene Simmons as they busily enacted roles firmly rooted in the imagination of their fans" (Performance Magazine).

February 21 - Nassau Coliseum, Uniondale, NY
Promoter: Phil Basile / Concerts East
Other act(s): Sammy Hagar
Reported audience: (16,500 capacity)
Notes:
- This show was added when the Madison Square Garden show sold out.
- In his autobiography, Peter recalls deliberately crashing his Camaro in his parking structure in a fit of rage, resulting in a visit to hospital and the postponement of the next show to allow him time to recuperate.

February 23 - Hampton Roads Coliseum, Hampton, VA **POSTPONED
Promoter: Entam, Ltd.
Notes:
- Rescheduled to March 7 when Peter broke his nose in an automobile accident and was prevented from being able to apply his make-up for a few days.

February 24 - Winston-Salem, NC **TEMP HOLD DATE

February 26 - Freedom Hall, Johnson City, TN
Promoter: Entam Ltd.
Other act(s): The Dictators
Reported audience: ~8,500 **SOLD-OUT
Set list: Detroit Rock City / Take Me / Let Me Go, Rock 'N' Roll / Ladies Room / Firehouse / Makin' Love / I Want You / Cold Gin / Do You Love Me? / God of Thunder / Nothin' To Lose / Rock And Roll All Nite / Shout It Out Loud / Black Diamond
Notes:
- Freedom Hall came under fire in 1977 for the sorts of rock acts that were being booked at the venue, even though those events were providing the venue with nearly 50% of its revenue, allowing many other non-musical events to be held there.
- Paul sings "Black Diamond" during this show while "Beth" wasn't performed.
- An average AUD recording circulates though it's affected by a bit of tape-drag in parts, and chattering children in the audience near taper.
- At 3 a.m. on the morning of this show Ace was arrested in Dobbs Ferry and was "charged with driving while intoxicated... [He] allegedly struck two parked cars on Cedar Street" (Tarrytown Daily News, 2/28/77). He was scheduled to appear in court on March 10 after being bailed at 5:30 a.m.

February 27 - Carolina Coliseum, Columbia, SC
Promoter: Beach Club Promotions
Other act(s): The Dictators
Reported audience: (13,500 capacity)

March 1 - Civic Center Auditorium, Asheville, NC
Promoter: Kaleidoscope Presents
Other act(s): The Dictators
Reported audience: 7,901 / 8,000 (98.76%)
Notes:
- While the capacity of this venue, using the reserved seating arrangement, was 7,654, the local Fire Marshall allowed the venue to sell 8,000 tickets due to the use of festival seating (no seating on the main floor). Future Asheville Mayor Ken Michalove, then acting City Manager, had to defend the concert to the Vice-Mayor and Civic Center Commission. In his response to 8 questions levied concerning the concert he was adamant that the challenges any public event had been well planned for and handled both by staff and in conjunction with local police (one ejection for drugs possession, one reported case of public urination). He was equally adamant that the facility was for the benefit of all citizens of Ashville and the surrounding communities, regardless on any particular view of the suitability of such entertainment other than protecting the well being of the attendees — in other words that personal judgment shouldn't require imposing personal morality on others. He went so far as to offer his resignation if his managerial philosophy was deemed incompatible.

March 3 - Birmingham-Jefferson Civic Center Coliseum, Birmingham, AL
Promoter: Ruffino & Vaughn
Other act(s): The Dictators
Reported audience: (18,903 capacity)

March 5 - Rupp Arena, Lexington, KY

Promoter: Entam Ltd. & Sunshine Promotions
Other act(s): Legs Diamond
Reported audience: 16,701 / 18,500 (90.28%)
Reported gross: $109,935
Set list: Detroit Rock City / Take Me / Let Me Go, Rock 'N' Roll / Ladies Room / Firehouse / Makin' Love / I Want You / Cold Gin / Do You Love Me? / Nothin' To Lose / God of Thunder / Rock And Roll All Nite / Shout It Out Loud / Beth / Black Diamond
Notes:
- "Legs Diamond" purportedly crashed a KISS after-show party and persuaded Gene to check them out. Gene apparently liked them enough for them to get the final three shows of the tour.
- A generally poor AUD recording circulated for years prior to a reasonable 2nd generation upgrade surfacing in 2007.

March 6 - St. John Arena, Steubenville (Columbus), OH

Promoter: OSU Pep Board Presents
Other act(s): Legs Diamond
Reported audience: (14,000 capacity)
Notes:
- The Dictators were originally scheduled to open this show.
- From a local review: "After their Sunday evening show in St. John Arena, I am convinced that three straight hours of 'KISS Alive' would be lethal; it's a wonder the Food and Drug Administration hasn't nailed them yet. They ought to be deported to Uganda. These guys are not entertaining; they are obnoxious. There is no content to their music or their lyrics, and the special effects aren't even what they are built up to be. They jump up and down, stick out their tongues, spit all over the stage; they use smoke and concussion bombs and strobe, but it's all so cheaply utilized I'm sure a sixth grader choreographed it all. And they don't even have the courtesy to bring a laser show. That's gall. Their performance is the utmost in poor taste and empty musical force; they call it rock and roll, but I'm certain Buddy Holly is writhing in his grave" (Ohio State Lantern, 3/7/77).

March 7 - Hampton Roads Coliseum, Hampton, VA

Promoter: Entam, Ltd.
Other act(s): Legs Diamond
Reported audience: 9,949 **SOLD-OUT
Reported gross: $67,928
Partial set list: Detroit Rock City / Take Me / Firehouse / Cold Gin / Nothin' To Lose / God of Thunder / Rock And Roll All Nite / Shout It Out Loud / Beth / Black Diamond
Notes:
- Last show of the U.S. "Rock And Roll Over" tour. This show was reported as sold-out in trade magazines even though the venue's maximum capacity was 1,000 more than the audience figure stated (many factors could explain the discrepancy — such as the staging).
- From a local review: "An average rock concert crowd packed the Hampton Roads Coliseum Monday night for KISS, one of America's heaviest and most exotic bands. Paul Stanley, Gene Simmons, Peter Criss and Ace Frehley not only play music but give their fans a show as well. There was a strong presence of KISS's early music, which seemed to be more pleasing to the

crowd. Of the 15 songs performed, seven were from their 'KISS Alive' album, a collection of earlier hits" (Newport News, 3/10/77).

- From another review: "It would take a great deal more theatrics than KISS alread employs to mask the fact that they are foremost a very credible band... KISS' live appeal, once a somewhat frightening nature, is graphically displayed in the revenue of their catapault to the top of the commerical market. Anticipatory cries from the audience, compost largely of early and even pre-teenagers, revealed just how regimented the group's grab bag of trick has become. This was KISS' third appearance in the area and all the illusions have been the same each time... Like them or not, they are always a lot of fun" (The Marquee, 5/77).

March 21 - Osaka Bampaku Hall, Suita City, Japan **SOUND-CHECK
March 22 - Osaka Bampaku Hall, Suita City, Japan **REHEARSALS
March 23 - Osaka Bampaku Hall, Suita City, Japan **REHEARSALS
Notes:
- KISS flew out of New York's JFK Airport on March 17 on a Pan-AM 747 named "Clipper KISS." After the long flight they took a couple of days off to sightsee and recuperate from the long flight. On March 21, after flying to Osaka, the band held a press conference at Osaka Bampaku Hall in Suita City, before getting on with the work at hand: press interviews and rehearsing for the concerts. The band had worked hard in preparation for their first tour to Japan and approached it with a great deal of respect. They asked Udo reps for Japanese language translations of many of their raps and phrases, to be able to communicate more effectively with the audience. While it was deemed that the phrases would be better understood in the band's native language, some things (such as KISS album titles!) simply do not translate well into Japanese in conjunction with the challenges in enunciation and inflection so central to that language.
A new stage, including the platforms over the amplifiers, lighted stairs, and new drum riser was constructed for a cost of $46,000 for the tour. The backline was constructed from Marshall amps, Perkins cabinets and Crown amplifiers.
- The tour had originally been planned to also encompass both Australia and New Zealand, though these markets would have to wait a few more years for KISS to visit.

March 24 - Kosei-Nenkin Hall, Osaka, Japan
Promoter: Udo Artists
Other act(s): Bow Wow
Reported audience: 2,400 **SOLD-OUT
Set list: Detroit Rock City / Take Me / Let Me Go, Rock 'N' Roll / Ladies Room / Firehouse / I Want You / Makin' Love / Cold Gin / Do You Love Me? / Nothin' To Lose / God of Thunder / Rock and Roll All Nite / Shout It Out Loud / Beth / Black Diamond
Notes:
- Final rehearsals were held in the show venue in the morning. Show time was scheduled for 6:30pm with (unusually for Japan) the services of an opening act being utilized.

March 25 - Kosei-Nenkin Hall, Osaka, Japan
Promoter: Udo Artists
Other act(s): Bow Wow
Reported audience: 2,400 **SOLD-OUT
Set list: Same as March 24.
Notes:

- The Japanese "Sneak Attack" tour was an extension of the U.S. tour with no changes to the set lest. However, the "Love Gun" stage debuted while the previous tours costumes were retained.
- A low-generational very good AUD recording of the show circulates. The best version of this show is noted to have come from a 3rd gen tape, which was originally thought to be a better version of 3/29 rather than the new show it turned out to be.

March 26 - Kyoto Kaikan Dai Ichi Hall, Kyoto, Japan
Promoter: Udo Artists
Other act(s): Bow Wow
Reported audience: 2,000 **SOLD-OUT
Set list: Same as March 24.
Notes:
- The band took the hour-long drive from Osaka to Kyoto at lunch time on the day of this show.
- An excellent AUD recording by Mr. Peach from this show titled "Kabuki Beasts — Kyoto 1977" surfaced via Tarantura Records in 2012.

March 28 - Aichiken Taiiku Hall, Nagoya, Japan
Promoter: Udo Artists
Other act(s): Bow Wow
Reported audience: 6,000 **SOLD-OUT
Notes:
- The band travelled via bullet train from Kyoto to Nagoya the afternoon prior to this show.

March 29 - Osaka Festival Hall, Osaka, Japan
Promoter: Udo Artists
Other act(s): Bow Wow
Reported audience: 2,800 **SOLD-OUT
Set list: Same as March 24.
Notes:
- The band travelled via bullet train from Nagoya to Osaka the afternoon prior to this show.
- A low-generational very good AUD recording circulates. The best version of this show is noted to have come from a 3rd gen tape.
- Rap after "Take Me:" Whoa! How ya doin' Osaka? Whoa! Alright, I'll tell you... I'll tell you... It's been a while... It's been a while since we saw some people like you that really want to rock and roll! Do you want to rock and roll? Then I'll tell you we better get goin' 'cause this is gonna be a rock and roll party!"

March 30 - Kyuden Taiiku Hall, Fukuoka, Japan
Promoter: Udo Artists
Other act(s): Bow Wow
Reported audience: 4,000 **SOLD-OUT
Notes:
- The band flew into Fukuoka from Osaka at lunchtime on the day of show.
- After the show several members of the crew and band were invited to a private club, Honey Pot #2, across the road from the Fukuoka hotel the band were staying in, for an after-show party. An impromptu jam ensues with Paul taking lead, Gene on rhythm, roadie

Barry taking bass, and Fritz on drums. The band stumble through "Honky Tonk Woman," "Wild Thing," and "Louie, Louie" before being ended by the prospect of a police raid (Playboy, 12/1/77).
- March 31 was something of a day off for the band, though they did fly back to Tokyo in the afternoon.

April 1 - Budokan Hall, Tokyo, Japan
Promoter: Udo Artists
Reported audience: 11,000 **SOLD-OUT
Set list: Same as March 24.
Notes:
- Usually sourced from the "Mama Weer All Crazee Now" bootleg which some indicate is a SBD, but certainly is not.
- A low-generational very good AUD recording circulates.

April 2 - Budokan Hall, Tokyo, Japan **two shows
Promoter: Udo Artists
Other act(s): Bow Wow
Reported audience: 22,000 **SOLD-OUT (Both Shows)
Set list: Same as March 24.
Notes:
- The band played two shows, one at 3pm and the other at 7pm, with television station NHK filming both for domestic broadcast. The shows were also recorded by Eddie Kramer for a planned, but later abandoned, Japanese only live album then titled "Rock And Roll Party In Tokyo."
- The mixed audio was used for the TV broadcasts, on NHK's "Young Music Special" and later HBO (See Below).
- AUD from both shows circulates.
- The video from these shows is stunning, and was broadcast in both Japan and the US. It was officially released as part of the "KISSology Vol. 1" DVD package in complete form, though fans debate whether other unofficial versions are better.

April 4 - Budokan Hall, Tokyo, Japan
Promoter: Udo Artists
Other act(s): Bow Wow
Reported audience: 11,000 **SOLD-OUT
Set list: Same as March 24.
Notes:
- The band enjoyed a day off on Apr. 3. Prior to the show Peter toured Pearl's Japanese drum factory.
- Paul references the show as the bands "last night in Japan" during the show (after "Take Me"). The Japanese tour was expected to lose some $150,000, though much of the cost was underwritten by Victor and Casablanca.
- A below average rather muffled AUD recording circulates.
- The band entourage returned to the U.S. on Apr. 5.

Love Gun

Lisa Robinson, in her syndicated "Rock Talk" newspaper feature reported what was ultimately to become the road-map for the band for the rest of 1977 in early June: "In July, the band begins a Canadian tour. Then in August, KISS will perform all over the West Coast — they missed it last time around — with a possible four shows at Los Angeles' Forum. One of those Forum dates may be recorded for their next live album, to be released in the fall and backed by a giant promotional tour" (Springfield Union, 6/2/77). And thus things pretty much were... The "Love Gun" album would be the band's highest charting of their original incarnation, hitting #4 on the Billboard Top-200. The period, both album and tour, marked the beginning what is generally considered to the "Super KISS" era; the band's halcyon days of grandeur, the days and image most desirous of being replicated when a reunited band reconvened for the originals line-up reunion in 1996. And yet, in some ways, what was and what was later recreated are two completely different beasts in terms of performance and the scale and how each was ultimately utilized. The 1977 "Love Gun" tour (and following tour supporting "Alive II") show was impressive and majestic, and certainly represented the band at the zenith of their live performance. But it was also smaller in scale and scope than the magnified bloated-version recreated in 1996 to meet the demands in the minds of the fans of reliving what they remembered; larger than life from a time when many were much younger, smaller, less experienced, and utterly transfixed by the "show."

It seems rather strange to consider that the "Love Gun" tour run covered a meager 32 performances! A plan, that the band would attempt to implement more fully during the 1979 "Return of KISS" tour, meant that they scheduled seven dates as multiple engagement in three cities, being consecutive multi-date stands at three venues (the two dates in Edmonton were separated by a visit to Lethbridge). A large chunk of the tour, some 14 dates, took place across Canada and somewhat further skews the tour's overall appearance. As a result the "Love Gun" tour run appeared particularly short and seems more designed as a set up for the longer "Alive II" tour that followed. It certainly wasn't particularly arduous, with plenty of rest/travel days between most shows (other than a 5 day stretch in early August) though for the Canadian leg some of those travel days were particularly long for the ground crew involving drives of 1,000 – 1,600 miles. From Halifax to Salt Lake City some 7,000 road miles were covered. The band flew. Having paid their dues the band were no longer killing themselves on the road and compared with the 1976/77 North American touring cycle for "Rock And Roll Over," which ran some 60 dates, followed by 9 dates in Japan, it was a positive vacation (as much as being a touring musician on the road can be).

The finances of the tour were much more challenging, even in June before the cancellation of several dates. At the band's financial meeting on June 21, "The Canadian tour budget was reviewed and it was agreed by all concerned that we would be operating on a very tight budget on the summer tour and that cancellations of concerts would be extremely costly. As it is, the tour may well lose $100,000 and while this was discussed, the partners approved it." Within the next few weeks several dates would be removed from the itinerary... In May the band's tour rider was finalized growing to some 25 pages of requirements; technical, professional and personal, for promoters and venue operators.

Outside of the professional the personal comforts for the dressing room required "one and a half cases of Heineken, one and a half cases of Budweiser, one and a half cases of Fresca (cans), one case of ginger ale, on case of 7-Up, two gallons of real orange juice, one gallon of milk, three gallons of tomato juice, two bottles of champagne (Mums or Moet), two bottles of Soave Bolla (White Wine) second choice Muscadet, once case of Pepsi. Additionally two (2) cases of Budweiser warm. In cities where available one case of Molson Ale (Red Label)." In terms of food a meat main course for band and crew was deemed sufficient with cold-cuts and sandwich fixings also available. No demands such as "no brown M&Ms."

The accompanying tour saw a wholesale reinvention of the band's stage presence and costuming fully implementing the cost-saving measures and deployment lessons learned the hard way during the previous year with the "Destroyer" stage. While it most certainly took a step back from the complexity that that stage had represented in terms of stage-production, it leaped forward with the visual shock and awe that was married to the bombastic audio assault the band had become legendary for. It was in some ways a brute force reaction to Jules Fisher's intimation that KISS' road crew had been "incapable of operating some of this stuff," in relation to the "Destroyer" stage — everything challenging was dropped to make things as simple and problem-free, not that it required any fewer people to set it up or move it from venue to venue. It might seem trite to suggest the show was little more than a giant horizontal lighting truss rigged with explosives designed to melt the brains of the audience with a highly choreographed performance. Whatever the case, both Gene and Paul were proud of it: "The summer gigs are being staged on a sleek, future-styled chrome set which Paul Stanley deems 'ten times more effective' than the B-movie Boris Karloff backdrop of last year's Destroyer tour. 'It's streamlined,' says Paul, 'but still a bigger show.' 'The drum riser,' Gene continues, 'is an animal all its own. It can move forward and levitate. The balconies can place us down on stage. The steps light up as we walk. There are lots of hidden hydraulics in the set'" (Circus, 8/4/77). The new stage was based on the $150,000 initial version used during the Japanese tour earlier in the year which had provided the ideal opportunity for its deployment due to the required trans-Pacific shipping for those shows. I'm some ways it provided a trial run for the overall concept and avoided the costs of shipping the existing production with lead times required.

Overall the new show was an assault on all of the senses, but it was also a tour where the performance became very much "paint by numbers" losing any organic traits. With a footprint measuring 60' wide by 44' deep the 6' tall stage had plenty of space. Costs for the stage were around $46,000 including the "platform over the amplifiers, the stairs with treads that light up, the platform in front of the amplifiers which light up, the drum riser facing, and automation to make it go up and down-stage" (KA Memo, 3/4/77). An additional $55,200 was required for scissor-lifts, road boxes, the amplifier backline, and other elements. Additional elements to be incorporated following the Japan tour were anticipated to exceed $36,000. A flown 48' lighting truss was also central to the show and it was critical for venues to be able to meet this technical requirement. The show wasn't all about the lighting — visual presentation was bolstered by the use of hydraulics, elevators (walking down the stairs in platform boots was particularly tricky for those with issues with gravity) and cherry-pickers. When completed in June the final cost of the new show, including $38,064 for new costumes and instruments, came to $194,910. Stage props, in the form of "Sam the Serpent" remained, and the band made their entrance one elevators in front of the amplifier walls, to the left and right of Peter's drum riser.

For the second time in a year the band's costumes underwent a major redesign. While Gene continued to use a boot based on the gargoyle platform, instead of a scaled shaft overlay a pyramid metal stud covered one was used. A flat-metal stud cod-piece was integrated into an open chest vest with cross-chains across the breast attaching to a choker. Similar flat-stud gauntlets adorned both wrists. Gone was at armor shoulder-ware, replaced with a cape with flat-metal stud "ribs." Occasionally he'd wear horned shoulder pads similar to those he'd used in the early years. Paul continued with a basic black leotard with stars down the sides of the legs, but the chest cut-out was bordered with rhinestones. A vertically sequined vest was worn over, but like Gene, the black sequined jacket harkened back to an earlier era. Accessories used included a silver garter and feathered cuffs. Paul's boots were initially sketched as part of Gene's costume and are simple black leather affairs with silver chain adornments.

When most think of Peter Criss in this era, they are likely to recall his visually striking faux silver bandoliers worn in a cross pattern. He also wore a choker and bicep band, both bordered with small round studs. Similar studs bordered his black leather gauntlets and provided a cross design on them and his boots. Occasionally he'd use a black leotard with chest closed by laces and his ubiquitous "3" embroidered on the rear. Accessories included a black leather belt, again bordered with studs with cross designs. Ace's new design was also visually striking, with his black leotard peppered with rhinestones as "star" allusions. His upper body puffy silver covering appeared to be a metallic spacesuit shoulder covering with matching cuffs and "moon" boots. His leotard continued down the arms to the wrist to allow free movement. Accessories included the occasional use of a choker made of silver material matching the rest of the costume. It would be these costumes that would essentially provide the basis for those used on the 1996 reunion tour.

With the success of the Marvel comic, and the third cartoonish album cover, the band's audience demographic was inevitably shifting to a younger crowd. This change in dynamic was something that would become a common feature in reviews of their concerts; with many attendees being noted as having chaperones. This trend would continue until the band's ultimate fall from grace (in the U.S.). Venues selected for the tour also stayed away from the stadia of the previous summer. The band, or promoters, knew their place and the zone they could operate in. In a piece called "An Outrage Called KISS," it was made clear where KISS stood, at the time, in the rock hierarchy: "In most places, KISS makes $20,000 a concert — $40,000 in big cities. 'Forty thousand a night is still not exactly superstardom in our business,' says Aucoin's vice president-finance, Marvin Mann, poor mouthing it a bit because after all, he used to be comptroller for International Creative Management, the biggest talent agency in the world, and he knows what real rock-and-roll money is all about. 'The Beach Boys,' he says. 'For three straight nights in Madison Square Garden, the Beach Boys will net $80,000 a night'" (New York Times, 6/19/77). Yet, as the article also pointed out, The Rolling Stones and other massive draws wouldn't play 7,500-seat venues. KISS saw no shame in doing so and would more than willingly roll into town, set up shop, and add new members to the KISS Army.

Musical rehearsals were held for the tour in New York City in late-June before the band and crew headed to Theatre Techniques facilities at Stewart Airport in Newburgh, NY for the final production rehearsals before the set was transported to Halifax for the start of the tour. Unlike the previous tour, filmed rehearsals for the "Love Gun" tour do not circulate. One "work in progress" set list salvaged from a dumpster included the oddity, "Got Love for Sale" in the set, prior to "Christine Sixteen." Dated June 29, this set seems to counter any suggestion of the long-standing rumor that "Almost Human" was performed at the first show of the tour — the rest of the set list exactly matches what was actually performed in Montreal on July 12 (the earliest existing recording). If any additional song from the new album was performed at that first show, and reviews mention little specifically, then it seems more likely to have been "Got Love for Sale." The first leg, a jaunt through Canada, was essentially uneventful. Several dates needed to be cancelled as the schedule was finalized in early July with the tour expected to be run at close to a loss. Net income from the tour was reduced from $299,000 to 234,000 on the Canadian leg. Similarly, projections for percentages were reduced from the loss of shows and overly optimistic ticket sales projections. One plan to mitigate the financial impact was to replace later Canadian dates with shows in the U.S. since they were expected to result in higher grosses. Whatever the case, the dates did not match financial projections and not all of the shows sold-out or resulted in the additional percentages forecast. Most interesting during this part of the tour (with publicity about the band's plans for solo albums already circulating in the press) was Gene being reported as staying over in Vancouver to work on solo material with Doucette drummer Duris Maxwell at Pinewood Studios.

Like the solo albums, the band's next album "Alive II" was well publicized as they hit the road. Once the tour reach U.S. soil it continued in a very workmanlike manner heading towards those planned dates in Los Angeles. In late July negotiations were still under way with Filmways Heider Recording Studios for the use of their Mobile Unit One, equipped with 2 twenty-four track recording machines, and requisite engineering staff of three, for the Los Angeles concerts, at a cost of $6,400. Wally Heider's firm was one of the premier West Coast remote recording facilitators. Mobile Unit 1 was the largest vehicle in their fleet boasting 40 inputs. The double machines provided a fail-safe redundancy for critical remote recording — though the machines could also be used in tandem for complex recording operations handling the inputs of an incredible 120 microphones. The 35' vehicle was particularly impressive with its Ampex MM/1200 24/16-track, 3M M79 24-track, 3M M56 16/8-track, Ampex 440 4/2-track, and ATR -100 stereo machines (PR). Utilizing a API 40/24 with two AM-10 6x1 sub-mixers for console and Altec monitoring it could be equipped for all recording requirements, whether capturing an orchestra at the Hollywood Bowl or being driven to Lake Shasta to record Merle Haggard at his cabin retreat. Perhaps in anticipation of the live album the tour is underrepresented by bootleg recordings, other than the legendary Daly City show that has circulated for many years.

Fortunately, one of the Los Angeles dates, and Fresno, were also captured, and there is likely still material extant that has yet to surface (two additional partial soundboards do exist). For collectors, for many years, the pro-shot video recordings from both nights at Houston's Summit have been the keys from this tour. As a result there was little else to include visually on the "KISSology Vol. 1" DVD package in 2006. Within days of the final date of the tour, in Ft. Worth, TX, the band arrived in New Jersey to start rehearsals at the

Capitol Theater for the recording of the studio songs that would appear on "Alive II." No rest for the wicked...

June 20, 1977 - Star Sound Studios, New York City, NY **REHEARSALS
June 21 - Star Sound Studios, New York City, NY **REHEARSALS
June 22 - Star Sound Studios, New York City, NY **REHEARSALS
June 23 - Star Sound Studios, New York City, NY **REHEARSALS
June 24 - Star Sound Studios, New York City, NY **REHEARSALS
June 25 - Star Sound Studios, New York City, NY **REHEARSALS
June 26 - Star Sound Studios, New York City, NY **REHEARSALS
Notes:
- Musical rehearsals for the "Love Gun" tour at 419 Lafayette Street.

June 27 - Hanger E, Stewart Airport, Newburgh, NY **REHEARSALS
June 28 - Hanger E, Stewart Airport, Newburgh, NY **REHEARSALS
June 29 - Hanger E, Stewart Airport, Newburgh, NY **REHEARSALS
June 30 - Hanger E, Stewart Airport, Newburgh, NY **REHEARSALS
July 1 - Hanger E, Stewart Airport, Newburgh, NY **REHEARSALS
July 2 - Hanger E, Stewart Airport, Newburgh, NY **REHEARSALS
Set list: Detroit Rock City / Take Me / Calling Dr. Love / Hooligan / Love Gun / Firehouse / Got Love for Sale / Christine Sixteen / I Stole Your Love / Shock Me / I Want You / Makin' Love / God of Thunder / Rock And Roll All Nite / Shout It Out Loud / Beth / Black Diamond
Notes:
- Production rehearsals. Two days would have been required to transport the production to Halifax, plus tear down and setup time at both locations. Peter was involved in an auto accident the evening of June 30 "when their van overturned at Stewart Airport... [He] suffered cut knees that required several stitches... Police spotted the overturned vehicle on a winding roadway that runs along the perimeter of the airport Thursday night" (Poughkeepsie Journal, 7/2/77).

July 7 - Forum, Halifax, NS, Canada **REHEARSALS
Notes:
- The crew flew into Halifax on July 5 with load-in starting early the following day. While the band had rehearsed in Newburgh, this extra time allowed any last minute road kinks to be worked out. This day served as the final production rehearsal before the show hit the road.

July 8 - Forum, Halifax, NS, Canada
Promoter: Concert Productions International (CPI)/Donald K. Donald
Other act(s): Cheap Trick
Reported audience: 6,000 / 6,200 (96.77%)
Notes:
- Likely Ace Frehley's live lead vocal debut with "Shock Me."
- "Almost Human" has long been rumored to have been played at this show. Unfortunately, no evidence to substantiate that rumor has yet surfaced, even if the song might have made sense as a replacement for "God of Thunder." The local review of the show is generic enough to not add any particularly useful information about a KISS concert other than the obvious.
- From a local review: "They aren't pretenders to the title of the world's most talented rock band. What they are is theatre. In a grand sense. The whole show reeks of money, big money, but is nonetheless impressive. One can't ignore what's happening when one goes to a performance by these painted reptiles even if he wants to. The show doesn't ask for

attention, it demands it. And the kids love it. Here on stage is the embodiment of every spark of social rebellion even the most frustrated kid could imagine in his wildest dreams... Messages in their songs are simple and straightforward. None of that ethereal folderol or heavy social protest of the 60s, just power chords in the mega-watt range... KISS is an experience. Anyone who can stand loud rock, even for a half hour or so should see them once. Once is enough, you won't get anything more from a second or third concert except a few vicarious kicks. But all in all it is about as safe as anything else in life, and although Baden Powell would probably disagree, I doubt that it makes people any crazier than they already are" (Halifax Chronicle Herald, 7/11/77). The only song mentioned in the review is "I Want You."

July 9 - Coliseum, Moncton, NB, Canada
Promoter: Concert Productions International (CPI)
Other act(s): Cheap Trick
Reported audience: (8,916 capacity)

July 10 - Forum, Halifax, NS, Canada **CANCELLED
Notes:
- Originally scheduled for this date, with Moncton being the first night of the tour, this date was moved to become the first night of the tour. By changing the order of the Halifax and Moncton shows, the travel distance and time to Montreal was reduced by roughly 170 miles, a distance difference reasonably considered negligible.

July 12 - Forum Concert Bowl, Montreal, QC, Canada
Promoter: Concert Productions International (CPI)/ Donald K. Donald/Treble Clef
Other act(s): Cheap Trick
Reported audience: ~12,000 / 18,000 (66.67%)
Set list: Detroit Rock City / Take Me / Calling Dr. Love / Hooligan / Love Gun / Firehouse / Christine Sixteen / I Stole Your Love / Shock Me / I Want You / Makin' Love / God of Thunder / Rock And Roll All Nite / Shout It Out Loud / Beth / Black Diamond
Notes:
- From a local review: "KISS is a rock group that is depressingly indicative of what the tock music business has become. The quartet are at the zenith of costume rock — what with their comic book science-fiction make-up and their smoke and fire bombs. They are a commodity, a package that combines a hyped-up approach to costumes and gimmickry, and brutally loud rock sound. The combination pays off for KISS" (Montreal Gazette, 7/13/77).
- Joe Owens, Quality Records' (Casablanca's Canadian distributors) promotion director, presented the band members with their Canadian Platinum awards for "Love Gun" at this show.
- A very reasonable AUD recording circulates from this show, which provides the currently earliest known set list from the tour.

July 14 - Civic Center, Landsdowne Park, Ottawa, ON, Canada
Promoter: Concert Productions International (CPI)/Treble Clef
Other act(s): Cheap Trick
Reported audience: ~6,000 or ~10,000 / (10,120 capacity)
Partial set list: Firehouse / Christine Sixteen / Love Gun / Rock And Roll All Nite / Beth / Shout It Out Loud / Black Diamond

Notes:
- From a local review: "As musicians, the KISS characters are smash and grab artists - as subtle as a baseball bat to the back of the head. There's no sense trying to analyze or evaluate their musicianship — that'd be like looking for artistic merit in a broken muffler... When a band plays super loud like KISS did and lets it distort all over the place — one suspects to camouflage the lack of musicianship — then the audience is left physically and mentally stunned" (Ottawa Citizen, 7/15/77).
- From a local review: "KISS deals in the outrageous and they are unequaled in their field. KISS has done bigger and brighter and louder than ever before... The relentless drone pins you to your sea and the vibrations rattle the ribcage. It's a feeling that quickly is lost among a light and sound barrage of all your senses. At the show's end, ears were burning and hearing was impaired. KISS had come to Ottawa and did in the flesh what so many magazines have described... KISS really isn't a band. It is theatre. It's not conventional theatre. It's more like theatre of the grotesque and obscene. But it involves its audience like few other theatre forms. It is impossible to make it through a concert and not be swept up in the tidal wave of rhythm that grips the KISS crowds" (The Ottawa Journal, 7/15/77).

July 15 - Memorial Auditorium, Kitchener, ON, Canada **TEMP HOLD DATE
Notes:
- This date was held, but not put on sale when ticket sales didn't warrant a second show.

July 16 - Memorial Auditorium, Kitchener, ON, Canada
Promoter: Concert Productions International (CPI)
Other act(s): Cheap Trick
Reported audience: ~5,800 / 7,800 (74.36%)
Notes:
- A mention of the then forthcoming show in the Globe & Mail: "There is no group that combines blood, deviant sex and neo-Nazism the way KISS does, all wrapped into a cutesy-pie rock show that thrills and chills" (7/13/77).
- From a local review: "How could anyone be expected to feel human in a cacophony of ear-splitting noise the likes of which would make an air-raid siren tranquil? And could you help feeling a little less than your best when the temperature inside the auditorium threatened to break the equatorial record?... It was so hot the walls were sweating... But what had the listeners really heard? Did they even care? If only they realized they're more important than a group of non-musicians who clutter up a stage and make loud sounds. Then perhaps they'd put those groups out of business, and do everybody's ears a favor" (Kitchener-Waterloo Record, 7/17/77).

July 18 - Treasure Island Gardens, London, ON, Canada
Promoter: Concert Productions International (CPI)
Other act(s): Cheap Trick
Reported audience: ~4,400 / 5,800 (75.86%)
Notes:
- From a local review: "They served up a little more than an hour of the sounds and sights (heavy on the sights) that have made them wealthy and fairly popular throughout the world. But they are not by any stretch of the imagination the world's best band, a claim they make before launching their on-stage assault" (Free Press).

July 19 - Arena, Sudbury, ON, Canada
Promoter: Concert Productions International (CPI)/Donald K. Donald
Other act(s): Cheap Trick
Reported audience: (7,000 capacity)
Notes:
- Transport for the ground crew following the tear down at this show involved a grueling 1,061 drive to Winnipeg the following day.

July 21 - Arena, Winnipeg, MB, Canada
Promoter: Concert Productions International (CPI)
Other act(s): Cheap Trick
Reported audience: ~8,000 / 9,000 (88.89%)
Notes:
- While the standard capacity of this venue was around 10,700 patrons, KISS' staging requirements were reported to have reduced it to 9,000 for the show.
- Tickets for the show did not sell as quickly as had been anticipated. On commentator suggested, "Several factors seem to have contributed to the less-than-overwhelming response for the show. Whereas last year's performance utilized rush seating — which enables anyone who purchases a ticket as late as the day of the show to have a shot at a seat in the first 10 or 20 rows — all the dates on the current Kisstruction of Canada tour feature reserved seating. After the initial response when tickets first went on sale, sales have been sluggish" (Winnipeg Free Press, 7/20/77).
- From a local review: "KISS gave an enthusiastic crowd of more than 8,000 young people more than their money's worth Thursday night in the Winnipeg Arena. Although there was a delay of about 30 minutes from the time warm-up act Cheap Trick left the stage until KISS began its performance, the audience, made up mainly of teen-agers, waited patiently and the 13 Winnipeg policemen and 24 security guards on hand for the show had little to do except to try to keep the aisles clear of ever-present throngs of amateur photographers... They are a bizarre act, no doubt about it, but they are bizarre in an amusing, good humored way. Everything about them and their show (an incredibly intricate, technically precise bit of P.T. Barnum space-age showbiz) is done with just the right touch of camp excess, but not overdone" (Winnipeg Free Press, 7/22/77).
- Two days were required to get the ground equipment to Vancouver, a trip of over 1,500 miles crossing the northern stretches of the Rocky Mountain range.

July 24 - Pacific Coliseum, Vancouver, BC, Canada
Promoter: Concert Productions International (CPI)/Donald K. Donald
Other act(s): Cheap Trick
Reported audience: ~10,000 / 15,571 (64.22%)
Notes:
- According to the promoter, "The cops heard of KISS' so-called reputation and they ordered four squads to the show. They played poker all night and billed us $8,000 for overtime" (Montreal Gazette, 8/2/77).
- From a local review: "Hype? Not really. KISS promise nothing less than the greatest spectacle in rock and nothing less is exactly what they provide. From that it is easy for the unaware parent or pundit to mistake KISS for a threat to our civilized way of life. But understand this, KISS are not self-pitying, humorless nihilists like the punk rockers. If anything, they are a fantasy for an age that has seen just about everything. Of course they

appeal to the escapist stripe. It would be fun to stand seven feet tall, spit fire, deafen everyone within a 1,000 yard radius and make a million bucks doing it" (Vancouver Sun, 7/25/77).
- From another local review: "The KISS concert Sunday night was better than the fireworks display the Sea Festival holds annually. The Coliseum took on all the aspects of kid's day at the PNE's Playland with harried parents leading offspring by the hand up into the stands, plopping their plump selves down into the same seats they had at The Ice Capades or The Shriner Circus, and stopping up their ears with cotton... KISS was perfunctory as you please, well rehearsed, but musically deadening and the sound from the press box was, as usual, muddy except when Ace Frehley took off into one of his solos. Frehley appeared to be bored, or tired, or sick, or drunk, or all four, while batman, Gene Simmons and Paul Stanley did their best to whip up a surprisingly complacent audience which eventually succumbed and went nuts when the hits and the gimmickry got into gear" (Georgia Straight, 7/28/77).
- Around 7 minutes of silent Super8 footage was filmed at this show.

July 25 - Victoria Arena, Victoria, BC, Canada **CANCELLED
Reported audience: (6,500 capacity)
Notes:
- Purportedly cancelled due to the venue being too small to handle the show; though since the tour was projected to carry a loss on the Canadian dates losing a smaller market would only have been beneficial for bottom-line adjustments.
- It was questionable in terms of travel logistics how much sense the venue would have made. Just 70 miles from Vancouver, travel involved a ferry to reach Victoria.
- Additionally, the schedule for the Victoria and Vancouver shows were initially reversed.

July 27 - Northlands Coliseum, Edmonton, AB, Canada
Promoter: Concert Productions International (CPI) / Edmonton Exhibition Association
Other act(s): Cheap Trick
Reported audience: 11,494 / 17,000 (67.61%)
Notes:
- From a local review: "KISS, you see, is a group whose members figured out long ago that as only average players they would never get noticed by doing what everybody else was doing. That by pounding at their guitars and drums, like every other rock band in North America, they'd get nowhere fast. So, KISS looked around. They saw Alice Cooper doing turn-away business with his freak-rock show. KISS, or whatever powers-that-be created them, decided to go one better. With Wednesday's show, they displayed how they have actually gone several steps better. Or father, if you prefer" (Edmonton Journal).

July 28 - Sportsplex, Lethbridge, AB, Canada
Promoter: Gold & Gold/Concert Productions International (CPI)/Donald K. Donald
Other act(s): Cheap Trick
Reported audience: ~7,000 / 8,000 (87.50%)
Notes:
- From a local review: "Billed as the Demons of rock and roll, the quartet burst on stage amidst a fiery display of lights and an explosion of sound, the likes of which have never before been witnessed in Lethbridge. Their professionalism shone through in every song they performed. In one word KISS was fantastic. KISS put on a show that will not soon be forgotten... But the special effects were only a small part of what went on. Between all the

lights and smoke, there was some darn good, foot stompin' ear-piercing rock and roll" (Lethbridge Herald, 7/29/77).

July 29 - Northlands Coliseum, Edmonton, AB, Canada
Promoter: Edmonton Exhibition Association/Concert Productions International (CPI)
Other act(s): Cheap Trick
Reported audience: (17,000 capacity)
Notes:
- KISS' performances were part of Edmonton's Klondike Day's at the Ex "Coliseum of Stars '77" celebrations.

July 31 - Stampede Corral, Calgary, AB Canada
Promoter: Brimstone/Concert Productions International (CPI)
Other act(s): Cheap Trick
Reported audience: ~7,000 / 7,265 (96.35%)
Notes:
- From a local review: "Whatever else KISS might not be, they certainly are crowd pleasers... It was an amazing spectacle. These macabre clowns, jumping about and clicking heels with surprising grace on stilts, were mesmerizing the under-13 crowd and shell-shocking the older one. But none of it means much. The songs were build around the stunts, or in the case of Simmons puking his prerequisite quart of blood while kneeling at the front of the stage, having the bass guitar play itself while he goes about his business flicking his tongue and grinning" (Calgary Herald, 8/1/77).

August 1 - Stampede Corral, Calgary, AB, Canada **TEMP HOLD DATE
Promoter: Concert Productions International (CPI)
Other act(s): Cheap Trick
Notes:
- Only one date in Calgary was mentioned in local press, so it is likely that this date was never booked.

August 2 - Saskatoon Arena, Saskatoon, SK, Canada **CANCELLED
Promoter: Concert Productions International (CPI)
Other act(s): Cheap Trick
Reported audience: (7,000 capacity)
Notes:
- This show had been cancelled by early July, along with the first Halifax date.

August 2 - Agridome Star Theatre, Regina, SK, Canada
Promoter: Concert Productions International (CPI) / Donald K. Donald / Star Command Productions
Other act(s): Cheap Trick
Reported audience: ~6,800 **SOLD-OUT
Notes:
- This show had originally been scheduled for Aug. 3. Part of the Regina Buffalo Days Exhibition celebrations, other acts scheduled during the week included Kenny Rogers, Paul Anka, the Bay City Rollers, and Bob Hope.

- From a local review: "There's no denying KISS puts on a theatrical show. They use every trick in the book and play them to the hilt. But all the sirens, flashing lights, screaming and stage blood in the world can't disguise the fact that musically KISS is a very mediocre band. Theatrics can only carry anyone so far. Somewhere, beneath all of the glitter and razzle-dazzle there has to be something more of a group becomes a bore. Scrape away the KISS glitter and there's nothing. That's why the group grates on the nerves after the initial amusement of their appearance and outrageous antics wears off. KISS has been trying desperately of late to improve its music and to broaden its base of popular support. They gave little indication that they're ready to do that" (Regina Leader-Post, 8/3/77).

August 4 - Arena, Winnipeg, MB, Canada **TEMP HOLD DATE
Notes:
- This show was never put on sale, but formed part of the early itinerary for the Canadian tour. Some newspaper reports suggested that if the July 21 show had sold-out that the band would return for a second visit on this date. "Concert Productions International — promoting the tour — had an option for a second and even a third show. But it wasn't about to exercise that option until the original show was a sellout" (Winnipeg Free Press, 7/20/77).

August 4 - Salt Palace, Salt Lake City, UT
Promoter: United Concerts
Other act(s): Cheap Trick
Reported audience: (13,075 capacity)
Notes:
- From a local review: "KISS do things big, there are no two ways about it. They also run the risk of being dwarfed by their monstrous stage and gimmicks, and of having the squeeze put on [how to] make each tour more spectacular than the last. How much further can the theatrics be taken?" (Summer Chronicle, 8/9/77).
- From a local review: "Kids of all ages, from six to 39, came wearing everything from KISS belt buckles to homemade black KISS costumes. All were up for what was about to happen. I say happen, because going to see KISS is more than going to a concert. It is going to an event" (Deseret News, 8/5/77).
- Opening act Cheap Trick was interviewed by journalist Charles M. Young for a Rolling Stone magazine feature prior to this show. Rick declares "Gene Simmons, Paul Stanley, Robin Zander and Tom Peterson are four of the most eligible bachelors in rock!" Charles describes the audience: "I have anticipated wide-eyed Donny and Marie types; they do appear healthier than the average Madison Square Garden crowd, but they quickly reveal themselves as typical KISS worshippers, out for a night of good fun and human sacrifice when the firecrackers and smoke bombs start exploding" (New Orleans Times-Picayune, 9/10/77).

August 6 - Adams Fieldhouse, Missoula, MT **CANCELLED
Promoter: Amusement Conspiracy
Other act(s): Cheap Trick
Reported audience: (7,321 capacity)

August 7 - Yellowstone Metra, Billings, MT
Promoter: Amusement Conspiracy

Other act(s): Cheap Trick
Reported audience: 9,971 / 11,500 (86.70%)
Notes:
- From a local review: "A KISS concert is probably a great way to fight the peacetime bias. It almost resembles an electronic Hitler youth rally. But there is little danger of KISS' launching a new wave of fascism. If they could play, sing and/or write 'heavy' lyrics, they might be dangerous... KISS is good theatrics, as long as the foursome has its expensive gimmicks. But a bunch of major chords chunked through a mega-decibel wall of amplifiers will never pose much of a threat to serious musicians — or political systems" (Billings Gazette, 8/8/77).

August 8 - MSC Fieldhouse, Bozeman, MT **TEMP HOLD DATE
Reported audience: (8,900 capacity)
Notes:
- This show appears in early Casablanca PR and Performance Magazine itineraries, but was either never booked or put on sale.

August 8 - Rushmore Plaza Civic Center, Rapid City, SD
Promoter: Amusement Conspiracy
Other act(s): Cheap Trick
Reported audience: (8,800 capacity)
Notes:
- There hadn't been many concerts at this venue by the time KISS performed there. The first show was Elvis' appearance June 21, 1977, as part of the venue's grand-opening, which was filmed and later broadcast as part the "Elvis In Concert" TV special in October of that year.

August 11 - Spokane Coliseum, Spokane, WA
Promoter: Concerts West
Other act(s): Cheap Trick
Reported audience: 8,500 **SOLD-OUT
Reported gross: $60,000
Notes:
- From a local review: "Their acronym might mean 'Keep It Simple, Stupid,' because that's exactly what they do. The only thing hidden or complex about the noise-rock band is their make-up. The rest is as straight-forward and simple as a punch in the mouth... But like Alice Cooper before them, KISS did put on a show. Those four vaudevillians, dressed as a prehistoric bird, a cat, a spaceman and a rock star, belched fire, burned guitars and performed assorted gyrations and leaps to the crowd's pleasure" (The Spokesman-Review, 8/12/77).
- This show generated $14,384 for the Spokane city's coffers. The promoters rented the Coliseum for $6,654. One patron, who couldn't get in to the sold-out show, threw a rock through one of the venues glass doors and was quickly arrested (Spokesman-Review, 8/17/77).

August 12 - Coliseum, Seattle, WA
Promoter: Concerts West
Other act(s): Cheap Trick
Reported audience: ~14,000 / 14,405 (97.19%)
Notes:

- From a local review: "The last time KISS was in town, in February of 1976 at Paramount Northwest, I dumped on them unmercifully, calling them 'dumb' and 'weirdoes,' among other things. A short time later I kept hearing a song on the radio called 'Shout It Out Loud' that I liked a lot. To my surprise, it turned out to be by KISS. Then there was another song called 'Beth,' a touching little ballad, quite unlike anything KISS has ever done before, that I liked, too. And then there was a Marvel comic book starring KISS that wasn't bad and a couple of great articles in Creem magazine... It wasn't enough to turn my head around completely but at least I wasn't dreading the thought of the concert last Friday at the Coliseum — I was actually looking forward to it. In terms of pure theatrics, it didn't disappoint. There was something going on every minute that was worth watching... The carnival sideshow was amusing but the music took a very distant back seat. Everything sounded so much alike I didn't even notice 'Shout It Out Loud' until it was half over. There was no 'Beth' in the show — everything was hard rock... All that seemed to serve to hid the band's obvious limitations musically. For all the praise Frehley gets, his guitar-playing was incredibly lame. The rest of the band performed blandly for the most part, going through their routines as if they were bored... I still think the band is weird but they aren't so dumb. The show was nearly sold out and their albums sell like crazy. They know how to make money. But I wonder how long before the novelty wears off" (Seattle Times, 8/15/77).

August 13 - Memorial Coliseum, Portland, OR
Promoter: Concerts West
Other act(s): Cheap Trick
Reported audience: ~12,000 / 13,200 (90.91%)
Notes:
- Backstage, interview and brief live performance footage was aired by local television KATU-TV.
-From a local review: "Each tune was a production unto itself. The really big ones were accented by flash pots, pillars of fire, sparks, sirens and plenty of loud 'cracks' from explosive devices. KISS is, then, a visual act. Face it: The music keeps the adrenalin flowing but it's the show that keeps the crowd on edge... Perhaps the most important factor of all in KISS is its impact on young folks. It's like watching 'Godzilla Meets the Lone Ranger' on Saturday afternoon TV. The kids watch it and when it's over, all they can think of is what's to eat and drink. The aggressive tendencies seem to be diluted in either instance. While the kids are rowdy at KISS shows, it comes off as a goodtime sort of behavior that doesn't manifest in fighting" (Sunday Oregonian, 8/14/77).

August 14 - Memorial Coliseum, Portland, OR **TEMP HOLD DATE
Notes:
- A second show for August 14 was considered but not booked.

August 16 - Cow Palace, Daly City (San Francisco), CA
Promoter: Bill Graham Presents
Other act(s): Cheap Trick
Reported audience: 14,500 **SOLD-OUT
Set list: I Stole Your Love / Take Me / Ladies Room / Firehouse / Love Gun / Hooligan / Christine Sixteen / Makin' Love / Shock Me / I Want You / Calling Dr. Love / Shout It Out Loud / God of Thunder / Rock And Roll All Nite / Detroit Rock City / Beth / Black Diamond
Notes:

- "Rock And Roll All Nite" was dedicated to Elvis, who had died that day.
- A great recording of this show circulates, though it's open to debate whether it's a SBD or a SBD-mix. Regardless, it's great, though it is missing "Beth!" Unfortunately, some silver CDs, which sell for irrational prices, are sourced from MP3s.
- From a local review: "A concert by KISS is more of a sideshow than a musical presentation. The special effects are the real attraction; the music just provides a context. Consequently, reviewing a performance by KISS, who played Tuesday before a sold-out Cow Palace audience, is somewhat futile... KISS purveys a rudimentary, unadorned brand of rock that owes a lot to more traditional rock bands like the Rolling Stones and the Who. In concert, the band's more recent compositions stick out like sore thumbs, as KISS has become much more adept at fashioning tunes with slick guitar parts and tightly arranged, repeating choruses... Lead vocalist Paul Stanley suffered from a throat made hoarse, undoubtedly, through a grueling tour schedule. Each member had his moment in the spotlight and each sang lead on at least one tune, including Ace Frehley, who has a terrible voice and is barely able to use it anyway" (SF Chronicle, 8/18/77).
- From another local review: "It happened some years back with Grand Funk Railroad, too. After vowing never to subject my ears to musical trash at high volume again, I sat through two Grand Funk Railroad concerts (I'll do anything to see Traffic perform). The music was straight noise; dregs, and Grand Funk was destroyed by rock critics, but they became the heavy metal kings. Likewise, the teens of late have picked a band that plays in a class with Grand Funk as the most popular group in America (according to the Gallup Youth Survey). Last night's Cow Palace show (before a sold-out crowd of 14,500 KISS Army recruits) was a real destroyer. The volume was so high that I may never hear again. The musicianship was so poor I shudder when I think about it. But then I'd be shuddering anyway; the KISS show was akin to experiencing an earthquake and the neutron bomb simultaneously.

Smoke, explosions, enough flashing lights (including one high above the stage spelling out the, group name) to open a used car lot, and that deafening noise of KISS opened the 90-minute show. The three guitar players stood on platforms flanking the drummer before hydraulic lifts brought them to stage, level from their 15-foot high perches. The quartet was dressed to kill in black with chrome attachments and 18-inch platform boots. But the best part was the painted faces I which rendered the boys anonymous, superhuman symbols of teen rebellion, aggression, sex and violence. 'Firehouse' had sirens blaring, guitars feeding back, and flames shooting from the mouth of bassist Gene Simmons. When not mouthing off, Simmons would jump around in motions akin to a grasshopper or lizard, his long tongue darting in and out of his face. Guitarist-vocalist Paul Stanley was hoisted on one lift in 'Love Gun,' Simmons on another as he sang 'Calling Dr. Love,' with fog machines turned on high. My favorite part was the guitar solo in 'Shock Me,' when lead guitarist Ace Frehley finds himself holding a flaming, smoking guitar, finishes out his solo before setting the Gibson Les Paul on a stand where it appears to be consumed in a ball of smoke and flame.

'Hooligan' and 'Sweet Sixteen' got a big response, as did 'Shout it Out,' featuring 20-foot flames leaping from various flash pots. Between sets a Bill Graham employee had announced an upcoming Cow Palace concert to feature 'the king of rock and roll: Ted Nugent' But Paul Stanley set the record straight when he dedicated 'I Want to Rock and Roll All Night' to 'The King of rock and roll: Elvis Presley.' Ignore the negative qualities of the show, and think of the positive ones: KISS' concert allows teens to act out their aggressiveness in socially acceptable form. The group puts on what must be one of the best shows on the concert circuit (no doubt about it, every kid there got his money's worth). And the group has risen quickly from second-string to starting team in the big hall competition" (Oakland Tribune, 8/17/77).

August 17 - Selland Arena, Fresno, CA

Promoter: Avalon Attractions
Other act(s): Cheap Trick
Reported audience: 7,333 **SOLD-OUT
Reported gross: $51,296
Set list: Same as Aug. 16
Notes:
- A reasonable AUD recording circulates from this show with an upgrade having surfaced in 2014. A common poor incomplete version circulated for many years before prior to the upgrade.

August 19 - San Diego Sports Arena, San Diego, CA

Promoter: Fun Productions
Other act(s): Cheap Trick
Reported audience: 11,925 / 14,500 (82.24%)
Reported gross: $104,779
Notes:
From a local review: "A surprising show of popular support was displayed Friday night at the Sports Arena for KISS, a rock quartet that has parlayed a reputation for plebeian visual aesthetics into a multi-million dollar business that offers for sale everything from KISS records to KISS comics, makeup, belt buckles, T-shirts, posters and jewelry. A packed arena with the majority pubescent teens was showered with a boggling spectacle of pyrotechnics and rock theatrics... A huge KISS logo that flashed in synch to the music's beat was suspended in midair above and behind the stage. With such flashy visual diversions, the music became a secondary consideration. KISS delivers a crude, thoroughly forgettable metallic symphony... Compared to their peers of the hard sledgehammer-rock genre, KISS still is mired in the Stone Age, a sort of modern day Cro-Magnon skiffle band" (San Diego Union, 8/21/77).
- This show was noted as being sold-out in Billboard, but not Performance Magazine.

August 21 - Tucson Convention Center, Tucson, AZ

Promoter: Avalon Attractions
Other act(s): Cheap Trick
Reported audience: 6,561 / 9,400 (69.8%)
Reported gross: $49,407
Notes:
- From a local review: "KISS poured on the theatrics, noise, smoke screens, flame throwers, high-energy rock, flash pots, bombs, simulated blood and a touch of fire eating. An evening delightfully determined to scare the hell out of any adults who might have happened by accidentally. The kids loved it. The same way they love grotesque horror movies, comic books and freak shows. KISS is all of that... Musically, if that's the appropriate word for such a theatrical production, the songs were done with enough high volume enthusiasm to make them exciting at a very fundamental level" (Tucson Citizen, 8/22/77).

August 22 - Memorial Coliseum, Phoenix, AZ
Promoter: Fun Productions
Other act(s): Cheap Trick
Reported audience: ~13,000 **SOLD-OUT
Reported Gross: $103,000
Notes:
- For comparison, Alice Cooper and Peter Frampton drew 9,816 (July 7) and 12,525 (July 9) at the same venue, respectively.
- From a local review: "So now we have KISS, at this point the No. 1 rock band in the U.S., if not the world. The average age of its fans is 14. Millions of kids love KISS. Phoenix kids apparently are no different. I have seen many concerts in my time, but I've yet to see one in which the performers so dominated their audience as KISS did the other night. It captured and enthralled 10,000 screaming, maniacal young people — 9 and 10-year-olds bedecked in mock-KISS costumes, their faces painted to match the white masks of their idols. They even aped the hand and arm movements of the on-stage theatrical antics of the four KISS members.

Those social conditions Steppenwolf decried in such vile language KISS glorifies, romanticizes and tarns into millions of dollars: Blood and guts connotations of the supernatural, overt displays of implied eroticism, extravagant lighting and fireworks demonstrations and the outrageous cat, vampire, space suit and sex-starved costumes which make up KISS are employed solely for their fans" (Chris Shuey, Scottsdale Progress, 8/25/77).
- The $103,000 gross was a record for the venue resulting in $14,750 rent. While the above review notes 10,000 attendees, the reported gross would not be possible figure. With a mix of $7.50–8.50 tickets, a sell-out or near sell-out is more plausible.

August 25 - Forum, Inglewood, CA **STAGING / TEMP HOLD DATE
Notes:
- This date, appearing on itineraries, was strictly for staging and set-up for the "Alive II" shows. Pre-sets were also conducted on all of the recording equipment that was to be used to capture the shows. On both the 26th and 27th it was planned to record at both rehearsals and the actual shows.
- During the day the band participated in a financial meeting with all of the principle figures at Glickman/Marks and Aucoin Management. Item #6, "When questioned by the Partners when they would become millionaires, Carl estimated that with their next set of royalty statements it was a good possibility that they would each be worth $1 million."
- In his review of the "Love Gun" album in this day's issue of Rolling Stone magazine (Issue #246), Charles Young commented, "I'm told their next album will be a double live set. If history repeats itself, that album will contain the definitive versions of everything potentially worth hearing on Love Gun."

August 26 - Forum, Inglewood, CA
Promoter: Fun Productions
Other act(s): Cheap Trick
Reported audience: 17,763 **SOLD-OUT

Set list: I Stole Your Love / Take Me / Ladies Room / Firehouse / Love Gun / Hooligan / Makin' Love / Christine Sixteen / Shock Me / I Want You / Calling Dr. Love / Shout it out Loud / God of Thunder / Rock And Roll All Nite / Detroit Rock City / Beth / Black Diamond
Notes:
- According to a KISS Army fan club postcard, sharing the info that the shows would be recorded for "Alive II" and that "I Was There" pins would be handed out to attendees, the new tour book debuted at this show.
- Super KISS: "There were a few of us at the KISS concert at the Fabulous Forum Friday night (and probably a few on the following nights) who weren't particularly glad to be there. Some of us were there to satisfy a curiosity, which was satiated seconds after the group began its first number (none dare call it a song). Teenagers and pre-teens were packed in the restrooms throwing up (and this was before the music even started), and one impatient youth looked concerned and asked, 'Is it all out yet?' as he watched his partner losing a pint of whisky and a pizza on the steps. In the lobbies the fans squandered the remainder of their allowance money..." (Long Beach Independent, 8/31/77).
- From a mainstream review: "If you asked a kid in the audience — most were 12–20 — what they liked best about KISS, which opened here Aug. 26 for a series of shows, they usually replied that they liked the makeup and the visual effects, especially 'when he started spitting blood and when the guitar started smoking.' Stage effects aside, KISS is a middlingly decent progressive rock group, neither any worse nor any better than the dozens that used to exit in the heyday of progressive rock acts such as Cream, Mountain and others. But when it comes to a show, KISS gives 100% entertainment, interspersing 14 tunes such as 'I Want You' and 'Rock 'n' Roll All Night' with fire-eating and roaring bursts of flame and pounds of confetti tossed out over the audience. There was constantly something going on. And the sold-out crowd ate it up. Many of them wore greasepaint like their onstage heroes" (Billboard, 9/10/77).
- A very reasonable AUD recording circulates from this show, generally known as the legendary "Sneak Attack" vinyl bootleg. Roughly 10 minutes of non-consecutive 8mm footage was also filmed and sold contemporaneously as the 3 part "Gun" series of mail-order films.
- A few of Paul's stage raps from this show:

After "Take Me:" "Whoa! How ya doin' Los Angeles? Does everybody feel alright? Whoa! And I know... I know, by God, it's gonna be a hot night for rock and roll! And I know. I know we're gonna have a couple of girls, pretty girls, coming back and meeting us in the ladies room..."

After "Ladies Room:" "Alright! This being Los Angeles, and this being summer time, you know, you know we're gonna get this place hot tonight! Are you ready to get this place hot? 'Cause I know... I just know that if everybody loosens up a little bit, we're gonna get this place so hot we're gonna have to call out... call out the 'Firehouse'!"

After "Firehouse:" "Alright! Does everybody feel good? Alright, this is the title track... title track off the new album... 'Love Gun!'"
- Rock journalist Sylvie Simmons reviewed the show: "What KISS lack in musical subtlety, they more than make up for in special effects... The KISS set-up boasted five truck-sized trailers, necessary when you're lugging giant mirror-balls, giant lighting rigs, giant KISS logo, giant kinetic meccanno set, more amps than any other group has used on stage (so says

their record co.), altogether a million dollars worth of chrome, glass and wires and a cast of thousands to operate it, round the country. KISS are nothing if not visual... Unless it gets a good deal of mixing afterwards, the album doesn't look like stunning anyone with its musical quality though. If you closed your eyes to the visual distractions and concentrated on the tunes it was all rather flat. The backing music especially had a definite unreal quality, often sounding distant and blurred, a bit like a tape. Their guitars weren't visibly connected to the amps, so it's possible they were using the equivalent of radio mikes. It might help them play while suspended 30 feet in the air, but if that was the reason for the fuzzy sound it's quite a risk to take when recording live" (Sounds, 9/17/77).

August 27 - Forum, Inglewood, CA
Promoter: Fun Productions
Other act(s): Cheap Trick
Reported audience: (17,763 capacity)

August 28 - Forum, Inglewood, CA
Promoter: Fun Productions
Other act(s): Cheap Trick
Reported audience: (17,763 capacity)
Notes:
From a local review: "Before Bob Dylan and the Beatles gave it respectability, rock 'n' roll was dismissed by most adults as shrewd but untalented musicians preying on the prurient interests of a young, unsuspecting audience. A quick glance at KISS' three weekend concerts at the Inglewood Forum was enough to make most of those grouchy detractors from two decades ago seem like prophets. Picking up where ghoulish Alice Cooper left off, KISS mixed demonic makeup, fire-spitting antics and flashy stage effects for some sideshow hokum that would have made even P.T. Barnum take note. Often theatrics cause an audience to overlook a band's solid musical capabilities, but that's not the case with KISS. The vocals are undistinguished, the songs are rarely more than passable and the musicianship isn't likely to win its members a place on anyone's all-star poll. But it's hard to take offense at KISS. That's largely because the band has a good-natured, unpretentious stance on stage. They don't pretend to be anything more than comic-book figures. And, yes, there is a KISS comic book on the market... Despite its somewhat ominous overtones, KISS is no more dangerous or perverse than a walk through the haunted house at Disneyland. And it's a lot more lively. The concert is like an extension of the barroom scene from 'Star Wars.' It's not as imaginatively staged, but just as teasingly bizarre... Emphasizing materials from its last three LPs, KISS wasted little time in getting to the music. More precisely, it wasted little time getting to the special effects. Though many in the audience knew the songs well enough to sing along the words, the songs often seemed like time-killers as the next effect was being readied" (LA Times, 8/30/77).
- Gene attended one of the AC/DC shows at the Whiskey (Aug. 29 – 30) and invited the band to open up for KISS on their next tour.
- Part of this show is purportedly part of the "KISS Takes Los Angeles" bootleg.

September 1 - The Summit, Houston, TX
Promoter: Pace Concerts/Concerts West
Other act(s): Styx
Reported audience: 14,950 **SOLD-OUT

Reported gross: $255,520 **both nights
Set list: Same as Aug. 26
Notes:
- From a local review: "Interesting? Colorful? You bet, but then (no doubt) so was Sodom and Gomorrah... or the burning of Atlanta... or any one of a hundred other disasters. I mean, KISS doesn't just 'play music' (actually, that's what they do the least of!); togged out in their bizarre costumes and painted faces, the rip, snort and breathe fire all over the stage, push their powerful amps to the limit and, these days — now that they've been successfully sold as the 'hottest rock group in the land' — they work large concert halls full of young people into absolute hair-whipping frenzies" (Houston Chronicle, 9/2/77).
- "Black Diamond" from this show was released as part of the "KISSology Vol. 1" DVD package. Both nights were filmed by John Crow TV Productions with a SBD audio mix for in-house use (the venue famously had 4 "telscreens" and full capabilities for filming and recording). Because the video was filmed for the house-screens there are blank gaps between songs where nothing would have visible during the show.

September 2 - The Summit, Houston, TX
Promoter: Pace Concerts/Concerts West
Other act(s): Styx
Reported audience: 14,950 **SOLD-OUT
Set list: Same as Aug. 26
Notes:

- Provides the bulk of the show released as part of the "KISSology Vol. 1" DVD package, with the exception of "Black Diamond." "Rock And Roll All Nite" is also missing Ace's solo on that release. Like night one it's a pro-shot video with SBD audio mix. It's generally felt that this show has the edge over the previous night visually, though the performance certainly wasn't better.

September 4 - Tarrant County Convention Center, Ft. Worth, TX
Promoter: Concerts West
Other act(s): Styx
Reported audience: ~10,690 **SOLD-OUT
Set list: Same as Aug. 26
Notes:
- Tickets for this show went on sale Aug. 6.
- From a local review: "Welcome ladies and gentlemen and children between the ages of six and 16. The circus is back in town. Now this is not the greatest show on earth. It's not even a 3-ringer. No, this is a 1-ring, 1-dimensional affair featuring Gene 'Tongue' Simmons, the fire-breathing bass player, and his three equally grotesquely painted clowns, collectively known as KISS. KISS, however, is a misnomer. The word implies tenderness, love and affection. After seeing the band's concert Sunday night, the first of two consecutive nights they will appear at the Tarrant County Convention Center, I think a name better suited to this foursome is Rape. A kid in back of me had a portable tape recorder; destroying the illusion that no one comes to see KISS for the 'music.' I thought the only thing that dragged them here was theatrics" (Dallas Morning News, 9/5/77).
- A partial SBD exists from this show. Paul sings "Black Diamond."

September 5 - Tarrant County Convention Center, Ft. Worth, TX
Promoter: Concerts West
Other act(s): Styx
Reported audience: (10,690 capacity)
Set list: Same as Aug. 26
Notes:
- The final date of the "Love Gun" tour.
- While the previous night's show was reported as a sell-out, tickets were still available on the day of show for the final engagement. Box office reports suggest an attendance of around 7,000, though some press articles also reported that the second night had also sold-out by Sep. 2. The first show had nearly sold-out by Aug. 12, and this second date was added on Aug. 18.
- A partial SBD exists from this show.

KISS Alive II

Even with the adjustment of the set list, the "Alive II" tour was little more than an extension of the "Love Gun" tour with it starting off where the latter had left off. However, it is firmly burned into the psyche as the ultimate tour the band conducted during their original era. Simply put, the "Alive II" represented the band at its visual height and domestic popularity as they prepared for an extended hiatus from the road in order to pursue the solo albums and TV projects. During this period merchandising grew, as did the band's overexposure. But for a few months the band put on some of their strongest performances on this tour, which still stands as one of their best attended averaging 13,900 attendees per show.

When compared with the "Love Gun" tour set, the "Alive II" set was generally static (as far as available sets suggest) and saw "Hooligan" and "Take Me" being replaced with "King of the Night Time World" and "Let Me Go, Rock And Roll." At a single show "Deuce" made a return to the set following a delay, quickly to disappear again. As had been the case the in 1977 the band returned to Japan, though not for a tour but a five-night stand at the Budokan. It is likely that the venture, unlike the previous year which lost money (with most of the tab being picked up by Victor Industries, Casablanca's Japanese distributor), made a profit of over $250,000. And for hype value, beating the Beatles record at the Budokan was probably worth it any way. Following the conclusion of the tour the band would play a final show at Magic Mountain, primarily for radio contest winners, in order to film performance sequences for the "KISS Meets the Phantom of the Park" TV movie. They'd not perform together again until the "Return of KISS" tour kicked off the following year...

November 1 - Stewart Air Base, Newburgh, New York **REHEARSALS
November 2 - Stewart Air Base, Newburgh, New York **REHEARSALS
November 3 - Stewart Air Base, Newburgh, New York **REHEARSALS
November 4 - Stewart Air Base, Newburgh, New York **REHEARSALS
November 5 - Stewart Air Base, Newburgh, New York **REHEARSALS
November 6 - Stewart Air Base, Newburgh, New York **REHEARSALS
November 7 - Stewart Air Base, Newburgh, New York **REHEARSALS
November 8 - Stewart Air Base, Newburgh, New York **REHEARSALS
November 9 - Stewart Air Base, Newburgh, New York **REHEARSALS
Notes:
- One day was scheduled to be set aside during the rehearsals for the filming of songs for promotional use and the E. Newman interview for the "Land of Hype and Glory" NBC documentary.

November 15 - Myriad Convention Center, Oklahoma City, OK
Promoter: Concerts West
Other act(s): Detective
Reported audience: 14,885 **SOLD-OUT
Set list: I Stole Your Love / King of the Night Time World / Ladies Room / Firehouse / Love Gun / Let Me Go, Rock 'N' Roll / Makin' Love / Christine Sixteen / Shock Me / I Want You / Calling Dr. Love / Shout It Out Loud / God of Thunder / Rock And Roll All Nite / Detroit Rock City / Beth / Black Diamond
Notes:
- This show was reported in local press as being sold-out (11/14/77). The band flew into Oklahoma City, from New York's LaGuardia airport, the day prior to the show following a band business meeting where the were advised that Carl Glickman would close the coal mining deal that would require each partner to invest $185,000.
- From a local review: "KISS — rock and roll's answers to comic book super heroes — exploded onto the Myriad stage Tuesday night with a dazzling display of predictable theatrics and borrowed rock riffs... But to their rabid fans, KISS can do no wrong. The near sellout crowd was on its feet throughout, cheering wildly at everything from a mere change in lighting to an occasional genuine show of musicianship... Their music alone is sometimes painfully boring, unimaginative, brain-pounding hard rock, but their visual antics are always interesting" (Oklahoma Journal, 11/17/77).
- Detective was more than a vehicle for former Silverhead singer Michael Des Barres. The band's line-up included original Steppenwolf guitarist Michael Monarch and original Yes keyboard player Tony Kaye. They were completed by bassist Bobby Pickett and drummer John Hyde. The band was supporting their second and final studio album, "It Takes One to Know One" (Swan Song/Atlantic).
- An AUD recording from this show exists.

November 17 - McNichols Arena, Denver, CO
Promoter: Feyline Presents, Inc.
Other act(s): Detective
Reported audience: 10,586 / 18,949 (55.87%)
Reported gross: $94,852
Notes:
- The band flew from Oklahoma City the day prior to the show.

- Roughly 4 minutes of silent 8mm footage circulates from this show which was also released on "The Vintage" DVD in 2001.

November 19 - Taylor County Coliseum, Abilene, TX
Promoter: Stone City Productions
Other act(s): Detective
Reported audience: 9,082 **SOLD-OUT
Notes:
- KISS broke the attendance record that they'd set at this venue in January. Only 2,300 tickets sold the first couple of weeks on sale, and by the day before the concert sales were reported in the local press as standing at 5,200.
- From a local review: "With repeated shouts of 'Abuleeene, we love you!' KISS triumphantly returned to the Big Country, setting a new attendance record of 9,082 while turning 600 people away from Taylor County Coliseum Saturday night. KISS seems to have reached the point where they can no longer be viewed as merely a popular rock and roll band, but must be examined as a cultural phenomenon. The average age of the crowd was probably 15 and most of the teen-agers sported the demonic KISS logo silk-screened on T-shirts, molded into belt buckles and printed on their skin with rub-on tattoos. Rut the crowd wasn't all teen-agers. A few parents braved the crowd and the noise to chaperone their pre-teenagers to their first rock concert probably the first for both the parents and their children in some cases. And the show itself lived up to the advertising slogan labeling it 'The Show of Shows.' KISS made a grand entrance complete with dry-ice fog swirling on stage, a mirror ball reflecting the light of four spotlights and deafening explosions while the band was lowered to the stage by a hydraulic lift.

KISS is a band made up of four distinctive personalities. The most popular is Gene Simmons, a deadly-looking vampire figure who eats fire and spews blood during the show. Paul Stanley pranced around the stage on eight-inch platforms in his role as the bisexual sex-symbol. Peter Criss crouched catlike on his drummer's platform and Ace Frehley stumbled around the stage like a spaced-out spaceman. Critics have consistently lambasted KISS for playing inane three-cord rock and roll and generally intuiting the intelligence of serious rock fans. But no band can remain as popular as KISS without having some kind of talent. Although the members of KISS concentrated primarily on their campy, glittering stage show; their music was clean and loud obviously designed to complement the stage show and maintain a high-energy level. Using the latest in rock and roll technology — including radio pick-ups on their guitars so they aren't tripping over wires and the largest assemblage of amplifiers of any rock group KISS put on a hard rock show that appealed directly to the crowd's primal instincts. One theory lays that KISS is essentially a bar band. They have shown the world that it doesn't take talent to be a superstar. It just takes a gimmick. But I have long been a fan of bar bands. Bar bands put on no-nonsense shows uncluttered with overproduction and maudlin ballads. A bar band's goal is to entertain, and that is exactly what KISS does. They play exactly what the crowd wants to hear.

However, Frehley played a stinging lead guitar and although his solos may not have been as fast as Ted Nugent's, they were just as exciting. With land mines bursting around them, pulsating sirens and lights flashing overhead and 40-foot-tall fountains of flame beside them, KISS performed songs that may become rock and roll classics 'Rock and Roll All Nite,' 'Shout It Out Loud,' 'Love Gun' and others. The show included a lot of theatrics as Simmons glared from his perch on a 20-foot high hydraulic lift above the crowd as he dramatically pointed at the fountains of flame onstage. Frehley's guitar literally caught fire and blew up during his solo. (Jimi Hendrix's pouring lighter fluid on his guitar at the Monterey Pop Festival seems incredibly tame by comparison.) The finale was pure spectacle. Criss calmed the crowd down with the popular ballad 'Beth.' But after about a 10-minute ovation with Bic lighters and burning Coke cups lighting up the coliseum, Simmons came out and started the intro to 'Black Diamond,' one of the group's most powerful songs. He was joined by the rest of the group and each member was raised up on hydraulic lift as explosions went off all over the stage, fireworks spun over the stage, confetti was dumped onto the audience and the KISS logo flashed brilliantly in the background. The drummer's platform raised to reveal an gold and silver tapestry of two ferocious-looking cats.

And then with a final 'We love you, Abuleeene!' the cultural phenomenon was over. After the concert, small kids scurried around the coliseum picking among the mounds of confetti, loose bottles and coke cups trying to find souvenirs. The scene looked like a battleground with the ominous KISS logo with the lightning 'SS' of Hitler's secret police adding to the eerie atmosphere. Approximately 20 people were arrested, a surprisingly small number for such a large crowd. Traffic control was again a problem, but no major accidents were reported. The concert proved there's a Big Country concert-going crowd. Hopefully it will enable Dennis Templeton, coliseum manager, to book more major acts" ("KISS Spectacle Sets Coliseum Record," Dannay Goddard, Abilene Reporter-News, 11/21/77).
- Another feature: "Tight security surrounded the KISS concert Saturday night and backstage passes were rare as snow in July, but Jeanne Henninger of Abilene got an insider's view of the operation. Her cousin, Laurie Greenan of New York, is the band's costume mistress, and Ms. Henninger was hired as the show's 'go-fer' for the day. 'They try to hire somebody local who knows the town everywhere they go, I worked all day sewing costumes and going for different things,' Ms. Henninger said Ms. Henninger, who has just finished a tour in the Air Force and works for a local private nursing firm. She met the band members, but only briefly. 'I met them very briefly when they came in for a sound check around 4 or 4:30 p.m. (Saturday),' she said. They were not wearing makeup, she said. 'They were fairly friendly. They said hello. But they were nothing great to look at. The long hair really shocked me but I guess that was just an Air Force thing,' she said. She said 'none of the band members was particularly handsome. I can see why they wear the makeup. I don't think all the girls would be crazy about them if they didn't wear the makeup onstage.'

The stage crew impressed Ms. Henninger the most. 'They were a very professional group. They all pitched in and got the job done.' The road crew includes 22 people. Ms. Greenan is the only female. Two stages are transported on two separate flatbed trucks. Alternate stages are used at each show. The rest of the equipment is transported in five 43-foot Lo-Boy air-ride trucks. The gear is estimated at $250,000. The crew travels in two plush buses complete with carpet, bunks, a shower, kitchenette and stereo system with headphones in each bunk. It takes 10 men and a forklift operator four hours to erect the stage. They are assisted by 22 local people hired for each show. The KISS road crew moved into Taylor County Coliseum about 1 a.m. Saturday and had the stage ready by 4 p.m. Most of the crew was up all night putting up the stage. 'When we came in that morning, there were huge trunks waiting for us that held the costumes. I couldn't believe those costumes. I stood next to one of the guy's boots and it came up to my hip. They must have had eight-inch platforms on them.'

Her cousin has been with the group for about two years, but this is her first time to travel with the road crew. Ms. Greenan had worked for a costume company in New York and free-lanced for awhile as a stylist for television commercials until Ken Anderson, KISS' production manager, and an old friend asked her if she wanted to design costumes for the group. 'She went to high school with Gene Simmons at Newton High School in Queens, but she doesn't remember him. Gene said he remembered her though,' Ms. Henninger said. Ms. Henninger watched the show from the mixing stage the central control board set up at the back of the coliseum floor. 'I'm not really into that hard rock music, but I got all excited at the show. The guys on the mixing stage laughed at me, but they see the show every night. It was definitely exciting and very theatrical.' However, there were a few problems with the staging. The explosions didn't all go off at the right time, and at one point Simmons was pointing at a fountain of flame that wouldn't work.

'But I don't think any of the kids noticed,' Ms. Henninger said, after the concert. KISS, still in costume and make up, jumped into the limousines and roared off. A bodyguard drove the limousine back with the costumes and Ms. Henninger helped pack the costumes into the huge trunks. 'I washed all their makeup brushes and my cousin and I talked about picking up all the dirty Kleenexes and selling them. I bet you could make good bucks doing that,' she said. 'It was all a real kick for an aged teenybopper like me.' Ms. Henninger said she worked 17 hours and was paid 'handsomely'" ("Abilenian gets behind the scenes with KISS," Danny Goddard, The Abilene Reporter-News, 11/22/77).

November 20 - Coliseum, Lubbock, TX
Promoter: Stone City Attractions
Other act(s): Detective
Reported audience: 10,300 **SOLD-OUT

November 22 - Joe Freeman Coliseum, San Antonio, TX
Promoter: Stone City Attractions
Other act(s): Detective
Reported audience: 7,500 **SOLD-OUT

November 23 - Joe Freeman Coliseum, San Antonio, TX
Promoter: Stone City Attractions
Other act(s): Detective
Reported audience: 7,500 **SOLD-OUT
Notes:
- Both dates were reported as sold-out in the local press.

November 26 - Assembly Center, Tulsa, OK
Promoter: Stone City Attractions
Other act(s): Detective
Reported audience: ~8,300 / 8,994 (92.28%)
Notes:
- From a local review: "KISS is more than a night out for teenagers. It is a chance to, as the psychologists put it, 'act out;' it is a Saturday night bath that, at least for the space of a few hours, removes the gritty clay of authority... KISS is the after effects. Unlike some groups

that start riots, KISS leaves a crowd exhausted and feeling strangely relieved and satisfied" (Tulsa World, 11/28/77).

November 27 - Kemper Arena, Kansas City, MO
Promoter: Contemporary Productions/Chris Fritz Productions
Other act(s): Detective
Reported audience: 13,613 / 19,252 (70.71%)
Reported gross: $100,151

November 29 - Veteran's Memorial Arena, Des Moines, IA
Promoter: Celebration Productions
Other act(s): Detective
Reported audience: 13,000 / 14,500 (89.66%)
Reported gross: $100,000
Set list: Same as Nov. 15
Notes:
- Concerts at this venue were under threat following U.S. District Court Judge William C. Hanson ruling that searches of concert attendees without cause prior to shows was unconstitutional and issued a permanent injunction against them. Venue operators were concerned about contraband, bottles and weapons often leading to poor behavior by attendees. The venue manager threatened this show (and others) with cancelation if concert-goers at an Oct. Blue Oyster Cult show misbehaved in light of the new rules. Fortunately it went smoothly enough.
- A generally poor AUD recording circulates. It's heavily muffled with static in parts and cuts during Peter's drum solo.
- From a local review: "Any estimation of the rock group KISS must be made in two parts, the music and the act. The music part can be dispensed by quoting the advertising slogan that underground cartoonist Robert Crumb dreamed up to sell his joke 78-rpm recording of 'Wisconsin Wiggle: A high standard of standardness.' KISS drew 13,000 to Veterans Auditorium Tuesday night, after attracting a record crowd of 14,500 to Vets just 10 months ago. One hopes the music is not the attraction that induced the sub-voting age population of central Iowa to empty its pockets of roughly $100,000. If not the music, then it must be the act, right? Well, that's hard to believe. The act just wasn't that good. A little history is perhaps in order. The first rock & roll acts were staged by Ben Jonson, a poet laureate of England, and Inigo Jones, an architect, for King James I about 375 years ago. These included almost everything that modern rock acts have, except incandescent light bulbs and loudspeakers: Fireworks, loud music, dancing and prancing, smoke, sets that opened up to reveal volcanoes, dancing girls, wildlife, you name it. Thus, a good rock act depends more on style and pace than on originality.

KISS has a lot of trouble with pace. Although it records both heavy metal songs and ballads, the stage act is almost all heavy metal; none of it varied enough to create a pace. The style is warmed over Alice Cooper, though that probably means little enough to the KISS crowd, which is hardly old enough to remember Alice Cooper. For example, KISS has a big, fiberglass snake that breathes smoke; Alice had a real snake he wore around his neck. KISS uses lots of smoke; Alice used even more smoke, and bubbles too. (Credit Lawrence Welk on that one?) KISS has lots of flames and moving drummer's thrones and stuff like that. So did Alice. Alice also had a sense of humor, and KISS will never have that. KISS doesn't even have a sense of respect. Late in the show, lead vocalist Paul Stanley asked the crowd to show some respect by rising for 'the rock 'n' roll national anthem,' which a lot of people did. Well, you could have fooled me. I thought the rock 'n' roll anthem was 'Roll Over, Beethoven,' or maybe 'On Broadway.' KISS turned out to mean a song of its own that went, 'I-I-I-I want to rock and roll all ni-i-i-i-ght,' that wasn't even the second best rock anthem played at Vets Tuesday.

I'll get to the other one in a minute. So, KISS is musically routine and theatrically uninspired. Still, you can't dislike the band. They play simple, derivative music for an unsophisticated audience of children who have not had the chance of seeing a real rock show, like Rod Stewart or Ike and Tina Turner (alas, they'll never see Ike and Tina together again, probably). KISS at least is introducing them to the concept of rock 'n' roll, and some of those children will graduate to the Kinks or Frank Zappa someday. (As for the considerable proportion of adults on hand, there is no hope for them.) Summing up, the show was no fun to anyone who's seen top rock acts live, but the evening did have its moment. It came at the end of the set by Detective, the warm-up band. Detective played so loud — like early Uriah Heep, but without the stage presence - that it was hard to tell whether the band was any good or not. But for its last number the group turned the volume down and broke into a nice arrangement of 'Good Rockin' Tonight,' which really was some kind of rock 'n' roll anthem" (Des Moines Register, 11/30/77).

November 30 - Omaha Civic Auditorium, Omaha, NE
Promoter: Schon Productions

Other act(s): Detective
Reported audience: 11,800 / 12,000 (98.33%)
Reported gross: $84,700
Notes:
- Reported in trades as not being sold-out.
- From a local review: "A bizarre stage show separates KISS from the rest of rockdom, but the band's hard-driving sound ultimately moves the audience... The show's the thing with KISS, and it was there Wednesday. Every musical number had its share either of fire shooting into the air, or smoke, or confetti, or fireworks" (Omaha World-Herald, 12/1/77).
- Detective were not well received by the audience who chanted "We want KISS" throughout their set promoting Des Barres to offer to give the audience a kiss. "He was refused by some rude gestures." Barres was later cut by an object thrown from the audience prompting a warning to the audience that KISS would leave the stage if assaulted similarly.

December 2 - Civic Center Arena, St. Paul, MN
Promoter: Schon Productions
Other act(s): Detective
Reported audience: 16,000 **SOLD-OUT
Reported gross: $115,250
Notes:
- Roughly 4 minutes of audience 8mm footage was filmed at this show.

December 3 - Dane County Coliseum, Madison, WI
Promoter: Stardate Productions
Other act(s): Detective
Reported audience: 10,100 **SOLD-OUT
Reported gross: $80,800
Notes:
- Paul was reportedly hit by a bottle thrown from the audience at this show.

December 4 - Milwaukee, WI **TEMP HOLD DATE

December 6 - Henry Levitt Arena, Wichita, KS
Promoter: Contemporary/Chris Fritz Productions
Other act(s): Detective
Reported audience: 10,724 **SOLD-OUT
Reported gross: $76,318
Set list: Same as Nov. 15
Notes:
- An incomplete poor AUD recording circulates. It's missing "King of the Night Time World," "Shout It Out Loud" and "Black Diamond."

December 7 - Checkerdome, St. Louis, MO
Promoter: Contemporary Productions
Other act(s): Detective
Reported audience: 13,478 / 13,744 (98.06%)
Reported gross: $98,912

Notes:
- This show was not sold out. It had also initially been scheduled for Kiel Auditorium (which instead hosted two Waylon Jennings/Jessi Colter shows instead).
- From local preshow press: "Picture fire-breathing and blood-vomiting by weirdoes in drag with painted faces, outrageously attired in platform boots and skin-tight jumpsuits embellished with scales, studs and feathers. Their show is big on circus sideshow fare: fire pods, a hydraulically levitating drum stand, showering confetti and colored smoke bombs. All this accompanied by a pulsating and hypnotic rock sound... KISS is coming to town" (St. Louis Post-Dispatch, 12/1/77).
- It's probably not surprising that a venue originally built as a livestock hall (aka "The Barn") was notorious for its terrible acoustics. While a KISS show may have come close, the venue was finally blown up on Feb. 27, 1999 with 133lbs of TNT.

December 9 - Mid-South Coliseum, Memphis, TN
Promoter: Mid-South Concerts/Beaver Productions/Electric Factory Concerts
Other act(s): AC/DC
Reported audience: 11,493 / 11,500 (99.94%)
Reported gross: $91,944
Notes:
- Show was not reported as sold-out in trade magazines, but was close enough in terms of the venue's capacity! In a TV interview lead singer Bon Scott was asked about KISS and commented that he'd seem them at the 1976 London show and that Gene had attended one of the Whiskey shows in August and invited the band to do some shows with them. Gene has also placed AC/DC as one of his favorite opening acts.
- From a local review: "The white-haired old man, who said he could remember Warren Harding's presidency and Lindbergh's solo flight across the Atlantic, admitted he drove from Oklahoma City to Memphis yesterday to see what this KISS stuff is all about.' And after watching the rock group KISS put on a performance last night at the Mid-South Coliseum that included flashing colors, exploding fireworks, flaming guitars, crashing cannons and unuttered rock-and-roll, Bert Williams rubbed his forehead and said, 'All I can say is all those weird effects must cost a bundle.' Williams, who said he was a life insurance salesman, conceded that the nine-hour drive was 'something I did on an impulse. I'd read a lot about them, but I had no idea, just no idea. I haven't been to listen to music since right after World War II. It's just amazing. Do kids today always listen to music so loud? O mean, is it always turned up so high? Oh, well, I've got to admit it's pretty exhilarating, especially when all the people are clapping and stomping their feet like this'" (Commercial Appeal, 12/11/77).

December 10 - Municipal Auditorium, Nashville, TN **TEMP HOLD DATE

December 11 - Market Square Arena, Indianapolis, IN
Promoter: Sunshine Productions
Other act(s): AC/DC
Reported audience: ~18,165 **SOLD-OUT
Set list: Same as Nov. 15
Notes:
- Initially scheduled for Dec. 13 this date was moved when the third New York (14th) date was added.

- Tour manager Fritz Postlethwaite was given a feature in local press due to him having graduated from Brebeuf High School in 1968. The feature ran through the daily challenges of setting up the show.
- From a local review: "Its music may smell like a New York City garbage strike, but ya gotta hand it to — KISS them boys sure know how to put on a show... No matter what critics may say about the band's music, KISS concerts are a hallmark in rock 'n' roll... KISS undeniably is the best theatrical group in rock 'n' roll today. Mixing a heavy combination of smoke, fire, explosions, levitating platforms, outrageous makeup and costumes with overbearing, high-voltage rock, KISS displayed why its concerts sell out worldwide. The brightly burning KISS sign etched the band's famed logo deeply into the retina... The audience response was warm, but not as overwhelming as at some of the arena concerts this year. Even the encore calls were weak by KISS standards" (Indianapolis News, 12/12/77).

December 12 - Freedom Hall, Louisville, KY
Promoter: Sunshine Productions
Other act(s): AC/DC
Reported audience: ~19,000 / 19,400 (97.94%)
Notes:
- From a local review: "KISS' appeal is to a very young audience, and a sizeable segment of the Freedom Hall audience was parents accompanying small children... As for the music itself... KISS comes on like a sideshow freaks, not serious musicians, and their hard-driving selections are virtually interchangeable. The flip side of that criticism is that the audience — or at least 90 percent of the audience — could not have cared less about the music quality and I doubt very much that KISS cares either. It is, after all, difficult to approach the guitar as a serious musical instrument when said guitar has a built-in smoke bomb. The fans and the curiosity seekers attend, I think, for the visual aspect of the program and admittedly that's pretty darn spectacular" (Lexington Leader, 12/16/77).
- From a local review: "KISS, the slickest of the shocker rockers, deadened the eardrums of a near-capacity crowd last night in Louisville's Freedom Hall. When you can see the firecrackers going off in the crowd around you, but nobody's flinching — when you can smell the sulfur from the explosions, but you can't hear them, you know it's loud" (Courier-Journal, 12/13/77).

December 14 - Madison Square Garden, New York City, NY
Promoter: Ron Delsener
Other act(s): Detective
Reported audience: 18,000 **SOLD-OUT
Set list: Same as Nov. 15
Notes:
- This was the third New York show added after the other two sold out.
- A lower quality AUD recording from this show circulates.
- From a mainstream press review: "When the lights dimmed, I threw my coat over my head and screamed at the woman next to me, 'Here they come!' Only they never came. No M80s from the upper tier. No cherry bombs. No finger-poppers. No nothing. The woman, who had never been to a hard-rock concert before, thought I was a damn fool. 'Listen, you gotta believe me,' I begged. 'I've seen six KISS concerts in the last year and it's never been like this. The crowd is the most docile since I saw Crosby, Stills and Nash last summer.' And they

stayed that way through the show — barely bothering to stand for the encores, making little noise of any kind. Possible explanations:

1. New York is a bad town for KISS. It was one of the last areas to break for the band. This being a media center, it is possible that some people read critics and want to fell sophisticated.

2. The word is finally getting out that the firecrackers are blowing people's heads off. KISS is hereby commended for having some guy come out before the shows and berate the fans for kilting each other.

3. The thrill is gone. Much as I enjoy watching Gene Simmons puke blood; he's been doing it every night for three years.

4. The real fanatics were elsewhere. They went to the following nights' concerts. This show was added only after two others had sold out.

5. Their demographics are changing. Through overexposure, KISS seems no longer Forbidden Fruit. They are losing their traditional support among proletarian teenage boys and picking up children impressed by costumes. A third of the crowd appeared to be parents with little kids. KISS records are selling phenomenally well, but maybe to Shaun Cassidy weenie bops.

6. KISS got demoralized when I compared their music to buffalo farts last spring. But I compared it favorably. Most popular music I rank lower than buffalo farts.

7. Even though they are better than buffalo farts, Gene Simmons' latest love songs to his dick are dumb. Unless you are a fourteen-year-old virgin with zits. But then you don't want to be sitting next to your mommy and five-year-old brother while you think macho.

8. The show wasn't that good. Even with all the explosions, flame throwers and hydraulic lifts, the band seemed tired. Peter Criss was so hoarse during "Beth" that he broke up laughing. Ace Frehley, whose mind is supposedly on Mars, looked more as if his mind were on getting it over with.

9. Detective stunned the crowd into silent awe. Since these guys don't do anything but clone late-period Zeppelin and Bad Company licks, it must have been the two avocados the singer seemed to have stuffed in the crotch of his white satin stretch pants" (Rolling Stone Magazine #258, Feb. 1978).

December 15 - Madison Square Garden, New York City, NY
Promoter: Ron Delsener
Other act(s): Piper
Reported audience: 18,000 **SOLD-OUT
Set list: Same as Nov. 15
Notes:
- During the day Gene and Paul attended the band's scheduled business meeting at the Drake Hotel. Reports indicate that the tour has resulted in $270,000 profit to date with a projection of about $500,000 for all dates through February.
- Piper was an act, fronted by Billy Squier, also managed by AMI. They were supporting their second album, "Can't Wait," which had been co-produced by Sean Delaney (with Chris Kimsey). Additionally, pre-KISS band member Neil Teeman (Uncle Joe) was credited as the tape operator for the sessions at Electric Lady Studios.

December 16 - Madison Square Garden, New York City, NY
Promoter: Ron Delsener
Other act(s): Piper

Reported audience: 18,000 **SOLD-OUT
Set list: Same as Nov. 15
Notes:
- From a national press review: "Maybe the glitter-rock band KISS should change its name to 'Smack.' KISS, they of the painted faces and outrageous costumes, smacked a full house at Madison Square Garden recently with something close to 180 decibels and outrageous visual effects which were eaten up by the teen-age 'KISS Army' fans. (Those over the age of 21 seemed to have a 'what-am-I-doing-here' look on their faces). KISS opened with 'I Stole Your Love,' a driving foot-stomping number that may have sounded better than it was because the band kept the opening night audience waiting more than an hour past the billed starting time. Ensuing numbers included 'Doctor Love,' 'Christine Sixteen,' and 'Love Gun,' but only the names indicated any individuality in the songs. Bassist Gene Simmons, the tongue-thrusting vampire figure, breathed smoke throughout 'Firehouse' and drooled blood in a guitar solo. 'Space' Ace Frehley's lead guitar smoked and exploded in a shower of sparks at the conclusion of 'Shock Me.' Paul Stanley, the rhythm guitarist and lead singer, broke his instrument over his knee and tossed it to the crowd after 'Rock & Roll All Night.' Peter Criss, the feline-faced drummer, played a long solo to the accompaniment of fireworks in 'God of Thunder.'

The music was pretty good, the guitar playing talented, the drumming fair, and the singing ranged from below average (Frehley) to above average (Stanley and Simmons). KISS' appeal lies in two areas. First, any member of the audience who ever picked up a guitar or beat a drum gets the feeling watching them that all he needs is a smidgen of talent and a load of gimmicks for him too to be a superstar. Secondly, and most importantly, the group truly appreciates its fans and strives to show them a good" (William Cahill - UPI, 12/77).
- The band celebrated after the show at the Harkness Ballet School on East 75th Street.
- A party was held for the road crew at JP's on First Avenue on December 17.

December 19 - Capital Centre, Largo (Landover), MD
Promoter: Cellar Door Presents
Other act(s): AC/DC
Reported audience: 17,561 **SOLD-OUT
Notes:
- From a local review: "Mass hysteria, usually reserved for the last few songs that climax a rock concert, raged among last night's Capital Centre crush and greeted KISS as they appeared on stage. And appear they did, amidst flashing colored lights and minor explosions. The fusion of music and theatre on stage is nothing new — remember Little Richard; and if there is a forum for outlandish overstatement, it is in the rock arena. But this is ridiculous. KISS' two-to-three-chord melody-less, lyric-less music is so loudly repetitious as to be almost characterless... KISS plays rock and roll with a heavy handedness that is supposed to be mistaken for energy but which has all the subtlety of a lead pipe" (Washington Post, 12/20/77).
- From another local review: "It was a scene straight from Hell; a living, medieval panorama of the Inferno. A sea of writing, uplifted arms waved in torment in the stormy darkness, holding up flickering matches and cigarette lighters as a revolving prism reflected starry patches of dancing light space-tripping over furry young moronic heads with constantly-moving jaws chewing purple gum. On stage their hellborn, malefic leader — a fire-eating devil dressed in black with bizarre whiteface makeup and a wildly-flapping, pointed serpent

tongue — was throwing up fake blood in a nightmare alley of evil, billowing smoke, crashing cannon fire, blinking strobe lights, dazzling fireworks, confetti snow-storms, wailing police sirens, booming pillars of fire, and an elevator platform raising him up and down.

And there was, incidentally, the sound of music in concert as practiced by the demoniacal group called 'KISS.' *Music*? It was an explosion of amplified, fuse-blowing sound that moves the eyebrows from the inside of your skull out; a throbbing, pulsating beat that backs you down into your seat and twangs the very bones in your body that have withered to rubber; a riotous torture of sound; a damaging entry through the tympanic membrane that exits through curled toes, leaving a battered head exhausted, ringing and spinning. There is hardly a way to describe such a sound run amuck, such a creation of man's electronic genius that somehow borders on the insane. It is a terrifying exercise in electrical limits" (Washington Star, 12/20/77).

December 20 - Capital Centre, Largo (Landover), MD
Promoter: Cellar Door Presents
Other act(s): Piper
Reported audience: 17,561 **SOLD-OUT
Set list: Same as Nov. 15
Notes:
- This second date was an addition to the itinerary. Aerosmith was queued up for two nights immediately following KISS' stand.

- This show had circulated as a below average AUD recording. Perhaps because the video version of this show had not generally been available, or even known of (other than the material that had been broadcast on TV as part of Dick Clark's American Music Awards), it staggered many fans when included partially as a "KISSology Vol. 1" DVD bonus for retailer Wal-Mart. The full version, albeit with timestamp, was soon circulating, and offers fans a look back at KISS at the visual zenith of the originals era. Of course, with KISS fans seldom being satisfied, the question remains whether the previous night's show was also archived. Additional audience filmed 8mm footage is known to exist.
- Audio from "Love Gun", "Christine Sixteen", and "Shock Me" (with Ace's solo) were included on the 2014 "Love Gun" deluxe edition release, albeit with triggered drum samples and audio work designed to enhance the inferior quality of the original tape.
- Members of the band were scheduled to be interviewed by DC101's David Brown in Ric Aliberte's room following sound-check.

December 22 - Spectrum, Philadelphia, PA

Promoter: Electric Factory Concerts / Spectrum Concerts
Other act(s): Piper
Reported audience: 19,500 **SOLD-OUT
Set list: Same as Nov. 15
Notes:
- AC/DC was originally scheduled as the opening act.
- Interesting though poor AUD recording circulates from this show. Strangely, Paul raps following "I Stole Your Love," rather than the band immediately segueing into "King of the Night Time World." Heavily muffled and distorted — for diehards only. This show could equally be from the Jan. visit.
- From a local review (though "Beth" was indeed performed): "KISS does not need songs to be an exciting stage act. The foursome, which is ranked at the top of the rock pile, has blazed a path in the musical world with its outlandish garb and hard-driving rock music. It's set records which put it in a league with the Beatles as far as audience appeal is concerned. Last night was another example of the group's drawing power. It sold out the Spectrum — a claimed attendance of 15,500 persons — many weeks in advance of the performance. And the performance itself... the music was passable, but the staging and the theatrics were the equal to any legitimate stage production. KISS has admitted in the past that its music is not its strongest point. The four have become competent musicians during the long years they have spent touring and playing together but they are far from being super musicians. The draw of KISS is its features four average musicians who are above-average actors. Not only actors but technicians in the art of generating a crowd magnetism.

Last night's staging for the group's concert fell somewhere between the futuristic and the fantastic. The group played from a multi-level stage. It opened with guitarists Paul Stanley and Ace Frehley and bassist Gene Simons standing on platforms above the stage level. Drummer Peter Criss was on a platform of his own which remained more or less on one level throughout the show but even the drummer's platform was rigged for some exciting activity. As the band started to play, the upper platforms of the guitarists and bass player began to move toward stage level through their hydraulic systems and the stage simultaneously was layered with fog, blazed by a multitude of lights and was resounding with the after-shocks of planned stage explosions. The chrome and glass stage never ceased to be a marvel with its intricate lighting and design. A snake, coiled around a pole, would alternately spew fog and fire over the stage. Sections of the stage would rise 10-feet-or-more above its base to accentuate a band member's solo. Guitars exploded, lights flashed, confetti rained from above, blood flowed... there never was a point during the concert when the audience even could think of being bored. If anything, it was more like a three-ring circus and if you did not watch the show closely, you stood the chance of missing one of its more subtle nuances, although subtlety was a rarity.

If the staging, pyrotechnics and related stage business does not sound flashy enough, you still have to take into consideration the costuming of the group. The members never have been pictured out of makeup. On stage, Criss is a whiskered feline; Simmons is a lizard with a long snaking tongue; Frehley is a surrealistic spaceman, and Stanley, the on-stage group leader, is the star-eyed sex symbol with an exposed hairy chest. They all dress in black, with silver accents, and wear platformed shoes of nose-bleed proportions. During the course of the show, all of the group members, with the exception of Criss, took the band's helm for solo vocals. If it seems that this review is giving the music second-billing to the show, it is because the music was secondary to the show. KISS will continue to draw astronomical numbers to its concerts as long as it, too remembers, music is not its primary message — the show's the thing" (Bucks Co. Courier Times, 12/23/77).

December 27 - Riverside Centroplex, Baton Rouge, LA
Promoter: Beaver Productions
Other act(s): Piper
Reported audience: 15,327 **SOLD-OUT
Notes:
- From a local review: "The most talented members of their company don't ever appear on stage — they are the faceless miracle-workers in charge of the special effects, who provide fireworks on cue and ever-changing lights in multitudes of colors, and giant signs that say 'KISS' with two Nazi SS marks providing part of the word (much like the swastikas and German helmets of the motorcycle gangs — anything to outrage the old establishment, and the farther out the better). As for the actors — and indeed they are actors, for at the end they come out and give bows much like a troupe — they have their own identities after a fashion... It is quite a show. There is sound and color and movement. There are fireworks, strobe lights, lights that flash on and off, smoke bombs, Roman candles. But now we come to the music. And, alas, for all their flash and glitter and noise and light shows and smoke and fancy costumes, KISS isn't a very good band" (Morning Advocate, 12/28/77).
- An AUD recording of this show exists but does not widely circulate.

December 29 - Birmingham-Jefferson Civic Center Coliseum, Birmingham, AL
Promoter: Ruffino-Vaughan Productions
Other act(s): Piper
Reported audience: (18,046 capacity)

December 30 - The Omni, Atlanta, GA
Promoter: Alex Cooley Productions
Other act(s): Piper
Reported audience: 14,417 / 16,500 (87.38%)
Reported gross: $116,201
Notes:

- This show was originally to be promoted by Beach Club Bookings.
- From a local review: "Anyone who has ever listened to a KISS record knows that music is not the group's strong suit, but during the five years that Gene Simmons, Paul Stanley, Ace Frehley and Peter Criss have been touring the country extensively, they have built up a reputation for putting on quite a show. Unfortunately, that reputation appeared to be unwarranted Friday night. Not that they didn't put a lot of effort into it, because they did... But while it might have had a certain childish, circus-like appeal to some, it was hardly sophisticated or even particularly exciting showmanship. The stage patter of the group was particularly infantile and inane" (Atlanta Journal & Constitution, 12/31/77).

December 31 - Coliseum, Greensboro, NC
Promoter: Entam, Ltd. & Beach Club Promotions
Other act(s): Piper
Reported audience: 13,185 / 13,500 (97.67%)
Reported gross: $119,424
Partial set list: Calling Dr. Love / Firehouse / Christine Sixteen / God Of Thunder / Shout It Out Loud / Beth / Rock And Roll All Nite
Notes:
- On the same evening KISS were profiled on a pilot episode of the Allison Steele's "Night Bird" television show, including her classic 1974 San Francisco interview with the band.
- From a local review: "KISS, an outrage disguised under the label of rock 'n' roll, broke into its eleventh straight grinding song Saturday night, entitled, 'Calling Dr. Love.' But the prescription the crowd came to have filled wasn't written for rock 'n' roll. If the doctor's handwriting could be read at all, the prescription read: 'One heavy dose of escape for an hour and a half.' And escape they did, into a fantasy-filled New Year's Eve of blood, fire, smoke and lights" (Greensboro Daily News, 1/1/78).

January 3, 1978 - Memorial Auditorium, Jacksonville, FL **TEMP HOLD DATE

January 3 - Sportatorium, Hollywood, FL
Promoter: Cellar Door Productions
Other act(s): Piper
Reported audience: 16,500 **SOLD-OUT
Set list: Same as Nov. 15
Notes:
- Originally scheduled for Jan. 5.
- A below average AUD recording circulates from this show.

January 5 - Coliseum, Charlotte, NC
Promoter: Kaleidoscope Concerts
Other act(s): Nantucket
Reported audience: (13,000 capacity)
Notes:
- This was Nantucket's first of several opening slots for KISS through the following year's "Return of KISS" tour. They were proud when a promoter told them after one show that they'd done a better job than most opening acts opening for KISS. The southern rock band were about to release their debut album featuring the hit single "Heartbreaker."

January 6 - Carolina Coliseum, Columbia, SC
Promoter: Beach Club Promotions
Other act(s): Nantucket
Reported audience: (12,542 capacity)
Set list: Same as Nov. 15
Notes:
- From a local review: "For rock and roll fans in Columbia, KISS may have presented the greatest show since childhood memories of the circus Friday night at the Carolina Coliseum. And they loudly thanked them with applause and cheers. Even before the four men decked in black and silver costumes and sporting decorative make-up came on stage, the fans bristled with excitement. Security was tight with police monitoring the aisles... As soon as the show began, everyone was on their feet, dancing and jumping around. This was one show where the audience didn't sit by and listen quietly... The group had the Coliseum in the palms of their hands" (Columbia State, 1/7/78).
- A generally poor partial AUD recording circulates from this show. It omits the center of the show from "Makin' Love" through "Shout It Out Loud," and "Beth."

January 8 - Richfield Coliseum, Cleveland, OH
Promoter: Belkin Productions
Other act(s): Rockets
Reported audience: 17,500 **SOLD-OUT
Set list: Same as Nov. 15
Notes:
- The show was reported in local press as sold-out prior to date of show.
- From local press: "Plans to make snowbound visitors to the Coliseum more comfortable when weather-related emergencies occur in the future have been developed by Coliseum officials. The changes in several aspects, including security, were designed after many persons attending the KISS concert Jan. 8 were trapped by that day's blizzard... KISS fans had complained about their treatment by Coliseum guards after that concert, when 258 persons had to spend the night and most of the next morning in the building because of the snow. Since that concert the new firm has been hired" (Elyria Chronicle Telegram, 2/17/78). Other press reports indicated as many as 400 sheltered in the venue. Some also took sanctuary at the Bedford Heights Police station.
-"Beth" not present on the average AUD recording. Unfortunately, the recording quality of the recording declines as the show progresses.

January 9 - Riverfront Coliseum, Cincinnati, OH **POSTPONED
Notes:
- The show, scheduled for this date, was postponed due to poor weather that was affecting the region making it impossible for travel. The band performed the following night.

January 10 - Riverfront Coliseum, Cincinnati, OH
Promoter: Electric Factory Concerts
Other act(s): Rockets
Reported audience: 18,239 **SOLD-OUT
Reported gross: $127,484
Notes:

- From a local review: "When a great artist is born with talent, especially if he is an Italian, he'll tell you he was kissed by God. Whether or not the rock group KISS was born with talent, it's pretty clear that God and the Establishment looked the other way. The group was kissed instead by a Genius of Packaging and Promotion. And the results are pretty spectacular. As long as you don't pay too much attention to the music, that is... There were times when the music, in all its mediocrity, slipped through. But KISS' stage show is bizarre enough, outrageous enough — and more than varied enough — to keep anyone listening with his eyes more than his ears. For those who did bother to listen, KISS foiled them with the First Rule of Aural Camouflage: The difference between first-rate and second-rate music is detectible in inverse proportion to the noise level. If you play loud enough, most people won't be able to discern anything, except possibly that their ears hurt. But back to the stage show, which trades exclusively in the fantastic. And in this, KISS knows exactly what it is about. Using giant, weird, aggressive and absolutely unequivocal gestures, the four-member band immediately established its command of the stage and the audience" (Cincinnati Enquirer, 1/13/78).

- On the night of this show Edwin Newman's "Land of Hype and Glory" was broadcast on NBC Reports: "After wryly noting the program is 'unprecedented, compelling and superlative,' he dwells at length on how publicity helped make millionaires out of four distinguished rockers called KISS. They are distinguished because they wear face paint, occasionally destroy guitars, breath fire, vomit fake blood and even sing via a sound rig sporting only 40 amplifiers and 150 speakers. In inspecting this gonzo group and their guru, Bill Aucoin, Newman deftly establishes that suckers are still born every minute, and thanks to hype, many of them are KISS fans" (AP).

January 11 - Civic Center, Huntington, WV
Promoter: Entam, Ltd.
Other act(s): Rockets
Reported audience: 11,934 **SOLD-OUT
Reported gross: $101,438
Notes:
- From a local review: "They stood in temperatures near 10 degrees (-12C) in Huntington yesterday, all for the sake of rock 'n' roll. Not just any rock 'n' roll, however. It was KISS, the most popular concert group in America, that brought them to the gates of the Civic Center about noon yesterday, 6 1/2 hours before the doors opened to allow the first customers in" (Huntington Herald-Dispatch, 1/12/78).
- Super8 video footage was filmed at this show.

January 13 - Civic Arena, Pittsburgh, PA
Promoter: DiCesare-Engler Productions
Other act(s): Rockets
Reported audience: 17,053 / 17,500 (97.45%)
Reported gross: $128,198
Partial set list: Ladies Room / Firehouse / Love Gun / Christine Sixteen / Calling Dr. Love / God of Thunder / Rock And Roll All Nite / Detroit Rock City / Beth / Black Diamond
Notes:
- From a local review: "Four New York boys — in drag and wearing whiteface makeup such as Marcel Marceau might devise on LSD — lured 17,000 cheerful fanatics into the Civic Arena Friday night for a mixed media performance featuring fireworks, 10-foot flames, lasers, exploding guitars, instant fog, the throwing-up of artificial blood and allegedly 'more amplifiers than have ever been assembled on one stage in Pittsburgh... Their canny combination of hard-rock music plays Barnum-&-Bailey-meets-Dracula has propelled them in just four years to the top of the rock 'n' roll heap, thanks to a massive public relations campaign which modestly bills them as the embodiment of the new rock and the Symbol of the Seventies here to fulfill all our fantasies once and for all... KISS — public relations aside — is a talented and professional rock group which specializes in entertainment as opposed to plain old-fashioned music. Or even new-fashioned music. The group's dazzling road show operates on a magic formula in which music is but one of several equally vital elements: costumes, makeup, sets, lights, choreography, dialogue and — most of all — special effects" (Pittsburgh Post-Gazette, 1/16/78).
- In a letter to the edition, one local resident described the above review in amusing terms: "I was horrified and shocked to find the horrendous Jan. 16 article about KISS on the front page of your paper. The page, usually reserved for more urgent, important news items, was marred somewhat by the editorialized critique of the group's performance. Mr. Paris, it seems, retained more from the erotic display of the 'phallic imagery' than he did from the 'good, but not great' musicianship of the rock group. It is both disgraceful and appalling that the music field has regressed to the point of annihilation of human dignity... It is a frightening thought that 17,000 of tomorrow's citizens are exposed to this violent mockery of the arts which dwells more on the morose and the macabre than the aesthetic... Excuse me while I vomit" (Pittsburgh Post-Gazette, 1/24/78).

January 14 - War Memorial, Syracuse, NY **TEMP HOLD DATE
Notes:

- This date appears in the advance calendar from Performance Magazine, but was not booked.

January 15 - Chicago Stadium, Chicago, IL
Promoter: Jerry Weintraub / Concerts West
Other act(s): Rockets
Reported audience: (18,250 capacity)
Notes:
- From a local review: "No one was asking for any signifying, only a good loud time at the old concert hall, and that is what KISS delivers. Throwing in leaping guitar athletics, a wide assortment of facial grimaces and at least a dozen mentions of our fair city (the easiest way to get a response, it seems), it kept the crowd standing on chairs from the opening blast of fireworks" (Chicago Sun-Times, 1/17/78).
- The show that circulates, attributed to this date, is the same as January 16, a generally poor AUD recording. Audience 8mm footage was filmed at this show.

January 16 - Chicago Stadium, Chicago, IL
Promoter: Jerry Weintraub / Concerts West
Other act(s): Rockets
Reported audience: (18,250 capacity)
Set list: Same as Nov. 15
Notes:
- The show that circulates is the same as January 15, a very poor AUD recording.

January 18 - Rupp Arena, Lexington, KY
Promoter: Entam, Ltd. / Sunshine Productions
Other act(s): Rockets
Reported audience: 10,500 / 18,500 (56.76%)
Reported gross: $87,143
Notes:
- Poor weather likely resulted in this subpar attendance (likely impacting last minute walk-ups); a winter storm warning had been issued across the state.
- From a local review: "Rebellion can take many forms. Wednesday night, about 10,500 area young people showed they could not be intimidated by the foul weather that has virtually closed Lexington. The horde defied the weather gods to participate in that pagan ritual known as a KISS concert at Rupp Arena and they were temporarily warmed by a murderous barrage of danger lever decibel rock and roll and pyrotechnics" (Lexington Herald, 1/20/78).

January 20 - Olympia Stadium, Detroit, MI
Promoter: Belkin Productions
Other act(s): Rockets
Reported audience: (16,500 capacity)
Set list: I Stole Your Love / King of the Night Time World / Firehouse / Love Gun / Makin' Love / Christine Sixteen / Shock Me / I Want You / Calling Dr. Love / Shout It Out Loud / God of Thunder / Rock And Roll All Nite / Beth / Detroit Rock City / Black Diamond
Notes:
- Paul was presented with a cake and trophy on stage in celebration of his birthday.

- From a local review: "Everything previously said about the things the outrageous rock band KISS does on stage is true — these guys are mad! KISS displayed its spectacular yet bizarre stage show to a packed Olympia Stadium Friday night" (The Michigan Daily, 1/24/78).
- An average AUD recording circulates from this show.
- The setup of this show was featured in a 5-page Detroit Free Press article on band roadies on Feb. 26.

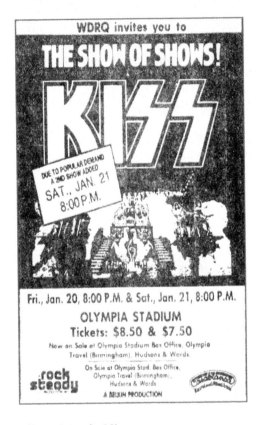

January 21 - Olympia Stadium, Detroit, MI
Promoter: Belkin Productions
Other act(s): Rockets
Reported audience: (16,500 capacity)
Notes:
- Second show added due to demand.

January 23 - Roberts Stadium, Evansville, IN
Promoter: Sunshine Promotions
Other act(s): Rockets
Reported audience: 14,144 **SOLD-OUT
Reported gross: $109,298
Set list: I Stole Your Love / King of the Night Time World / Ladies Room / Firehouse / Love Gun / Let Me Go, Rock 'N' Roll / Makin' Love / Christine Sixteen / Shock Me / I Want You / Calling Dr. Love / Deuce / Rock And Roll All Nite / Detroit Rock City / Beth / Black Diamond

Notes:
- "Deuce" makes a rare return to the set list as a treat following a delay in the set — it hadn't been performed since 1976. Paul announced it after set interruption: "Alright, since you people have been so patient, we've got something we haven't done in a long time so you might want to hear it!"
- From a local review: "An accident on stage temporarily dimmed the intensity of the concert, the third for KISS in Evansville. A spotlight tower, approximately 40 feet high, collapsed on stage about three-fourths of the way through the concert. Only when the lights went on several minutes later, and the announcement was made of the accident, did many fans realize that it was not part of the show. Two persons were reported as injured in the accident" (Evansville Courier, 1/24/78). One of those people was spotlight operator Thomas Mills, who required stitches. The other was Lydia Criss, who was taken to hospital as a precaution. She was identified in the review as "Ledia Criscuola."
- A below average partial AUD recording circulates from this show. It cuts during "Beth."

January 25 - War Memorial Auditorium, Buffalo, NY
Promoter: Festival East/Hooke Productions
Other act(s): Rockets
Reported audience: 17,500 **SOLD-OUT
Reported gross: $112,636
Notes:
- Roughly 8 minutes of silent 8mm footage circulates from this show.

January 27 - Civic Center, Springfield, MA
Promoter: Cross Country Concerts
Other act(s): Rockets
Reported audience: 10,395 **SOLD-OUT
Reported gross: $72,765
Set list: Same as Nov. 15
Notes:
- Mayor Theodore E. Dimauro attended the show and later comments, "I couldn't hear a thing. Were they playing music?" (North Adams Transcript, 1/31/78). He was there to witness firsthand the behavior of attendees that had been disorderly at other events resulting in his threat to ban concerts.
- An above average AUD recording circulates from this show, though the intro cuts and starts with "field! You wanted the best..." leading to the assumption that the show is indeed Springfield, until Paul confirms the location in his post "King of the Night Time World" rap. There are a couple of minor cuts, but otherwise the recording is pretty solid.

January 28 - New Haven Coliseum, New Haven, CT
Promoter: Cross Country Concerts
Other act(s): Rockets
Reported audience: 10,407 **SOLD-OUT
Reported gross: $76,000
Notes:
- From a local review: "KISS gives the illusion of being demonic hell-benders but essentially they are harmless. The sing mostly about love and rock and roll rather than drugs and blowing up the First National Bank. They invite screams but giggles usually follow as well.

There isn't the threat that punk rock demonstrates — there are no safety pins in the ears and the KISS tattoos come off in the bubble bath. At worst, the amps may give the family migraines, the makeup may aggravate the pimples and everybody knows you shouldn't wear black at night. They're not rebels with or without causes. They're not rebels at all. They're party people representing rock and roll at its most innocent and insipid level" (New Haven Journal Courier).

January 29 - Nassau Coliseum, Uniondale, NY **TEMP HOLD DATE
January 30 - Nassau Coliseum, Uniondale, NY **TEMP HOLD DATE
Notes:
- On early itineraries these dates were penciled in as possibilities, but were ultimately never booked.

January 30 - The Spectrum, Philadelphia, PA
Promoter: Electric Factory Concerts
Other act(s): Rockets
Reported audience: 19,500 **SOLD-OUT
Notes:
- It's amazing to consider that KISS had just performed at the same venue a month previously (12/22/77) and tickets for that second show had gone on sale the week of the first show.

January 31 - Civic Center Baltimore, MD **TEMP HOLD DATE

February 2 - Civic Center, Providence, RI
Promoter: Frank J. Russo Presents
Reported audience: 13,082 **SOLD-OUT
Set list: Same as Nov. 15
Notes:
- Bill Aucoin personally requested that these Providence shows be added to the band's itinerary at their Nov. 14 business meeting in New York.
- An average AUD recording, attributed to this date, circulates.

February 3 - Civic Center, Providence, RI
Promoter: Frank J. Russo Presents
Reported audience: 13,082 **SOLD-OUT
Notes:
- The end of the "Alive II" tour, and KISS' last U.S. public performance (excludes the Magic Mountain filming concert) until June 1979.
- A dreadful AUD recording from this show circulates.

March 28 - Budokan Hall, Tokyo, Japan
Promoter: Udo Artists, Inc.
Other act(s): Bow Wow
Reported audience: 11,000 **SOLD-OUT
Set list: Same as Nov. 15
Notes:

- KISS arrived in Tokyo on March 24. They had some rehearsal time scheduled at Victor Record studios on March 25 and 26, with Gene doing some solo recording there as well.
- Sound check was scheduled for 3PM with Bow Wow's 30-minute set starting at 6:30. KISS hit the stage at 7:30PM.
- Dating most of the 1978 Japan shows is a difficult task. This show was thought to circulate as a muffled and below average AUD recording. A far better AUD version (Mr. Peach) was released on the unofficial CD "Heartbreaker from Hell" in 2011, though some keen-eared critics have noted that the show was recorded in line with Ace's amp resulting in less definition of Paul's guitar. Mr. Peach is an unknown private archivist who captured some 300 Japanese shows, including the five 1977 shows (some with multiple tape decks) and these 1978 shows.
- However, differences can be noted via Paul's raps to at least denote different performances.
- Paul's raps:
King of the Night Time World: "Whoa! Whoa! Alright! Whoa! I know. I know, we're all after some Rock 'N' Roll. So I want to, I want to tell ya... With all those pretty girls. With all those pretty girls we've got. I want to meet you in the ladies room!"

Ladies Room: "Domo Arigato. You like that, huh? I'll tell ya. I'll tell ya. This place is gonna get so hot tonight. We're gonna have to call out... We're gonna have to call out the firehouse!"
Firehouse: "Firehouse. Whoa! Alright! Alright! I'm gonna shoot you... with my... Love Gun!"

Love Gun: "Ah! Alright everybody? Let me hear you say, Whoa! Whoa! Whoa! Whoa! Rock and roll!"

Let Me Go, Rock 'N' Roll: "Nice, uh, huh, huh? I tell ya what I wanna do! Uh! Uh! Uh! I wanna make love to you!"

Makin' Love: "Okay! Alright, I wanna... I wanna tell everybody, we're really happy to be in Tokyo tonight. Here's a song for all the girls! Girls! Girls! Christine Sixteen!"

Christine Sixteen: "Alright now, since everybody's feeling good. Are you feelin' good? Alright then, we've got a surprise for you. Are you ready for a surprise? Alright, we're gonna turn the microphone over to... When I count to three I wanna here everybody say Ace Frehley, one... two... three... Ace Frehley!"

March 29 - Budokan Hall, Tokyo, Japan
Promoter: Udo Artists, Inc.
Other act(s): Bow Wow
Reported audience: 11,000 **SOLD-OUT
Set list: Same as March 28.
Notes:
- A muffled and below average AUD recording circulated for many years. Additionally tape-flip issues result in the loss of the first half of "I Want You" and "Black Diamond" fades out prior to conclusion. A far better version (Mr. Peach) was released on the unofficial CD "Makin' Up! Makin' Love!" in 2011.
- Dating most of the 1978 Japan shows is difficult. This show was originally circulated for years as a muffled and below average AUD recording. Tape-flip issues resulted in the loss of

the first half of "I Want You" and "Black Diamond" faded out prior to conclusion. The Mr. Peach source is superior sonically with minimal distortion and crown interference.
- Paul's raps:

King of the Night Time World: "Whoa! Whoa! Alright! Alright! Rock and roll! Rock and roll! Whoa! Hello Tokyo! I tell ya, I tell ya this is gonna be a hot night for rock and roll! So all you girls, all you girls, let me hear all you girls say 'Hello! Hello!' Meet us in the ladies room!"

Ladies Room: "Whoa! Domo Arigato. You like that, eh? I tell ya, I tell ya this gonna get so hot tonight. We're gonna have to call out... [drum beat] We gonna have to call out... the firehouse!"

Firehouse: "Firehouse! Whoa! Alright! Alright! I'm gonna shoot you... With my... Love Gun!"

Love Gun: "Uh! Alright everybody? Let me hear you say 'Whoa! Whoa! Whoa! Whoa! Rock and roll!"

March 31 - Budokan Hall, Tokyo, Japan
Promoter: Udo Artists, Inc.
Other act(s): Bow Wow
Reported audience: 11,000 **SOLD-OUT
Set list: Same as Nov. 15
Notes:
- Extremely good AUD recording (Mr. Peach) released on unofficial CD "Fab Four from Hell." Considered by some to be the best of the Mr. Peach recordings from 1978 with excellent definition of each player's instruments and a somewhat raw sound.
- Paul's raps:

King of The Night Time World: "Whoa! Whoa! Hello Tokyo! Does everybody feel alright? Alright? Whoa! Then I tell ya, I'll tell ya, all the pretty girls... All you pretty girls... We wanna meet you in the ladies room!"

Ladies Room: "I wanna tell ya! I wanna tell ya I think this is gonna be a hot night for rock and roll. Rock and roll! And I know we're going to get this place so hot we're gonna have to call out... We're gonna have to call out! The firehouse!"

Firehouse: "Firehouse! Domo! Domo arigoto! You like that, huh! I want you all to know I've got my gun... I'm gonna get you... with my Love Gun!"

Love Gun: "All...right! All...right! Alright, I wanna hear everybody? I want to hear everybody say 'Rock and Roll!' (rock and roll!) 'Rock and Roll!' (rock and roll!) 'Rock and Roll!' (rock and roll!)"

Let Me Go, Rock 'N' Roll: "Ah! Uh-huh! I tell ya what I wanna do! I wanna make love to... You!"

Makin' Love: "Aw! Ooh! Here's a song for all the girls. Let me hear all the girls say, 'Hello!' (hello!) 'Hello!' (hello!) 'Hello!' (hello!) Christine Sixteen!"

Christine Sixteen: "Okay! Okay, we got, we've got a surprise. We got a surprise for everybody tonight! We're gonna let... Ace Frehley's gonna sing 'Shock Me!' Shock me!

I Want You: "Alright! (alright) Alright! (alright) Does everybody feel good? Does everybody feel alright? Alright, we're gonna... we're gonna listen now to Dr.. Dr... Dr... Dr. Love!"

Calling Dr. Love: "Thank you! We're going to do a song now. The song... The song says if you wanna have good time. If you want to have a good time and have a party. Shout it out loud!"

God of Thunder: "Let's rock and roll all night and party every day!"

Rock and Roll All Nite: "Alright! (alright) Alright! (alright) Alright! (alright) Rock and roll! (rock and roll) Rock and roll! (rock and roll) We're going to do a song now. This song's about a city in America... It's called 'Detroit Rock City!'"

April 1 - Budokan Hall, Tokyo, Japan
Promoter: Udo Artists, Inc.
Other act(s): Bow Wow
Reported audience: 11,000 **SOLD-OUT
Set list: Same as Nov. 15
Notes:
- KISS was interviewed by the Japanese music magazine Music Life prior to this show. This is the only 1978 show to currently not known to circulate.

April 2 - Budokan Hall, Tokyo, Japan
Promoter: Udo Artists, Inc.
Other act(s): Bow Wow
Reported audience: 11,000 **SOLD-OUT
Set list: Same as Nov. 15
Notes:
- KISS' set started at 5PM.
- An average AUD recording circulated from this show and seems to have only started circulating widely in late-2006. An upgraded AUD source was released in December 2014, the Mr. Peach recording "Maiko Girls from Hell" (Tarantura). "Maiko" girls are apprentice Geiko, usually in the 15 to 20-year-old range, who are learning the skill of song, dance, and samisen (a traditional Japanese musical instrument) performance.
- This is the only show from the 1978 Japan tour that can definitively be dated, since Paul mentions such following "Love Gun". Paul's raps:
King of the Night Time World: "Whoa! Whoa! Hello Tokyo! Does everybody feel... alright? Alright! Well then, here's a song about the beautiful girls of Tokyo. Meet us in the ladies room!"

Ladies Room: "Thank you! Domo! Domo Arigato. Here's a song... about getting this place hot tonight. We're gonna get this place so hot. We're gonna have to call out... <drum beat> I think we better call out... the firehouse!"

Firehouse: "Firehouse! Whoa! Okay! Okay! Here's a song about... I'm gonna shoot you with my... Love Gun!"

Love Gun: "Alright! Alright! I want to tell ya, tonight is our last show in Tokyo. I want you to know, we love you. Now I want everybody to say Rock and roll! Rock and roll! Rock and roll!"

May 18 - Magic Mountain, Valencia, CA
Promoter: Hanna-Barbera/Aucoin Productions
Reported audience: ~7,000
Set list: I Stole Your Love / King of the Night Time World / Ladies Room / Firehouse / Love Gun / Let Me Go, Rock 'N' Roll / Makin' Love / Christine Sixteen / Shock Me / I Want You / Love Gun (lip synch) / Love Gun (lip synch) / Shock Me (lip synch)
Notes:
- Filmed for live concert sequences for the "KISS Meets the Phantom of the Park" television movie that was being filmed at the time... The invitation made clear what sort of event guests could expect: "The concert will not go on as a regularly scheduled KISS concert. There will be breaks in between the songs as additional filming, equipment and scenes are set. The foundation for special effects that will be added later in the film will be laid at this time... There will be a lot happening for you to see! Remember, if you see a man running out on stage yelling, 'CUT!'... It's only a movie" (PR)!
- Musically, highlights for many from the movie are the live performance sequences of songs such as "Shout it Out Loud," "I Stole Your Love," "Rip & Destroy" and "Rock And Roll All Nite." They give a tantalizing glimpse at what a proper multi-cam professionally filmed concert of KISS at their height could have looked like. And, perhaps, leave tears at the prospect of the unused footage that might simply have been discarded as part of the film making process.
- Many of the attendees were West Coast radio contest winners.
- A marginal and choppy AUD recording circulates from this show.

Dynasty: The Return of KISS

Planning for the "Return of KISS" tour had commenced in November 1978 with two primary, and quite reasonable, albeit obvious, objectives: 1) Make money; and 2) Take the most spectacular show ever seen on the road. Within the context of KISS, neither of those objectives were particularly shocking or interesting. It was essentially what the band had been doing since 1974. However, after the break taken in 1978 for the TV movie and solo albums the band knew that it was time to get back on the road. Regardless of the hit Ace had with "New York Groove," which could have easily justified a second single from his album, the band had 1979 mapped out long before the calendar ticked over from 1978. Whether it was recording a new studio album, planning new animated specials or exploring the idea of a different type of KISS movie, KISS knew that they would be back on the road following the first long break they'd been allowed since the set off in support of "KISS" back in 1974. Gene stated the obvious: "We decided it was time to get back out there and show everybody what rock 'n' roll shows should be like. If we have done nothing else, we've made sure that people's expectations of rock 'n' roll have going up. It's no longer enough to just get up onstage and strum your instruments... I think the real winners are the audience" (Fort Worth Star-Telegram, 10/25/79). For their return to the stage they wanted to ensure that the audience remained in awe of the show that had really only evolved slightly since the band's earliest days.

However, as a February production meeting minutes noted, there were challenges as the band developed their ideas for exactly how they were going to present themselves to audiences. And how! Few acts wanted to open for the band, due to their perceived popularity, but the band knew that they needed the additional drawing power of an opening act. Gene went so far as to suggest The Cars or Van Halen as prospective openers. Obviously nothing came from that idea! Even at that early stage the band's concert entry had been considered: "coming out of the stage as opposed to walking onstage... [And] the band should be in action as soon as the audience has the first view of the band in the opening of set" (Production Memo, 2/5/79). This evolved into the band rising from below the stage via an elevator mechanism. It was also hoped that the band could do four shows per week with at least one multiple engagement stop. This layover would cut down on the transportation and staging (setup and stage strike) costs resulting in more cash flowing into the bottom line. The band also looked into out-sourcing as much of the production as possible to minimize costs and sought the advice of large touring entities such as "Ice Capades" and the "Peter Pan Road Show."

An "in the round" staging format was envisaged to maximize the number of seats in each venue that could be sold, along with a higher per-ticket pricing. Avoiding obstructions on stage would make the design clean. Howard Marks had suggested using silver-colored Formica "for all trimmings that would look like steel in appearance," and the use of an off-white surface to "pick up the lights well." This was almost a minimalist approach relying more on the lighting to impress. A massive truss would be used to allow the sound gear to be removed from the stage and hung with the lighting to keep the stage as unobstructed as possible. Gene in particular wanted to take the use of lifts to a new level, employing Simon-

Grause Giraffe long-neck lifts that would allow the band to be projects from the back of the stage out over the audience. Obviously there were concerns over safety and liability, but the schemes considered were designed to do what KISS did best: Impress. In essence, they were also simply evolutions of much of what already existed. The show needed more than just a new coat of paint in order to entice the public to pay higher than average ticket prices in a challenging economy. Peter also had ideas, wanting the band to either rent equipment or have sell-back agreements in place for the major show hardware so that the band did not get stuck with the equipment following the conclusion of the tour.

To create that most spectacular show many new effects were considered: A laser-light curtain that would run the perimeter of the stage using the band's signature colors individually or combined. Gene recalled, "We were expecting a laser curtain that would be — you know what the sluts wear — the see through stuff? It was supposed to actually look like the material, a real curtain that would completely surround the stage; then, as we ran down the ramps, it was supposed to part and then close up and/or disappear and/or turn into bars — it was supposed to do everything a quarter-of-a-million-dollar laser show was supposed to do" (Grooves). But it didn't, and to be fair, Peter Criss had rightfully been against the idea of using lasers from the beginning. Peter Criss has mixed feelings about using lasers because he feels that ELO already has the best laser show, and that it would be difficult to top" (Production Memo, 2/5/79). However, his concerns were shot down by the others who felt "the KISS show was, and will be the most exciting show on the road, and any form of competition would not affect them." This attitude is illustrative of the delusional state the KISS organization had essentially fallen into. They had in essence trapped themselves into believing that just because they did something that it would be successful. It might even seem odd, considering the often rewritten view on Peter Criss' contributions to the band, particularly on the business side, that he did have useful contributions to make. No wonder he became frustrated during the tour in conjunction with his personal challenges.

Effects for the band included a 360-degree rotating drum-riser for Peter. Harkening back to 1974 Peter would use enlarged 2' long neon-illuminated drum sticks that would strobe or be continuously lit. A 600lb animatronics lion would serve as his stage prop, and one proposal had Peter morphing into the lion and back. Sam the serpent would "start out coiled up on the stage, then slithering up the torch, igniting the torch by breathing fire on it, and then turning his head away" (Ken Anderson concepts letter, 12/21/78). Ace would get spark-firing effects that would appear to shoot from his hands or guitar and the flying rig for his guitar would be modified to have it fly around the stage until he gestured to it — having it explode. Paul was not going to be left out of the fun either. He "was going to shoot a laser beam from his eye to the back of the hall. Ace was going to shoot lasers from his guitar. In fact, everything has always been possible, it's just that nobody's willing to spend millions. This new show without the lasers still cost a million and a half dollars to build and put together. Next time, if it's going to work, we'll use it; if not, we just will not use it. A beam of light is not enough. It's got to do something" (Grooves). Paul, naturally, was very concerned about the laser eye-piece though any consideration for an "unsafe laser radiation" or "applicable regulations" must have had some in the organization blanching at not only the cost but the possible costs of attempting such gimmicks! One particular downside to the eye effect was that it was deemed "much too expensive to have a model made for testing only. All decisions must be final" (Production Memo, 2/5/79). The band was invited to witness elements of Dick Sandhaus' Science Faction Corporation (SFC) laser show at the Xenon disco. Sandhaus was actively developing a laser system, known as the SFC 2000 that he had attempted to place on the 1978 Foreigner tour.

Whatever reservations there were about the lasers, the band signed a contract with SFC in March 1979 and the company commenced work on the laser show for the tour at a cost of $130,000.00 plus an additional $5,000.00 for each week of the tour. Development ran through final production rehearsals in June and the show was demonstrated to the band in Lakeland. It failed to perform properly and the band refused to take the equipment on tour, perhaps by that stage sensing the overall economic challenge the tour was facing. According to Gene, "We invested a quarter of a million dollars in a laser show that is pretty miserable. We're either going to sue the company of try and get our money back, but it simply wasn't as good as the rest of the show, so we didn't use it. Oh, it would have gathered the usual 'ohs' and 'ahs,' but nothing like the 'Oh-my-Gods' that the rest of the show has. If something doesn't have the effect of "Oh-my-God," then it's not worth using" (Grooves). The band certainly did sue SFC, but only recouped the additional $10,000 that had been paid the company rather than the monies that had been used for three months worth of development (Weinreich v. Sandhaus, No. 83 Civ. 3966). That meant the development costs were a waste.

Fire, naturally, played a part with Gene with his fire-breathing gimmick being proposed to be changed to having him engulfed in flames and disappearing or floating across the stage. Alternatively, having him breathe multiple bursts of flame through a flame-thrower attachment to his face — similar to moving his jaw and spewing flame in the movie was seen as a possibility. Having members disappear on stage and then re-appear in another location was considered, either using smoke tricks or a Star Trek inspired transport illusion via a clear Plexiglas cylinder. One area, that would be attempted in 1998, was a video magnification system to use during parts of the show, or as an alternative a 35mm projection system, to embellish the performance. The lasers were chosen over the projection system due to being deemed more cost effective. Also implemented later was the use of inflatable props. While the 1996 tour would use inflatable figures, for the 1979 tour a morphing inflatable KISS logo was considered to be constructed by the same firm that built the inflatable furniture for the KISS movie the year prior.

What the band did take on the road was certainly most impressive. The massive 400,000 watt lighting grid was "hexagonal measuring 67 feet from point to point, by 57 feet parallel side to parallel side, with spokes running to the middle. It holds 104.000 watts and weighs just under 12,000 pounds" and even fit into a single trailer (Billboard, 8/11/79). The staging, built by Theatre Techniques, was equally impressive: "It is multi-tiered, 12 feel at its highest point. It has five elevators, lights, fog machines and guitar amps built into it. The drum kit is motorized so it can roll down to the front of the stage, as well as rotate and elevate. The various levels of the stage are connected by ramps, so the performers don't trip while running up and down There are also ramps beneath the stage, where there are dressing room areas, so any of the four musicians can go there between numbers to touch up the makeup, if needed" (Billboard, 8/11/79). And while appearing somewhat sparse, when fully in use with that fog and lighting it was impressive.

Apart from cost, both monetary and development and staffing, many of the ideas would prove technically challenging or require too much power or attention. Many of the ideas were unrealistic (such as Gene's idea for a helium-filled spaceship for large stadiums), other than the basic premise of the tour: maximizing routing, though it soon became clear that even the best-planned routing couldn't work if there weren't enough patrons for multiple engagements, or to fill a single visit. What was described as "economies of scale" (KISS & Sell) didn't occur with a soft touring and record sales marketplace. The super-KISS tour encompassed that superlative: "Defying the current malaise that has hit the touring as well as the record market, KISS has gone out on the road with a mammoth 80-date arena tour, which, with a reported production cost of $2.2 million, not including salaries, is the biggest such musical show on record. The tour began on Father's Day and is expected to run until about Christmas. Sources say it is doubtful if the hand recovers its investment before the fall" (Billboard, 8/11/79). As shows began to be cancelled it was clear that even a successful tour would have a difficult time breaking even with staffing and hotel bills in excess of $30,000 per week. Why were so many shows cancelled? According to Gene, "Gas. Arabs. Carter. America. I mean, I don't have to go into explaining the way things are. If there's no gas, you can't go to a concert that's 30 miles out of town. We could have waited six months until there was gas. We don't have to tour; we have enough money to buy Argentina, but that's not exciting, and it's not exciting to play it safe. People tell us, don't release four solo albums, wait until the gas crisis is over, don't spend $1 million on a stage, but we did it" (Grooves). Throwing down the cards and challenging fate with an unwavering self-belief, that all of the contributing factors, affecting the rest of society, could somehow be held from entering the band's orbit by the strength of that self-belief or power of ego. Wrong, though for Ace the mission was clear: "What we're trying to do is just go out there and play some rock and roll and entertain people. That's all there is to it. The kids understand it. There's no underlying meaning in our show. It's just a rock and roll show that's meant to entertain the ears and the eyes as well. Yeah, we put a lot of money and time into the visual side. But we're gonna put out the biggest and best rock and roll show there is, no matter what it costs" (Oklahoman Journal, 10/12/79).

While the start-up costs for the 110 day process it took to create the stage show may have seemed staggering, the production costs were a necessity for getting a KISS-sized show on the road. According to Bill McManus, "head of the Philadelphia-based McManus Enterprises which is responsible for the overall lighting, sound, transportation, staging, logistics, rigging and personnel for the tour. 'KISS doesn't tour to make money on a tour, so much as it tours to sell records... It takes about six months on the road before there is enough profit to pay back the original capitalization.' This is the beginning of the tour and we have just spent $1 million putting together a new show. Maybe by the end of the summer, we will wind up paying for everything. But the point is that at the beginning of going into a new venture, you do not see dollar one for a while" (Billboard, 8/11/79). Throughout the tour the economics would become a common theme in interviews. Even Ace had to address them: "To an extent, y'know? I mean the tour is a success at this point. Ticket sales are good, but not as good as the last four, but nobody is doing as good as their last tours. It's the economy, y'know? A lot of places we used to do two nights we're only doing one now. Initially, when we started this tour we thought it was us. We thought, 'wow, we've been away from the concert circuit too long.' We weren't selling out every night. But then we started to hear these horror stories about other groups... People cancelling whole tours because they were losing money" (Oklahoman Journal, 10/12/79).

Early on during the tour Gene was admitting the challenges: "The tour has gotten off to a little bit of a slow start because we're not sure yet about the effects. It's like anything else when you're away for two years; it takes a while to get back into it. But these Capitol Centre shows were numbers eight and nine, and I think we're getting around once again to being the spectacle of the century, the veritable greatest show on earth. I'm not humble or anything, I think we'll blow anybody off" (Grooves). Paul tried to paint a bigger picture that reflected the state of the economy within the context of what KISS were attempting to do; commenting, "As far as I know a lot of hands on the road are being hurt a lot worse than we are (by the gas shortage, and subsequent slower ticket sales). There are some who are just going off the road. Talk to enough booking agents and they are advising some of the bands not even to go out. But as bad as the situation is we are out there. People are cautious now, they want to see what happens with the economy, with the dollar, and they are waiting. But we can't wait. We have a new album out, and we haven't been out there for a long time, so we want out" (Billboard, 8/11/79). There was no way to take the band on the road without the necessary support: "Like a circus, the KISS tour is a self-contained unit that includes six carpenters, six electricians, four band roadies, four soundmen, two wardrobe persons, three pyro-technicians, three riggers, a production manager, a tour coordinator, a tour manager, four security men, eight truck drivers, one accountant, two bus drivers, four personal assistants to the hand members, and three others doing the concessions, in addition to the four musicians who make up KISS. Also, says McManus, there are five persons, under the direction of Ken Anderson who work In the New York offices of Aucoin Management coordinating tour activities" (Billboard, 8/11/79).

To a certain extent, that was the crux of the matter — a cycle of spending with hopes that the totals column would be in the black rather than the red at the end. Advances had been received and spent to feed the insatiable appetite of the machine. Touring and the attached merchandising were required to make contributions. But a show requiring a 12-hour setup by 56 workers simply had too many costs associated with it in the 1979 economy. Where two dates in some cities, became one, nowhere demonstrated the tour's contraction as much as the band's hometown. New York was supposed to be the band's grand home-coming, the return of the conquering heroes of rock. In April a minimum of four dates were envisaged, July 24 & 25 and 27 & 28. Hold dates were added for two additional dates, on July 26 & 29, though realistically a six consecutive night stand would have been brutal on the band. Promoter Ron Delsener dealt all in for the promotion planning to run teaser ads in the local press from May 20th and opening up a telephone hotline that mimicked what Peter Frampton had done. The plans for promotion also included an aerial assault, with a flying banner over the regions beaches on the Memorial (May 28) and Independence Day (July 4) holidays weekends. There would also be a radio campaign and the usual TV advertising. For radio contests even the grand prize of attending a KISS recording session or "backstage before the concert to watch the make-up going on" were considered. The scope of consideration was Super KISS at its biggest, no expense spared, before the reality of the touring situation was really known and understood. Only two of these shows took place, even backed with a massive local publicity campaign that had included advertizing on the ass-end of over 200 city busses. The massive gamble had essentially failed.

36 shows from the tour grossed an average $100,000 per show with 382,911 of 478,055 tickets sold, or roughly 82%. From that perspective the tour wasn't a failure in terms of

attendance; however the high production, staging, and running costs, multiple cancelled dates, abandoned effects, national economics, etc, had the opposite effect. What was clear was there was a step-down from the 1977-8 touring years and that KISS had over-estimated the drawing power of their "Return." By the time the band came off the road the true cost of the tour was yet to be realized with the departure of Peter Criss. He had simply deteriorated during the tour, and while things would not come to a head until the following year the damage had been done.

May 1979 - Nassau Community College, Long Island, NY **STAGING & PRODUCTION
Notes:
- According to CK Lendt, two weeks of rehearsals were held at this venue, where the "Return of KISS" stage was constructed in the gym before being shipped to Florida. Philadelphia-based McManus was contracted to provide "overall lighting, sound, transportation, staging, logistics, rigging and personnel for the tour" (Billboard, 8/11/79).

June 9 - Superdome, New Orleans, LA **TENTATIVE
Notes:
- In February 1979, when the band and management met to plan touring activities for the next album cycle, this date was noted as one that was tentative. More interesting, from the meeting notes, was Gene's suggestion that either Van Halen or The Cars should be engaged as the opening act for the tour. However, it was noted, "the majority of the groups do not want to open for KISS due to their popularity" (Memo, 2/5/79).

June 10 - Civic Center, Lakeland, FL **STAGING & REHEARSALS
June 11 - Civic Center, Lakeland, FL **REHEARSALS
June 12 - Civic Center, Lakeland, FL **REHEARSALS
June 13 - Civic Center, Lakeland, FL **REHEARSALS
Notes:
- During pre-staging two "sub-contracting" members of the road crew were arrested during a cocaine purchase sting at a Holiday Inn hotel. Gene, Paul and Ace were guests at WRBQ radio in Tampa on the afternoon of the 13th (unmasked) while Peter had the stitches in his hand removed.

June 14 - Civic Center, Lakeland, FL **CANCELLED
Promoter: Beach Club Bookings
Set list: King of the Night Time World / Radioactive / Move On / Christine Sixteen / Firehouse / New York Groove / Calling Dr. Love / Tossin' and Turnin' / Love Gun / 2,000 Man / I Was Made for Lovin' You / God of Thunder / Shout It Out Loud / Rock And Roll All Nite / Beth / Detroit Rock City / Black Diamond
Notes:
- While the show scheduled for this date was cancelled, the band performed the show's closing number/sequence (just "Black Diamond") for the press. The date also had appeared on itineraries as questionable as either rehearsals or a show, so likely was first a hold-date, then a show, and then rehearsal. "A concert scheduled for Thursday was cancelled earlier in the week; the official word for the cancellation was that drummer Peter Criss needed an extra day to heal a cut hand. Observers speculate the concert was canceled because only 8,000 tickets had been sold for the two shows in the 10,000 capacity arena. Center officials said Wednesday there were approximately 1,000 tickets left for Friday" (Lakeland Ledger, 6/15/79).
- A recording from the "Dynasty" tour rehearsals is often attributed to this date, but was more likely made during earlier rehearsals for the tour due to the nature of Paul's raps; They're obviously not being directed towards any "audience." It's rather ominous, considering what would later occur, to hear Paul telling Peter to pick up the beat and hear him obviously having issues.

- Production costs for the tour were a staggering $2.2 million in a music industry that was suffering a major touring and sales slump. There was no shortage of chutzpah in hitting the road at the time with such a massive show.
- Gene Simmons appeared on Orlando's BJ-105FM lunch-time radio from June 14, 1979, amusingly using the "Jumpin' Gene Simmons" moniker. Gene attempts to get people who call in to talk, discusses the cancellation of that day's show (which would have been the first night of the "Dynasty/Return of KISS" tour), and more...

June 15 - Civic Center, Lakeland, FL
Promoter: Beach Club Bookings
Other act(s): Nantucket
Reported audience: 8,136 **SOLD-OUT
Notes:
- The band's first public live performance in more than a year (since the Valencia, CA live concert as part of the filming of "KISS meets the Phantom of the Park" in May 1978).
- From a local review: "At show time the 10,000 capacity arena was packed, but it wasn't a typical rock crowd — many of the KISS fans were between 8 and 14 years old; and many came with one or both parents... One tolerant father stood for hours with his 8-and 10-year-old sons so they could get a place up front, then alternately lifted each son to his shoulders so they could see the band. He said he didn't understand the music or the costuming, however... KISS-watchers are still wondering why Thursday night's concert was cancelled. Drummer Criss' injured paw was said to be the reason, but his dynamic performance makes that hard to believe" (Lakeland Ledger, 6/16/79).

June 17 - Sportatorium, Pembroke Pines (Hollywood), FL
Promoter: Beach Club Bookings
Other act(s): Nantucket
Reported audience: 7,300 **SOLD-OUT
Set list: King of the Night Time World / Radioactive / Move On / Calling Dr. Love / Firehouse / New York Groove / Tossin' and Turnin' / I Was Made for Lovin' You / 2,000 Man / Love Gun / God of Thunder / Shout It Out Loud / Black Diamond / Detroit Rock City / Beth / Rock And Roll All Nite
Notes:
- Too much equipment was apparently hung from the venue's superstructure resulting in bending. Additionally, KISS apparently left their trinket distribution ball at the venue since the effect hadn't worked properly during the show.
- From a local review: "Their stage show was incredible. The special effects, dazzling. They have fireworks that would put many cities' Fourth of July celebrations to shame... Technically the show was a masterpiece" (Boca Raton News, June 24, 1979).

June 19 - Savannah Civic Center, Savannah, GA
Promoter: Beach Club Bookings
Other act(s): The Sweet
Reported audience: 7,950 **SOLD-OUT
Notes:
- Ace was arrested after refusing to pay a $150 charter boat cruise bill after the captain had trouble starting the engine and delaying his return from Hilton Head, SC.

- Only Andy Scott, Steve Priest, and Mick Tucker remained in the line-up of the classic glam band that opened for KISS at this one show. They were supporting their "A Cut above the Rest" album, their final U.S. charting release. That night the band included "Fox On The Run" in their set, a song later covered by Frehley on his 2009 "Anomaly" album.

June 20 - Savannah Civic Center, Savannah, GA **CANCELLED
Notes:
- Even though the second night's show had been cancelled the band filmed their performance videos for "I Was Made for Lovin' You" and "Sure Know Something" (directed and produced by John Goodhue) at this venue. John, who had a strong advertizing background, led him into commercial production and then the video production industry in 1978. His first work was on Bruce Springsteen's "Darkness at the Edge of Town" tour performance in Phoenix that year. He also produced videos for Cheap Trick. As videos caught on as a standard promotional tool, there was some thought within the music industry that "video albums" would become the next big thing. John spoke against the idea, due to the inherent cost of production, for which single song videos for promotional use were seen as an effective write-off by the record companies. John mentioned the reaction to the KISS videos, "With a group like KISS the initial reaction from a lot of people is that it's something for the kids. After seeing the video, though, people are more interested" (Billboard, 9/20/80).
- Local press reported that a paltry 700 tickets had been bought for this second show, prior to its cancellation, and that the tickets would be honored at the remaining Tuesday show (Savannah Morning News, 6/17/79).

June 22 - Carolina Coliseum, Columbia, SC
Promoter: Beach Club Bookings
Other act(s): Whiteface
Reported audience: (12,401 capacity)
Notes:
- June 21 was designated as a travel day.
- Multi-camera, possibly local news footage, of at least part of "Radioactive" was filmed at this show suggesting that the first two songs may have been archived.
- The day of this show Ace was in court: "A charter-boat cruise that cost $150 carried a price tag of $257 by the time Ace Frehley, lead guitarist for the-rock-group KISS, left Savannah. Frehley pleaded guilty Friday to a theft of services charge and was fined $107 after he refused to pay the cost of a cruise to Hilton Head, SC, Thursday. According to Municipal Judge Victor Mulling, the captain of the boat had trouble starting the engine, delaying the return. 'His attitude was that his day was spoiled and the captain should have paid him, not the other way around,' said Mulling. 'He paid the fine and made restitution, and I presume got the dust of Chatham County off his feet'" (AP).

June 24 - Charlotte Coliseum, Charlotte, NC
Promoter: Beach Club Bookings
Other act(s): Nantucket
Reported audience: ~10,000 / 13,000 (76.92%)
Notes:
- From a local review "But whether they strike you as drooling dream-demons or slick satin supermen gone kinky, KISS leaves a harsh mark on your eyes and ears, pressing to the limits theatrics to give the audience as much excitement as they can handle. And they can handle a lot" (Charlotte Observer, 6/25/79).

June 26 - Memorial Auditorium, Greenville, SC
Promoter: Beach Club Bookings
Other act(s): Nantucket
Reported audience: ~6,600 / 7,500 (88%)
Notes:
- From a local review: "For KISS, tricks are part of the show. Maybe all of the show. By the time they whisked themselves off stage they had blasted confetti from the ceiling, lit firepots on stage, performed on elevated platforms, lit one guitar and drew smoke from another, used strobe lights and fog as if it were going out of style, and unveiled a couple of jackass-like gargoyles (not to be confused with members of the band). By now, everyone must have heard of KISS... Their stage show is well known throughout the world and their outfits remain practically indescribable — something like an unsubtle cross between a John Belushi samurai nightmare and the Daniel Building's Christmas light display" (Greenville News, 6/28/79).

June 28 - Asheville Civic Center, Asheville, NC
Promoter: Kaleidoscope Productions
Other act(s): Nantucket
Reported audience: ~5,000 / 7,646 (65.39%)
Notes:

- From a local review: "The performance of rock groups KISS and Nantucket in Asheville's Civic Center Thursday night was exactly what the promoters and sponsors promised it work be, a rock and roll show. It was not what some city government officials and many other folks thought it would be, a melee" (Asheville Citizen, 6/29/79). There had been concerns, following numerous arrests at previous rock concerts that the same would reoccur. However, organizers put on extra security for the event.

June 30 - The Omni Auditorium, Atlanta, GA
Promoter: Rich Floyd Productions
Other act(s): New England
Reported audience: (16,700 capacity)
Set list: King of the Night Time World / Radioactive / Move On / Calling Dr. Love / Firehouse / New York Groove / I Was Made For Lovin' You / Love Gun / 2,000 Man / Tossin' And Turnin' / God Of Thunder / Shout It Out Loud / Black Diamond / Detroit Rock City / Beth / Rock And Roll All Nite
Notes:
- This was the first show with New England as opening act. Paul had produced their self-titled album for Infinity Records.
- A reasonable AUD recording from this show exists.

July 1 - The Omni Auditorium, Atlanta, GA **CANCELLED
Notes:
- This second show was cancelled, presumably due to ticket sales issues.

July 3 - Coliseum, Greensboro, NC
Promoter: Entam, Inc. / Beach Club Booking
Other act(s): Nantucket
Reported audience: 10,336 / 15,000 (68.91%)
Reported gross: $101,280

July 5 - Coliseum, Hampton, VA
Promoter: Entam, Inc.
Other act(s): New England
Reported audience: 8,682 / 13,800 (62.91%)
Reported gross: $85,430

July 7 - Capital Centre, Largo (Landover), MD
Promoter: Cellar Door Productions
Other act(s): New England
Reported audience: ~12,000 / 20,476 (58.61%)
Set list: King of the Night Time World / Radioactive / Move On / Calling Dr. Love / Firehouse / New York Groove / I Was Made for Lovin' You / Love Gun / 2,000 Man / Tossin' and Turnin' / Shout It Out Loud / Black Diamond / Detroit Rock City / Beth / Rock And Roll All Nite
Notes:
- From a local review: "Unfortunately, KISS did not let the weekend performances go with the stage effects alone. The quartet insisted on playing music, such as it was. It also insisted on doing so at such a volume that it probably effected the earth-quake equipment in

California. Rarely has the Capital Centre come closer to simply shaking apart. In some ways, KISS' rock 'n' roll amusement park for 13-year-olds is fun. The special effects are terrific, superior in ways to those used by the likes of Parliament-Funkadelics. Each tour there's something new to be admired even if the overall thrust is the same... It didn't seem to make one bit of difference that the music was appalling bad. KISS makes three-chord buzz put out by the Ramones positively complicated. There was only one change of pace during the entire show with all the other songs falling squarely into the grunt and drone category" (Washington Star, 7/9/79).

- Another local review: "At its central metaphor, KISS has chosen the rock 'n' roll quartet, the epitome of exuberant ephemera. The actors have learned enough to play the basic chords and rely on a loud, distorted sound system to cover their further deficiencies. The fact that the music is oppressively loud and boring fits in with their theme of technological dominance" (Washington Post, 7/9/79).

- A below average AUD recording circulates from this show. However, like the following night, this show was archived on in-house video. Interference and linear artifacts are more noticeable on this video, than the following night, though some footage from the concert film was used promotionally by stage designer Bill McManus & Associates, first shown at the December 1979 International Entertainment Expo.

July 8 - Capital Centre, Largo (Landover), MD
Promoter: Cellar Door Productions
Other act(s): New England
Set list: King of the Night Time World / Radioactive / Move On / Calling Dr. Love / Firehouse / New York Groove / I Was Made for Lovin' You / Love Gun / 2,000 Man / Tossin' and Turnin' / God of Thunder / Shout It Out Loud / Black Diamond / Detroit Rock City / Beth / Rock And Roll All Nite
Notes:
- Pro-shot video with mixed audio had long circulated. The show was partially officially released as the bonus disc included with initial pressings of the "KISSology Volume II" DVD package sold through Wal-Mart. Sadly, the quality of this recording is worse than many collectors already have. That "official" version excludes "King of the Night Time World," "2,000 Man," and "Beth."
- The following day the band took a day off lounging at their hotel in New Carrollton, MD. Charlie Crespo recounted the shows and day in a piece for Grooves Magazine, "KISS Blasts New Dynasty."

July 10 - Roanoke Civic Center, Roanoke, VA
Promoter: Entam, Inc.
Other act(s): New England
Reported audience: 11,000 **SOLD-OUT
Reported gross: $108,670
Set list: King of the Night Time World / Radioactive / Move On / Calling Dr. Love / Firehouse / New York Groove / I Was Made for Lovin' You / Love Gun / 2,000 Man / Tossin' and Turnin' / God of Thunder / Shout It Out Loud / Black Diamond / Detroit Rock City / Beth / Rock And Roll All Nite
Notes:
- This show circulates as a partial and generally poor AUD recording (through "Tossin' and Turnin'"). Songs in the set following that are probable.

July 13 - Pontiac Silverdome, Pontiac, MI
Promoter: Belkin Productions/WABY
Other act(s): Cheap Trick, New England (opener)
Reported audience: ~40,000 / 75,000 (53.33%)
Set list: King of the Night Time World / Radioactive / Move On / Calling Dr. Love / Firehouse / New York Groove / I Was Made for Lovin' You / Love Gun / 2,000 Man / Tossin' and Turnin' / God of Thunder / Shout It Out Loud / Black Diamond / Detroit Rock City / Beth / Rock And Roll All Nite
Notes:
- Tickets were still available on the day of the show, at a steep $12.50 each, which may have gone some way to explaining the turnout.
- From a show attendee: "During Rick Nielsen's guitar solo he was hit by a Frisbee and left the stage. Tom Petersen came out with Gene's Axe Bass and threatened to cut the balls off of whoever had thrown the Frisbee. Rick finally came back out and finished his solo" (FAQ Forum Member pdennis1).
- A below average AUD recording circulates from this show.

July 14 - Pontiac Silverdome, Pontiac, MI **CANCELLED

July 16 - Rupp Arena, Lexington, KY
Promoter: Entam, Inc. & Sunshine Productions
Other act(s): New England
Reported audience: 9,480 / 11,809 (80.28%)
Reported gross: $92,500
Set list: King of the Night Time World / Radioactive / Move On / Calling Dr. Love / Firehouse / New York Groove / I Was Made for Lovin' You / Love Gun / 2,000 Man / Tossin' and Turnin' / God of Thunder / Shout It Out Loud / Black Diamond / Detroit Rock City / Beth / Rock And Roll All Nite
Notes:
- From a local review: "For those who like rock music, KISS is good. Their music is vibrant and alive. Every member carries his weight in the performance while offering a unique approach to rock music. It's a shame, however, that so much hype has to be used to sell good music" (News-Enterprise, 7/20/79).

July 18 - Richfield Coliseum, Cleveland, OH
Promoter: Belkin Productions
Other act(s): New England
Reported audience: 14,100 **SOLD-OUT**
Set list: King of the Night Time World / Let Me Go, Rock 'N' Roll / Makin' Love / Calling Dr. Love / Firehouse / New York Groove / I Was Made for Lovin' You / Love Gun / 2,000 Man / Tossin' and Turnin' / God of Thunder / Shout It Out Loud / Black Diamond / Detroit Rock City / Beth / Rock And Roll All Nite
Notes:
- From a local review: "Far from running for cover, the Coliseum crowd only screamed for more, gleefully accepting a 90-minute barrage of aural shrapnel launched from the stage and proving that the sound and the fury did, indeed, signify something after all..." (Akron Beacon Journal, 7/19/79).

- The show was reported as sold-out, though press reports place the attendance nowhere near the 20,000 total capacity of the venue, even with staging and production considerations. Though, for comparative purposes many other similar scale rock shows of the period are noted as sold-out in the 14,000 attendance range.
- This show circulates as an average AUD recording. Parts of this show were also filmed by local TV for news broadcast use.

July 19 - Richfield Coliseum, Cleveland, OH
Promoter: Belkin Productions
Other act(s): New England
Reported audience: (14,100 capacity)
Set list: King of the Night Time World / Let Me Go, Rock 'N Roll / Makin' Love / Calling Dr. Love / Firehouse / New York Groove / I Was Made for Lovin' You / Love Gun / 2,000 Man / Tossin' And Turnin' / God of Thunder / Shout It Out Loud / Black Diamond / Detroit Rock City / Beth / Rock And Roll All Nite
Notes:
- This second show was added when the first appeared to be selling well.
- An incomplete generally poor AUD recording from this show circulates.

July 21 - Civic Arena, Pittsburgh, PA
Promoter: DiCesare-Engler Productions
Other act(s): New England
Reported audience: 13,873 / 13,900 (99.81%)
Reported gross: $142,352

July 22 - Civic Arena, Pittsburgh, PA **CANCELLED
Promoter: DiCesare-Engler Productions
Other act(s): New England
Notes:
- This was another multiple engagement city to be reduced to a single show.

July 24 - Madison Square Garden, New York, NY
Promoter: Ron Delsener / Ardee Productions
Other act(s): New England
Reported audience: ~15,000
Set list: King of the Night Time World / Let Me Go, Rock 'N' Roll / Move On / Calling Dr. Love / Firehouse / New York Groove / I Was Made For Lovin' You / Christine Sixteen / 2,000 Man / Love Gun / God of Thunder / Shout It Out Loud / Black Diamond / Detroit Rock City / Beth / Rock And Roll All Nite
Notes:
- A "Dial-A-KISS" hotline was set up with messages from each of the band members to promote the shows. Gene's: "This is Gene Simmons and I'm all fired up and ready to get hot for the hometown KISS fans. It's gonna be the rock and roll party of the year — new songs, new show, spectacular new magic, and I'll be looking for you!" Following the message information is given about the shows, then fades out with the respective member's song playing: "I Was Made For Lovin' You," "Charisma," "Hard Times," and "Dirty Livin'."
- From a local review: "A KISS concert is a little like a circus, a little like a Saturday morning cartoon show on television, a little like an exhibition of parlor magic improbably blown up

to arena proportions and a little like rock 'n' roll. It's loud, but otherwise it's safe family entertainment, and the audience that packed into Madison Square Garden on Tuesday for the first of two evenings with the group included numerous groups of father, mother and children, all clapping their hands on the beat with cotton stuffed in their ears. One suspects KISS would never have got very far on its musical merits alone..." (New York Times, 7/26/79).

- From a mainstream press review: "Let us put KISS in a humane perspective; that is, if I had been writing magazine articles for seven years and were only known for puking blood on my desk and having skyrockets go off in my typewriter, I would be real depressed. Even if millions of twelve-year-old boys bought belt buckles emblazoned with my face painted like a tree toad, I would have to question my professional competence to write a sentence. So let's all help keep KISS off lithium and not say their music is lame. We know it. They know it. Millions of twelve-year-old boys don't know it, but they aren't going to figure out music until their pubic hair grows in anyway. Let us instead praise the KISS Stage show, which has too many neat special effects that your pubic hair retracts and you become twelve-years-old again and the music doesn't matter. Get this, man: Gene Simmons does this weird bass solo and vomits blood all over himself, just like he always does, but then they hoist him about fifty feet over the audience, where he sings 'God of Thunder' with a good imitation of the Christmas bombing of Hanoi exploding all around him. And Ace Frehley shoots skyrockets out of his guitar, man, and Paul Stanley clocks the heels of his eight-inch platforms in, the air, man, and Peter Criss does a drum solo on a hydraulic lift that is lifts him almost as high as Simmons is over the stage lights, man.

Okay, not that much was new (only Simmons' hoist, really) and nothing was spontaneous, but that has always been, the KISS philosophy: Give 'em what they want, only more of it. KISS would label this democracy. Critics call it demagogy. Whatever it is, it works for the same reasons religion does: it's mystical and awe inspiring, and twelve-year-old boys don't get that in church. Unlike past KISS stage sets this one is built low to the ground, presumably so they could sell seats behind the stage in large auditoriums. Since they didn't sell seats behind the stage at Madison Square Garden (KISS' booking agent says this was intentional; the Garden's box office says it wasn't), one can assume there was no demand. Kids on Long Island and New Jersey still buy the myth of instrumental prowess and go for macho jack-off guitar work. Through maximum macho jack-off, KISS is minimal prowess and must look elsewhere for their strongest audiences.

The opening act, New England, was yet another loathsome attempt by KISS' management, Aucoin, to generate a second KISS without makeup. Naming the band after a geographical area (I can think of ten others offhand) is as close as these shitheads have come to originality. I didn't see any licks, aural or visual, that weren't copped directly from Boston. This is, of course, the way KISS, started cashing-in on a trail blazed by Alice Cooper. You gotta give these half-wits credit for tenacity" (RS #300, Sep. 1979, Charles M. Young).

July 25 - Madison Square Garden, New York, NY
Promoter: Ron Delsener / Ardee Productions
Other act(s): New England
Reported audience: ~15,000
Set list: King of the Night Time World / Let Me Go, Rock 'N' Roll / Move On / Calling Dr. Love / Firehouse / New York Groove / I Was Made For Lovin' You / Christine Sixteen / 2,000 Man

/ Love Gun / God of Thunder / Shout It Out Loud / Black Diamond / Detroit Rock City / Beth / Rock And Roll All Nite
Notes:
- Peter has issues with the canned music during "Beth" leading to him missing part of the song.
- A partial-but-reasonable AUD recording circulates from the show (there's nothing in the raps to indicate either show), missing the first two songs and starting with the intro to "Move On" and excluding the end of "God of Thunder." Unfortunately the master tape seems to have been affected by variable tape-speed issues so areas of the tape drag in areas. Parts of one of the MSG shows were also filmed by local TV for broadcast use.

July 27 - Madison Square Garden, New York, NY **CANCELLED
July 28 - Madison Square Garden, New York, NY **CANCELLED
Notes:
- Additional planned dates from the early itinerary that were also cancelled.

July 28 - Cumberland County Civic Center, Portland, ME
Promoter: Ruffino & Vaughn / Govatsos Presentations
Other act(s): New England
Reported audience: 9,300 **SOLD-OUT
Reported gross: $93,000
Partial set list: King of the Night Time World / Let Me Go, Rock 'N' Roll / Move On / Calling Dr. Love / Firehouse / New York Groove / I Was Made For Lovin' You / Christine Sixteen / God of Thunder / Shout It Out Loud / Black Diamond / Detroit Rock City / Beth / Rock And Roll All Nite
Notes:
- From a local review: "The KISS concert had been viewed by many in the community as a possible crowd control problems, but none were witnessed inside. Instead, a youthful crowd cheered and shouted as one of the most bizarre groups in rock music went through an 80-minute set with a maximum of flare" (Dyke Hendrickson, Portland Press Review, 7/29/79).
- The circulating above average AUD recording from this show is missing "Love Gun," "2,000 Man" and Ace's solo.
- KISS briefly held the venue gross record, before being surpassed by an $113,791 Frank Sinatra concert in October (though he only played for 7,593 fans).

July 29 - Madison Square Garden, New York, NY **CANCELLED
Notes:
- An additional fifth planned date from the early itinerary that was also cancelled.

July 31 - Civic Center, Providence, RI
Promoter: Frank J. Russo/Gemini Concerts
Other act(s): New England
Reported audience: 18,436 / 26,592 (69.33%) **both nights
Reported gross: $181,698 **both nights
Set list: King of the Night Time World / Let Me Go, Rock 'N' Roll / Move On / Calling Dr. Love / Firehouse / New York Groove / I Was Made For Lovin' You / Christine Sixteen / 2,000 Man

/ Love Gun / God of Thunder / Shout It Out Loud / Black Diamond / Detroit Rock City / Beth
/ Rock And Roll All Nite
Notes:
- One concert attendee made an attempt to sell drugs to a Rhode Island assistant attorney general and was arrested for his efforts.
- A first generation above average AUD recording circulates from this show (assumed to be the first show because there's nothing to indicate which show it comes from, other than the lack of any mention of "last night"), though "Love Gun" is missing as is the city introduction (though Paul mentions the city in his rap following "Let Me Go, Rock 'N' Roll").

August 1 - Civic Center, Providence, RI
Promoter: Frank J. Russo/Gemini Concerts
Other act(s): New England
Reported audience: (13,246 capacity)
Set list: King of the Night Time World / Let Me Go, Rock 'N' Roll / Move On / Calling Dr. Love / Firehouse / New York Groove / I Was Made For Lovin' You / Christine Sixteen / 2,000 Man / Love Gun / God of Thunder / Shout It Out Loud / Black Diamond / Detroit Rock City / Beth / Rock And Roll All Nite
Notes:
- An average AUD recording circulates from this show.

August 2 - Civic Center, Providence, RI **CANCELLED
Promoter: Frank J. Russo/Gemini Concerts
Notes:
- A third planned date from the early itinerary that was cancelled (on July 3). In light of ticket sales for the first two shows it wouldn't have made economic sense.

August 4 - Maple Leaf Gardens, Toronto, ON, Canada
Promoter: Concert Productions International/CHUM
Other act(s): New England
Reported audience: 14,000 / 18,411 (76.04%)
Set list: King of the Night Time World / Let Me Go, Rock 'N' Roll / Move On / Calling Dr. Love / Firehouse / New York Groove / I Was Made For Lovin' You / Christine Sixteen / 2,000 Man / Love Gun / God of Thunder / Shout It Out Loud / Black Diamond / Detroit Rock City / Beth / Rock And Roll All Nite
Notes:
- From a local review: "For the most part, a good many in the audience of 14,000 would have been too young for a Donny Osmond concert, the exceptions being the parents who had been conned into bringing their kids along. And the con-job didn't stop with the tickets" (Sunday Star, 8/5/79).
- A partial very poor AUD recording from this show (from "2,000 Man" to the conclusion) circulates.

August 6 - Forum de Montreal, Montreal, QC, Canada
Promoter: Donald K. Donald
Other act(s): New England
Reported audience: ~15,000 / 18,000 (83.33%)

Set list: King of the Night Time World / Let Me Go, Rock 'N' Roll / Move On / Calling Dr. Love / Firehouse / New York Groove / I Was Made For Lovin' You / Christine Sixteen / 2,000 Man / Love Gun / God of Thunder / Shout It Out Loud / Black Diamond / Detroit Rock City / Beth / Rock And Roll All Nite

Notes:

- Members of the local Young Communist League of Canada handed out material outside of the show denouncing the band as promoters of "violence, crime, war, fascism, hedonism, sadism, obscurantism and mysticism" (Montreal Star, 8/7/79).

- From a local review: "In an age of rock as product KISS is building a dynasty with non-stop gimmickry, costuming so elaborately splendiferous it wouldn't be out of place on a Shakespearian stage, and with the mind-numbing, simple but, very insistent heavy metal attack, the very sound that's taking over the charts and teendom turntables as we slide into the 80s" (Montreal Star, 8/7/79).

- From a local review: Those begging for the group KISS last night found them cavorting upon center stage at the Forum, picking up money and running. True, the New York group was accompanied by one of the most expensive stage acts in the business — a $1.5 million set-up. However, the show was about as exciting as a fireworks display on a rainy night. Their costumes did them no good, either; they simply looked like guys in weird clothes trying to impress. Of course, they had the expensive set-up to get them through. Nevertheless, while it barely rose above a simple circus act, there was no denying the group's shock appeal" (Montreal Gazette, 8/7/79).

- A couple of AUD recording sources circulate from this show though one is missing the last two songs.

August 8 - War Memorial Auditorium, Buffalo, NY

Promoter: Festival East Inc. / Hooke Productions
Other act(s): New England
Reported audience: 8,900 / 13,422 (66.31%)
Reported gross: $86,792
Set list: King of the Night Time World / Let Me Go, Rock 'N' Roll / Move On / Calling Dr. Love / Firehouse / New York Groove / I Was Made For Lovin' You / Christine Sixteen / 2,000 Man / Love Gun / God of Thunder / Shout It Out Loud / Black Diamond / Detroit Rock City / Beth / Rock And Roll All Nite

Notes:
- A very poor AUD recording circulates from this show.

August 10 - Market Square Arena, Indianapolis, IN

Promoter: Sunshine Promotions
Other act(s): Michael Stanley Band
Reported audience: 13,283 / 18,250 (72.78%)
Reported gross: $130,240
Set list: King of the Night Time World / Let Me Go, Rock 'N Roll / Move On / Calling Dr. Love / Firehouse / New York Groove / I Was Made for Lovin' You / Christine Sixteen / 2,000 Man / Love Gun / God of Thunder / Shout It Out Loud / Black Diamond / Detroit Rock City / Beth / Rock And Roll All Nite

Notes:
- From a local review: "It is capable of good rock — but most of it is remotely adequate at best... Mostly, though, the music was a side effect for the special effects. And, like the

music, when they were good, they were spectacular. Otherwise, they seemed simply silly... What seems likely is that the kids identify with KISS the same way as they do with the cartoon characters on Saturday morning television" (Indianapolis Star, 8/11/79).
- From local press: "Police records show 77 arrests outside the arena Friday and 15 inside during the concert. In addition, a police spokesman said there was much smoking of marijuana inside the concert but the crowd was very orderly" (Logansport Pharos-Tribune, 8/12/79).
- A low quality AUD recording circulates from this show.

August 12 - Mid-South Coliseum, Memphis, TN
Promoter: Mid-South Concerts/Beaver Productions
Other act(s): New England
Reported audience: 11,999 **SOLD-OUT
Reported gross: $112,250
Notes:
- From a local review: "'We can't stand KISS, but we came to see what they look like,' Jody said. 'I can't stand them because they worship the devil,' Jody added, pointing out, 'That's what everyone on my street says.' That view wasn't shared by the majority of the band's fans" (Memphis Commercial Appeal, 8/13/79).

August 14 - Municipal Auditorium, Nashville, TN
Promoter: Sound Seventy Productions
Other act(s): New England
Reported audience: 9,900 **SOLD-OUT
Reported gross: $113,148
Notes:
- A "KISS Festival" was held at the auditorium plaza from 1 to 6PM offering prize drawings, T-shirts, and other merchandise opportunities.
- From a local review: "KISS did little last night to dispel the criticism that makeup comes before music for the four-piece band. The group's latest albums show that they want to be taken seriously — that their makeup may eventually only be used to protect their private lives. But they resorted in last night's Municipal Auditorium concert to the same by-now old standbys of garish garb and special effects... KISS' appeal to children is presumably based on appearance, so a lack of attention to [the] music is understandable" (The Tennessean, 8/15/79).
- Alan Nelson from local Channel 4 provided a dour TV report on the show that included footage from "King Of The Night Time World" and "Let Me Go, Rock 'N' Roll:" "Before a capacity crowd of pre-pubescents. KISS performs what music trade people disdainfully call bubble-gum music — Music designed for ages 8 to 14. The KISS crowd was comprised largely of people in that age group... Despite the slurs on KISS' age-orientation the four musicians are really pretty competent on their instruments. Unfortunately, when you push a guitar with 10,000 watts of power, it tends to sound like the soundtrack from the apocalypse and it's difficult to tell an augmented G-chord from a falling trash can... The aluminum-foil costumes, the smoke machine and the mirror ball make for a highly visual performance — sort of like watching a slow-motion instant replay of an explosion in a tinsel factory."

August 16 - Jefferson County Coliseum, Birmingham, AL
Promoter: Ruffino & Vaughn Productions
Other act(s): New England
Reported audience: 12,213 / 19,000 (64.28%)
Reported gross: $112,341
Notes:
- Ian Hunter was initially scheduled as the opening act for this show.
- From a local review: "Twelve thousand, eight hundred Birmingham children were 'robbed' of their allowances last night. Willing accomplices in the 'theft' were a legion of parents who either stuffed cotton in their ears and braved the KISS concert at Birmingham-Jefferson Coliseum, or waited for three hours in cars out sides while the kids saw the show" (Birmingham News, 8/17/79).

August 18 - Riverside Centroplex, Baton Rouge, LA
Promoter: Beaver Productions
Other act(s): New England
Reported audience: 15,327 **SOLD-OUT
Notes:
- The band was interviewed backstage and footage filmed during the show. A resulting 10 minute feature was broadcast on local TV station WNOE's show "The Journal." Footage from this broadcast was shared online in 2010. The closing remarks for the feature indicate that the show was sold-out.

August 20 - Civic Center, Mobile, AL
Promoter: Beaver Productions
Other act(s): Eli
Reported audience: ~13,000
Notes:
- Eli, a last minute replacement for New England, was a Tallahassee based southern rock band. Nantucket had also been advertised as the opening act in local ads the day prior to the show. According to Eli drummer Chaz Darling, "Apparently they [the scheduled opener] were unable to make the show for one reason or another; and the promoters were forced to shop around for a group that was close enough to get there and put on a halfway decent show. I was awakened that morning by a phone call from the leader of the band asking if, on our first day of vacation (ELI took two weeks off at the end of August), I'd like to open for KISS that evening in Mobile. It took a few logistical phone calls back and forth with the promoter... yes, we're going... no, we're not... yes, we are... All the band members had to change vacation plans, but we were able to make the commitment to go. We sent our road crew and equipment over in the late morning and the band followed later, arriving just after KISS' sound-check had ended. The road crew got to witness this, the band did not. We had one interaction with Gene Simmons as we were preparing to go onstage, he was standing with two attractive young women (go figure) and no words were spoken; apparently he was highly amused at the lead singer's outfit (deerskin loincloth and thigh high spats). I remember as we walked to the stage and passed by KISS fans, we were not welcomed very enthusiastically, as calls of 'We want KISS' and a couple of middle fingers were lifted to us in salute. However, it was an incredible experience... some tech glitches on our part kept it from being stellar."

- From a local review: "The power for the show, so intense, complicated, contrived and truly intricate in its programming, must give Jimmy Carter nightmares for the not-conserved energy. It is rivaled by July 4th fireworks, some of which were included in the routines" (Mobile Register, 8/21/79).
- Parts of this show were filmed by local TV for news broadcast use.
- During the break that followed this date, Peter vacationed in the Caribbean which was hit by Hurricane David, something he'd comment about in the press following the restart of the tour.

September 1 - Nassau Coliseum, Uniondale, NY
Promoter: Ruffino & Vaughn/Delsener Productions
Other act(s): Judas Priest
Reported audience: 11,278 / 13,564 (83.15%)
Reported gross: $114,620
Set list: King of the Night Time World / Let Me Go, Rock 'N' Roll / Move On / Calling Dr. Love / Firehouse / New York Groove / I Was Made For Lovin' You / Christine Sixteen / 2,000 Man / Love Gun / God of Thunder / Shout It Out Loud / Black Diamond / Detroit Rock City / Beth / Rock And Roll All Nite
Notes:
- One fan made the national press for attempting to get passes by impersonating a county prosecutor and calling the ticket agency and offering to dismiss criminal charges if tickets were provided to him!
- Backstage, before the show, the band presented AMI's Jack Tessler with a special cake in appreciation of his efforts on their behalf.
- An average AUD recording from this show circulates.

September 3 - Veterans Memorial Coliseum, New Haven, CT
Promoter: Cross Country Concerts
Other act(s): Judas Priest
Reported audience: 8,008 / 9,800 (81.71%)
Reported gross: $79,640
Notes:
- There was an hour delay between acts due to "technical issues."
- Judas Priest's set at this show was AUD recorded.

September 5 - Civic Center, Springfield, MA
Promoter: Cross Country Concerts
Other act(s): Judas Priest
Reported audience: 7,650 / 8,514 (89.85%)
Reported gross: $73,079

September 7 - The Spectrum, Philadelphia, PA
Promoter: Electric Factory Concerts
Other act(s): Judas Priest
Reported audience: 13,524 / 19,567 (69.12%)
Reported gross: $123,334
Set list: King of the Night Time World / Let Me Go, Rock 'N' Roll / Move On / Calling Dr. Love / Firehouse / New York Groove / I Was Made for Lovin' You / Christine Sixteen / 2,000 Man

/ Love Gun / God of Thunder / Shout It Out Loud / Black Diamond / Detroit Rock City / Beth
/ Rock And Roll All Nite
Notes:
- The band received a $50,000 guarantee for this show.
- A generally good AUD recording from this show circulates.

September 10 - Civic Center, Huntington, WV
Promoter: Entam, Inc.
Other act(s): Judas Priest
Reported audience: 9,798 **SOLD-OUT
Reported gross: $97,980
Notes:
- The venue had been forced to turned down a KISS concert previously, due to the technical
requirement for staging a KISS show — something the venue were able to work around for
the "Dynasty" tour. During the show audiologists from Marshall University monitored the
volume of the show, which reportedly topped out at nearly 110 decibels. The group handed
out some 4,500 pairs of earplugs.
- Huntington Holiday Inn refused the band services: "The hotel's manager, Philip Bernard,
declined to comment. However, Ted Lewis, manager of the Huntington Civic Center, said
Bernard had told him KISS would not be allowed to stay at the hotel unless it posted a
$5,000 bond against damages. The group refused, he said. 'Phil told me that he wasn't
going to let KISS stay there because the last time there were a lot of kids hanging around
and some pictures were stolen, and he said members of the KISS group were rude to him
and his staff,' Lewis said. Lashinsky said KISS would leave Huntington immediately after the
concert for their next performance in Tennessee" (Bluefield Daily Telegraph, 9/7/79).
- From a local review: "Civic Center Manager Ted Lewis reported that 8,483 people paid to
see KISS. That's 17 short of a full paid house. The gross takes was $84.830 from tickets.
Lewis said the city made an estimated $20,500 from the show" (Huntington Herald-
Dispatch, 9/11/79).
- Roughly 10 minutes of 8mm footage were filmed at this show.

September 12 - Coliseum, Knoxville, TN
Promoter: Entam, Inc.
Other act(s): Judas Priest
Reported audience: 9,442 **SOLD-OUT
Reported gross: $94,420
Notes:
- Backstage interview footage for a Veronica's Countdown (Holland) TV episode was filmed
at this show.

September 14 - Riverfront Coliseum, Cincinnati, OH
Promoter: Electric Factory Concerts
Other act(s): Judas Priest
Reported audience: 17,820 **SOLD-OUT
Notes:
- This show was reported as sold out in the 11/79 edition of "Cincinnati Magazine." KISS was
also involved in a deal to purchase 196 acres of land in Butler County to build an industrial

park. The day before this show Lydia's divorce from Peter Criss was finalized at Stamford Superior Court.

- From a local review: "KISS wasn't playing any gems either. The 40 minutes this writer sat through before catching a final-edition deadline showed that KISS' vacation from touring did nothing to improve the group musically. Peter Criss still approaches the drums with a beginner's gingerliness. The concept of a backbeat continues to elude him and he uses the cymbals as often as donkeys fly. What Criss lacked in finesse he more than topped with his ill-timed tempos. He rushed so terribly it became obvious he couldn't keep the beat if it were locked in Ft. Knox. Gene Simmons' tentative bass guitar work was right at home with Criss' drumming. The same went for the outrageously out-of-tune guitar musings of Paul Stanley and Ace Frehley. In concerts past, KISS attempted to temper its wretched rock with on-stage wanderings which bordered on theater. Theater of the absurd, but theater nonetheless. Friday evening, the theater was gone. KISS was merely a rock and roll band in grotesque mime makeup. Thus, the band's performance could only be judged on the basis of its music and... its dancing. Oh, yes. There was dancing. As Simmons garbled his way through "Calling Dr. Love," Stanley bounded across the stage. In his high-heels and mincing, one-and-a-two-and-a-three steps, he cavorted like a reject from a Lawrence Welk polka contest" (Cincinnati Enquirer, 9/15/79). The harshness of the review is hardly surprising in the context of the critic's preshow interview and piece that ended, "That's great, Gene. You're just what the world needs, and old school teacher who preaches nihilism and sticks out his tongue" (Cincinnati Enquirer, 9/9/79) as a response to Gene's comments that being awed by a show experience was more important than searching for meaning in art.

September 16 - Freedom Hall, Louisville, KY
Promoter: Sunshine Promotions
Other act(s): Judas Priest
Reported audience: ~7,000 / 13,500 (51.85%)
Partial set list: King of the Night Time World / Move On / Black Diamond / I Was Made For Lovin' You / Detroit Rock City / Beth / Rock And Roll All Nite
Notes:
- Gene didn't fly during this gig, which reportedly had a bad sound quality.
- From a local review: "A little less than half a house showed up, for one thing. And many of them just didn't seem to care enough to respond between the band's numbers. Each song got only one or two seconds of applause, followed by a long, silent lull. Even when the group left the stage — only to return for three short, completely programmed encores — the audience didn't seem to notice the absence for a minute or two. But then this was not the ordinary rock concert audience. There were parents and even grandparents. There were children small enough not to have to worry about school this morning" (Louisville Times, 9/17/79).

September 18 - Memorial Coliseum, Ft. Wayne, IN
Promoter: Sunshine Promotions
Other act(s): Judas Priest
Reported audience: 7,669 / 10,480 (73.18%)
Reported gross: $76,690
Set list: King of the Night Time World / Let Me Go, Rock 'N' Roll / Move On / Calling Dr. Love / Firehouse / New York Groove / I Was Made For Lovin' You / Christine Sixteen / 2,000 Man

/ Love Gun / God of Thunder / Shout It Out Loud / Black Diamond / Detroit Rock City / Beth / Rock And Roll All Nite

Notes:

- The bands had a travel day/day off in Ft. Wayne on the 17th. Peter was caught sans makeup in a local restaurant, The Sands, by a fan resulting in a news article on the encounter.

- From a local review: "The theatrics used by KISS make the show. All four band members seem to really enjoy the show they are giving, but their individuality makes them each yearn for the spotlight, and receive it, at some point in the show" (Fort Wayne News-Sentinel, 9/19/79).

- Rob Halford on KISS: "I know that in terms of money in this business they're worth an absolute fortune, but that doesn't mean they can't even come around and say hello. There's been no real mutual contact, which to me is a letdown, because if you take away all the effects, the glamour and the costumes, you've basically got four musicians playing music" (Melody Maker, 9/29/79).

- Priest guitarists KK Downing and Glenn Tipton, along with journalist Steve Gett and members of KISS' crew, went clubbing in Ft. Wayne on 9/17 and were mistaken for KISS. Glenn pretended to be Ace, "KK, who's usually mistaken for Rod Stewart was safe — no one in KISS has blond hair" (Melody Maker, 9/29/79).

- A below average partial AUD recording from the show circulates excluding "Firehouse" and "Calling Dr. Love."

September 20 - Roberts Stadium, Evansville, IN

Promoter: Sunshine Promotions
Other act(s): Judas Priest
Reported audience: 8,220 / 12,732 (64.56%)
Reported gross: $82,200
Notes:

- From a local review: "The concert never let up from that high intensity pace from then on. People were standing in the aisles screaming to every movement the band made throughout the evening. The people themselves were half the fun of the evening... KISS is not purely a rock and roll band, they are an entertainment package. It just so happens that their package is based on entertainment. The show combined bombs, sparks, explosions, flame pots, burning guitars, and a semi-rotating drum platform to provide the concertgoer that something extra" (Mount Caramel Daily Republican, 9/21/79).

September 22 - International Amphitheater, Chicago, IL

Promoter: Celebration Concerts/Flipside Production
Other act(s): Judas Priest
Reported audience: (11,513 capacity)
Set list: King of the Night Time World / Let Me Go, Rock 'N' Roll / Move On / Calling Dr. Love / Firehouse / New York Groove / I Was Made for Lovin' You / Christine Sixteen / 2,000 Man / Love Gun / God of Thunder / Shout It Out Loud / Black Diamond / Detroit Rock City / Beth / Rock And Roll All Nite
Notes:

- The night before this show Paul and Ace appeared on WALS Chicago FM radio.

- Atlanta-based merchandising company, Colton/Sedrish Associates, won a restraining order in Chicago's Cook County Court resulting in the confiscation of thousands of bootleg T-shirts

and other merchandise. The company's GRABEM division (Get Rid of All Bootleggers And Evil Merchandise) activities were directly tied to an increase in merchandise sales at the Chicago Amphitheatre venue (Billboard, 10/13/79).
- Around 10 minutes of silent 8mm footage was filmed at this show. An average AUD recording also circulates.

September 24 - MECCA Arena, Milwaukee, WI
Promoter: Stardate Productions
Other act(s): Judas Priest
Reported audience: 9,200 / 12,000 (76.67%)
Set list: King of the Night Time World / Let Me Go, Rock 'N' Roll / Move On / Calling Dr. Love / Firehouse / New York Groove / I Was Made for Lovin' You / Christine Sixteen / 2,000 Man / Love Gun / God of Thunder / Shout It Out Loud / Black Diamond / Detroit Rock City / Beth / Rock And Roll All Nite
Notes:
- From a local review: "This may sound crazy, but there something very likable about KISS. Not that the bandsmen are charming or anything. Certainly no one would call them cuddly. But their travelling colossal rock extravaganza smacks of the same sentiments that made Disneyland or 'Star Wars' successful. It's great, if you're a willing believer... It's the bandsmen's seeming delight with themselves and their act that allows KISS the success it has enjoyed" (Milwaukee Journal, 9/25/79).
- This show circulates as an average AUD recording.

September 26 - Dane County Memorial Coliseum, Madison, WI
Promoter: Stardate Productions
Other act(s): Judas Priest
Reported audience: ~7,000 / 10,231 (68.42%)
Notes:
- From a local review: "Watching the KISS concert Wednesday night at the Coliseum was really quite entertaining, even educational. Especially for an 8-year-old. Now the kid understands why mom and dad said college was the best years of their lives: All these no-no's were suddenly no longer out of reach... The staging was masterful, and all those fireworks! Why, it was just like an intergalactic battle and the Fourth of July all rolled into one. There were guitars that shot off skyrockets and smoke screens that enveloped the four musicians. And Peter Criss, whose drum solo made him sound like a graduate of the primate school of drumming, played this solo while being lifted above the stage" (Wisconsin State Journal, 9/27/79). The first 5,000 tickets were sold at a discount of $1 off the $10.50 price.

September 28 - Met Center, Bloomington, MN
Promoter: Schon Productions
Other act(s): Judas Priest
Reported audience: ~15,000 / 16,000 (93.75%)
Notes:
- The band conducted an autograph signing at the 494 & Lyndale Great American Music store in Bloomington the day prior to the show.
- From a local review: "Some have seen KISS's popularity in psychological terms, as an acting-out and perhaps purging for the more gruesome fantasies lurking beneath the layers

of your average 15-year-old's psyche... Others see the phenomenon as harmless escapism" (Minneapolis Tribune, 10/1/79).

September 29 - Met Center, Bloomington, MN **CANCELLED

September 30 - Municipal Auditorium, Kansas City, MO
Promoter: Contemporary Productions
Other act(s): Judas Priest
Reported audience: 10,000 **SOLD-OUT
Reported gross: $99,092
Notes:
- While in town Gene conducted an interview with the Knight News Wire for a syndicated article covering the band's history through the current tour that appeared in many papers in November.

October 2 - The Checkerdome, St. Louis, MO
Promoter: Contemporary Productions
Other act(s): John Cougar & The Zone
Reported audience: 12,333 / 20,000 (61.67%)
Reported gross: $116,345
Set list: King of the Night Time World / Let Me Go, Rock 'N' Roll / Move On / Calling Dr. Love / Firehouse / New York Groove / I Was Made for Lovin' You / Christine Sixteen / 2,000 Man / Love Gun / God of Thunder / Shout It Out Loud / Black Diamond / Detroit Rock City / Beth / Rock And Roll All Nite
Notes:
- Gene and Paul were interviewed unmasked, though facing away from the cameras, by local TV station KSDK. Additionally, at least "King of the Night Time World" was filmed for the program and news footage use.
- From a local review: "When I talked with Gene Simmons of KISS last week, he promised a spectacle filled with gimmicks. And there were gimmicks galore as the New York rock quartet performed for a large crowd Tuesday night at the Checkerdome. The crowd deserves mention, too, because it has grown younger and older simultaneously. Simmons and the other members of the group — Paul Stanley, Ace Frehley and Peter Criss — have become comic book heroes. Consequently, they have captured the preteen crowd. And when you have preteens at a rock concert, you have their parents. KISS has retained a lot of its audience between the preteens and their parents, as well, so it was a real mix" (St. Louis Post-Dispatch, 10/3/79).
- John Mellencamp recalled those early days, "We were the worst band in the world at that time. We approached it from a different aspect, we were young and wild then ... We were just happy to meet people and happy to get out there ... The dough and songs weren't that great, that's for sure" (Aiken Standard, 3/6/88). Often his band would be mismatched with acts, the fans of whom didn't necessarily hate the Zone, but wanted a different band on stage opening for their favorite band.

October 4 - Veteran's Memorial Auditorium, Des Moines, IA
Promoter: Celebration Productions
Other act(s): John Cougar & The Zone
Reported audience: ~7,000 / 9,000 (77.78%)

Notes:
- KISS performed the same day Pope John Paul II visited the town, at a time when the religious-right was attacking their concerts. Irony.
- From a local review: "I really knew they were bad when they started to play. It's too bad they use the words rock 'n' roll so loosely in their act, for they are not rock 'n' roll, but an obscure music form known as 'Trend-ola.' Everything about KISS has been borrowed, piece by piece, from some other music group, and then badly assembled into a wall of noise" (Des Moines Register, 10/5/79).

October 6 - Arena Auditorium, Duluth, MN
Promoter: Schon Productions
Other act(s): John Cougar & The Zone
Reported audience: (8,000 capacity)
Notes:
- Judas Priest appeared on many print ads for this show.

October 8 - Civic Auditorium, Omaha, NE
Promoter: Schon Productions
Other act(s): John Cougar & The Zone
Reported audience: (10,960 capacity)
Notes:
- The following day, Ace Frehley was interviewed by phone by Gene Triplett of the Oklahoma Journal where he addresses the state of the tour and expresses surprise that the album is doing well both domestically and in international markets.

October 10 - Five Seasons Center, Cedar Rapids, IA
Promoter: In-house/Amusement Conspiracy Productions
Other act(s): John Cougar & The Zone
Reported audience: 9,030 **SOLD-OUT
Reported gross: $90,030
Partial set list: 2,000 Man / God of Thunder / Shout It Out Loud
Notes:
- KISS received "$35,000 as a guaranteed fee, plus $10,000 for providing its own stage, lighting and sound system, and another $1,865.10 as its percentage split, as stipulated in the contract. That's a total $46,865.10. Cougar and his band, The Zone, got a flat $750 for their performance. Other expenses incurred by the acts and by the Five Seasons Center are also included in the total expense figure of $66,895.97. Center manager Mike Gebauer said the $11,702.06 the city received from the show does not include the center's percentage from the sale of concessions during the performance, or the fee charges for the tickets" (Cedar Rapids Gazette, 10/12/79).
- From a local review: "Yes, KISS did do a few of their sexually suggestive numbers, but for the most part, they promoted having a good time. At one point in the show, a few fisticuffs broke out in the crowd in front of the stage, which caused Simmons to point a finger at the culprit and stare him down for several minutes. Stanley, the only member who talks outside of the songs, told the combatants to cool it by saying, 'Listen muscles, we're not here to fight. We're here to have a good time.' Things then cooled down" (Cedar Rapids Gazette, 10/11/79).
- 2,457 signed a petition asking the Cedar Rapids City Council to ban the concert on the grounds that it would "have a negative influence on young people and the community as a

whole" (Cedar Rapids Gazette, 10/3/79). 7,000 tickets selling in 75 minutes seems to indicate the public thought otherwise: "The tickets didn't go on sale until 6 p.m. Wednesday, but the lines began to form at 8 a.m. And they grew throughout the day. The attraction was the Oct. 10 concert of the rock group KISS at the Five Seasons Center. One woman, who drove from Des Moines to buy tickets, told Five Seasons' officials that she left the capital city at 4:30 a.m. The tickets, all general admission, were sold inside the center's arena by six ticket sellers. Center manager Mike Gebauer said 7,000 of the $10 tickets were sold in 75 minutes and that most of the lines had been taken care of by 7:15 p.m. The center remained open until 9 p.m. and about 500 more tickets were sold. Gebauer said the lines went fast because the six ticket sellers sold only KISS tickets and nothing for other upcoming events at the center. All ticket sales were for cash only" (Cedar Rapids Gazette, 9/13/79).

October 12 - Britt Brown Arena @ Kansas Coliseum, Wichita, KS
Promoter: Contemporary Productions

October 14 - Convention Center Arena, Pine Bluffs, AK
Promoter: Pace Concerts
Other act(s): John Cougar & The Zone
Reported audience: 8,257 / 9,000 (91.74%)
Reported gross: $71,818

October 17 - Lloyd Noble Center, Norman, OK
Promoter: Little Wing Productions
Other act(s): Breathless
Reported audience: 10,500 **SOLD-OUT
Reported gross: $98,325
Notes:
- Scheduled opening act John Cougar was replaced by Breathless, who included drummer Kevin Valentine (later a session player on "Psycho Circus" and "Revenge"), for this show.

October 19 - Convention Center Arena, San Antonio, TX
Promoter: Stone City Attractions
Other act(s): Breathless
Reported audience: (12,800 capacity)
Set list: King of the Night Time World / Let Me Go, Rock 'N Roll / Move On / Calling Dr. Love / Firehouse / New York Groove / I Was Made for Lovin' You / Christine Sixteen / 2,000 Man / Love Gun / God of Thunder / Shout It Out Loud / Black Diamond / Detroit Rock City / Beth / Rock And Roll All Nite
Notes:
- Footage was filmed at this show for the syndicated show "PM Magazine" feature on the day in the life of a KISS concert, notably the assembly of the stage prior to the show.

October 21 - The Summit, Houston, TX
Promoter: Pace Concerts / Louis Messina
Other act(s): Breathless
Reported audience: 17,572 / 18,000 (97.62%)
Reported gross: $182,359

Presumed set list: King of the Night Time World / Let Me Go, Rock 'N Roll / Move On / Calling Dr. Love / Firehouse / Christine Sixteen / I Was Made for Lovin' You / 2,000 Man / Love Gun / New York Groove / God of Thunder / Shout It Out Loud / Black Diamond / Detroit Rock City / Beth / Rock And Roll All Nite

Notes:

- Cleveland band Breathless included a former member of previous KISS-opener, the Michael Stanley band, vocalist Jonah Koslen, and drummer Kevin Valentine. The band was touring in support of their debut album on EMI Records.

- A generally poor and chopped AUD recording attributed to, but not confirmed as definitively being from this show, circulates.

October 23 - Tarrant County Convention Center, Fort Worth, TX

Promoter: Concerts West

Other act(s): Jon Butcher Axis

Reported audience: ~13,000 / 14,000 (92.86%)

Notes:

- Both John Cougar and Breathless were mentioned in separate press reports as opening acts for this show.

- Peter played his part in managing the furor affecting the Lubbock show in the press commenting, "We were in a town recently where an organized religious organization called us demons from hell. I'm no demon from hell and neither is anyone else in the band... Our songs aren't about sex. We don't sit down and day, 'Hey, let's write a song about sex.' We write about life on the road, living in different hotel rooms every night. Look, money's tight. Some of these kids may have fathers who are out of jobs. School is getting rough for 'em. All we try to do, our one single aim, is to help them forget about all their problems for an hour and a half. This has been a hard tour for us. We're playing cities groups of our stature wouldn't normally play because there's not any money to be made there. But we feel the kids want to see our show, and we don't want them to miss it. We work this hard and there here things like this, and it hurts, I mean it really hurts" (Dallas Morning News, 10/23/79).

- From a local review: "The rock 'n' roll circus has come and gone. And all the time it was just a KISS away. It was a circus for the young and for the young at heart — but mostly for the young. The very young. The very, very young... They heard what sounded like a tamer KISS from years past; a slightly older KISS; a KISS that relies more on vocalization, particularly vocal harmonies. Yes, the rock 'n' roll circus has come and gone for another year. And all the time it was just a KISS away" (Dallas Morning News, 10/25/79).

October 27 - Taylor Coliseum, Abilene, TX

Promoter: Stone City Attractions

Other act(s): Breathless

Reported audience: ~9,000

Notes:

- From a local review: "The KISS crowd was comprised of a jillion (at least it seemed so) kids and, believe this or not, parents. Some of the kids were so young that parental guidance (by hand) was necessary. Because of the dominance of these two age groups, there was little of that famous 'blue haze' that tends to fog the lights when the first chords are struck" (Hardin Simmons University, The Brand, 11/2/79)

- Live, backstage, and fan footage was filmed at this show for 321-Contact on public television (PBS).

October 29 - Tulsa Assembly Center, Tulsa, OK
Promoter: Stone City Attractions
Other act(s): Breathless
Reported audience: ~7,500 / 9,500 (78.95%)
Notes:
- While in Oklahoma City Gene conducted a phone interview with press in Lubbock to address the growing satanic accusations against the band. He didn't mince his words: "I've got a couple of comments. First let me say that I am ashamed that these men, these supposedly grown-up men, are acting like complete idiots. If these religious groups would just take some time out and try to think of what they could do to make their time a little more worthwhile. I shudder to think about all the work and energy these people have put into these supernatural accusations, this nonsense, when they could be working toward getting money for the poor or getting housing for the displaced. They could be doing really constructive work that would really help people instead of spending so much time blowing their own horn. I'm just really embarrassed for them, and I apologize to the sensible people in Lubbock being embarrassed by them. I'm just completely embarrassed by grown-up people living in the 20th century who are acting like idiots. That's my first reaction. My second reaction is this: If you can pick on Gene Simmons, why can't you pick on Superman? I mean, what's the difference? What's wrong with these people? What about Santa Claus, who flies through the air with reindeer? Is he a demon or something" (Lubbock Avalanche Journal, 10/28/79).
- From a local review: "What happened Monday night proved captivating to thrill-seekers. It sickened those with a musical ear... The four-man group's live performance in Tulsa Monday night was completely devoid of musical talent. Their patented hard-driving sound drove nowhere but under the skin... The idea is to keep everyone looking at Simmons when the west of the show slows down. He holds attention for the initial 20 minutes, but soon grows old and trite. Some might think him vulgar... A gross lack of harmony and cracking falsettos made the songs more of a chore than a treat to sit through" (Doug White).
- Police made some 41 arrests during the show for offenses ranging from drugs to attempted robbery.

October 31 - Municipal Coliseum, Lubbock, TX
Promoter: Stone City Attractions
Other act(s): Breathless
Reported audience: 6,723 / 9,589 (70.11%)
Notes:
- A local Lubbock church member organized a protest against the band, and gained quite a bit of press, on the grounds: "Take no part in the unfruitful works of darkness" after admitting in the press that he didn't really know anything about the band other than them being "gross." The accusations against the band went to levels of strangeness: "Goff claimed that Simmons worshipped Satan. An evangelist's assistant said Simmons was 'normal' off stage, but drummer Peter Criss worshipped demons. Again, the question of sources came up. 'Well, People Magazine said that several times,' she said. 'But I think it was all considered a rumor until the band was interviewed a couple months ago on the 20/20 program on ABC. That's when the drummer said he worshipped Satan, and the band said their name stood for Kings in Service of Satan.' These accusations have no foundation in truth. Contacted at ABC's 20/20 offices in New York City, Pam Spall, 20/20 host Hugh Downs' personal secretary, revealed that the KISS interview in question was conducted by

reporter Sam Donaldson and aired on August 18, 1979. She then read the entire transcript of the interview and at no time was mention made of Satan, demons or blood rituals. At no time did the band say that KISS stood for anything. At no time did the subject even come up" (Lubbock Avalanche Journal, 10/21/79).

- Later this night the band's infamous appearance on Tom Snyder's "Tomorrow Show" on NBC television was broadcast. The late-night talk-show, replaced by David Letterman in 1982, had moved its filming back to a studio in New York City in June, so the band flew there on their day-off on October 30 to film their appearance. Right from the start things got off to a poor start with Tom introducing Gene as the "bass" (as in fish) player. A clearly drunk Ace responds hysterically claiming that he's actually the trout player. Peter, on the other hand, appears disheveled and disoriented while Gene and Paul attempt to dominate the conversation. Ace and Peter repeatedly attempt to interject to participate with tangents and embellishments while Gene and Paul stolidly attempt to keep things moving along safely. Unfortunately, even with those attempts Ace and Peter manage to get in comments about guns and drugs and the animated Ace utterly steals the limelight by cackling maniacally.

Decades later, Paul was still not amused: "It wasn't that big of a fun time because you have to respect your position. You have to respect your job. You have to respect the people that you're trying to communicate with. It may seem funny that somebody is drunk... but the fact is that the root of it was, I believe, a contempt and a lack of respect for the audience and the fans. So, sure, can you look at it and chuckle? Yeah. I can, too, but I see deeper. And I look at it and say, what a shame to take this lofty position that somebody gave us and spit in it. Spit in its face. By showing up inebriated or unable to connect a sentence. It may be funny on the surface, but what's below the surface is a lack of appreciation for a gift that you've been given" (LA Weekly, 2012).

November 2 - Al G. Langford Chaparral Center, Midland, TX
Promoter: Stone City Attractions
Other act(s): Breathless
Reported audience: (5,500 capacity)
Notes:
- KRIG & Winwood Mall held a KISS look-alike contest on October 31 with two winners being awarded backstage passes for autographs and pictures with the band.
- Another source suggests John Cougar opened this show, but that would seem unlikely with the scheduling.

November 4 - McNichols Arena, Denver, CO
Promoter: Schon Productions/Concert Group
Other act(s): Breathless
Reported audience: 10,543 / 18,000 (58.57%)
Reported gross: $113,487

November 6 - Convention Center, Anaheim, CA
Promoter: Avalon Attractions
Other act(s): Breathless
Reported audience: ~10,000
Notes:

- From a local review: "Tuesday night's concert at the Anaheim Convention Center was billed as 'The Return of KISS,' a title too melodramatic for a 'reunion' that was clearly predestined from the moment the band parted ways to record last year's solo albums. The audience treated KISS as it would an old, familiar face, not a long-lost friend, and the group responded with a predictable set. The four-piece group still has the biggest bag of tricks in rock, and this year's music industry slowdown may have changed the scale of the evening slightly, but the overall tone remains the same" (LA Times, 11/8/79).

November 7 - The Forum, Inglewood (Los Angeles), CA
Promoter: Avalon Attractions
Other act(s): Breathless
Reported audience: 15,822 **SOLD-OUT
Reported gross: $187,240
Set list: King of the Night Time World / Let Me Go, Rock 'N Roll / Move On / Calling Dr. Love / Firehouse / New York Groove / I Was Made for Lovin' You / Christine Sixteen / 2,000 Man / Love Gun / God of Thunder / Shout It Out Loud / Black Diamond / Detroit Rock City / Beth / Rock And Roll All Nite
Notes:
- A Casablanca Records reception what hosted at the Forum Club following the performance.
- An average AUD recording circulates from this show.

November 10 - Veterans Memorial Coliseum, Phoenix, AZ
Promoter: Beaver Productions
Other act(s): Breathless
Reported audience: ~12,750
Notes:
- From a local review: "KISS is not so much and rock 'n' roll band as a Saturday morning cartoon show come to life... They did not come to hear the music, the came to see the show. And it was a show they got, complete with dazzling lighting effects, fire, fireworks and smoke... The show is everything, because KISS' heavy metal theater-rock lacks the humor and wit of Alice Cooper and the cutting satirical edge of the Tubes, two other practitioners of the genre" (Arizona Republic, 11/11/79).

November 19 - PNE Coliseum, Vancouver, BC, Canada
Promoter: Perryscope Concert Productions
Other act(s): Loverboy
Reported audience: 14,271 / 17,500 (81.55%)
Reported gross: $145,399
Set list: King of the Night Time World / Let Me Go, Rock 'N' Roll / Move On / Calling Dr. Love / Firehouse / New York Groove / I Was Made for Lovin' You / Christine Sixteen / 2,000 Man / Love Gun / God of Thunder / Shout It Out Loud / Black Diamond / Detroit Rock City / Beth / Rock And Roll All Nite
Notes:
- This show circulates as an incomplete AUD recording.

November 21 - Seattle Center Coliseum, Seattle, WA
Promoter: Concerts West

Other act(s): The Rockets
Reported audience: 14,000 **SOLD-OUT
Reported gross: $133,000
Notes:
- An average AUD recording from this show circulates.
- The Rockets were a Detroit band formed by guitarist Jim McCarty, who had two minor hits from their Capitol Records album, "Turn Up The Radio" and "Oh Well" (a Fleetwood Mac cover) in 1979. Jim had been the original guitarist in the Detroit Wheels, Mitch Ryder's backup band, a band that Ace had seen in his teens.
- From a local review: "KISS outdid itself this time. The outrageous comic-book quartet had so many new gimmicks it its show at the Coliseum Thanksgiving Eve that there was something happening every minute. Just when you'd get tired of the music — about every seven and a half minutes — BOOM! An explosion would go off or fireworks would spurt from the drum rise or lights would flash and sirens wail... The audience was an interesting one. There probably were more parents there with kids than at any other rock show this year. There were a lot of young kids — 6 through 11 — but quite a few adults. Of course, most of the crowd were teens" (Seattle Times, 11/23/79).

November 23 - Coliseum, Portland, OR **CANCELLED
Other act(s): The Rockets
Notes:
- This show was cancelled: "The KISS show at the Portland Coliseum was called off after the Oregon fire Marshall refused to issue a permit, despite appeals by Pyro Tech Inc., a federally licensed special effects company, which does KISS' effects" (Billboard, 12/22/79).
- Newspaper reports indicated that 12,000 tickets for the show had been sold.

November 25 - Cow Palace, Daly City (San Francisco), CA
Promoter: Bill Graham Presents
Other act(s): The Rockets
Reported audience: 14,500 **SOLD-OUT
Reported gross: $123,250
Notes:
- From a local review: "Whether or not KISS, 1979, was the all-time, absolutely best show any human being or reasonable facsimile thereof has ever experienced, now, and forevermore, never to be out done come hell or high water blah, blah, blah as it was hyped to be, is a matter of opinion. In terms of aerials alone, KISS outdid any other band that comes to mind, if one gives that subject at least 10 seconds of thought" (Gail S. Tagashira).

November 27 - Selland Arena, Fresno, CA
Promoter: Avalon Attractions
Other act(s): The Rockets
Reported audience: 7,333 **SOLD-OUT
Reported gross: $60,690
Set list: King of the Night Time World / Let Me Go, Rock 'N Roll / Move On / Calling Dr. Love / Firehouse / New York Groove / I Was Made for Lovin' You / Christine Sixteen / 2,000 Man / Love Gun / God of Thunder / Shout It Out Loud / Black Diamond / Detroit Rock City / Beth / Rock And Roll All Nite
Notes:

- A partial AUD show, often from the "Show Us Your Tits" bootleg, omits the encores. A complete version also circulates. Some 8mm footage also exists from this show.

November 29 - Sports Arena, San Diego, CA
Promoter: Avalon Attractions / Marc Berman Concerts
Other act(s): The Rockets
Reported audience: 7,180 / 13,325 (53.88%)
Reported gross: $88,967
Set list: King of the Night Time World / Let Me Go, Rock 'N Roll / Move On / Calling Dr. Love / Firehouse / New York Groove / I Was Made for Lovin' You / Christine Sixteen / 2,000 Man / Love Gun / God of Thunder / Shout It Out Loud / Black Diamond / Detroit Rock City / Beth / Rock And Roll All Nite
Notes:
- This show is a good illustration of the vagaries involved in touring, and the risks a promoter takes on when booking an act. With a gross potential of $173,226 for a sold-out house of 14,217, the actual attendance came nowhere near and with the costs of the show exceeding $100,000 it's likely the promoter took a hit. KISS' guarantee, on the other hand, was $40,000.
- An average AUD recording from this show circulates, though the sound quality progressively deteriorates.

December 1 - Tingley Coliseum, Albuquerque, NM
Promoter: Feyline Presents
Other act(s): The Rockets
Reported audience: 10,656 **SOLD-OUT
Reported gross: $91,564

December 3 - Civic Center, Amarillo, TX
Promoter: Stone City Attractions
Other act(s): The Rockets
Reported audience: ~5,800 / 7,800 (74.36%)
Notes:
- More than 700 people, led by 30 ministers, protested at the concert, part of a "pray in to protest... demon worship, sexual perversion and promiscuity... protesters carried lighted candles and formed a cross while they sang and held a worship service. A flashing arrow pointed to a lighted sign which said: 'A KISS betrayed Jesus'" (UPI).

December 6 - Civic Center Coliseum, Lake Charles, LA
Other act(s): The Rockets
Reported audience: (7,781 capacity)
Notes:
- This concert took place fresh in the aftermath of the Who's concert at Riverfront Coliseum in Cincinnati where 11 fans died in a crowd crush when the gates to the venue were opened. Many venues, not least those hosting Who concerts on their tour, took stock of the concerns raised by the assorted factors that had led to the tragedy.

December 8 - Hirsch Coliseum, Shreveport, LA
Promoter: Beaver Productions

Other act(s): The Rockets
Reported audience: 10,150 **SOLD-OUT
Notes:
- CK Lendt, in his book "KISS & Sell," suggested that Peter delibertly sabotaged the set at this show: "Peter had unexpectedly shifted from his normally intense staccato beat. The song then started to slow down. Everyone in KISS seemed confused, glowering at Peter. He just kept beating the drums, slower and slower." This event apparently ended the show with Paul screaming "Good Night" and leaving the stage while the confetti canons went off. A local review also suggests a delay between the opening act's set and KISS taking the stage.
- From a local review: "Drummer Peter Criss has deteriorated. Criss' one extended solo during 'God of Thunder' sounded rather like a watery version of John Densmore's classic opening to the Doors' version of 'Who Do You Love?' for a while and then fizzled out entirely. The band saved Criss by going into 'Shout It Out Loud' and the closing tune, 'Black Diamond.'... KISS' appearance after an hour-long break put fire in the crowd, but the relative shortness of the set — just over an hour — and the exclusion of popular numbers like 'Beth' and 'Rock And Roll All Nite' was keenly felt. There wasn't an encore, which disappointed many of the fans who paid $10 for tickets. KISS put on a good, solid show Saturday, which is all they were paid to do" (Shreveport Bossier City Times, 12/9/79).

December 10 - Jackson Coliseum, Jackson, MS
Promoter: Beaver Productions
Other act(s): The Rockets
Reported audience: (7,500 capacity)
Notes:
- Peter stops playing during "Move On" and leaves the stage, leaving the rest of the band to finish. They also leave the stage after the song, with the house lights coming on. After a 15-minute delay the whole band return to the stage with Paul providing a cover story that Peter had been hit in the eye with a drumstick fragment. He storms off again following "Beth."

December 12 - Mississippi Coast Coliseum, Biloxi, MS
Promoter: Beaver Productions
Other act(s): The Rockets
Reported audience: (15,000 capacity)
Notes:
- Peter throws a drumstick at Gene on stage resulting in a scuffle between the two backstage after the show.
- News footage including part of the first song circulates (often attributed to the previous night).

December 14 - Von Braun Civic Center Arena, Huntsville, AL
Promoter: Sound Seventy Productions
Other act(s): The Rockets
Reported audience: 9,113 **SOLD-OUT
Reported gross: $90,610

December 16 - Sports Arena, Toledo, OH
Promoter: Belkin Productions

Other act(s): The Rockets
Reported audience: 7,500 **SRO
Notes:

- A local news crew filmed before and during the concert for a report.
- From a local review: "KISS, according to a recent Gallup Youth Survey of American teenagers, has fallen from the most popular rock group each of the last three years to fourth this year. But such a survey would have been hard to sell to a boisterous, standing-room-only crowd at the band's concert at the Sports Arena Sunday night. The crowd, made up of mostly teenagers, was on its feet whistling, cheering, and lighting lighters from the first song to the last. The group's extensive special effects only served to add to the audience frenzy... This being the group's first American tour in more than a year, drummer Criss added, 'We couldn't wait to get back on the road again and show the people who's boss.' Sunday at the Sports Arena, KISS proved that they still are, in Toledo at least" (Toledo Blade, 12/17/79).
- This show was Peter Criss' final concert with KISS during his original tenure with the band.
- A week following the end of the tour (12/23) Peter married Debra Lynn Svensk in Los Angeles. The other members of the band, plus Bill Aucoin (Peter's best man) and Neil Bogart, attended. By the end of the month he was demoing solo material with Stan Penridge, with Vini Poncia producing, which would become his first post-KISS solo album "Out of Control."
- Peter would only play with the band one more time, during an unsuccessful rehearsal at S.I.R. Studios in New York City the following year.

Unmasked

Touring activities for KISS in 1980 were initially intended to be very different to those that later occurred. Following the conclusion of the "Return of KISS" North American tour there had been plans to start work on the next studio prior to embarking on a European tour, that would see the band continuing to support the "Dynasty" album which was doing well internationally. Concurrent with the touring plans was a proposal for the filming of a 90–100-minute "docu-theatrical-musical" for possible broadcast as a back-to-school television special. The John Goodhue (director of the two "Dynasty" promo videos) written/directed film would be interspersed with material filmed during the spring/summer tour, notably dates in Holland and Belgium, and backed with hit songs from the KISS catalog. The proposal noted, "It combines the exciting and graphic look at this most unusual and highly successful group, both onstage and backstage operation, with a compelling and entertaining theatrical story running parallel with the concert tour... The basic theme of Behind The Mask is a pursuit, or chase, in which two attractive and wholesome teenage girls set out to see if they can discover the real, in person, identity of the four masked KISS stars. As the tour passes through a nearby city, the chase is on... And so is the fun, excitement, adventure and spectacle. The pursuit is fun, and the ending is a double surprise which satisfies the girls' challenge and entertains the audience" ("Behind the Mask" proposal). Communications suggest that there were ongoing negotiations for the project leading right up to the time when Peter Criss quit the band (and other matters). While nothing came of the proposal, a feature, "Jutta, KISS & The Big Show," was filmed for German youth TV program "Schüler Experess" in September. However, it should be noted that broad elements of the script were utilized in the "Shandi" video, where a fan is thwarted in her attempts to spy the unmasked visages of the band members as they emerge from their dressing room.

The planned European summer tour was initially announced in February 1980, though details about the dates had started leaking in late January. In the UK, Wembley dates went on sale on April 17 at a time when the band were actively negotiating a new six album contract with Phonogram. However, the whole European tour would be cancelled before the end of the month. The reason given to the press was the time-honored "unexpected delay" excuse: "Due to the extended studio time KISS need to complete the recording of their next album, 'KISS Unmasked...' The decision to postpone the tour was made by the management and the group when they realized they wouldn't have time to record the album and rehearse their show before the tour started" (Sounds, 4/26/80). However, it had also been rumored at the time that "KISS has been re-negotiating their contract with Casablanca and was unable to do their UK and European tours as planned because of this (ongoing?) label limbo situation" (Sounds, 5/10/80). Additionally, adding to the problems facing the band, merchandiser Ron Boutwell had sued various parties, including AMI and Niocua Merchandising, alleging "he was wrongfully cheated out of royalty money" (Billboard, 2/16/80). The obvious conclusion is likely a combination of these various challenges along with the more immediate issues with Peter. An internal memo simply stated, "Due to the fact that the new KISS album cannot be released in time to coincide with the European Tour, the tour is being postponed until later on in the summer" (Memo,

4/16/80). Whatever the case, CK Lendt revealed in "KISS & Sell" that Phonogram was later heavily on the hook for expenses related to the rescheduled tour. There would be a period where all of these issues were resolved, the recording of "Unmasked" was completed, and ultimately Eric Carr was hired to replace Peter Criss. The album was released on May 30.

The first show of the "Unmasked" era, and Eric's first with the band, took place at the Palladium in New York City on July 25. Originally named the Academy of Music, the venue was where KISS had made their professional industry debut back on New Year's Eve 1973/4; and it was also a venue where Eric's pre-KISS bands had opened for established acts. In some ways it was a homecoming of sorts, reestablishing contacts with their roots, but ultimately a simple baptism of fire for the new drummer. Local press noted that there could be a perception that the venue was a major step down for the band, "Tonight at the Palladium, KISS will give a single show, which is a far cry from the series of sold-out spectacles the band offered at Madison Square Garden not so long ago. This is in part a testimony to the notion that all fads must pass. But there is another, less pessimistic reason: this is a showcase for the band's new member" (New York Times, 7/25/80). In the United States the band's fortunes had certainly declined and the date would be the last full concert in their own country for more than two years. By the time this show took place the album had reached its high position at #35 on the Billboard album charts. Within days it would also scrape to what would have been considered paltry RIAA Gold certification (July 30, 1980). Internationally, at least, the band and management possibly saw a savior in the stronger performance of the album. It hit #1 in Norway and New Zealand, #3 in Austria and Australia, #4 in Germany, #5 in Holland, #11 in Italy; #12 in Canada, #15 in Japan, #17 in Sweden, and #48 in the United Kingdom. Those chart positions translated into European album sales of just over 250,000 by early August 1980, and provided a glimmer of hope for the band on the continent they'd not visited since 1976.

In Australia the band sold an impressive 110,000 copies of "Unmasked" on the first day of release (Sydney Morning Herald, 6/22/80) while in Germany it took until September 30 to reach that same level! Likewise, "Shandi," a single that had flopped at #47 in the U.S., was a top-10 hit in several markets: Norway (#4), Australia (#5, with sales of 75,000 copies), New Zealand (#6) and Austria (#10). Even though it was perceived as the best single option by Phonogram for the European markets, it struggled to gain any traction elsewhere. In Germany the single sold a respectable 52,000 copies helping it reach #28 while a follow-up, "Talk To Me," failed to make it higher than #32 in any market other than Switzerland (#10). From those album and single positions it was clear that certain markets were worthy of exploration and exploitation. KISS too were motivated to tour Europe, according to C.K. Lendt, because "Phonogram was especially anxious to see KISS on the continent since they were about to commit to another six KISS albums to the tune of $15 million" ("KISS & Sell"). Additionally, the fact that the summer tour had been cancelled, aggravating promoters and the band's booking agency, persuaded the band to focus on those markets. Japan had also tentatively been scheduled for a run of seven concerts during the last 10 days of October, but those were ultimately abandoned.

Paul reduced the band's plight to a purely clinical appraisal: "'Unmasked' tanked in the States and we spent most of 1980 inactive... The single 'Shandi' was a hit abroad, however, and we booked a tour of Europe and Australia for the fall" ("Face The Music"). As a result the band took their show on the road internationally and even the U.K., with its general rejection of all things KISS to that point, was included in the itinerary and used as a base of operations. The prospects of the European tour were not economically optimistic from the onset. Tour budgets projected a loss of some $675,000. When revised, with dates in Lisbon being cut and staffing being reduced, the loss was still expected to be somewhere near $474,000. Playing to half-filled venues across Europe, in many cases much smaller than their American counterparts, must have been depressing following years of excess in their homeland and reminiscent of the less than spectacular debut on the continent in 1976. Economically, the band also failed to sell merchandise, and in the case of Italy no merchandise was even on-hand for sale. The band also threw themselves off a cliff into financial oblivion with uncontrolled spending during the tour continuing to live the rock 'n' roll lifestyle to which they'd become accustomed. C.K. Lendt has recounted the band's $70,000 hotel bill for one week in London, and him running around the city trying to cash the American Express letters of credit he carried with him.

If the "Unmasked" tour is remembered for anything then it would be for the band's first visit to Australia. However, the reception and KISS-mania that the band experienced in Australia was not indicative of some wildly successful "Unmasked" touring cycle. The band were highly aware of that fact and hoped to use it to their advantage: "Let the press know what went on in Australia during the tour, and to make them aware of the continuing super-star status the band enjoys in places outside of the United States. It reinforces that, despite current feelings in the press in America about KISS, the band is still creating mob scenes and hysteria around the world, and maybe the press should take a second look" (KISS publicity campaign proposal). The Australia tour was more about hype than substance, and while the tour did take on epic proportions when compared with the previous two U.S. outings, there was enough evidence that a house of cards was being constructed. Regardless of the reality, it certainly was a time of excitement for the Australian fans.

Initially scheduled to arrive on November 8 and play their first show three days later, the band arrived in Australia early on the morning of November 1, 1980. At the Town Hall appearance with the Lord Mayor in Sydney the following day, of the "100,000 expected by the KISS public relations machine, [only] about 4,000 turned out" (Sydney Morning Herald, 11/3/80). So brief was the band's appearance, to throw out some trinkets to the natives and pose for some photos that minutes later they departed for their press conference at the Sebel Town House Function Centre. Reality was severely skewed from the months of press coverage the prospective "cosmetic disco-rock group" (The Age, 6/20/80) touring had received following the initial rumors in June until the actual announcement. That announcement finally came on Tuesday, July 15, the anniversary of the release of "Dynasty," at the Pavilion on the Park Restaurant in Sydney. For comparison, a crowd of more than 300,000 greeted the Beatles on their arrival in Adelaide in 1964...

The likes of Neil Bogart or Malcolm McLaren would have been proud of the magnificent manufactured hype, affectionately referred to as "KISSteria." It was most certainly a matter of selling to the Australian public something that wasn't actually reflected in reality. Perhaps it was a need from the consumer side to embrace something perceived as exciting, a "Beatles" experience for a new generation. According to Glenn A. Baker, "the Australian editor of America's 'Billboard' magazine, a misleading image of KISS as 'the biggest band in the world' has been thrust down our throats by the media. Mr. Baker, himself a KISS fan who wouldn't miss the concert, describes KISS as a second level act which has had one big album... 'The average kid probably thinks KISS are number one in America. They're a great band but somebody should tell the media moguls that KISS have a few notches to get on their belts yet,' Mr. Baker said" (The Age, Melbourne, 11/13/80). It wouldn't be fair to suggest that the hype was all of the band's own making. The Australian press hopped on the bandwagon with aplomb, and with promoter Kevin Jacobsen having rolled the dice to the tune of $2 million, all the hype possible was needed — expecting the tour to service 150,000 patrons at $13 a ticket was going to take some doing in a country with a population of less than 15 million, even one that pre-tour economic analysis indicated had a per capita entertainment expenditure of $14.28, the second highest globally. Ultimately Jacobsen would take out a trade ad thanking the band for servicing 250,000 people and grossing over $3 million.

By early August sales of "Unmasked" had reached 139,146 in Australia, particularly impressive compared with Europe and the U.S. (Japan had only reached 40,000 at the same time). By the end of 1980 the album had reached 206,475 copies (4X platinum) buoyed by a combination of the band's exposure and a hefty dose of merchant discounting. However, even before the tour had ended the hype had commenced its inevitable dissipation. That there were 8,000 tickets remaining unsold two days prior to the second Sydney show is only partially illustrative of that fact. An article in the Sydney Morning Herald pointed to the over-merchandising and lack of consumer demand. One manufacturer, Plough Australia, had produced 200,000 KISS make-up bags, but had only sold half. One licensee for KISS coins had manufactured 20,000 units, selling only 419 pieces. Even the "Unmasked" sales figures were becoming tarnished by heavy discounting of the album (Sydney Morning Herald, 11/20/80). C.K. Lendt, in his excellent "KISS & Sell," suggested that the band played to over 250,000 fans and grossed in excess of $3 million, yet the tour still apparently lost $250,000. The band may have had the time of their lives during the tour, but the excesses approached legendary levels. According to one article, "Backstage at venues he [promoter Kevin Jacobsen] built them a swimming pool, a games tent with mini-golf and pinball machines and the obligatory hospitality tent. Each plane they flew on was stocked with enough Dom Perignon to serve everyone in it. 'It was insane, there was a party every night,' he recalls. 'We would go out to dinner and take over a restaurant.' Jacobsen says he lost a lot of money (about $200,000) on the KISS Tour. He refers to it as a milestone in history: The last example of outrageous rock star extravagance in Australia" (The Age, Melbourne, 11/6/87). Departing Australia, there might well have been the mystical aroma of burning bridges wafting through the subconscious of the participants...

Much of the excess was rooted in the need to maintain the mystique of the masked band, therefore preventing them from being able to play "normal" tourists during their periods of downtime. The band had become prisoners of their fame, more so in an unfamiliar environment than they were at home. Having to pay for 4 charter planes to New Zealand and increasing security at shows following the press reports of injuries at one of the Adelaide shows also contributed to the costs of the tour borne by the promoter. Bomb threats also added to the siege mentality while keeping the band in the press. While KISS received around $800,000 for the tour Jacobsen suggested, "We cut even, and the band didn't make any money either" (The Sydney Morning Herald, 3/22/81), taking into account its large personal touring entourage and "Super-KISS" expenses. The touring entourage, outside of the staging staff, included Bill Aucoin, George Sewitt, John Harte, Ken Anderson, Jack Tessler, Chris Lendt, Doug Hull, Ernie Bostock, Warren Linney, Wally Andrews, Mick

Chiodo, Ron Blackmore, Pixie Esmonde, Robert Franco, Robbie Robertson, Patti Mostyn and often Kevin Jacobsen. Outside of hotels were the massive costs involving staging, sound, lighting, and transport, 15 trucks worth according to some press reports. However, the hype and hysteria had also worked against the promoter. The promoter "Had to spend an extra $28,000 on security after an exaggerated newspaper story claimed that 200 people were injured at the Adelaide concert. And he was forced to charter four flights across the Tasman at $27,000 a tip" (The Sydney Morning Herald, 3/22/81). Sydney rock journalist Glenn Baker perhaps sums up the tour best, "It was the result of a remarkably adept and stunningly successful marketing campaign. Kevin [Jacobsen] did something in the best traditions of showbiz — he gave people a lot of fun and was successful."

Little would KISS have known that Ace Frehley had performed his last full concert with the band (until the 1996 reunion) at the final 1980 tour date in Auckland, New Zealand, on December 3 — though there may well have been signs that were either missed or ignored. While there may have been interpersonal challenges within the band, matters had yet to come to a head. Fortunately a soundboard of that show was captured for posterity and circulates for collectors to enjoy. For the band catalog sales throughout the markets the band toured were reasonable. In Germany, the clearance of Bellaphon product was strong as was demand for the new Phonogram distributed releases. The same was the case in Australia where Astor had been supplanted by PolyGram distribution. While not a financial windfall, the visibility and intensity of the tour would have left the band at least hopeful for the new decade having survived their first tour with a replacement member.

May 19, 1980 - Ekeberghalle, Oslo, Norway **CANCELLED
May 21 - Broendbyhalle, Copenhagen, Denmark **CANCELLED
May 23 - Eriksdalshallen, Stockholm, Sweden **CANCELLED
May 24 - Scandinavium, Gothenburg, Sweden **CANCELLED
May 27 - Ernst Herck Halle, Munich, Germany **CANCELLED
May 28 - Ysselhal, Zwolle, Holland **CANCELLED
May 30 - Ahoy, Rotterdam, Holland **CANCELLED
Notes:
- These two dates, and the two following as contingencies, were planned to be professionally filmed and recorded for inclusion in a proposed television project titled "Behind The Mask."

May 31 - Forest National, Brussels, Belgium **CANCELLED
June 3 - Saarlandahlle, Saarbrucken, Germany **CANCELLED
June 4 - Pavillion de Paris, Paris, France **CANCELLED
June 5 - Palais des Sports, Lyon, France **CANCELLED
June 7 - Parc des Expositions Chateaublanc, Avignon, France **CANCELLED
June 8 - Arenes, Frejus, France **CANCELLED
June 10 - Padalon, Bacelona, Spain **CANCELLED
June 11 - Real Madrid, Madrid, Spain **CANCELLED
June 14 - Hallenstadion, Zürich, Switzerland **CANCELLED
June 15 - Messehalle, Stuttgart-Sindelfingon, Germany **CANCELLED
June 16 - Festhalle, Frankfurt, Germany **CANCELLED
June 18 - Rhein-Neckar-Halle, HD-Eppelheim, Germany **CANCELLED
June 20 - Sporthalle, Cologne, Germany **CANCELLED
June 21 - Westfallenhalle, Dortmund, Germany **CANCELLED
June 22 - Stadthalle, Bremen, Germany **CANCELLED
June 23 - Ernst-Merck Halle, Hamburg, Germany **CANCELLED
Notes:
- Cancelled continental dates. There are likely other dates in markets that the band ultimately visited in the autumn. Posters and tickets for many of the Mama Concerts promoted German dates are regularly available. The planned European tour was postponed when it became impossible to release the album in time for the dates.

June 25 - Brighton Centre, Brighton, England **CANCELLED
June 27 - Wembley Arena, London, England **CANCELLED
June 28 - Wembley Arena, London, England **CANCELLED
July 1 - Bingley Hall, Stafford, England **CANCELLED
July 3 - Royal Highland Showground, Edinburgh, Scotland **CANCELLED
Notes:
- The impact on British fans with the cancellation of the tour was negligible — Wembley had reportedly only sold £200 worth of tickets, and only 7 Edinburgh tickets had been sold due to that show having gone on sale the day prior to cancellation and having only been advertized locally. Dates were rescheduled in May, though negotiations for concerts in Brighton and Edinburgh were not successful.

July 25 - The Palladium, New York City, NY
Promoter: Ron Delsener Presents

Other act(s): The Rockats
Reported audience: 3,385 **SOLD-OUT
Set list: Detroit Rock City / Cold Gin / Strutter / Calling Dr. Love / Is that you? / Firehouse / Talk to Me / You're All That I Want / 2,000 Man / I Was Made For Lovin' You / Love Gun / Shout It Out Loud / God of Thunder / Rock And Roll All Nite / New York Groove / King Of The Night Time World / Black Diamond
Notes:
- Eric Carr's live debut with KISS wearing the first version of his "Fox" makeup. While heavily featuring the 1979 and 1980 studio albums, it is somewhat strange to consider that the set included three covers: "2,000 Man," originally recorded by the Rolling Stones; "New York Groove," originally recorded by Hello; and "King of the Night Time World," originally performed by the Hollywood Stars (though never commercially released). "Is That You?" while not written by the band had also not been commercially release by the writer or other artists.
- The only United States "Unmasked" era concert and contemporary performance of material from that album. This show marked the live debut of three songs from "Unmasked" including "Is That You?," "Talk To Me," and "You're All That I Want."
- The Palladium was the renamed Academy of Music, where KISS had made their industry debut in December 1973. KISS spun their appearance at a smaller venue: "It was a night of nostalgia for Ace, Paul and Gene. And a dream come true for Eric Carr. KISS planned a special performance at the Palladium (formerly The Academy of Music) in New York to introduce Eric to its staunchest home town fans. There was very little publicity. The one-night-only show was mostly a word of mouth affair. Although small for KISS today, the hall was chosen for sentimental reasons. Most of the fans, as well as the band, were remembering the historic night KISS played its first important New York performance on that very stage... the show was a resounding success" (KISS Army News).
- From local press: "KISS performed at the Palladium on Friday night, which was unusual; the group usually plays venues the size of Madison Square Garden. Slipping popularity may account for the Palladium date to some extent, but KISS could certainly have filled the theater several nights running and chose not to do so. The show's primary purpose seems to have been the introduction of Eric Carr, the new drummer, to the band's hard-core fans. A few diehards yelled for the departed Peter Criss, but not for long. This listener kept trying to remember what Mr. Criss used to sound like, but the effort proved fruitless. Before long, he became accustomed to Mr. Carr, who played a somewhat elaborate drum kit and was sometimes a little floppy but kicked the music along nicely.

The band had installed its flashy stage set and resorted to a number of its tried and true visual gimmicks, but with the scale of the event reduced, one tended to focus more on the music. It wasn't bad. It was heavy-handed, macho to an almost comical degree, rife with bombast and excess, everything one expects heavy metal to be, but the playing was tight — much tighter than the last time the reviewer heard KISS, at the Garden — and most of the songs weren't padded with unnecessary solo noodling. Whether KISS fans will take to Mr. Carr remains to be seen; one would think they'd be satisfied with Gene Simmons's tongue-wagging and fire-breathing and Ace Frehley's flaming guitar. In any event, and for what it's worth, Mr. Carr's addition to the band seems to have been a positive step, though it isn't likely to make KISS' music 'genuinely important to life'" (New York Times, 7/27/80). Another: "Carr proved to be a capable drummer but no Peter Criss. The show wasn't quite the visual extravaganza I'd anticipated, nor was it the Sodom and Gomorrah meets 'The

Night of the Living Dead' I'd feared. Instead, it seemed like the 'Wizard of Oz' gone awry" (Aquarian).

- From a mainstream review: "It was apparent from the appearance and playing of Carr that KISS, one of the most successful rock acts of all times, was not taking any chances with the music or the formula now that original drummer Peter Criss has departed for a solo career... So it was almost the typical KISS show. But with the new drummer now more in the background, the focus was more on the front three... And although performing on a smaller stage than usual, the show was basically the same" (Billboard, 8/9/80).
- From a regional review: "KISS concerts are a little like Christmas. The anticipation is half the fun, and everyone was up for this one... KISS crashed through their 20-song set with the delicacy of a chain gang" (London, CT, The Day, 8/1/80).
- An average AUD recording circulates from this show, as does a limited amount of 8mm and news video footage.

August 9 - Mexico City, Mexico **CANCELLED
August 10 - Mexico City, Mexico **CANCELLED
August 11 - Mexico City, Mexico **CANCELLED
August 12 - Guadalajara, Mexico **CANCELLED
August 14 - Monterrey, Mexico **CANCELLED
Notes:
- KISS' tour was being organized by promoters Promociones Artisticas y Espectaculous Internacionales to play three dates in the Federal District August 9–11, plus additional dates at soccer stadiums in Monterrey and Guadalajara. Some press sources mention an unidentified sixth show.
- The tour was cancelled when the promoter couldn't obtain the necessary permits for the shows in Mexico City. As a result, the dates in Monterrey and Guadalajara also had to be cancelled since they wouldn't have made economic sense with the cost of bringing the show to Mexico without all of the dates occurring (Billboard, 8/9/80).

August 24 - Cascais Hall, Lisbon, Portugal **CANCELLED
August 25 - Cascais Hall, Lisbon, Portugal **CANCELLED
Notes:
- The scheduled first dates of the tour. These were ultimately cancelled for simple economic reasons.

August 29 - Castel Sant'Angelo, Roma, Italy
Promoter: Francesco Sanavio / David Zard
Other act(s): Iron Maiden
Reported audience: 10,000 / 20,000 (50%)
Set list: Detroit Rock City / Cold Gin / Strutter / Calling Dr. Love / Is That You? / Firehouse / Talk to Me / You're All That I Want / 2,000 Man / I Was Made for Lovin' You / New York Groove / Love Gun / God of Thunder / Rock And Roll All Nite / Shout It Out Loud / King of the Night Time World / Black Diamond
Notes:
- First night of the "Unmasked" World Tour. Iron Maiden performed an eight-song set for most of the tour, including an encore, "Drifter." In most of the countries visited the dates on this tour marked Iron Maiden's debut in those markets.

- Francesco Sanavio and David Zard were Italy's top rock promoters during the 1970s and 80s. Castel Sant'Angelo is an incredibly historic location right next to the Vatican and has more recently featured centrally in Dan Brown's "Angels & Demons" book/movie.
- Ace has guitar issues during the beginning of "New York Groove" forcing an extension of the intro section.
- A couple of average AUD recordings circulate from this show though one is marred by cut-outs and missing Eric's drum solo, and the second source is incomplete. The show was pressed on picture disc as the "KISS This" title.
- Brief news footage from the opening song circulates.

August 30 - Stadion Communale, Perugia, Italy **CANCELLED
August 31 - Stadion Communale, Bologna, Italy **CANCELLED

August 31 - Pallasport, Genova, Italy
Promoter: Francesco Sanavio / David Zard
Other act(s): Iron Maiden
Reported audience: 10,000 / 20,000 (50%)
Set list: Same as August 29.
Notes:
- The band arrived in Genoa on August 30 and stayed at the Colombia Excelsior under the names Don Dot, Dr. Van Helsing, Mike Rohone, and Rusty Blades.
- A below average AUD recording circulates from this show which cuts out sections of the raps/breaks between songs.
- Local TV filmed part of the show, backstage, and attendee interviews for a broadcast TV report.

September 1 - Munich, Germany **TV FILMING
Promoter: ZDF
- The filming of the band's RockPop TV appearance miming "She's So European" and "Talk to Me." The recordings were first broadcast on RockRop #27 on September 13. Apparently, "Is That You?" and "Tomorrow" are filmed during the 4 hour session. According to Gene, while the performance was lip-synched to backing music, Eric was playing the drums live making the songs something of a hybrid. However, like many European music shows it was policy on "Pop Rock" for bands not to perform live and a close inspection of Eric's performance leaves it clear that Eric isn't playing live... Magazine Bravo (a co-sponsor of the tour) attended the filming and it is from this session that many quality photos from the period originate.

September 2 - Velodromo Vigorelli, Milano, Italy
Promoter: Francesco Sanavio / David Zard
Other act(s): Iron Maiden (opener)
Reported audience: 20,000 / 30,000 (67%)
Set list: Same as August 29.
Notes:
- From an UPI news article "Police used tear gas and baton charges to control rowdy fans during a concert of the American rock KISS. The rock group, which performs in black leather costumes and macabre facial makeup, had not yet mounted the stage when young fans without tickets crashed through entrance gates to the Vigorelli Stadium where they were

playing. After controlling the scuffling youths with tear gas, police finally opened the gates and allowed everyone waiting outside into the arena, officers said. But the scuffling broke out again inside the arena after the concert began, with youths hurling empty bottles, milk cartons and fruit onto the stage and nearby rock fans. Police moved in again and threw out about a dozen youths. One young woman was slightly injured by a flying bottle, police said."
- During the show Molotov cocktails were thrown on stage forcing a 30 minute delay in the show.
- Multiple average AUD recordings circulate from this show. Roughly 10 minutes of Super8 footage also exists featuring parts of six songs.

September 5 - Bingley Hall, Country Showground, Stafford, England
Promoter: Kennedy Street Enterprises/MCP Presents
Other act(s): Girl (opener)
Reported audience: 8,711 **SOLD-OUT
Set list: Same as August 29.
Notes:
- Iron Maiden, who had then recently toured the UK in support of their debut album, took a break for KISS' UK leg. KISS conducted a UK press conference on September 4 after arriving in country on the 3rd. The band was invited to a dinner at Legends on Old Burlington Street on the evening of the 4th. The guests included representatives from Phonogram including managing directors, product and marketing managers, and A&R/press staff.
- A below average AUD recording circulates from this show omitting the first song and a half.

September 6 - Deeside Leisure Center, Queensferry, Wales
Promoter: Kennedy Street Enterprises/MCP Presents
Other act(s): Girl (opener)
Reported audience: 3,086 / 6,000 (51.43%)
Set list: Same as August 29.
Notes:
- A very poor AUD recording from this show circulates.

September 8 - Wembley Arena, London, England
Promoter: Kennedy Street Enterprises/MCP Presents
Other act(s): Girl (opener)
Set list: Same as August 29.
Notes:
- From a mainstream review: "From the wonders of Wonder to the overblown kitsch of KISS — anyone monitoring events at Wembley over the past few days may be forgiven for questioning what extremes, from the truly sublime to the truly ridiculous, currently coexist under the banners of pop music. Of Stevie represented the heights of black American music in the Seventies, then KISS represent if not quite the total depth, then at least an overemplified vaudeville circus that has done wonders for the band balance of white American 'theatrical heavy metal...' Gene Simmons — whose unlikely friend Diana Ross was the only attractive sight at Wembley last night — wore a cloak, a sci-fi Roman costume and makeup that was somewhere between Chinese Emperor, clown and a vampire bat. He also stuck out his tongue a great deal. If that's what gives little American girls erotic nightmares, then my profound condolences to all little American girls.

The problem with the band's performance was not a lack of music but that there was far too much of it in between the expensively cheap and jolly garish special effects. KISS played with thunderous slick professionalism and no feeling, with a deafening sound that easily disguised their few reasonable songs like 'I Was Made For Loving You.' But music didn't sell this band, as you might have guessed, and after the first minute I was hoping for the much-publicised special effects if only to relieve the painful tedium. When they came these included Simmons breathing fire (very briefly), and a guitar that started belching smoke and was then hauled above the stage where it was shot down by another guitar apparently firing rockets. I staggered out, musing on the devotion that must have led Ms. Ross to sit through such a tacky show more than once" (The Guardian, 9/9/80).
- A below average AUD recording circulates from this show.

September 9 - Wembley Arena, London, England
Promoter: Kennedy Street Enterprises/MCP Presents
Other act(s): None
Reported audience: 10,028 / 15,600 (64.28%)
Set list: Same as August 29.
Notes:
- No Other act for this show; Girl had been "removed" from the tour. It would have been their final show any way, so nothing was really lost and the guitarist in that band, Phil Collen, went on to bigger and better things with Def Leppard.
- A near excellent AUD recording circulates from this show and is the definitive recording from the early part of the tour and was bootlegged early on with the infamous "Egos at Stake" title.
- Back at home, Peter Criss' "Out of Control" album was released this day.

September 11 - Messehalle, Nürnberg, Germany
Promoter: Mama Concerts
Other act(s): Iron Maiden (opener)
Reported audience: 3,037 / 3,500 (86.8%)
Set list: Same as August 29.
Notes:
- The band flew into Germany from England on the day of the show.
- First appearance of the modified logo in concert (it had been used in print from August). The controversy concerning KISS' use of their logo, due to its incorporation of the runic "SS" (that had connotations to the Nazi Schutzstaffel - SS), became an issue in May 1980 when a an opponent of politician Franz Josef Strauss was convicted of violating German anti-Nazi laws for "glorifying Nazi emblems and symbols" for using the lightning bolts in an advertizing campaign "Stoppt Strauss." While KISS' German labels had taken varying views on the logo. EMI in 1975/6 had replaced the logo with a normal rendition of the band's name while Bellaphon (1976-80) had used the standard logo. With KISS' change to the Phonogram label in 1980, complaints by lawyers that KISS had been using a logo incorporating features banned by law forced them to change the logo to the "ZZ" version as a matter of safety. "The 12 German concerts pulled a total 100,000 fans, the only hassle being over the use of the usual KISS logo. But the band readily agreed to change it, because of its similarity to the Nazi insignia, now unlawful to display in Germany" (Billboard, 10/25/80). Gene, though, had addressed that issue with some indignation during press

while on the UK leg of the tour: "I can't see how we can have any form of Nazi connection with two members of the band are Jewish... Obviously being a Jew myself I abhor that kind of system" (Record Mirror, 9/13/80).
- A below average AUD recording circulates from this show.

September 12 - Philipshalle, Dusseldorf, Germany
Promoter: Mama Concerts
Other act(s): Iron Maiden (opener)
Reported audience: 4,732 / 5,800 (81.6%)
Set list: Detroit Rock City / Cold Gin / Strutter / Calling Dr. Love / Firehouse / Talk To Me / Is That You? / 2,000 Man / Ace Frehley Guitar Solo / I Was Made For Lovin' You / New York Groove / Love Gun / Gene Simmons Bass Fart / God of Thunder / Eric Carr Drum Solo / Rock And Roll All Nite / Shout It Out Loud / King Of the Night Time World / Black Diamond
Notes:
- It's not clear whether "You're All That I Want" was performed at this show, but it was certainly dropped by the following day.

September 13 - Rebstock-Gelände, Frankfurt, Germany (Open Air)
Promoter: Mama Concerts / Abendpost-Nachtausgabe Presents
Other act(s): Iron Maiden (opener)
Reported audience: 5,906 / 10,000 (59.1%)
Set list: Detroit Rock City / Cold Gin / Strutter / Calling Dr. Love / Firehouse / Talk To Me / Is That You? / 2,000 Man / I Was Made For Lovin' You / New York Groove / Love Gun / God of Thunder / Rock And Roll All Nite / Shout It Out Loud / King Of the Night Time World / Black Diamond
Notes:
- Out door show. First definitive set list following the dropping of "You're All That I Want."
- Gene was featured as a full-color illustration on this day's issue of the UK music magazine, Record Mirror.
- A below average AUD recording circulates from this show.

September 15 - Westfalenhalle, Dortmund, Germany
Promoter: Mama Concerts
Other act(s): Iron Maiden (opener)
Reported audience: 5,357 / 12,000 (44.6%)
Set list: Same as Sept. 13.
Notes:
- This was the only show, to that point, that had earned a percentage ($3,033.07).
- The following day the band conducts an in-store appearance at Main Records in Frankfurt which reportedly caused major traffic jams with some 2,000 fans attending (Billboard, 10/25/80).

September 17 - Messehalle, Stuttgart Sindelfingon, Germany
Promoter: Mama Concerts
Other act(s): Iron Maiden (opener)
Reported audience: 3,466 / 6,000 (57.8%)
Set list: Same as Sept. 13.

September 18 - Olympiahalle, München, Germany
Promoter: Mama Concerts
Other act(s): Iron Maiden (opener)
Set list: Same as Sept. 13.
Notes:
- The band departed the following evening via overnight train to Kassel. It's interesting to note that the band generally reserved 8 singles, 1 double (for Ace), and two tourist rooms for the touring entourage.
- Austrian TV Program "Okay" used parts of Eric's drums solo, "I Was Made For Lovin' You," "Black Diamond," "Talk To Me," along with interview and backstage footage for a feature on the band.

September 20 - Eisstadion, Kassel, Germany
Promoter: Mama Concerts
Other act(s): Iron Maiden (opener)
Set list: Same as Sept. 13.

September 21 - Westfalenhalle 1, Dortmund, Germany **CANCELLED

September 21 - Forest National, Brussels, Belgium
Promoter: Make It Happen Productions / Joepie Magazine
Other act(s): Iron Maiden (opener)
Set list: Same as Sept. 13.
Notes:
- The band flew from Frankfurt to Brussels during the afternoon. During their visit the band took a striking photo with the gold-clothed pop trio Babe.
- This show circulates as an average AUD recording.

September 23 - Parc Des Expositions, Avignon, France
Promoter: Koski-Cauchoix Productions (KCP)
Other act(s): Iron Maiden (opener)
Set list: Same as Sept. 13.
Notes:
- A near excellent AUD recording circulates from this show, though it is missing "King of the Night Time World."

September 24 - Palais Des Sports, Lyon, France
Promoter: Koski-Cauchoix Productions (KCP)
Other act(s): Iron Maiden (opener)
Notes:
- With an extra day off in Lyon, due to the cancelled show in Lille, Ace apparently entertained himself by trashing his hotel room, resulting in the hotel manager chasing down the band, and blockading their travel van, to prevent them from leaving without paying for the damage.

September 26 - Parc Des Expositions, Lille, France **CANCELLED
Promoter: Koski-Cauchoix Productions (KCP)
Notes:

- Because this show was cancelled the promoter booked a replacement date in Paris on October 16.

September 27 - L'Hippodrome de Paris, Porte de Pantin, Paris, France
Promoter: Koski-Cauchoix Productions (KCP)
Other act(s): Iron Maiden (opener)
Reported audience: ~20,000
Set list: Same as Sept. 13.
Notes:
- One review suggests that it was literally raining from the sweaty roof of the tent (Rock & Folk Magazine)! The venue was essentially a permanent circus-styled tent which had been the home of the Jean Richard Circus. The city's large concert facility, the Pavillon de Paris, had closed in mid-1980 leaving this as the primary concert venue until the Le Zénith de Paris was completed in 1983.
- A partial version of this show was broadcast on local radio though an excellent AUD version also circulates.

September 28 - St. Jacob's Halle, Basel, Switzerland
Promoter: Good News Agency
Other act(s): Iron Maiden (opener)
Reported audience: 6,000 **SOLD-OUT
Set list: Same as Sept. 13.
Note:
- This show is purportedly available on the "Swiss KISS Collection I" bootleg CD, but the recording is not from this date.

September 30 - Sporthalle, Köln, Germany
Promoter: Mama Concerts
Other act(s): Iron Maiden (opener)
Set list: Same as Sept. 13.
Notes:
- An incomplete SBD recording from this show circulates (though the current version is lossy) — it's missing "New York Groove" and "Black Diamond."
- Interviews and part of this show was professionally filmed for a feature, "Jutta, KISS & The Big Show," on German youth TV program "Schüler Experess" for ZDF. The broadcast incorporated a fictional movie featuring a star struck female fan yearning for Paul and breaking up with her boyfriend to attend a KISS concert. Parts of "Firehouse," "New York Groove," "Rock And Roll All Nite," plus Gene's bass solo were featured.

October 1 - Stadhalle, Bremen, Germany
Promoter: Mama Concerts
Other act(s): Iron Maiden (opener)
Set list: Same as Sept. 13.
Notes:
- A below average AUD recording from this show circulates.

October 2 - Eilenriedehalle, Hannover, Germany
Promoter: Mama Concerts

Other act(s): Iron Maiden (opener)
Set list: Same as Sept. 13.

October 4 - Ernst-Merck-Halle, Hamburg, Germany
Promoter: Mama Concerts
Other act(s): Iron Maiden (opener)
Set list: Same as Sept. 13.
Notes:
- The band arrived in Hamburg on October 3 and stayed at the Intercontinental under the names Don Dot, Dr. Van Helsing, Mike Rohone, and Rusty Blades. Two members received suites.
- While in Hamburg the band conducted an autograph signing attended by over 2,000 fans.

October 5 - Groenoordhalle, Leiden, Holland
Promoter: Wim Bosman
Other act(s): Iron Maiden (opener)
Set list: Same as Sept. 13.
Notes:
- Some live footage from this show, and an interview, were broadcast on local TV. The intro and parts of "Firehouse" (with Gene's fire-breathing) and Ace's guitar solo are included.

October 6 - Schwarzwaldhalle, Karlsruhe, Germany
Promoter: Mama Concerts
Other act(s): Iron Maiden
Set list: Same as Sept. 13.
Notes:
- This final date of the German 1980 tour did take place. KISS performed to nearly 100,000 fans in the country during their visit (Billboard, 10/25/80)...
- The band travelled back to Frankfurt and flew to Stockholm the following morning.
- A generally poor AUD recording of this show circulates. Sadly, due to a tape break, the recording is missing "New York Groove" through "Rock And Roll All Nite," a substantial part of the concert.

October 9 - Erikdalshallen, Stockholm, Sweden
Promoter: EMA-Telstar
Other act(s): Iron Maiden
Reported audience: 3,300
Set list: Same as Sept. 13.
Notes:
- The band conducted press and TV interviews during their day off on October 8. Gene and Paul invite Maiden guitarist Dennis Stratton out to dinner to celebrate his birthday.
- An incomplete and below average AUD recording from this show circulates which excludes the final song.

October 10 - Scandinavium, Göteborg, Sweden
Promoter: EMA-Telstar
Other act(s): Iron Maiden
Reported audience: 5,443 / 14,000 (38.88%)

Set list: Same as Sept. 13.
Notes:
- The band flew from Stockholm on a lunchtime flight.
- An excellent AUD recording from this show circulates. 6 minutes of mediocre 8mm also exists, often attributed to Stockholm.

October 11 - Broendbyhalle, Copenhagen, Denmark
Promoter: International Concert Organization A/S
Other act(s): Iron Maiden
Set list: Same as Sept. 13.
Notes:
- KISS flew in from Sweden in the afternoon.
- Two known AUD recordings from this show circulate.

October 13 - Drammenshallen, Drammen, Norway
Promoter: Gunnar Eide, Internasjonal Konsertdireksjon/ICO
Other act(s): Iron Maiden
Reported audience: ~5,500 / 6,000 (91.67%)
Set list: Same as Sept. 13.
Notes:
- Drammen 25 miles southwest from Oslo.
- The final show of the European tour. This show marked Iron Maiden guitarist Dennis Stratton's final show with the band (though he didn't know it at the time). Dennis remained in the band long enough to appear in the "Women in Uniform" music video, filmed at the Rainbow soon after the band returned to London, but was gone by the time the band performed the song on Top of the Pops on November 13. He was replaced by Adrian Smith.
- During Maiden's encore, Paul ran on stage and cakes one of the guitarists (Dave Murray or Dennis Stratton), quickly followed by Ace who cakes singer Paul Di'Anno. Maiden's revenge appears innocuous - having a roadie dressing in drag parading on the stage during KISS' set. However, during "King of the Night Time World" they rush the stage with cake and buckets of confetti.
- The band attends an after-show disco party and flies to London the following day.
- A couple of AUD recordings circulate from this show.
- According to CK Lendt, the European tour lost money with Phonogram taking a major hit. 56 days on the road netted KISS $796,000 with costs in excess of $1 million. Iron Maiden benefitted from a successful outing on the continent, a foundation that they would build on in the years to come.

October 16 - L'Hippodrome, Porte de Pantin, Paris, France **CANCELLED
Promoter: Koski-Cauchoix Productions (KCP)
Notes:
- This late addition to the tour, as a replacement for the previously cancelled date in Lille, was also ultimately cancelled. Gene and John Harte returned to the U.S. on October 14 with Ace, Eric, and Paul following on the 15th.

October 20 - Tokyo, Japan **CANCELLED
October 21 - Tokyo, Japan **CANCELLED
October 24 - Tokyo, Japan **CANCELLED

October 27 - Kyoto, Japan **CANCELLED
October 28 - Nagoya, Japan **CANCELLED
October 29 - Osaka, Japan **CANCELLED
October 30 - Osaka, Japan **CANCELLED
Promoter: Udo Artists, Inc.
Notes:
- Or not booked, these dates were included on a May 9 itinerary. A visit to Japan at that time ultimately wasn't feasible.

November 5 - Entertainment Centre, Perth, Australia **REHEARSALS
November 6 - Entertainment Centre, Perth, Australia **REHEARSALS
November 7 - Entertainment Centre, Perth, Australia **REHEARSALS
Notes:
- The crew departed JFK on October 29, arriving in Sydney via Los Angeles and Auckland on October 31. The band flew into Sydney on November 2 via Los Angeles and Honolulu for the tour press conference. They departed for Perth the following day.
- Three days of rehearsals on the new stage were scheduled. The band was "keen to practice on an American stage which has been imported for the four-week tour. The stage is larger than the one they used on a recent European tour" (The Sydney Morning Herald, 11/4/80).
- On the afternoon of this final day of rehearsals the band were scheduled to record their appearance on Countdown at Perth's ABC Studios.
- KISS had been rumored to tour Australia back in 1976, but it took several more years for plans to come to fruition. When a tour was finally announced in 1980 it was supported with hype reminiscent of The Beatles Antipodean visit in 1964, and certainly more merchandising. It should be noted that 300,000 took to the streets of Adelaide for the Beatles, while 2-3,000 showed up for KISS' arrival in Sydney. KISS arrived in Australia on November 1 and enjoyed a week of press and hype as they prepared for their first concert. KISS flew to Perth on the evening on November 3 to take care of final preparations for the first shows.
- The band held their press conference at the Sebel Town House Function Centre in Sydney the following day.
- The Eyes were named as the sole opening act for the Australian leg. They were supporting a recent single, "City Living."
- During the tour the band members used aliases such as "John Baron," "Noah Cortez," "Earl Grey," and "Gerry Ford," "Art Deco," "Robert Hall," "Dr. Van Helsing," and "Rusty Blades" for their hotel reservations. Unlike Europe, the band and Bill Aucoin were housed in suites.
- In October, the New York Production Company had proposed a motion picture based on the band's tour of Australia and New Zealand, if the company was able to raise the necessary funding (the proposed budget was $651,637). Starting out in almost 2001: A Space Odyssey fashion albeit with Aboriginals witnessing the KISS members walking along edge of Ayers Rock, "silhouetted against the Australian sky." From the proposed script the movie would track the band from their arrival, press conference, fans and backstage, to the performance while travelling the country. In essence, this was similar to what later was condensed as "KISSteria" in 2008. Nothing came from the film, at the time, and Gene denied knowledge about the proposal when asked by a fan in 1995. However, there are some similarities with the Bill Aucoin produced "The Inner Sanctum," which discarded much of the art and presented instead the performance and hype.

- The manufactured hype, which Neil Bogart or Malcolm McLaren would have been proud of, was selling something to the Australians that wasn't reflected as reality. Perhaps it was a need from the consumer side to embrace something perceived as exciting. "According to Glenn A. Baker, the Australian editor of America's 'Billboard' magazine, a misleading image of KISS as 'the biggest band in the world' has been thrust down our throats by the media. Mr. Baker, himself a KISS fan who wouldn't miss the concert, describes KISS as a second level act which has had one big album... 'The average kid probably thinks KISS are number one in America. They're a great band but somebody should tell the media moguls that KISS have to a few notches to get on their belts yet,' Mr. Baker said" (The Age, Melbourne, 11/13/80).

November 8 - Entertainment Centre, Perth, Australia
Promoter: Kevin Jacobsen Concerts & Michael Edgely International
Other act(s): Eyes
Reported audience: 8,003 **SOLD-OUT
Notes:
- From a local review: "A fire-breathing, blood-spitting demon who 'flies' across the stage, a flaming guitar that fires rockets and a swirling shower of silver rain brought the KISS fantasy to life for 8,000 people at the Entertainment Centre on Saturday night. It created a vision of four supermen acting out rock's wildest dreams in a world of fire and light inhabited by painted monsters" (The West Australian, 11/10/80).
- The band clowned around with Aussie fast-bowler (cricket) Dennis Lillee backstage prior to this first show (which was a late addition to the itinerary).

November 9 - Entertainment Centre, Perth, Australia
Promoter: Kevin Jacobsen Concerts & Michael Edgely International
Other act(s): Eyes
Reported audience: 8,003 **SOLD-OUT

November 10 - Entertainment Centre, Perth, Australia
Promoter: Kevin Jacobsen Concerts & Michael Edgely International
Other act(s): Eyes
Reported audience: 8,003 **SOLD-OUT

November 11 - Entertainment Centre, Perth, Australia
Promoter: Kevin Jacobsen Concerts & Michael Edgely International
Other act(s): Eyes
Reported audience: 8,003 **SOLD-OUT

November 15 - V.F.L. Park, Waverley, Melbourne, Australia
Promoter: Kevin Jacobsen Concerts & Michael Edgely International
Other act(s): Eyes
Reported audience: ~35,000
Notes:
- According to a press report very few of the 35,000 tickets were still available two days prior to the show. A figure of 45,000 was used in advertizing the Auckland show.
- From a local review: "When the super heroes finally appeared on the stage in spinning light and clouds of smoke, the crowd went predictably wild. It might have come as an

anticlimax, to anyone but a KISS fan, that the center of all the cleverly-timed fireworks, lights, and jets of flame were four people doing nothing more diabolical than playing guitars and drums and singing. True, they swayed band and forth a bit, and gave the crowd such speeches as 'alright!,' 'Oh yeah,' and 'we're going to sweat our butts off for you...' It must be said that the Rock magazine critic who described the KISS sound as 'a herd of buffalo breaking wind' was a bit unfair. Buffalos do not break wind in four-four time. None of this mattered to the KISS brigade, of course" (The Age, Melbourne, 11/17/80).

November 18 - Adelaide Oval, Adelaide, Australia
Promoter: Kevin Jacobsen Concerts & Michael Edgely International
Other act(s): Eyes
Reported audience: ~20,000
Set list: Detroit Rock City / Cold Gin / Strutter / Shandi / Calling Dr. Love / Firehouse / Talk To Me / Is That You? / 2,000 Man / I Was Made For Lovin' You / New York Groove / Love Gun / God Of Thunder / Rock And Roll All Nite / Shout It Out Loud / King Of The Night Time World / Black Diamond
Notes:
- While in Adelaide a bomb hoax was called into the hotel forcing its evacuation on the night of November 16. The following night a dinner at the private "Ballroom" of Ayers House for the touring entourage was scheduled.
- This is the first known set from the tour, which was essentially the same Europe with the addition of "Shandi," due to the success of the single and "Unmasked" album on the Australian charts.
- From a local review: "After months of expectation, KISS was on-stage at Adelaide Oval, despite early fears the concert might be cancelled due to the weather... Most of what we had been promised came true... The music was a well-rehearsed, if sometimes scratchy, soundtrack for the KISS special-effects show... Given the trying conditions, it was a commendable effort" (Tim Parker).
- One newspaper reported that 200 fans were injured during the concert. The police denied the rumor which had "incensed member of the band" (The Sydney Morning Herald, 11/21/80).
- An average AUD recording circulates from this show.

November 21 - Sydney Showground, Sydney, Australia
Promoter: Kevin Jacobsen Concerts & Michael Edgely International
Other act(s): Eyes
Reported audience: ~20,000 / 20,000
Set list: Same as Nov. 18.
Notes:
- The band arrived back in Sydney on November 19, the same day an ad ran in local press notifying the public of ticket availability. At that time there were around 4–8,000 unsold tickets for the second show. Media overhype was blamed for that lack of sales, but oversaturation was being seen in other areas including merchandising. "Mr. Tony Higgins, the marketing director of Plough Australia, which distributes a range of cosmetics, described his company's KISS effort as a failure. 'We made up 200,000 KISS bags containing make-up and have sold a little over half of them...' While KISS have sold more than 1 million albums in Australia, their latest album, Unmasked, which was released mid-year, is not doing as well as expected" (The Sydney Morning Herald, 11/20/80).

- From a local review: "The KISS phenomenon is all it's hyped up to be. Its sheer size and daunting professionalism almost puts it beyond critical analysis... With KISS the predominant smell is cordite. However apt the surface metaphor is, KISS, certainly don't perform without a new. They are chilling in their calculation. But for all that, bloody good fun... In some sophisticated circles it is considered chic to not like KISS. But how can you hate a musician who fires rockets at you from his instrument" (Sydney Morning Herald, 11/22/80).

November 22 - Sydney Showground, Sydney, Australia
Promoter: Kevin Jacobsen Concerts & Michael Edgely International
Other act(s): Eyes
Reported audience: ~16,000 / 20,000
Set list: Same as Nov. 18.
Notes:
- This second show was announced in late August. Just days before the show there were still around 4,000 tickets unsold to this show. Weather and an assumption that both shows were sold out were excuses offered in the press.
- During the afternoon CK Lendt and Roadshow Licensing (Australian representatives for 20th Century-Fox) presented a display of all of the merchandising options that had been available in Australia during the tour.
- This show was professionally filmed. It was heavily edited and condensed, and combined with interview and backstage footage, to become the "Inner Sanctum" documentary broadcast in early 1981.

- This show was scheduled for release as an unofficial DVD, as "Live at the Sydney Showground," in June 2003, featuring the concert, backstage and TV footage. It was ultimately pulled from distribution. The Showground concert was officially released on "KISSology, Volume 2" after circulating in collector's circles for decades (though it is missing Gene's bass solo and the start of "God of Thunder").

November 25 - Lang Park, Brisbane, Australia
Promoter: Kevin Jacobsen Concerts & Michael Edgely International
Other act(s): Eyes
Notes:
- The band arrived in Brisbane on the day of the show.
- In July, when tickets for this show had gone on sale, fans nearly rioted while waiting overnight for the ticket office to open: "Almost every building on the block was covered with some form of obscene language and broken bottles and wine flagons littered the streets" (The Sydney Morning Herald, 7/27/80).
- The day prior to the show the promoters ran an ominous ad stating, "We are not sold out - still plenty tickets available."

November 30 - Athletic Park Stadium, Wellington, New Zealand
Promoter: Kevin Jacobsen Concerts/Michael Edgley International
Other act(s): Techtones
Reported audience: ~20,000
Notes:
- The crew flew to Wellington from Brisbane on November 28. The band flew to Auckland from Sydney on a morning flight on November 29 and then on to Wellington in the evening.
- The show took place on a wet and windy evening with local press reporting an attendance of 12-15,000.
- Presenter Roger Gascoigne hosted a feature on the band's arrival and show, incorporating concert footage, for his Today and Tonight show.

December 3 - Western Springs Arena, Auckland, New Zealand
Promoter: Kevin Jacobsen Concerts/Michael Edgley International
Other act(s): Techtones
Reported audience: ~20,000
Set list: Same as Nov. 18.
Notes:
- KISS flew to Auckland from Wellington on December 1, arriving 7:45PM.
- From a local review: "So this is a KISS concert. Four guys dressed as Japanese monsters from outer space who sing about such healthy subjects as firehouses, conversation, and teenage lust. Paul Stanley's introductory patter is probably identical to that used by the likes of Van Halen and Wet Willy" (Joe Wylie).
- Another era ends: Ace Frehley's final full concert with KISS until 1996. The soundboard from this show is stunning and the definitive recording from the "Unmasked" era...
- The KISS Australian/NZ tour played to over 250,000 fans and grossed in excess of $3 million, but still apparently lost $250,000 (CK Lendt). According to one article, "Backstage at venues he built them a swimming pool, a games tent with mini-golf and pinball machines and the obligatory hospitality tent. Each plane they flew on was stocked with enough Dom Perignon to serve everyone in it. 'It was insane, there was a party every night,' he [promoter

Kevin Jacobsen] recalls. 'We would go out to dinner and take over a restaurant.' Jacobsen says he lost a lot of money (about $200,000) on the KISS Tour. He refers to it as a milestone in history: the last example of outrageous rock star extravagance in Australia" (The Age, Melbourne, 11/6/87). Having to pay for 4 charter planes to New Zealand and increasing security at shows following the injuries press report also contributed to the costs of the tour borne by the promoter. KISS received around $800,000 and Jacobsen suggested, "The band didn't make any money either," (The Sydney Morning Herald, 3/22/81) taking into account its 45 person touring entourage and "Super-KISS" expenses.

- KISS departed New Zealand for the USA on the evening of December 4, arriving in Los Angeles.

1981/2 "Elder" Intermission

KISS didn't perform live in public in 1981. However, they did make several television appearances... The first preceded the release of "The Elder," and had been intended to be a vehicle for promoting the album and announcing a Jan. 1982 Latin American tour. Planning for this excursion had been underway since July and the promoter had, at least, gone as far as to retain the services of Gerry Stickells, president of GLS Productions, based in Los Angeles, as an advisor for the tour. Gerry had "previously coordinated a 1981 Latin American tour by Queen" ("Billboard, Jan. 5, 1985) and would later coordinate for the 1985 "Rock In Rio" festival. Queen's Feb. / Mar. 1981 tour had included many of the same venues that were being suggested for KISS. The president of The Twenty Eighth Company (which references the longitudinal line that separates the U.S. from every territory south of the Texas border), José Rota, was also not an unknown quantity within the South American touring industry and was a proponent for bringing international acts to Latin America. He used the economic argument that the Latin American market was not being properly exploited by many acts. In relation to the Queen tour he suggested, "Before the tour, Queen's sales in Argentina, Brazil, Venezuela and Mexico were only 100,000 units. Three months after the tour they had reached 700,000. What are the record companies waiting for"; however he did admit, "You have to know that it takes half a day just to have cup of coffee" (Billboard, Aug. 7, 1982). From this perspective, it was clear that there was a different way of doing business in the market and that acts needed to be particularly flexible and understand the differences in the market.

The proposed tour was not particularly onerous from a scheduling perspective. The band would fly into Buenos Aires on January 5, 1982 and conduct a press party two days later. They would then perform concerts in that city on Jan. 9–10. While not detailed the band would likely fly via charter to Porto Alegre for a concert there on Jan. 13 followed by two concerts in São Paulo on Jan. 16–17. The South American leg would culminate with a single show in Rio de Janeiro on Jan. 20, following which the band would fly to Monterrey, Mexico for a show on Jan. 24. The Mexican leg would include a show in Guadalajara on Jan. 27, and end with two shows in Puebla, sixty miles from Mexico City, on Jan.30–31. Even with a mix of air and ground transportation the proposed schedule was not particularly arduous, though the logistics of touring equipment movement are naturally far more complex. Even more complex and crucial are the financial and organization aspects of touring: Concerts needed permits. Concerts needed contracts. Concerts needed a finely tuned and properly executed plan by people who knew exactly what to do or knew the people who did. And facilities. While it would be highly insular to suggest that expected venues mirror what the band had become accustomed to in the U.S., Europe (for which there was more than enough criticism), and Japan. However, according to Chris Lendt, the band had already had a highly negative encounter with Mexican promoters who had tried to bring the band to that country in 1980: "What they call stadiums in most Latin American countries are simply enormous concrete shells with tiers of concrete slabs for people to sit on. There aren't any seats, and the facilities backstage, if there are any, are more suited to the cattle than people. The stink of manure from the animal stalls was nauseating. I doubt there was enough electrical power in any of those places to run a toaster let alone 400,000 watts of sound and lights. They're built to house huge crowds of 100,000 and 200,000 to watch soccer matches or bullfights, not high-tech stage productions" ("Kiss & Sell"). Of more concern was the manner in which business was conducted, primarily late-night meetings in police station basements...

The 1980 experience goes some way towards explaining any perception of wariness the band had for touring Latin America. From a business perspective it was clear that they lacked the experience to deal with the promoters from those markets, or at least that the people and systems they encountered when doing so were totally alien. They also clearly lacked understanding of the cultures of those markets, but rapidly learned to protect themselves financially against the endless "no problem" responses to any concerns. The approach in 1981 for the early 1982 tour was conducted in a far more professional manner. In fact there were two approaches, the first of which, through promoter Carlos Espadone, made it as far as a $100,000 deposit being paid and contracts signed at AMI's offices in New York. According to Lendt, "the proposed deal was worth over $1 million — to come to South America... These would be big events, broadcast live on local TV. Half a million or more people would be at the shows" ("KISS & Sell"). Lendt dates the meetings surrounding the 1982 tour as occurring in October 1981; however other documents seem to contradict that timeline, with the separate promoter, Rota, having been in contact earlier in the year. In fact, a photograph of Aucoin, Jeff Franklin, Rota, and Espadone was published in Cashbox Magazine in July 1981 noting a 10-date tour.

Whatever the case, soon after the contracts were signed the tour fell apart and AMI never heard from Espadone again. Rota stepped in and attempted to pick up the pieces using his more suitable connections. Ultimately, his efforts met the same fate and he disappeared along with the prospect of a $1 million payday for a band that was in dire need of financial injections. Within AMI the party line was as general as non-descript as possible when dealing with the press. Ric Aliberte stressed, "When referring to touring in South America and Mexico, please be very general. I would suggest that you say we will be touring sometime in early 1982 in Latin America" (memo, 9/22/81). This, in turn, suggests that touring plans outside of the U.S. were not completely dead in late-September while the Mexican promotional tour was being organized. Gene expanded on the possible touring configuration in October: "One idea is to have two segments in the show, do all the standards and then do 'The Elder'. We have some interesting ideas and we won't be using tapes; anything you hear, you'll see in front of you, I don't think there's anything wrong with having extra people onstage. Tapes don't give you the freedom to let the music breathe, but [there are] lots of plans on how we're going to do it and if we tell you now, we're going to put our boots in our mouths" (Sounds, 2/13/82).

As late as March 1982 the band met with Mark Ravitz to discuss the design of the stage for a proposed tour. He was given no details about what the band would be specifically touring, though his designs included many elements that would have been specifically geared towards that album, rather than the new one the band were about to embark on. According to Mark, "The basic themes I was getting into, or at least the words, let me put it that way: One was "timeless," another "fantastical," another is "high-tech/militaryesque," another was "compact" and "portable," for the movement, and "powerful" and [finally] "variation in scale." Those are the themes that I was moving forward on. They're not like pictures, per se, but, [for example] "timeless" can be about a lot of different things, but it's not [just] today.

"Fantastical" is the range of what is fantasy and bringing that [style] to life. For me, I like to do a lot of things in fantasy. When I bring fantasy to life I make it a fantastic reality, just like the politicians! Then "high-tech/militaryesque" was something that I was looking around at the day and wanted to combine "Star Wars" and the kind of fantasy around the time" ("Odyssey"). Some elements, such as the dreadnaught gun turret were used by the band for their "10th Anniversary Tour" at the end of the year.

May 31, 1981 - Vienna Town Hall, Vienna, Austria **STAGE APPEARANCE
Promoter: Rennbahn Express Starparty
Reported audience: ~13,000
Notes:
- In the middle of recording "The Elder," Gene and Eric travelled to Austria for what would be their final appearance wearing the "Unmasked" costumes. Having already cut their hair, they had to wear wigs in order to appear somewhat as expected costumes and not give away any of the planned changes. They received the Golden Otto award for "Best Rock Band in the World" award from Rennbahn-Express and conducted an onstage interview at the Town Hall in Vienna at a multi-artist event for 13,000 music fans. Gene was reticent to discuss the new album other than commenting that fans would be in for all new surprises when the project was completed later that year. The visit was brief with the party (Gene, Eric, Bill, George Sewitt, John Harte and Laurie Greenan) arriving in Vienna on May 30th. With the promotion being held on the afternoon of the following day there was little time available to schedule other events though there was a meeting with Phonogram.
- Video from the appearance exists but does not widely circulate.

(Screen capture of Gene & Eric in Vienna, 1981)

September 27 - Channel 13 Studios, Mexico City, Mexico **TV FILMING
Promoter: Show Aplausos / Channel 13
Set list: Charisma / I Was Made For Lovin' You
Notes:
- Planning for this excursion had been underway since July, and it had originally been intended to promote both the album and announce a Jan. 1982 Latin American tour.
- Irreverently known internally as the "Don't Drink The Water Tour." While south of the border the band were interviewed by Jimmy Forson. Oddly, for their performance, the band was incongruously dressed in their "Elder" outfits, and lip-synched "Charisma" (which the band chose over the recommended "Talk to Me") and "I Was Made For Lovin' You," rather

than perform anything from the then-forthcoming album. While those tracks had been popular in Mexico — the "I Was Made For Lovin' You" 7" single had sold 252,803 copies in that country by September 1981, plus an additional 121,354 copies of the 12" backed with "Charisma" — it doesn't really explain why the band ignored "The Elder," even if it certainly helps explain the song selection.

- With the release of the album slipping from the intended Oct. 1982 date and the touring plans remaining in limbo, other than debuting the new costumes the band's current affairs were ignored during the Mexican visit. A scheduled appearance on "Hoy Mismo," originally scheduled for the morning of Sept. 27, was cancelled due to the early start time needed and the audience demographic being deemed unnecessary to the band's PR efforts. While in Mexico the band visited an orphanage at Chimalhuacan to distribute toys and candy. The orphanage visit was a concerted PR effort to "dispel any negative rumors about KISS being socially unacceptable. It will help our image greatly" (Memo, 9/15/81) and assist in the plans for concert dates in the country and in South America. The entourage returned to the States on Sep. 28.

December 7 - KTLA Studios, Hollywood, CA **TV FILMING
Promoter: Solid Gold
Set list: I
Notes:
- On the promotional trail for the album the band agreed to appear on "Solid Gold," a lip-synched appearance taped on Dec. 7, 1981. Segments of the band's appearance were later incorporated into the second version of the "I" music video.
- Hosted by Andy Gibb and Marilyn McCoo, the show was taped on Stage 6 at the former Warner Bros. Studios. The show was broadcast the following month.

January 9 - SIR Studio C, New York City, NY **REHEARSALS
January 10 - SIR Studio C, New York City, NY **REHEARSALS
January 11 - SIR Studio C, New York City, NY **REHEARSALS
January 12 - SIR Studio C, New York City, NY **REHEARSALS
Notes:
- The band had time at SIR booked, but all was not necessarily used, to rehearse for the Friday's filming. It's likely they rehearsed the songs that were performed live on that broadcast. It's also not clear if all of the members of the band were present at each session.

January 14 - ABC Studio 55, Hollywood, CA **REHEARSALS
Notes:
- Final rehearsals for the following days filming.

January 15 - ABC Studio 55, Hollywood, CA **TV FILMING
Promoter: ABC TV / Fridays
Set list: The Oath / A World Without Heroes / I
- Filmed for episode 13 of season three of the show, hosted by Tab Hunter, this was the only contemporary live performance of "Elder" material, for ABC-TV's "Fridays" television show. "Fridays" was a West Coast alternative to "Saturday Night Live," which by the time KISS performed was midway through its final season of a short three-year run. As the singular contemporary live performance of "Elder" material, this broadcast has become very popular in collector circles. The footage was finally officially released as part of the

"KISSology Vol. 2" DVD released in 2007, and as part of the "Best of Fridays" DVD. As an interesting side note, in the audience for that performance was one Blackie Lawless, of the early '80s metal band W.A.S.P. fame. Lawless was a childhood friend of Ace's and was readying his own musical assault in Los Angeles.

- The band rehearsed each song three times prior to the performance, with "I" containing the "balls to stand alone" lyric, which was changed to "guts" for the actual broadcast.

January 28 - Studio 54 Soundworks Soundstage, New York City, NY **TV FILMING
Promoter: San Remo Music Festival

- Directed by Michael Bernhaut and produced by Bill Aucoin, this filming of a lip-synced performance was for a satellite appearance to the San Remo Music Festival in Italy where the band were being presented with the "Golden Cat" award for the "Most Important International Artist Of The Year." The band had been invited to attend in person, but were unable to do so, resulting in the first ever live satellite performance for that event — reaching a purported audience of 32 million on the Eurovision Network ("Record World," Feb. 13, 1982). In that country, at least, the album continued to perform well into mid-1982.

- Ace had gone AWOL and/or couldn't be bothered to show up, though at the time Paul used the standard excuse that Ace was sick. In reality, Ace had simply lost all interest in the band and was preparing to transition out.

10th Anniversary Tour

Touring in support of the "Creatures of the Night" album was always going to cause KISS no small amount of trepidation. They had essentially been off the road in the U.S. for three years, their popularity had sunk to a level which wasn't clear if it was the nadir, and they'd lost their relationship with their lead guitarist and record label. And the economy was less than stellar. The ramifications of years of poor choices magnified the effects of natural changing musical tastes. KISS had climbed the mountain and reached the top, and were being rolled down the other side by a constant line of emerging acts ready to take their crown in a multitude of ways. Paul had commented that he felt that many acts were borrowing heavily from the show KISS had put on, so it was time to take the real deal out on the road. It was time to stop the rot, and, as needs must, so too did the band need to hit the road and prove to the masses that they were still alive, still relevant, and more importantly had gotten over their artistic dalliances of the previous three albums. In those basic terms, the band more than delivered with the metallic assault of "Creatures of the Night," a tour that revived the bombast of the "Return of KISS" era, without the overwrought scheduling, excessive scale, and mixed material to draw from. The band were certainly under no illusions about the challenges they faced, nor the depths to which they'd fallen — though the depth would only be defined by certain markets during the tour, markets that had once been economically solid for them. Gene commented, "Sure there'll be a falloff in three years, there won't be as many people. So what? We've got the best show in the world... In '79 we were in Europe, where we played to half a million people, and we went to Australia in '80 for some massive outdoors shows, filling soccer stadiums two times over in city after city, and then we wanted a rest. We'd been touring every single year for eight years and we were tired... But you get hungry. You get to the point where you want it again. I want it now. I want to eat 'em up and spit 'em out" (Providence Journal, 1/21/83). However, things weren't in their control, and they couldn't control whether the public still wanted KISS.

Touring in support of "The Elder" had been an impossible proposition due to the public reception it received (and the resulting fallout). And the debut of "Creatures of the Night" on the U.S. charts, at a paltry #155, was hardly an immediate portent of the band's resurrection. While the album would ultimately climb to a more respectable #45 by Jan. 29, where it lingered for several weeks, before starting an inevitable plummet off the charts, it wasn't a commercial supernova even if it did improve on the performance of "The Elder." Supported by the "I Love It Loud," which maxed out in the U.S. at just #102 on Feb. 5 (though like the album it hovered around the Top-100's nether regions for a few weeks before capitulating), the band simply didn't get the airplay they had once enjoyed. Even the video, directed by Philip Davey and produced by John Weaver only managed to get into light rotation on MTV getting one or two airings per day. Better than nothing, but certainly not what was hoped for. Fans in Richmond, VA were the first to see the band in their new costumes when the band made an appearance at Much More Records on Broad Street on Oct 22. Some 300 fans turned up for the event, which started two-hours late due to Ace missing his flight from New York. Following a brief Q&A and signing session the band participated in an interview on radio station WRXL-FM 102, who had heavily promoted the band.

As had been the case following the band's touring hiatus in 1979, they knew they had to take the "show of shows" out on the road, and not only to meet the expectations of fans old and new. But "Dynasty" had resulted in a harsh lesson learned in terms of both routing and scale. The reality was that the band was in no position to scale things up, and instead had to do more with less. Paul explained the situation, "You constantly figure that you have to top yourself each time you go on tour. And I know this from other bands too, because I was with some friends a few nights ago that are about to go on tour. What happens is when you start thinking each tour has to be bigger — not necessarily better, but somehow you equate bigger and better as the same thing — you dig yourself into a hole that almost makes it impossible to tour. We wound up in the position where we were in Australia with a huge tour and eleven trucks — and you just can't do that" (Sounds, 12/18/82). The band debuted the new stage during their Oct. 28 press conference at Zoetrope Studios in Hollywood. The declared intention for the tour was simple: According to Paul, "We're going to be going out and blowing more bombs; be louder than ever, do the show everybody expects from us" (Press Conference). Ace, though he was present and actively participated at the press conference, seemed unsure about the band's prospects. When asked about whether the tour was timed with the slump in the industry, Paul responded, "This new tour is timed with our 10th anniversary and with a new album. This album seemed really ideal to go out with on tour because pretty much it's the ballsiest thing out there, so it's ideal for playing live." Gene chimed in, "I say, 'The Hell with bad times.' We're going to go out on tour whether or not the times are good or bad. And fuck the bad times." Perhaps most telling was Ace's follow-up: "Even though we're going to lose millions, right? Who cares? It's only money." With his body language, the quip seems more serious than the attention a seemingly flip comment was given and is perhaps indicative of some of the internal conflict affection the band. At that time the band were under the impression that the tour would be starting in Dallas.

The stage built on ideas originally designed by Mark Ravitz earlier in the year for an unnamed KISS tour. Even though it was essentially a simple design, the militaristic stage exuded "heavy metal" with a central tank-turret drum riser and tank-tread side stages. Additional dead space on the stage was filled with amplifiers and numerous flash-pots, while the omnipresent lighted KISS logo filled the background. As would be noted throughout the tour, the lighting was, as was expected from the band, impressive when combined with the other elements of the show. The stage became a regular selling point for the tour, "The simplest way to describe it (the staging) is that it's the biggest (military) tank you've ever seen in your life. The entire stage is a tank, with the drums on a revolving turret and treads that run from the front of the stage to the back. We've got a guy who designs tank simulators for the Army and we're using some of the effects that they use to simulate combat" (Indianapolis Star, 12/5/82).

The "Creatures of the Night" era was an illusion, one designed to placate and in equal matter mislead Phonogram, with whom the band didn't have a particularly strong relationship following the disaster of "The Elder." According to CK Lendt, "They were trying to maintain the illusion that Ace was still in the band and they had to do that in order to keep the record company from thinking that Ace was out of the band in which case their contract would be voided, which happened anyway, it just happened latter rather than sooner, that was a business decision" (KISS Hell, 1998). Ace, for his part, must be viewed somewhat admirably during the period. While he may have not have participated in the recording of the album, he was willing to go on tour with the band — the European promotional tour conducted in late-November. He'd also participated in the October press conference and appeared on the cover of the album. But according to Paul, he was in a fragile state. Paul recounted, "He said to me, 'I'm on the verge of a nervous breakdown. I can't do this anymore'" ("Face The Music"), even if he'd kept things together during Europe. Returning to the U.S. on December 3 there were less than three weeks before the scheduled start of the tour. For Ace, there was no other option. In his mind his future was clear, were he to remain in the band: "I knew that if I didn't leave the group, I was going to die. Everything about my life was in disarray at that time. I felt no connection to KISS anymore and wasn't happy with the direction the band was taking" ("No Regrets").

While Ace's departure was masked with misinformation, being presented as temporary, the new guitarist's involvement was not secret. Industry press reported, "Guitarist Vinnie 'Wiz' Vincent is replacing Ace Frehley on the current 100-date KISS tour, though Frehley may do some isolated concerts with the group and will continue to play on KISS albums. According to a release from the band, Frehley has not yet recovered enough from an auto accident last year to undergo the rigors of the road. In the KISS shows, Vincent wears a costume based on an ancient Egyptian motif" (Billboard, 1/15/83). Ace had explained at the band's October press conference that he'd been involved in a wreck in July 1982 and that the crash had resulted in injuries and that at that time he was an active member of the band with no intention of leaving... As had been the case with the recording of the album, Vinnie appeared to get the job touring with the band by default. As Paul succinctly put it, "nobody else was on the horizon" ("Face The Music"). With Vinnie "in," shows in many markets still advertized shows using older stock photos available to the newspapers — some including Ace, and some even with Peter era lineups. But many used an accurate lineup photo that included Vinnie. There is no doubt, still, that many fans would have been shocked and confused to see a strange unknown figure on stage as the band they thought they knew performed.

From the beginning the tour had issues, with the first show being cancelled due to weather preventing the band and equipment from converging in the same place at the same time. Religious protests, which the band had previously experienced and were becoming more *en vogue*, and being targeted at rock groups in general, followed the band through many of the markets they visited. As the saying goes, any press is good press, though the accompanying news articles did little to raise interest in the tour. Nor did the inclusion of the Plasmatics, adding an extra level of schlock/shock with Wendy O. Williams' stage antics, entice more prospective patrons to purchase tickets. In some markets she received more press coverage than the headliner. The first month of the tour was certainly affected by an overall touring slump throughout the industry, though it had started to ease the following month (Billboard, 2/12/83). From available stats, the tour averaged 59.12% attendance. That sort of mediocrity was not what the band were looking for. Even their first visit to South America, which should have provided a pleasurable adventure, turned into an unpleasant struggle; one pitting the band against the climate and culture, judges, and promoters — even if the tour saw the band playing to some of their most massive audiences in years, if not their career. According to Paul, "the Creatures tour did horrendously in most markets. Before we went onstage, we'd hear 'You wanted the best, you got the best, the hottest band in the land...' and we'd walk out to find nobody was there. Sometimes there would be only a thousand people in an arena that could hold eighteen thousand. We had packed the same venues a few years before, but now, if I threw my guitar pick too far, it sailed over people's heads and landed on the floor" ("Face The Music"). It wasn't much of a celebration of the band's 10th anniversary; though by the end of the struggle there was a new clarity for the band...

November 21, 1982 - Stockholm, Sweden **PROMOTIONAL TOUR

Notes:

- Following their arrival in Europe, the band conducted press interviews and photo sessions (for Okej magazine) on Nov. 22. During the European promotional tour there were no live performances by the band at events, but several TV performances were filmed with Ace (still using his "Elder" outfit) and numerous photo shoots took place in addition to various local press/media interviews. This short tour would mark Ace's final contributions to the band.

November 22 - London, England

Notes:

- Arriving late in the day, on Nov. 23 the band conducted an in-store appearance at Virgin Records in London.

November 24 - Amsterdam, Holland

Notes:

- With Nov. 25 being spent rehearsing, during their Dutch visit the band filmed a lip-synced performance of "I Love It Loud" for "Top of the Pop" in Hilversum on Nov. 26. They returned to England on Nov. 27. Nearly 30 minutes of footage from the rehearsal sessions circulates, showing the band working with the directors and interacting with the fans attending the filming. Eric plays the opening drum part to "I Love It Loud" live for audience participation.

November 28 - Madrid, Spain

Notes:

- The day following their arrival (29th), the band filmed a lip-synced performance of "Creatures of the Night" and "I Love It Loud" for TV program "Applauso" along with recording "Merry Christmas" in Spanish messages for later use.

November 29 - Munich, Germany

Notes:

- Arriving late in the day, the band had a full schedule for Nov. 30... After conducting the requisite press functions the band filmed a lip-synced performance of "I Love It Loud" for the Vorsicht Musik television show (which would be broadcast on ZDF on Dec. 13). In the afternoon the band conducted an in-store appearance and signing at Karstadt in the Fußgängerzone at Stachus.

December 1 - Rome, Italy

Notes:

- The band filmed lip-synced performances of "Creatures of the Night" and "I Love It Loud" at RAI TV for the Discoring program. The following day they participated in the "Blue Room" photo session and filmed "I Love It Loud" for Channel 5. Ace and Paul returned to the U.S. on Dec. 3, ending his association with the band. The rest of the band would convene in Dallas, TX, with Vinnie Vincent, for final rehearsals for the tour.

December 27 - Rushmore Plaza Civic Center, Rapid City, SD **CANCELLED

Promoter: Concert Company Presentations
Other act(s): Unknown.
Reported audience: (10,000 capacity)

Notes:
- The Christmas week western U.S. snow storm caused the late cancellation of this concert. According a press report, "Some of their [KISS's] equipment was stranded in Denver and they couldn't get it out." An inauspicious start to the tour...

December 29 - Bismarck Civic Center, Bismarck, ND
Promoter: Contemporary Presentations
Other act(s): Hotz
Reported audience: 3,335 / 8,200 (40.67%)
Reported gross: $30,011
Notes:
- This show marked Vinnie Vincent's live debut with the band in addition to it being their first U.S. concert since July 25, 1980.
- As a result of ensuing travel problems, caused by the weather challenges facing the band and western states, it has long been rumored that KISS were forced to perform this first show using slightly modified "Love Gun" era costume pieces that were flown in from the East Coast. No photographic evidence has yet surfaced.
- A shake up of the set list was always planned with six songs from the new album replacing older material. However, the band also considered "I" and "The Oath" from "The Elder," "Is That You?," "Rock Bottom," and "2,000 Man;" and even toyed with the idea of bringing back "Go Now" (a Moody Blues song they'd performed live in 1973) as an encore.

December 30 - Municipal Auditorium, Sioux City, IA
Promoter: Terry Drea Productions
Other act(s): Dare Force
Reported audience: 4,934 / 5,200 (94.88%)
Set list: Creatures of the Night / Strutter / Calling Dr. Love / Firehouse / I Love It Loud / Cold Gin / Keep Me Comin' / War Machine / I Want You / Rock And Roll Hell / I Still Love You /

Shout It Out Loud / God of Thunder / Love Gun / Black Diamond / Rock And Roll All Nite / Detroit Rock City

Notes:

- It is likely that this is the same set list as performed the previous night.

- The final live performance of "Keep Me Comin'" (until the 2016 KISS Kruise VI).

- There were local protests against the concert in advance though the Board of Auditorium Trustees declined at a meeting to cancel the concert and lose a possible $5,000 income. Gene continued his press response against the protestors: "If they want to hunt for witches, let them go ahead. I'm always wary, though, of groups who proclaim to speak for others, particularly when what they really care about is if you spell their names right. If mom or dad says kids shouldn't listen to us, [and] that's fine. But let us make up our own minds first" (Sioux City Journal, 12/31/82).

- From a local review: "Thursday's KISS concert smacked of success as far as promoter Terry Drea was concerned. Despite 30 letters of protest and weather delays, the post-Christmas 'Creatures of the Night' performance went without a hitch. With nearly 5,000 teen-agers and adults crowding into the Municipal Auditorium, Drea termed the KISS appearance one of the city's most successful music events to date... Monday's blizzard nearly halted the advance of the KISS Army. Appearing in Bismarck, N.D., Wednesday night, the rock group had to bring a special rigging crew in to Sioux City early Thursday morning to assure that the stage would be set by 8 p.m... Appearing in makeup and employing flash-pots, fog and an arsenal of amplifiers, KISS has widely been regarded as one of the groups that changed the face of rock and roll. Indeed, its 'Creatures of the Night' show (believed to be the nation's costliest road production) has set a standard few — if any — groups have been able to duplicate" (Sioux City Journal, 12/31/82).

- A generally poor AUD recording circulates from this show which is also missing part of "Rock And Roll All Nite."

December 31 - MetroCentre, Rockford, IL

Promoter: Jam Productions
Other act(s): Shoes
Reported audience: 3,500 / 9,213 (37.99%)
Set list: Creatures of the Night / Strutter / Calling Dr. Love / Firehouse / I Love It Loud / Cold Gin / War Machine / I Want You / Rock And Roll Hell / Shout It Out Loud / I Still Love You / God of Thunder / Love Gun / Black Diamond / Rock And Roll All Nite / Detroit Rock City

Notes:

- Uriah Heep were originally announced in mid-November 1982 as the second act on the bill, where they remained until late-December. Gene attempted to sign opening act Shoes to his $immons Records label in 1988, though in 1982 they were reaching the end of their signing with Elektra Records, with whom they'd released three albums.

- The final live performance of "Rock And Roll Hell" (until the 2016 KISS Kruise VI).

- From a local review: Nope, the main Rockford Register Star seldom reviewed rock concerts, though KISS' performance was noted with a single photo of Gene Simmons, by paper reporter/photographer Fred Hutcherson, with a brief tag-line, "KISSing off 1982" appeared in their January 1 edition. Total word count, 34: " A KISS guitarist loudly bands out the old year as the rock group said goodbye to 1982 and welcomed 1983 to Rockford late Friday and early Saturday with a concert at the Metro Centre" (Rockford Register Star, 1/26/83). This show actually made a profit ($8,748) during a period when many concerts at the venue were losing money (Rockford Register Star, 1/26/83).

- A reasonable AUD recording from this show circulates.

January 1, 1983 - Hulman Civic University Center, Terre Haute, IN
Promoter: Sunshine Promotions
Other act(s): Why on Earth
Reported audience: 3,944 / 10,000 (39.44%)
Set list: Creatures of the Night / Detroit Rock City / Calling Dr. Love / Firehouse / I Want You / I Love It Loud / Cold Gin / God of Thunder / Love Gun / War Machine / I Still Love You / Shout It Out Loud / Black Diamond / Strutter / Rock And Roll All Nite
Notes:
- This was the tour's first "standard" set list with it being performed through the second week of the month (through the Montreal show).
- An average AUD recording circulates from this show.

January 4 - Civic Center Coliseum, Charleston, WV
Promoter: Future Entertainment & Belkin Productions
Other act(s): The Defectors
Reported audience: 4,466 / 10,195 (43.81%)
Set list: Same as Jan. 1
Notes:
- From a local review: "4,500 screaming, hip-rocking fans at the Charleston Civic Center joyfully submitted to the ear-splitting cacophony that has become the trademark of the rock group, KISS... Their visit to Charleston is part of a six-month, 100-city tour that began last month. The group, which saw better times in the late 1970s, is now just one of several acid rock bands with a mostly pubescent following. But fans that showed last night felt no less adoration for the group... Many of them aren't interested in rock 'n' rollers who preach morality. They want hard-driving, high-volume irreverent rock and roll. And to their delight, KISS gave it to them" (Charleston Daily Mail, 1/5/83).
- A very decent AUD recording circulates from this show. 8mm video footage also exists. While it's shot from the floor it does at least capture some of Vinnie's violin bow assault on his guitar solo and early use of his gold RR guitar. The roughly 10 minutes of disjointed footage captures various parts of the show.

January 6 - Rupp Arena, Lexington, KY
Promoter: Future Entertainment & Belkin Productions
Other act(s): Night Ranger
Reported audience: 3,305 / 9,500 (34.79%)
Notes:
- This show was sold in a "half-house" configuration for 9–10,000 maximum seats. However, the promoters only expected to sell around 5,000 tickets.
- From a local review: "Maybe this would be a good time for KISS to call it quits. The heavy metal rock theater group brought its act back into Rupp Arena last night to a less than spirited reception from about 2,500 survivors of the 'KISS Army.' As predicted by early tour reports, the crowd was a little older and less weirdly dressed than previous KISS contingents, and also a good deal quieter... Only half of Rupp arena was used for last night's performance, but less than half of the available seating was filled. The highly touted tank-shaped stage was nicely rendered but disappointingly unimposing in size and function. The

fog, pyrotechnics and light show were merely standard rock fair" (Lexington Herald-Leader, 1/7/83)...

January 7 - Wendler Arena, Saginaw, MI
Promoter: Belkin Productions
Other act(s): Night Ranger
Reported audience: 5,409 / 7,169 (75.45%)

January 8 - Sports Arena, Toledo, OH
Promoter: Belkin Productions
Other act(s): Night Ranger
Reported audience: 4,739 / 7,500 (63.19%)
Partial set list: God of Thunder / I Still Love You / Calling Dr. Love / Shout It Out Loud / Firehouse / I Love It Loud / Rock And Roll All Nite
Notes:
- From a local review: "If KISS proved anything Saturday night at the Toledo Sports Arena, it was that without its theatrics, the band could not exist... Without the extravagant lighting, the pyrotechnic stage show, and the outlandish costumes, KISS would be hard-pressed to find an audience for its macho, head-banging heavy metal which comes dangerously close to a musical wasteland" (Toledo Blade, 1/11/83).

January 9 - UD Arena, Dayton, OH
Promoter: Belkin Productions
Other act(s): Night Ranger
Reported audience: 4,430 / 13,278 (33.36%)
Set list: Same as Jan. 1
Notes:
- A couple of below average AUD recordings circulate from this show.

January 12 - Colisée de Quebec, Quebec, QC, Canada
Promoter: Donald K. Donald
Other act(s): The Headpins
Reported audience: 8,893 / 11,285 (78.80%)
Set list: Same as Jan. 1
Notes:
- The day before this show the band conducted a press conference (at the Saenger Theater in New Orleans) and then participated in an afternoon in store appearance at Warehouse Records and Tapes in Kenner, LA, to promote their Mardi Gras concert appearance the following month.
- An average AUD recording circulates from this show.

January 13 - Forum de Montreal, Montreal, QC, Canada
Promoter: Donald K. Donald
Other act(s): The Headpins
Reported audience: 8,217 / 12,500 (65.74%)
Set list: Same as Jan. 1
Notes:

- From a local review: "Take away the volume and the music has little to offer unless you add a little visual burlesque of your own, which is exactly what KISS has done. You want a circus? KISS members reasoned, 'we'll give you a circus.' But because it's 1983, and because we're talking about a generation that knows a lot more about rock than about wild animals, KISS mount a rock 'n' roll circus, and it attracts kids of all ages. KISS bring in an army tank that becomes the Forum stage, complete with gun turret, end-to-end treads, and a gun barrel that fires honest-to-war-games tank blanks. They bring in jet-propelled lighting trusses that turn the stage into a subterranean never-never land, they throw fireballs 25 feet into the air, they make it rain fire and they power the whole fantasy with enough sound to turn you into a mental midget in minutes" (Montreal Gazette, 1/14/83).
- A complete average AUD recording, and more importantly a reasonable partial audience video, circulate from this show. While the quality of the video certainly isn't the greatest, it is shot high and from distance allowing a good overall view of the stage. It's generally stable and the filmer does a decent job zooming in and out appropriately. "Love Gun" is cut from the video with the disjointed end to the video occurring after part of Eric's drum solo, though you get a great look at the rotating tank-turret drum riser. The end of that solo is cut, fortunately still including the band's explosive show culmination prior to the first notes of "Rock And Roll All Nite." With so little else from the tour it's a decent enough archival relic to have in one's collection. The complete AUD recording has some fade-outs/ins, but is very listenable.

January 14 - Maple Leaf Gardens, Toronto, ON, Canada
Promoter: Concert Productions International (CPI)
Other act(s): The Headpins
Reported audience: 9,565 / 10,000 (95.65%)
Reported gross: C$124,100
Set list: Creatures of the Night / Detroit Rock City / Calling Dr. Love / Cold Gin / I Want You / I Love It Loud / Firehouse / War Machine / Love Gun / God of Thunder / I Still Love You / Strutter / Black Diamond / Shout It Out Loud / Rock And Roll All Nite
Notes:
- First set list change since the beginning of the month: "Cold Gin" and "Firehouse;" "God of Thunder" and "War Machine;" and "Strutter" and "Shout It Out Loud" switch order.
- In conjunction with the Toronto Sun sponsored a KISS look-alike contest resulting in coverage on TV.
- From a local review: "Even 10 years down the road, a KISS concert is still a KISS concert... Doing exactly what they've always done, exactly as they've always done it. No surprises, no disappointments, just pure and simple, mindless and harmless... KISS... The faithful who were in attendance got exactly what they came for, 90 minutes of trashy, explosive, high-decibel theatrics, the slickest rock circus ever created, performed by men who have been doing it so long they are masters of musical manipulation" (Toronto Star, 1/16/83).
- An average AUD recording circulates from this show.

January 15 - Civic Centre, Ottawa, ON, Canada
Promoter: Concert Productions International (CPI) / Donald K. Donald / Bass Clef
Other act(s): Headpins
Reported audience: 4,919 / 7,000 (70.27%)
Reported gross: C$59,028

Set list: Creatures of the Night / Detroit Rock City / Cold Gin / Calling Dr. Love / I Want You / I Love It Loud / Firehouse / War Machine / Love Gun / God of Thunder / I Still Love You / Shout It Out Loud / Black Diamond / Rock And Roll All Nite

Notes:

- From a local review: "KISS was once described as the greatest act since death, but it now appears to be gasping its last breathe of air. Judging from the display of tedious drama Saturday night at the Civic Centre the one-time fearsome foursome has chosen not to exit kicking and screaming but merely wait patiently for the arrival of the grim reaper... Despite the arsenal of fireworks, smoke bombs, and towering torches of fire that were set off, KISS had no life, no real excitement. The band didn't seem to be having so much fun and so it wasn't much of a party for the audience either" (Ottawa Citizen, 1/17/83).

- An above average AUD recording circulates from this show.

January 16 - Civic Center, Glen Falls, NY

Promoter: Magic City Productions / TCA
Other act(s): Night Ranger
Reported audience: 4,637 / 7,713 (60.12%)

Set list: Creatures of the Night / Detroit Rock City / Cold Gin / Calling Dr. Love / I Want You / I Love It Loud / Firehouse / War Machine / Love Gun / God of Thunder / I Still Love You / Shout It Out Loud / Black Diamond / {cuts}

Notes:

- Poor weather conditions likely affected this show's attendance with some 19" of snow falling over the weekend. An early article in the Post-Star, about the concert tickets going on sale, incorrectly noted Jan. 9 as the show date — a correction would appear in the following day's newspaper.

- From a local review: "They set the tone for Sunday night's concert when they sang a tune from their new album entitled 'I Love It Loud.' And loud it was as the outrageous group KISS took the stage before 4,400 people at the Glens Falls Civic Center. The group, best known for its facial makeup design and unique costumes, gave a 90-minute performance and lived up to their claim of being 'the loudest band in rock 'n roll...' KISS is a consummate show band, meant to not only blast their music to their 'army' of fans but to entertain as well. They group has been described as one of the last of the pyrotechnic performing acts" (Glens Falls Post-Star, 1/18/83)...

- An incomplete and poor AUD recording circulates from this show. It's missing "Rock And Roll All Nite" and possibly "Strutter" (it's unknown if the song was performed at this show after being dropped the previous night).

January 18 - Onondaga War Memorial, Syracuse, NY

Promoter: Magic City Productions/TCA
Other act(s): Night Ranger
Reported audience: 4,902 / 7,908 (61.99%)

Notes:

- Plenty of seats were still available on the day of show with local press suggesting that the show was only two-thirds sold by that point (Syracuse Post-Standard, 1/18/83).

- Local TV WIXT Channel 9 news filmed backstage and concert footage at the show which was broadcast including clips of "Creatures of the Night." Superior, but shorter, footage of the same song was filmed (also with backstage interview) and broadcast by WSTM Channel 3 news.

- From a local review: "KISS has been called Disneyland on acid, and the description isn't far from the truth. The band is a showbiz extravaganza that Disney himself might have concocted had he been born forty years later. Introduced as 'The Greatest Band in the World,' KISS walked onstage to flashing lights, jets of smoke pouring from the ceiling, and a hall full of kids standing on their chairs, fists in the air, cheering the band's arrival. The audience itself was somewhat incongruous for a War Memorial concert. Seated here and there among leather and T-shirt clad, long-haired rockers and face painted KISS enthusiasts were a sizeable number of middle-aged people with young children, looking at times bewildered and besieged. Then again, their presence shouldn't have been entirely unexpected. After all, how many other rock bands have become the basis for such a wholesome American institution as the comic book... The band's movements were highly exaggerated, and when these were absorbed along with the rest of the stage, the show began to look like a Kabuki presentation some crazed individual had turned inside out.

Musically, the concert was a disaster, distorted and garbled, noise with a driving beat. It was heavy metal music in its purest form: volume. That this didn't matter to the audience proves one person's noise may be another's ecstasy. Although lyrics were indistinguishable, when the crowd wasn't cheering and dancing it was singing right along. They knew all the words. Close your eyes and KISS becomes just another heavy-metal band. Open them, and you enter a world of fantasy. P.T. Barnum would be proud" (Syracuse Post-Standard, 1/19/83).
- From a local review: "But the fans at the War Memorial last night were obviously not there to hear good music. KISS was what they wanted and KISS is what they got. KISS's music is the same tinny, metal-grinding music that it was during the band's heyday. The glitter costumes and makeup have remained virtually unchanged. Except for drummer Peter Criss, who left the group in 1981, the band has remained the same, although guitarist Vinnie "Wiz" Vincent has taken over for Ace Frehley on this leg of the 100-city tour. Today's KISS, as witnessed last night, is the same old KISS. The band's stage theatrics and antics have always outshone their unremarkable heavy metal sound. And last night was no exception" (Syracuse Herald Journal, 1/19/83).

January 20 - Rochester Community War Memorial, Rochester, NY
Promoter: John Scherr Presents
Other act(s): Night Ranger
Reported audience: 4,267 / 4,900 (87.08%)
Set list: Creatures of the Night / Detroit Rock City / Cold Gin / Calling Dr. Love / I Want You / I Love It Loud / Firehouse / War Machine / Love Gun / God of Thunder / I Still Love You / Shout It Out Loud / Black Diamond / Strutter / Rock And Roll All Nite
Notes:
- Paul's birthday was celebrated during the show. The venue had a normal capacity of 10,200, but was configured with half-house seating. Regardless of the downsizing, the day prior to the show it was reported that only 1,100 tickets had sold.
- This set may actually have first been performed in Glens Falls on January 18.
- An incomplete average AUD recording circulates from this show. It's missing the first three songs.

January 21 - Cumberland County Civic Center, Portland, ME
Promoter: Larry Vaughn Productions

Other act(s): Night Ranger
Reported audience: 4,338 / 4,500 (96.4%)
Reported gross: $45,549

January 22 - The Centrum, Worcester, MA
Promoter: Frank J. Russo Productions
Other act(s): Night Ranger
Reported audience: 10,147 / 11,000 (92.25%)
Reported gross: $94,652
Set list: Same as Jan. 20
Notes:
- On the day of show the band made an appearance at Strawberries Records & Tapes.
- A January 20 TV clip on WSMW Channel 27 indicates that Gene was prevented by city and state fire codes from performing his fire-breathing routine and using other pyro. Newspaper articles also suggest that Gene was told that the band would be prosecuted if they violated the order. With the strong ticket sales at the show it was impossible for the band to cancel.
- From a local review: "KISS, the resident clowns of arena rock's travelling circus, were being put to the test. Strict enforcement of state and local fire codes prohibited KISS from using their arsenal of flame-throwing theatrical devices. After 10 years and 2,000 concerts, KISS agreed to play for the first time without pyritechnics... The question was: Could the unexpectedly *revealed* KISS muster the rock 'n' roll spirit needed to pull off a concert without their visual and instrumental aces-in-the-hole? Well, not quite. The sound was right — loud and clear, and the band panted and puckered as best they could. But the concert was as satisfying as being kissed by one lip... Like actors in a corny disaster film, the band members were really little more than human props. Each struggled to compensate for the loss of visual fire, but their clumsy, costume-heave movements and repertoire of silly sub-teen anthems were dull and dated in the context of today's faster, more streamlined heavy metal rock. KISS also failed to project an attitude of emotion that went beyond their painted-face persona" (Boston Globe, 1/24/83).
- A couple of AUD sources circulate from this show. Both are below average.

January 23 - Civic Center, Providence, RI **CANCELLED
Promoter: Frank J. Russo Productions
Other act(s): Night Ranger
Reported audience: (14,197 capacity)
Notes:
- While this show was cancelled due to poor sales (less than 2,000) the promoter "arranged free bus service for ticket holders from Providence to the Centrum and back" (Providence Journal, 1/18/83) and offered exchanges for tickets to the Worcester show. An employee of the promoter attempted to exchange tickets with fans returning their tickets at the venue, but was thrown out. Exacerbated by then recent opening of the Centrum in Worcester, the Civic Center saw a marked decline in business, more so than it had already been suffering. Russo had been concerned in November 1982 that the venue would be at a disadvantage, so it's hardly surprising he cut his losses when his fears were realized.

January 25 - The Scope, Norfolk, VA
Promoter: Whisper Concert Productions

Other act(s): Night Ranger
Reported audience: 5,191 / 13,800 (37.62%)

January 27 - Von Braun Civic Center Arena, Huntsville, AL
Promoter: Cumberland Concert Company
Other act(s): Night Ranger
Reported audience: 5,025 / 10,106 (49.72%)
Reported gross: $49,959
Notes:
- An employee of the promoter, working on the production of the show, was arrested en route to this show and held on charges of drugs and gun posession.

January 28 - Boutwell Auditorium, Birmingham, AL
Promoter: Tony Ruffino & Larry Vaughn
Other act(s): Night Ranger
Reported audience: 4,635 / 5,778 (80.22%)
Notes:
- From a local review: "KISS — the gladiator rockers who make up what they lack as musicians with a titillating extravaganza of blinding lights, rat-a-tat fireworks and fiery flash-pots — was back in town... Without the Halloween makeup, minus the imposing platform shoes, the tough-guy prances and iron-man stances and the boom-boom-boom of assorted stage props — KISS is just another loudmouth rock band, without the roll. No better, no worse. This is not meant to imply that Friday night was not worth its while. To the contrary, if this sort of thing turns your meter — and obviously, it does an ample job for many — well, enjoy. To call it a concert, though, might be a bit much. But it is a show. Indeed. And with all due respect to the Clash, KISS is the real king of Combat Rock. Lizzard-tongued Gene Simmons and his mates drove that point all the way home — and into the ground — Friday night" (Birmingham News, 1/29/83).

January 29 - UTC Arena, Chattanooga, TN
Promoter: Cumberland Concert Company
Other act(s): Night Ranger
Reported audience: 4,451 / 11,000 (40.46%)
Reported gross: $43,533
Notes:
- This city became something of a ground zero for the religious protests that seemed to follow the band during the tour. According to Gene, "There's an ordinance before the city of Chattanooga that we must make a declaration that we're not Satan worshippers in order to play there. I won't. It's none of their business. You know, when we take them to court for slander, they usually lose... We're still KISS, the loudest rock band in the world. If you want Lawrence Welk, stay home" (UPI). He further addressed the furor: "A lot of the publicity that preachers give us actually brings people out to see us. Besides, a lot of what those preachers are saying has nothing to do with religion. They just want to bring some attention to themselves. It's a self-promotional thing" (Chattanooga Times, 1/28/83).

January 30 - Municipal Auditorium, Nashville, TN
Promoter: Cumberland Concerts Company
Other act(s): Night Ranger

Reported audience: 8,936 / 9,900 (90.26%)

Reported gross: $92,841

Set list: Same as Jan. 20

Notes:

- In preshow press Gene addressed the Satanist protests popping up again: "I'm sure they'd all love to know we're Jewish as well. Then they could call us Christ-killers... It's so they can get their names in the paper; and I think it's an insult to use religion that way" (Tennessean, 1/30/83).

- From a local review: "Lead singer/guitarist Paul Stanley sported a black furry tail, a right shoulder tattoo, huge gobs of fringe on his boots, and a bare-midriff ensemble designed to show off his physique. Lest anyone miss the point, studded Stanley did a mini-strip in mid-show. Bassist Gene Simmons wore his usual metallic medieval arm and leg plates and leather codpiece. We waved his top-knotted hair and stuck out his famous tongue a lot. The two of them stalked the stage in impossibly-high platform boots. New guitarist Vinnie 'Wiz' Vincent seemed a tad tiny to be in this league of giants, but he was fetching in his silver knee-plates, matching arm bands, and black lipstick nonetheless... The quartet worked the crowd into a frenzy with musical skill as much as with showmanship. A good portion of the audience remained on its feet throughout the performance, arms waving above heads in time" (Tennessean, 1/31/83).

- An AUD recording circulates from this show.

February 1 - Civic Coliseum, Knoxville, TN

Promoter: Sunshine South Promotions

Other act(s): Night Ranger

Reported audience: 4,391 / 10,000 (43.91%)

Set list: Same as Jan. 20

Notes:

- From a local review: "About 5,000 Knox-area youngsters paid to see a band which would have filled the hall to overflowing a few years ago. Touring behind its 'Creatures of the

Night' album, KISS was loud, rowdy, obnoxious and fairly spectacular... No protest was mounted; the concert got little publicity... Today, KISS is just another heavy metal rock band... All in all, KISS gave a competent performance at the volume the audience wanted. What KISS didn't give was any indication why they should still be considered a vital force in rock 'n' roll after 10 years and 50 million album sales" (Knoxville Journal, 2/4/83).

- A below average AUD recording circulates from this show. It does, however, provide the final confirmed appearance of "Shout It Out Loud" on the tour.

February 3 - Auditorium, West Palm Beach, FL
Promoter: Fantasma Productions
Other act(s): Plasmatics
Reported audience: 5,202 / 6,200 (83.9%)
Reported gross: $58,588
Notes:
- Member's hotel rooms at the Palm Beach Hilton were ransacked during the concert resulting in the reported loss of some $350 in cash, $6,500 in jewelry, and Gene's legendary photo collection (UPI).
- The Plasmatics were reportedly booed off stage at this show.

February 4 - Civic Center Arena, Lakeland, FL
Promoter: Beach Club Productions
Other act(s): Plasmatics
Reported audience: 5,287 / 10,000 (52.87%)
Notes:
- From a local review: "Ten years ago four guys painted their faces black and silver, donned weird outfits and platform boots, and exploded onto the rock music scene... Now, KISS is on the last leg of their 10th anniversary tour, and, apparently, their career. They are no longer a novelty and are no longer selling out concerts... Their three-year absence from touring hasn't helped... KISS has been reduced to wringing rock 'n' roll for all it's worth. And they are sparing no expense doing it" (Lakeland Ledger, 2/7/83).

February 6 - Charleston County Hall, Charleston, SC **CANCELLED
Notes:
- Cancelled due to "production manager illness."

February 8 - Civic Center, Asheville, NC **CANCELLED
Promoter: Kaleidoscope Productions
Notes:
- There was no mention of any opening act in the Jan. 28 Hendersonville, NC Times-News article announcing the show, though it would likely have been the Plasmatics. Some sources

indicate that this was only a temp hold date. However, the show was publically cancelled on Feb. 1 due to poor ticket sales, according to the venue manager (Hendersonville Times-News, 2/1/83).

February 11 - Convention Center, Pine Bluff, AR
Promoter: Mid-South Concerts
Other act(s): Plasmatics
Reported audience: 3,173 / 10,000 (31.73%)
Reported gross: $29,905
Notes:
- From a local review: "Going to the KISS/Plasmatics concert at the Pine Bluff Convention Center Friday night was much like watching a *National Geographic* television special, musical speaking. The 'music' was so far to the heavy metal side of the spectrum, the stage act was so outrageous — onlookers couldn't avoid out and out gawking. It was an enlightening cultural experience in a strange sort of way... The drone finally reached that unusually unattainable depth at which point it was no longer music — a musical absolute zero of sorts" (Arkansas Gazette, 2/13/83).

February 14 - Super Dome, New Orleans, LA
Promoter: Barry Mendelson Presents
Other act(s): Zebra
Reported audience: 10,421 / 15,000 (69.47%)
Reported gross: $107,866
Notes:
- The "Mardi Gras Eve Spectacular." Prior to the show the band conduct a press conference with various news outlets.
- A feature on "PM Magazine" TV program is broadcast noting the band's return to touring the US. A brief comedy clip of the news presenter trying to interview the band, and being thwarted by security chief Big John Harte, as they exit a New Orleans hotel is included. Backstage footage detailing the application of make-up and costumes is shown along with a brief interview with Gene and Paul. Sadly, no footage from the actual show is included.

February 16 - Five Flags Center, Dubuque, IA
Promoter: Jam Productions
Other act(s): Plasmatics
Reported audience: 3,319 / 6,700 (49.54%)

February 17 - Duluth Arena, Duluth, MN **CANCELLED
Other act(s): Plasmatics
Notes:
- This show was cancelled due to poor ticket sales.

February 17 - LSU Assembly Center, Baton Rouge, LA **POSTPONED
Other act(s): Plasmatics
Notes:
- This show was postponed until Mar. 17, which was then cancelled. The reason for the initial postponement was "a shift in management and PR agencies necessitated the delay" (Baton Rouge Advocate, 1/28/83).

February 18 - Met Center, Bloomington, MN
Promoter: Schon Productions
Other act(s): Plasmatics
Reported audience: 5,370 / 12,731 (42.18%)
Notes:
- Video and audio footage was filmed at this show by the Peter's Brothers for their "The Truth about Rock" anti-rock series. The first three songs from the set can be heard in the background of their audio cassette, while video footage is used in the background to the ministry's 1-hour video production. Gene conducted a phone interview with Dan Peters which was released by the ministry as "KISS Exposed" in 1983.

February 19 - Arena, Sioux Falls, SD
Other act(s): Plasmatics
Reported audience: 2,020 / 8,000 (25.25%)

February 20 - La Crosse Center, La Crosse, WI
Promoter: Stardate Productions
Other act(s): Plasmatics
Reported audience: 3,613 / 8,000 (45.16%)
Notes:
- Paul used a crutch for the first couple of songs in the set, due to spraining his ankle during the previous night's show.

February 22 - Richfield Coliseum, Richfield (Cleveland), OH
Promoter: Belkin Productions
Other act(s): Plasmatics
Reported audience: 10,212 **SOLD-OUT
Reported gross: $102,120
Set list: Same as Jan. 20
Notes:
- From a local review: "It was excitement and movement and unexpected sounds and outrageous doings they came for. And of all the heavy metal groups, KISS still does it best... One of the surprises was a softer song. Stanley sang 'I Still Love You' from the latest LP, 'Creatures of the Night.' You might not have expected the group to do this one. All right, it wasn't a real ballad, but it was as close as this group is going to get. Soulful, almost... At first pairing KISS and the Plasmatics seemed like the mismatch of the decade, as bad as the Beatles' opening for Roy Orbison..." (Plain Dealer, 2/23/83).
- From another local review: "About the best thing that can be said of KISS' 90-minute performance is the fact it didn't include Ms. Williams and company. Although it did feature some spectacular effects — fiery explosions, billowing smoke, big-time lighting and a stage designed to resemble a 60-foot-wide tank — and some occasionally hot heavy metal (most notable I Love It Loud and War Machine from the new Creatures of the Night LP) — the group seemed relatively tame and predictable... KISS seems to have worn out the ghastly novelty that elevated it to superstar bucks in the mig-'70s, back when fire-breathing and blood-spitting were not so much a way of life" (Akron Beacon Journal, 2/23/83).
- A poor incomplete AUD recording circulates from this show. It's missing the final four songs from the set which are presumed to have been the same as the Jan. 20 set (since both "Strutter" and "Rock And Roll All Nite" are specifically mentioned in a local review).

February 23 - Cobo Arena, Detroit, MI
Promoter: Belkin Productions
Other act(s): Plasmatics
Reported audience: 7,620 / 12,191 (62.51%)
Set list: Same as Jan. 20
Notes:
- From a local review: "You remember KISS, the costumed, concussive, controversial band parents once loved to hate. That honor may not hold today. The man sitting behind me in sparsely-populated Cobo Arena last night busied himself buying ice cream for his 4-year-old boy. A touching sight, father and son sharing a generational bond. While the majority of the crowd was comprised of the fuzzy-cheeked heavy metal males who have always been foot soldiers of the 'KISS Army,' their ranks didn't halt a recurring doubt about this band 10 years after. The worst possible thing has happened to KISS: It has become ordinary. Its sideshow no long holds thrills and danger... In the end KISS was the old sound and fury, signifying nothing" (Detroit News, 2/24/83).
- An average AUD recording circulates from this show.

February 24 - Market Square Arena, Indianapolis, IN
Promoter: Sunshine Productions
Other act(s): Plasmatics
Reported audience: 5,426 / 11,000 (49.33%)
Notes:
- Gene's old flame, Diana Ross, performed at the same venue the night before KISS's engagement.
- From a local review: "The band roared through about 90-minutes of tunes that, despite what most critics and parents might think, have made it onto the charts many, many times. The band proved why it's been able to last so long even though it's met with such resistance over the years: It appeals strongly to teen-age rock tastes and caters to its audience with top-notch playing and volume. Lots of volume... Though the audience was on the small side, it was nonetheless devoted" (Indianapolis Star, 2/25/83).

February 25 - Prairie Capitol Convention Center, Springfield, IL
Promoter: Len Trumper / Whatever Production
Other act(s): Plasmatics
Reported audience: 3,384 / 6,888 (49.13%)
Notes:
- From a local review: "Both groups demonstrated their ability to wrench the crowd's attention Friday — but showed little musical ability... KISS showed a little more taste, but were guilty of an even more serious offense for a rock performance — they were just plain dull. Despite throwing in every gimmick — from torches to shooting six-foot spark showers and more explosions than a state fair fireworks finale — their heavy metal pounding was more plodding than rocking" (State Journal-Register, 2/26/83).

February 27 - Kiel Auditorium, St. Louis, MO
Promoter: Contemporary Productions
Other act(s): Plasmatics
Reported audience: 2,802 / 5,646 (49.63%)
Notes:

- The band turned this poorly attended show into a benefit concert for baby Amy Lynn Hardin who was in dire need of a liver transplant, but whose family didn't have the $175,000 needed. Amy received the transplant on May 10, but passed away 2/27/88 in Cahokia, IL (exactly 5 years to the day of the KISS concert).
- From a nasty local review: "KISS is a show band. They wear funny clothes, ruin their complexion with lots of makeup and make loud, disagreeable noises — on purpose. I fame that up after junior high. Some parts of the spectacle were entertaining. I liked when Gene Simmons breathed fire. I liked when he spat blood. I liked the dry ice, the flash-pots, the moving light trellises, the tank turret with ... Ho-hum. I liked when Paul Stanley interrupted one of his stupid, sexist monologues to dare a youth to come onstage... It didn't matter that only Simmons and Stanley were original KISS cretins" (St. Louis Post-Dispatch, 2/28/83).
- Brief video footage, possibly from this show, was broadcast as part of a Channel 2 news feature.

March 1 - Municipal Auditorium, Kansas City, MO
Promoter: Chris Fritz Concert Promotions
Other act(s): Molly Hatchet
Reported audience: 3,929 / 10,372 (37.88%)

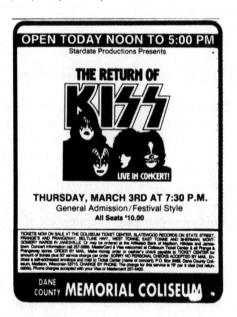

March 3 - Dane County Coliseum, Madison, WI **CANCELLED
Promoter: Stardate Productions
Reported audience: (10,400 capacity)
Notes:
- This show was cancelled on Feb. 22 due to "scheduling problems," or as a Coliseum spokesman stated, "due to circumstances beyond our control." During the break between tour legs Gene attended a Bette Midler preview concert, at Radio City Music Hall, with beau Diana Ross on Mar. 7.

March 9 - Convention Center Arena, Dallas, TX
Promoter: 462, Inc.
Other act(s): Plasmatics
Reported audience: 5,468 / 7,475 (73.15%)
Notes:
- Riot listed as the opening act on some flyers/tickets.
- From a local review: "Equipped with army tanks and loud music, KISS and the Plasmatics battled it out at the Dallas Convention Center Wednesday night. The question of which band is the most outrageous evolved into a full-fledged 'musical' war... If Neanderthals had had access to electronic instruments, they probably would have sounded a lot like the Plasmatics... KISS' show seemed to be too slow-paced because each member of the band performed a lengthy, often uninteresting solo, perhaps to give the other band members a rest from the exhausting chore of being bigger than life... For all the rough and ravaged gestures of KISS' performance, it was obvious that their show was as carefully staged as a ballet" (Dallas Morning Mail, 3/11/83)...

March 10 - Sam Houston Coliseum, Houston, TX
Promoter: Pace Concerts
Other act(s): Plasmatics
Reported audience: 5,975 / 6,969 (85.74%)
Notes:
- Houston Music News WLOL 101-FM filmed backstage interview and performance footage at this show. Clips of "Detroit Rock City" were included in the broadcast. The full show is rumored to exist in some form and be the best from the tour.

March 11 - Convention Center Arena, San Antonio, TX
Promoter: Stone City Attractions
Other act(s): Plasmatics
Reported audience: 8,474 / 8,694 (97.47%)

March 13 - Civic Center, Beaumont, TX
Promoter: Three Phase Productions
Other act(s): Plasmatics
Reported audience: 2,663 / 6,300 (42.27%)
Notes:
- At the protests preceding this show Gene was accused of being a cannibal...

March 14 - Memorial Coliseum, Corpus Christi, TX
Other act(s): Plasmatics
Reported audience: 6,500 **SOLD-OUT
Notes:
- Religious groups petitioned for the concert to be cancelled and picketed the show when their efforts failed.
- From a local review: "Obligatory clouds of smoke filled the stage as the four KISS band members walked on to the roar of the crowd. The usual array of multi-colored lights pulsated with the hard rock beat" (Corpus Christi Caller, 3/15/83). Outside the venue protestors handed out leaflets and picketed, one carrying a cross — he got his photo in Billboard Magazine (4/9/83)...

March 17 - L.S.U. Assembly Center, Baton Rouge, LA **CANCELLED
Promoter: Barry Mendelson Presents
Other act(s): Plasmatics
Reported audience: (15,327 capacity)
Notes:
- This show was cancelled the day prior to its scheduled date, even after having originally been rescheduled from its initial Feb. date, "through mutual agreement of the promoter and the group's management." Tickets were honored at the Biloxi show, some 150 miles away, the following night.

March 18 - Mississippi Coast Coliseum, Biloxi, MS
Promoter: Barry Mendelson Presents
Other act(s): Plasmatics
Reported audience: 4,645 / 7,000 (66.36%)

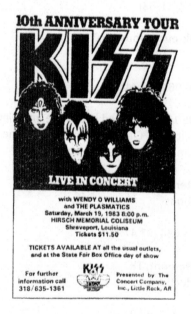

March 19 - Hirsch Memorial Coliseum, Shreveport, LA
Promoter: Concert Company, Inc.
Other act(s): Plasmatics
Reported audience: 4,059 / 10,200 (39.79%)
Notes:
- Public reception to the news Wendy was coming to town was not exactly positive: "Well, I see where KISS and Wend Williams are coming to town. All I have to say is don't we have enough weirdos around here... I just got finished reading an article about Wendy Williams coming to concert with KISS and I'm trying to figure out why they put a punk band with a heavy metal band because people who want to go see KISS don't want to hear this kind of music. I for one will be booing them instead of cheering them" (Shreveport Times, 3/13/83).
- From a local review: "The band was much improved since its last time here, a change due, it seemed, to the substitution of guitarist Vinnie Vincent for Ace Frehley and of drummer Eric Carr for Peter Criss. The band's show, as usual, featured a lot of fire and smoke, flash-

pots, special effects, superb lighting and a drum set that resembled a tank turret, with all the attendant effects. It spat fire, belched smoke, turned to and fro and was very menacing, indeed. That was really the only menacing thing about the show... Beneath the veneer of volume and the layers of greasepaint, there lurked something new, something critics of the group have been quick to point out the lack of, and something fans should be equally as quick to note. And that is a sense of melody and musical identity. The days of jokes about KISS as all bluster and no music are over" (Shreveport Times, 3/20/83). However, for all the adoration in the review for KISS, it was Wendy who made the front page of the paper...

March 21 - Lloyd Noble Center, Norman, OK
Promoter: Little Wing Productions
Other act(s): Plasmatics
Reported audience: 3,699 / 12,260 (30.17%)
Set list: Creatures of the Night / Detroit Rock City / Cold Gin / Calling Dr. Love / Firehouse / I Want You / I Love It Loud / War Machine / Love Gun / God of Thunder / I Still Love You / Black Diamond / Strutter / Rock And Roll All Nite
Notes:
- Gene was unapologetically positive in the face of KISS's 1983 situation in preshow press: "I am thrilled that people are turning up at all. To be completely honest about it, it's nowhere near the size that the group used to be. You know, we used to play just stadiums. Now, what with... a lot of complications, the group is not anywhere near as big as it used to be. But that's okay. It's still the best band in the world... and they'll come back to see us again" (Oklahoman, 3/20/83).
- A fan reportedly suffered third-degree burns at the concert when someone squirted lit lighter fluid into the crowd (Lubbock Evening Journal, 3/23/83).
- Photographer Richard Galbraith shot photos at this show included in his "KISS" photo book in 2009.
- An incomplete poor AUD recording circulates from this show. It's missing the final two songs from the set which are presumed to have been the same other sets from around the same time.

March 22 - Civic Center, Amarillo, TX
Other act(s): Plasmatics
Reported audience: 3,419 / 7,850 (43.55%)
Notes:
- A fan was reported burned at this concert when someone squirted lighter-fluid in the audience (UPI).

March 23 - Civic Center, El Paso, TX
Other act(s): Plasmatics
Reported audience: 5,171 / 8,000 (64.64%)
Set list: Same as Mar. 21
Notes:
- From a local review: "Words can't do justice to a spectacle of this magnitude. The KISS concert Wednesday night in the El Paso County Coliseum sizzled and seethed with plumes of smoke, cannon fire, showers of sparks, four Visigoths dressed to the nines and the clamor of nuclear war... The attraction of a KISS show lays not so much in musical proficiency as in energy, urgency and razzmatazz. What the players lack in melodic

coherence they compensate for with visual excess... Generally, the music was more loud than skillful, bearing more vigor than versatility. But the band is not devoid of talent" (El Paso Times, 3/24/83).

- Another review suggested that Gene had jumped off the stage to confront a fan who had been throwing stuff at him. Following "Strutter" Paul can clearly be heard threatening a fan for throwing a drink on stage.

- The band would be banned from future concerts at the venue due to their fans being accused of being too obnoxious and causing damage to the venue (New Braunfels Herald-Zeitung, 6/9/83).

- This show circulates as an average AUD recording as does the Plasmatics' opening set — it was the band's last show opening for KISS.

March 26 - Irvine Meadows Amphitheatre, Irvine Meadows, CA
Promoter: Avalon Attractions
Other act(s): Mötley Crüe
Reported audience: 5,786 / 5,969 (96.93%)
Set list: Same as Mar. 21
Notes:
- First show with Mötley Crüe opening.
- From a local review: "During Saturday night's Irvine Meadows stop of KISS' 10th anniversary tour, it became apparent that history has come full circle. KISS was upstaged by its opening act, Mötley Crüe, an outrageous band that mixes the transsexual posing of the New York Dolls with a suggestion of Satanism and plenty of thundering heavy metal riffs. Although the energy and excitement Saturday night was with the rising stars, Mötley Crüe, KISS proved that it is still a master of rock 'n' roll extravaganza. Theater and entertainment always have been KISS' strong suit. Unlike most rock acts in which the novelty of the special effects wears off in the first five minutes, KISS managed to keep the thrills coming for the duration of the show. KISS' 95-minute set featured a constant barrage of fog, smoke bombs, fireworks, cannon shots, flashing lights and fire pots" (Santa Ana Orange County Register, 3/28/83).
- From another local review: "It's doubtful that anyone over the age of 10 has ever really cared about KISS's cartoonish, essentially juvenile approach to rock. Still, the group's performance Saturday at Irvine Meadows Amphitheatre (to open the facility's 1983 season) showed there's nobody who deals with gee-whiz pop any better than KISS. Putting on one of the most elaborate state productions since the days when money was no object in the music business, KISS had the entire stage decorated as an armored tank and turret. This left the audience (gulp) looking down the barrel of the tank's cannon. Throughout the 90-minute performance, the band employed a slew of special effects including (wow) fireworks, explosions and a quartet of industrial-size flame throwers... While KISS' jackhammer brand of heavy metal offers little of lasting value, the group delivers it with some degree of imagination, and believe it or not, a lack of pretentiousness. For all the outlandish costumes and exaggerated behavior, this is a group that doesn't take itself too seriously" (Los Angeles Times, 3/28/83)...
- An average AUD recording circulates from this show.

March 27 - Universal Amphitheatre, Universal City (Los Angeles), CA
Other act(s): Mötley Crüe
Reported audience: 6,251 **SOLD-OUT

Set list: Same as Mar. 21
Notes:
- An average AUD recording circulates from this show.

March 28 - Veteran's Memorial Coliseum, Phoenix, AZ
Promoter: Evening Star Productions
Other act(s): Mötley Crüe
Reported audience: 5,734 / 10,000 (57.34%)
Reported gross: $58,418
Set list: Same as Jan. 20
Notes:
- From a local review: "KISS was even willing to give pre-concert interviews to counteract any religious demonstrations that might have occurred outside the Coliseum. Unfortunately for KISS, Bible-thumpers — like most rock listeners — seem to have had more pressing engagements Monday. The auditorium was half empty. Like other groups that were in their prime in the '60s or '70s, KISS is finding that popularity, like youth, is not to be depended upon. Dismissed by some critics from their outset as the low ebb of glamour rock, the quartet may be *passe* even for the listening public. Unlike Mötley Crüe and its ragged, impoverished fundamentals, KISS at least provided a spectacle of some interest. Their stage set was designed to look like a tank. The turret was the platform for the drum kit, and Carr's competent solo was coordinated with flashes, bands and belching smoke from the gun barrel... The playing was rudimentary, and the sound quality suffered from the Coliseum's usual pattern of distortion. By and large, though, the set seemed to satisfy the fans' expectations" (Arizona Republic, 3/30/83).
- A below average AUD recording circulates from this show.

March 31 - Sports Arena, San Diego, CA **CANCELLED
Promoter: Marc Berman Concerts / Talent Coordinators of America
Other act(s): Mötley Crüe
Reported audience: (8,300 capacity)
Notes:
- This show was cancelled about a week prior to the date due to "lagging ticket sales."

April 1 - Aladdin Theatre, Las Vegas, NV
Promoter: Evening Star Productions / Michael Schivo Presents
Other act(s): Mötley Crüe
Reported audience: 4,702 / 7,240 (64.95%)
Reported gross: $65,832
Notes:
- Some late-1982 newspaper reports about the tour suggest that Vegas as the intended first date, scheduled for Dec. 26. However, obviously no show took place at that time, nor does it appear that any booking was advertised.

April 3 - Civic Auditorium, San Francisco, CA
Promoter: Bill Graham Presents
Other act(s): Mötley Crüe
Reported audience: 7,299 / 8,500 (85.87%)
Set list: Same as Mar. 21

Notes:

- KISS' final U.S. concert in make-up until the reunion in 1996.
- There has long been the suggestion that Mötley Crüe were kicked off KISS' tour after the five dates. Nikki has commented, "We had played a few dates with KISS after 'Too Fast For Love,' and not only were they excruciatingly boring but Gene Simmons had kicked us off the tour for bad behavior" (The Dirt). That comment is in direct contrast to something Nikki said in 1986: "They're the greatest! We had a blast on tour! They taught us the importance of treating an opening act with respect and consideration" (Faces Metal Muscle No. 1)... The accusation that KISS' shows were boring cannot be substantiated, though with Ace Frehley and Peter Criss departed from the band by 1982 there was a lack of toxic craziness from the band with Gene Simmons and Paul Stanley being notorious straight-arrows, unless women were counted. Regardless, KISS would provide Mötley Crüe with their first major national tour exposure" (excerpt from an unpublished work)...
- From a local review: "Disguised and with enough bombs, smoke, sparklers and flame-throwers on stage to recreate the Normandy Invasion, KISS thunders into the show like a troupe of circus clowns, which, in many ways, they are. In recent years the heavier-handed Bible pounders have declared KISS to be agents of the devil and reported 'authentic' stories of backstage blood-rituals. KISS, of course, has responded by selling many more records and acquiring millions of new heavy metal fans. Last night, in front of the Civic Auditorium, a group of Christian youths paraded with placards on sticks condemning the 'devil's music' of KISS. As the fans went into the show many shouted 'right on' when they saw the signs" (San Francisco Examiner, 4/4/83)...
- An average AUD recording circulates from this show.

June 18 - Maracanã Stadium, Rio de Janeiro, Brazil
Promoter: Arteshow / Starship Productions
Other act(s): Herva Doce
Reported audience: 100,000 – 1,000,000,000 ;)
Set list: Same as Mar. 21
Notes:
- Local band Herva Doce, fronted by Renato Ladeira, was supporting their self-titled debut album.
- This show was performed to the largest audience in the band's history though the number in attendance fluctuates wildly depending upon source. The band had arrived in Brazil on June 14 and were contracted to conduct a maximum of four concerts over a two week period.
- 40 minutes of local TV archival video footage was officially released on "KISSology". It's not perfect, but it's as close as possible to representing the tour currently available. 1 hour of reasonable AUD excludes "I Still Love You" and "Strutter."

June 20 - Mineirão Stadium, Belo Horizonte, Brazil **POSTPONED
Notes:
- Electrical challenges forced the last-minute postponement of this show until the following day.

June 21 - Mineirão Stadium, Belo Horizonte, Brazil
Promoter: Arteshow / Starship Productions
Other act(s): None.

Reported audience: ~30,000
Notes:
- A local judge's ruling that children under 16 could not attend the show, without parents, on moral grounds (CK Lendt).
- Reportedly, more than 250 fans were injured at the concert, "as thousands of fans poured from the bleachers of a soccer stadium after organizers invited them down to the nearly empty expensive section on the playing field. Eight of the fans were seriously hurt, including one woman who suffered a broken back. The worst injuries, including fractured skulls, were suffered by people who tried to jump from the bleacher seats and fell into the concrete ditch that rings the field. Most of those hurt were trampled by the surging mob" (AJB News Agency).
- Brief chopped video footage from this show circulates featuring Paul wearing a local football team's jersey.

June 24 - Estádio do Morumbi, São Paulo, Brazil **CANCELLED
Notes:
- This show was cancelled due to lack of ticket sales though tickets were honored for the second show (CK Lendt).

June 25 - Estádio do Morumbi, São Paulo, Brazil
Promoter: Arteshow / Starship Productions
Other act(s): None.
Reported audience: ~60,000
Set list: Creatures of the Night / Detroit Rock City / Cold Gin / Calling Dr. Love / Firehouse / I Want You / I Love It Loud / War Machine / Love Gun / God Of Thunder / I Still Love You / Black Diamond / I Love It Loud / Rock And Roll All Nite
Notes:
- KISS' final concert in make-up until 1996. Originally two shows were planned at this venue. The band flew back to the U.S. the following day, but not before the promoter unsuccessfully attempted to organize a final last-minute show in Porto Alegre (CK Lendt). While the three Brazilian shows were performed to massive audiences, far greater attendances were expected and tour was a disaster for the promoter.
- Heavily chopped video footage and audio circulate from this show, though far from the best quality. It's unknown if "Love Gun" or "Strutter" were performed, but "I Love It Loud" was performed twice. Footage of the band conducting a press conference prior to the show also circulates.

Summer - Starlight Bowl, Stough Park, Burbank, CA **NOT BOOKED
Notes:
- KISS was banned from scheduling a summer concert at the 6,000 seat Starlight Bowl by city officials and a citizen's advisory group. They were in good company: Bette Midler, The Clash, Toto, and other bands were banned (AP). It's not clear whether the band had actually tried to book a concert at the venue, or were simply listed as being *persona non grata*. The banning of rock groups from the city-owned venue, a policy dating back to 1979, eventually went into the courts ultimately resulting in a ruling by the U.S. Supreme Court that over-turned the ban on the grounds that the U.S. Constitution's First Amendment's "free speech" principle applies to rock concerts.

August 19 - Estadio Del C.A. Boca Juniors, Buenos Aires, Argentina **CANCELLED
August 20 - Estadio Del C.A. Boca Juniors, Buenos Aires, Argentina **CANCELLED
August 21 - Estadio Del C.A. Boca Juniors, Buenos Aires, Argentina **CANCELLED
Promoter: Democrs Proudocciones / Ruben Mollo
Notes:
- Other reported dates for the aborted Argentine dates included August 12–14.
- There's a certain amount of debate concerning how far in actual planning this tour had reached. In the 1981–2 period there had been several attempts at booking tours south of the border, but local promoters had ultimately disappeared and nothing come from the efforts. CK Lendt certainly travelled to Buenos Aires in July 1983 to meet with the promoter eager to book KISS. KISS would perform three shows over two weekends. C.K., in his "KISS And Sell" book, is adamant that nothing was ever signed, simply because it was far too soon in the negotiations for anyone in the band's organization to possibly tie them to a still unclear event; or more importantly provide a third-party with credibility for some still unplanned and uncommitted event. Regardless, the promoters put tickets on sale for the event and continued selling tickets after the tour was cancelled on August 9.

Whatever the case, several factors seem to have killed the Argentine tour for the "group of degenerate Anglo-Yankees:"
1) KISS was having enough issues getting their equipment from the June shows released from Brazil. This tour had been a challenge for all associated on the KISS side, so it may simply have made them less interested in another South American touring adventure with the unique negotiation and business practices;
2) A group of former Falkland Islands war veterans, the Center for Ex-Combatants in the Malvinas, also protested the proposed tour using the "savagery and depravation" (UPI) argument that "could destroy the values of Argentine youth" (UPI);
3) The "Captain Giacchino" commando right-wing nationalist group threatened to blow up Boca Stadium if KISS performed, calling the band "bunch of degenerates and homosexuals" (UPI). The promoter was not concerned, commenting, "All we know is what we read in the papers, but we believe these threats are not very serious. And besides, it would take very specialized experts about 10 days to arrange to blow up Boca Juniors stadium into a thousand pieces."

It was apparent after the Brazil experiment that the payout simply wasn't worth it, particularly with a new album to finish up...

"KISS ON TOUR" CONTINUES IN...

KISS
ON TOUR
1983 - 1997

JULIAN GILL

CPSIA information can be obtained
at www.ICGtesting.com
Printed in the USA
BVOW11*2302191017
498043BV00015B/72/P